The Economics
of Education

To
Sharon, David, and Klara

and
In Loving Memory of
My Mother and Mother-in-Law

The Economics of Education

Revised Edition

Elchanan Cohn
University of South Carolina

Ballinger Publishing Company ● **Cambridge, Massachusetts**
A Subsidiary of Harper & Row, Publishers, Inc.

Copyright © 1978 by Ballinger Publishing Company. All rights reserved. No part of this publication may be reproduced, stored in a retrieval system, or transmitted in any form or by any means, electronic mechanical photocopy, recording or otherwise, without the prior written consent of the publisher.

International Standard Book Number: 0-88410-185-1

Library of Congress Catalog Card Number: 78-13277

Printed in the United States of America

Library of Congress Cataloging in Publication Data

Cohn, Elchanan.
  The economics of education.

  Includes bibliographies and index.
  1. Education—Economic aspects—United States. 2. Education—United States—Finance. I. Title.
LC66.C6 1978   338.4'7'370973   78-13277
ISBN 0-88410-185-1

Contents

List of Figures

List of Tables

Preface

This is a thoroughly revised and updated version of the original edition first published by Heath Lexington Books in 1972 and reprinted by Ballinger in 1975. The revision was motivated by the excellent reception that the profession accorded the book, along with a tremendous upsurge in the volume of literature in the area. It was necessary not only to update the tables on the costs of education, teachers' salaries, the internal rate of return to education, and so forth, but also to incorporate findings from numerous studies that have altered the structure of the economics of education.

One significant editorial change is the much-expanded Bibliography coupled with the Literature Guides at the end of each chapter. These provide the reader with a large (even if not exhaustive) selection of references from which additional insight and details may be obtained. In fact, a serious student of the economics of education *must* go beyond this volume and explore the field through journal articles, monographs, books, and unpublished studies.

The purpose of this volume, like its predecessor, is to provide a survey of the major topics in the economics of education. It is intended for both students and professionals. Knowledge of economics or advanced mathematics is not a prerequisite for comprehension of the material, though readers with better backgrounds in economics, mathematics, and statistics will surely have an advantage. It may be used as a primary text in courses on the economics of education; as a secondary or supplementary text in courses on educational finance or economics of human resources, manpower, or labor economics; or as a reference book for professionals in government, academe, or school administration.

There are only minor changes from the first edition in the sequence of the chapters. Chapter 1 provides a brief introduction, followed by a short discussion in Chapter 2 of the role of human capital and the economics of education in early writings.

Chapters 3 through 7 present the "human capital" approach, beginning with Chapter 3 (where other approaches to income distribution are also discussed), which provides an examination of the benefits of education. Chapter 4 follows, with a detailed analysis of the costs of education. Chapter 5 is devoted to a brief introduction to the theory of benefit-cost analysis, which is followed in Chapter 6 by applications of the benefit-cost analysis to the educational scene. Chapter 7 provides an examination of the role of education in promoting economic growth.

Production and cost functions in education, a topic devoted to a discussion of the internal efficiency of educational systems, are discussed in Chapter 8. The level and structure of teacher and faculty salaries and compensation are examined in Chapter 9.

Educational finance follows in Chapter 10. Topics include the role of government in education, federal and state aid to education, and the voucher plan. Educational planning, both for centralized (macroplanning) and decentralized (microplanning) systems, is the topic for Chapter 11. An overall summary, major conclusions, and some suggestions for research conclude the volume in Chapter 12.

This edition is a product of approximately ten years of work (which includes work on the first edition). The enormous expansion in published and unpublished material on the economics of education requires a full-time effort to seek, examine, select, and interpret the various contributions. Despite our effort, we surely have missed many items worthy of inclusion here. The only reasons for excluding an item are either lack of awareness of its existence or inability to locate it.

Many individuals provided assistance in bringing this volume to light. A searching review of the original edition by Henry M. Levin provided excellent insights and suggestions for the revision. Also, reviews of the original work, especially the one by E.G. West (in the *Journal of Economic Literature*), provided helpful guidance in the revision. In addition, I have used material from two of my books (Cohn, 1974a, and Cohn with Millman, 1975) in which the contribution of Stephen D. Millman is apparent. I have also benefited from comments on Chapter 7 by Edward F. Denison. Also, a number of graduate students at the University of South Carolina provided able assistance in library research, data tabulation, and, in one case (Margaret M. Capen), literature survey. And comments by students at Penn State and the University of South Carolina were quite helpful.

The grueling task of typing the manuscript fell on the shoulders of Allyson K. Hearn and Mary W. Hoskins whose admirable efforts deserve a special thanks. Also, the Ballinger staff, in particular Mr. Geoffrey S. Gunn, deserve appreciation for their patience and speedy production of the manuscript.

Last, but not least, I owe a debt of gratitude to my wife, Sharon, for making personal sacrifices so that I could complete the book on time and for providing editorial assistance and helping to prepare the Bibliography.

Elchanan Cohn
Columbia, South Carolina
June 1978

 *Chapter 1*

Introduction

There is only one good, knowledge, and one evil, ignorance.

Socrates

ECONOMICS, EDUCATION, AND THE ECONOMICS OF EDUCATION

Economics defined: As Professor Samuelson (1961) has pointed out, there is no single definition of economics. However, he developed "an informative introductory description" as follows: "*Economics* is the study of how men and society *choose*, with or without the use of money, to employ *scarce* productive resources to produce various commodities over time and distribute them for consumption, now and in the future, among various people and groups in society" (p. 6; italics in original). In essence, then, economics is the study of the production and distribution of all scarce resources—whether physical goods or intangible services—that individuals desire. The key words are (1) *scarcity* and (2) *desirability*—that is, economics is concerned only with resources that are available in limited quantities (and that includes virtually every good and service that comes to mind—including air, water, and other so-called plentiful resources, which, in many cases, are no longer plentiful) and with the goods and services that people want, namely, for which a demand exists (at least potentially).

Economics is inevitably connected with the allocation of resources among competing uses. The economist is thus charged with the responsibility of overlooking the functioning of the economic system from either a broad view (such as the functioning of the entire U.S. economy) or a narrow one (such as a specific firm).

Although some controversy exists as to what role an economist should play in society, it is agreed by all that he should be engaged, at least, in an analytical role. That role is limited to suggesting the consequences of various courses of action (which includes, of course, an outline of all relevant alternatives to any given choice) without taking an active part in offering normative policy solutions. A number of writers have argued for a more active role on the part of economists in normative matters, suggesting that economists present not only alternative choices and implied consequences but also their opinion regarding which of these choices is "best." The emphasis in this book will be on the analytical aspect.

Education defined: According to *Webster's New World Dictionary* (1962), education is "the process of training and developing the knowledge, skill, mind, character, etc., especially by formal schooling" (p. 461). Educational activities, then, involve the production and distribution of knowledge, whether they are undertaken in regular institutions of learning or elsewhere. Since the majority of such activities take place in institutions of learning (the public and private elementary and secondary schools and the public and private institutions of higher learning), the emphasis in this volume will be on formal education. However, it is recognized that substantial educational activities are carried out in other institutions, such as the military, churches, civic and other clubs, and business firms.

The economics of education defined: Based upon the definitions of economics and education, a definition of the economics of education emerges: The economics of education is the study of how men and society choose, with or without the use of money, to employ scarce productive resources to produce various types of training, the development of knowledge, skill, mind, character, and so forth—especially by formal schooling—over time and to distribute them, now and in the future, among various people and groups in society. In essence, then, the economics of education is concerned with (1) the process by which education is produced; (2) the distribution of education among competing groups and individuals; and (3) questions regarding how much should be spent by society (or any of its component individuals) on educational activities, and what types of educational activities should be selected.

It has been argued by Beeby (1966) that economists should be involved only in those aspects of education that may be considered to be "outside the classroom and into the market-place, where the quality of education is measured by its productivity." But where such matters as the "three R's" or "the acquisition of a given fact about history, geography, hygene and the like" are concerned, Beeby argues that no role should be played by the economist (pp. 10-13).

That position is contrary to the definition presented above. For while no economist, *qua* economist, would consider the proper technique of teaching speech, for instance, as his domain, there are certain aspects of such matters that could benefit from the economists' involvement. For example, a study of the entire educational process, involving all relevant inputs and outputs—as well as current and potential teaching techniques influencing inputs and outputs—might result in suggesting to the teacher the adoption of different teaching techniques so that the educational effort could be improved. Of course, it is expected that the educational expert will furnish the necessary information regarding inputs, outputs, and the process by which inputs might be converted into educational outputs—the latter being a most difficult task. So although the economist is not expected to be involved in the educational process as such, his tools might facilitate an improvement in the educational process. Limiting the economist to the marketplace will result in limiting the potentialities for improved analysis of decisionmaking in education.

EDUCATION AS AN INDUSTRY

Education is a gigantic industry in the United States, certainly one of the largest, if not *the* largest. In 1975-1976 it employed at least three million teachers, involved nearly sixty million pupils in all levels of formal education, and cost the American people more than 12 percent of their (adjusted) gross national product (GNP). The magnitude and components of the educational industry are explored in this section in some detail.

Enrollments

Total fall enrollment in formal education increased from approximately forty-five million in 1959-1960 to more than fifty-nine million in 1975-1976. As may be seen from Table 1-1, however, 1975-1976 enrollments in elementary and secondary education have decreased relative to 1969-1970, attributed to declining birth rates. Further declines in K-12 enrollments are projected until 1983

Table 1-1. Enrollments in Regular Educational Institutions, 1960–1980 (thousands).

Type and Control	1959–1960	1969–1970	1975–1976	1979–1980 (projected)	Percent Changes	
					'59–60 to '69–70	'69–70 to '79–80
K–12, Public	36,087	45,909	44,837	41,924	27.22%	–0.09
K–12, Private	5,675	5,400	5,300	5,300	–0.05	–0.02
IHEs, Public[a]	1,832	5,800	7,426	8,545[b]	226.59	+47.33
IHEs, Private[a]	1,384	2,120	2,306	2,417[c]	53.18	+14.01
Total	44,978	59,229	59,869	58,186	31.68	–0.02
High School Graduates	1,864	2,896	3,135	3,080	55.36	0.06

Sources: Grant and Lind (1976), Tables 1, 3, and 59; and Frankel and Harrison (1977), Tables 1, 4, 5, and 6.

[a]Degree credit only.

[b]Estimated by subtracting 2,417 from projected total IHE degree credit enrollments (10,962).

[c]Estimated by multiplying the 1975–1976 enrollment estimate by the factor of increase in total projected enrollments (including nondegree credit) in private IHEs.

(Frankel and Harrison, 1977, Table 4). At the same time, enrollments in higher education continue to increase, especially in the public sector, and are expected to peak around 1983 (Frankel and Harrison, 1977, Table 5).

Given the birth rate, enrollment gains may be achieved by increasing attendance rates in the population. As may be gleaned from Table 1-2, there is not much that can be done to increase enrollment rates for ages five to fifteen years. Beyond that, considerable gains could be made by reducing high school dropouts and/or increasing college attendance rates.

Employment

The educational industry employs a large number of workers. In addition to the nearly three million teachers and instructional staff reported in Table 1-3 for the year 1973-1974, many more workers are employed in noninstructional positions. The National Education Association estimated that about six million workers were employed in the education industry in 1969-1970.

It is interesting to note that 24.2 percent of the professional and technical workers employed in the United States are teachers or instructional staff members. Also, teachers comprise a very significant proportion of state and local government employees.

Table 1-2. Percent of the Population Five to Thirty-four Years Old Enrolled in School, by Age—United States, Selected Years, October 1947 to October 1974.

Year	Total 5–34 years	5 years[a]	6 years[a]	7–9 years	10–13 years	14–15 years	16–17 years	18–19 years	20–24 years	25–29 years	30–34 years
1947	42.3	53.4	96.2	98.4	98.6	91.6	67.6	24.3	10.2	3.0	1.0
1960	56.4	63.7	98.0	99.6	99.5	97.8	82.6	38.4	13.1	4.9	2.4
1970	58.9	77.7	98.4	99.3	99.2	98.1	90.0	47.7	21.5	7.5	4.2
1974	55.2	87.0	98.7	99.1	99.5	97.9	87.9	43.1	21.4	9.6	5.7

Source: Grant and Lind (1976), Table 5.
[a]Includes children in kindergarten, but excludes those enrolled in nursery schools.

Table 1-3. Number of Teachers in Elementary and Secondary Schools and Instructional Staff Members in Institutions of Higher Education (IHEs)— United States, 1949-1950 to 1973-1974.

	1949– 1950	1959– 1960	1969– 1970	1973– 1974
Elementary	665,665	953,431	1,271,467	1,327,980
Secondary	366,277	577,160	970,786	1,058,468
IHEs	190,353	281,506	546,000[a]	600,000[a]
All Levels	1,222,295	1,812,097	2,786,253	2,986,448

Source: Grant and Lind (1976), Table 7.
[a]Estimated.

Expenditures

Total expenditures by regular schools for current expense, capital outlay, and interest charges have increased from $24.8 billion in 1959-1960 to $108.4 in 1974-1975. A breakdown of the expenditures for the years 1959-1960, 1969-1970, and 1974-1975 is given in Table 1-4. It is noteworthy that expenditures have increased much faster than both enrollment and instructional staff. Possible explanations for the rise in educational expenditures will be explored in succeeding chapters.

Resources Entering Education. Total expenditures do not provide a complete view of the magnitude of investment in education. It is now widely recognized (through not entirely undisputed) that an important element in educational cost is represented by the earnings students forego while attending school. In addition, the costs of educational effort by the military and other nonregular schools should enter the calculation of total resource costs. Finally, an imputation for tax exemption, books and supplies, and depreciation and "rent" is also made. Table 1-5 provides a summary of the calculations for 1950, 1960, 1970, and 1975. The second column in the table contains data indicating that total educational costs are nearly twice the expenditure estimates provided in Table 1-4.

Comparison with GNP. The magnitude of the investment in education becomes more apparent when it is compared to total resources produced by the economy, measured by GNP. To facilitate comparison with column 2 of Table 1-5, figures for GNP were taken from the *Economic Report of the President* (1977) and have been adjusted upward to include some of the imputations made in estimating edu-

Table 1-4. Educational Expenditures, by Level and Control, in Regular Educational Institutions—United States, 1959-1960 to 1974-1975 (billions of current dollars).

	1959–1960	1969–1970	1974–1975
Elementary and Secondary			
Public	15.5	41.0	61.6
Private	2.4	4.4	6.6
Total	17.9	45.4	68.2
Institutions of Higher Education			
Public	3.7	15.8	26.8
Private	3.2	8.9	13.4
Total	6.9	24.7	40.2
All Levels			
Public	19.2	56.8	88.4
Private	5.6	13.3	20.0
Total	24.8	70.1	108.4

Source: Cohn (1977b), derived from various editions of the *Digest* and *Projections of Educational Statistics.*

Table 1-5. Resources Entering Education Compared to GNP—United States, 1950-1975 (billions of current dollars).

Year	Adjusted GNP[a]	Investment in Education	Investment in Education as a Percentage of Adjusted GNP
1950	294.2	18.3	6.2
1960	524.9	47.0	9.0
1970	1,030.6	125.0	12.1
1975	1,592.8	195.6	12.3

Source: Cohn (1977b), Table 7.
[a]Includes earnings foregone of students plus depreciation and implicit rent on school buildings and property.

cational investment. The adjusted GNP figures are given in column 1. It emerges that investment in education increased from 6.2 percent of GNP in 1950 to 12.3 percent in 1975. Further analysis indicates that the relative share of educational investment has reached its peak in recent years and is not likely to go much beyond 12 percent of GNP.

Revenues

Public Elementary and Secondary Schools. Traditionally, the local level of government has been responsible for public schooling. In recent years, however, a trend toward greater participation by state governments in support of public schools has occurred. Yet in 1975–1976, almost one-half of public school revenues originated in the local sector. It is expected, however, that the states will soon surpass local governments in public school support. With regard to federal support, although there has been a continuing trend of increased support, federal aid in 1975–1976 was still only 7.9 percent of total revenue. Some data are reported in Table 1-6.

Institutions of Higher Education. Total revenues have increased more than sixfold between 1960 and 1975, but the shares of federal, state, and local governments remained relatively constant. The federal share has, in fact, declined between 1960 and 1973, and in 1975 it was almost equal to what it was in 1960. The states' share increased slowly but steadily from 24.1 to 30.5 percent of the total. The share of local governments has been very small and has not changed materially during the period (from 3.4 to 3.9 percent). Most interestingly, tuition and fees have remained a steady 20–21 percent of total revenues throughout the period. Other sources, including private gifts, income from auxiliary enterprises, and endowment earnings, comprised approximately 35 percent of total revenues for the years 1960, 1970, and 1973. In 1975 the share was only 28 percent, largely replaced by greater federal grants. Relevant data are displayed in Table 1-7.

MAJOR ISSUES IN THE ECONOMICS OF EDUCATION

Given that the process of education involves the use of a substantial amount of scarce resources, a number of questions arise for which answers may be sought within the domain of economic analysis. It should be emphasized that while the tools of the economist may be used to assist in such matters, the cooperation of educationists, sociologists, psychologists, and others is needed if an adequate solution to these questions is to be found.

The issues that will concern us in this volume are conveniently grouped into five major categories:

1. Identification and measurement of the economic value of education,

Table 1-6. Revenue Receipts of Public Elementary and Secondary Schools, by Source—United States, 1959-1960 to 1975-1976 (billions of current dollars).

School Year	Total	Federal	State	Local	Local as a Percentage of Total Revenues
1959–1960	14.7	0.6	5.8	8.3	56.5
1969–1970	40.3	3.2	16.1	21.0	52.1
1973–1974	58.2	4.9	24.1	29.2	50.2
1975–1976	67.1	5.3	29.3	32.5	48.4

Source: Grant and Lind (1977), Table 69.

Table 1-7. Current Fund Income of Institutions of Higher Education: United States, 1959-1960 to 1974-1975 (billions of current dollars).

School Year	Total	Federal	State	Local	Tuition and Fees	Other
1959–1960	5.8	1.0	1.4	0.2	1.2	2.0
1969–1970	21.5	2.7	5.8	0.8	4.4	7.8
1972–1973	28.6	3.4	7.9	1.1	6.0	10.2
1974–1975	35.7	6.1	10.9	1.4	7.2	10.1

Source: Grant and Lind (1976), Table 118, and Grant and Lind (1977), Table 123.

2. The allocation of resources in education,
3. Teachers' salaries,
4. The finance of education, and
5. Educational planning.

A brief explanation of each issue follows.

The Economic Value of Education. Both individuals and society at large have a stake in educational investment. It is therefore desirable that the value of a given investment in education both to the individual and to society be calculated. This involves the estimation of educational costs and educational benefits. A historical description of such efforts is given in Chapter 2. A discussion of benefits is given in Chapter 3, followed by an analysis of costs in Chapter 4. The techniques of benefit-cost analysis are discussed in Chapter 5, followed by their application to educational investments in Chapter 6. Another common measure of educational benefits—the relation between education and economic growth—is described in Chapter 7.

Allocation of Resources in Education. The process of education involves the production of educational outputs from sets of inputs. Systems analysis techniques may be used to evaluate the functioning of educational institutions and to examine the possibilities for increased efficiency. Also, cost functions for public schools, from which it is possible to determine the existence of scale economies, are explored in Chapter 8.

Teachers' Salaries. The level and determinants of teachers' salaries are of particular concern to the nearly three million instructional staff associated with educational institutions. In Chapter 9, changes in salaries overtime, factors that might affect teachers' salaries, and the much-debated effect of collective bargaining are documented.

Educational Finance. Who should pay for education? Should the government support public and private education? If so, which level of government should take what share of the burden? And what share of total costs should be borne by the taxpayer as opposed to direct beneficiaries of the educational endeavor? Also, if subsidies are justified, should they be given to educational institutions or to individuals in the form of a voucher? These and other issues are explored in Chapter 10.

Educational Planning. Since education is not a private good and is not subjected to the full rigor of market competition, it has been argued that there is a need to institute educational plans to insure the optimal use of resources. A discussion of the rationale for planning, various approaches to planning, and some macro- and micromodels of planning is provided in Chapter 11.

SUMMARY AND CONCLUSIONS

This chapter has been devoted to three main topics: (1) a definition of the economics of education; (2) a demonstration of the magnitude of the educational industry; and (3) a discussion of the topics to be covered in this volume.

The definition of economics of education in the first section is designed to provide an informative introductory description of the subject matter area. Our concern here will be with the magnitude of and the manner in which scarce resources are diverted from other uses to produce educational outputs. Since it has been shown that the magnitude of current investment in education is clearly staggering, rational analysis of educational investment is likely to result in substantial savings of scarce resources.

Finally, the broad issues that will be covered in this volume include the economic value of education, the allocation of resources in education, teachers' salaries, the finance of education, and educational planning.

LITERATURE GUIDE

Texts or Broad-based Readings Collections
Texts in the economics of education include Benson (1978), Blaug (1970), O'Donoghue (1971), Perlman (1973), Rogers and Ruchlin (1971), Sheehan (1973), Vaizey (1962, 1973), and Woodhall (1972). A French language text by Hallak (1974) has been highly recommended by Windham (1976a).

Collections of essays include Benson (1963), Blaug (1968, 1969), Bowman et al. (1968), Froomkin, Jamison, and Radner (1977), Joint Economic Committee (1969), Kiker (1971), Mushkin (1962b), Sirageldin (1978), and Wykstra (1971a, 1971b).

Bibliographies
Bibliographies in the economics of education include Blaug (1976d), Deitch and McLoone (1966), Hüfner (1968), Windham (1976c), and for benefit-cost analysis, Wood and Campbell (1970). Earlier editions of Blaug are also available.

Other
Other publications providing descriptive or statistical overviews of the economics of education include Bureau of Labor Statistics (1976), Cohn (1976a), Golladay (1976), Hansen (1977b), Nollen (1975), and Windham (1976c).

Chapter 2

Education and Human Capital in The History of Economic Thought

> When a man shall clearly utter a vow of persons unto the Lord
> according to thy valuation, then thy valuation shall be for the
> male from twenty years old even unto sixty years old, even thy
> valuation shall be fifty shekels of silver . . . . And if it be a female, then thy
> valuation shall be thirty shekels. And if it be from five years old even unto
> twenty years old, then thy valuation shall be for the male twenty shekels
> and for the female ten shekels.
>
> (Leviticus, XXVI: 3-6)

The valuation of human capital dates back at least to early biblical times. The above-quoted passage from Leviticus suggests the valuation of a person's "human capital" according to age and gender, on the apparent presumption that males have greater labor market value than females and that persons aged twenty to sixty have the greatest value.

The evaluation of human capital has advanced considerably since that time. Additional variables have been taken into account, and the stream of expected earnings has been investigated in more detail. However, recognition of the need to evaluate the economic value of man can be traced to very early economic thought. At the same time, human resources, except for raw labor, were not generally incorporated in economic models until very recently. This chapter provides a very brief outline of the role of human capital and education in early literature. Readers desiring a more complete account should consult the literature guide at the end of this chapter.

The chapter is divided into six sections. The first presents a brief discussion of alternative methods to estimate the value of human capital. The second section presents a brief account of the use of human capital in early doctrines. Section three follows with a discussion of early views on the role of government in education. Next we bring an account of early writings on the relationship between education and income. After a brief summary, we conclude with a literature guide.

THE VALUE OF HUMAN CAPITAL

We have already shown that "there is no novelty in the idea of setting a price on a human individual" (Dublin and Lotka, 1946: 6). In addition to the biblical example already cited, one may mention the sale of slaves and the setting of a system of "fines" imposed on persons responsible for loss of human life during the time of Alfred the Great.

The first to attempt a serious estimation of the value of a human being was Petty (1699). His procedure was based on two critical assumptions:

1. The total earnings of labor are the residue remaining of total national expenditures after the profits from land and other sources are subtracted.
2. The value of mankind is worth twenty times the present annual earnings of labor.

As Nicholson (1891) pointed out, these assumptions are difficult to accept, and moreover, the estimation procedure neglects a host of factors that ought to be taken into account. It served, however, as a catalyst for further work in the area.

A better understanding of the early literature would be facilitated by classifying the valuation of human capital into (1) the cost of production approach and (2) the capitalized earnings approach (Kiker, 1966).

The Cost of Production Approach

The basic feature of the approach is the assumption that the value of man is equal to the value of resources expended in his "production." Such resources would include natal and prenatal care, cost of food, clothing, shelter, education, recreation, and so forth from birth to the age at which the evaluation is made. According to Ernst Engel (1883), who was one of the first to use this procedure, the individual is "fully produced" at age twenty-seven. Engel also assumed that the costs of production increase each year by a constant amount, an assumption that is clearly questionable. (A discussion of Engel's method is provided in Cohn, 1970b.)

Another formulation of the cost of production approach was presented by Theodore Wittstein, writing in 1867. His formulas improve on Engel's in so far as they take into account the rate of interest as well as maintenance costs and the number of men living at a given age in a life table. Finally, Dublin and Lotka (1946) conducted a thorough investigation of the costs (as of 1930) involved in bringing up a child. A portion of their data is used in Cohn (1970b) to test various hypotheses about the "proper" cost of production approach.

The Capitalized Earnings Approach

The main objection to the first approach is that there is no a priori connection between the value of resources spent in behalf of a person and the market value of the person. The second approach, therefore, disregards any past (sunken) costs and concentrates on the person's current and future (expected) market value (It should be emphasized that the analysis does not in any way attempt to measure the total worth of an individual, only his market value.)

The first rigorous formulation of the capitalized earnings approach was presented by William Farr in 1853. In his computational method, which remains the core of present value computation to this date, the present value of an individual's future net earnings is computed, after deducting the cost of living and allowing for deaths according to an appropriate life table. This method was somewhat improved by Dublin and Lotka (1946). In their formulation, V_x, the gross of an individual can be computed by the following equation:

$$V_x = \frac{1}{P_x} \sum_{t=0}^{\infty} v^t L_{x+t} \, w_{x+t} \, g_{x+t} \qquad (2.1)$$

where P_x is the number, in a life table, surviving from birth to exact age x; $v^t = (1 + i)^{-t}$ is the present value of $1 due t years hence at an interest rate of i per annum; L_x is the average number in a life table, living in the year of age x to $x + 1$; w_x is the annual earnings in wages, per head, in the year of age x to $x + 1$; and g_x represents the proportion of males employed in the year of age x to $x + 1$. If we let c_x denote the cost of living during the year of age x to $x + 1$, a similar formula for the net value of a human being can be constructed:

$$V'_x = \frac{1}{P_x} \sum_{t=0}^{\infty} v^t L_{x+t} \, (w_{x+t} g_{x+t} - c_{x+t}) \qquad (2.2)$$

where V'_x denotes the net value of an individual at age x, based upon the future stream of earnings less the cost of living of the individual.[1]

HUMAN CAPITAL IN EARLY ECONOMIC DOCTRINES

We have argued that human capital was considered by few early writers to be of paramount importance. Only a few economists included human capital in their definition of capital, and with the exception of Adam Smith, none have considered human capital to be the center of economic theory and the main source for economic strength and growth. As Eli Ginzberg (1966) points out, human resources did not seem to be of much import:

> Ricardo, writing in the early days of the industrial revolution, saw no reason to be concerned with the availability of labor. There was a great number of rural workers at the doors of the new factories looking for employment. The mills of that day had no difficulty of absorbing illiterate, unskilled workers so long as they were able and willing to submit to discipline. In Ricardo's view the strategic element in the economy was capital. (P. 2)

Ginzberg goes on to assert that the old economic philosphy in which a man was considered to be "a calculating individual interested in maximizing his pleasure and minimizing his pain" was at the heart of the neglect of human capital. It was only the "revolution in psychology" that has "exercised a major influence on contemporary views about the potentialities of education and training and therefore on the acquisition of skill, talent, and competence" (pp. 3–4).

Adam Smith

Already in 1776, Adam Smith considered the skills of the labor force to be the predominant force for economic progress. In his definition of fixed capital, human capital is also included. It consists

---

1. The reader not familiar with present value calculations should consult Chapter 5. For further elucidation of the two approaches consult Kiker (1968b: ch. 1).

of the acquired and useful abilities of all the inhabitants or members of the society. The acquisition of such talents, by the maintenance of the acquirer during his education, study, or appreticeship, always costs a real expense, which is a capital fixed and realized, as it were, in his person. Those talents, as they make a part of his fortune, so do they likewise of that of the society to which he belongs. The improved dexterity of a workman may be considered in the same light as a machine or instrument of trade which facilitates and abridges labour, and which, though it costs a certain expense, repays that expense with a profit. (Smith, 1952: 119-20)

Although Adam Smith did not go as far as attempting to estimate the value of human capital, he strongly believed that the production of human capital yields a considerable return in the form of greater lifetime income. His comparison between man and a machine highlights this view.

When any expensive machine is erected, the extraordinary work to be performed by it before it is worn out, it must be expected, will replace the capital laid out upon it, with at least the ordinary profit. A man educated at the expense of much labour and time to any of those employments which require extraordinary dexterity and skill, may be compared to one of those expensive machines. The work which he learns to perform, it must be expected, over and above the usual wages of common labour, will replace to him the whole expense of his education, with at least the ordinary profits of an equally valuable capital. It must do this, too, in a reasonable time, regard being had to the very uncertain duration of human life, in the same manner as to the more certain duration of the machine. The difference between the wages of skilled labour and those of common labour, is founded upon this principle. (Pp. 42-43)

Those economists who, like Adam Smith, included human capital in their definition of capital generally referred to the value of human skill and other acquired abilities rather than to the individual himself. Senior, for example, held this view, asserting that the value of human capital "exceeded the value of the stock of all Great Britain's 'material capital'" (Kiker, 1966: 487). And John Stuart Mill held a similar view: "The human being himself I do not class as wealth. He is the purpose for which wealth exists. But his acquired capacities, which exist only as means, and have been called into existence by labor, fall rightly, as it seems to me, within that designation" (Mill, 1909: 47).

Von Thünen
Heinrich von Thünen, writing in 1875, accepted the notion of human capital wholeheartedly:

There is no doubt about the answer to the very controversial question of whether the immaterial goods (services) of mankind form part of national wealth or not. Since a more highly schooled nation, equipped with the same material goods, creates a much larger income than an uneducated people, and since this higher schooling can only be obtained through an educational process which requires a larger consumption of material goods, the more educated nation also possesses a larger capital, the returns of which are expressed in the larger product of its labor. (Von Thünen, 1968: 393)

Von Thünen attacked the "reluctance to regard human beings as capital" on many grounds. In his own words:

An inner reluctance appears to prevent writers (and also others) from considering the question of what a man costs, what capital is contained in him. A human being appears to be too sublime, and we fear to commit a degradation if we apply to him such a method of an analysis.

But from this reluctance stems lack of clarity and confusion of concepts on one of the most important points of political economy. Moreover, it may be proved that freedom and dignity of man may be successfully preserved, even if he is subject to the laws of capital. It is politeness which one renders to the species to which one belongs onself, by so apparently elevating its status. (Pp. 393-94)

A particularly interesting application of human capital and the costs of its neglect is presented by Von Thünen with respect to the effects of a war:

The reluctance to regard human beings as capital becomes especially pernicious in the wars of mankind; for here one preserves physical capital, but not human beings, and one will sacrifice in a battle a hundred human beings in the prime of their lives without thought in order to save one gun.

But with the hundred persons, a capital at least twenty times as large is lost as would result from the loss of one cannon. But the purchase of the cannon causes an outlay of public funds, whereas human beings are to be had for nothing by means of a mere conscription decree. The state will take any man suitable for military service where it finds him without giving the least compensation to his family who lose in him perhaps their only source of support. Citizens miraculously do not protest against this practice, whereas, if the state confiscated without compensation oxen and cows, a general revolt would break out immediately. Hence, we regard capital as much more valuable than human beings. (P. 394)

Von Thünen goes on to propose schemes by which soldiers and their families be compensated for loss of life, injury, and the use of the soldier's labor during his military life "equal to what he could have earned while in service" (p. 394).

Other "Classical" Writers

There were several other writers in the "classical" school who considered the issue of human capital. They include David Ricardo, Jean-Baptiste Say, Nassau Senior, Frederich List, Henry Maclead, William Roscher, Léon Walras, Walter Bagehot, and Henry Sidgwick. For example, Walras (1954) treated human capital in much the same manner as any other capital good. Realizing that "consideration of justice and practical expediency" hinder viewing humans "exclusively from the point of view of value in exchange," he argued that one should abstract from such consideration and include all humans in the capital concept (p. 216).

Alfred Marshall

Alfred Marshall, while excluding human capital from his definition of "wealth" and "capital," still accepted the notion of human capital for many purposes. He even proceeded to discuss the capitalized earnings (net) approach to the estimation of human capital. His views on "personal wealth" can best be described by his own words:

> We have already defined Personal Wealth to consist firstly of those energies, faculties and habits which directly contribute to making people industrially efficient . . . if they are to be reckoned as capital. Thus Personal Wealth and Personal Capital are convertible; and it seems best to follow here the same course as in the case of wealth, . . . to raise no objection to an occasional broad use of the term, in which it is explicitly stated to include Personal Capital . . . . (Marshall, 1961: II, 204-205)

As Blandy (1967) points out, Marshall "accepted the basic Smithian position that an educated man may be compared to an expensive machine" (p. 874). Marshall also assumed that the profit motive operates in personal investment in the same manner as it operates in any other investment decision:

> The motives which induce a man and his father to invest capital and labour in preparing him for his work . . . are similar to those which lead to the investment of capital and labour in building up the material plant and the organization of a business. In each case the investment . . . is carried up to that margin at which any further investment appears to offer no balance of gain . . . and the price, that is expected for all this investment, is therefore a part of the normal expenses of production of the services rendered by it . . . . (I: 619)

That investment in human capital stems fundamentally from the profit motive is not incontroversial. Senior, for example, held the following view:

> Neither the labour which the boy undergoes, nor the expense borne by his father, is incurred principally in order to obtain future profit. The boy works under the stimulus of immediate punishment. It never occurs to the father that . . . he is engaging in a speculation which is likely to be unprofitable. To witness a son's daily improvement is, with all well-disposed men . . . one of the sources of immediate gratification. The expense incurred for all that purpose is as much repaid by immediate enjoyment as that which is incurred to obtain the most transitory pleasures. It is true that a further object may also be obtained but the immediate motive is ample. (Senior, 1939: 203–206)

Similar views were held by other early writers, noting that not all of the investment in humans is undertaken for future profit.

EDUCATIONAL BENEFITS AND THE ROLE OF GOVERNMENT IN EDUCATION

Much of the analysis concerning the value of education to the individual and to society is far from new. And although a new emphasis has been placed upon the economics of health, education, and other human resources, it had been well understood by Adam Smith in 1776, as well as by Marshall in the 1890s, that education confers both direct and indirect benefits upon the individual receiving the education and the society to which this individual receiving the education belongs. Adam Smith (1952) believed that without ample education, the masses of working people would be so alienated from society that the principle of the "division of labor" would be threatened. He therefore proposed that public attention be given to the education of the poor "in order to prevent the almost entire corruption and degeneracy of the great body of the people" (pp. 340–43). The best system of schooling, according to Smith, was the Scottish system of parish schools where compulsory education was established. Regarding the costs involved, Smith had the following to say:

> The expense of the institutions for education . . . is . . . , no doubt, beneficial to the whole society, and may, therefore, without injustice, be defrayed by the general contribution of the whole society. This expense, however, might perhaps with equal propriety, and even with some advantage, be defrayed altogether by those who receive the immediate benefit of such education and institution, or by the voluntary contribution of those who think they have occasion for either the one or the other. (P. 357)

Marshall (1961) made an explicit differentiation between the direct and the indirect benefits:

> It is true that there are many kinds of work which can be done as efficiently by an uneducated as by an educated workman: and that the higher branches of education are of little direct use except to employers and foremen and a comparatively small number of artisans. But a good education confers great indirect benefits even on the ordinary workman. It stimulates his mental activity; it fosters in him a habit of wise inquisitiveness; it makes him more intelligent, more ready, more trustworthy in his ordinary work; it raises the tone of his life in working hours and out of working hours; it is thus an important means towards the production of material wealth; at the same time that, regarded as an end in itself, it is inferior to none of those which the production of material wealth can be made to subserve. (I: 211)

He then pointed out that education not only helps the individual to improve life within each social class but also acts as a buffer between social classes. It is the means to achieve social mobility and to the discovery of "latent abilities" of those who would otherwise "have died unknown." His argument for public support of education is based, in part, on the alleged existence of indirect, or external, benefits:

> We may then conclude that the wisdom of expending public and private funds on education is not to be measured by its direct fruits alone. It will be profitable as a mere investment, to give the masses of the people much greater opportunities than they can generally avail themselves of . . . . And the economic value of one great industrial genius is sufficient to cover the expenses of the education of a whole town . . . . All that is spent during many years in opening the means of higher education to the masses would be well paid for if it called out one more Newton or Darwin, Shakespeare or Beethoven. (I: 216)

Another benefit of education was considered to be its effect on limiting the growth of population. Malthus was particularly concerned about the "population explosion," which, if unchecked, would keep the masses at a mere subsistence level. Hence it was Malthus who regarded education as a worthwhile investment if it could, indeed, provide the "means of inculcating habits which would lead to family limitation." Malthus also maintained that education is necessary to assure "civil liberty" and thus "generate prudential habits" (cited in Vaizey, 1962: 19). John Stuart Mill followed the same avenue:

> For the purpose therefore of altering the habits of the labouring people . . .
> an effective national education of the children of the labouring class, is the

first thing needful. . . . It may be asserted without scruple, that the aim of all intellectual training for the mass of the people should be to cultivate common sense; to qualify them for forming a sound practical judgment of the circumstances by which they are surrounded. . . . An education directed to diffuse good sense among the people, with such knowledge as would qualify them to judge of the tendencies of their actions, would be certain, even without any direct inculcation, to raise up a public opinion by which intemperance and improvidence of every kind would be held discreditable. (Cited in Vaizey, 1962: 20)

Even earlier writers saw great benefit in public education. As E.A.J. Johnson (1964) points out, Sir William Petty held the view that "talent . . . is widespread, not necessarily concentrated in a politically-favored elite." Accordingly, Petty believed that "schools and universities ought therefore to be made 'a Publick Charge' so that the really able might be selected as scholars rather than let the 'fond conceits' of privileged parents flood the schools and colleges with dullards. However, to be certain that no talent is lost by family misfortune, the state should support and properly educate all orphans" (Johnson, Rpt. in M.J. Bowman et al., 1968: 27).

Neither did the question of efficiency in schooling escape the attention of early economists. Smith in particular was concerned over the problem of efficiency. The lack of competition among the universities resulted, in Smith's view, in poor instruction. To combat the problem, Smith suggested restoring "competition by a system of basic stipends augmented by payments from the pupil's families." With competition, circumstances will insure that "nothing but what is useful will be taught" (Vaizey, 1962: 16).

EDUCATION AND INCOME

So long as the availability of reliable data on incomes of persons classified by education, age, sex, and so forth was limited, no useful studies of the monetary return to education could be made. Around the turn of the nineteenth century, a number of studies appeared in which the authors attempted to isolate the effect of education on earnings. Such studies were limited in scope and quite crude, but they serve nevertheless as the forerunners of subsequent work in this area of endeavor. A listing of some such studies was prepared by E.A. Caswell (1917). It describes numerous works in which the money value of education to different socioeconomic groups in various locations was assessed. For example, there is a study by James Dodge (1904) in which the monetary value of different grades of schooling was assessed by comparing the earnings of various employees of several large factories differentiated according to common laborers, shop-apprentice-trained men, trade school graduates, and technical school graduates.

The common denominator of all of those studies, according to Gorseline (1932), is their failure explicitly to account for factors other than education. He objected to Caswell's conclusion that "the figures show conclusively that the schools are giving their pupils a greater earning power than even the strongest advocator of education had claimed" (Caswell, 1917: 44) on the ground that most of the studies listed in Caswell's work *"failed to reveal the slightest attempt scientifically to eliminate from the effect of schooling the influence of the other disturbing factors having a bearing on individual income"* (Gorseline, 1932: 19; italics in original).

Gorseline's Study

It is strange, said Gorseline, that Caswell could come to such a strong conclusion while, at the same time, indicating that perhaps an appreciable portion of the monetary returns to education are due to factors other than education. For this reason, Gorseline attempted to provide a method by which the returns to education could be assessed after sufficient account had been taken of "other disturbing factors."

These factors include the native ability of the educated, the opportunities open to him by virtue of family and other connections, age, sex, residence, inheritance, "the money gains due to 'good luck,' the money losses due to 'bad luck,' and the money losses due to bad health." To account for some of these factors, Gorseline undertook to examine a group of Indiana blood brothers, whom he classified into two groups: the "most schooling classes" and the "least schooling classes." By a special technique, he classified those families where there were more than two brothers, still maintaining just two groups as noted above. The use of blood brothers supposedly corrects for differences in inheritance, opportunities, and so forth, but differences due to residence (urban-rural), "good luck," ability, and other factors must be taken into account by a different method.

His methods of taking these factors into account are rather dubious. He compared, separately, his "most schooling classes" with the "least schooling classes" with respect to school grades, success on standard tests, age, change of occupations, residence, marital status, and other factors. And while in almost every comparison the conclusion was "no measurable difference," he merely tested gross differences and not the effect of one factor net of changes in the remaining ones. In other words, although he was conceptually correct in trying to "correct" for various factors, his statistical design was rather primitive.

Comparing incomes of the two groups (one with more schooling than the other) for 1927, the conclusion was that the "most schooling classes" had significantly higher incomes than the other group (both when the mode and when the median were used as a proxy for "central tendency").

Walsh's Study

Another early study on the effects of education upon income was carried out by J.R. Walsh (1935). His study "considers schooling alone (not all education), and schooling of a particular kind—that which trains a man for a career. It attempts to determine whether money spent in acquiring such training is, in a strict sense, a capital investment in a profit-seeking, equalizing market, in response to the same motives which lead to the creation of factories, machinery, and the like" (Walsh, rpt. in M.J. Bowman et al., 1968: 453).

His choice of studying professional training stems from his belief that much of presecondary education is undertaken without much regard to economic returns. "The purpose is to provide political and cultural education in the widest sense." But postsecondary school "is more apt to be undertaken for definitely economic reasons." And although he concedes that some individuals undertake education "for reasons of custom, social prestige, affection, and the like," he contends that the high costs of education to the individual or his parents increase the liklihood that consideration of cost and returns will loom large in the individual's decision on whether and how much additional education ought to be undertaken (pp. 453–54).

To test this assertion, he made use of a study made for the Alpha Kappa Psi fraternity in 1926. This study provided information on some 15,000 persons of various educational levels and occupations concerning the age, annual earnings, and educational levels of these individuals. In addition, data on age and earnings of 23,000 graduates of the land grant colleges (up to 1929) were also available. Three other sources of data were also used in his study.

Walsh then proceeded to estimate both the returns and the costs of the educational investment. Using a discount rate of 4 percent, the stream of future incomes was discounted, account being taken of mortality in accordance with an appropriate life table (this is, essentially, the same method as presented above in Equation [2.1]).

Next, Walsh computed the "average cost of the various grades of education whose values have been computed. . . . The expenses included:

1. Tuition, fees, and the like, paid to the school.
2. Board and room.
3. Equipment, such as books, and the like.
4. Personal expenses: clothes, recreation, travel.
5. Loss of that income which would, on the average, have been earned if the individual had not continued in school. From this amount was deducted the estimated average earnings of students during the school year and vacation periods.
6. Annual cumulative interest at 4 per cent on the sum of the above."
   (P. 456)

Although some of the costs included in this impressive list (in particular, items 2 and 4) present some conceptual difficulties, Walsh's treatment of costs is quite comprehensive.

The results of the empirical work are conflicting. For some professions and educational investments, the benefits exceed the costs. In others, the reverse is true. And instead of questioning the initial hypothesis—namely, that market forces operate in the market for education in much the same manner as they operate in other markets—Walsh preferred to justify the cases where negative returns occur by attributing nonpecuniary values to those professions. In essence, then, he contended that positive returns are due to equalizing market forces, whereas negative returns are due to the existence of nonmonetary benefits. For example, "the training represented by the M.A. and Ph.D. degrees has a value less than cost. This is to be expected when only monetary returns are considered. The holders of these degrees are for the most part teachers. Their vocation possesses special satisfactions and 'net advantages'" (pp. 460–61). A similar argument is made with respect to physicians.

SUMMARY AND CONCLUSIONS

Although we have only touched upon early doctrines concerning education and human capital, it may be concluded that while the importance of human capital was recognized by most writers, few had come to accept human capital as "wealth" in the same sense that material capital was accepted.

The early attempts to estimate the monetary value of humans were inherently inadequate, due in large measure to a fundamental misconception about the relationship between value and cost. But the capitalized earnings approach utilized by Farr, Petty, and Dublin and Lotka is, in principle, the very same approach used now by various writers to estimate the value of various investments in human capital.

The discussion of educational benefits and the role of government began centuries ago and continues unabated to this date. Early views in large measure reflect current controversies on the same issues, although the issues themselves have become much more complex.

Gorseline's and Walsh's studies indicate early interest in the economic value of education, where the latter is measured by the observed income differentials that exist, allegedly, due to education. Walsh's methodology, involving discounting of earnings streams and deduction of costs, together with Gorseline's attempt to adjust earnings differentials for various "disturbing factors," constitute a major portion of present-day effort in the same area of endeavor.

In conclusion, it appears that current ideas in the economics of education are not novel. Nor are they new; rather, it is the refinement of tools, data, and concepts—as well as the intensification of study in the area of human resources—that has so revolutionized modern economic thought.

LITERATURE GUIDE

The single best reference on this topic is Kiker (1966). A somewhat more expanded analysis (but more difficult to find) is Kiker (1968b). Other relatively general accounts of the topic include Dublin and Lotka (1946), Kiker (1967), W.L. Miller (1966), Tu (1969), Vaizey (1962: ch. 1), and West (1975b).

More specialized analyses include Cochrane and Kiker (1970), Kiker (1968a, 1969, 1974), Kiker and Cochrane (1973), Lord (1928), Spengler (1977), Thurow (1970: ch. 1), and West (1964, 1967, 1970b, and 1975a). See also selections of classical excerpts in M.J. Bowman et al. (1968).

Chapter 3

The Benefits of Education

> The direction in which education starts a man will determine his future life.
> Plato

> Educated men are as much superior to uneducated men as the living are to the dead.
> Aristotle

> Education is the best provision for old age.
> Aristotle

The importance of education has been emphasized since days of old. Education is often regarded as the single most important determinant of a person's economic and social success. A recent study of occupational prestige (reported in an NBC Nightly News program) placed highly educated persons (doctors, professors, etc.) at the top of the prestige ranking.

Our task here is not to question the intrinsic (moral, religious, as well as material) value of education but rather to provide an evaluation of the economic benefits of education. It is also necessary to provide an impartial description of views critical to the prevailing assertion that education is highly related to income and success.

The chapter begins with a discussion of alternative models employed to explain labor income variations in the population. We then provide a more detailed analysis of the "human capital" approach, beginning with a classification of educational benefits and followed by approaches to measuring the benefits of education and a discussion concerning the problems in providing complete and reliable measures of educational benefits.

THEORIES OF INCOME DISTRIBUTION

It is no secret that different people earn different amounts of labor income. The obvious question is, Why? The answer, unfortunately, is not quite so obvious, and scholars have been at odds on which theory provides the most plausible explanation. We will discuss four theories: human capital, credentialism, labor market segmentation, and radical views.

The Human Capital Approach

The basic premise of the human capital approach is that variations in labor income are due, in part, to differences in labor quality in terms of the amount of human capital acquired by the workers. Therefore, if one wishes to reduce income inequality, one method to achieve this would be to reduce inequality in the investments people make in human capital (health, education, on the job training, other vocational training, etc.). A simple description of the process is illustrated in Figure 3-1, where A (investment in human capital) leads to B (higher productivity of workers) which in turn causes C (higher earnings). This is consistent with "orthodox" economic theory, better known as the marginal productivity theory, which argues that wages are determined according to the worker's marginal contribution to the revenues of the firm, implying that more productive workers will be paid more, other things equal.

Another important facet of the human capital approach deals with investment in on the job training and the criteria determining who will pay for such training and who will benefit therefrom. Based on the pioneering work of G.S. Becker (1962, 1964), a distinction is made between "general" and "specific" training. "General" training refers to training that provides valuable knowledge and skills to workers usable both within the present employment (where training takes place) and in other employments. On the other hand, "specific" training has value only within the current employment and is totally irrelevant for the worker's productivity in other firms. In the first instance, the theory predicts that the worker will be willing to pay for general training (in the form of reduced income during the training period) and that the employer would be willing to (in fact he must) pay the worker a higher wage following training. On the other hand, the worker is not likely to agree to pay for specific training, and likewise, the employer is not likely to pay a higher wage to a worker trained in such a manner. This last conclusion is altered to some extent when it is recognized that employers investing in the specific training of workers would be reluctant to let them go and

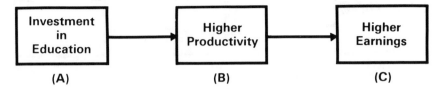

Figure 3-1. The Human Capital Approach.

thus are likely to pay them a wage somewhat higher than the competitive wage (how much higher depends on the relative bargaining strengths of the two sides). Similarly, the worker may not object to paying for some of this specific training when it is realized that such training would bring a return in the form of greater job security and higher wages. Empirical corroborations of this view are numerous. The work of Mincer (1970, 1974) is particularly worthy of mention here.

The Screening (Or Credentialism) Hypothesis

A book was published in 1970 by I. Berg in which the human capital approach was branded as a "Great Training Robbery." Joining Berg, Arrow (1973), Spence (1973), Taubman and Wales (1973), and Stiglitz (1975) have argued that a different connection between education and income might exist, as illustrated in Figure 3-2. The main difference between Figures 3-1 and 3-2 is the "connecting" stage B. In the human capital approach, it is greater labor productivity; in the screening approach, it is just the acquisition of a diploma or a credential. It is argued that educational achievement—or the acquisition of training—may not have a significant effect on productivity. However, since persons selected for an educational (or training) program possess the kinds of attributes sought by employers, higher earnings are paid even if no productivity effect is descernible. Education thus becomes merely a selection or signaling device (Spence, 1973), and a correlation between education and earnings is no proof of the human capital theory.

A number of writers have questioned the relevance of the screening hypothesis. Layard and Psacharopoulos (1974) contend that the persistence of the education-income relationship over the life cycle of earnings contradicts the screening hypothesis, and that the signaling argument, if true, would surely call for the development of far less expensive means by which ability and other personality traits could be discovered. Similar arguments are raised by Psacharopoulos (1974) and Chiswick (1973), and evidence of a positive relationship between educational achievement and job performance is presented

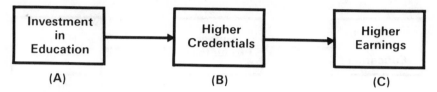

Figure 3-2.   The Screening (Credentialism) Hypothesis.

by D.A. Wise (1975). Work by Wolpin (1974, 1977) brings further evidence against the screening hypothesis. These arguments are seriously challenged, however, by Lazear (1977a). At this writing, the argument is far from being settled.

The Dual Labor Market Hypothesis

Another challenge to the human capital approach comes from the proponents of the labor market segmentation theory. The argument brought here is that the human capital approach is correct only for certain segments of the labor force. For other segments, mainly minorities and poor persons, the theory does not apply. The segmentation hypothesis, in its simplest form known as the "dual" theory after the works of Piore and Doeringer, argues that the labor market is segmented into two parts: the "primary" and "secondary" labor markets.[1] The primary labor market consists of individuals who are admitted to training slots and job ladders holding promise of economic and job mobility. The secondary market consists of workers who are hired, usually on a temporary basis, for whom good training slots are not open and who are not likely to receive good ladder type positions no matter what their stock of education and training happens to be.

According to the dualists (or segmentists), the connection between education and income, as described in Figure 3-1, is not related to worker productivity per se, but rather to some key characteristics that distinguish workers who are admitted to the primary labor market from those who are not so fortunate. The result, again, is some kind of a "screening" process, but the implications differ. In the screening hypothesis, education and income are related, albeit not because of changes in productivity but rather due to the use by employers of educational credentials as a selection device. In the segmentation hypothesis, on the other hand, the very relationship between education and income is questioned, since such a relationship does not hold for persons admitted only to secondary labor markets.

1. See, e.g., Doeringer and Piore (1971, 1975), Piore (1971, 1972), and Reich, Gordon and Edwards (1973). Critical reviews of this theory are summarized in Cain (1976).

Programs such as federal training, compensatory education, and the like would do little to alleviate the disadvantageous position of blacks and other groups.

Even proponents of the human capital approach, such as Albert Rees (1968: 11), appear to recognize the validity of the segementation hypothesis. Rees describes the Chicago labor market area as a single labor market but with a number of geographic submarkets, marked by wage differences related to patterns of residential and nonresidential areas, concentrations of particular kinds of industry, and concentrations of nonwhite population. He is not persuaded, however, that a depressed secondary labor market is an inevitable feature of America's capitalism, believing instead that a free enterprise economy with full employment and without discrimination in employment "could perhaps wipe out much of the present low-wage, dead-end job syndrom" (Rees, 1973: 143).

In a critical evaluation of the labor market segmentation (LMS) hypothesis, Cain (1976) discusses a number of conceptual and statistical difficulties with that approach. He argues that LMS proponents have examined what he terms the "intensive margin" (that is, the relationship between educational resources and labor market success, when years of education are held constant) but have not successfully refuted the human capital theory in terms of what he calls the "extensive margin" (that is, the relationship between years of schooling and labor market success). He proceeds to cite several studies that have tested the LMS hypothesis using recent data,[2] concluding that there is no hard empirical evidence in support of the LMS theory other than anectodal information. Moreover, Cain claims that the use of truncated samples, in which the education-earnings relationship is examined separately for low and high earners, biases the results and may be the reason why some of the studies by LMS theorists show a weak education-income relationship for low earners.

The Radical Approach

A totally different explanation, in a neo-Marxist style, is provided by proponents of the radical approach. Notable among such proponents is Bowles (1972a, 1972b; also Bowles and Gintis, 1975, 1976), who has argued repeatedly that the main explanatory factor of income inequality is family background, or as he prefers to call it, social class. Education is viewed as a vehicle by which the wealth of

---

2. See, for example, Freiman (1976), Leigh (1976a, 1976b), and Wachter (1974).

the upper classes is transmitted from generation to generation. Rather than serve as equalizer of opportunity, public education trains the masses to act according to the wishes of the capitalists (and therefore schools teach discipline, punctuality, and mannerism while eschewing independent thinking and creativity). Since members of the elite typically attend private schools (where such norms are not emphasized), public education serves the interests of the elite and therefore cannot be considered as a medium of social and economic change.

In his 1972 papers, Bowles argues that the effect of education on income is very small when "social class" is appropriately taken into account. Thus, not only do the radicals question the education-income mechanism, they seem to be questioning the very existence of the relationship. A critic of the radical approach, G.S. Becker (1972) claims (in a comment on Bowles's 1972 paper) that the evidence presented by Bowles is rather shaky and that the term "social class" is not sufficiently accurate to support a Marxist interpreation of income inequality. Marshall, Cartter, and King (1976) claim that the radical approach is not amenable to empirical verification—unlike the preceding theories—because it is based on a dialectical interpreation of history. Therefore, it is impossible to either prove or disprove the validity of the radical theory.[3]

Conclusion

Although we are unable to refute the theories presented by credentialists, labor market segmentists, or radical economists, the evidence in support of the conventional human capital theory is so overwhelming that we think it proper to concentrate our attention on that approach. That is not to say, however, that we can afford to overlook the important questions and issues raised by critics of the human capital approach. In any event, a thorough understanding of the human capital approach and the evidence accumulated in its support is a prerequisite for analyzing the three theories which have been presented as alternatives to the human capital approach.

TAXONOMY OF EDUCATIONAL BENEFITS

In his outstanding book, *The Economic Value of Education*, T.W. Schultz (1963) lists a number of categories of educational benefits. These include the benefits the economy obtains from educational research, the cultivation and discovery of (potential) talent, increased

---

3. See also Blaug (1976a) for a critical review of Bowles and Gintis (1976).

"capability of people to adjust to changes in job opportunities," the preparation of teachers (a self-sustaining activity), and the provision of manpower for sustained economic growth (pp. 39–42). In addition, schooling provides for better citizenship, the ability to appreciate and recognize a wider range of cultural and other services, reduced reliance on the market for such services as the filing of income tax returns, and a chance to give the next generation better education and, therefore, a better future.

The benefits that education bestows on an individual can conveniently be classified into "consumption" and "investment." A product or service is considered to belong to the consumption category when it yields satisfaction (or utility) in a single period only. It would be called a pure investment good (or service) when it is expected to yield satisfaction in future periods only. In between we have goods and services that are both consumption and investment goods—that is, they yield satisfaction now and expect to yield some satisfaction in the future as well. Education is a product that is best characterized by the "in between" classification. It yields satisfaction to the student at the time the education is given, and it also provides for increased utility over time in the form of increased productivity, greater capacity to enjoy things, and so on.

The Consumption Component

Even a young child who is forced by law to attend school receives consumption benefits from education. Indeed, the child might state that he "hates school." But when compared to the alternatives to being in school, the latter is most likely to be strongly preferred. This is not necessarily true of everyone, but for large groups of pupils, the consumption element is probably significantly positive. The magnitude of the consumption element is likely to increase as the student begins his college education. We take pains to emphasize this point because all too often studies on educational benefits have excluded consumption effects.

The Investment Component

Most studies on the economic benefits of education have emphasized the investment component. But here, too, there has been an important omission. Indeed, the increased capacity to earn income is a very real benefit of education. Schooling and training increase one's productivity and as such increase his chances, in a free market, to obtain higher wages—and certainly increase his contribution to the social product. An individual who obtains more schooling, general education in particular, is more flexible in adapting to new job opportunities, thus providing him a "hedge" against unemployment. But another form of investment exists—namely, the future stream of "consumption" that a given amount of education could be expected to produce. That is, since education opens new horizons to the student, introducing him to hitherto unknown works of literature, music, and the arts and enabling him to comprehend material that he could not be expected to master otherwise, a student is likely to experience increased consumption in the form of greater utility derived from his leisure. This may be offset, in some measure, by reduced leisure time associated with the increased demands that his job and position in the community entail (these would have been much different had he chosen to undertake less education.)[4] But on the whole it seems probable that significantly positive returns would accrue in the form of future consumption benefits (another such benefit is the enjoyment one gets from his job, which would, no doubt, be different if the individual did not reach the same educational level).

Private Versus Social Benefits

Educational benefits may be further classified according to the incidence of the benefits. "Private" benefits are those benefits that are retained by the individual being educated. Social benefits, on the other hand, also include benefits that the individual cannot appropriate and that are therefore absorbed by other members of society. Generally, since the person being educated is a member of society, the private benefits are included in the social benefits. The social benefits, then, are the sum of the private benefits and other benefits (which the individual cannot capture).

There are basically two types of benefits that belong in the social but not to the private domain. They include (1) tax payments associated with the educational benefit (i.e., income taxes paid out of one's lifetime income stream), and (2) "external" benefits, which are those benefits that are due to the educational investment but that the individual cannot capture.

An example of the external benefits of education is the ability of the government to rely on individual filing of income tax returns, which would be impossible to achieve without general literacy. Similarly, mass production of books and magazines, resulting in the availability of a great variety of such media at a relatively low per unit cost, is another result of education. One could continue to

---

4. Morgan and David (1963) assert that with more education people also tend to enjoy more leisure time.

enumerate numerous other daily functions that are taken for granted but that would be impossible to accomplish without an educated population. Perhaps the most important external benefit of education is the development of an informed citizenry, without which democratic institutions could not survive.

There is little argument about the *types* of external benefits associated with elementary and secondary education. An excellent discussion of this topic is contained in two studies by Weisbrod (1962, 1964; see also J.R. Davis, 1970.) The externality argument in Weisbrod's work is not limited to a discussion of the difference between educational benefits to an individual as opposed to society, but also of the difference between educational benefits derived by a single local community as opposed to society in a more aggregated sense (i.e., school district versus the state, or the state versus the nation). There is growing discontent among economists, however, with the assumption that higher education bestows unusually large external benefits (when compared to noneducational activities), placing the burden of proof on those who argue that such external benefits do exist.

The problem is not confined to estimating external benefits of education. Although some attempts have been made to illustrate the magnitude of the external benefits of education,[5] it is not clear whether such external effects are really external. As Hansen (1973) points out, it is possible that when an individual obtains an education that this activity will benefit other individuals in society. But if such benefits are generally confined to persons who also have completed the same educational level, the aggregate external benefits are totally captured by the group of educated persons and are therefore, in a sense, really private (or internalized) benefits. Hansen argues, therefore, that we need estimate not only what external benefits are but also how they are distributed among different groups in society.

Whether external benefits exist or not, they are rarely included in empirical estimates of educational benefits. Thus, in practice, the difference between social and private benefits amounts to tax payments that, although a part of an individual's earnings, represent a portion of society's returns to education in that the individual is unable to retain them and therefore they are not included in *private* benefits.

---

5. There are very few empirical studies on external effects. Weisbrod's work (1962, 1964) provides the first attempt at measuring indirect and external effects. Two other studies contain data illustrating the decline in crime rates for persons possessing more education (see Spiegleman, 1968, and Webb, 1977).

Other Educational Benefits

There are a host of additional benefits of education that most studies neglect to mention. One such benefit is what Weisbrod terms the financial option open to students. This option refers to the fact that the completion of one level of schooling gives the student the opportunity to undertake the next step in education. (According to Mincer [1962], increased amount of schooling is also associated with the option of getting increasing amounts of on the job training.)

A second class of options is Weisbrod's nonfinancial options. For instance, a college professor has some nonfinancial advantages associated with his position. These include not only the degree of freedom and flexibility in work, but also the daily contact with students, the joy of teaching and research, and so on. It is not surprising that a large number of individuals who have the capacity for both teaching and industrial work (research, management, etc.) choose teaching in a college or university despite the generally lower salaries (i.e., financial return) in the latter. The monetary value of these nonfinancial options could conceptually be measured by the difference between the wage that the individual could have earned and that which he actually earns. Other options of this sort include the "hedging option" (i.e., the flexibility of educated individuals in adapting to new job opportunities) and the "nonmarket option" (i.e., the fact that with education an individual can perform a variety of activities that he could not have done without it). Weisbrod's example is the filing of income tax returns, for which sufficient competence in arithmetic and other skills is required. Weisbrod (1962: 114) performed some interesting calculations indicating that the savings to the total population in the United States realized in this manner amounted to at least $250 million in 1956, suggesting "a current-year return of 3.2 per cent of current investment" (p. 114) in elementary school. Other activities falling within the nonmarket category include typewriting and driving.

Intergeneration Effects

In addition to the various direct and indirect returns, one must consider possible educational benefits that will be felt only a generation later. The alleged intergeneration effects of education stem mainly from studies showing that persons are more likely to complete a given level of education if their parents are (or were) more highly educated. The intergenerational effect is the increment in a person's education that can be ascribed to the incremental education of the parent. As we shall soon observe, increased education results in increased potential income. Hence, we could trace some of the higher expected earnings of the children back to their origin in the increased educational investment by the parents. Therefore, if we confine our investigation of the benefits of education to the parents only, some (perhaps serious) underestimation of benefits would result. One needs to guard, however, against the possibility that double counting on a person's educational benefits will take place—once in the calculation of one's own educational investment and then once more in claculating intergenerational benefits.[6]

We have elaborated on many aspects of educational benefits in the foregoing pages. We have stressed the economic benefits (monetary or nonmonetary) that education bestows. Surely there are many noneconomic considerations. This is not to deny the applicability of such factors in any decisionmaking model of education. As stated earlier, however, the emphasis here is on economic benefits.

APPROACHES TO MEASURING THE BENEFITS OF EDUCATION

Three general approaches to measuring educational benefits are considered here: (1) the simple correlation approach; (2) the residual approach; and (3) the returns to education approach.

The Simple Correlation Approach

A number of scholars have noted a striking correlation between measures of educational attainment or expenditures and income. Such results are obtained both for cross-country studies and for time series (longitudinal) and cross-sectional (state-by-state, for example) studies for the United States. Such studies suggest that education and income are somehow associated with one another. They do not explain why such a relation exists. It is not clear whether higher income permits a country, a state, other political subdivisions, or individuals to spend more on education or whether higher investments in education are, in part, a cause of higher income in future years. It is possible that both are true: higher incomes permit more education; and more education results, in time, in higher incomes. A careful analysis will have to take into account a complex model that explains such interactions and allows for lags in the effect of education on income.

Another possible avenue for research is to study the effect of the education of workers on the profitability and productivity of enter-

6. For discussions of intergenerational effects consult, e.g., Brazer and David (1962), Morgan et al. (1962), Swift and Weisbrod (1965), and Ribich (1968: 101-107).

prises or industries. Several attempts at measuring the effect of labor quality (education) on productivity were undertaken in recent years, showing a clear and positive relationship between education and productivity. Examples of such studies include Besen (1968), Griliches (1970), Welch (1970), and D.A. Wise (1975).

Although quite important, the simple correlation approach does not provide the data necessary for the selection of "optimal" educational investments among sets of alternative strategies. Since economists have focused attention on educational decisionmaking and financial strategies, it is not surprising that this avenue has not been much pursued.

The Residual Approach

A number of scholars, in studying the dynamics of economic growth, noted that a large portion of economic growth remains unexplained when classical inputs (land, labor, and capital) are enumerated. One possible explanation for this "residual" phenomenon is that classical inputs include only the quantity of labor, not its quality. Changes in output due to changes in labor quality (and other unspecified factors) would then be left unexplained.

The relationship between education and economic growth is sufficiently important to warrant a comprehensive treatment. In addition, a number of studies on the contribution of education to economic growth are based on the returns to education approach. We shall therefore devote a complete chapter to this issue (Chapter 7), after we have described in some detail the direct returns approach, the costs of education (Chapter 4), and benefit-cost analyses (Chapters 5 and 6).

The Direct Returns to Education Approach

This approach is based upon the premise that education results in direct, measurable returns to the individual and society. Although returns to individuals should be measured according to satisfaction derived now and in the future, data and conceptual problems have forced researchers to define returns in terms of income or earnings alone.

Age Earnings Profiles: In his famous book, G. S. Becker (1964) argues that earnings vary over an individual's life cycle according to a typical age-earnings profile. Such a profile typically suggests low earnings while the individual is young and inexperienced, higher earnings up to a peak in middle life, and lower earnings afterwards. More importantly, the height of the age-earnings profile would vary according to the educational level of the individual, with successive upwards shifts in the profile being associated with higher levels of education.

It should be noted that higher educational levels do not result in an upward shift of the profile uniformly for all relevant ages. Consider two educational investments: high school versus college. Suppose the person under discussion has completed twelve years of schooling and has an expected age-earnings profile as shown in Figure 3–3. If he decides to undertake four more years of schooling, he will have little or no income during the next four years (ages eighteen to twenty-one. It is possible that earnings at age twenty-two would be higher for the high school graduate, when on the job experience and training more than compensate for the completion of four years of college education. The Current Population Survey (CPS) data, depicted in Figure 3–3, show this to be true, and other studies (such as Blaug, 1970: ch. 2) clearly illustrate the strong likelihood of such an occurrence.

We note that the peak of the higher profile is at a higher age (fifty-seven) than is the case for the lower profile (age forty-seven). This might be explained in at least two ways. First, occupations involving higher levels of education require less physical stamina and more intellectual ability. People face greater depreciation of "human capital" in the physical than in the mental sense as time goes on. Second, as Mincer (1974) shows, higher educational levels also

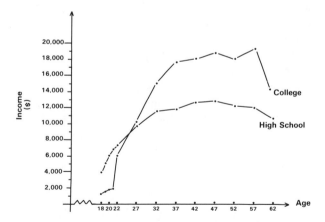

Figure 3–3. Age-Earning profiles, in current income, for white males, United States, 1973.
Source: Freeman (1976), Table A-1, derived from Current Population Report Survey Tapes, March 1974.

imply increasing amounts of on the job training. In consequence, the individuals with higher levels of education continue to receive a return on their education and subsequent training long after less-educated persons reached their peak earnings.

Earnings Differentials: The age-earnings profile can be used to derive the difference between the earnings of the higher education group and the earnings of the lower education group. In Figure 3-3, for example, we can calculate, for each age, the difference between the earnings of a college graduate and the earnings of a high school graduate. For ages eighteen to twenty-one the earnings differentials are negative—that is, earnings of high school graduates exceed earnings of college graduates. This is as one would expect it to be. The same is also true for age twenty-two, and the result is plausible as explained earlier. The "breakeven point"—that is the age where incomes of the two groups are equal—is around age twenty-five, when both graduates expect to earn (in 1973) approximately $9,000. Beyond that age, we get positive earnings differentials, and these differentials increase in magnitude (except at age forty-two) till age fifty-seven. Income differentials for 1973 are provided in column 3 of Table 3-1.

Lifetime Income Differentials: Using the income differentials in Table 3-1, one can calculate the lifetime income differentials associated with college education. Since we do not have income data for each age, but rather for age groups (thus, for example, age twenty-seven in Figure 3-3 represents average income for the age group twenty-five to twenty-nine), it will be necessary to make some simplifying assumptions. Specifically, we will assume for the sake of this exercise that earnings for ages twenty-three and twenty-four are equal to the average of the earnings for ages twenty-two and twenty-seven and that the average income for the other age groups is relevant for each of the ages within that age group. The calculation of lifetime incomes associated with college education, assuming that no income is earned after age sixty-four, is given in column 5 of Table 3-1. The total lifetime earnings differential associated with completion of four years of college, for white males in 1973, using Census cross-sectional data, is $174,055. This compares with $144,280 for 1968. Similar calculations may be performed for other educational investments, using data on income that are cross-classified by age and education.

The most comprehensive sources of such data have been the decenial *U.S. Census* and *Current Population Reports.* The Bureau

Table 3-1.   Income Differentials by Age, and Lifetime Income Differentials for College Versus High School Education—United States, White Males, 1973 (in current dollars).

Age Group	Income College	Income High School	Income Differential (1) - (2)	Years at Age Group	Total Income Differentials for Age Group (3) × (4)
	(1)	(2)	(3)	(4)	(5)
18	$ 1,244	$ 3,907	$-2,663	1	$ -2,663
19	1,523	5,188	-3,665	1	-3,665
20	1,824	6,100	-4,267	1	-4,267
21	1,963	6,954	-4,991	1	-4,991
22	6,107	7,265	-1,158	1	-1,158
23-24[a]	8,175	8,483	- 308	3	- 924
25-29	10,242	9,702	540	5	2,700
30-34	15,113	11,618	3,495	5	17,475
35-39	17,684	11,827	5,857	5	29,285
40-44	18,265	12,680	5,585	5	27,925
45-49	18,806	12,945	5,861	5	29,305
50-54	18,194	12,315	5,879	5	29,395
55-59	19,459	12,059	7,400	5	37,000
60-64	14,356	10,860	3,496	5	17,480
Total				48	$174,055

Source: Columns (1) and (2) from Freeman (1976), Table A-1.
[a]Income for this age group is not given in source and was derived by linear interpolation (see text).

of the Census also makes available survey tapes from which various configurations of lifetime income (including Table 3-1) may be derived. A summary of Census Bureau estimates of lifetime earnings by education, for the years 1957-1972, is provided in Table 3-2. We note that the lifetime earnings differentials associated with completion of four years of college in 1972 (in comparison to completion of four years of high school) are $231,696, a figure considerably larger than what we derived on the basis of Freeman's data for 1973. One reason for the difference is that the data in Table 3-2 are from age eighteen to death, whereas Table 3-1 is for age eighteen to sixty-five. (The median income differential per year for the age group sixty-five and over is $2,771 for 1974.) In addition, there are differences in the composition of the samples used to derive the two data sets, and differences in income are therefore likely to arise.

We note that the data in Table 3-2 are not suitable for calculating lifetime income differentials associated with every educational investment represented in this table. For example, additional

Table 3-2.   Lifetime Income of Men, Age Eighteen to Death, by Years of School Completed—United States, Selected Years, 1956-1972 (in current dollars).

Years of School Completed	1956	1961	1964	1968	1972
Elementary:					
Less than 8 years	$131,432	$151,881	$170,145	$213,505	$279,997
8 years	178,749	205,237	223,946	276,755	343,730
High school:					
1 to 3 years	201,825	235,865	255,701	308,305	389,208
4 years	244,158	273,614	311,462	371,094	478,873
College:					
1 to 3 years	278,227	335,100	355,249	424,280	543,435
4 years or more	372,644	454,732	478,696	607,921	757,923
4 years	a	432,617	459,482	584,062	710,569
5 years or more	a	475,116	500,641	636,119	823,759

Source: Reproduced from Grant and Lind (1977), Table 18. Based upon Bureau of Census data of sample surveys of households.
[a]Data not available.

lifetime earnings associated with completion of four years of high school (in comparison with only eight years of elementary education) should be calculated from age fourteen, not age eighteen. And the benefits of postgraduate college training (in comparison with only four years of college) require estimation of lifetime income from age twenty-two. The data in Table 3-2, therefore, provide only general orders of magnitude regarding lifetime income associated with completion of various levels of education. One must use the raw data for specific studies.

PROBLEMS IN THE MEASUREMENT OF EDUCATIONAL BENEFITS

The direct returns to education approach is based on the presumption that one could calculate ex post or ex ante lifetime income differentials due to education. Of particular interest to individuals contemplating educational investment or to government agencies is the expected returns to education. A number of qeustions arise concerning the use of census and other survey data in providing such estimates, including the use of cross-sectional data, adjustments for "ability" and other nonschool variables, measurement of nonpecuniary and external benefits, and other conceptual and statistical problems.

Cross-Section Versus Life Cycle Data

Most studies on the economic returns to education are based on cross-sectional analysis. In essence, a snapshot of the income-age-education relationship is taken at a given moment, let us say, 1973. We observe, in 1973, numerous individuals of different ages, schooling, and income and tabulate a cross-classification of income by age and education. We then develop lifetime income differentials associated with a given level of education (as was done in the preceding section) by assuming that the cross-section could be projected into the future. For example, if the average income of a person sixty-two years of age who completed four years of college was $14,356 in 1973, it is assumed that a person who was eighteen in 1973 can expect to earn $14,356 when he will reach age sixty, in the year 2015, provided he obtained four years of college education.

The life cycle (also known as cohort) approach, on the other hand, is based on longitudinal income data for the same individual or group of people. One could use successive census data (for example, from 1930 to 1978) for individuals who were eighteen in 1930 and sixty in 1978 to derive data on income by age and education and thence lifetime income differentials due to education. Such lifetime income differentials could then be projected into the future.

Each method has advantages and disadvantages. The cross-sectional approach is deficient because it presupposes a constant age-education-income relationship over time. In a dynamic world, one would expect this relationship to change over time in response to changes in relative supplies of educated labor and relative demand for them. Specifically, it is likely that economic growth would shift the age-earnings profile upward over time. An example of such an occurrence has been documented by H.P. Miller (1965), and Figure 3–4 illustrates his findings. Whereas a cross-sectional approach, based upon the 1950 census, would lead one to expect the income of a college graduate aged forty to be $9,853 in 1960, the 1960 census data show that his income should be $11,590. We observe a significant shift in the cross-section between 1950 and 1960, illustrating the degree to which cross-sectional studies are likely to under-estimate lifetime earnings by education during periods of economic growth.

At the same time, not only are longitudinal data unavailable at this time for the construction of complete life cycle income-age profiles, there are also significant conceptual problems associated with their use. First, it is necessary to adjust such income data for changes in the price level. Although there are a number of price indexes available for this task, the longer the period for which such indexes are used, the less reliable will the adjustment be. Second,

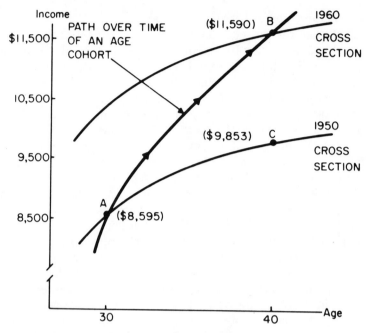

Figure 3-4. A Comparison of Cross-Section and Cohort Methods for Estimating Lifetime Earnings.
Source: Adapted from H.P. Miller (1965), Figure 1; and Ben-Porath (1966), Figure 1.

longitudinal data are affected by fluctuations in the business cycle, by the effect of wars and domestic crises, and by various other variables that may not be easily isolated. Some adjustment is certainly possible using multivariate analysis, but longitudinal data will contain a significant potential of error that is totally absent from cross-sectional data.

There is a lack of sufficient life cycle data to estimate complete age-earnings profiles. However, there is no reason why one may not attempt to combine cross-sectional and longitudinal data, to the extent available, to derive superior estimates. As a matter of fact, a number of recent studies have already done so to a greater or lesser extent, and additional use of the idea is certain to continue in the future, especially due to the fact that new and improved microdata sets are being made available on a longitudinal basis.

Education, Ability, and Earnings

Supposing that we are able to estimate lifetime income associated with different levels of education, can we also argue that these income differentials are due to education? Is it not possible that a portion (or all) of the earnings differentials are due to differences in ability, motivation, socioeconomic and environmental characteristics of individuals, and other nonschool factors—all of which happen to correlate with years of school completed?

The Earnings Function. These questions imply the need to specify what economists call an "earnings function." The earnings function is a mathematical expression relating earnings to variables that are likely to affect them, the shape of the function being determined by a priori formulation based on the theory of human capital.

Let Y denote earnings. Then a generalized earnings function is given by

$Y = f$ (age, sex, race, education, experience, ability, motivation, socioeconomic background, religion, veteran status, region of birth and current residence, quality of education received, parental background, health status, and other relevant variables).

In practice it is difficult to obtain sufficient information to estimate such an equation, so that a more modest subset of variables is typically included.

Much of the empirical work published during the last ten years has been aimed at improving the specification of the earnings function. In particular, a good deal of effort has been expended to include measures of "ability" in the earnings function. Table 3-3 presents a summary of ability measures employed by several researchers (no attempt is made here to be exhaustive.)

A serious question, posed by Arrow (1973), is whether "ability" measures, such as IQ or other mental ability tests, also reflect an individual's ability to earn a higher wage in the job market. Welch's analysis (1970) would seem to support the alleged relationship between mental ability and labor market performance, but the connection between mental ability and ability to earn higher wages has not been fully explored to date. Nevertheless, measures of mental ability must be used simply because no viable alternatives have as yet been made available.

In recent years, a considerable amount of new empirical information has been gathered from which new and improved earnings functions have been estimated. In addition to census data, longitudinal information is now available from the Michigan Income Dynamics Survey (collected by the Survey Research Center of the University

Table 3-3. Some "Ability" Measures Employed in Estimating the Benefits of Education.

Author(s)	Ability Measure(s)
Wolfe and Smith (1956)	IQ and class rank
Hunt (1963)	Achievement tests
Ashenfelter and Mooney (1968)	Mathematical aptitude
Weisbrod and Karpoff (1968)	Class rank
Husén (1969)	IQ
Rogers (1969)	IQ
Danière and Mechling (1970)	SAT scores
Griliches and Mason (1972)	Armed Forces Qualifying Test (AFQT)
Hause (1972)	AFQT, IQ, and "ability and achievement" scores, using four different samples
Taubman and Wales (1973)	Mathematical ability

Note: A good discussion of some of these studies is contained in Solmon (1973a).

of Michigan) and the National Longitudinal Survey (NLS; collected by the Ohio State University's Center for Human Resource Research). In addition, Chamberlain and Griliches (1975, 1976) and Taubman (1976a, 1976b), have examined data on twins in which case earnings differentials by education are not affected by environmental differences among individuals.

Estimates of the bias resulting from omission of ability and other pertinent variables vary from 0 to 65 percent. The latter figure was obtained by Taubman (1976a) in a study of male twins forty-five to fifty-five years old. He shows that the bias is only about 12 percent when the earnings functions include variables typically employed in income-education studies of the Mincer (1974) variety, but increases to 65 percent when environmental and genetic factors are removed through the use of identical twins. Griliches (1977a), on the other hand, argues that the bias is not greater than 10 percent and that studies obtaining a larger bias are deficient because they do not consider measurement error and interactions between education, ability, experience, and income. Moreover, estimating the bias in percentage terms is "somewhat misdirected," because it is impossible to generalize across samples and the population at large. If the bias is the same in absolute value, it could be much different in relative value and vice versa. "The point . . . is . . . that one's estimate of the 'percentage bias' is model-dependent and hence not generalizable easily across different data sets and formulations" (p. 6). Furthermore, Griliches shows that when one allows for interaction between education, experience, ability, and income, the effect of education can actually be greater than in a simple cross-tabulation. "This is consistent with the view that [other variables] were 'robbing' the schooling coefficient" in other models (p. 16).

The truth of the matter is that no one really knows what proportion of the observed education-income relationship is strictly due to education. Despite all of the work that has been completed in this area, we are a long way from arriving at the final destination. It is doubtful, moreover, whether this problem will ever be solved unambiguously. As long as it is not certain what portion of the earnings differentials are due to a given educational investment, it would be wise to calculate the economic value of education using both low and high estimates of the ability bias. Such information could then be evaluated by private or public users on the basis of their respective value judgement.

Average versus Marginal Benefits

The calculation of lifetime income differentials by level of education provides an estimate of the "average" benefit of education. Such an average benefit would be relevant, at best, for an individual with "average" characteristics. Students with greater ability, motivation, or other favorable attributes are likely to gain more, and those with below average characteristics are likely to gain less. Use of well-specified earnings functions would make it possible to estimate different age-earnings profiles for persons with different characteristics.

Use of the Mean versus the Median in
Aggregate Census Data

The U.S. Census Bureau publishes aggregate data on income cross-classified by age and education. Typically, median incomes are given, rather than mean income. Since the distribution of income tends to be skewed, with mean income exceeding the median, use of the latter might produce a downward bias in age-earnings profiles.

A number of authors have devised methods to estimate means from the census medians. The main problem arises with respect to an "open-ended" classification, such as "income over $25,000." The emerging use of Census Public Use Samples, along with the Michigan Income Dynamics, the NLS, and other microdata sets, reduces the severity of this problem, since both means and medians may be estimated directly from such samples.

Social versus Private Benefits

Lifetime income differentials are used as an index of the social benefits of education on the presumption that higher earnings represent greater productivity. Such a presumption is based upon the neoclassical theory of income distribution—namely, that each productive factor is paid a wage equal to the value of its marginal contribution to output. As noted earlier, some writers question the validity of the assumption that education is responsible for increased productivity of individuals. Moreover, others question the validity of the neoclassical theory of income distribution, arguing that bureaucratic wage scales are frequently totally unrelated to one's productivity. Such an assertion is clearly more relevant in countries where the private sector is relatively weak. In the United States, the neoclassical wage theory is more likely to be approximately accurate, though studies of the U.S. government sector (e.g., S.P. Smith, 1977) clearly illustrate the deviation from the neoclassical world in organizations where wages are determined in a bureaucratic setting.

Private benefits, on the other hand, are not affected by the alleged lack of correlation between higher wages and higher productivity. One must take into account, however, the portion of the lifetime income differentials that is not included in one's disposable income, especially income tax payments to federal, state, and local governments. (Contributions to social security are more difficult to handle. On the one hand, the more one earns, the more social security benefits one gets. On the other hand, the social security system is not based on actuarial principles, so that the relationship between payments to the fund and benefits received from it may not be symmetric. It is not surprising, therefore, that studies of private benefits typically deduct income tax payments but do not deduct payments for social insurance.)

A study by Houthakker (1959) serves to illustrate the impact of taxes on lifetime income. As may be gleaned from Table 3-4, the difference between before tax and after tax lifetime incomes is relatively insignificant for the lower education levels. For the education category "16 or more" the inclusion of the tax reduces lifetime income by 15 percent.

Annual Income versus Hourly Wages

The benefits of education are said to include both an increase in productivity, measured by the hourly wage, and an increase in employability, measured by the number of hours one is employed. Multiplying the wage rate by the number of hours worked, we get annual income. This is a justification for the use of annual income. (Of course, since census data typically provide only annual income data, and not hourly wage rates, users of census data had no choice but to employ annual income data!) A number of writers, beginning with

Table 3-4. Lifetime Income from Age Fourteen, by Level of Education—
United States, 1949.

Years of School Completed	Before Tax (1)	After Tax (2)	Ratio (2) ÷ (1) (3)
0	$ 64,132	$ 60,785	.95
1-4	79,386	75,021	.95
5-7	100,430	93,571	.93
8	124,105	115,277	.93
9-11	142,522	130,933	.92
12	175,160	157,940	.90
13-15	198,268	175,206	.88
16 or more	280,989	238,761	.85

Source: Columns (1) and (2) from Houthakker (1959), Table 3.

Morgan and David (1963), have argued that the number of hours worked represents a choice by the individual between leisure and income and has no relation to the benefits of education. They calculate lifetime income, therefore, by multiplying hourly wages (cross-classified by age and education) by 2,000 hours (assuming one works 40 hours per week for fifty weeks per year). Lifetime income estimates are therefore not sensitive to individual choices regarding work versus leisure.

It may be argued, however, that not only does education make it possible for persons to be employed (i.e., results in less involuntary unemployment), but also it conditions people to seek full employment. That is, education affects both productivity and individual preferences in favor of work. If this is true, then the hourly wage method would not capture all of the relevant benefits of education.

Again, it is difficult to settle the argument unequivocably. Both procedures have advantages and disadvantages. A good compromise would be to estimate lifetime income according to both methods and to compare their magnitudes. This will make it possible for users of the results to choose for themselves whichever set of figures they prefer.

Quality versus Quantity of Education

Most of the studies on the economic value of education use years of schooling or completion of a given level of schooling as the focus of the analysis. A few studies have also examined the extent to which variations in the quality of a given educational program contribute to variations in lifetime earnings. One of the first studies of which we are aware is J.N. Morgan and Sirageldin (1968). Using survey data, they find that each dollar increase in per pupil expenditures per year in public education was associated with an increase in earnings of $0.0024 per hour. Assuming a 2000-hour work year, this translates into an increase per worker of $4.80 per year—a rather large return on the investment. Morgan and Sirageldin also employed an index of college quality to obtain estimates of the returns to college education which are not clouded by the effect of college quality on lifetime earnings.

Further analysis of the Morgan-Sirageldin data was performed by G.E. Johnson and Stafford (1973). They obtain a differential impact of an increase in per pupil expenditure on hourly wages depending on the number of years of school completed and the level of per pupil expenditures. "The authors find high but diminishing marginal returns to investment in expenditures per pupil per year" (p. 139), and recommend increases in per pupil expenditures in low-expenditure districts as a substitute for increasing the number of years of school completed.

Other studies of the effect of per pupil expenditures on income include Link (1975b), Link and Ratlege (1975), Ribich and Murphy (1975), and Rizzuto (1977). All of these studies show some impact of school quality on income, but the degree of impact varies from study to study. Ribich and Murphy (1975), for example, conclude that the main impact of higher per pupil expenditures is through their effect on years of schooling completed, implying that students attending high quality schools are more likely to pursue additional educational investment. Link and Ratlege (1975) and Rizzuto (1977), on the other hand, emphasize the importance of school quality in enhancing the income of blacks, arguing that much of the improvement in the income of blacks may be traced to improvements in school quality as opposed to quantity.

Mention should also be made of studies of college quality. In addition to the Morgan and Sirageldin (1968) study cited above, there are studies by Weisbrod and Karpoff (1968), Danière and Mechling (1970), Solmon (1973b), and Leibowitz (1976). Solmon used different measures of college quality in his study, demonstrating that SAT scores of the student body and average salaries of the faculty show a strong influence on earnings of college graduates. The study indicates that college quality is especially important for students with either low or high ability (measured by IQ). The Leibowitz study, measuring "intensity" of schooling by college costs, also indicates that quality of college is an important variable and argues that quality is a good substitute for quantity, with higher college quality making it possible for students to enter the labor market earlier.

It is clear from most of these studies that school quality can serve as a substitute for the quantity of schooling (years of schooling). This is true, however, only up to a point, as there are diminishing returns to school quality. It is possible, however, that studies on the quality of schooling are misdirected, by merely pointing out that better schools attract better students. As Astin (1973) shows, increases in cognitive skills of college students are not affected by variations in college quality, even though average levels of cognitive skills do vary by school quality (Taubman, 1973: 2).

Education and Income Distribution

Education has been viewed for many years as a vehicle for economic and social mobility. Social policy regarding education has been based, in part, on the premise that one way (perhaps the best) to fight poverty is to give the poor an education (help the poor to be able to help themselves). In recent years, however, that premise has come under intense fire. A number of writers have claimed that education does not improve the distribution of income (i.e., reduce inequality), and, in fact, some have argued that it has increased the inequality of income (for example, see Hansen and Weisbrod, 1969a, 1969b; and Staff and Tullock, 1973). Writers such as H.M. Levin (1972, 1977a, 1977b), Jencks et al., (1972), and Thurow (1975), claim that education is simply not capable of meeting the expectations that society has placed upon it.

On the other hand, Rivlin (1975) indicates that recent experience in the United States does show a narrowing of wage differentials, so that education may yet be able to play the role of income equalizer. Also, a study by Marin and Psacharopoulos (1976) shows that more schooling is positively related to improved income distribution. Likewise, Pechman (1970, 1971) questions the validity of the Hansen-Weisbrod (1969a, 1969b) results and claims that higher education subsidies can be shown to lead to improved income distribution.

This issue, like so many others in this field, has not yet been solved satisfactorily. The point, however, is that the social benefits of schooling are not confined to the total extra lifetime income generated, but relate also to the manner by which such extra income is distributed. So long as society desires to improve the economic conditions of the poor, the ability of the educational system to reduce income inequality will have to be investigated.

External and Nonpecuniary Benefits

Additional lifetime income is the simplest available measure of the economic benefits of education. It is, however, an incomplete measure. Regarding private benefits, the main omission is nonmonetary (also known as nonpecuniary) benefits. They may be of the consumption variety (i.e., benefits to the individual while attending college) or of the investment variety (benefits received in later years). For example, the choice of occupations is likely to be broadened by more schooling, hence the potential for greater job satisfaction. Alternatively, education could influence lifestyles and the productivity of individuals at home or in other nonmarket settings. Also, education could influence an individual's health and, hence, the probability of a longer life.

There are a few studies that throw light on the existence of such nonpecuniary benefits. For example, Hettich (1972) discusses a Michigan study showing that more educated individuals usually seek more information about consumer goods. Hettich then calculates the savings an individual can reap from a more efficient buying strategy, using the buying guide of the *Consumer Reports*. Also, Michael (1972, 1973a, 1973b) demonstrates the effect of education on home production and fertility, arguing that more educated persons are more productive in nonmarket activities. The evidence on job satisfaction is not strong, but Quinn and Mandilovitch (1975) do show a relatively small payoff in job satisfaction resulting from increased education. Finally, Duncan (1976) shows that improved working conditions (healthy and safe work, overtime hours control, and employment stability) are related to one's educational attainment and that, when included in the earnings function, they make it possible to predict earnings more accurately.

The relationship between education and health has also been investigated. For example, Lefocowitz (1973) argues that there is a causal relationship between the levels of education and individual health status and that the observed correlation between income and medical deprivation appears to be a consequence of education's relationship with both variables." Likewise, Lando (1975) shows that higher levels of education are associated with lower rates of work disability, age being taken into account, and that about four-fifths of racial differences in work disability can be seen to be due to educational differences between the races. Lando concedes that this relationship may be due, in part, to the relationship between education and occupational choice and to possible discrimination against persons with disability. On the other hand, as G.S. Becker (1964) points out, much of the educational effect is through occupation, so that there is no reason to be too agnostic about the empirical relationship found between education and health. Finally, Orcutt et al. (1977) show that the probability of death declines as one's educational level is increased.

The social benefits of education include, in addition to private benefits, those benefits that may be attributable to education but that are so diffused among the population that individuals are unable to appropriate them. For example, if an educational investment makes a person more prone to participate in political and civic functions, the benefits from such a participation accrue to the community as a whole. Such benefits are not included in the usual calculus of educational returns. A study by Stapleton (1976) indicates that high school and college graduates are generally more likely to participate in political activities (campagning, voting, and communal activities). He cautions, however, that increased campaign activity may not be a social benefit if the individuals are "motivated by a desire to influence the government in a way which will benefit a special interest group at the expense of the majority" (p. 29).

There is some evidence that more educated persons are less prone to commit crime. Spiegleman (1968) presents some data regarding juvenile crime, and Webb (1977) provides some information on the educational background of inmates in correctional institutions versus that of the general population. She calculates the cost of crime attributable to inadequate education to range between $7 billion and $14 billion in 1970. Additional data on the relationship between education and crime is given in Ehrlich (1975). Finally, Phillips, Votey, and Maxwell (1972) show that labor market status is a sufficient factor to explain rising youth crime rates. Since education is associated with higher labor force participation rates, it can be argued that increased education could help in reducing the crime rate.

It should be pointed out that the positive external and nonpecuniary benefits of education could be offset by negative effects. For example, as Berg and Freedman (1977) argue, increased education in the United States has not always been matched by increased job opportunities commensurate with the higher skill levels of the work force. As a result, many educated persons find it difficult to find suitable jobs, and the ensuing frustration could more than offset any nonmonetary benefits attributable to education. This view is contradicted, however, by an Associate Press (1976) report. Also, it has been argued by Goffman (1977) that the external effects of education could contain negative elements. For example, the student unrest of the late 1960s and early 1970s may be considered as a negative external effect of higher education. "Some have even blamed education for the generation gap itself. In the employment field, while we tend to regard education as enhancing opportunities and productivity, the 'education echos' may be inimical to productivity because it has tended to downgrade more mundane and materialistic activities to a much lower status than cultural, intellectual, artistic or similar activities" (p. 83).

Discounting

Tables 3-1, 3-2, and 3-4 provide data on lifetime earnings due to education. These lifetime earnings are undiscounted; they are based on the premise that it is proper to sum future expected benefits without regard to when such benefits are expected to accrue. Essentially, it means that $1 of benefits expected fifty years from now is equal to $1 of benefit expected next year. We need not elaborate on the obvious; these two expected benefits are clearly unequal, with the earlier expected benefit being worth a good deal more than the expected benefit in the more distant future. The process by which such expected benefits can be brought together under a common denominator is known as discounting, which will be explained in more detail in Chapter 5. The main problem in the discounting process is the choice of the rate of discount, which will influence the degree to which passage of time from the present reduces the present value per dollar of expected benefits.

To illustrate the impact of discounting on additional lifetime income, by level of education, data taken from the 1950 census and reported by Hansen (1963) are presented in Table 3-5 (data for zero rate of discount represent undiscounted lifetime income differentials). It is quite clear that additional lifetime income for any educational

Table 3-5. Present Value of Additional Lifetime Income by Level of Education (Before Tax)—United States, 1950.

	Rate of Discount (percent)				
Investment In	0	3	6	8	10
High School					
2 years	$16,802	$ 7,756	$ 2,301	$1,190	$ 545
4 years	46,038	18,156	6,488	3,601	1,949
Final 2 years	29,236	10,400	4,187	2,411	1,404
College					
2 years	20,725	5,644	864	-386	-953
4 years	95,430	31,273	10,764	5,121	2,186
Final 2 years	74,705	25,692	9,900	5,507	3,139

Source: Hansen (1963), Table 6.

level becomes successively smaller as a higher rate of discount is applied. In fact, the additional lifetime income associated with the completion of two years of college, relative to completion of four years of high school, becomes negative at discount rates of 8 percent or higher.

Nonformal Education

The foregoing sections dealt exclusively with formal education. One should also consider the economic benefits of nonformal education, such as education in the home, on the job training, or other unconventional forms of education. Although it is important to consider such educational endeavors, nonformal education is outside the scope of this volume and will not be discussed further. Some recent literature on nonformal education includes Ahmed (1975) and Coombs and Ahmed (1974).

SUMMARY AND CONCLUSIONS

This chapter provided a comprehensive discussion of educational benefits. We first described the types of benefits that education is expected to produce, among which we included the potential increase in individual productivity and income, the immediate and future increase in consumption, other direct effects, external benefits, and possible intergeneration benefits. In all, it would appear that the benefits from a given educational investment are quite large. Different methods have been presented here to determine the quantitative significance of such benefits—namely, the correlation method, the residual approach, and primarily, the returns to education approach. Any of these methods is subject to a host of conceptual and statistical problems. An attempt was made to describe these difficulties and, when feasible, to suggest possible solutions. Prominent among these problems is the question of the impact of ability upon earnings or productivity. Several different possible solutions were listed for the treatment of education, ability, and income. Other problems involve such matters as the use of cross-section versus life cycle data, the identification of the "investment" and "consumption" components, the quantification of external and other direct benefits, and other conceptual or statistical difficulties.

Since this chapter did not take into account the costs of education, no conclusions as to the profitability of education can as yet be made. The focus of the next chapter will, therefore, be on the costs of education.

LITERATURE GUIDE

It is particularly difficult to provide a literature guide for this chapter because there are so many items that are pertinent to some extent, yet most of these items also involve material that we cover in later chapters. The focus here will therefore be on literature that is primarily concerned with the value of education and problems associated with measuring the returns to education.

Value of Education-General

Early studies on the economic value of education include H.F. Clark (1937), Gorseline (1932), and J.R. Walsh (1935). The most celebrated work in the area is clearly G.S. Becker (1964). The contributions of Theodore W. Schultz are also well known, such as Schultz (1961a, 1962, 1973, 1967, 1971, and 1972a). Excellent introductory essays on the economic returns to education include Alexander (1976), Bolton (1969), M.J. Bowman (1962), and Weisbrod (1966). Another study receiving wide acclaim is Mincer (1974), reviewed by Blaug (1976c).

There a number of good collections of essays printed in single volumes. They include Carnoy (1972), Juster (1975), and Solmon and Taubman (1973).

Readers interested in relatively simple treatments of the topic may wish to examine the following studies: Fiske (1977), Fogel (1966), R.B. Freeman (1977a), Gilpatrick (1975), Gilroy (1975), C.R. Hill (1976), Houthakker (1959), Kastner (1964, 1976), Lassiter (1965, 1966), H.P. Miller (1960, 1965), Morgan and David (1963), Morgan and Sirageldin (1968), Ribich (1968, 1970), Thurow (1970), Withey (1971), Witmer (1970), Wolfle (1973), and Wolfle and Smith (1956).

More complex models are presented in the following studies: G.S. Becker (1962, 1967), Carnoy (1975b), Fane (1975), Freeman (1973, 1975, 1976, 1977b), Mincer (1962, 1970), Psacharopoulos (1975), Ribich and Murphy (1975), W.H. Sewell and Hauser (1976), J.P. Smith and Welch (1977), Solmon (1973a, 1973b), Taubman (1973, 1975, 1976a, 1976b), Tabuman and Wales (1974), Wales (1973), Weisbrod (1961, 1962), L. Weiss and Williamson (1972, 1975), R.D. Weiss (1970), Welch (1970, 1973b, 1975), and D.A. Wise (1975).

Educational benefits in other countries are included in a number of studies. Examples are Selby-Smith (1969) for Britain, Sen (1966b) for Canada, Senna (1975) for Brazil, and Stroup and Hargrove (1969) for Vietnam.

Ability and Earnings Function

One of the earliest studies attempting to measure the bias in the education coefficient due to omission of ability is Denison (1964b), based on the data in Wolfle and Smith (1956). The study by Griliches and Mason (1972) has received considerable attention, and the work by Hause (1971, 1972) provides evidence based upon a number of surveys. A good discussion of the ability issue is Hartog (1976). Other studies, or discussion of ability studies, include Ashenfelter and Mooney (1968), M.J. Bowman and Anderson (1969), Chamberlain (1977), Chamberlain and Griliches (1975, 1976), Conlisk (1971), Danière and Mechling (1970), Fägerlind (1975), Griliches (1970, 1974, 1976, 1977a, 1977b, 1977c), Hunt (1963), Husén (1969, 1972), Kiker and Liles (forthcoming), Reed and Miller (1970), Rogers (1969), Taubman (1972, 1976a), Taubman and Wales (1973), Weisbrod (1972), and Weisbrod and Karpoff (1968). A summary of many of these and other studies is contained in Psacharopoulos (1975: ch. 3).

Other studies, in which allowance is made for nonschooling factors in a context of an earnings function, include Birnbaum (1976), Chiswick and Mincer (1972), G.E. Johnson and Stafford (1973, 1974a), Klevmarken and Quigley (1976), Knapp (1977), Knapp and Hansen (1976), Lazear (1976), Leigh (1976a), Link (1975b, 1975c), Link and Ratledge (1975), Long and Liles (1976), Park and Bielefeld (1976), Parsons (1975), and Tannen (1976).

Education and Income Distribution

Among the studies in this area are included Chiswick (1970, 1971), Chiswick and Mincer (1972), Jencks (1972), H.M. Levin (1977a), Marin and Psacharopoulos (1976), Mincer (1970, 1974), Rivlin (1975), Staff and Tullock (1973), Taubman (1975), Thurow (1972, 1975), and Weintraub (1973).

Nonpecuniary and External Effects

The classical studies on indirect and external benefits of education are Weisbrod (1962, 1964). Additional studies on external benefits include a summary by J.R. Davis (1970), a critique by Goffman (1977), a study of political participation by Stapleton (1976), and studies relating education to crime by Ehrlich (1975), Spiegleman (1968), and Webb (1977).

A study by the Associate Press (1976) indicates that college graduates are generally satisfied with their position, contrary to what Berg and Freedman (1977) argue. Studies on the relationship between education and health include Baldwin and Weisbrod (1974), Grossman (1972), Lando (1975), Manheim (1975), and Orcutt et al. (1977). The relationship between education and migration is investigated in Grubel and Scott (1966), Ledebur (1977), E. Lee (1969), McInnis (1970), Schwartz (1976), Shryock and Nam (1965), Suval and Hamilton (1965), and Weisbrod (1964). And Solmon (1975) describes the positive effect of education on savings behavior, acceptance of risk, and knowledge of traditional hedges against inflation.

Duncan's (1976) study on nonwage benefits has already been discussed in the text. K. A. Feldman and Newcomb (1969) present evidence on nonmonetary effects of college education. Bowlby and Shriver (1970) discuss nonwage benefits, and Featherman and Hauser (1976b) show that the narrowing occupational differentials between blacks and whites may be attributed in a large measure to education. The studies by Hettich (1972), Leibowitz (1974), and Michael (1972, 1973a, 1973b) have already been discussed. Morris (1976) agrees with Michael (1972) that education changes one's lifestyle, but finds evidence contrary to Michael's contention that education increases productivity at home. Standing (1976) provides data on the relationship between education and female labor force participation. Finally, Hill and Stafford (1974, 1977) show that more educated parents spend more time with their preschool children.

Critiques of the Human Capital Approach

Theoretical discussions of the screening hypothesis include Arrow (1973), Lazear (1977a), Spence (1973), and Stiglitz (1975). Berg (1970) is probably the first study to suggest the existence of screening. See also Berg and Freedman (1977) and Berg, Freedman, and Freeman (1978). Empirical studies that suggest the existence of screening include Dick and Medoff (1976), W.R. Johnson (1977), Riley (1976a, 1976b), and Taubman and Wales (1972a, 1973). Empirical studies suggesting the opposite include Chiswick (1973), Layard and Psacharopoulos (1974), Psacharopoulos (1974), and Wolpin (1977).

For studies on the dual labor market, consult Doeringer and Piore (1971, 1975), Piore (1971, 1972), and Reich, Gordon, and Edwards (1973). Critical of this approach are Cain (1976), Freiman (1976), Leigh (1976b), and Wachter (1974).

Radical views are given by Bowles (1972a, 1972b, 1974), Bowles and Gintis (1975, 1976), Gintis (1971), B. Harrison (1970, 1972a, 1972b), H.M. Levin (1977b), Steinberg (1976), and Thurow (1972, 1975). A critical review of Bowles and Gintis (1976) is given by Blaug (1976a), in contrast to a rather sympathetic review by B.W. Brown and Saks (1977). Further criticism of the radical approach is contained in E.G. West (1976).

Other Areas

The cross-section versus time series controversy is discussed in Ben-Porath (1966), Danielsen (1970), David (1969), and H.P. Miller (1965). The intergeneration effect is expounded in Parsons (1975), Swift and Weisbrod (1965), and Ribich (1968). Barnow and Cain (1977) and Cicirelli et al. (1969) discuss the economic benefits of the Headstart program. And Renshaw (1960) provides a varied discussion of problems in measuring the economic returns to education.

Readers interested in the IQ controversy (regarding the argument that intelligence is based on heredity, and hence, that education could not bridge the gap between various segments of society) should consult Conlisk (1976), Goldberger (1976a, 1976b, 1976c), Herrnstein (1973), and Jensen (1969, 1972, 1973, 1975).

Chapter 4

The Costs of Education

All taxpayers in the United States (and in most other countries as well) undoubtedly know that outlays on education have soared over the past decades. But even so, one is likely to consider only the burden of educational expenditures that could be felt through increasing outlays by the local school systems. Yet school costs may not be identical to outlays. First, educational spending includes not only expenditures on current activities (such as payment for teacher services rendered during the particular period under consideration), but also outlays for future periods—what is usually termed the "capital" account. Outlays on new buildings and equipment, improvements and renovation of old structures, and so on must not be counted as current costs—unless part or all of such outlays are in fact used up during the period. On the other hand, depreciation of building and equipment (including actual wear and tear as well as depreciation due to obsolescence) during the current period ought to be added to current costs. As we shall see later, inclusion of capital outlays in the current period would have the effect of overestimating current costs so long as the value of the physical assets of the schools is increasing.

At the same time, current costs should, in principle, include not only direct outlays but all opportunity costs, some of which are implicit rather than explicit costs. For example, the social costs of high school education include, in addition to direct expenditures by the schools or the students, the cost of earnings foregone by the students as well. Time spent in school or in preparation for school is not cost-less. The student could have utilized this time to earn income in occupations open to individuals of his age, education, and ability. Other hidden (opportunity) costs may also exist.[1]

The analysis presented in this chapter has two main purposes: (1) to analyze the extent of the investment in education, at all levels, in the United States over time; and (2) to study the relationship between the changes in benefits from schooling and investment (cost) in education. The second purpose underlines the need to assess the nature of both the costs of and returns from education. For what may seem an "alarming" rate of increase in educational costs may not be so alarming after all—provided that the benefits accruing to the investment are sufficiently large. For example, if $1 of investment in high school education is shown to yield a larger return than one could earn from investing in physical capital or other earning assets, we might want to conclude that investment in schooling may be more productive than other forms of investment. Of course, the value of education is too complex a concept to be completely measurable; still, the costs of education must be compared to some variant of a measure of educational benefit before rational conclusions about the merits of the investment could be formulated. We shall limit our discussion in this chapter to the consideration of the costs only. Benefit-cost analysis, applied to educational investments, is left for a subsequent chapter.

DIRECT COSTS

As mentioned above, the costs of education include both direct costs (by the school, the student, and/or the student's family) and indirect costs (such as earnings foregone). Direct costs have received by far the bulk of attention, perhaps because the consequences of such costs are directly and strongly felt by the taxpayer—and, of course, because statistics on direct school outlays are readily available (or estimable), whereas indirect costs must be imputed.

The majority of the direct costs are incurred by the school systems themselves. This is especially true for the public school system, since tuition and fees in the elementary and high schools are virtually nil; in public colleges and universities, these are far smaller than in private institutions. Yet some direct costs are also incurred by students and/or their families. Examples are (1) the additional costs of room, board, and clothing; (2) transportation costs to and from

---

1. There is considerable disagreement among experts in the field of educational costs as to what can be regarded as a "true" cost. See, for example, Vaizey (1962: ch. IV) and M.J. Bowman (1966a).

school; and (3) costs of supplies, such as books, art and gym equipment, and so forth. Further, since student charges are also included in the category of school costs, there will be no need to separate private and institutional costs in this respect. Also, since statistics on other direct costs (as outlined above) are not directly available, an imputation is necessary.

Our discussion concerning the costs of education will necessarily concentrate on formal schooling. This includes elementary and secondary (private and public) schools (K-12) and public and private institutions of higher education. There are a multitude of other formal and informal educational programs, but because of substantial difficulties in providing satisfactory estimates of costs, they will not be included in the present analysis.

Expenditures of Elementary and Secondary Schools

Let us begin with the expenditures of public elementary and secondary schools. As may be observed from Table 4-1, column 2, expenditures have increased from $5.8 billion in 1950 to an estimated $72.9 billion in 1977, an increase of 1,157 percent. Of course, enrollments have increased, too, during the period—by 76 percent—and inflation increased the price level by 264 percent (implying that $3.64 in 1977 would buy the same commodity bundle that could have been purchased only for $1 in 1950). Nevertheless, expenditures on public education have increased considerably in real terms even on a per pupil basis, indicating increased investment in public education during the period.

Expenditures of private elementary and secondary schools are more difficult to estimate, but the figures provided in column 3 of Table 4-1 are the best available. While the total magnitude is much smaller than in the public sector, relative costs are quite similar (that is due, in part, to the manner by which private costs are estimated). Thus we find an increase of 1,125 percent in expenditures between 1950 and 1977.

Average Daily Attendance (ADA) and Per Pupil Expenditures. Data on average daily attendance (ADA) for public and private elementary and secondary schools are presented in columns 1 and 2 of Table 4-2. On the basis of the data in Tables 4-1 and 4-2, expenditures per pupil in ADA for public and private elementary and secondary schools are provided in Table 4-3 (columns 1 and 2). We observe that per pupil expenditures are very similar in the two

Table 4-1. Educational Expenditures, by Level and Control—United States, 1950-1977 (billions of current dollars).

Year	Elementary and Secondary Schools			Colleges and Universities			All Levels		
	Total	Public	Private	Total	Public	Private	Total	Public	Private
	1	2	3	4	5	6	7	8	9
1950	6.6	5.8	.8	2.6	1.4	1.2	9.2	7.2	2.0
1960	17.9	15.5	2.0	6.9	3.7	3.2	24.8	19.2	5.6
1970	45.7	41.0	4.7	24.7	15.8	8.9	70.4	56.8	13.6
1975	68.7	61.1	7.3	38.9	26.3	12.6	107.6	87.6	20.0
1977[a]	81.9	72.9	9.0	49.2	33.5	15.7	131.1	106.4	24.7

Sources: Grant and Lind (1977); Frankel and Harrison (1977), Table 30; and earlier editions of the Digest and Projections.
[a]Projected.

Table 4-2. Average Daily Attendance in Elementary and Secondary Schools, and Full-time Equivalent Enrollments in Institutions of Higher Education, by Control—United States, 1950-1977 (in thousands).

	Average Daily Attendance (K-12)		*Full-time Equivalent Enrollment in Institutions of Higher Education*	
	Public	*Private*	*Public*	*Private*
Year	*1*	*2*	*3*	*4*
1950	22,284	2,000	1,294[a]	1,139[a]
1960	32,477	5,351	1,749	1,194
1970	41,934	5,055	4,973	1,783
1975	40,310	4,765	6,523	1,958
1977[b]	39,305	4,765	7,070	2,009

Sources: Various editions of the *Digest* and *Projections.*
[a]Estimated by extrapolation.
[b]Projected.

Table 4-3. Per Pupil Expenditures, by Level and Control—United States, 1950-1977 (current dollars).

	Elementary and Secondary Schools		*Institutions of Higher Education*	
	Public	*Private*	*Public*	*Private*
Year	*1*	*2*	*3*	*4*
1950	260	261	1,082	1,054
1960	477	451	2,115	2,680
1970	978	930	3,177	4,545
1975	1,479	1,553	4,032	8,018
1977[a]	1,855	1,889	4,738	7,815

Sources: Tables 4-1 and 4-2.
[a]Projected

sectors, having increased from $260 and $261 in 1950 to $1,855 and $1,889 in the public and private sector, respectively. In both cases, this represents more than a six-fold increase in per pupil costs during the period.

Adjustment for Inflation. It is no secret that the price level has increased substantially during the period, so that $1 of expenditures in 1950 cannot be compared to $1 of expenditures in 1977. Using the implicit price deflator for government purchases of goods and services in the state and local sector, we find in Table 4-4 that per pupil expenditures, in 1972 dollars, increased from $666 in 1950 to $1,307 in 1977, an increase of 96.2 percent. This is, of course, a much smaller increase than that obtained without adjustment for increase in the number of pupils and the effect of inflation, but still represents almost a doubling of the investment per pupil by public elementary and secondary schools.

Components of Expenditures. Table 4-5 provides a breakdown of expenditures by public elementary and secondary schools for the 1975-1976 school year. Current expenditures account for almost 88 percent of total expenditures, the remainder being spent on transportation (3.1 percent), capital outlay (3.3 percent), and debt service (5.7 percent). Of particular interest is the fact that more than 70 percent of current expenditures are for instruction, the majority of which are for teacher salaries and other wages and salaries. These figures highlight the highly labor-intensive nature of the public school system (and education in general).

Institutions of Higher Education (IHEs)

Tables 4-1, 4-2, and 4-3 contain expenditure data for public and private institutions of higher education (IHEs). Whereas the relative increase in expenditures of private IHEs during the period (1,135 percent) was very similar to the record of elementary and secondary schools, public IHEs expanded much faster (by 1,378 percent). The expansion of public IHEs was particularly rapid during the 1960s.

Table 4-4. Per Pupil Expenditures in Public Elementary and Secondary Schools, Adjusted for Inflation—United States, 1950-1977.

Year	*Per Pupil Expenditures Unadjusted* *1*	*Implicit Price Deflator, 1972=100* *2*	*Adjusted Per Pupil Expenditures* *3*
1950	$ 260	39.0	$ 666
1960	477	56.8	840
1970	978	88.3	1,106
1975	1,479	129.8[b]	1,168
1977	1,855[a]	141.9[b]	1,307

Sources: Column 1, from Table 4-3; column 2, from *Economic Report of the President* (1977), p. 191, "Government Purchases of Goods and Services, State and Local" column; Column 3 = (col. 1 ÷ col. 2) × 100.
[a]Projected.
[b]Data are for fourth quarter, 1976.

Table 4-5. Components of Educational Expenditures, Public Elementary and Secondary Schools—United States, 1975-1976.

Expenditure Category	Expenditures per Pupil	Percent of Current Expenditures	Percent of Total Expenditures
	1	2	3
Instruction	$ 901	70.2	61.7
Teachers Salaries	$675	52.6	46.2
Other Professional Salaries	115	9.0	7.9
Other Instruction	110	8.6	7.6
Noninstruction, Current	383	29.8	26.2
Plant Operation and Maintenance	167	13.0	11.5
Fixed Charges	108	8.5	7.4
Other	107	8.3	7.3
Total Current Expenditures	$1,284	100.0	87.9
Transportation	46	—	3.1
Capital Outlay	48	—	3.3
Debt Service	84	—	5.7
Grand Total	$1,461	—	100.0

Source: National Comparison of Local School Costs, 1975–1976 (1975).

Note: Figures may not add to totals because of rounding.

Based upon data for full-time equivalent enrollment in IHEs (Table 4-2, columns 3 and 4), per pupil expenditures for public and private IHEs are reported in columns 3 and 4 of Table 4-3. In current dollars, per pupil expenditures increased by 438 percent for public IHEs and by 641 percent for private IHEs. We note a widening of the gap between per pupil expenditures in private and public IHEs (actually public institutions spent more per pupil in 1950 than did private IHEs) between 1950 and 1975, although estimates for 1977 indicate a considerable narrowing of the gap, with public IHEs spending more and private IHEs less per pupil in 1977 relative to 1975.

When adjusted for inflation (as was done in Table 4-4), per pupil spending in public IHEs increased from $2,774 in 1950 to $3,339 in 1977 (in 1972 dollars)—an increase of 20 percent. For private IHEs, per pupil expenditures rose from $2,703 to $5,507—an increase of 104 percent. We thus observe only a modest increase in educational investment per student in the public sector, the bulk of the increase in expenditures being due to increased enrollments (by 446 percent) and inflation, in contrast to private IHEs, where investment per student more than doubled but enrollments increased only modestly (by 76 percent).

Other Direct Costs

There are direct costs not incurred by schools or IHEs, such as transportation costs borne by pupils, costs of books and supplies, and other out of pocket costs. Since we do not have reliable data on their magnitude, we must impute them. The particular method of imputation used here is related to estimates of earnings foregone discussed in the next section; hence, we postpone calculation of other direct costs to that section.

Total Direct Costs

Total direct costs, excluding the "other direct costs" category, are summarized in columns 7-9 of Table 4-1. It is estimated that, in 1977, total expenditures in public and private elementary and secondary schools and IHEs amounted to $131.1 billion, 81 percent of which was spent in the public sector. This contrasts with a total expenditure of $9.2 billion in 1950, 78 percent of which was spent in the public sector. There is some evidence, then, on the increased involvement of the public sector in education, although the increase is quite small in magnitude.

INDIRECT AND IMPUTED COSTS

Economic costs include not only those costs that represent a direct outlay. The notion of cost is basically one of opportunity cost. That is, a given activity will have a cost of x dollars if, and only if, x dollars are thereby unavailable for an alternative activity. To illustrate, spending $10 million on elementary education in a given town precludes the use of these funds for other desirable activities. But if these funds do not cover such items as "imputed rent" (i.e., the fact that if elementary education were not provided in the school other productive activities could have taken place there), the true cost will exceed $10 million.

The notion of opportunity costs can be applied in our case to provide estimates for certain hidden costs. We shall concentrate in this section on (1) earnings foregone by students attending school; (2) the value of tax exemption commonly enjoyed by all nonprofit institutions; and (3) the imputed costs of depreciation and interest (regarding buildings and equipment).

Earnings Foregone by Students

Time spent by students in school or in preparation for school is not costless. So long as jobs are available for individuals with no or relatively little education, some income could have been earned had the student chosen to work rather than go to school. Since individuals under the age of fourteen are prohibited by law from obtaining most types of jobs (except for some restricted part-time employment), earnings foregone for that age group are practically nonexistent. However, children could substitute school work for help in the home, the farm, or in some instances, in the father's job—in which case there would be some foregone earnings.

As a compromise solution, we may follow Schultz's treatment of the problem by assuming that pupils in elementary schools forego no income, whereas secondary and college or university students forego a certain portion of the income earned by individuals of their age group. Schultz's method for estimating the amount of earnings foregone by students is best described in his own words:

High school students were treated separately from college and university students. The year 1949 was taken as a base year in determining the "earnings" per week of young people, both males and females, for each of the four age groups (14-17, 18-19, 20-24, and 25-29). Students' foregone earnings were calculated on the assumption that, on the average, students forego 40 weeks of such earnings, and then expressed in earning-equivalent weeks of workers in manufacturing in the U.S. The results . . . indicate that high school students forego the equivalent of about 11 weeks and college or university students about 25 weeks of such earnings. These 1949 earnings ratios were applied to particular years between 1900 and 1956; an adjustment was then made for unemployment. . . . (1960: 573)

Estimates of foregone earnings, using the Schultz method, are presented in Table 4–6. Note that our methodology differs from that of Schultz in two respects. First, adjustment for unemployment is based upon annual rates of unemployment published by the federal government for young workers (age sixteen to nineteen)—regarding high school students—and for adult workers (age twenty and over)—regarding students in IHEs—in contrast to Schultz's method of using an average unemployment rate for an entire period (1900–1965). Second, we use full-time equivalent enrollments for students in IHEs rather than total enrollments as used by Schultz.

The figures in Table 4–6 show a more than sevenfold increase in earnings foregone of high school students and more than a twelve-fold increase for students in IHEs. Total foregone earnings increased almost tenfold. When adjusted for inflation, the increase was almost 200 percent (from $17.9 billion in 1950 to $53.3 billion in 1977, in 1972 dollars).

A number of conceptual problems are encountered when an application of the Schultz method is attempted. First, although it may be correct to argue that an individual student, or a relatively small group of students, could possibly earn what we called the average weekly equivalent salary of manufacturing workers in the United States, the influx of a large number of students into the labor market would probably have changed the entire earnings pattern in the particular segment of the labor market (with repercussions likely on the entire labor market). This is known as the "aggregation" problem. Serious as this problem may be, the proportion that high school and college or university students are of the total labor force is sufficiently small so that they could have been absorbed into the labor force without affecting average earnings too severely in the long run. More likely, an influx of such students would lead to the replacement (at least temporarily) of other workers who are likely to possess less ability and training than the average student. In all, while we must be aware of the possible bias due to aggregation, it is not clear, as some theorists would argue, that our estimates are entirely meaningless. If it were possible to account for an aggregation effect, we would have certainly modified our estimates; how-

Table 4-6. Estimated Earnings Foregone by Students in Current Prices—United States, 1950-1977.

	Average Weekly Earnings in All Manufacturing (per worker)	Rate of Unemployment		Earnings Foregone per Student in				Total High School Enrollment (thousands)	Total Earnings Foregone (millions of dollars)		
				High Schools		IHEs					
		Workers 16-19 Years Old	Workers 20 Years and Older	Unadjusted	Adjusted for Unemployment	Unadjusted	Adjusted for Unemployment		High Schools	IHEs	Total
Year	1	2	3	4	5	6	7	8	9	10	
1950	$ 58.32	12.2	4.8	$ 641.52	$ 563.25	$1,458.00	$1,388.02	6,453	3,635	3,377	7,012
1960	89.72	14.7	4.8	986.92	841.84	2,243.00	2,135.34	9,689	8,157	6,284	14,441
1970	133.73	15.2	4.0	1,471.03	1,247.43	3,343.25	3,209.52	14,632	18,252	21,571	39,823
1975	189.51	19.9	7.2[a]	2,084.61	1,669.27	4,737.75	4,396.63	15,694	26,205	37,288[b]	63,493[b]
1977	215.34[a]	19.0[a]	6.7[a]	2,368.74	1,918.68	5,383.50	5,022.81	15,658[b]	30,043[b]	45,602[b]	75,645[b]

Sources: Columns 1-3 from Economic Report of the President (1977); Column 4 = 11 × col. 1; Column 5 = [(100 − col. 2)/100] × col. 4; Column 6 = 25 × column 1; Column 7 = [(100 − col. 3)/100] × col. 6; Column 8 from Biennial Survey of Education and various editions of Projections of Educational Statistics; Column 9 = col. 5 × col. 8; Column 10 = col. 7 × (col. 3 + col. 4, Table 4-2).
[a]Data are for fourth quarter, 1976.
[b]Projected.

ever, in the absence of a method that could account for such an effect, we have chosen to use the estimates provided in Table 4-6.

Another difficulty relates to the general level of intelligence and ability of students. If, as we believe is the case, students are generally endowed with more intelligence and ability than individuals of comparable age in the labor force, using the latter's earnings as a proxy for what the former could have earned represents a serious downward bias in earnings foregone by students.

On the other hand, we have overlooked the fact that many students work part-time during the academic year. Thus, any such part-time earnings ought to be deducted from the estimated foregone earnings. This phenomenon is probably most serious in the estimation of earnings foregone for students in IHEs.

Finally, the adjustment for unemployment deserves special scrutiny. First of all, it is not clear which unemployment rate should be used in the adjustment. Regarding high school students, should we use the rate for ages sixteen to nineteen or the adult rate (for ages twenty and over). On the one hand, the sixteen to nineteen rate may seem to be the more reasonable of the two, since age discrimination in employment is likely to prevail across economic classes and ability lines. Yet employment of individuals sixteen to nineteen years of age is mostly restricted to school dropouts who, as a group, exhibit much higher unemployment rates than graduates. Further, since college and university students represent the elite of society, the average adult unemployment rate is probably too high. Studies on unemployment have revealed that unemployment among professional and other white collar workers is substantially below the average for all adults.[2] Therefore, it seems that the choice of the two unemployment rates tends to underestimate earnings foregone.

In summary, the utilization of schultz's method, together with the adjustment for unemployment, reflects both upward and downward biases in the estimation of foregone earnings. Which of the biases predominates is impossible to tell at this point. We shall therefore adhere to that method with the (hopeful) expectation that, over all, the estimates are not severely biased in one or the other direction.

An alternative formulation for estimating earnings foregone is presented by Blitz (1962b). He objects to Schultz's method on the ground that census data do not reflect the true opportunity costs of students. In the first place, he contends that census data used by Schultz include casual workers who could not "realize their full potential in the labor market" and who are working, on the average,

2. See, for example, Bloom and Northrup (1969: 406-14).

less than forty hours per week. These two factors lead to a downard bias. Second, as we have already mentioned above, "racial and environmental factors or the lower intelligence of the full-time workers of high school age will reduce their income potential in comparison with that of students" (p. 391). In addition, Blitz argues that a further downward bias in Schultz's estimates has resulted from his use of median earnings (i.e., the earnings of the person in the fiftieth percentile of the income distribution), whereas mean earnings (the arithmetic average) would have been more appropriate. All in all, Blitz believes that Schultz's estimates were far too low.

Blitz presents a number of studies of the earnings of youth in five different locations and at different time periods. The advantages of these studies is that they deal specifically with the earnings of youth and not of the labor force in general. Further, Blitz found the studies to corroborate one another quite closely. Leaving unchanged the assumption made by Schultz regarding the eleven and twenty-five weeks of foregone earnings by high school and college or university students, respectively, the weekly wages used to compute annual earnings foregone are much different. Consequently, Blitz's estimates, for 1956, of earnings foregone by high school and college or university students, respectively, amount to $11,581 and $7,041 million compared to Schultz's figures of $6,784 and $6,601 million. The Blitz estimate of earnings foregone by high school students is, therefore, 70 percent higher than that reported by Schultz. For college and university students, Blitz's figures are only 17 percent larger than those reported by Schultz.

On the other hand, a study by Solmon (1971) compared earnings foregone for 1959 according to the Schultz method and an alternative method in which foregone earnings were calculated as the difference between earnings of school age individuals not enrolled in school and earnings of individuals of the age group who were enrolled. The Schultz method yielded earnings foregone estimates of $10.7 billion and $7.0 billion, respectively, for high school and IHE students, whereas the respective figures for the alternative methodology were much lower: $5.0 billion, and $1.98 billion. If the alternative methodology were correct, then our calculations of foregone earnings are substantially overestimated.

Schultz argues that Blitz's method is suspect because he uses localized studies to generate estimates for the population in general. The problem with Solmon's estimate, on the other hand, is that it depends too much on earnings of individuals out of school, without properly adjusting for level of ability and other important variables. A possible solution to the problem is the use of a well-specified earnings function supplemented by detailed enrollment data cross-classified by age, sex, mental ability, labor market experience, and so on. Until such data become available, it will not be possible to judge the accuracy of the data in Table 4-6.

Costs of Tax Exemption

All nonprofit educational institutions are exempted from payment of property, income, and also in many instances, sales taxes. Consequently, schools have an advantage over other enterprises in that they can buy inputs at a lower price. In other words, the total expenditures reported by a school for supplies, equipment, and the like would have been somewhat higher had the school not been exempted from tax payment. Consider the state and local property tax, for example. If schools were subject to property taxes, total educational costs would have risen. Exempting schools from tax payment does not lower the social cost of the tax; rather, it shifts the burden from exempt to nonexempt property owners. (Some social cost in the form of "excess burden" could, of course, occur if such a shift in the tax burden creates distortions in the prices of goods and services.)[3]

Although the above argument carries much force, it is not foolproof. In the first place, even some of the most avid proponents of the "subsidy" argument (namely, Blitz, Machlup, etc.) point out that in the event that schools would have been subject to the tax, the tax rate (per dollar of assessed valuation) would have been lower than otherwise. Therefore, any calculation of the tax foregone must take this possibility into account. Moreover, since about 75 percent of the local property tax is earmarked for the support of education itself, it could be argued that, since taxes are collected for the very purpose of financing school operations, it would be improper to add all of the foregone taxes to school costs. Since such a sizable proportion of local taxes is designed to support school activities, in the absence of public education, only a reduced tax would have been necessary (to support other local services: fire and police protection, highways, sanitation, etc.). Consequently, the true extent of the opportunity costs is much less than it would appear to be. In summary, our analysis agrees with the basic postulate that tax exemption does represent an opportunity cost. However, when all or part of the tax is designed for the support of education, only that portion of it that does not apply to education could strictly

3. For an excellent treatment of excess burden, see R.A. Musgrave (1959: 140ff).

be regarded as a hidden cost. For example, if the property tax rate is currently set at $1.90 per $100 of assessed property valuation, and if the value of the school property is estimated to be $1 billion, the proponents of the "subsidy" doctrine would add $19 million to total school costs. However, if 75 percent of the tax is earmarked for education, it seems that the true subsidy amounts to only $4.75 million.

Similarly, since a portion of sales tax revenues is also used to support educational activities (through state aid to education and other state programs for education), allowance should be made for the tax exemption of schools only insofar as the noneducational portion of the tax is concerned.

An argument against the tax exemption allowance has been made by Hu et al. (1969). The essence of the argument is that it is improper to compare private and social goods, since the production and the distribution of the two are fundamentally different. Tax exemption is but one characteristic of a social good. Correcting for this difference only—leaving all other fundamental differences unchanged—cannot by itself render the two types of goods comparable. In other words, since education is a social good, it is erroneous, according to this argument, to apply the criteria of a private good to it. Thus, earnings foregone need not be calculated—only the explicit costs of producing and distributing the product "education" (pp. 22-26).

This argument, however, really misses the point. Our aim is not necessarily a comparison between private and social goods, but rather, an inquiry into the nature and magnitude of the investment in education. Thus, if the tax exemption could be construed as a (hidden) social investment in education, it, too, must be added to total resource costs. All economic costs must be estimated; the criterion is not whether a good is a social or a private one, but rather, whether or not the educational activity results in any economic costs.

Due to data limitations, the present analysis is confined to estimating the costs of exemption from payment of local real property taxes. Since approximately 75 percent of local property taxes go to school districts, we count only 25 percent of the tax loss for elementary and secondary schools. On the other hand, since IHEs are almost never financed through property taxes (in Richland County, South Carolina, approximately 0.2 percent of property tax revenues go for the support of the local community college), we count all of the tax loss for IHEs.

The main problems arise with respect to the measurement of the taxable value of school property and the effective tax rate that should apply thereto. For the first problem, data for IHEs are taken from the *Digest* (see, for example, Grant and Lind, 1977, Table 139). For later years, property value was estimated by adding to the previous year's value the amount invested in capital outlays. For elementary and secondary schools, we find data on property values per student for some states, based upon the Office of Education publication *Statistics of State School Systems.* Using these data, we obtained an estimate of average values per pupil (based on a weighted average) in reporting states and multiplied the result by total enrollment in the United States. Data for years for which such information was lacking were derived by adding to property value the amount invested in capital outlay during the previous years.

Derivation of the effective tax rate is explained in Table 4-7. *Census of Government* data were used to compute the total market value of property, and data from the *Statistical Abstract* were used to derive total tax revenues for each year. From these, the effective tax rate (equal to the ratio of property tax revenue to market value) was derived for the census years 1956, 1961, 1966, and 1971. Linear interpolation and extrapolation was used to derive the effective tax rates for other years.[4]

The estimation of the property tax exemption costs is given in Table 4-8. Due to rising market values and tax rates, the tax exemption cost rose nearly 1,750 percent from 1950 to 1977—considerably faster than other educational costs. We estimate the cost of property tax exemption to be more than $1.9 billion in 1977.

Implicit Rent and Depreciation

As noted earlier, the costs of implicit rent and depreciation are another example of economic costs that must be imputed. Implicit rent represents foregone opportunities of renting school buildings, grounds, and equipment for noneducational uses, while depreciation reflects the wear and tear or obsolescence of physical assets owned by the school system. Both represent current educational costs.

Since our earlier figures of school costs included an item called "capital outlays" (on new buildings and equipment), we must clarify

4. These effective tax rates differ somewhat from estimated average effective tax rates for single family homes with FHA-insured mortgages, for fifty large SMSAs, reported by the Advisory Commission on Intergovernmental Relations (ACIR). The rates reported by the ACIR are 1.42, 1.71, 1.95, 2.13, and 2.02 for the years 1958, 1962, 1966, 1971, and 1975, respectively. The differences, however, are not sufficiently large to warrant any adjustments in our data. See ACIR (1977a, Table 72, p. 108).

Table 4-7. Estimation of Effective Property Tax Rates—United States, 1956-1971.

	Net Assessed Value (millions)	Ratio of Assessed Value to Sales Price	Estimated Market Value (millions)	Property Tax Revenues (millions)	Effective Tax Rate (percent)
Year	1	2	3	4	5
1956	$272,444	.303	$ 899,155	$11,749	1.31
1961	353,968	.308	1,149,247	18,002	1.57
1966	484,057	.308	1,571,614	24,670	1.57
1971	694,575	.327	2,124,082	37,852	1.78

Sources: Columns 1-2 from various editions of the U.S. Bureau of the Census, Census of Governments; Columns 3 = col. 1 ÷ col. 2; Column 4 from various editions of U.S. Bureau of the Census, Statistical Abstract of the U.S.; Column 5 = (col. 4 ÷ col. 3) X 100.

the compatibility of the latter category with that of implicit interest. It might be argued that if a school follows a procedure by which capital outlays are added to current costs when incurred, there seems to be no need to add either depreciation charges or estimates of implicit interest costs. Adding both of these categories would appear to result in "double counting." Machlup (1963) argues that the criteria for including the two together or only one of the two depend upon the purposes for which these costs are computed in the first place. If our purpose is to assess the true opportunity cost of education in any year, regardless of whether the costs represent investment in humans or in physical assets, one must deduce (1) the opportunity costs of releasing old resources from education (thus necessitating the computation of implicit interest and depreciation) and (2) the costs of releasing new resources (such as those devoted to the building of new structures and equipment)—in addition to the current costs of education represented by teacher salaries, wages of noninstructional personnel, and so on. Thus the summation of both capital outlays and depreciation and implicit interest does not represent, in this case, double counting. On the other hand, if our interest lies with the investment in human capital only, the summation of both capital outlays (i.e., investment in new physical capital) and depreciation and implicit interest (a part of the investment in the education of humans—hence, an investment in human capital) would be quite inappropriate. It is for that reason that Schultz (1960) excluded the costs of capital outlays from his figures (his purpose being to measure the investment in human capital), whereas Blitz (1962a) included both (his purpose being to measure total

Table 4-8. Estimated Costs of Property Tax Exemption by Educational Institutions—United States, 1950-1977 (in millions of current dollars).

	Elementary and High Schools					IHEs			
	Value of Property		Total (1) + (2)	Tax Rate (Percent)	Tax if All Property Tax Is Included (3) × (4)	25 Per-cent of Column 5	Value of Property	Tax (all Property Tax Is Included) (4) × (7)	Total (6) + (8)
Year	Public	Private							
	1	2	3	4	5	6	7	8	9
1950	11,400	1,948	13,348	1.30	173.50	43.4	4,800	62.4	105.8
1960	27,285	4,437	31,722	1.53	485.35	121.3	13,448	205.6	327.1
1970	53,522	5,598	59,120	1.70	1,005.00	251.3	42,093	715.6	966.9
1975	95,643	8,935	104,578	1.90	1,986.98	496.7	62,183	1,200.1	1,696.8
1977	107,372	10,031	117,403	1.93	2,265.88	566.5	72,108	1,391.6	1,958.1

Sources: Columns 1 and 2 derived by multiplying estimated per pupil property values as given in *Statistics of State School Systems* by respective ADAs; Column 4 from Column 5, Table 4-7 (linear extrapolations); Column 7 from Grant and Lind (1977), Table 139. Data for 1977 are derived by assuming that property value in 1977 is equal to property value in 1975 plus capital outlays in 1975 and 1976.

resource costs in education). Since we attempt to provide a comprehensive measure of total educational costs, the inclusion of both capital outlays and depreciation and implicit interest costs seems warranted.

We shall follow once again the procedure developed by Schultz (1960) to estimate the costs of depreciation and implicit interest. First, regarding the estimates for elementary and secondary schools, suppose that "the distribution of physical assets is placed at 20 percent land, 72 per cent buildings, and 8 percent equipment" (Table 3, note). Further, assume that there is no depreciation on land, and 3 percent and 10 percent depreciation on buildings and equipment, respectively. Also assume that implicit interest equals 5 percent of the value of all physical assets. Then the combined rate of depreciation and interest is 8 percent per year of the assets owned by the public schools.

Second, if we accept Robert Rude's (1954) figures—as reported by Schultz—which indicate that the assets of colleges and universities "were distributed 15 percent to land, 70 percent to buildings and 15 percent to equipment"; and given that the rate of depreciation is assumed to be equal to 0 percent on land, 2 percent on buildings, and 10 percent on equipment; then, if the implicit interest is assumed to be 5.1 percent, the rate of depreciation plus implicit interest on the property of colleges and universities will also be 8 percent. A summary of our calculations is presented in Table 4-9.[5]

The figures in Table 4-9 reveal a ninefold increase in imputed costs of implicit rent and depreciation during the period 1950-1977. The assumption of a constant percentage of property value (8 percent) over time reduces the increase in costs relative to, say, our estimates of the tax exemption. Since interest rates have increased in recent years, the estimates in Table 4-9 are probably biased downward.

Imputed Direct Costs

A final category of costs is the imputed direct costs of books and supplies. Lacking a direct measurement, we continue to follow

5. An alternative formulation that may account for both depreciation and implicit interest may be employed by using the "capital recovery factor" (CRF). Let C_O denote the present value of capital (given by the discounted stream of capital costs in past years), n the expected life of the buildings or equipment, and i the "proper" rate of discount. Then the CRF, denoted by c, is derived from the formula $c = C_O i (1 + i)^n / [(1 + i)^n - 1]$. The CRF, it should be noted, is not a measure of the true capital consumption costs during a given period. Rather, it "is the level end-of-year annual amount over the life of the project necessary to pay interest on and recover the capital costs in full" (see Hirshleifer et al., 1960: 158-59).

Table 4-9.   Imputed Costs of Implicit Rent and Depreciation in U.S. Educational Institutions, Selected Years (millions of current dollars).

	Elementary and High Schools		Institutions of Higher Education		
	Value of Property	Implicit Rent and Depreci- ation (0.08 X Column 1)	Value of Property	Implicit Rent and Depreci- ation (0.08 X Column 3)	Total (2) + (4)
Year	1	2	3	4	5
1950	13,348	1,068	4,800	384	1,452
1960	31,722	2,538	13,448	1,076	3,614
1970	59,120	4,730	42,093	3,367	8,097
1975	104,578	8,366	62,183	4,974	13,340
1977	117,403	9,392	72,108	5,769	15,161

Sources: Columns 1 and 3 are taken from Table 4-8.

Schultz (1960), by assuming that costs of books and supplies are 5 percent of earnings foregone for high school students and 10 percent of earnings foregone for college students. One might also include in our estimates the cost of private transportation and other out of pocket costs, since a comparison with a study by Carroll and Ihnen (1967) indicates that costs of books and supplies are only approximately 4 percent of earnings foregone for students attending a post-secondary vocational school in Gastonia, North Carolina, for the years 1959 and 1960. Our results are reported in Table 4-10.

RESOURCES ENTERING EDUCATION

Total resources entering formal education are summarized in Table 4-11. Examining total costs by type, we find that approximately 43 percent of the costs in 1977 are indirect, the rest being direct costs. Similarly, about 54 percent of 1977 costs were due to elementary and secondary education and 46 to IHEs. All in all, the costs of education have increased from slightly over $18 billion in 1950 to nearly $230 billion in 1977.

The contrast between the increase in costs in current dollars as opposed to costs in real terms (1972 dollars, in our case) is, again, quite obvious. Whereas costs in current dollars increased by approximately 1,160 percent between 1950 and 1977, costs adjusted for inflation increased by only 245 percent. The increase of 245 percent, however, still reflects a considerable expansion in the investment society has chosen to make in education.

Table 4-10. Imputed Costs of Books and Supplies of Students in All Levels of Education in the United States, Selected Years (millions of dollars).

Year	High Schools 1	Colleges and Universities 2	Total (1) + (2) 3
1950	182	338	520
1960	408	628	1,036
1970	913	2,157	3,070
1975	1,310	3,729	5,039
1977	1,502	4,560	6,062

Sources: Column 1 = 0.05 $\times$ col. 9, Table 4-6; Column 2 = 0.10 $\times$ col. 10, Table 4-6.

Table 4-11. Resources Entering Education, by Type of Cost and Level of Schooling—United States, 1950-1977 (billions of dollars).

	By Type of Cost		By Level of Schooling		Total	
Year	Direct Costs[a] 1	Earnings Foregone and Imputed Costs[a] 2	Elementary and High Schools[a] 3	IHEs[a] 4	In Current Dollars 5	In 1972 Dollars 6
1950	9.2	9.1	11.5	6.8	18.3	46.9
1960	24.8	19.4	29.3	14.9	44.2	77.8
1970	70.4	51.6	69.6	52.4	122.0	138.2
1975	107.6	83.6	105.1	86.1	191.2	147.3
1977[b]	131.1	98.8	123.3	106.6	229.9	162.0

Sources: Column 1 from Table 4-1; Column 2 from Tables 4-6, 4-8, 4-9, and 4-10. Columns 3 and 4 from Tables 4-1, 4-6, 4-8, 4-9, and 4-10. Column 5 is the sum of columns 1 and 2 *or* of 3 and 4. Column 6 = (Col. 3 $\div$ Col. 2, Table 4-4) $\times$ 100.
[a]In current dollars.
[b]Projected.

Measured against the growth of income and investment in physical capital in the United States during the same period (Table 4-12), we find educational investment to have grown both absolutely and relatively. As a proportion of gross national product (adjusted to include earnings foregone and implicit rent and depreciation), investment in education increased from 6.2 percent in 1950 to 12.5 percent for 1977. Some slippage in the relative position of investment in education occurred during 1973-1975, and only time will tell whether the improved 1977 projections will be sustained.

Table 4-12. Investment in Education Compared to GNP and Gross Investment in Physical Capital—United States, 1950-1977.

	GNP	Adjusted GNP	Investment in Education	Gross Physical Investment	Col. 3 ÷ Col. 2 (percent)	Col. 3 ÷ Col. 4 (percent)
			(billions of current dollars)			
year	1	2	3	4	5	6
1950	286.2	294.7	18.3	53.8	6.2	34
1960	506.0	524.0	44.2	76.4	8.4	58
1970	982.4	1,030.3	122.0	140.8	11.8	87
1975	1,516.3	92.8	191.2	183.7	12.0	104
1977	1,748.5[a]	1,839.3	229.9[b]	249.0[a]	12.5	92

Sources: Columns 1 and 4 from *Economic Report of the President* (1977); Column 2 = col. 1 + col. 11, Table 4-6, + col. 5, Table 4-9, following Machlup (1963).

[a]Data are for fourth quarter, 1976.
[b]Projected.

Alternatively, we find that the proportion that gross investment in education is to gross investment in physical capital has increased substantially from 34 percent in 1950 to 92 percent in 1977. We also note the relative stability of the educational investment as opposed to the great instability of gross physical investment, especially during the period 1972-1976,[6] suggesting the potentially stabilizing influence that educational investments are likely to have on the business cycle.

Some International Comparisons

It would be quite interesting to compare the extent of educational investments in different countries. Such comparisons are, by their very nature, hazardous, as national statistics are compiled in various manners in different countries. Moreover, such extensive computations as we have carried out for the United States cannot be undertaken in many other countries because of the lack of data. The only somewhat comparable figures are those for expenditures on education in formal schooling (not including any indirect and/or imputed costs). The most extensive work on comparative costs of education in different countries is that of Edding (1966). Table 4-13 presents a brief summary of some of his findings. Needless to say, such

6. Gross physical domestic investment, in the United States, during the period 1972-1976 was as follows (in billions of current dollars): 1972—188.3; 1973—220.0; 1974—215.0; 1975—183.7; and 1976—241.2 (see the *Economic report of the President*, 1977, Table B-1, p. 187).

Table 4–13. Expenditures on Education Related to National Income in Twenty-three Countries, 1950 and 1960 (U.S. dollars).

Country	National Income per Capita 1960	Educational Expenditures per Capita 1960	Educational Expenditures as Percent of National Income 1960	Educational Expenditures as Percent of National Income 1950	Percent Increase in Educational Expenditures Relative to National Income 1950–1960
	1	2	3	4	5
United States	2,237	138.48[a]	6.19	4.04	53
Canada	1,528	89.65	5.87	3.21	83
Sweden	1,470	73.74	5.02	3.20	57
New Zealand	1,301	49.55	3.81	2.40	59
Australia	1,187	41.41	3.49	2.06	69
United Kingdom	1,036	45.64	4.41	3.65	21
West Germany	985	37.37	3.79	3.21	18
Belgium	981	57.20	5.83	3.35	74
Denmark	979	44.03	4.50	2.65	70
France	968	33.87	3.50	1.90	84
Norway	909	49.78	5.48	3.37	63
Finland	806	53.32	6.61	2.57	157
Netherlands	735	43.04	5.85	3.34	75
Ireland	528	18.00	3.41	2.62	30
Italy	510	26.56	5.19	3.03	71
Japan	342	18.28	5.34	4.78	12
Portugal	234	5.17	2.21	1.35	64
Colombia	216	4.36	2.02	1.21	67
Ecuador	179	4.38	2.45	1.27	93
Honduras	167	3.66	2.20	0.60	207
Ceylon	122	5.37	4.39	2.96	48
Brazil	107	2.90	2.70	1.26	114
India	64	1.18	1.85	1.20	54

Source: Edding (1960), Tables 2 and 3.

[a]Using our estimates, as given in Column 7 of Table 4–1, total educational *expenditures* in the United States in 1960 amounted to $24.8 billion. United States population in 1960 was 180,684,000. Therefore, per capita expenditures on education were approximately $137.26. This is quite close to Edding's estimate in Column 2.

figures are at best suggestive. Not only are the figures on educational expenditures subject to error, but also, national income implies different things in different countries. Since only market transactions are recorded in the national accounts, for those countries in which informal markets exist and/or in which home production is more significant, the national income accounts will grossly underestimate total production. Further, since the criteria for the inclusion of items in the national income accounts differ between nations, one should be cautious in interpreting the data.

In any event, Table 4-13 suggests that the United States spends the largest amount per capita (among the countries considered) and, in addition, invests a relatively high proportion of its national income in education. Moreover, such investment in education has markedly increased in the United States between 1950 and 1960. In the main, Table 4-13 suggests that the richer nations spend more on education. It is not clear whether nations become rich because they invest more in human resources or whether richer nations spend more on education because they can afford more. All we can say is that national income and expenditure on education seem to be correlated.

In addition to Edding's results we have some data assembled by Ritzen (1977) from UNESCO (1975) and other data sources for 1967 (see Table 4-14). Costs per pupil in six countries are compared by level of schooling completed. Uganda appears to have the lowest costs per pupil in any level. Whereas Nigeria has the next lowest costs for primary and secondary education, the costs of higher education are lower in Mexico. The two developed nations—the Netherlands and the United States—lead the rest in per pupil costs, with the United States having the highest costs in elementary and secondary education, whereas the Netherlands tops the list for IHEs.

Table 4-14. Direct Costs of Education per Graduate and Per Capita Income in Six Countries—U.S. Dollars, 1967.

Country	*Level of Education*			*Per Capita Income*
	Primary	*Secondary*	*University*	
Colombia	270	1,140	6,000	250
Mexico	260	1,000	3,110	520
Netherlands	1,330	4,420	21,440	1,230
Nigeria[a]	170	930	6,130	95
Uganda	8	380	1,470	130
United States	4,448	8,650	19,700	2,570

Source: Ritzen (1977), Table A-1.
[a]Data for 1964.

Since these data are not supplemented by information on the quality of education per pupil, inferences about the desirability of obtaining an education in a given country cannot be drawn.

EXTERNAL COSTS, COSTS OF NONFORMAL EDUCATION, AND OTHER ISSUES

The costs of education estimated in the foregoing sections include both direct and indirect costs but exclude external costs. External costs occur when the educational endeavor results in losses to the economic system or any individuals in society, where such losses are not taken into account either in the social or the private calculus. For example, when a school becomes a staging point and/or a refuge for youth gangs who terrorize a neighborhood, some external costs occur. Or when students, teachers, or other individuals are victims of crime within the school perimeter, the costs of such crimes may be attributable to the educational enterprise. Likewise, noise, unsightly buildings and grounds, or other undesirable effects may be associated with schools, the costs of which should be taken into account.

One should also consider the proper placement of the costs of various services given to school children. For example, many schools in urban areas provide police protection around the clock, particularly in high schools. Yet if such services are performed by the local police force, the costs of the service would not constitute a part of educational costs. But these are definitely educational costs, and so a proper adjustment in school costs is in order.[7] On the other hand, costs of medical services performed in school may be recorded as school costs, despite the fact that these are definitely not educational costs. Other types of services may likewise belong to a cost category different from that to which they are currently assigned.[8]

Finally, our estimates of the investment in education centered on formal schooling. No similar estimates were made for informal education (at home, on the job, etc.). The difficulties in securing reliable data need not be belabored. Moreover, one encounters the difficulty of separating informal education from leisure: Is the reading of an interesting book (fiction or nonfiction) to be taken as education or

7. This point has been suggested to me by Thomas G. Fox.
8. There is some evidence, however, that improved nutrition is associated with improved learning ability. Thus, costs of food given to poor children may be considered, indirectly, as educational costs. Also, to the extent that better health is associated with greater learning ability, reduced absenteeism, and so forth, medical costs may also be regarded, at least in part, as educational costs (see Cohn, 1971c).

as leisure? All seems to depend on the intent of the person reading the book.

Informal education on the job is probably quite important. General and specific training is usually informal. In many cases, an individual replacing an employee will be hired some time before the latter leaves so that the latter can provide the former with necessary "tips" connnected with the position. This represents an educational activity, the cost of which is the difference between the new employee's marginal productivity (or contribution to the firm) and his or her wage during the training period, plus the cost of maintaining that portion of the time used by the retiring employee to conduct the informal training, plus the cost of whatever other supplies and materials are used in the training process. Estimates of such training activities are extremely difficult to obtain. Figures on training costs are virtually nonexistent. The exceptions are generally in the larger employer groups where formal training courses are conducted, but even these are based on such heterogeneous and largely unreliable sources that they are best neglected.

CONCLUSION

The bulk of this chapter focused on the estimation of the costs of education in the United States during the period 1950-1957. Our data indicate a substantial growth in educational investment in the United States, both in absolute terms and relative to GNP and gross physical capital formation. The continuation of such a trend is not assured however. There are signs that society is shifting its priorities toward other goals, such as health, income maintenance, environment, energy, and above all, reduction in taxes. Since enrollments are likely to decrease at all levels in the near future, it will not be surprising if real expenditures on education level off or even decrease. The educational sector will be pressed to translate enrollment reductions into cost savings so that reduced or even constant total real expenditures will not result in the deterioration of educational quality.

It should be emphasized that the educational costs presented herein are estimates. Problems arise with the data used and the methods adopted. Serious questions arise with respect to earnings foregone. Omitted from the calculations are expenditures on libraries, education in the home, religious and civic institutions, news media, books and magazines, and many more. What is certain is that educational costs are very high, probably about as high as $230 billion in 1977, if not more. Questions needing further study are (1) To what ends are such costs incurred? (2) How can we reduce the costs of education without reducing the amount and quality of education we get? and (3) Are the costs of education more than offset by educational benefits, both in the aggregate and for each educational program? It is the last question to which we turn in the next two chapters.

LITERATURE GUIDE

Comprehensive studies on the costs of education in the United States include Schultz (1960), Blitz (1962a, 1962b), Machlup (1963), Kendrick (1974), and Cohn (1975b, 1977b). Other widely known works are Vaizey and Chesswas (1967) and M. J. Bowman (1966a).

International comparisons are discussed in Edding (1966), Palm (1968), and Ritzen (1977). Historical studies of educational costs include J.R. Walsh (1935), Fishlow (1966), and Solmon (1970a).

Specific studies include Stromsdorfer, Hu, and Lee (1968) on the costs of vocational education; Carroll and Ihnen (1967) on the costs of postsecondary vocational education; Ewald and Kiker (1971) on the costs of higher education by degree program; Witmer (1972) on the costs of higher education; Cohn, Hu, and Kaufman (1972) —also Cohn and Hu (1973)—on costs of secondary education by program in Michigan; and Marriner (1977) on the costs of programs to educate handicapped pupils.

Earnings foregone are discussed in numerous studies, many of which deal with costs and returns. Three studies deserve to be mentioned at this time—Solmon (1971), Parsons (1974), and Crary and Leslie (1977).

While Sharma and Ram (1974) contend that it is not proper to adjust earnings foregone for the level of unemployment, it is argued in Cohn (1977c) that the adjustment *is* appropriate.

Finally, data sources for educational costs include the *Biennial Survey of Education* (until 1958), the *Digest of Educational Statistics* (annual), the *Projections of Educational Statistics* (annual); *National Comparison of Local School Costs* (1975, 1977), National Education Association (1975), Organization for Economic Cooperation and Development (1974–1975), and UNESCO (1975).

✳ *Chapter 5*

An Introduction to Benefit-Cost Analysis

The enumeration and quantitative estimation of educational costs and benefits that we have performed in preceding chapters are certainly of paramount importance to those who are interested in formulating rational decision rules for investment in education. This is true for both private and public decisionmakers, although the former will search for costs and benefits different from those of the latter. But enumeration and evaluation of costs and benefits are not sufficient (they are necessary, of course): To formulate rational decision rules, we must be able to specify our ultimate objective, the constraints (physical, technological, financial, and legal, among others) that must be taken into account by the decisionmaker, the alternative choices open to us, and various other considerations—in addition to the specification and quantification of the relevant costs and benefits. To make the policymaking process more manageable, we might want to suggest simple, but correct, decision rules that will satisfy our prime objectives, the various constraints, and so forth. As we shall soon see, this is not a simple matter. Ostensibly "correct" criteria often lead to incorrect decisions; it is therefore important that sufficient space be devoted in this volume to the theoretical underpinnings of optimal investment decision.

Although the utilization of benefit-cost techniques has received a great deal of attention only in recent years, its application dates as far back as the early 1900s, as a result of the River and Harbor Act of 1902, which "required a board of engineers to report on the desirability of Army Corps of Engineers' river and harbour projects, taking into account the amount of commerce benefited and the cost " (Prest and Turvey, 1965: 683). The methods used then were much cruder and far less satisfactory than the ones we are about to review here, but the basic idea of a benefit-cost analysis is certainly not new.

A very general definition of benefit-cost analysis is given by Prest and Turvey: It is "a practical way of assessing the desirability of projects, where it is important to take a long view (in the sense of looking at repercussions in the further, as well as the nearer, future) and a wide view (in the sense of allowing for side-effects of many kinds on many persons, industries, regions, etc.), i.e., it implies the enumeration and evaluation of all the relevant costs and benefits" (p. 683). From the apparent simplicity and generality of this definition, we shall move in the direction of explaining the complexities involved as well as describing specific problems and situations that do not manifest themselves in a composite definition.

THE MAXIMUM SOCIAL WELFARE CRITERION

It is convenient to assume that policymakers (individual and/or government) seek to maximize something. The assumption of profit maximization by entrepreneurs, utility maximization by consumers, and so forth leads to convenient and relatively simple sets of decision rules. Whether or not individuals strive to maximize is really an empirical question. Further, a slight deviation from the maximization assumption may be ignored without undue loss, since there are, after all, costs in the specification of alternative assumptions of individual behavior (unless we can empirically establish behavioral assumptions such as offered by Herbert Simon [1957a, 1957b] that individuals are "satisficers" rather than maximizers, i.e., that firms, for example, only stirve to earn a given satisfactory" return over cost).

We may therefore assume that the decisionmaker attempts to maximize economic welfare. His "objective function" may give a greater weight to increases in welfare achieved by, say, individuals with incomes under \$3,000 per year than to all other individuals, or it may favor one geographic location over another. In general, however, we may write the function as:

$$W = f(W_1, W_2, \ldots W_n) \tag{5.1}$$

where W is "social welfare" (the maximand) and W_i refers to the welfare of individual i. (We assume that "society" is composed of n individuals.) Formula (5.1) does not tell us precisely how changes in the welfare of individuals 1, 2, and so forth affect W. Nor is there any indication of the time period in which W and W_i occur. Formula (5.1) may also be expressed in a marginal form:

$$\Delta W = h(\Delta W_1, \Delta W_2, \ldots \Delta W_n) \qquad (5.2)$$

where the symbol Δ means a "change in . . . ." The letters f and h are symbols for a functional form (we use different letters for (5.1) and (5.2) to indicate that the two functions may not be identical; i.e., the effect of W_i on W may not be the same as the effect of ΔW_i on ΔW).

Presumbly, any new investment project will produce discernible effects on the welfare of individuals. For instance, the authorization of a college scholarship fund by a state legislature will produce changes in the respective welfare of the individuals so affected. At the same time, the money for the fund must come from somewhere: either it means less expenditures on other state projects, or it may imply higher taxes, or perhaps it would come from funds that otherwise would have been used to reduce the state's debt. In any event, the opportunity cost of the fund will certainly have an effect on the welfare of some or all of the n individuals in society. Now, suppose we were able to measure all such repercussions. Could we suggest a course of action to the state? Not knowing the exact form of Formula (5.2), we could offer an unabiguous policy prescription only if (1) the effects of said policy would increase some or all of the W_i and decrease none; or (2) the effects of the policy would be to increase none of the W_i and to decrease some (at least one). In the first case, the project is obviously worthwhile; the second case it is obviously undesirable.[1]

Rarely, if ever, would projects fall clearly into one or the other categories mentioned above. As in the case of a scholarship fund, it is most likely that some would benefit (in particular, the recipients of the funds) and some would suffer (if the alternative to the scholarship were an improvement in the housing of low income families in the state, the group of low income families would suffer, as would construction companies that would have benefited thereby). An explicit objective function is needed to decide what the net effect upon social welfare is when a project results in net benefits to some and net losses to others.

---

1. The situation in which any new policy would benefit some individuals but only at the expense of at least one other individual, i.e., no one could be made better off without, at the same time, making someone else worse off, is termed "Pareto optimal." The choice between two Pareto optimal "states" requires an explicit social welfare function (see, e.g., Bator, 1957).

One plausible (though not perfect) form of the social welfare function assumes that income and welfare are identical.[2] Then:

$$W = f(Y_1, Y_2, \ldots Y_n) \tag{5.3}$$

where Y denotes income. In marginal form,

$$\Delta W = h(\Delta Y_1, \Delta Y_2, \ldots \Delta Y_n) \tag{5.4}$$

That is, social welfare is determined, according to the functional form h, by the impact of the proposed program on individual incomes, Y_i. Further, we might specify that an extra dollar earned by any one individual increases social welfare by the same amount that an additional dollar earned by any other individual would. Moreover, assume that total welfare is simply measured by total national income. Then

$$\Delta W = \Delta Y_1 + \Delta Y_2 + \ldots + \Delta Y_n = \sum_{i=1}^{n} \Delta Y_i \tag{5.5}$$

On the basis of Formula (5.5), it is now possible to formulate an investment decision. For those programs for which the sum of the positive increments in income exceed any negative increments—namely, where $\Delta W > 0$—the project would be deemed worthwhile. Conversely, if $\Delta W < 0$, the project would not be recommended. If $\Delta W = 0$, the formula would not provide any guidance, and decision must be based on additional evidence or value judgement.

Formula (5.5) assumes that changes in the distribution of income have no welfare implications. This is certainly an oversimplification. Few would argue that a project that would add $2 to a rich person and subtract $2 from a poor one is desirable. Therefore, it might be desirable to weight each ΔY_i in Formula (5.5) according to society's preferences concerning the distribution of income.

Economists have shied away from attaching such weights to the welfare function. The principal reasons for this are: (1) Some economists consider the redistributional aspects of a project to be entirely irrelevant to efficiency considerations, since they involve only transfers of income, which could easily be corrected through opposite transfers. (2) Other economists who consider redistributional effects to be relevant still choose to ignore them because they simply do not

2. Our analysis here draws upon, but is not identical to, Eckstein (1961).

know which weights should be attached to whom; that is, they consider the attachment of distributional weights in the objective function to be a value judgement, which, as economists, they refuse to make. (3) The consideration of redistributional effects would complicate the analysis considerably; as long as the redistribution effects appear to be relatively unimportant, they may best be ignored in the analysis itself. (They could, and should, however, be described separately as an additional "exhibit," to use the phrase in McKean, 1958.)

Weisbrod (1968) believes that "grand efficiency" includes both pure efficiency (changes in total income, in our case) as well as distributional effects (changes in the distribution of income). He proposes a way in which the distributional weights attached to different groups of individuals may be determined on the basis of an ex post analysis of sets of water resource projects that were considered by the Corps of Engineers in 1950. Since some of the projects were undertaken before others, it may be concluded that Congress viewed the projects undertaken earlier as being at least as worthy as the others. Since it can be shown that the project that was undertaken last (among a set of four) had the highest benefit-cost ratio (to be explained below), Weisbrod concluded that it was not undertaken earlier because Congress included distributional effects in its global decision process. Using some data on the distribution of income in the regions where the impact of the various projects was to be felt, Weisbrod constructed a model that makes it possible to determine implicitly the weights Congress assigned to a dollar of benefits expected for each of four race-income groups.

Although Weisbrod's idea is extremely interesting, it suffers from both theoretical and practical difficulties, which reduce its usefulness, given the present state of the art and availability of relevant data. It is not surprising, therefore, that Weisbrod's formulation has not been replicated in any benefit-cost study of which we are aware.

Another shortcoming of Formula (5.5) is that it does not provide explicitly for the treatment of intertemporal effects. It is not clear what the effect of a given policy on welfare would be when net income will be increased in some future period, where net losses are incurred at present. For example, it is a project that reduces current (net) income by X dollars but which increases income ten years from now by $X + 1$ dollars worthwhile? Further, suppose we must choose between two projects, one with a net income stream of $(-1, 0, 1.5)$ and the other with $(-1, 1.2, 0)$.[3] Which project is better? Using For-

3. The net income stream $(-1, 0, 1.5)$ implies that costs exceed benefits by 1 during the first (initial) period, costs and benefits cancel each other in the ensuing period, and benefits exceed costs by 1.5 in the final period. This notation could be used to describe net income streams for any number of finite periods.

mula (5.5), the answer to the first question is in the affirmative, and regarding the second question, the project with the net income stream (-1, 0, 1.5) would be preferable, since total net income is 0.5, compared to only 0.2 for the other project. But the wisdom of such choices is questionable when it is realized that net benefits are expected to occur at different times.

The problem of intertemporal allocations would not exist if individuals were indifferent between a dollar now and a dollar t years hence. For many reasons, this is not the case. First, there is the consideration of possible "myopia," meaning that individuals are not certain that they would live to enjoy that dollar in the future—hence, they would always prefer a dollar today to a dollar in the future. In addition, it has long been observed that a dollar saved and invested today could be transformed into a larger sum in the future because of the productivity of capital. One of the classical examples is the aging of wine: If I sacrifice a given amount of grapes today, the value of my investment will increase (up to a point) when the grapes are being transformed into the more valuable wine.[4] Or, if I consent to leave a newly planted tree alone for some time, its value is almost certain to increase as time goes on (again, only up to a point).[5] In addition, physical assets used as capital goods could, in time, lead to the production of far more valuable goods and services than the initial resources sacrificed. In sum, capital has a positive marginal productivity; hence, individuals will be reluctant to sacrifice a dollar today unless they are promised a return greater than a dollar (how much greater is another question) in the future.

More concretely, individuals who so choose have the option of placing their resources (savings) in a variety of relatively safe investments. Suppose that a "safe" savings account yields 5 percent per annum. Then a dollar saved today will be worth $1.05 next year, $1.1025 the following year (assuming that the interest of $.05 is reinvested), and in general, the value of a dollar t years hence, when the rate of interest is i, can be deduced from the following:

$$P_t = (1 + i)^t \tag{5.6}$$

where P_t is the value of $1 t years hence. The implications of this discussion should be quite clear: to increase individual or social welfare,

---

4. This is the Böhm-Bawerk example (the "Austrian School"). See, for example, Haavelmo (1960: 27–37).

5. This type of "productivity" was considered by Frank Knight. For a simple but authoritative analysis of this and other theories of capital, see Dewey (1965).

W, a project that costs X dollars today must yield a net benefit over time in excess of X dollars.

To take account of intertemporal allocations, Formula (5.4) could be rewritten as follows:

$$\Delta W = g(\Delta Y_{11}, \Delta Y_{12}, \ldots \Delta Y_{1T}; \Delta Y_{21}, \Delta Y_{22}, \ldots, \Delta Y_{2T};$$
$$\ldots; \Delta Y_{n1}, \Delta Y_{n2}, \ldots, \Delta Y_{nT}) \tag{5.7}$$

where Y_{it} is income received by individual i at time t ($t = 1, 2, \ldots, T$). Formula (5.7) implies that the social welfare resulting from any proposed project depends on the stream of net benefits (income in this case is equivalent to benefits) over the horizon of T periods for all n individuals. But since a dollar expected t years in the future is not equivalent to one received at present, the stream of expected benefits must be reduced to a present value. Instead of maximizing the change in total income—as Formula (5.5) implies—our objective becomes the maximization of the present value of net income over the period in which the (positive or negative) income stream is expected to occur.

The present value, V_o, of a dollar earned t years hence, when the applicable rate of interest is i, is given by:

$$V_o = 1/(1 + i)^t.$$

Similarly, the present value of P_t ($\$P$ expected in year t) is:

$$V_o = P_t/(1 + i)^t.$$

If we expect a stream of future earnings to occur between period 0 and period T, the present value of such a stream is given by:

$$V_o = \sum_{t=0}^{T} P_t/(1 + i)^t.$$

Instead of Formula (5.5), we will then use the following (where T is the "horizon," and W^* is the new measure of welfare):

$$\Delta W^* = \sum_{t=1}^{T} \left[\sum_{j=1}^{n} \Delta Y_{jt}/(1 + i)^t \right] \tag{5.8}$$

Example 1. Suppose we have a society composed of two individuals. A certain project is proposed with the following effects: in period 1, net income to both individuals will decrease by $2 each (that is $Y_{11} = Y_{21} = -\$2$); in period 2, net income will increase by $10 for Mr. One and decrease by $2 for Mr. Two (i.e., $Y_{12} = +\$10$, $Y_{22} = -\$2$). Assuming that net income in all subsequent periods for both individuals is nil, we can calculate ΔW^* on the basis of Formula (5.8), (assuming an interest rate of 4 percent):

$$\Delta W^* = \frac{-2 + (-2)}{1.04} + \frac{10 + (-2)}{1.0816} = -4(0.96154) + 8(0.92456) = 3.55$$

Note that if the interest rate were, say, 100 percent, the results would have been quite different:

$$\Delta W^* = -4(0.50) + 8(0.25) = 0$$

Furthermore, had we chosen an interest rate in excess of 100 percent, ΔW^* would have turned negative. It was shown earlier that the choice of the interest (or discount) rate is quite crucial, as the outcome of many investment decisions may be quite sensitive to (even small) changes in i. In addition, this example clearly illustrates the redistribution problem in that Mr. One appears to receive a net gain (even at a very high discount rate), whereas Mr. Two is certain to lose.

In summary, the general criterion for investment decisions is the maximization of net present value of income (or "present worth," as some authors refer to it), the choice of interest rate, the distribution of income, and other considerations notwithstanding. A project would be considered worthwhile when the present value of expected benefits (income to individuals) exceeds the present value of costs (loss of income).[6] Alternatively, when two or more projects compete for investment, those with higher present worth should be undertaken first, provided, of course, that present worths of the chosen projects exceed zero. In what follows, we shall attempt to provide decision rules that will satisfy this general criterion and, in addition, discuss a number of conceptual problems that are likely to be encountered in benefit-cost applications.

DECISION CRITERIA

The Criteria

The criteria of public expenditures most widely used in recent years are outlined below.[7]

6. A general criterion of this sort is also expounded by McKean (1958) and many other scholars.

7. Much of the following is based on Prest and Turvey (1965: 703) and Hirshleifer et al. (1960: 152–157).

1. *The net present value rule:* "Select all projects where the present value of benefits exceeds the present value of costs" (Prest and Turvey, 1965: 703). Denote annual benefits by b_t and annual costs by c_t; then, if the rate of discount to be used is i and the lifespan (horizon) of the project n years, our rule implies that we select all projects for which

$$\sum_{t=0}^{n} b_t/(1 + i)^t > \sum_{t=0}^{n} c_t/(1 + i)^t \qquad (5.9)$$

For simplicity, we may denote the lefthand side of Formula (5.9) by B_o (the present value of gross benefits) and the righthand side of the inequality by C_o (the present value of costs); then the net present value rule requires that $B_o > C_o$, or that $B_o - C_o > 0$.

2. *The internal rate of return rule.* "Select all projects where the internal rate of return exceeds the chosen rate of discount" (Prest and Turvey, 1965: 703). If r denotes the internal rate of return, then r is obtained by solving the following equation:

$$\sum_{t=0}^{n} b_t(1 + r)^{-t} = \sum_{t=0}^{n} c_t(1 + r)^{-t} \qquad (5.10)$$

where $(1 + r)^{-t} = 1/(1 + r)^t$.
In other words, the internal rate of return is simply that rate of discount that makes $B_o - C_o = 0$. The solution of r is straightforward only when n approaches infinity. When a project has a finite life, the computation of r requires successive approximations.

3. *The benefit-cost ratio rule:* "Select all projects where the ratio of the present value of benefits to the present value of costs exceeds unity" (Prest and Turvey, 1965: 703). Using our previously defined symbols, a project will be worthwhile whenever $B_o/C_o > 1$.

A Comparison of Investment Criteria
Before we proceed to analyze these rules in more detail, let us provide an illustration so that the reader can visualize how these rules could be used.

Example 2.[8] Suppose that a project involves the outlay of $1,000 at its inception (time period 0) and an annual (equal) benefit stream

8. This example is based on a similar example given by Hirshleifer et al. (1960: 153–54).

of \$100 per year lasting for twenty years. Then we calculate the following (assuming a discount rate of 5 percent):

$$B_O = \sum_{t=0}^{20} 100(1.05)^{-t} = 100 \sum_{t=0}^{20} (1.05)^{-t}$$
$$= 100(12.462) = \$1,246.2$$
$$C_O = 1000$$

The benefit-cost ratio is B_O/C_O = 1,246/1,000 = 1.246. The computation of the internal rate of return, r, is more complicated. Using successive approximations, we get r = 7.75 percent. (In this case the task of computing r is reduced to finding that rate of discount that would result in B_O = 1,000.)

In this example, all of the above-mentioned rules would lead to identical policy prescriptions. Since the net present value exceeds 0, rule 1 would lead to the acceptance of the project. Similarly, the ratio of B_O to C_O exceeds unity, suggesting that the project is worthwhile. Finally, since the internal rate of return exceeds the discount rate (5 percent), recommendation of the project would follow.

Insofar as the determination of which project is altogether worthwhile, the three rules would generally provide equivalent answers. Further, except for the internal rate of return rule, these rules would lead to optimal decisions in all instances in which the question posed is simply, Should the project be adopted or not? However, when we make a choice among projects (determining which of a set of projects is best), or when a ranking of projects is called for, then it matters a great deal which of the rules is utilized.

There are a number of possible circumstances when these three rules may not yield identical results. It is possible, for example, that the stream of benefits fluctuates from negative returns in early periods to positive returns later, followed by negative returns further in the future. Then, there could be more than one solution to Equation (5.10); that is, there might be multiple rates of return.[9] Under such circumstances, it is necessary to know the net present value for a variety of rates of discount if maximization of social welfare (as defined in Equation (5.8) is desired. Furthermore, when investments are mutually exclusive such that undertaking project A might exclude

9. The possibility of such an occurance in the area of educational investment is not farfetched. See, for example, Blaug (1967b, Figure 6:344) and Hanoch (1967: 310–29).

the possibility of undertaking another project, B, the internal rate of return may not lead to the selection of the optimal projects.[10]

Furthermore, when it is desired to rank projects, there is a good likelihood that the three investment criteria will lead to different conclusions. An example taken from the economic value of education and described in Cohn (1972b) demonstrates that the internal rate of return rule could, in some cases, lead to the selection of projects different from those to be selected by the net present value rule. Concerning the benefit-cost ratio rule, the ranking of projects depends to an important extent on the manner by which costs and benefits are defined. For example, earnings foregone may be deducted automatically from educational benefits (measured in terms of additional earnings due to education), or alternatively, they may be considered a part of total costs. It is almost certain that the ratio B_o/C_o will not be identical in both cases, and moreover, it is not unlikely that the ranking of educational investments will differ according to the method used to account for such foregone earnings.[11]

In sum, although there are cases in which the internal rate of return or the benefit-cost ratio rules are appropriate, they do not always provide a satisfactory policy prescription. The fact that these two rules are often used in the literature reflects, to a large extent, the intuitive appeal that these rules generate—rather than a methodological superiority. Given this intuitive appeal, and given the fact that in most cases the rules yield identical policy implications, a compromise may be suggested: (1) use any of these rules as your purposes dictate; (2) to make sure that Equation (5.8) is maximized, compute the net present value of benefits for as wide a range of discount rates as seems relevant to insure that the results obtained in step 1 are indeed commensurate with the maximization of social welfare; and (3) always present the entire schedule of net present values (as a function of the rate of discount), so that the reader can see for himself the sensitivity of the results to the choice of the discount rate.

SOME PROBLEMS IN BENEFIT-COST ANALYSIS

A straightforward application of the rules may not always be possible. For the sake of completeness, we shall discuss some problems that may be encountered in benefit-cost analysis.

10. For an example, and further discussion, see McKean (1958: 89-92).
11. Further elucidation of this point can be found in McKean (1958: 108-11).

Capital Rationing[12]

Most government bodies must adhere to a budget stipulation. Consequently, even if a dozen projects are judged to be worthwhile (in accordance with, say, the net present value criterion), there are likely to be sufficient funds to support only a few of these. Alternatively, a student who considers investment in himself through education is subject to imperfect capital markets, since he would find it quite difficult to borrow funds for that purpose, the collateral for which is his (uncertain) expected lifetime income. Such a situation is (operationally) similar to capital rationing.

There are a number of types of "capital rationing." Most common of these is the fixed budget to which the decisionmaker must adhere in the short run (current period). This means that c_0, the costs of the project during the current period, is the constraining variable. Further, even the fixed budget can be of two types, the one in which the entire budget must be exhausted (specific rationing), the other in which the decisionmaker can use no more than the fixed budget (maximum rationing). Other types of rationing also involve funds in the future, such as long-run educational projects in which governmental funds are to be used over a number of years. When a condition of capital rationing exists, the use of the present value rule as presented above breaks down, since it is quite possible that a set of some projects might be chosen that would not maximize social welfare as defined above. To avoid such a possibility, it has been suggested by McKean and others that the marginal rate of return (the IROR[13] on the next best project) be used to discount the stream of net benefits. Hirshleifer et al. (1960), however, remind us of the difficulties with the IROR and propose another rule, which, they contend, is always correct. First they define the "present value as of time 1 (the value of the time stream for periods 1 through n, discounted back to time 1)" as:

$$V_1 = s_1 + \sum_{t=2}^{n} s_t(1 + i)^{-(t-1)} \tag{5.11}$$

where $s_t = b_t - c_t$ is the net annual benefit. Then, under the condition of capital rationing applicable to the current period, the procedure is "to compare projects on the basis of their present value as of time 1

12. For a more complete analysis see Hirshleifer et al. (1960: 160-61, 169-74).

13. IROR = internal rate of return.

. . . *per dollar of current funds"* (p. 161; italics in original). That is, we compute V_1/c_0 for each project (where c_0 is the "fund input for the current period"), and "the rule is successively to adopt projects with the highest values of this ratio until the fixed budget is exhausted or until the alternative use of funds elsewhere becomes more desirable than further investments" (p. 161).

The Choice of a Discount Rate

In the computation of the net present value of a project, a discount rate (or a set of discount rates) must be specified. The reason for discounting has already been explained: it accounts for the potential return that one could receive from investing funds in alternative sources (other than the project itself). But alternative returns are different for different individuals in different locations and in different time periods. The alternative rate of return to an entrepreneur who considers a new plant may be the rate of return on spending the money on the old plant. The entrepreneur has other alternatives as well—buying corporate stocks, bonds of different issues and maturities, and so on. On the other hand, an individual with relatively meager resources and opportunities has far fewer options than the above entrepreneur; consequently, the former's alternative rate of return is most likely to be higher than the latter's. Similarly, the social rate (to be applied to public projects) may differ significantly from the private rate.

Some authors prefer the rate of return on "safe," long-term, federal bonds for use in public projects. Others contend that we must use the marginal internal rate of return on the next best alternative investment. Still others seem to prefer the pure time preference rate (which is quite low indeed). The only consensus in this controversy is that there is a lack of consensus. Consequently, many authors propose that a sensitivity analysis be carried out in each decisionmaking process. That is, instead of computing the net present value of a project for only one discount rate (4 percent, for example), we calculate the present worth of each project for a number of discount rates (for example, 2, 3, 6, 8, and 10 percent). Then we could rank projects according to their present worth for each of the chosen discount rates. In some cases, the choice of projects would not at all vary with changes in the discount rate. In others, particularly when some projects are expected to have a long life whereas others are of shorter duration, changes in the discount rate could change the attractiveness of some projects with respect to the alternatives and/or with respect to the criterion of acceptability (i.e., that $V_o > 0$). Note that the utilization of the internal rate of return rule, although simplifying the analysis, still cannot dodge the question of which rate of discount is the "proper" one, since the resulting rate of return must be compared to the chosen rate of discount (unless the purpose of the analysis is merely to rank projects, regardless whether or not $V_o > 0$ for any of them).

Risk and Uncertainty

Since most decision processes involve expected future costs and benefits, there is always a chance that such expected streams of net benefits will not materialize at all or will be different from expectations. In such cases, we have to deal with the problems of risk or uncertainty. A situation of risk is said to occur when the probability distribution of such chances is known. When no knowledge of the probability distribution exists, we are in a situation of uncertainty.

A number of ways by which risk could be incorporated into our decision models have been suggested in recent years. One of the most common procedures is to add a "risk premium" to the discount in the present value formula. This amounts to an increase in the discount rate commensurate with the degree of riskiness attached to each project. As Eckstein (1961) points out, risk has also traditionally been accounted for by (1) "contingency allowances, which arbitrarily raise certain categories of costs by a certain percentage or reduce benefits through price assumptions which are below expected prices"; and (2) "a limit to economic life shorter than physical life but also shorter than expected economic life" (p. 469). Eckstein goes on to illustrate how pure risk could be taken into account by incorporating the probability distribution of outcomes into the objective function, resulting in modified decision rules for investment. Regarding uncertainty, Eckstein is forced to conclude in his survey of the problem that "judgment methods must be used, whether verbal or formal, with the identification of the major contingencies and some provision being made against them constituting a minimum program for the design of reasonable decision procedures in the face of uncertainty" (p. 478).

The Redistribution of Income

We have already pointed out earlier that an objective function in which redistributive effects arising out of any project are ignored is something less than satisfactory. Some authors believe that the redistributive problem should be handled separately from the efficiency question. That is, we first calculate present values of each project, with no regard to possible redistributive repercussions, and then compile whatever information can be gathered concerning redistribution and present this to the policymaker as a special exhibit. The decision-maker is thus expected to make his decision on the basis of these two separate pieces of information.

Such a method as outlined above has been recommended by most authors. An objection to this method was recently raised by Weisbrod (1968), who argues that as long as redistribution of income is an important goal of government—as it certainly is in this day and age—it should not be excluded from the objective function itself. In other words, Weisbrod refuses to accept the definition of "efficiency" as excluding redistributive effects. Instead he proposes a "grand efficiency" scheme in which both ordinary efficiency and distributive effects are combined. Then our goal becomes to maximize this grand efficiency function, with the policymaker receiving just one set of exhibits.

Whether or not we choose to follow Weisbrod's formulation (whenever such a formulation is feasible), we cannot neglect the question of income distribution in the decisionmaking process. This is true for educational policy as much as it is for water resource projects, urban and slum renewal, and other public projects.[14]

Ex Post and Ex Ante

A final qualification to the analysis suggested in the earlier parts of this chapter is concerned with the fact that in many cases, ex post information is used as if it were ex ante. This is not true for all decisionmaking processes; in many cases no ex post information is available at all, and estimates of costs and benefits are purely of the ex ante variety. In the case of education, however, most studies of the cost-benefit variety have utilized ex post information to test ex ante hypotheses. Prominent among these are studies on the value of college (and other levels of) education in which the benefits to be derived from the educational investment are computed on the basis of past censuses, surveys, and so forth. All that we want to emphasize here is that such reliance on past data is apt to admit some serious uncertainty into our calculations. This uncertainty could possibly be converted into risk by capitalizing on whatever information now exists to show the probability that past information will also truly represent future conditions. In any event, it would be wise to recognize such shortcomings in the benefit-cost procedure and to explicitly state any such use of ex post data in the context of the decision model.

---

14. For further discussion, see Musgrave (1969: 803–805).

PROBLEMS IN THE MEASUREMENT
OF COSTS AND BENEFITS

The previous section concentrated on problems in the application of cost-benefit analysis, assuming that we can measure the costs and the benefits without difficulty. Such is not the case, however. In this section we shall discuss some of the more common problems involved in the measurement of costs and benefits.

Externalities

The possible existence of external economies or diseconomies in production and/or consumption has concerned many economists, and much has been written on the subject in recent years.

The distinction between "internal" and "external" costs and benefits is quite important. Internal costs are those costs that accrue directly or indirectly to the individual or entity whose costs we measure. Likewise, external costs are those costs that accrue to individuals or entities other than those whose costs we attempt to measure. An illustration might serve to clarify the nature of external costs. Suppose that a new secondary school is built in a predominantly residential area. The school has a marching band, a football squad, and a machine shop. The marching band begins practice early in the morning and meets again in the evening. The football games are scheduled mainly during the weekends. And the machine shop is operated only during the regular school hours. The costs of all of these activities to the school are assumed to be measurable. But what about the added cost to the community in the form of (1) excessive noise from the marching band, (2) traffic congestion and disruption of a weekend's rest due to football games, and (3) noise and/or industrial waste and pollution from the machine shop? Although it may not be easy to calculate these costs to the community in dollars and cents, they are real costs to society and should be included in the balance sheet of educational costs.

Similarly, private educational benefits may differ markedly from social benefits. For example, the private returns to an individual undertaking advanced education in nuclear physics may be substantially less than the benefits derived by society as a whole to the extent that the individual may not be able to collect revenues from all those who will enjoy the fruits of his labor. Or, the educational effort may result in side effects—such as greater involvement of persons in community affairs—that benefit all of society, not only those who undertake an educational investment.

It is convenient, and theoretically fundamental (according to many authors), to distinguish between two types of externalities: (1) technological or real effects, and (2) pecuniary effects.[15] This distinction is akin to the one between efficiency and income redistribution, as we shall soon see. The technological effects refer to changes in the production and/or consumption opportunities in the economy resulting from any project or policy. Pecuniary effects are related to changes in the prices of goods, services, and factors of production. For example, when firm A expands, it hires additional factors of production. If the economy is fully employed—or even nearly so—additional resources (workers, raw materials, etc.) can be obtained only by offering them higher wages. As a consequence, prices for these factors of production will also go up in other firms, resulting in external pecuniary costs. Also, an expansion of production by one firm is likely to reduce prices received by producers of substitutable products. Another type of pecuniary externality is the benefits spilled over to producers of complementary goods when more of a product is being produced by a firm. Finally, if a firm's expansion is large enough to affect prices in its industry, an increase in its output is most likely to result in lower output prices for the industry as a whole, which will, of course, have repercussions on the profitability of other firms in the industry.[16]

As McKean points out, the distinction between the two types of externalities may become obscured, since technological spillovers could result in pecuniary ones, and vice versa. Nevertheless, it is often argued that only technological externalities be taken into account—pecuniary effects are to be ignored. The reason for this position is that pecuniary effects only cause changes in the distribution of income—not in the physical opportunities of production and consumption. If redistributional effects are irrelevant for the efficiency criterion, so are pecuniary effects.

Secondary Effects and Overcounting

Secondary effects are quite similar to what we termed previously "pecuniary external" effects. An example, related to water resource projects, is given by McKean (1958):

"Secondary benefits" is the name applied to the increased incomes of various producers, from dry-cleaners to sugar-beet processors, that stem from water-resource projects. When we include secondary benefits, we go beyond counting both the value of the crops and the value of the cattle that

15. See, e.g., McKean (1958: ch. 8); Weisbrod (1968, Appendix); and Prest and Turvey (1965: 688–89).

16. For more detail see McKean (1958: 136–41).

eat the crops. For secondary benefits embrace the value of the meat-packing, for example, that springs up because of the cattle industry, and the value of the haircuts that the new barbers sell to the meat-packers. (P. 154)

McKean goes on to emphasize that only the incremental income arising from such effects should be considered in this category of secondary effects.

These types of effects are "secondary" because they involve changes in the demand for and supply of goods, services, resources, and factors of production that arise from a particular project. As such, they are quite similar to pecuniary externalities, although as McKean points out, secondary effects "do not fall squarely into any of the categories" of external effects (p. 156). For example, the increase in wages that results form a project hiring scarce labor was considered previously to be an external cost to other firms who must now pay more for that type of labor. Yet the laborers receive higher wages. As a result, they obtain a secondary benefit. In this instance, external effects and secondary effects operate in opposite directions. This need not, however, always be the case.

McKean also takes pains to emphasize the possibilities for over-counting of costs and benefits. In water resource applications, counting the increase in grain production and the increase in the value of finished products such as livestock and milk—in addition to the imputed value of the extra water generated by the project—is clearly a case of overcounting. Caution must be exercised in all cases—including education—to avoid overcounting of costs and/or benefits, just as it is important to avoid undercounting of costs and benefits.

Employment Effects

We refer here to the possibility that a project of a significantly large size may have important ramifications on aggregate employment —locally or even nationally. For example, the construction of a huge project such as the space program (NASA), TVA, and the like is almost certain to have repercussions on aggregate employment in the United States. But even smaller projects could have employment effects in localities, and indeed, such effects are often cited to justify the selection of certain areas for a given project.

It should be quite clear that employment effects depend on what we assume would transpire if the program under consideration were not approved. For example, when we are to decide on whether or not manned flights to the planets should be attempted, what should we assume about the alternative use of the funds requested for the project? Should we assume that they will be used for other projects, that a tax cut is the alternative, or that the funds will be used to create a budgetary surplus? Moreover, even if we knew for certain that the funds will be used in alternative projects, it is quite important to know what types of projects the alternatives are, since the employment effects of two projects, using the same total amount of funds, may not be the same. Whereas one project may use resources that are already scarce (and hence will have negligible employment effects), another may use relatively abundant resources (resulting in important employment effects). In all, while employment effects should enter the calculus of costs and benefits, one must be quite clear as to what the alternatives to the project are. Only when these alternatives are known with a reasonable degree of certainty would it be useful to consider such effects.

Other Problems

A number of other problems may arise in undertaking benefit-cost analyses, such as discontinuities, interdependencies, and indivisibilities. The first, discontinuities, refers to a situation where some projects under review may require a large expenditure of resources, requiring an examination of alternative combination of projects before it is possible to determine the optimal mix. Interdependencies refer to cases where any one project (A) is likely to affect the profitability of another (B), so that a comparison of costs and benefits requires further calculations. And indivisibilities occur when a project requires a massive infusion of productive resources of a particular type, causing large increases in prices of factors of production, and hence complicating the calculation of the true costs of a project. These topics are discussed briefly in Cohn (1972c) and more thoroughly in Hirshleifer et al. (1960), McKean (1958), and Prest and Turvey (1965).

RECAPITULATION

The purpose of this chapter has been to provide the reader with some rudimentary notions of benefit-cost analysis. A presentation of empirical cost-benefit analyses in education without an understanding of the underlying theoretical foundations is both misleading and incomplete. Yet it should be made clear that no attempt was made here to survey the literature exhaustively or to consider every possible direct, indirect, internal, or external effect that the decision-maker should take into account.

The following chapter explores the empirical application of benefit-cost analysis in education. The theoretical analysis presented above was intended not only to enable the reader to comprehend the material more easily, but also to stimulate a critical examination of the studies, where the purpose of such a critical examination is not to dismiss studies that are understandably imperfect, but rather to opt for studies that will take into account more and more of the long list of considerations enumerated above.

LITERATURE GUIDE

It is clearly outside the scope of this volume to provide a comprehensive list of benefit-cost studies. The list provided herein is therefore only partial, and readers interested in the topic are advised to examine such works as Mishan (1976), Layard (1972), and R.A. Musgrave (1969) for additional literature. In addition to these three surveys, one may wish to review Burkhead and Miner (1971), Eckstein (1961), Haveman (1976b), Henderson (1968), McKean (1958), Prest and Turvey (1965), Turvey (1968), and Krutilla and Eckstein (1958)—all of which provide excellent general surveys of the topic. Also of interest are a volume on the planning-programming-budgeting system by Lee and Johnson (1973), a study of cost-effectiveness edited by English (1968), and a critique of cost-benefit analysis by Merewitz and Sosnick (1971).

Considerable discussion has appeared in the literature concerning the "proper" decision criteria and their relevance for policy. For example, consult the following works: Cohn (1972a, 1972b), Flemming and Wright (1971), Hirshleifer et al. (1960), McKean (1958), Mishan (1970, 1976), Moody (1974), Oakland (1970), Ramsey (1970), and Samuelson (1976, esp. p. 490).

For a discussion of the "proper" discount rate, see, for example, Henderson (1968); Eckstein (1961); Sandmo (1972); Seagraves (1970); and articles by Feldstein, Harberger, Marglin, and Sen in Layard (1972: pt. 3).

The topic of risk and uncertainty is discussed in Arrow (1971), Arrow and Lind (1970), Hirshleifer (1966), Hirshleifer and Shapiro (1970), Mayshar (1977), Pauly (1970), Sandmo (1972), and Zeckhauser (1970).

Other relevant studies include Acharya (1971), Haveman and Margolis (1970, 1977), Haveman (1976a), Haveman and Weisbrod (1975), and Maass (1966). Denison (1971) and Weisbrod and Hansen (1968) discuss the relevance of GNP as a measure of welfare, and Lipsey and Lancaster (1956-1957) provide the basic theory of the "second best," characterizing much of the benefit-cost literature.

Chapter 6

Benefit-Cost Analysis in Education

The most Valuable of all capital
is that invested in human beings.
Alfred Marshall, *Principles of Economics*

An investment in knowledge
pays the best interest.
Benjamin Franklin, *Poor Richard's Almanack*

The benefit-cost techniques summarized in the preceding chapter, along with the enumeration of benefits and costs discussed previously, provide a basis for testing the empirical validity of the above-quoted statements by a noted classical economist and a great American statesman. In fact, whereas such statements may have been taken for granted in the not too distant past, in recent years they have come under severe scrutiny. For example, in *The Overeducated American*, R.B. Freeman (1976) documents the decline in the economic value of college education in recent years, while critics such as Berg (1970) and Freedman (see Berg and Freedman, 1977) claim that the American educational system has produced an inflation in degrees and educational attainment unmatched by the needs of employers, so that more education could do more harm than good as more highly educated workers cannot find jobs commensurate with their talents and training.

Moreover, even if college education may be profitable in general, it may not be profitable for everyone in the United States or for anyone in a number of countries across the globe. In addition, college education may have different economic value at different levels of investment, for example, four years versus graduate or professional degree programs. We shall therefore endeavor to explore the economic returns to education by type of investment, ability groupings, minority status, and country. But before a survey of benefit-cost studies is attempted, a brief "how to do it" introduction is provided in the next section.

AN INTRODUCTION TO BENEFIT-COST ANALYSIS IN EDUCATION

One of the earliest comprehensive studies on the economic returns to education is Hansen (1963). In that study, the returns to various levels of education are documented. We will focus here only on the returns to high school education.

The first set of data consists of lifetime earnings cross-classified by age and years of schooling, which Hansen obtained from the 1950 census summaries. Using the procedure described in Chapter 3, Hansen developed a series of additional lifetime income estimates for the first two years, the final two years, and all four years of high school education. The undiscounted additional lifetime income by level of education is given in Table 6-1 for zero rate of discount. Applying positive rates of discount—3, 6, 8, and 10 percent—Hansen obtained the present (or discounted) value of gross benefits (i.e., additional lifetime income) due to education, as summarized in Table 6-1. Note that educational benefits are extremely sensitive to the rate of discount used.

On the cost side, Hansen calculated the cost per pupil to be $385 in 1950. Assuming that the cost per pupil was $385 in each of the high school years, the costs for each of the four high school years have been calculated, employing the discount rates of 0, 3, 6, 8, and 10 percent (see Table 6-2).

Based on these benefit and cost data, it is possible to derive (1) the net present value of benefits (NPV), and (2) the benefit-cost

Table 6-1. Present Value of Additional Lifetime Income Associated with High School Investment—United States, 1950 (discounted to age fourteen).

Invest-ment In	0	3	6	8	10
First 2 years	$16,802	$ 7,756	$2,301	$1,190	$ 545
4 years	46,038	18,156	6,488	3,601	1,949
Final 2 years	29,236	10,400	4,187	2,411	1,404

Source: Hansen (1963), Table 6.

Table 6-2. Present Value of Total Resource Costs of High School Education—United States, 1950 (discounted to age fourteen).

Years	*0*	*3*	*6*	*8*	*10*
First 2 years	770	759	748	741	735
4 years	1540	1474	1414	1377	1342
Final 2 years	770	715	666	636	607

Source: Calculated on the basis of Hansen (1963), Table 2.

ratio (B/C). The NPV, we recall, is the difference between discounted benefits and discounted costs. Table 6-3 gives the NPVs for the discount rates 0, 3, 6, 8, and 10. We see that the investment in either the entire four-year high school program or the last two years is socially worthwhile, since NPV > 0 at all rates of discount (up to 10 percent). The investment in only two years of high school, however, is worthwhile only for discount rates under 10 percent. If the "appropriate" rate of discount is 10 percent or more, then an investment in only two years of high school is not profitable.

The benefit-cost ratios are reported in Table 6-4. Again, the B/C decline as a higher discount rate is applied, and the investment decisions are identical to the ones suggested by the NPV rule. The ranking of the investments, however, differs in accordance with the decision rule employed. Based upon the NPV rule, the four year investment is best for discount rates under 10 percent, followed by the final two years and the first two years. At rates of discount of 10 percent or higher, the final two years become superior to a four-year investment. Using the B/C rule, the final two years are always best, followed in order by the four-year and first two-year investments. Of course, the three investments are not mutually exclusive, so the policy implications of such rankings are highly suspect. But it is not uncommon that the two rules will provide different rankings.

Finally, Hansen calculated the internal rates of return (IROR) for the two-year, four-year, and final two-year high school investments to be 9.5, 11.4, and 13.7 percent, respectively. The ranking of the investments based upon the IROR rule is consistent with the ranking produced by the benefit-cost ratio rule, but not with the NPV rule. The IRORs were estimated by successive approximations, varying the rate of discount in the NPV formula until NPV is approximately zero. A graphical representation of the NPV schedules is provided in Figure 6-1. Note that the IROR is the discount rate at which the NPV graph cuts the discount rate axis.

Table 6-3. Net Present Value of Additional Lifetime Income Attributed to High School Education—United States, 1950.

Invest-ment In	0	3	6	8	10
First 2 years	$16,032	$ 6,997	$1,523	$ 449	$ -190
4 years	44,498	16,682	5,974	2,224	607
Final 2 years	28,446	9,985	3,522	1,775	797

Source: Table 6-1 and 6-2.

Table 6-4. Benefit-Cost Ratios of Investments in High School Education—United States, 1950.

Invest-ment In	0	3	6	8	10
First 2 years	21.8	10.2	3.1	1.6	0.7
Entire 4 years	29.9	12.3	4.6	2.6	1.5
Final 2 years	38.0	14.5	6.3	3.8	2.3

Source: Tables 6-1 and 6-2.

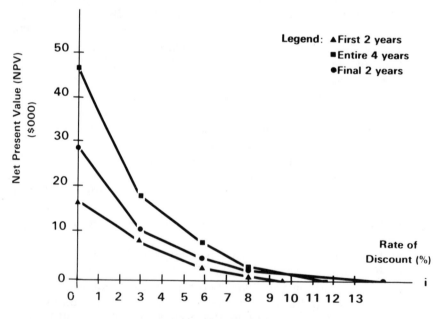

Figure 6-1. Net Present Value of Additional Lifetime Income Attributed to Years of High School Education, U.S., 1950.
Source: Table 6-3; and Hansen (1963), Table 3

When presented with complete information, the policymaker should be able to decide on an appropriate action—whether to invest in a given level of education and how much to invest. The tables provided in this example include complete information concerning the relevant data set. We still lack information about returns to education by race, sex, ability, and other factors. Some of the studies that will be discussed below do provide such information. Most of them, however, do not provide complete information, generally reporting only internal rates of return. To the extent that the IROR rule is inappropriate, the information provided is less than satisfactory.

It should be noted that Hansen provided information on both "private" and "social" returns. "Private" returns were defined as the difference between after tax income differentials and "private resource costs," whereas the "social" benefits were defined as the difference between before tax income differentials and "total resource costs." Although before tax income exceeds after tax income, the much larger "social resource costs" cause private returns to exceed social returns. In the case of elementary education, private resource costs are considered nil, hence the IROR is nearly infinite. At higher levels of education, the major cost of education has been foregone earnings—which is both a social and a private cost—hence, the IRORs do not differ much between the social and the private calculus.

Another point is worthy of note. Hansen's estimates of the benefits (additional lifetime income) are already net of earnings foregone, since the earnings stream of the lower education group was subtracted from that of the higher education group for all ages up to age fourteen, when the high scholl enrollment decision was to be made. Since earnings foregone should properly be counted as costs, our B/C ratios are clearly overestimates. Such overestimates do not invalidate the basic decision on whether one should invest in any one of these programs, but could considerably alter the ranking of the three programs.

RETURNS TO EDUCATIONAL INVESTMENTS IN THE UNITED STATES

Following the pioneering efforts of Houthhakker (1959), H.P. Miller (1960), G.S. Becker (1960, 1964), and Hansen (1963), numerous studies appeared concerning the economic returns to investment in schooling. Since the majority of studies used the interal rate of return (IROR) as the investment criterion, much of the discussion will focus on the IROR. For expository purposes, we divide this section into discussions of investment payoff by level and type of education.

Elementary Schooling

Since the private costs of attending public elementary schools are virtually nonexistent, the private return to elementary schooling is astronomical. A number of authors claim it is infinite (e.g., Hansen, 1963; and Hanoch, 1967). An IROR of 155 percent (!) is calculated by Hines, Tweeten and Redfern (1970). For students enrolled in private schools, the returns would be considerably lower, depending on the tuition charged.

The social returns take into account the social costs of elementary schooling. Estimates of the social IROR to elementary schooling vary from 7.2 percent for 1970 to 17.8 for 1960 (see Table 6-5). Except for the 7.2 rate, which appears rather low, all other estimates of the return to elementary schooling suggest that investment at this level is profitable both for the individual and for society.

Secondary Schooling

Although public secondary schools do not charge tuition, earnings foregone are not inconsequential, hence private returns to secondary schooling are much lower than private returns to elementary schooling. By all accounts, however, the private returns are substantial, with the estimated IROR varying from 13.0 percent for 1960 (Mincer, 1974) to 49.1 percent for 1940 (Carnoy and Marenbach, 1975). The estimate for 1970 by Carnoy and Marenbach (1975) is 18.9 percent—well over what most people can earn in alternative investments. It should be emphasized that rates of return vary by individual attributes, program of study, and other fac-

Table 6-5. Social IRORs to Elementary Schooling in the United States.

Author(s)	Sample Year	IROR (percent)
Hansen (1963)	1950	15.0
Carnoy and Marenbach (1975)	1940	11.6
	1950	12.7
	1960	13.2
	1970	7.2
Hines, Tweeten, and Redfern (1970)[a]	1960	17.8[a]

[a]For male whites. IRORs for other race-sex groupings vary substantially.

tors, so that a rate of 18.9 percent is certainly not applicable for everyone.[1]

The social rate is much lower, with an estimate for 1970 of 10.7 percent. Given a 10 percent discount rate currently used for federal projects, secondary education, on the average, still appears to be a good investment. The Carnoy and Marenbach (1975) estimates indicate that the IROR to secondary education has declined from 1940 to 1960 and remained relatively stable between 1960 and 1970.

It appears, therefore, that secondary education is, in general an excellent investment for an individual and a reasonably profitable investment to society, too. Furthermore, if it can be shown that significant external benefits are associated with secondary education, then the conclusion is greatly strengthened. A summary of private and social IRORs to secondary schooling is provided in Table 6-6.

Four-Year College Education

Economists have been much more interested in the returns to college education than in lower education levels. There are, in consequence, a good many studies on the subject.

Table 6-6. Private and Social IRORs to Secondary Schooling in the United States.

Author(s)	Sample Year	IROR (percent)	
		Private	Social
Hansen (1963)	1950	14.5	11.4
Becker (1964)	1940	16.0	
	1950	20.0	
	1956	25.0	
	1958	28.0	
Hanoch (1967)[a]	1960	16.1	
Hines, Tweeten, and Redfern (1970)[b]	1960	19.5	14.0
Mincer (1974)	1960	13.0	
Carnoy and Marenbach (1975)	1940	49.1	18.2
	1950	22.7	14.2
	1960	14.6	10.1
	1970	18.9	10.7

[a]Northern whites only.
[b]Male whites only; rates for other race-sex groups vary substantially.

1. Hansen, Weisbrod, and Scanlon (1970) show, for example, that for a group of low achievers (scoring below the thirtieth percentile on the Armed Forces Qualification Test), job training is "considerably more attractive than more schooling" (p. 415). In fact, their calculations appear to imply an IROR much below 5 percent for investment in secondary schooling.

A summary of results obtained by several authors is presented in Table 6-7. Results vary because of differences in methodology; data base; adjustments for ability; other nonschooling variables; and expected growth in earnings differentials and estimates of private and public costs. The results in the table show that, in general, private returns exceed social returns (in one instance by more than 10 percentage points), although in recent years there appears to be a convergence of the two rates. Some reduction in the IROR to college education is apparent between 1940 and 1973, although Raymond and Sesnowitz (1975) argue that the 1970 rate is higher than what Becker (1964), Carnoy and Marenbach (1975), and others obtained for earlier years. R.B. Freeman (1976, 1977b) argues that economic returns to college education have decreased in recent years, and the data reported in Table 6-7 are indicative of the magnitude of the decline in the five-year period, 1968-1973.

Whether the decline in IRORs is temporary or not cannot as yet be ascertained. But the general level and trend of IRORs for investment in college education also indicate that, in general, such an investment is profitable both for the individual and society, unless the lower IRORs reported by Freeman are accurate.

A number of authors argue, furthermore, that even an IROR as low as 7.5 percent is sufficient to justify investment in higher education because of the existence of nonmonetary benefits. In addition,

Table 6-7. Private and Social IRORs to Investment in Four Years of College Education in the United States.

Author(s)	Sample Year	IROR (percent)	
		Private	Social
Hansen (1963)	1950	11.4	10.9
Becker (1964)	1940	14.5	
	1950	13.0	
	1956	12.4	
	1958	14.8	
Hanoch (1967)[a]	1960	9.6	
Mincer (1974)	1960	10.0	
Carnoy and Marenbach (1975)	1940	21.4	10.7
	1950	13.2	10.6
	1960	17.6	11.3
	1970	15.4	10.9
Raymond and Sesnowitz (1975)[b]	1970	17.9	14.3
Freeman (1977b)[c]	1968	11.0-12.5	12.0-13.0
	1973	7.5-10.0	8.5-10.5

[a,b]See Table 6-6.

[c]IRORs differ according to method used to estimate growth in income over time.

the low rates of return to college education reported by Freeman may be due to temporary adjustments in the supply of and demand for college graduates. A recent report by the conference board, summarized in Fiske (1977d), questions Freeman's results and argues that future supply-demand conditions would maintain college education as a highly profitable investment. It cannot be overemphasized, however, that college education is not universally profitable, with rates of return varying considerably by "ability" and other factors.

Graduate Education

The economic returns to postgraduate programs are generally much lower than for lower level programs. Hanoch (1967) obtained an IROR of 7.0 percent for the category 17+ (at least some graduate education), for Northern whites for the year 1960. Similar figures were also obtained by Mincer (1974). On the other hand, Bailey and Schotta (1972) report very low, even negative, returns to graduate education for academicians for 1966—and according to the Commission on Human Resources of the National Academy of Sciences (1976a), nearly three-fifths of the working doctoral scientists and engineers in the United States were employed by educational institutions in 1975. Their results are disputed by Tomaske (1974), who claims that when summer and outside earnings are taken into account, the private IROR climbs to around 10 percent. A summary of such results is reported in Table 6–8.

Other studies demonstrating low, and sometimes negative, IRORs to graduate education (such as Rogers, 1969, and Maxwell, 1970) raise some interesting questions about (1) the forces motivating individuals to seek graduate education and (2) the desirability of providing public subsidies to graduate education. In fact, without public subsidies (in the form of tuition rebates, assistantships, fellowships, etc.), the private IROR to graduate education is extremely low and probably negative. Concerning the first question, there are a number of possibilities. First, it is possible that individuals place a relatively higher weight on future income as opposed to present income foregone. As Ashenfelter and Mooney (1968) point out, expected income at any age after completion of graduate school is uniformly higher for postgraduate students. Also, studies on returns to graduate education often omit student income while in school, as well as outside earnings, which tend to create a downward bias in the IROR estimates. Finally, the expectation of nonmonetary benefits in the form of greater leisure time, more attractive work environment, greater social prestige, and the like could influence one's decision to invest in postgraduate schooling.

Table 6-8.   Private IRORs to Graduate Education in the United States.

Author(s)	Sample Year	17+	Masters	Ph.D.	Other
			IROR (percent)		
Hanoch (1967)[a]	1960	7.0			
Rogers (1969)	longitudinal				neg.-6.0[g]
Ashenfelter and	1958-			3.5-	
Mooney (1969)	1960		4.8	10.5[b]	
Maxwell (1970)	1967 (males)		neg.	12.6	
	(females)		6.3		
Agnello and Hunt	1959-		6.0-		
(1976)	1974		10.0[c]		
Siegfried (1971)[d]	1964			5.3-	
				23.6	
Weiss (1971b)[e]	1966		12.2	12.3	
Bailey and Schotta (1972)	1966	neg.-1.0			
Tomaske (1974)[f]	1966	10.0			
Mincer (1974)	1960	7.3			

[a]Northern whites only.
[b]IRORs vary depending on number of years in school.
[c]Lower rate for full-time MBA students; higher rate for part-time MBA students.
[d]Rates are for Ph.D. economists; rates differ by type of employment and by type of financial aid while individuals were in graduate school.
[e]These are "average IRORs"; "marginal" IRORs are somewhat lower. Also, considerable variation of IRORs by field is observed.
[f]This is a recalculation of Bailey and Schotta (1972), allowing for summer and outside earnings.
[g]Negative rates are found for some graduate schooling with no degree earned; IRORs of 0-6 percent are obtained for the "any degree" category, varying according to method used and assumptions made regarding private costs of education.

With regard to the second question—concerning the social value of graduate education—one could again cite the downward bias in the IRORs as one possible justification for social support. If it can be shown, however, that social IRORs are low even after proper adjustments are made, then the support argument will rest squarely on the "external benefits" argument. Bailey and Schotta (1972) refuse to accept the argument, claiming that other occupations, including plumbers, create similar external benefits. Other economists have become increasingly skeptical over the alleged existence of substantial external benefits due to college graduate education, citing the lack of any empirical verification of the argument.

The data reported in Table 6-8, along with data from other studies, indicate, generally, insufficient returns in the form of lifetime earnings to justify either private or public investment in graduate education. There are some exceptions, such as the IROR for a three year Ph.D. program calculated by Ashenfelter and Mooney (1969)—10.5 percent—the higher rates estimated by Siegfried (1971) for Ph.D. economists employed in business (as high as 23.6 percent), and the average IRORs (over 12 percent) calculated by Weiss (1971b). Additional information, in the form of nonmonetary and/or external benefits, is needed to supplement the IROR data for private and social policy purposes. Also, as Ritzen (1977) demonstrates, increased investment in graduate education could be justified on egalitarian grounds.

Vocational Education

Interest in vocational education has been intensified in the United States since it was recognized that unemployment may be due, in part, to "structural" unemployment—that is, to the persistence of job vacancies along with a large number of unemployed individuals who lack the required skills to qualify for these vacancies. Federal programs, such as the Area Redevelopment Act, the Manpower Development and Training Act, and more recently, the Comprehensive Employment and Training Act, symbolized the apparent need to provide the required education and vocational training to bridge the gap between labor supply and demand. Evaluations of vocational programs sprung out of these and other federal acts, among which are included a number of benefit-cost studies.

One of the better known works is the study by Hu, Lee, Stromsdorfer, and Kaufman (1969; see also Hu, Lee, and Stromsdorfer, 1971), in which the returns to a vocational track in high school was compared to the academic track for three large cities. The results showed a very high return to vocational education, with an estimated IROR of 56.8 percent.

On the other hand, studies by Corazzini (1968) for Worcester, Massachusetts, and Taussig (1968) for New York City, indicate much lower returns to vocational education. Both studies suggest that the extra costs of vocational education are generally not fully covered by additional estimated benefits. In contrast, Watson (1977) obtained generally high IRORs for postsecondary vocational schooling in public and proprietary institutions (with the exception of one out of five schools examined). Similar results for postsecondary vocational schooling were obtained earlier by Carroll and Ihnen (1967), obtaining net present values of benefits ranging from $5,157 (using a 10 percent discount rate, relatively low earnings projections, and total resource costs) to $36,157 (using a 5 percent rate of discount, relatively high earnings projections, and private resource costs).

The variability of returns to vocational education is representative of the many different vocational education programs offered across the United States. The results summarized here clearly indicate the need to evaluate each program on its own merit.

Educational Returns by Race, Sex, and other Groups

The results reported in the preceding paragraphs are, for the most part, "average returns," combining the returns to education by a host of disparate race-sex-ability groups. Some of the studies were specifically focused on a particular race-sex group, such as male whites. It has been claimed that the returns to education differ significantly among various groups in society, and considerable evidence has been accumulated to support such a contention.

Black-White Differences. One common allegation is that the IROR to education for blacks is considerably below that for whites. For example, Hanoch (1967) provides IRORs by race (white versus nonwhite) and region (north versus south), and the IRORs for each region are generally lower for blacks (who comprise the majority of the nonwhite group) than for whites—in many cases much lower. Similarly, Hines et al. (1970) obtain, in most instances, higher IRORs for white males than for males of other races (although the returns to four years of high school are greater for nonwhites). On the other hand, they obtain generally higher IRORs for nonwhite females than for white females.

Further results are reported by Adams and Nestel (1976), who used the National Longitudinal Survey as their data base. For young males, they find that whites have much higher returns to education than blacks. Blacks have small returns to secondary education and virtually no return to some high school (eight to eleven years). For college education, the return to young blacks approaches the return to young whites.

For older males, whites have about double the returns to high school or some high school education and about three times the returns to college education as compared to older blacks.

Much of the discrepancy in black-white returns is attributed to the quality of education received as well as to the area where an individual lives. Living in a black ghetto is alleged to be the main reason why black returns to education are low. What Adams and Nestel imply is that improved education cannot serve as the only vehicle for social and economic advancement of minority groups. At the same time the results appear to imply that education has the potential to improve the earnings status of all races when problems of urban isolation, racial discrimination, and other social ills are removed.

An interesting question is whether the economic returns to blacks have increased in relative terms during the recent past, as efforts toward integration, affirmative action, and other programs in behalf of minorities have taken hold. A positive answer is given by Welch (1973b). Concurring with Welch are Niemi (1974, 1975a, 1976); Link, Ratlege, and Lewis (1976); and Weiss and Williamson (1972, 1975). Other writers, notably Thurow (1975), Jencks et al. (1972), and H.M. Levin (1977a, 1977b), continue to argue that education has not improved the plight of the poor, especially blacks.

Male-Female Differences. A similar analysis with respect to males and females is also of interest. Again, some evidence on differential returns by sex are available. Hines et al. (1970), for example, provide IRORs by sex-race groupings. For whites, returns to education are almost uniformly higher for males. For nonwhites, however, returns are higher for males in the lower educational levels and higher for females in the higher educational levels. The claim that females receive a lower return than males is, however, disputable. A study by Carnoy and Marenbach (1975) does show differences in IRORs by sex, but in 1969, white females had higher IRORs for both high school and college education than white males, whereas black females had a higher IROR for college education while black males had a higher return to high school.

Although studies have shown differences in returns to education by sex, it does not necessarily follow that such differences are due to discrimination. Such differences may be due to various attributes of the male-female groups under examination, such as labor market experience, commitment to full-time participation in the labor force, continuity in employment, or types of skills and professions for which individuals are qualified. Moreover, the Carnoy and Marenbach (1975) study does not demonstrate substantial differences in educational returns between males and females of the same race, reinforcing the supposition that educational investments may be equally beneficial to both sexes.

Region. Differences in the returns to education by region are observed in a number of studies: for example, Hanoch (1967), Lassiter (1966), and Adam and Nestel (1976). Because wages are generally higher in urban areas, residence in such areas implies higher lifetime incomes and, hence, higher returns to education. Also, wages in the

North generally exceed those in the South, again suggesting higher returns to education in the North. Although it is also true that educational costs are generally lower in the South and in rural areas, most studies find higher overall returns to education in the urban north. Hanoch's (1967) results, for instance, show almost uniformly higher IRORs for Northern whites than for Southern whites, whereas the North-South comparison for blacks is mixed. And Adams and Nestel (1976) obtain results that indicate that wages in the urban North exceed those for the urban South for both whites and blacks. In contrast, Lassiter (1966) obtains higher returns for Southern whites and lower returns for Southern blacks (for 1960).

Other Minorities. Of interest, too, are possible differences in return by national origin of large groups of American citizens. A study by Carliner (1976) compared educational returns for blacks, Anglos, and five Spanish groups. The author concludes that, in 1970, men of Cuban or other Central or South American origin obtained returns 30 percent higher than those of Anglo (non-Spanish, nonblack) men. On the other hand, black and Chicano men received returns about 70 percent of those for Anglo men, with the lowest returns found for blacks, followed by Chicanos, "other Spanish," Puerto Ricans, Anglos, Cubans, and Central or South Americans. Interestingly, returns to Anglos were almost identical to those of Puerto Ricans. These results were obtained after marital status, region, and age were taken into account.

We may also mention a study by Neimi (1974) in which IRORs were derived for three levels of education (high school, college, and postgraduate) for California and Texas individuals by race (white, black, and Mexican). Niemi's results (for 1960) show some differences in IRORs by race, but the differences are relatively minor and, in some cases, show higher IRORs for nonwhites (especially for postgraduate education). A recalculation of the IRORs, using a different methodology, by Raymond and Sesnowitz (1976b) produces different results but preserves the pattern of relatively small differences in returns to education by whites, blacks, and Mexican Americans.

Educational Returns for Specific Occupations or Programs
The literature is replete with benefit-cost analyses regarding specific occupations or programs. Examples are medical and dental education, MBA-ETV programs, dropout prevention programs, and nursing education.

Medical Education. Estimates of the economic benefits of investment in the MD program were obtained, among others, by Sloan (1970) and Lindsay (1973, 1976). Using different methodologies, Sloan obtained estimates of the net present value of lifetime earnings for physicians, using a 10 percent discount rate, of $33,542 for 1955 and $39,841 for 1959. The respective figures for Lindsay's estimates are $6,740 for 1955, $11,720 for 1959, and $4,660 for 1966. Sloan and Lindsay disagree about the magnitude of the returns to medical training, but figures obtained by these and other authors generally confirm that medical education is highly profitable.

Dental Education. Economic returns to dentistry were calculated by Maurizi (1975). Private IRORs for dentistry are estimated as follows: for 1948, 17.6; for 1958, 13.6, and for 1970, 25.5. The respective social IRORs are 13.5, 11.3, and 19.9. The results show a decline in IRORs between 1948 and 1958, followed by a significant increase in the private and social profitability of dentistry from 1958 to 1970. If the 1970 figures are still relevant, then the economic returns to dentistry are clearly very high, both to the individual and to society.

Nursing Education. Data assembled by Despain (1975) from Mesa Community College (Arizona) indicate very high IRORs to nursing education, with a private IROR of 27 percent and a social IROR of 21 percent, for nurses working till age sixty-five. Moreover, the private and social IRORs exceed 12 percent even if the nurses work only six and eight years, respectively.

MBA-ETV. A sample of students enrolled in both the traditional MBA and MBA-ETV (Masters of Business Administration, Educational Television) programs administered by the University of South Carolina, during the period 1969–1973, were assembled by Kiker and Wilder (1975). Although the net present value of the traditional BMA program exceeds that for the MBA-ETV for students with undergraduate majors in business, engineering and nontechnical arts and sciences (the opposite is true for those with undergraduate majors in technical arts and sciences), the calculated benefit-cost ratio for MBA-ETV exceeds all benefit-cost ratios obtained for the traditional MBA-ETV. The main reason for this is the very low foregone earnings experienced by MBA-ETV students, who are able to complete the degree while remaining at their current jobs. The data show high returns to both the traditional and the ETV-MBA programs.

Drop Out Prevention.   A study by Weisbrod (1965b) provides estimates of the value of a dropout prevention program conducted in St. Louis, Missouri, during 1960–1962. An important element in the calculation of benefits and costs is the fact that only 8 percent of the students enrolled in the program were prevented from dropping out. Therefore, the costs per dropout prevented were about $7,300, even though the costs per enrollee were only $580. Because of the large rate of failure, the net present value of the program was negative, and Weisbrod was forced to conclude that a dropout prevention program, for students aged sixteen or older, is not likely to succeed. "Prevention seems to be difficult at that stage; even when extensive counseling and work-study programs are tried, attitudes and motivations may be too solidified. Dropping out of school is, after all, symptomatic of other problems" (pp. 147–48). Adjustments by Ribich (1968: 51–60) to Weisbrod's calculations—including adjustments for growth in income differentials and ability—result in even lower estimates of net benefits.

These results are in contrast to the findings by Kastner (1964) and others that the dropout problem is very costly to society. For example, using 1960 Census data, Kastner calculates the income loss due to the lack of universal secondary education to be at least $33 billion per year in 1960, and further losses are calculated due to the fact that able students do not go as far as possible in acquiring higher levels of education. The point made by Weisbrod is that, although the income loss is very large, it might be too expensive to reduce the number of dropouts sufficiently to justify the investment.

Compensatory Education.   Ribich (1968) analyzed a number of compensatory education programs, including the Higher Horizons program in New York City, which began in 1959. Ribich's calculations of the costs and benefits imply that the program was not economically worthwhile. For a number of other programs, however, positive net present values (for a 5 percent discount rate) are obtained.

Another compensatory education program, originally initiated by the Office of Economic Opportunity, was studied by Garms (1971). He shows positive net present values, at discount rates of 5 and 10 percent, for private returns, and positive social returns at 5 percent. However, at a 10 percent rate, social returns were negative. Garms questions the value of the program in increasing college attendance among those otherwise not likely to attend college, since a large number of the Upward Bound students who finally attended college also had siblings attending college (which indicates that they might have attended college anyway).

Finally, a good deal of attention has been placed on Head Start, with evaluative studies by Cicirelli et al. (1969) and Barnow and Cain (1977). The general conclusion obtained in both studies is that the long-run benefits of Head Start are very small and that the economic profitability of the program is in doubt. The major disappointment with Head Start has been the disappearance, over time, of any short-run gains made by the program.

Returns to Increased Expenditures. If additional years of education are a good investment, would additional expenditures on education per year also be profitable? In his 1968 study, Ribich concluded that the answer is negative. He shows that Project Talent students enrolled in schools in which per pupil expenditures in 1960 were $100 higher than in other schools obtained a 19 percent gain in scholastic achievement. Using data on the present value of schooling per year, he obtains benefits per pupil of $417, while discounted costs are estimated to be $749, so that the net present value is negative.

Using Project Talent followup data, Ribich and Murphy (1975) provide additional estimates of the profitability of increased expenditures. They show that the main impact of increased expenditures is through the effect on increasing the number of years a student is likely to remain in school. As was the case in the initial study, however, the authors conclude that "the time-discounted lifetime gain that is associated with increased spending is estimated to be less than the amount of the increased spending" (p. 56).

Cost-Effectiveness Studies. In a number of cases, it is virtually impossible to measure the monetary benefits associated with a given program, although some measure of "effectiveness" can be constructed. In such cases we cannot assess the value of a program to an individual or to society (unless the "effectiveness" is nil), but given that it is decided that a particular service or product be provided, the technique of cost-effectiveness can help identify the program(s) that would achieve the objective at minimum cost.

A good example of how cost-effectiveness may be employed is provided in Webster (1976). Using multiple educational outcomes, especially cognitive learning, Webster demonstrates how a school system could make decisions about expansion, retention, or elimination of school programs. Webster describes the process by which cost-effectiveness data, along with some value judgement, are combined to produce a final choice. Other studies employing the cost-effectiveness model include Hu, Kaufman, Lee and Stromsdorfer (1969), H.M. Levin (1970), and Wolfe (1977).

RETURNS TO EDUCATIONAL INVESTMENT IN OTHER COUNTRIES

Interest in the profitability of education has not been confined to the United States alone. Similar studies have appeared for thirty or more other countries. In the interest of brevity, only a summary of such studies appears here. Much of the discussion is based upon the excellent compilation by Psacharopoulos (1973), which is a required reading for those interested in the returns to education in other countries (see also Carnoy, 1975a). A sample of IRORs for thirteen countries is presented in Table 6-9.

Because of considerable differences in the data base, educational structure, and methodology, the IRORs produced in Table 6-9 are not strictly comparable. Although the majority are based upon unadjusted earnings profiles, in some instances (e.g., New Zealand), adjustment for ability and nonschooling factors was made. Also, the IRORs to primary education have not been calculated in six out of the thirteen countries surveyed. The reasons for the omission of primary education are at least twofold: (1) Since studies on the returns to education are typically motivated by the desire to influence educational policy, the existence of compulsory education laws removes primary education from the focus of public policy

Table 6-9.   IRORs in Thirteen Countries.

| Country | Sample Year | Social (Private) IRORs (percent) | | |
		Elementary	Secondary	Higher
Canada	1967	na	9 (11)	12[a] (13)
Brazil	1962	11 (11)	17 (21)	15 (38)
Mexico	1963	25 (32)	17 (23)	23 (29)
Ghana	1967	18 (25)	13 (17)	17 (37)
Nigeria	1966	23 (30)	13 (14)	17 (34)
India	1960	20 (25)	17 (19)	13 (14)
Israel	1958	17 (27)	7 (7)	7 (8)
Japan	1961	na	5 (6)	6 (9)
Thailand	1970	31 (56)	13 (15)	11 (14)
Greece	1964	na	3 (5)	8 (14)
Sweden	1967	na	11 (na)	9 (10)
United Kingdom	1966	na	4 (6)	8 (12)
New Zealand	1966	na	19 (20)	13 (15)

Sources: Canada from Stager (1972a), Table 17. Other countries, compiled from Psacharopoulos (1973), Table 4.1.
[a]IROR is for 1961.
na = not available.

debate. (2) In addition, the paucity of earnings data for persons completing less than primary education makes it very difficult to estimate income differentials due to primary education.

Although there is a good deal of variability in the IRORs presented in Table 6-9, the similarity of the IRORs is much more striking. The average social IROR for a larger sample of nineteen countries reported by Psacharopoulos (1973, Table 4-2) is 25.1 percent, which is higher than the respective rates found for the United States (see Table 6-5, above). The average social IROR for secondary education in a sample of twenty-six countries is 13.5, which is highly comparable to the rates found by Hines, Tweeten, and Redfern (1970). And the average social IROR to higher education for a sample of twenty-eight countries is 11.3, which is identical to the IROR found by Carnoy and Marenbach (1975) for the United States. When the IRORs derived by Hines et al. (1970) are used instead, the other countries average is higher than the respective social IROR in the United States (9.6).

Some data on postgraduate education are also available for other countries. For example, Dodge and Stager (1972), using 1966 data, show that the returns to a Masters degree in Canada vary from negative to 16.3 (private) or to 9.0 percent (social). Social and private returns to the doctorate degree in Canada vary from negative to 9.6 (private) or to 1.3 percent (social). And benefit-cost ratios are estimated by Selby-Smith (1975) for a variety of graduate and postgraduate degrees in Australia. For example, social benefit-cost ratios (when the rate of discount is 8 percent and an adjustment of 25 percent is made for nonschooling factors) vary from 0.803 for a B.A. in agricultural science to 2.337 for a first professional degree in dentistry; from 0.321 for a Masters degree in science to 5.785 for a Masters in law; and from 0.290 for a Ph.D. in science (compared to a Masters degree) to 0.659 for a Ph.D. in engineering (compared to an honors degree). Private returns to graduate education are significantly greater due to substantial subsidization of university education in Australia, and hence, most educational investments appear to be profitable for the individual.

The low returns to secondary education in a number of countries (including Israel, Japan, Greece, United Kingdom, Netherlands, and Norway) may be due to specific socioeconomic conditions prevailing in the countries concerned. For example, in Israel's egalitarian society, high school graduates do not earn much more than primary school graduates. It is not surprising, therefore, that both social and private returns to secondary education are rather low. Moreover, a study by Borus (1977) shows that apprenticeship programs in Israel are more "cost-effective" than formal vocational education programs, because earnings do not differ much between graduates of the two programs, whereas costs of formal education are much higher than those of an apprenticeship program. Similar explanations may be found with regard to low IRORs to secondary education in other countries.

It should be noted that the data in Table 6-9 are rather old and that additional evidence must be gathered for policy purposes. Moreover, the need to adjust for nonschooling factors cannot be satisfied by merely applying a standard correction (known in the literature as the alpha factor), because the effect of ability and other nonschool variables could vary significantly among countries and groups within each country.

EXTERNAL EFFECTS, "OPTION VALUES," AND INTERGENERATIONAL EFFECTS

Most of the studies on the economic returns to education omit any calculations of external or other indirect returns. Benefits are almost universally defined as income differentials associated with a particular educational investment. Extension of the studies to include external effects, option values, and intergenerational benefits are rare. In addition to numerous data problems, there are a host of methodological problems that explain the reluctance of researchers to examine such additional returns.

External Benefits

As noted in Chapter 3, Weisbrod (1962, 1964) has provided the earliest attempt to measure some of the external benefits of education. Others, including Ribich (1968), Spiegelman (1968), and Webb (1977) also provide data that shed some light on the existence and magnitude of external returns. We are left, however, with relatively little information regarding external returns, and the field is wide open for pioneering research.

The Financial Option

Completion of one level of schooling (e.g., level a) enables one to pursue additional levels of schooling ($a + 1$, $a + 2$, etc.). The returns that one might expect to receive for a higher educational investment (say $a + 1$) might induce him to invest in a lower educational level (e.g., a), even if the expected return on the latter (a) would not be sufficient to justify the necessary expenditure. Weisbrod (1962) went even further, arguing that the returns to elementary education are actually higher than customarily estimated because a portion of the returns to higher levels of schooling are due to the completion of primary schooling. As Ribich (1968) points out, the Weisbrod exercise was not necessary, because the estimated returns to primary schooling were sufficiently high to justify private and social investment in any case. Nevertheless, the point made by Weisbrod is worthy of consideration, especially in cases where a consideration of two or more consecutive educational levels is at stake.

For example, it has been noted that a study by Hu and his associates (1969, 1971) shows much higher returns to students completing a vocational rather than comprehensive secondary program. The results are intuitively sound for those secondary students who do not contemplate going on to college. On the other hand, if a student has an aptitude for occupations for which a college diploma is required, then a choice of a secondary academic or secondary comprehensive program might be more profitable, taking into account both the private returns to the high school program and the expected returns to college (adjusted by the probability that the student will be accepted by a college).

An empirical study of the returns to education, using Canadian data, by Comay et al. (1976) is a case in point. They show that when option values are explicitly considered, the profitability of various early educational investment are strongly affected by the probability of completion of higher educational levels, so that one's decision regarding an educational investment is critically affected by the option value.

Intergeneration Effects

Both the private and social returns to education may be shown to depend on the transmission of educational values—in the form of the propensity to complete higher levels of education—to succeeding generations. There is evidence, both from United States' and other countries' data, that the probability of a person completing, for example, college education, is higher the more education was received by the parents. It may therefore be concluded that the returns to the investment in one's education should include both direct returns as normally calculated plus the expected benefits that the individual or society gains from increased education obtained by offspring.

The intergenerational effect is not likely to be very strong for the simple reason that such benefits must be discounted at least twenty-five years back. With i = 8 percent, a dollar expected twenty-five years hence will have a present value (PV) of only $0.1460, with lower PVs the higher the rate of discount, i. Nevertheless, a study by Swift and Weisbrod (1965) shows that the IROR to elementary and secondary education would be increased by up to 7 percent when intergenerational benefits are taken into account. On the other hand, the intergenerational benefit scheme employed by Swift and Weisbrod does not produce positive intergenerational benefits to college education of the parent. Some methodological refinements of the Swift and Weisbrod method are discussed by Ribich (1968), who provides additional data on the returns to compensatory education.

Another study in which the intergeneration effect was estimated was Spiegelman (1968). He considered two types of benefits: (1) the social benefits of increased income and productivity in the future, and (2) the private benefits—namely, the satisfaction that the first generation obtains from knowing that the second generation will be better educated. The social benefits are obtained by computing the present value of extra lifetime income for each educational level, multiplying each of these terms by the increased probability of attendance in that educational level due to the particular investment under consideration, and discounting this twenty years back, "in order to shift the starting point of earnings from the next generation to the present" (p. 448).

The computation of present values of additional lifetime income and the increased probability of school attendance by the next generation follows the same pattern as in the Swift-Weisbrod and Ribich studies. Special features of Spiegelman's work are: (1) the discounting of the intergenerational benefits twenty years back, instead of discounting them to the desired age; (2) the choice of a discount rate, which is of prime importance in the study; and (3) the computation of the private intergeneration benefits, assuming that the latter are a fraction, λ, of the social benefits. This fraction is estimated at 0.30.

The intergenerational effects in the Spiegelman study appear to be a great deal stronger than those suggested either by Swift and Weisbrod or by Ribich. For example, the sum of social and private intergeneration benefits amount to more than one-half of the direct benefits estimated for the Title I program of the Elementary and Education Act in California. The effect of the intergeneration benefits does not appear to tip the scales in one or the other direction, since the Title I program appears to be profitable with or without the intergeneration effect. But the latter does increase the profitability of the program by a wide margin, particularly when the social value of the program is considered.

SOME CRITIQUES OF THE CONCEPT OF HUMAN CAPITAL

It is important to consider some of the criticisms voiced at the type of analyses outlined above. Some self-criticism is certainly in order, the objective being to improve both the theoretical and empirical foundations of the benefit-cost framework. Some of the critics, however, do not stop here. They contend that the entire framework is extremely troublesome. They conclude that no more effort should be expended in this area of study.

Balogh and Streeten (1963) provide some interesting illustrations of the dangers involved in the publication of results such as reported in Chapter 3 and in this chapter. They quote a United Nations official who was translating the results of the cost-benefit studies of education in the United States into a policy statement regarding underdeveloped countries. They properly argue that what is true of the United States is not necessarily true of other countries—and, we might add, what is true of the United States today may not be at all true of the United States tomorrow. But this is hardly a criticism of the approach itself; misinterpretation of the published results is not necessarily the fault of the researcher, nor would such misuse of cost-benefit work justify curtailment of the research.

Yet some reasonably forceful criticisms could be leveled against the cost-benefit framework. For one, "the American data, which are mostly used, do not provide evidence as to whether expenditure on education is *cause* or *effect* of incomes" (p. 385). Also, the computation of economic returns omits a host of direct and indirect returns—as we have mentioned numerous times. There is also the knotty problem of the consumption-investment dichotomy, with consumption benefits evading measurement, with a few exceptions, at least up to this date. Moreover, it might be argued that the income differentials used to predict the return to educational investment are devoid of any significance, as conditions in a dynamic world are almost certain to change the requirements for skill levels and educational attainment, whereas the expected return to future investments must be derived from past income data. According to Balogh and Streeten, "to conclude from those returns anything about today's returns is like identifying a crystal radio set with a Telstar" (p. 387).

Another objection is that our analysis separates human capital from physical capital, hence ignoring the complementary relationship between the two.

Merrett (1966) presents a catalogue of objections—over and above those voiced by Balogh and Streeten. First he argues that the concept of earnings foregone could lead to absurd results when foregone earnings are measured not only for complete stages of training but also for part training. Second, he contends that a major omission in the benefit stream, aside from the omission of the consumption effect, is "that education changes the nature of our leisure activities. . . . This effect is simply outside the scope of economics and for this reason the use of the concept of human capital is justifiably criticized for the narrowness of its criteria" (p. 293).

Merrett also contends that the econometric methods used to derive income differentials, after correction is made for whatever variables are considered to be relevant, are inadequate. First, the frequent assumption that all variables are additive—that is, that there is no interaction among the variables—is rather absurd. Second, qualitative variables such as intelligence are so difficult to measure that errors in measurement are almost certain to occur. This, he argues, would result in an overestimation of the effect of education on income. Moreover, since the studies relating education and other variables to income fail to explain the full variation in income, Merrett argues that the residual education-income relationship could be spurious.

Some of the criticisms are difficult to counter. The econometric problems surely exist, although recent efforts by Griliches (1976, 1977a, 1977b), Taubman (1976a, 1976b), and others have reduced the sting of Merrett's criticisms. All the same, the possibility of purely spurious correlation between education and income cannot be summarily dismissed. Yet we have by now many studies, using different data bases, all showing substantial net education-income relationships. And until better methods become available, this is the best we can do. Further, the omission of some consumption, external, or indirect effects, though complicating the analysis, does not suggest, in our view, abandoning all efforts in the area, as suggested by Merrett. Rather, any policy statement emanating from our analysis must be carefully written, acknowledging the various omissions and problems involved in this analysis. In short, although we recognize the many pitfalls, shortcomings, imperfections, omissions, and whatever other problems are involved in educational cost-benefit manipulations, we reach a conclusion far different from Merrett's. For the admittedly imperfect results are still far better than no results, when the results are properly interpreted; and the utilization of cost-benefit frameworks will at least be of advantage in that "it forces those responsible to quantify costs and benefits as far as possible rather than rest content with vague qualitative judgments or personal hunches" (Prest and Turvey, 1965: 730).

SUMMARY AND CONCLUSIONS

The studies surveyed in this chapter indicate that, in the large majority of cases, the returns to investment in education are quite high. Exceptions were noted in regard to graduate education in the United States and a number of educational investments in other countries. It is, of course, tempting to argue that those cases for which educational investment does not appear to be profitable should be reconsidered in light of the many external, indirect, and nonmonetary returns—so that we can argue that in these cases, too, the returns exceed the costs. But this is precisely the type of argument against which we must guard. For the major purpose of the analysis is to demonstrate that some programs provide higher returns than others. If this is so, programs with low returns should be deemed inferior—unless we have good reasons to believe that the external and other returns associated with the latter are substantially larger than those of other (educational and/or noneducational) investments.

The methodology used in this chapter to assess the contribution of education to increased income and productivity is criticized by some authors. Although a good deal of the criticism is valid, the conclusions derived thereof are really a matter of judgment. An alternative to the benefit-cost analysis, known as the "manpower requirements" approach, is often suggested by critics of the benefit-cost technique (e.g. Eckaus, 1964). The manpower-forecasting method dispenses with the cost-benefit framework and argues for planning of education so that skill levels are geared to predicted needs in the future commensurate with stated objectives for economic growth. But this is an entirely separate topic, to which we will subsequently devote an entire chapter.

LITERATURE GUIDE

The Profitability of Educational Investments in the United States

General. Estimates of return to various levels of education are presented in G.S. Becker (1960, 1964), Carnoy and Marenbach (1975), Danière and Mechling (1970), R.B. Freeman (1975, 1976, 1977a, 1977b), Hanoch (1967), Hause (1971, 1972), Hines et al. (1970), G.E. Johnson and Stafford (1973), T. Johnson (1970),

Psacharopolous (1969, 1970), Rizzuto (1977), Rogers (1969), and J.R. Walsh (1935). Reviews of studies include K. Alexander (1976), Leiter (1975), J.R. Davis and Morrall (1974), and Cohn (1972a, 1972b, 1972c).

College Education. Studies concentrating on the returns to college education, in addition to those already included above, include Berls (1969), H.R. Bowen (1977), Fiske (1977d), Gwartney (1972), Heineman and Sussna (1971), Hodgkinson (1972), Hunt (1963), Koch (1975), Link and Ratledge (1975), Mantell (1973), McMahon (1974, 1975), Raymond and Sesnowitz (1975), and Rogers (1969). See also comments by Akin and Kniesner (1976) and Ross (1975).

Graduate Education. Studies providing information on the returns to graduate education include Agnello and Hunt (1976), Ashenfelter and Mooney (1968, 1969), Bailey and Schotta (1972), Butter (1966), Campbell and Curtis (1975), Danielsen (1970), Deane (1975), Hunt (1963), G.E. Johnson and Stafford (1974a), L. Maxwell (1970), Metcalf (1973), Rogers (1969), Siegfried (1971, 1975), Siegfried and Scott (1977), Tomaske (1974), Y. Weiss (1971b), and Wessel (1971).

Vocational Education and Training. Studies on the returns to vocational education include the following: Barsby (1972), Bloch (1977), Bowlby and Schriver (1973), Carrol and Ihnen (1967), Corazzini (1968), R.B. Freeman (1974), Hardin and Borus (1971, 1972), Hu, Lee, and Stromsdorfer (1971), Hu, Lee, Stromsdorfer, and Kaufman (1969), Somers and Stromsdorfer (1970, 1972), Taussig (1968), Watson (1977), and Ghazalah and Pejovich (1973).

Returns by Race, Sex, and Minority Group. In addition to information on these issues provided in the above studies, see Adams and Nestel (1976), Carliner (1976), Link (1975a), Link, Ratledge, and Lewis (1976), McMahon (1976), Niemi (1974, 1975a, 1975b, 1976), Raymond and Sesnowitz (1976b), L. Weiss and Williamson (1972, 1975), and Welch (1973a, 1973b, 1975).

Other Studies on Returns to Education in the United States. Studies on returns to education in the health professions include Lindsay (1973, 1976), Maurizi (1975), Scheffler (1975), Despain (1975), and Sloan (1970, 1976). Returns to (or losses due to) dropouts are discussed by Kastner (1964), Spiegelman (1968), and Weisbrod

(1965b). Returns to two-year and community colleges are presented by Raymond and Sesnowitz (1975), Heineman and Sussna (1971), and Kastner (1976). Of interest, too, are the study by Danière (1969) on financial aid and that by Kiker and Wilder (1975) on the MBA-ETV program; the cost-effectiveness studies by H.M. Levin (1970a, 1971b, 1975a), Webster (1976), and Wolfe (1977); the work by Ribich (1968) and Ribich and Murphy (1975) on compensatory education and the returns to additional expenditures in education; evaluation of the Upward Bound program by Garms (1971), of returns to low achievers by Hansen, Weisbrod, and Scanlon (1970); of returns to high school in farm areas by Gisser (1968), and of returns to continuing education by Babock (1975); and the work by Swift and Weisbrod (1965) on intergenerational benefits. See also Psacharopoulos (1969) on returns to education in Hawaii and Verdon (1974) for Nebraska.

The Profitability of Educational Investments in Other Countries

The best single source is Psacharopoulos (1973), which contains additional bibliography and a summary of returns to education in thirty countries. Other studies include the following: Magnusson (1973)—Sweden; Klinov-Malul (1966) and Borus (1977)—Israel; Nalla Gounden (1967) and Paul (1972)—India; Blaug (1965, 1967b), Selby-Smith (1969), and Ziderman (1969, 1973a, 1973b)—United Kingdom; Blaug (1971, 1974, 1976c) and Puntassen (1977)—Thailand; Senna (1975) and De Mello E Souza (1975)—Brazil; Dodge (1972), Dodge and Stager (1972), Stager (1972a, 1972b) and B.W. Wilkinson (1966)—Canada; Stroup and Hargrove (1969)—rural South Vietnam; Thias and Carnoy (1972)—Kenya; Danielsen and Okachi (1971)—Japan; Hoerr (1974)—Ethiopia; Krueger (1972b) —Turkey; and Carnoy (1967)—Latin America. Other studies of interest include Carnoy (1975a) and Carnoy and Levin (1975) on educational television; Comay (1970) on study abroad; and Comay et al. (1973, 1976) on the option value of education using Canadian data.

Other Areas

In addition, we have a few studies on the returns to quality and quantity of education, including Hines et al. (1970), Johnson and Stafford (1973), Rizzuto (1977), and Wachtel (1976).

Methodological points are discussed in Balogh and Streeten (1963), Gustman (1973), Merrett (1966), D.O. Sewell (1967), Shaffer (1961), Singer and Feldman (1969), and Wiseman (1965).

Finally, an alternative method to estimate the returns to education, known as the "life·cycle" method, is used by a number of writers, including Ben-Porath (1967), Blinder and Weiss (1976), C. Brown (1976), Heckman (1976), Rosen (1976), Stephan (1976), and Wallace and Ihnen (1975).

Chapter 7

Education and Economic Growth

By sowing seed, you will harvest once.
By planting a tree, you will harvest ten-fold.
By educating the people, you will harvest one-hundred-fold.
Kuan-tsu, Fourth-Third-Century B.C.E., China

There is ample evidence that educational investments are profitable both to the individual and to society. It would appear, therefore, that investment in education should foster economic growth. The questions that need to be answered are (1) How does investment in education affect economic growth? and (2) What is the magnitude of the effect? Answers to both of these questions are needed if a policy prescription is to be made regarding the use of educational investment as an instrument for growth.

Much of the literature has been focused on the second question, with much of the work dealing with the United States. The work related to the first question is generally descriptive in nature, although some authors have attempted to discern the nature of the growth process.

THE DIMENSIONS OF GROWTH

Before we discuss the various attempts to measure the contribution of education to economic growth, it may be useful to define "economic growth." According to Denison (1962), "economic growth" refers to "the increase in the national product, measured in constant dollars" (p. 3) If we wish to measure the economic growth from, say, 1975 to 1976, we need to obtain figures on the national product in the two years, measured in constant dollars, and calculate the change (in percent). Fortunately, such data are provided in numerous media, such as *The Economic Report of the President* (1978), *Survey of Current Business, Federal Reserve Bulletin,* Organization for Economic Cooperation and Development (OECD), United National publications, and many more.

Using the figures for national income in 1972 dollars (based upon *Economic Report of the President, 1978*), we find that national income increased from $956.9 billion in 1975 to $1,018.9 in 1976—an increase of $62 billion, or 6.5 percent. Similar calculations may be made for other years and for longer invervals, from which the growth rate in average annual terms is computed.

Alternatively, "economic growth" may be defined as the rate at which per capita national product in constant dollars grows over a given period of time. If national income again serves as the measure of national product, we must now divide the respective national income figures by the number of people in the U.S. population—213,559,000 in 1975, and 215,142,000 in 1976—which gives us per capita national income in 1972 dollars of $4,481 in 1975 and $4,736 in 1976. The growth in per capita income was $255, or approximately 5.7 percent. So long as the population increases, the rate of growth of GNP must be greater than the rate of growth of GNP per capita.

The above definition of economic growth does not go unchallenged. In the first place, national income (NI) includes only those products and services that are provided in the marketplace. Suppose that the economy has been experiencing an increase in the relative importance of marketplace activity as compared to home production (i.e., food processing, use of servants in households, etc.). Then some of the increase in NI would be only apparent. (It seems plausible, indeed, that the relative importance of home production in the United States has declined substantially from, say, 1930 to the present.) Furthermore, improvements in accounting procedures, installation of new and modern data processing equipment, and so forth may have contributed to a more extensive reporting of the extent of production. Hence, over a long period of time, the rate of growth in NI will overestimate the growth of the economy.

On the other hand, a number of factors exist that would appear to create a serious underestimate of economic growth as measured by NI. First, if we deflate the NI series by utilizing the implicit price deflator, we are likely to fail to fully take into account quality changes in products. For example, if the average price of an automobile increased from $4,500 in year t to $4,680 in year $t + 1$, all that we can say for sure is that automobile prices increased by 4 percent. Whether the entire price increase is due to "inflation" or whether some or all of this increase is actually due to improvements in the workmanship and materials invested in the car it is quite difficult to tell. Moreover, the absence of price increases may not at all prove that no changes in the pricing of the product took place. On the one hand, improving the quality of the product without changing its price represents, in effect, a decrease in the price. On the other hand, maintaining the same price in both years (t and $t + 1$) at the expense of product quality in year $t + 1$ (by substituting cheaper material, etc.) is nothing but a hidden price increase. Hence, the compilation of accurate price indexes is quite difficult. In sum, correcting NI for price movements may neglect changes in quality; moreover, since no corrections for quality improvement are likely to be made when the price of the product has not changed, even money NI (unadjusted) may be under-estimated.

A more fundamental issue relating to the general use of aggregate income figures to determine economic growth is centered on the proposition that NI provides a measure of economic welfare and well-being. That is, we assume that an increase in NI is synonymous with an increase in the overall well-being of society and that improvements in economic welfare will be approximated by similar improvements in NI. There are several reasons to suspect that these assertions do not necessarily hold. First, increases in NI—even if an accurate provision for sheer price movements were to be made—may represent the production of more goods and services, but perhaps not those goods and services that are desired by society. This is more likely to be true when a sizeable portion of the national product is produced and/or consumed by the public sector of the economy, since the demand for public goods cannot be measured very accurately. Second, improvements in consumer welfare do not necessarily reflect themselves in the NI accounts. For example, if resources are shifted from a high cost and inefficient production sector to a low cost, efficient one, NI might remain constant or even decrease. Yet consumers receive the goods they desire most (and, perhaps, at reduced prices), which indicates that consumers' welfare is almost certain to increase.

Moreover, even if it were likely that changes in NI and consumer satisfaction move in the same direction, a number of conceptual problems remain. First, there is the phenomenon of external effects (variously termed "third party effects," "spillovers," or simply "externalities"), which point to the fact that market prices do not necessarily represent consumer satisfaction. Second, prices reflect consumer satisfaction only to the extent that perfect competition prevails in all sectors of the economy.[1] The greater the number of industries in which some form of imperfect competition appears to predominate, the less reliable will the price system be in reflecting consumer welfare.[2] Finally, economic progress may lead to a situation in which the volume of production of year t can be accomplished at year $t + 1$ by an identical labor force but at much less effort. Then it is conceivable that $NI_{t+1} = NI_t$, but each laborer will have more leisure time, which yields a certain satisfaction over and above the enjoyment of goods and services.[3] So there may be some economic progress that could never be detected by measuring the change in GNP.

Despite all of its shortcomings, NI is one of the best empirical measure we have for the purpose of assessing the rate of economic progress in the United States. As will be shown later, other measures could be used (such as electricity production), but even these will be closely correlated with NI. Since NI will be used here as the most important proxy for economic welfare, it may be useful to provide the reader with some NI series reflecting the growth paths of the economy in recent decades. Table 7-1 provides such information. In column 1 we present unadjusted figures of NI for selected years (1929-1977). Column 2 gives the implicit price deflator. Column 3 has the figures for NI at 1972 prices ("Real" NI). Column 4 contains figures for total United States population. "Real" NI per capita is obtained by dividing column 3 by column 4 and is given in column 5.

Growth rates in gross national products, GNP are summarized in Table 7-2. They are average annual compounded rates of change in

1. An industry is said to be "perfectly competitive" if all of the following requirements are satisfied: (1) each firm or economic entity in the market is small relative to the market as a whole, and there exist many such small firms in the market; (2) there is no product differentiation—i.e., all firms in the industry produce one homogenous product; (3) all resources are perfectly mobile: there are no restrictions on exit from or entry into the industry; (4) all participants in the market possess full knowledge of prices, opportunities, and newest technologies pertinent to that industry. For more details, see Ferguson (1972: 250-53).

2. We may distinguish three main types of "imperfect competition": (1) *monopoly*, in which there is a single seller ("firm" and "industry" are synonymous); (2) *oligopoly*, in which there are several large firms, each of which could have some perceptible impact on market prices; and (3) *monopolistic competition*, in which there are many small firms, but each firm is still able to exert some influence on market prices because of product differentiation (See Ferguson, 1972: chs. 9-11).

3. More leisure may also provide increased satisfaction in that the individual would now have the time to enjoy fully the many goods and services available to him. Data from the *Economic Report of the President* (1978) indicate that average weekly hours in the private, nonagricultural sector have decreased from 40.3 in 1947 to 36.1 in 1977.

Table 7-1. National Income in Current and 1972 Prices, Implicit Price Deflator, Total U.S. Population, and Per Capita Income, Selected Years.

Year	National Income (billions of current dollars) 1	Implicit Price Deflator 1972 = 100 2	"Real" National Income (billions of 1972 dollars) [(1) ÷ (2)] × 100 3	Total U.S. Population (thousands) 4	"Real" National Income Per Capita (dollars) (3) ÷ (4) 5
1929	84.8	32.87	258.0	121,767	2,119
1933	39.9	25.13	158.8	125,579	1,265
1940	79.7	29.10	273.9	132,122	2,073
1950	236.2	53.64	440.3	152,271	2,892
1960	412.0	68.67	600.0	180,671	3,321
1970	798.4	91.36	873.9	204,878	4,265
1977	1,520.3[a]	141.32[a]	1,075.8[a]	216,817	4,962[a]

Source: Economic Report of the President (1978), Tables B-4, B-17, and B-26.
[a]Preliminary estimates.

Table 7-2. Rates of Economic Growth in the United States, 1929-1974.

Terminal Year	*Initial Year*					
	1929	*1940*	*1950*	*1960*	*1970*	*1973*
1941	2.2	16.1	—	—	—	—
1951	2.9	4.9	7.9	—	—	—
1961	2.8	3.8	3.1	1.9	—	—
1970	3.1	3.9	3.6	4.0	—	—
1974	3.1	3.9	3.6	3.8	3.2	-2.2

Source: Bureau of the Census, *The Statistical Abstract of the U.S.*, 1976, Table 618, p. 382.

GNP, expressed in constant dollars. The table shows a relative stability in the long period rates along with considerable volatility in the short run. We find that the American economy has been growing at a rate slightly over 3 percent per year during 1929-1974, with almost a 4 percent annual growth rate when the Depression years are excluded (1940-1974). Recently, the growth rate has been close to 4 percent, with the exception of 1973-1975, when the U.S. economy experienced a recession.

THE SOURCES OF ECONOMIC GROWTH

Economic growth does not occur in a vacuum. Something must propel it. It is not surprising, therefore, that some attempts to account for past growth have been made. It is equally tempting to project past rates of growth into the future or to specify conditions that must prevail if the rate of growth is to become x percent. Some attempt is made here to illustrate the theoretical and empirical relationships that allegedly affect the growth of our economy.

The Aggregate Production Function

One of the most important (yet controversial) tools for such an analysis is the so-called aggregate production function. For expository purposes, let us assume that all the factors of production can be lumped into three different input categories: labor inputs (L), capital inputs (K), and land inputs (A). If we designate the aggregate national product by X, a generalized production function would have the following form:

$$X = f(L, K, A) \qquad (7.1)$$

Formula (7.1) is completely static, that is, it involves no time dimensions. Also, no account is taken of the state of technology—unless it is already embodied in any one or all of the three inputs.[4] Equation (7.1) states that the quantities of L, K, and A employed affect output, X, in accordance with the process specified by the functional operator, f.

To make the production function more realistic, time subscripts (i.e., X_t) are added to underscore the fact that outputs and inputs are measured for a given time period. Also, an additional term is included to capture the effect of disembodied technical change and other structural changes occurring over time—symbolized by t. The new aggregate production function will have the following general form:

$$X_t = f(L_t, K_t, A_t, t) \qquad (7.2)$$

A very convenient explicit form for Equation (7.2) was advanced many years ago by C.W. Cobb and Paul H. Douglas.[5] Assuming that

---

4. The question of whether technical change manifests itself in improvements in the capital stock (the "embodiment hypothesis") or whether it occurs independently of that stock (the "disembodiment hypothesis") has been a controversial subject among economists in recent years. Much of the analysis requires a relatively high degree of mathematical sophistication (see, e.g., Jorgenson, 1966, and You, 1976).

5. See Cobb and Douglas (1928). Other relevant work includes Tinbergen (1959), Aukrust (1959), and Solow (1959). Alternative specifications of the aggregate production function have been suggested, notably the CES production function (see, e.g., Arrow et al., 1961; Bowles, 1970a; and Selowsky, 1969).

their function holds for the American economy, Formula (7.2) becomes:

$$X_t = e^{\phi t} A_t^\alpha L_t^\beta K_t^\gamma \qquad (7.3)$$

where ϕ, α, β, and γ are constants—provided that $\alpha + \beta + \gamma = 1$—and e is a constant whose approximate value is 2.71828. . . . After some mathematical manipulations[6], it can be shown that:

$$\frac{\Delta X}{X} = \phi + \alpha \frac{\Delta A}{A} + \beta \frac{\Delta L}{L} + \gamma \frac{\Delta K}{K} \qquad (7.4)$$

where Δ denotes a change in a variable over a given time period—so that, for example, $\Delta X/X$ is the rate of change in X over time. Note that ϕ represents the rate of growth in "technical change."

Equation (7.4) implies that the rate of growth in X is the result of the additive effects of growth in each of the inputs. The interpretation of Equation (7.4) may best be illustrated by an example. Suppose that $\alpha = 0.05$, $\beta = 0.73$, and $\gamma = 0.22$. This means that land's share of national income is 5 percent, labor's is 73 percent, and capital's is 22 percent. Then if, say, the rate of change of L were 2 percent, its contribution to growth would amount of $2 \times 0.73 = 1.46$ percentage points. Similarly, if the growth rate of capital were 1.5 percent, its contribution to growth would amount to 0.33 percentage points. If the amount of land under cultivation did not change at all, it will not contribute to growth (even though it will continue to share a certain percentage of national income). It can thus be seen that labor and capital together would contribute to an increase in the national product of 1.79 percentage points. Suppose, however, that national income increased at a rate of 3 percent (per year). What of the "residual" of 1.21 percentage points in the growth rate? This is precisely the reason for the inclusion of the trend term which, as a residual, will "explain" the remaining portion of the rate of economic growth. It will be noted that this example closely corresponds to Denison's results, which are summarized below.

6. Taking natural logarithms in (7.3) we get

$$\log X_t = \phi t + \alpha \log A_t + \beta \log L_t + \gamma \log K_t$$

Let $\dot{X} = dX_t/dt$. Then we have (deleting the subscripts for simplicity):

$$\frac{\dot{X}}{X} = \phi + \alpha \frac{\dot{A}}{A} + \beta \frac{\dot{L}}{L} + \gamma \frac{\dot{K}}{K}, \text{ since } d \log X/dt = \frac{dX/dt}{X} = \frac{\dot{X}}{X}.$$

The implications of such an analysis to economic policy are obvious. We could increase the rate of economic growth by accelerating the rate of capital accumulation and of growth in the labor force or by improving our technical capability. By far the most potent weapon for growth, according to this analysis, will be the technical progress approach as it appears to be the single most important tool of growth of national income per capita. However, the analysis must take into account a number of factors: first, the specification of Formula (7.3) may be in error. In fact, an alternative formulation has proven to be superior to the Cobb-Douglas formulation in that the former (1) is less objectionable on theoretical grounds and (2) provides better statistical fit to the data.[7] Some critics, moreover, object to the entire procedure of estimating aggregate production functions. They claim that capital cannot be considered as one single and homogeneous factor of production. Similarly, inputs of labor and land must be disaggregated if any meaningful results are to emerge.[8] Therefore, we must be very cautious in interpreting results based upon the model formulated in Equation (7.4), although such analyses, if properly conceived and interpreted, may serve a good purpose in advancing our knowledge about the mysteries of economic growth.

The Growth of Land, Labor and Capital

Although the relevance of such aggregate inputs is open to doubt, it would still be interesting to see the paths of growth of each of the three major inputs. Table 7–3 presents some figures that may be used as proxies for A, L, and K for selected years. Column 1 gives some indication of acreage utilization in the United States. Needless to say, the number of acres alone does not fully represent the input of land. Use of fertilizers, improved irrigation methods, and so forth all have contributed to improvement in the quality of land. In other words, a unit of land (acre) in 1976 may not at all correspond to the same unit of land in 1929, even though both encompass the same area. Similarly, column 2 presents data on the employment of civilian labor force during the same period. Once again, such data do not take into

7. This is the so-called CES production function (see Arrow et al., 1961). Let a, b, and c be constants, and q_1 and q_2 be two inputs (labor and capital). Then the CES function has the form:

$$X = a[bq_1^{-c} + (1 - b)q_2^{-c}]^{-1/c}$$

8. An outspoken critic of the aggregate production function is N. Kaldor. See, for example, his article in the February 1961 issue of *Oxford Economic Papers*. An interesting growth model with disaggregated inputs is presented by Svennilson (1964). See also Kaldor's comments on Svennilson in *Organization for Economic and Cultural Development* (1964: 138–43).

Table 7-3. Land in Farms, Civilian Labor Force Employment, and Fixed Nonresidential Business Capital (at constant [1972] cost), Selected Years.

Year	Land in Farms (in million acres)	Civilian Labor Force Employment (thousands)	Fixed Nonresidential Business Capital (billions of dollars)
	1	2	3
1929	987	47,630	623.8
1940	1,061	50,350	576.5
1950	1,202	58,920	693.6
1960	1,179	65,778	963.9
1970	1,102	78,627	1,421.6
1976	1,078	87,485	1,743.4

Sources: Column 1, Bureau of Census, *Statistical Abstract of the United States*, and figures obtained from the Department of Agriculture; Column 2, from the *Statistical Abstract* and *Economic Report of the President* (1978), p. 290; Column 3, from Musgrave (1976), and *Survey of Current Business* 57 (August 1977): 57.

account shorter hours, on the one hand, or improvements in the skill and education of the labor force, on the other. Finally, in column 3 we have pertinent data on the magnitude of the physical capital stock in the United States. Needless to say, such figures are subject to all sorts of errors and thus ought to be interpreted with much caution.

The Residual

Using a set of input proxies for land, labor, and capital, Denison (1962) observed the following rates of growth for the period 1929–1957: land, 0.00 percent; labor, adjusted for quality changes, 2.16 percent; and capital, 1.88 percent. Factor shares were estimated as follows: land, 4.5 percent; labor, 73 percent; and capital, 22.5 percent. On the basis of this information, if Formula (7.4) is assumed to hold, the contribution of these three inputs to growth would amount to 2 percentage points. Since national income increased at an annual average rate of 2.93 percent during the same period, this leaves 0.93 percentage points unexplained. This unexplained portion of growth has been called the residual. Once again, the existence of the residual has meant different things to different people. One school of thought has maintained that the very existence of such a large residual (which would become much larger if no adjustments for changes in the quality of the labor force were to be made), points to the conclusion that Formula (7.3) is inappropriate. At the other extreme are those who would attribute the entire residual to what they call technical change (encompassing improvements in technology, better skills and training of the labor force, etc.). A middle position is taken by such theorists as M. Abramovitz (1962), who, while accepting in general the concept of the aggregate production function, still point to the fact that at least a portion of the residual ought to be attributed to statistical errors of sorts and to possible errors of specification in Formula (7.3).[9]

If, indeed, we accept the position that Formula (7.3) is at least approximately correct, it is clear that such a very large residual cannot be dismissed as being due to a set of statistical errors. Clearly, the analysis indicates that land, labor, and capital as traditionally measured do not give the entire picture of the production process in a modern society. Instead, attention must be paid to improvements in the labor force through education, training, reduced hours, and so forth, and to improvements in production through economies of scale "disembodied" technical change, and the like.

Since the focus of this chapter is on the effect of education on economic growth, we shall not discuss the contribution of other factors to growth. Instead, a summary of the results obtained by Denison (1974) are reported in Table 7-4. The remainder of this chapter will be devoted to discussions of the role of education in economic growth.

THE CONTRIBUTION OF EDUCATION TO ECONOMIC GROWTH

In what ways could education affect economic growth? Further, how could such an effect be quantified? As W.L. Miller (1967) notes, the attempt to quantify the contribution of education to growth clearly requires an a priori explanation of why we ought to expect any contribution to growth from education. So before we proceed to discuss the various attempts at the quantification of the educational effect, we will present Miller's analysis pertaining to the first question of this paragraph.

To be sure, "not just any kind of education will" promote economic growth. "Education is a source of economic growth only if it is anti-traditional to the extent that it liberates and stimulates as well as informs the individual and teaches him how and why to make demands upon himself." Accordingly, a proper educational strategy would manifest itself in four "growth-producing capacities." The

9. It should also be noted that a recent study by R.J. Gordon (1969) indicates that estimates of the capital stock in the United States have neglected substantial government-financed structures and equipment that have been sold to the private sector at much less than actual value.

Table 7-4. Sources of Growth in Actual National Income and National Income per Person Employed in the United States, 1929-1969, 1929-1948, and 1948-1969 (in percentage points).

Source	Growth in Total Actual National Income			Growth in Actual National Income Per Person Employed		
	1929-69	1929-48	1948-69	1929-69	1929-48	1948-69
National Income	3.33	2.75	3.85	1.89	1.47	2.27
Labor	1.31	1.36	1.30	0.23	0.34	0.13
Employment	1.08	1.02	1.17	—	—	—
Hours	-0.22	-0.23	-0.21	-0.22	-0.23	-0.21
Education	0.41	0.40	0.41	0.41	0.40	0.41
Other	0.04	0.17	-0.07	0.04	0.17	-0.07
Capital	0.50	0.13	0.80	0.22	-0.06	0.48
Land	0.00	0.00	0.00	-0.05	-0.05	-0.05
Increase in Output per Unit of Input	1.52	1.26	1.75	1.49	1.24	1.71

Source: Adapted from Denison (1974), Tables 9-4 and 9-7.

first is the "development of a general milieu favorable to economic progress." The reference is to social mobility, a general increase in literacy necessary for improved communication, and "record keeping and deposit banking" (p. 281).

The second capacity emphasizes the development of "complimentary resources for factors which are relatively plentiful and substitutes for comparatively scarce factors" (id.). For example, the use of natural resources is augmented by education, as the latter provides managerial talents that can then exploit resources more effectively. At the same time, education may provide techniques to overcome the scarcity of some resources by substituting a plentiful resource for the scarce one. Without education, people would be far less adaptable to varying production needs.

The third capacity underscores the durability of educational investment. Miller argues that education "has greater durability than most forms of non-human reproducible capital," particularly in countries "with a long life expectancy at birth." Further, Miller contends that depreciation and obsolescence of human capital occurs at a much slower rate than that of physical capital on the grounds that "usually only specialized training of the lowest sort becomes completely obsolete." Therefore Miller asserts that "a given investment in education tends to be more productive, other things being equal, than the same outlay on non-human capital" (p. 283).[10]

Finally, "education is an alternative to consumption, private investment in non-human capital, or government outlay for other than educational ends." It may be argued that expenditures on education are made mostly at the expense of consumption (not savings).[11] Since investment in physical capital is conditioned upon the availability of savings, "within limits, additional expenditures upon education can make a net contribution to growth even if the internal rate of return is lower in education than for material capital, for it transfers to

10. See Rosen (1975) for an attempt to measure the obsolescence of knowlege.

11. This assertion can be explained as follows: (1) A large portion of the direct outlays on education are made by governmental units. If these outlays are financed by new taxes, there is a good likelihood that most of the tax revenue will come out of consumption. (If the marginal propensity to save is 10 percent, 90 percent of the new taxes will come out of consumption.) (2) Educational costs borne by students and their families consist of direct expenditures and foregone earnings. The latter reflect in most cases reduced consumption by students—although some parents may deplete savings to support their children's standard of living while in school. The direct outlays by students and their families are relatively unimportant and, in addition, are not likely to be financed mainly by reducing savings. See Chapter 4 for cost data; further explanation is given by Denison (1962: 77-78).

roundabout production the resources that would otherwise be con-sumed" (id.).

Supposing that the educational system has developed at least one of the four "growth-developing capacities," the problem of esti-mating the quantitative magnitudes of education's contribution to economic growth remains to be solved. In what follows, we shall present a number of attempts to solve this problem.

Schultz's Study

The first serious attempt to quantify the contribution of education to economic growth was made by Schultz (1961b). We may outline his methodology as follows. First, we must obtain data on the dis-tribution of the labor force by years of education, making adjust-ments for increases in the length of the school year. Also, we must concentrate on the labor force only, even though Schultz believes that increments of education to, say, nonworking mothers have a definitely positive impact on growth through informal education at home. Now it can be shown that labor, in 1957, "earned 226.5 bil-lion dollars or *71 billion dollars* more than it would have had the earnings per person in the labor force not risen" since 1929 (p. 300; italics in original).[12] Next, Schultz demonstrates that the stock of human capital, represented by the accumulation of investments in schooling, has also increased. While some of the increase was required to maintain the 1929 level of the stock of education per laborer, this stock rose by an additional amount of $286 billion.

The major methodological issue is the assessment of the contribu-tion of this $286 billion of increased educational stock to the $71 billion of increased labor income. Schultz calculates three different internal rates of return on the educational stock. Multiplying each of these rates by the $286 billion of additional stock of education, he gets three different estimates of the "income attributable to this addi-tional education." Dividing each of these estimates by 71 and multi-plying by 100 gives us the "proportion of 'unexplained' increase in national income." Schultz thus obtains three estimates of this pro-portion, varying from 36 to 70 percent. That is, between 36 and 70 percent of the increase in labor income is attributable to the increase in the educational stock (between 1929 and 1957).

Let us observe Schultz's quantitative analysis in a bit more detail. First, he presents detailed analyses on explicit and implicit school costs (i.e., costs of operation of elementary and high schools, colleges and universities, as well as "earnings foregone" while attending high

12. Page references correspond to the reprint in M.J. Bowman (1968).

school and college or university), summarized in column one of Table 7-6, which lists the value of "an equivalent year of school (in 1956 prices)". This value represents a weighted average of the investments in the various levels of education, adjustments being made for the changes in the length of the school year in the various decades. Next, the number of "school years equivalent" of the labor force were computed by Schultz as described in Table 7-5, and the results are summarized in column two of Table 7-6 (note that column 5 of Table 7-5 = column 2 of Table 7-6).

To obtain the total value of the educational stock, we need only multiply the number of "school years equivalent" of the labor force by the value of an equivalent school year. These results are presented in column 4 of Table 7-6. It can thus be seen that the growth of the educational stock of the labor force from 1929 to 1957, as measured by Schultz, was in the magnitude of $355 billion (column 4).

Now we see from Table 7-6 that the educational stock in 1929 was valued at $180 billion (in 1956 prices). "The labor force increased slightly more than 38 percent between 1929 and 1957. Accordingly, to keep the stock of education per laborer constant at its 1929 level, it would have required 69 billion dollars more, increasing it to 249 billion dollars." Since the stock of education increased by $355 billion, $286 billion (i.e., 355 - 69) represented an increase "beyond the 69 billion dollars required to keep the per laborer stock constant" (p. 300).

At the same time that the stock of education increased by a net amount of $286 billion, labor income increased from $112.5 to $226.5 billion (between 1929 and 1957). Since the size of the labor force in 1929 was 49.2 million persons, income per member of the labor force was $2,287. "If the earnings per person were held constant, the labor force of 68.0 million in 1957 would have earned 155.5 billion dollars" (p. 300). Since total labor income in 1957 was equal to $226.5 billion, labor income has increased by $71 billion beyond the level of earnings that would have kept the per person earnings constant over the period 1929-1957.

To complete the analysis, internal rates of return to the educational stock of capital must be computed. The rates of return presented by Schultz come from three different sources. The first, 9 percent, is the low estimate reported by G.S. Becker (1960), "which is for college education of white urban males adjusted for ability, employment, and mortality, for 1940 and 1950." The second rate, 11 percent, is Schultz's (1960) own estimate of the return to college education in 1958. The third estimate, 17.3 percent, reflects the fact that the rates of return, as well as the relative weights in the educa-

Table 7-5. Total School Years Completed of the Labor Force of the United States, 1900 to 1957.

Year	Labor Force (millions)	School Years Completed per Person	Total School Years Completed (millions)	Equivalent 1940 Completed School Years per Person	Total Equivalent 1940 School Years Completed (millions)
	1	2	3	4	5
1900	28.1	7.70	216	4.14	116
1910	35.8	7.91	283	4.65	167
1920	41.4	8.12	336	5.25	217
1930	48.7	8.41	410	6.01	293
1940	52.8	9.02	476	7.24	382
1950	60.1	10.10	607	8.65	520
1957	70.8	10.96	776	10.45	740

Source: Reproduced by permission from T.W. Schultz, "Education and Economic Growth," in *Social Forces Influencing American Education,* Sixtieth Yearbook of the National Society for the Study of Education, Part II (Chicago: University of Chicago Press 1961), Table D, p. 87.

Table 7-6. Value of the Stock of Education of the Labor Force and Population, Fourteen Years and Older, for the United States in 1956 Prices.

Year	Value of an Equivalent Year of School (in 1956 prices)	School Years Equivalent		Total Value	
		Labor Force	Population Fourteen Years and Older	Labor Force (1 X 2)	Fourteen Years and Older (1 X 3)
		(in millions of years)		(in billions of dollars)	
	1	2	3	4	5
1900	540	116	212	63	114
1910	563	167	299	94	168
1920	586	217	388	127	277
1930	614	293	535	180	328
1940	650	382	714	248	465
1950	690	520	951	359	656
1957	723	740	1,173	535	848

Source: Reproduced by permission from T.W. Schultz, "Education and Economic Growth," in *Social Forces Influencing American Education,* Sixtieth Yearbook of the National Society for the Study of Education, Part II (Chicago: University of Chicago Press (1961), Table F, p. 88.

151

tional stock, of the three levels of education are very much different. Schultz's computation of this rate is given in a note to Table 7-7.

The final results of Schultz's analysis are explained in Table 7-7. Column 1 contains the three rates of return discussed above. Column 3 contains the $286 billion of additional stock of education as explained above. Multiplication of columns 1 and 3 yields column 5, entitled by Schultz "income attributable to this additional education." Dividing column 5 by 71 and multiplying by 100 gives the final result—namely, the contribution of education to labor earnings (column 7).

It is evident that although Schultz concentrated on the earnings and educational stock of the labor force, education is considered as a separate productive factor. The stock of education is treated much like the stock of physical capital in so far as their productive capacities are concerned. Moreover, as the increase in the stock of physical capital leaves some of the return to capital in the "unexplained" category, Schultz provides an estimate of the contribution of education to both the increase in labor earnings and the increase in income of capital that is not explained by the growth of physical capital (see Table 7-7).

Denison's Study

The most complete analysis of the sources of economic growth and education's contribution to it has been made by Denison (1962, 1964a, 1967, 1974). Although his basic methodology was already exposed in his 1962 treatise, we shall report mainly the results of his latest investigation (1974), in which the "education index" was thoroughly revised.

The basic approach employed to estimate the effect of education contains six steps.

1. Using data from the 1960 census, Denison calculates a weighting factor (w_e) that indicates the relative earnings of persons with any one level of education in comparison to a base level of education. The base level chosen is eight years $(w_8 = 100)$. He calculates weights for seven additional classes of education, employing adjusted earnings of persons in the nonresidential business sector (where adjustments are made for various nonschooling factors). For example, the weight for no schooling (w_0) is 75, whereas the respective weight for five or more years of college is 219. This information is summarized in column 1 of Table 7-8 for the year 1970.

Table 7-7. Estimates of the Contribution of Education in the Labor Force to Earnings and to National Income Between 1929 and 1956 in the United States.

Estimate	Rate of Return	Stock of Education Added (in billions of dollars)		Income Attributable to this Additional Education (in billions of dollars)			Proportion of "Unexplained" Increase in National Income (in billions of dollars)	
		Part One	Part Two	Part One (1×2)	Part Two (1×3)	Total $(4 + 5)$	Of the $71 Billion Increase in Earnings of Labor $\frac{Col.\ 5}{71} \times 100$ (percent)	Of the $88.8 Billion Increase in Returns in Capital and Labor $\frac{Col.\ 5}{88.8} \times 100$ (percent)
	1	2	3	4	5	6	7	8
1	9	69	286	6.2	25.7	31.9	36	29
2	11	69	286	7.6	31.5	39.1	44	36
3	17.3[a]	69	286	11.9	49.5	61.4	70	56

Source: Reproduced by permission from T.W. Schultz, "Education and Economic Growth," in *Social Forces Influencing American Education,* Sixtieth Yearbook of the National Society for the Study of Education, Part II (Chicago: University of Chicago Press, (1961), Table 18. p. 81.

[a]Schultz based this estimate on the following weights:

	Weights in Educational Stock	Rates of Return (percent)	Total
	1	2	(1×2)
Elementary	0.28	35	9.80
High School	0.45	10	4.50
College	0.27	11	2.97
Total	1.00		17.27

Table 7-8. Weighting Factors (W_e), Percentage Distribution of FTE Employment (P_e) by Sex, and Initial Index $(w_e) \cdot P_e$.

Educational Level (highest school grade completed)	Weighting Factor (w_e)	Percentage Distribution of FTE Employment, March 1970 (P_e) Males	Percentage Distribution of FTE Employment, March 1970 (P_e) Females	Initial Index Males (1) X (2)	Initial Index Females (1) X (3)
	1	2	3	4	5
None	75	0.42	0.21	0.315	0.158
Elementary, 1–4	89	2.46	1.00	2.189	0.890
Elementary, 5–7	97	7.07	4.19	6.858	4.064
Elementary, 8	100	10.82	8.14	10.820	8.140
High school, 1–3	111	17.91	18.16	19.880	20.158
High school, 4	124	36.77	50.60	45.595	62.744
College, 1–3	147	12.67	12.70	18.625	18.669
College, 4	189	7.27	3.49	13.740	6.596
College, 5 or more	219	4.62	1.52	10.118	3.329
Total	...	100.00	100.00	128.140	124.748

Source: Columns 1–3, from Denison (1974), Table 4–6, p. 44. Columns 4 and 5 calculated by author.

Note: Details may not add to totals because of rounding.

2. Next, Denison calculates the percentage distribution of full-time equivalent (FTE) employment by level of education. If P_e denotes the proportion of workers with educational level e, then the sum of the Ps must be unity. Data for 1970 are displayed in columns 2 and 3 of Table 7–8 for males and females.

3. When the educational weights are multiplied by the employment distribution (i.e., $w_e \cdot P_e$), the initial index is obtained by summing the products $w_e \cdot P_e$ over all education groups (given by $\Sigma_{e=0}^{8} w_e P_e$). This is done for males and females in columns 4 and 5 of Table 7–8. The significant figures are the totals: 128.14 for males and 124.748 for females. The same procedure is used to derive annual indexes for all relevant years.

4. The initial annual indexes are adjusted to take into account the level of unemployment.

5. The annual indexes are further adjusted for days per year and rates of attendance. In Denison's 1974 volume, no adjustments are made for days per year for persons regularly attending city schools, for those having had no schooling, and for those with at least some college. For others, a proportionate adjustment is made. For example, if a person completed twelve years in a rural school where instruction was given only on 80 percent of the days considered

"normal" (180 days), then it was assumed that the person obtained the equivalent grade level equal to (0.8) · 12 = 9.6 years of schooling.

6. Steps 1 through 5 provide annual education indexes for males and females separately. To obtain a global index for each (for the period 1929-1969), the two indexes were "weighted by total earnings to obtain the final index for both sexes combined" (p. 46). The computed values of the indexes, for selected years, are reported in Table 7-9.

Denison emphasizes that the final indexes represent only the quantity of education, assuming that the quality of education per year or per day is constant across time and space. Also, it is pointed out that the index only captures the contribution of education in enhancing labor input and ignores the effect of education on the improvement of capital.

As may be observed from Table 7-9, the combined educational index increased from 83.71 in 1929 to 106.71 in 1969—an increase of 27.5 percent. This implies that the average worker in 1969 provided an input per day 27.5 percent greater than what was provided by the average worker in 1929. If labor represents approximately 75 percent of national income, the national income should have increased by (0.75) × (0.275) = 20.6 percent over the period. Therefore, if the annual rate of per capita national income growth between 1929 and 1969 was 1.89 percentage points, the contribution of education would be approximately 0.39 percentage points. This is quite close to Denison's figures as reported in our Table 7-4. Similar calculations were made by Denison for other periods (see Table 7-10).

What the results of Table 7-10 indicate is that education has been an important factor in national economic growth. Note that whereas it has been less important in recent years (1948-1969) than in earlier years (1929-1969) relative to the growth rate of total real national

Table 7-9. Final Indexes Derived by Denison for the Effect of Education on Labor Input in the Business Sector, Selected Years, 1929-1969.

Year	Males 1	Females 2	Combined 3
1929	83.18	86.79	83.71
1948	93.40	96.33	93.85
1969	107.08	105.01	106.71

Source: Denison (1974), Table I-21, p. 259.

Table 7-10.   Estimates of the Contribution of Education to Past Growth of Real National Income.

	1929-1948	1948-1969	1929-1969
Growth Rate of Total Real National Income	2.75	3.85	3.33
Amount of Growth Rate Ascribed to Education	0.40	0.41	0.41
Percent of Growth Rate Ascribed to Education	14.5	10.6	12.3
Growth Rate of Real National Income per Person Employed	1.47	2.27	1.89
Amount of Growth Rate Ascribed to Education	0.40	0.41	0.41
Percent of Growth Rate Ascribed to Education	27.2	18.1	21.7

Source: Table format taken from Denison (1964a), Table 8, p. 35. Data are from Denison (1974), Tables 9-4 and 9-7 (see Table 7-4 above).

income, in absolute terms the contribution of education to economic growth was quite stable.

The reader may have noticed that Denison's calculation of the role of education in economic growth only takes into account the increase in the educational level of the labor force, not the maintenance of a given level of education for new members of the labor force. It may be argued that the investment in education between 1949 and 1969 necessary to produce increments to the labor force possessing the same distribution of educational stocks as prevailed in 1948 should also be taken into account. Using a slightly different methodology, Selowsky (1969) shows that the contribution of education to economic growth from 1940 to 1965 is only 12.9 percent compared to 20.9 percent when expansion of the labor force is also taken into account. The impact of introducing the expansion of the labor force into the analysis has even more far-reaching implications for other countries.

International Comparisons

A number of studies have appeared in recent years extending Denison's original study (1962) to other countries. One of these studies was conducted by Denison himself (1967), in which the contribution of education to economic growth was calculated for eight northwest European countries and Italy for the period 1950-1962. These were compared to the respective results for the United States. The Denison results are summarized in Table 7-11.

The role of education in past economic growth in Europe appears

Table 7-11. Contribution of Education to Economic Growth in the United States and Europe, 1950–1962.

Country	Rate of Growth in		Contribution of Education (in percentage points)	Contribution of Education as a percentage of growth in	
	Total National Income (in percentage points)	National Income per Person Employed		Total National income	National Income per Person Employed
	1	2	3	4	5
United States	3.32	2.15	0.49	15	23
Northwestern Europe	4.78	3.80	0.23	5	6
Belgium	3.20	2.64	0.43	13	16
Denmark	3.51	2.56	0.14	4	5
France	4.92	4.80	0.29	6	6
Germany	7.26	5.15	0.11	2	2
Netherlands	4.73	3.65	0.24	5	7
Norway	3.45	3.27	0.24	7	7
United Kingdom	2.29	1.63	0.29	13	18
Italy	5.96	5.36	0.40	7	7

Source: Denison (1967), Tables 21–1 through Table 21–20.

much more limited than in the United States. The only countries with records roughly similar to the United States (Table 7-11, column 3) are Belgium and Italy. In the rest of Europe, education appears to have been less important in fostering economic growth. This may, of course, be due in part to the large physical capital requirements in Europe following the second World War, so that more recent data might resemble the United States experience more closely.

A similar analysis for Latin America was performed by Correa (1970), with results summarized here in Table 7-12. Except for Argentina, in which the contribution of education to growth is larger than what Denison found for the United States, the Latin American countries appear to reflect an even lower contribution of education to growth than was shown by Denison for Europe. It is quite possible, however, that the empirical results are quite sensitive to the approach used to measure the contribution of education to growth. As may be seen in Table 7-13, the contribution of education to growth in Chile and Mexico, as estimated by Selowsky (1969; for the period 1940-1964) is considerably higher than Correa's estimates for these two countries (for 1950-1962). Moreover, when the expansion of the labor force is taken into account, it can be shown that the total contribution of education more than doubles for both Chile and Mexico. For India, Selowsky calculates that 90 percent of the contribution of education to growth occurs via the expansion in the labor force.

A number of other studies were conducted to assess the role of education in economic growth. For example, McClelland (1966)

Table 7-12. The Contribution of Education to National Income Growth in Latin America, 1950-1962.

Country	Rate of Growth in Total National Income	Contribution of Education (percentage points)	Contribution of Education as a Percentage of National Income Growth
	1	*2*	*3*
Argentina	3.19	0.53	16
Brazil	5.49	0.18	3
Chile	4.20	0.20	5
Colombia	4.79	0.20	4
Ecuador	4.72	0.23	5
Honduras	4.52	0.29	6
Mexico	5.97	0.05	1
Peru	5.63	0.14	3
Venezuela	7.74	0.19	2

Source: Correa (1970), Table IX.

Table 7-13. Estimated Contribution of Education to Economic Growth in Chile, Mexico, and the United States (percent of rate of growth of national income).

Country	Years	Due to Rise in the Level of Education	Due to Expansion of Labor Force	Total
Chile	1940–1964	9.7	13.5	23.2
Mexico	1940–1964	3.4	6.7	10.1
United States	1940–1965	12.9	8.0	20.9

Source: Selowsky (1969), Tables IV through VII.

studied the correlation between electricity consumption and the "stock of education" (measured by the number of "years of secondary education available among adults age thirty or forty per 1,000 inhabitants in 1950") for a number of developed and underdeveloped countries and showed that the stock of education is related to growth in electricity consumption (which he regards as a good measure of development, uncomplicated by methods of computation, definitions, etc.). And Razin (1977) provides data showing a positive correlation between per capita gross national income and the "percentage of the population aged 15-19 enrolled in the secondary level of education for the years 1950 and 1960" (p. 319). His sample includes data for eleven developed countries for the period 1953-1965. His results indicate that "an increase in the population enrolled in secondary education from, say, 70 percent in one country to 80 percent in another country, other things being equal, will lead to an increase in the proportional annual rate of growth of per capita GNP from, say, 2 percent per year in the first to 2.1 percent per year in the other" (p. 322).

Other studies on the role of education in economic growth are discussed in Bowman and Anderson (1963), Malassis (1969), and Peaslee (1969). Further estimates of the contribution of education to growth in a number of countries are provided by Psacharopoulos (1973), using both the Schultz and the Denison frameworks.

CONCLUDING COMMENTS

Our ability to measure the role of education in growth depends critically on the accuracy of the framework employed in the analysis and the quality of data. Both are suspect in all of the studies mentioned above, so that the results are tentative. It is interesting, however, that no matter how one measures the role of education in economic growth, we find that in the United States that role has been consistently substantial. The same may be true for other countries as they reach a higher stage of development. It seems, however, that countries at a lower stage of development tend to gain less from education, although the gains may be indirect rather than direct, as measured here.

As Ritzen (1977: ch. 2) points out, the assumption regarding the "elasticity of substitution"[13] between different types of labor and between labor and other inputs is quite important. Denison, for example, in constructing his education index, assumed that the elasticity is virtually infinite—that is, any one type of educated labor is a perfect substitute for any other type of educated labor. Others (for example, Layard et al., 1971, or Psacharopoulos, 1973) have employed an approach in which the elasticity of substitution between types of educated labor is 1. In yet other studies (e.g., Bowles, 1970a, or Psacharopoulos and Hinchliffe, 1972), attempts were made to empirically investigate the nature of the elasticity of substitution using frameworks that permit the elasticity to be different than 1 (though still a constant). Such differences in methodology could explain some of the variance in results obtained by different authors (e.g., Selowsky, 1969, vs. Correa, 1970) regarding the role of education in economic growth.

So whereas most of the studies confirm the expectation that investment in education fosters economic growth, the exact magnitude of the education effect is far from certain. Improved data and methods are needed to generate more accurate estimates of the role of education, in order that government policy can be formulated in a more rational manner.

---

13. The elasticity of substitution is defined by the percentage change in the ratio of any two inputs divided by the percentage change in the marginal rate of technical substitution between the two inputs, where the marginal rate of technical substitution between the two inputs "measures the reduction in one input per unit increase in the other that is just sufficient to maintain a constant level of output." Denote the two inputs by q_1 and q_2 and the marginal rate of substitution by $MRTS$. Then the elasticity of substitution (σ) is:

$$\sigma = -\frac{\Delta(q_1/q_2) \div (q_1/q_2)}{\Delta\,MRTS \div MRTS}, \text{ where } \Delta \text{ refers to "a change in } \dots \text{ ."}$$

For further discussion see Ferguson (1972: 178-80, 416-18).

LITERATURE GUIDE

General

For a general discussion of the role of education in economic growth, consult M.J. Bowman (1970b), M.J. Bowman and Anderson (1963), Eckaus (1962), Groves (1961), W.L. Miller (1967), Nelson and Phelps (1966), Razin (1972), or Vaizey (1962: chs. X–XI).

Role of Education in Economic Growth

The best known works, Schultz (1961a) and Denison (1962, 1964a, 1967, and 1974), have already been described above. A synthesis of the two approaches is brilliantly described by M.J. Bowman (1964b). Other theoretical or empirical studies include: Delaplaine and Hollander (1970), Firestone (1968), Griliches (1970), S.C. Hu (1976), W.A. Lewis (1962), Machlup (1970, 1975), Malassis (1969), Maldonado (1976), OECD (1964a), Peaslee (1969), Ritzen (1977), K. Stephens (1972), and Vanzetti and Bessell (1974).

International comparisons are discussed by Bieda (1970, showing that the type of educational investment is important), Correa (1970), McClelland (1966), Psacharopoulos (1973), Razin (1977), and Selowsky (1969). Joshi (1973) argues that international comparisons based on a cross-section of countries are inappropriate.

Technical Aspects

Aukrust (1959) and Solow (1959) debate the issue of what proportion of productivity change is due to measured inputs and what is due to a "technical change" residual. See also Solow (1962). Jorgenson and Griliches (1967, 1972a, 1972b) argue with Denison (1969) about the appropriate measurement of capital inputs and other technical matters. The "embodiment hypothesis," is discussed in Jorgenson (1966) and You (1976) brings evidence in support of the contention that technical change is disembodied. Layard (1973) quarrels with Denison's calculation of the education index, while Svennilson (1964) argues in favor of a disaggregated approach to the measurement of the capital input. Norman (1976) shows that an interaction exists between physical and human capital in the context of economic growth. Concerning the elasticity of substitution, see Bowles (1970a), Psacharopolous and Hinchliffe (1972), and Fallon and Layard (1975). Finally, Mishan (1970) raises questions about the desirability of attaining more economic growth by comparing the benefits from growth to the "price we pay" for economic growth.

Production and Cost Functions in Education

Non multa sed multum
(Not quantity but quality)

Latin proverb

The discussion in Chapter 3–7 has focused on the profitability of educational investments, viewed from highly aggregative data sources. It has been observed that a number of educational investments are profitable, both to the individual and to society, and that education can be shown to account for (or at least be associated with) a significant proportion of United States' (and other countries') economic growth. Our discussion did not consider, however, how educational outcomes are produced by schools or which school inputs are more or less effective in producing the educational outcomes that generate future income streams. The purpose of this chapter is to fill this gap.

Another question of interest is whether economies of scale may be found in the operation of schools and colleges, and if so, what conclusions might be drawn with regard to optimum school size. In order that such issues can be addressed, it will be necessary to understand the concept of the "educational production function" and the "cost function." In addition to the discussion of these two functions and related empirical studies, we shall discuss briefly some uses that might be made of these concepts.

THE EDUCATIONAL PRODUCTION FUNCTION

The educational production function is, in principle, similar to any production function. The latter is a mathematical relation that describes how resources (inputs) can be transformed into outputs. In education, the production function likewise is some mathematical relation describing how educational resources (inputs) can be transformed into educational outputs (outcomes). To describe an educational production function, it is therefore necessary to define and measure the inputs, outputs, and (last but not least) the process by which the inputs are transformed into outputs.

In very general terms, it is commonly recognized that educational outputs are functions of a number of types of input. They include student characteristics, school-related factors, and other community influences. The school-related factors are of particular interest to economists because these are the inputs that typically can be manipulated by school administrators and hence influence resource allocation in education. The remaining inputs are also of concern and interest, and public policy can surely influence many such factors, especially over the long run.

Moreover, it has become apparent that an educational system cannot be assumed to produce a single output, such as basic skills in reading and mathematics, either to the exclusion, or entirely independently, of other outputs. This latter task is formidable, and very little progress has been made on this score, despite the recent surge of studies on educational production.

Inputs

Much progress has been made both in identifying and measuring educational inputs. At the secondary school level, we must distinguish between inputs provided by the schools and those externally determined. Among the school factors, we may wish to further distinguish between easily manipulable factors and those not easily manipulated by the administrators. Among the nonschool factors, we may wish to distinguish between those factors that affect a student directly and those affecting the student indirectly through a community's environment.

School Inputs.   The identification and quantification of school-related inputs is not an easy task. The school's environment includes both human and physical resources, and each of these categories is highly complex. Moreover, in attempting to evaluate the contribution of a given input to the output of a given student or class of students, it is often difficult to ascertain which portion of the input under discussion is relevant to the current investigation.

For example, if the present analysis is concerned with the educational output of students completing eleventh grade, should we evaluate teacher characteristics of those teaching eleventh grade only or should we also include other teachers in the measurement? Further, should we attach weights to the characteristics of the various teachers based upon the time they contribute to the eleventh graders (recognizing that many, if not most, are likely to teach in other grades as well)? Moreover, would average teacher characteristics be sufficient, or should one attempt to disaggregate the teaching staff into a number of components (e.g., vocational, science, language arts, etc.)?

To make things even more complicated, it has been argued that even successful measurement of such variables as teacher characteristics provides only proxies for the real inputs (Mood, 1970). For example, a variable measuring the educational preparation of teachers only indicates an average teacher attribute, not a teacher input. Its use in the production function is based on the assumption that once having such an attribute, an input into the production process is also likely to result. Thus, average educational preparation is used as a proxy for the organization and quantity of knowledge that teachers attempt to transmit to students. This, of course, is far different from the definition of inputs in ordinary production analysis, where an input is measured in real terms (such as tons of steel) and not through a proxy. One should, therefore, not be surprised if some of the input proxies do not appear to exert any statistical influence on the outputs. The conclusion is not necessarily that the input is ineffective but, perhaps, that the evidence does not support the contention that the proxy used is, indeed, a good index of the real input.

School inputs include both human and physical inputs. A comprehensive study would require an investigation of both. Among the physical inputs, one could distinguish building characteristics (the technological design with respect to both instruction and ease of communication among related groups of faculty members, general condition of facilities, etc.); quantity and quality of equipment, both for vocational instruction and teaching aids (audiovisual, etc.); and supply room and other supporting physical facilities. The human inputs typically emphasized in studies of this nature include teachers; administrators; secretarial, clerical, and other auxiliary staff; counselors; and paraprofessional teaching aides. Since a large fraction of schools' budgets is spent on the teaching staff, much attention has been directed to the efficacy of teachers, and various measures reflecting their attributes have been proposed and employed.

A popular variable measuring teacher input is average teacher salaries. Although it has considerable appeal, it is lacking in many respects. An average teacher's salary is typically based on a teacher's experience and educational preparation; thus, the assumption that teacher salaries are a good proxy for teacher input implies that salaries alone are a good measure of teacher productivity. It would be surprising if such an implication can be shown to be true, in light of the fact that salaries take no account of teachers' talents, enthusiasm, resourcefulness, and dedication to the profession (Cohn, 1971a, 1973b).

Moreover, teaching experience could serve as both a positive and a negative input proxy; on the one hand, experience is a proxy for "on the job training" and "learning by doing." An experienced teacher knows the ropes, as it were, and thus can save considerable time and energy with regard to lesson preparation and discipline problems. At the same time, experience may also be a proxy for professional obsolescence and depreciation of human capital (when other variables are held constant). The effect of experience on educational production will therefore depend on the extent to which one input represented by experience is offset by the other.

What the foregoing discussion implies is the need to examine various potentially productive attributes of teachers, including educational preparation, experience, resourcefulness, talents, attitudes, and classroom practices. Even if a school is successful in recruiting a staff with excellent productive attributes, teacher productivity would be reduced to the extent that teachers are overburdened in terms of excessive teaching load and the number of subject matter assignments they are required to handle each year. In consequence, input proxies measuring the extent of teaching load and subject matter preparation should be included in the system. These variables are all the more interesting as they may be manipulated relatively easily by the school principal (Cohn, 1971b).

In addition, one should not lose sight of the possibility that different class sizes might also influence teacher productivity. Other school-related variables include the breadth and depth of the curriculum, the sheer size of the school, the type and extent of extracurricular activities, and the nature and accessibility of students to the school library.

Nonschool Inputs. It is by now common knowledge that factors outside the school itself are likely to contribute substantially to a student's educational output. Peer influence is one such general factor. Interest may then be focused on the general characteristics of the student body—among them parental socioeconomic levels (measured by family income, educational level of mother and father, number of books at home, etc.). Race, sex, family size, and other attributes have all frequently been mentioned. In addition, general characteristics of the student environment (community indexes) are alleged to affect educational outcomes. They may be measured by degree of urbanization, extent of poverty and existence of substandard housing, racial composition, average educational attainment of adults, and average personal income and wealth. The attitude of the local community toward education may be captured by such variables as the voting record on school bond issues, or tax effort, as measured by the ratio of school tax receipts to total taxable property value.

Another input that conceptually should be included in the model is the initial educational endowment of the students. Inclusion of such a variable would permit analysis of the gain in output over a given time period. Although some of the variables discussed above regarding student socioeconomic characteristics are typically correlated with initial educational endowment, they are clearly a less than ideal alternative. As H.M. Levin (1974) points out, however, the innate endowment variable "is usually omitted for lack of a reliable measure" (p. 5).

Manipulable Versus Nonmanipulable Inputs. Quite obviously, some of the aforementioned inputs are not manipulable by school or any other government officials. A good example is sex, race, and age of students. In addition, some inputs are more easily manipulable than others. For example, parental education and socioeconomic status could, in principle, be manipulated, but this cannot be accomplished by school officials nor can it be accomplished quickly and easily by other government bodies. The conclusion of the Coleman report and various other studies regarding the strong effect of nonschool variables on educational output has ramifications for long-run social policy, but it provides little comfort to school officials who strive to increase educational output with a given budget.

Among manipulable inputs subject to control by various hierarchies in the school system, mention may be made of the following: (1) teaching load, (2) average number of subject matter assignments per teacher, (3) class size, and (4) number of curriculum units. These inputs may be manipulated to some extent by the school principal (and, of course, also by the superintendent). Given a fixed number of teaching positions, the principal can choose between a smaller class size and heavier teaching load and also between a smaller number of curriculum units per semester and a smaller number of subject matter assignments per teacher.

Although the principal is typically constrained in his decision-making process by rules requiring a ceiling on class size and/or a floor on curriculum units—as well as by collective bargaining agreements pertaining to such matters as teaching loads and assignments —there is likely to be a good deal of room remaining for maneuvering the four variables, so that significant improvement in educational output may result. What we wish to emphasize here is that although some inputs could be manipulated at the school level, in the absence of information relating inputs and outputs, gains from such manipulations are not likely to be reaped (see Cohn, 1971b and 1974b). A number of other inputs may be manipulated also, especially at the district level. These include teacher experience and training (through changes in hiring policies), teacher salaries, availability of equipment, supplies, library facilities, and so forth.

Outputs

The outcomes of education may be classified into two categories: consumption and investment (Schultz, 1963). The consumption aspect is related to the joy, pleasure, and similar benefits derived by students, their families, and society as a whole. The student might sometimes experience negative consumption (he or she would rather do something else), but activities such as music, sports, arts and crafts, and the like appear to contribute to a student's enjoyment of school and hence to consumption benefits. In addition, the family is relieved of responsibility toward the youngster during the school hours—a highly important consumption benefit often overlooked by teachers and parents alike (Weisbrod, 1962, esp. pp. 116–18). Society, too, gets consumption benefits in the form of reduced crime; the enjoyment people get from observing youngsters learning, playing, and behaving in an orderly fashion; and perhaps even the lessened competition for jobs created by keeping job-ready youth in school for an additional three to four years.

The investment component includes a variety of outputs related to the enhancement of an individual's or society's productive skills and future well-being. The distinguishing characteristic here is that some of the educational outputs will not provide benefits to society until some time in the future (some will come sooner, some later). Obvious examples are the acquisition of basic mathematical and verbal skills, vocational preparation, improved health habits, inculcation of social and moral values leading to improved citizenship, or improving one's attitudes toward self, family, peers, and society.

It is much easier to specify the kinds of educational outputs than to define them in precise terms. Not only is it not unanimously agreed how "citizenship" might be defined, but even for such outputs as increased knowledge in basic skills, it is not quite clear how a student's or a school's performance can be measured. Thus we find a number of different basic skills test batteries, all purporting to measure the same output.

The question posed most frequently is not merely what the present level of skill is, but rather what improvements in basic skills have taken place over a certain time period. Furthermore, even if only the present skill level is adequate, we must contend with the "ceiling" problem. That is, it becomes successively more difficult to increase a student's score as one approaches the maximum, so that statistical comparisons of the type described herein are likely to underestimate the ability of some schools to manipulate inputs to achieve higher skill levels (and, conversely, to overestimate it for other schools).

Educational outcomes are often referred to in the educational literature as cognitive or affective (noncognitive). This classification is especially important since few noncognitive outputs have been incorporated into educational input-output analyses to date. From an economic viewpoint, however, the distinction is of little value, as both cognitive and noncognitive aspects of the educational process provide consumption and/or investment benefits. One should attempt, therefore, to list as many of the relevant outputs as possible and to obtain reliable means by which such outputs may be measured. An illustrative list of outputs follows.

1. *Basic Skills.* A student's success in acquiring new mathematical or verbal skills has for long been the cornerstone of the analysis of educational performance. Many test batteries are available: the Iowa Tests of Basic Skills, the Iowa Tests of Educational Development, the Stanford Achievement Test, or the well-known college entrance tests, such as the ACT and SAT. All these tests have been utilized in one or more input-output studies of education.

2. *Vocational Skills.* Despite the fact that huge sums have been invested in vocational education, no systematic vocational tests of the type developed for basic skills have been used to assess the performance of vocational education. Instead, market-oriented studies have been undertaken to assess the contribution of vocational education to one's employment opportunities and/or earnings (see Chapter 6, above). Since vocational development is clearly an identifiable educational goal, its exclusion from a formal model of the educational process cannot be justified.

3. *Creativity.* This is another dimension of school output long

ignored in input-output studies. Yet some schools do attempt to foster creativity. Measures to assess the success of schools in that area should include both creative output (a measure of consumption benefits) and increasing creative potential (investment benefits).

4. *Attitudes.* Because attitudes are difficult to quantify and because, as noted earlier, society is not unanimous about the "proper" mix of individual attitudes, it is not surprising that student attitudes have rarely entered a formalized educational input-output model.[1] Yet one of the main functions of schools (frequently cited in state constitutions) is the inculcation of "proper" attitudes. These include attitudes toward oneself and toward one's peers, family, the community, society at large, the school, and the world in which we live. One might include in this category a school's attempt to influence a student's lifestyle, including career aspirations, health habits, and sex and family education.

Measurement of such outputs is clearly extremely difficult. It is not impossible, however. Just as tests of cognitive skills have been developed and utilized over a span of more than half a century, so too, instruments can be (and some have been) developed to measure attitudes. Psychologists have by now amassed an incredible amount of experience in measuring motivation, job satisfaction, and other types of attitudes, and similar effort can be directed to the measurement of attitudes that comprise educational outcomes. The implementation of the Pennsylvania Plan is illustrative of the direction that future studies might follow.[2]

5. *Other Outputs.* A number of other outputs should be mentioned. For example, Burkhead et al. (1967) used the inverse of the dropout rate as an output of the secondary school system. Also, the role of some schools as welfare stations should be studied, as students from poor homes receive hot meals, stay in a warm and a relatively sanitary place, receive counseling, and so forth.

In addition, a review of the literature indicates a general failure to measure students' knowledge in areas other than basic skills. It appears obvious that educational output includes knowledge gained in the humanities, the social and behavioral sciences, and the natural sciences.[3] Finally, the benefits to students and others from other activities such as music, arts, and sports have generally been

1. A notable exception is a study by Mayeske and his associates (1973b).
2. For a description of the Pennsylvania Plan see Associated Press (1977), Beers (1970), Russell (1971), Cohn with Millman (1975), and Kuhns (1972).
3. Although these subjects were included in the Equality of Educational Opportunity Survey, analyses of the survey data largely use a composite score for all areas tested, and many studies confine the analysis to achievement in basic skills.

ignored. Yet such activities represent important consumption benefits and, in some cases (such as for students who receive college scholarships in athletics or who become professional athletes, musicians, or artists), also investment.

It should be noted, however, that an analysis of all such outputs as outlined in this section is both too cumbersome and unnecessary, for the proxies that inevitably must be chosen to represent the various outputs are likely to be intercorrelated, so that a subset of all outputs is likely to provide as much information as the entire output set and at a lesser cost. The implication of this is that whereas all outputs mentioned here should be investigated, it is not recommended that all outputs be used in every empirical study. The choice of the ideal set of outputs will depend on the relative ease with which outputs may be quantified and the degree of intercorrelation among the various outputs consistently found in other studies.

The Input-Output Process

The description and quantification of the inputs and outputs is necessary but not sufficient for input-output analysis. It is also necessary to specify the manner by which inputs influence outputs—or, in economic terms, we need to know something about the shape of the educational production function.

Economic theory provides a number of useful theorems that guide the analyst in his attempt to specify a production function. For example, it is asserted that each factor of production should be subject to diminishing marginal returns, such that successive additions of any factor of production, when all other inputs are held constant, should result (at some point) in successively smaller increments to output.

Considerable work has been directed toward identification and estimation of the "best" production function, based on both theoretical developments and empirical investigation of various industries. One must remember, however, that the education "industry" is far different from most other industries in scope and character and that, furthermore, we are faced with the difficult problem of multiple outputs in the production process. It is therefore not too surprising to discover that few analyses of the educational sector have been patterned after the typical industry production model.

It would be worthwhile to restate the problem with the aid of mathematical notation. Let the vector of educational outputs be denoted by $Q:q_1, q_2, \ldots q_n$; the vector of school related inputs by $X:x_1, x_2, \ldots, x_k$; and the vector of nonschool inputs by $S:s_1,$

$s_2, \ldots, s_m$. We thus have a total of n outputs and $k + m$ inputs. The generalized educational production function is given by:

$$f(Q,X/S) = 0. \qquad (8.1)$$

That is, once the levels of the nonschool inputs are given, the determination of the expected levels of the outputs will depend on both the levels of the school inputs and the functional operator, f (which specifies the shape of the production function).

A linear relationship between the X inputs and the Q outputs would be empirically valid to the extent that the curvature of the total output function is only mildly violated by employing a linear approximation. This is illustrated in Figure 8-1, in which a total output curve is drawn for one input and one output. To the extent that the range of the data is given by the arc segments AB or BC, a linear approximation would appear to provide reasonably good

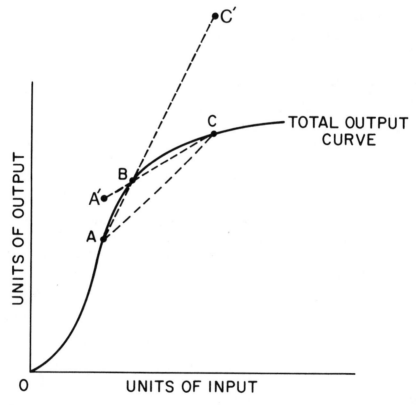

Figure 8-1. Total Product Curve and Linear Approximations.

estimates of the true production coefficients. However, if the range of the data is given by the arc segment AC, the linear approximation will seriously distort the true relationship between input and output. Moreover, conclusions derived from linear analysis should not be applied to input levels beyond the range of the sample observations, for use of the production coefficients for the purpose of extrapolation might result in predictions that are far off the mark (compare, for example, point C with an extrapolation of the line segment AB to C′, or point A with an extrapolation of the line segment BC to A′). These conclusions about extrapolation are no less pertinent to models that employ curvilinear analysis, because the shape of the production function may be different from that assumed or inferred at unobserved input levels, and the danger of extrapolation errors remains.

If a linear model is accepted, then the general form of the ith production function is given by:

$$q_i = a_i + \sum_{g=1}^{n} b_{ig} q_g + \sum_{h=1}^{k} c_{ih} x_h + \sum_{j=1}^{m} d_{ij} s_j + e_i, \qquad (8.2)$$

where a_i is the intercept (constant term), and the b_{ig}s, c_{ih}s and d_{ij}s are the (slope) coefficients we wish to estimate, with $b_{ii} = 0$, and e_i is a stochastic error term. This equation assumes linearity in all variables and that some of the outputs other than q_i might have coefficients different from zero (a good number of the b_{ig}s could, of course, be equal to zero). Of particular interest are the coefficients c_{ih}, which represent the marginal productivities of the school inputs.[4]

Since there are n outputs, n equations of the general form (8.2) should be specified. As long as not all the b_{ig}s are zero, it is apparent that the various equations will not be independent of each other. Thus the determination of the true effect of a given school input (e.g., x_1) on any one output (e.g., q_1) cannot be determined without finding out its effect on other outputs. For if that input (x_1) affects other outputs, which in turn have an impact on q_1, then the total effect of the input on q_1 would differ from what an isolated examination of the production function on q_1 would reveal. The n equations of the type (8.2) should therefore be considered as an

---

4. The marginal product of the hth input (x_h) with respect to the ith output (q_i), denoted by MP_{ih}, is defined by the change in q_i divided by the change in x_h, other things remaining equal. Mathematically:

$$MP_{ih} = \partial q_i / \partial x_h = c_{ih}.$$

interdependent system, and the coefficients in each of the equations should be estimated on the basis of techniques available for simultaneous equations (Johnston, 1972: chs. 12 and 13).

The major objection to the linear formulation of the educational production function is the constancy of the marginal products of the inputs. If, say, b_{11} = 2, then a one unit increase in x_1 will cause a two-unit increase in q_1 no matter how many units of x_1 are utilized and regardless of how many units of other inputs are employed by the school system. It is highly unlikely that such will be the case unless we are prepared to accept the results only for very small changes in x_1. If the analysis is to be used for relatively large changes in x_1 or other inputs, a nonlinear production function should be estimated. And while nonlinear educational production functions have been estimated, the popularity of the linear form derives from the relative simplicity of the approach.

EMPIRICAL ESTIMATES OF THE EDUCATIONAL PRODUCTION FUNCTION*

Interest in the effectiveness of schools is not new, but serious efforts to measure the relationship between inputs and outputs did not begin in earnest until the late fifties. Even then, most studies employed only a single measure of output, utilized relatively weak statistical techniques, and tended to concentrate measurement on school districts. As time progressed, so did the level and sophistication of the analysis. More studies began utilizing the more powerful technique of multiple regression, and multioutput models have appeared, along with new data bases at lower levels of aggregation (the schools and, ultimately, students). In the interest of brevity, we shall not attempt a complete review of production function studies, but shall instead provide a glimpse of a sample of the studies that have appeared since 1956 along with a general summary of the current state of the art.

Early Studies

It is generally recognized that the first large-scale input-output study, and one from which many later studies have profited, was undertaken for the Educational Testing Service by William G. Mollenkopf and S. Donald Melville (1956). The researchers selected 9,600 ninth grade students from 100 public schools and 8,357 twelfth grade students from 106 public schools; the schools were

*Portions of this section are taken from Cohn with Millman (1975: ch. 4).

selected from across the country. From answers to questionnaires administered to school principals, a list of thirty-four independent variables—including school, nonschool, and peer influences—was constructed. These inputs (independent variables) were compared with a test specially designed by Educational Testing Service as the output (dependent variable).[5]

Simple (Pearson) correlation techniques were used in this study to relate inputs to the specified components of output (vocabulary score, math score, science score, etc.).[6] Of the school factors, only one—library and supply expenditures—was consistently correlated with student achievement. This variable may have been serving as an inadvertent proxy for some other school, nonschool, or peer group variable. Other variables of some influence include number of special school personnel, class size, and student-teacher ratio.

Following the work of Mollenkopf and Melville, the state of New York instituted a study of some 70,000 seventh and eleventh graders in the state's public schools. As with the study before it, Samuel M. Goodman (1959) attempted (in what is popularly known as the New York Quality Measurement Project) to control as best he could for the effects of parents' socioeconomic status. As in some studies that were to follow his, Goodman found some distinct influence from a not too clearly specified variable he called "classroom atmosphere."[7] However, very much unlike certain succeeding studies, Goodman found the variable of teacher experience to have a potent positive effect on student achievement. Others, who will be discussed later, have also seen teacher experience or teacher training variables to significantly affect student output; however, the effect has not been as consistent as would be intuitively expected.

In 1962, James Alan Thomas (1962) conducted the first major study to rely on regression techniques as the primary means of statistical analysis. Using input and output data generated for Project Talent in over 200 schools in a national sample, Thomas found, from a list of twenty-seven input variables, the following three school variables to be of particular importance: starting teacher salaries, teacher experience, and number of books in the school library. A short time later, Benson and his associates (1965) conducted a

5. For clarity here, the input is pointed out to be the independent variable, and output the dependent. This is assumed in all the descriptions that follow, and the notation is thus simplified.

6. The seven individual test scores were eventually clustered into verbal and quantitative indexes.

7. Others have alluded to "environmental press," "empathic understanding," "nonthreatening atmosphere," and so forth.

study of California school effectiveness for a state senate fact-finding committee. After controlling for student background factors, they found a significant positive relationship between teacher salaries and student achievement.

The Equality of Educational Opportunity Survey

Perhaps the largest, most comprehensive, and most hotly debated study was published in 1966. Directed by James S. Coleman and his associates (1966), a study entitled *Equality of Educational Opportunity* attempted to determine the school and nonschool factors related to the achievement of over 600,000 students from coast to coast. Popularly known as the "Coleman report," the study found very little association between school factors (taken singly or collectively) in comparison to nonschool factors. Of the school factors, teachers' verbal ability seemed to be of most importance.

The Coleman report has been criticized along three basic axes. Frst, there is uncertainty as to whether the measurements used are sufficient for the task involved. Second, the handling of the data is thought by some to have been less than precise. Perhaps most damning, however, is the fact that many contend that the manner by which the regression technique was used in effect stacked the cards against any strong showing by school factors.

Basically, this latter argument is that stepwise multiple regression requires the statistical assumption of independence of variables. Where such independence is not present (i.e., multicollinearity is present), the first variables to be entered (in this case nonschool factors) will appear most potent. In fact, the nonschool and school factors may be so nested within each other that their effects cannot be so arbitrarily separated. This criticism has been expounded most persuasively by Bowles and Levin (1968a, 1968b).[8]

Nonetheless, the Coleman report stands as a benchmark for a number of reasons. More than any other study, it provided an impetus for theorists of all orientations to become more involved in what had previously been a very specialized and obscure branch of educational research. Because of its indictment of school effectiveness (whether that indictment was well founded or not), it also stimulated greater interest in other areas of school research and functioning.

By size of sample, number of variables, number of associates,

8. See also Cain and Watts (1968, 1970), Coleman (1968), Mood (1973), and M.S. Smith (1968).

wideness of distribution, and amount of data, Coleman's work is also distinguished from most other studies, past and future. The study used data from and about 645,000 individual students well distributed by type and location of school. Ninety-three separate input variables were delineated. The outcome measure consisted of ten scores, including a measure of nonverbal skill. To this day researchers continue to fill professional journals with research based on the Coleman data base, albeit alternatively supporting and debunking Coleman's conclusions. By any standard, the Coleman work is destined to be considered a classic in the literature of educational assessment.

Samuel Bowles, along with Henry M. Levin, had been among the most vocal and persistent of critics of the methodology and conclusions of the Coleman report, as was pointed out earlier.their basic disagreement has appeared in number of places (Bowles and Levin, 1968a, 1968b; and Bowles, 1970). In 1968 the two authors (Bowles and Levin, 1968b) reported results of a reanalysis of the Coleman data and found a significant positive influence of teacher verbal ability on both black and white student performance. Again, they also found teacher salaries and availability of adequate facilities (particularly science) to be positively related to achievement.

Employing a subsample of the Coleman data, Bowles (1970) obtained results that indicate that verbal achievement of black male twelfth grade students was affected significantly by science lab facilities, days in session, teacher's verbal ability score, and average time spent in guidance—in addition to nonschool factors such as parent's educational level and student attitudes regarding (1) central environment and (2) self-concept.

Henry M. Levin (1970c) presents another study that attempted to use the Coleman data pool while avoiding some of the methodological problems that plagued the original Coleman analysis. As the output measures, Levin specified, in addition to verbal score, student and parent attitudes and student grade aspirations. In the two stage least squares (TSLS) regressions, only teacher experience was positive and significant in terms of the verbal ability output.

Appearing in the same volume in which the above Levin study appeared is a report by Stephan Michelson (1970), also using the Coleman data. Michelson used the same dependent variables as Levin, but added test scores for reading and mathematics as well as verbal ability. Independent variables were similar to Levin's. Stratifying the sample on race, Michelson used both single and simultaneous equation systems. For whites, some school inputs were consistently positive using the TSLS approach for verbal ability. These include teacher verbal ability and experience. Results are less consistent for other outputs. No significant relationships are reported for blacks.

Another view of possible reinterpretation of the Coleman conclusions is presented in a study by James W. Guthrie and his associates (1971). Guthrie's team looked at the Coleman data for the state of Michigan. While the sample contained both blacks and whites, the group was not stratified by race, but rather by socioeconomic status regardless of race. The authors report a series of school inputs positively related to achievement under the general categories of facilities, materials, teacher characteristics, and peer environment. Significant teacher variables included verbal ability, experience, and job satisfaction.

In one of the earliest studies to look specifically at whether school and nonschool inputs might have a differential effect on blacks and whites, Hanushek (1968; see also Hanushek, 1972) examined the records of black and white sixth grade students in the northeastern and upper midwestern areas of the country. Hanushek's sample intentionally included students in predominantly white as well as predominantly black school situations. In this research, separate regressions were run for the black and the white samples. The data used were all drawn from the original Coleman data files for the geographical areas being studied.

Hanushek looked at a wide array of home and school variables, including parents' education, preschool exposure, racial mix, and school location. Teacher experience and teacher verbal ability were also measured. Hanushek found that basically the same input variables were operative for both black and white students. He found the two teacher variables to be significantly positive for both blacks and whites.

Considerable work has been underway for some years in the U.S. Office of Education to reanalyze the massive data supplied by the Equality of Educational Opportunity Survey (EEOS). The Coleman report was the first published document regarding the survey, but certainly not the last nor even the most significant. As Mood (1973) points out, the reanalyses by Mayeske and his colleagues "have viewed the survey information far more deeply and expertly than was possible in the limited time available to prepare the original [Coleman] report. Together they represent a giant step forward in understanding some of the most fundamental aspects of education in our public schools" (p. iii).

The three Mayeske reports (named after their major author, George W. Mayeske) were published during 1972 and 1973, although working papers providing much of the analyses had been made available in more limited quantities as early as 1969. The Mayeske reports may be distinguished from the Coleman study in two main respects: (1) the Mayeske reports study both schools and pupils respectively as the unit of analysis, and (2) the Mayeske reports have used more sophisticated statistical techniques in their analysis.

The first Mayeske report (1972) is focused on the schools as a unit of analysis. Within school variations are ignored. The main technique for analysis is termed "commonality analysis," which is used to divide the squared multiple correlation coefficient into portions of the variance uniquely explained by each variable (or sets of variables) in a multiple regression equation and the proportion of variance commonly explained by two or more (sets of) variables. For example, if the outcome (dependent variable) is designated by X, school factors by S, and nonschool factors by B (independent variables), then the analysis provides an equation such as:

$$R^2 (S,B) = U(S) + C(S,B) + U(B),$$

where $R^2(S,B)$ is the squared multiple correlation coefficient, derived by regressing X on S and B; $U(S)$ and $U(B)$ are, respectively, the unique variances attributed to S and B; whereas $C(S,B)$ is the residual variance of X explained by S and B together (exclusive of any error term).

The study employs factor analysis to generate indexes of school and nonschool variables. The latter were then studied in relation to a number of school outcomes, including achievement, students' expectations for excellence, attitude on life, educational desires and plans, and study habits. The major finding was that, on the whole, the unique contribution of school factors to explaining variations in outcomes was extremely small. At the same time, the common variance may be quite large, indicating the likelihood of a strong interactive effect of school and nonschool variables.

A number of other results deserve mention here:

1. A high correlation was found for schools among the various outcomes: "In other words, favorable performances tend to facilitate and reinforce one another" (p. 111).
2. Among school variables, those related to a school's personnel were shown to have greatest effect on outcomes, both in terms of the unique variance explained and the size of the commonality factor.
3. Expenditures, school facilities, and pupil programs and policies

are generally unimportant, measured both by the unique and common variance explained.

4. "Teacher attributes highly related to school outcomes were those reflecting a teacher's experiences in racially imbalanced educational settings" (p. 113). The authors cite the typical attendance of nonwhite teachers in predominantly nonwhite institutions (which are deemed less desirable) as a possible cause for lower output by students exposed to such teachers.

A major conclusion of the report echoes conclusions reached by Coleman and his associates, as well as by Jencks (1972) and other critics of the educational system: "For both students and teachers, the American educational system reflects the structure of American society. It, therefore, tends to perpetuate and even further increase the differential learning experiences that students bring to the educational setting by virtue of their birth" (Mayeske, 1972: 113).

The second Mayeske report (1973a) focused on student achievement. Two of the main findings should be mentioned.

1. "There were indications that the color-caste aspects of the social structure, as represented by Racial-Ethnic Group Membership, had a greater impact on achievement in the south, and would consequently be more difficult to overcome by means of educationally related childrearing activities" (p. 147).

2. The unique contribution of school factors to achievement was found to be quite low (4 percent). The effect of the school variables was thus seen to operate mainly through their interaction with variables representing background (socioeconomic status, family structure, racial-ethnic group membership) and family process (expectations, aspirations, beliefs regarding life, stimulation and support).

The third Mayeske report (1973b) is concerned with an explanation of variance in students' attitudes toward life. Most of the material in the report deals with nonschool factors. However, the authors conclude that a set of school inputs consisting of five teaching staff attributes did not show any independent influence on attitudes, but that the role of these variables was "completely confounded with that of the five student body variables" employed by the authors (p. 84). It is also noted that the association between school variables and attitudes was greater in the South than in the North and, finally, that there is once more considerable commonality with socioeconomic status, home background, and family process and achievement.

Further analysis of the EEOS data was conducted by Anthony Boardman and his associates (1973, 1974, 1977). In their 1973 study, they report on the results of a simultaneous equation model, where the endogenous (dependent) variables are various achievement measures obtained by the EEO survey. They include verbal, nonverbal, mathematics, reading, and general information achievement. The set of explanatory variables include a variety of peer-, environmental-, and school-related variables.

It is not clear why the authors chose the particular specification of the structural equations. Nevertheless, the study provides a number of interesting conclusions with regard to the impact of school variables. The first, and most important, significant variable is the average teachers' verbal score. The results here confirm previous results by H.M. Levin (1970c), Michelson (1970), and Bowles (1970c). Interestingly, the teacher-pupil ratio is "positively and significantly associated with each of the various measures of achievement" (Boardman, Davis, and Sanday, 1973: 64), a finding that makes a great deal of sense, yet one that, to date, most studies have failed to support.

Another significant school outcome is experience. The authors used a quadratic specification for that variable, indicating that the first few years of experience are negatively associated with achievement, but that as more experience is gained, the relation becomes positive. This is in contrast to the popular belief that experience is positively related to productivity during the first few years, after which the effect becomes zero or even negative.

A fourth significant factor is the number of teachers leaving. The positive correlation with verbal, nonverbal, and reading achievement may be explained by a process of "natural selection" whereby "dedicated teachers tend to be the ones who remain on the job . . . while those who really were not interested in this profession drop out" (p. 65). Also, "the perception on the part of teachers of the lack of effective administrative leadership is positively related to all measures of achievement" (p. 65). The authors explain this surprising result as follows: "Since the mean of this variable is low, one might speculate that only the better and more perceptive teachers are able to recognize such problems and these teachers perform well in any event" (p. 65).

It was also found that achievement tends to be higher in schools in which the administration of IQ and achievement tests is a matter of school policy. The authors do not elaborate, but it just might be that when such tests are administered year after year, and when schools pay attention to such results, teachers and pupils gain a certain degree of expertise in answering the questions (for students) and coaching students on the exam materials (for teachers). In consequence, this variable might be more appropriately considered as a control device rather than as a school factor.

Two other measures significantly related to achievement are school facilities and existence of problems in the school. As expected (though typically not found to be significant in other studies), the coefficient of facilities is positive, whereas the coefficient for the problems in schools variable is negative.

It should also be mentioned that factor analysis conducted by the authors indicates that all the achievement measures describe essentially the same characteristic, so that a single equation analysis based upon only one of the measures, or an index of the five measures (as was done by Mayeske et al., 1972), would probably result in similar conclusions. However, the case of simultaneous equation analysis is not seriously challenged by this finding, as the study was concerned exclusively with cognitive achievement, leaving aside attitudes and other outputs.

Other Studies

As another aspect of the New York Quality Measurement Project, Herbert Keisling (1967) assessed input and output in varying kinds of school districts in New York.[9] Keisling looked at large and small, urban and rural school systems. Keisling found significant relationships between the cognitive output measures and student-teacher ratio and expenditures for books and supplies. However, it must be stressed that the relationships were negative and that the variables had large coefficients. Keisling reports that none of the other variables was uniformly important.

The research team of Jesse Burkhead, Thomas G. Fox, and John W. Holland (1967) were able to conduct a unified study of thirty-nine Chicago schools, 22 Atlanta schools, and a subsample of 177 schools from the original Project TALENT sample. Although the independent and dependent variables were not identical in all three substudies, there was sufficient similarity to compare like items. In Chicago and Atlanta, family income was positively related to reading and verbal skills, respectively. Teacher experience and teacher salary, respectively, were both associated with positive outcomes. Using the Project TALENT sample, family income, teacher experience, and salary were significant positive variables.

9. The Keisling work was originally reported in a 1965 unpublished doctoral dissertation. Variations on the study appear in Keisling (1969). A somewhat different New York sample is analyzed in Keisling (1970). The results of all these efforts are discussed here collectively.

Thomas G. Fox, who earlier had collaborated with Burkhead and Holland (Burkhead, Fox, and Holland, 1967), reported again on an analysis of his thirty-nine Chicago schools in a separate paper (T.G. Fox, 1969). Using two of his original output measures—reading scores and school retention rate—he constructed a somewhat different set of school input measures, including school building utilization rate, capacity of building cross-footed by age, book expenditures, man years of teacher and support staff time committed to the school and to student time in specific vocational courses, and the employment status of students. These inputs reflected variables that had not been in the forefront of research on educational effectiveness. While book expenditures and building capacity by age were not significant, the other elements were found to be variously positive. The research shed some new light on additional variables of potential influence. Moreover, Fox's study presents the first simultaneous equation model of educational production.

In a second study by Eric Hanushek (1970), 1,000 students in a single school district in California are studied. In this research, the entire analysis proceeded from data at the individual student level of aggregation. In order to carry the procedure forward, it was necessary for Hanushek to delete all cases in which any information was missing. For example, if a student moved into or out of the system, and if characteristics of all previous and current teachers were not available, the case was removed. This requirement dropped the sample size from nearly 2,500 to just over 1,000 subjects.

Since the most visible minority in the school system was Mexican Americans, Hanushek compared these students with whites. He stratified the two groups into four subgroups depending on whether the student's father was in a manual or nonmanual occupation. In terms of school factors, it is interesting to note that teacher experience and teacher education level were found not to be significantly related to the output measure (Scholastic Aptitude Test scores) for any of the groups. Since this study is the first to operate at the individual student level, the lack of relationship of the output to the two most commonly used school input factors must cause a serious reevaluation of those studies that have shown these variables to be positive and significant.

Martin T. Katzman (1968) examined data from fifty-six Boston elementary schools. In addition to the typical input and output variables, Katzman also looked at student cultural advantage, degree of school overcrowding, attendance rate, school attrition, and size of school district. Results of overcrowding were not consistent, but economies of scale did appear in larger attendance area in terms of incremental reading ability and lessening of attrition. Teacher experience variables seemed inconclusive, although level of teachers' degrees was generally positive.

A study by this writer (Cohn, 1968) reports some of the findings obtained for a sample of 377 Iowa high schools, the overwhelming majority of which constituted the only public secondary schools in this districts. A significant negative relationship was found between the output measure (increment in scores on the Iowa Tests of Educational Development) and two inputs: (1) number of teachers' college credit hours, and (2) number of discrete teaching assignments per teacher. A significant positive relation was found between output and median teacher salary.

Richard Raymond (1968) examined the precollege educational backgrounds of in-state students who entered West Virginia University. Because of the time frame involved, Raymond used a very different set of criterion measures. He used college freshman grades, along with composite scores on the American College Test (ACT), as the output measure. By county of precollege attendance, he then compared the output with school inputs. He derived nonschool variables from 1960 census data for the various West Virginia counties. Of the school components, he found teacher salary positively significant, with the student's elementary school teacher salary being the most potent predicator.

Another study (Tuckman, 1971) made use of a current population study of 10,700 elementary and secondary schools. Tuckman chose a subsample of 1,001 senior high schools. For that sample, data were available on two inputs: percentage of teachers with ten or more years of experience and percentage of teachers holding at least a master's degree. Additional inputs included education of parents, sex, race, region, and the proportion of students who were behind in grade. On the output side, five measures were used: percentage of students completing high school, percentage continuing to any higher education, percentage attending a four year college, percentage attending a two year college, and percentage going on to other educational institutions.

The novelty of the Tuckman study is his attempt to study the effect of interaction between school and nonschool variables. His analysis indicates that the output effects of the school inputs, based on the typical linear regression analysis, differ from those obtained through the interactive model. His model and interpretation of the results are criticized, however, by Hambor et al. (1973).

Finally, a brief description of two studies using Pennsylvania data is given. One of these, using extensive data on twelve outputs and more than fifty inputs, was conducted by this writer (Cohn with Millman, 1975; and Cohn, 1976b) to estimate a simultaneous equation model for fifty-three Pennsylvania high schools. Most of the data were generated by the quality assessment division of the Pennsylvania Department of Education, while additional input data were obtained from Kuhns (1972), who earlier provided single equation estimates for each output, employing the technique of stepwise least squares to limit the number of inputs in each equation.

A brief description of the outputs used in the study is provided in Table 8-1. The outputs were developed in conjunction with the Pennsylvania Plan, and output measures were obtained from various sources, including the Coleman report, The Educational Testing Service, the Iowa and Stanford achievement tests, and other sources. Although imperfect, the list is clearly the most comprehensive yet developed, and efforts were made to obtain reliable indexes of the outputs in so far as possible.

The input list includes socioeconomic variables, various school-related variables (both teacher-related and others), and nonschool, environmental variables. A list of variables thought to be manipulable by the school administrators is given in Table 8-2.

Although the specification of the simultaneous equation model must be considered as tentative at best, the results, while not overwhelmingly encouraging, nevertheless show that key manipulable variables are statistically significant. A good example is teaching load, whose coefficient was statistically significant (negative) in ten out of the twelve equations, implying that a lower teaching load is associated

Table 8-1. Outputs in the Pennsylvania Educational Quality Assessment Model.

Output	Brief Description
1	Self concept
2	Understanding others
3	Verbal basic skills
4	Mathematical basic skills
5	Interest in school
6	Citizenship
7	Health habits
8	Creativity potential
9	Creativity output
10	Vocational development
11	Appreciation of human accomplishments
12	Preparation for change

Source: Cohn with Millman (1975), Table 6-1. For additional information consult Table A-1; and Beers (1970).

Table 8-2. Manipulable Inputs in the Pennsylvania Model.

Input	Brief Description
1	Average extracurricular expenditure per secondary school pupil
2	Administrative man hours per secondary school pupil
3	Auxiliary man hours per secondary school pupil
4	Library books available for checkout per pupil
5	Crowding: ratio of actual enrollment to state-rated capacity
6	Teacher classroom practices
7	Average class size
8	Curriculum units available for student registration per grade
9	Counselors per secondary school pupil
10	School usage of innovations
11	Accessibility of library
12	Preparation coefficient (teacher specialization)
13	Paraprofessional support
14	Students per academic faculty
15	Teacher's education
16	Teacher's teaching experience
17	Teacher load (instructional hours per week)
18	Average teachers' salary

Source: Cohn with Millman (1975), Table 6-2. For more information see Tables A-2 through A-4; Russell (1971); and Kuhns (1972).

with a higher output. Also, higher average teachers' salaries are positively related to output in seven out of the twelve equations. On the other hand, increased use of paraprofessionals, or more curriculum units per grade, are generally negatively related to output. In addition, the socioeconomic variables (lumped together in four variables that were obtained through factor analysis) are clearly not very important in the model, contradicting the Coleman (1966) and Jencks (1972) assertions. It should be noted, however, that socioeconomic variables were the first to enter the equations in Kuhns's (1972) study, which used the same data. Also, the nature of the model and the smallness of the sample should dissuade one from drawing far-reaching conclusions from the study.

The other Pennsylvania study is based on data for Philadelphia public schools by Summers and Wolfe (1975a). Like one of Hanushek's studies, this one, too, attempted to identify school resources, especially teachers, with the students who are directly affected by such resources. In addition, the Philadelphia study employed a longitudinal measure of output—growth in achievement scores over a period of two years for junior high school students and three years each for elementary and senior high school students. Another important characteristic of the study is its endeavor to study the effect of school resources on various student groups—disaggregated by race, sex, ability, and other variables.

The results of the study indicate that some school factors are significant, including class and school size, teacher experience, and quality of degree-granting institutions from which teachers graduate. Interestingly enough, these factors do not affect all students in a like manner: for example, class size appears to have an effect on elementary and senior high schools but not on junior high schools. The authors conclude that:

> In short, some school inputs can heighten student achievement: classes over certain sizes reduce learning; smaller elementary and senior high schools increase it. Net output may be increased by targeting teacher experience and higher rated college background to the appropriate students. Moreover, some of these school inputs can help offset the initial learning handicaps of race, income, and capability. (P. 14)

Additional analysis indicates that the student mix—both in terms of racial composition and ability levels—is likely to affect learning in some cases. This, once again, implies a role for school management in identifying the appropriate mixes for increasing output gains. The authors also advocate structuring teachers' salaries on the basis of the teachers' productive characteristics, as a suggestion proposed by the present author on several occasions (Cohn, 1971a; 1973b; and 1975b: 293-97).

Summers and Wolfe (1977) provide additional discussion of their results regarding sixth grade students in 103 Philadelphia elementary schools (for the year 1970-1971). They compare results obtained when the school is used as the unit of observation to results obtained when the student is used as a unit of observation (and teacher or other school data are related to each individual student). Their results indicate that at the higher level of aggregation, the data are too "noisy" to permit statistically significant results for the inputs to emerge. When students are used as the unit of observation, more school inputs are shown to be statistically significant.

Moreover, they employ an interactive model to study the differential impact of school and nonschool resources on achievement, and they show that the interactive model provides more positive results than one in which no interaction terms are employed. They contend that schools do matter, but that not every school input makes the same contribution to output as any other and that the types of inputs affecting achievement growth of low income or minority students are not necessarily identical to those of other students. These results, if correct, have far-reaching implications regarding any attempts to improve the "quality of education," especially for disadvantaged groups.

Production Functions in Higher Education

The basic structure of the educational production function in higher education is similar to what we have developed for elementary and secondary education, but the nature of outputs, inputs, and the input-output process is different. The major problem is estimating the production function of higher education is the definition and measurement of outputs. Since the mission of the university is not only to inculcate pupils with skills and affect their attitudes, but also to provide leadership in basic and applied research and public service and to serve as an example of "excellence," the output measurement problem becomes ever more difficult. Also, it is quite difficult to trace the effect of each input on the output of individual students, and thus highly aggregative studies must be employed.

It is not surprising, therefore, that very few studies on the production function of higher education have appeared. Moreover, the only one in which a qualitative dimension has been applied is the study by Astin (1968), in which the output measure was defined as the score on the Graduate Record Examination (GRE). Among the explanatory variables, students' inputs were estimated by (1) score on the National Merit Scholarship Qualifying Test; (2) high school grades; (3) nonacademic achievement ("for example, won a prize in a school science contest, elected to a student office" [p. 662]); (4) highest degree planned; (5) intended field of study in college; and (6) career choice. Socioeconomic variables such as sex, father's education, and father's occupation were also included.

A number of variables were included in the equation to capture "institutional quality." They include (1) index of selectivity; (2) per student expenditures; (3) number of books in the library; (4) number of books in the library per student; (5) faculty-student ratio; (6) percent of faculty with Ph.D. degree; (7) total affluence, based on items 2 through 6; (8) degree of competition for grades; (9) type of control; (10) type of institution; (11) geographic region; (12) type of college town; (13) total undergraduate enrollment; (14) percent of men in the student body; (15) curricular emphasis (for example, liberal arts versus science or business); and (16) measures of college environment derived from the Inventory of College Activities.

Astin was not satisfied with an equation in which only the independent effect of each of the inputs on output could be measured. He therefore explicitly introduced a number of "interaction" measures to study the interactive effect of some student and institutional inputs on output.

The input-output analysis was repeated for each of three broad areas—social science, humanities, and natural science. It was found that after measures of student input and socioeconomic variables were taken into account, few institutional quality variables were statistically significant. In the social sciences case, total affluence and library size were significant; for the humanities, only the expenditures variable was significant, but the sign of the coefficient was clearly in the "wrong" direction. And for the natural sciences, three variables were shown to be negatively related to output—ability level of the student body, academic competitiveness, and the interaction variable between student aptitude and ability level of student body. It should be noted, however, that when student inputs are excluded, all of the institutional quality coefficients have the expected signs and, further, that most of them are statistically significant.

The results of the study should be viewed in reference to the serious conceptual and statistical problems associated therewith. They include a small sample size; use of a single output, capturing at most only a portion of the university's total output; and the perennial multicollinearity problem. Nevertheless, the study provides a useful framework for additional work in the area.

Another study of production in higher education was conducted by Southwick (1969). Using time series data for the period 1957–1963 for sixty-eight land grant colleges and universities, he estimated a production function using enrollments by level and expenditures on contract research as outputs. Inputs include administrative staff, capital, library staff, senior teaching staff, junior teaching staff, and research staff. It is assumed that inputs are combined in fixed proportions to produce each of the outputs (number of undergraduates, number of graduates, and research expenditures), so that given the output levels, it is possible to estimate the input levels necessary to attain the outputs. Six equations are estimated for each of the seven years. The major conclusion is that most of the coefficients are not statistically significant. Southwick also discusses changes in the coefficients over time.

A reanalysis of the Southwick data was conducted by Sengupta (1975), who estimated production functions along the lines estimated by others for elementary and secondary schools. In addition, Sengupta combined (pooled) the time series and cross-sectional data, thus increasing his sample size, and also divided the sample into two (more homogeneous) groups. Further, some of the input variables were expressed in a "normalized" fashion (per 100 undergraduate students). Finally, he considered both linear and nonlinear (logarithmic) production functions.

The results of Sengupta's statistical analysis are more encouraging. Using an aggregate input measure for teaching staff (junior plus senior, full-time equivalent) and professional library staff as the only two inputs, he obtains positive, and highly statistically significant, coefficients for the teaching staff variable. Library staff has coefficients that are not statistically significant and are negatively related to output in three out of the four estimated equations.

The main problem with the Southwick-Sengupta analysis is the use of enrollment data as output measures. This implies that the quality of a year's education is invariant among the schools in the sample and for each school over time. It also implies that all the schools strive to attain the same output mix. Moreover, the lack of student-related data could result in a serious misspecification of the model, with results attributed to school inputs actually being the result of a correlation between student-related and school-related inputs (for example, good teachers might be attracted to schools where better students attend, and vice versa).

Estimates of the Educational Production Function in Other Countries

A number of studies on the effectiveness of schools were conducted in countries other than the United States. Some of the best early work in the area as was conducted by Husén (1969b). Also, work in the United Kingdom was done by Woodhall and Blaug (1965a, 1965b, 1968, 1969), along with the Plowden Report (1967), which arrived at conclusions quite similar to those of the Coleman Report (1966) in the United States.

The most impressive study, however, appears to be the massive effort by the Association for the Evaluation of Education and Achievement (IEA), as summarized by Simmons (1975). The research encompassed 258,000 students, 5,900 teachers, and 9,700 schools in twenty-three countries. Using multiple regression analysis to determine the effect of various inputs on output (cross-sectional studies for individual countries, with the school being the unit of analysis), the results show that, after nonschooling factors are netted out, *"very little consistent pattern is found in the school variable associated with differences in achievement"* (p. 57; italics in original). Simmons notes that in some countries, significant school variables are found, but that "the same variable may appear in reversed significance in some other country." He concludes that there does not appear to be sufficient variation in school inputs to show the effect of schooling on achievement: "It may merely be that schooling is relatively standardized, so that extreme variations in quality tend not to occur. These results are consistent with the view that more extreme variations occur in home and familiar backgrounds, and that the school is an aspect of society that provides more nearly standard experiences and opportunities" (p. 58).

The IEA and a number of other studies for developing countries are reviewed in Alexander and Simmons (1975). In summarizing the results, they note the lack of consistency across studies and the conflicting results. For example, in two studies (Kenya and Tunisia), a significantly positive influence on achievement was found for the provision of boarding facilities at the secondary school. An opposite conclusion was found in another study (Malaysia). Likewise, the use of double sessions in early grades (enabling the schools to use their facilities more efficiently) was shown to be positive in one study (Chile) and negative in another (Malaysia). Other school-related variables, such as class size, school size, and teacher characteristics, also are shown to be significant in some studies and nonsignificant (or negatively significant) in others. Again, nonschool variables appear to be especially important.

Alexander and Simmons (1975) clamor for more work in which educational outputs are analyzed simultaneously and report on one study (by Martin Carnoy) using the technique of two stage least squares with data for 182,000 Puerto Rican students in 1967. In that study, a number of teacher and school variables are statistically significant, although, they argue, the use of the school as the unit of analysis reduced the degree to which the study could produce useful results.

Finally, a study by Henderson et al. (1976) examined the effect of various variables on achievement in mathematics and language in Montreal's (Canada) Catholic, French language schools. The data were for primary school students (K-3). As most other studies conclude, the effect of family background and preschool IQ is quite strong. Among school variables, teacher and other school-related factors show a weak relation to achievement. The results indicate that the peer group variables, which have a strong effect on achievement, are the only group of factors that policymakers can influence.

Problems with Estimated
Production Functions

All of the estimated production functions suffer from a number of deficiencies. It is incontestable that they are imperfect, but it is arguable whether or not they are useful.

One critic of the estimated production functions is Henry Levin (1974, 1976). He claims that schools are inherently inefficient and that therefore production function coefficients obtained from a cross-section of pupils or schools do not represent what could be accomplished but rather what is accomplished. Inefficiency stems from three sources: (1) schools are not operating on what is known as the "production frontier"—that is, at the point where the best technology is employed; (2) given the technology used by the schools, resources are not combined in such a manner as to produce the maximum output from the available inputs; and (3) schools are not likely to respond to the true desires of society relative to the proper mix of educational outputs. If all these are true, then the observed data we gather from school systems are obviously inappropriate for generating data designed to improve resource allocation in schools. To these problems, we might add a host of statistical problems, such as the use of single equation estimation procedures where in fact some sort of a simultaneous equation method appears appropriate; the use of linear regression when nonlinearities might be more appropriate; the use of input or output proxies that do not properly capture the essence of real inputs or outputs; measurement errors in both inputs and outputs; "coaching" students on achievement tests, rendering the results meaningless; multicollinearity (the existence of substantial intercorrelation among the independent variables), which reduces the reliability of each regression coefficient; and the omission of important input and/or output variables from the models.

As Hanushek (1976) points out, the allegation of the existence of different kinds of "inefficiency" is not altogether indisputable. Hanushek argues that the main problem with past studies has been the lack of complete specification of the production function (especially with regard to omitted input and output variables).

Moreover, whether schools do or do not operate on the production frontier is an academic question. Empirical production functions are never based upon an idealized version of what production could be, but always on what production is exhibited by managers in real life. What the empirical production functions provide is information that can be used to improve resource allocation within the context of current technology in use. What would happen if new technologies are introduced or when educational administrators adopt new policies or production procedures is another question.

An interesting argument against the customary production model in education is presented by B.W. Brown and Saks (1975). They argue that schools strive not only to increase average output (call it $\bar{Q}$) but also affect the distribution of student outputs. If the standard deviation (σ) is used to represent the distribution of outputs, then it is argued that the "welfare function" (or the objective function) that schools attempt to optimize may be given by:

$$w = f(\bar{Q}, \sigma)$$

That is, "welfare" (w) is affected by both the average outcome ($\bar{Q}$) and the distribution of outcomes (σ). Taking account of various constraints, they show that multiple regressions for, say, scholastic achievement, should be run twice—once for the average output, $\bar{Q}$, and again for the standard deviation of output, σ. They contend that when an input is statistically significant either in the equation for $\bar{Q}$ or in the equation for σ, then it follows that the input does matter in production of Q. Using Michigan Assessment Survey Program data for 1971, they show that all of the school inputs used in the study (average experience of instructional staff, ratio of students to teachers and professional staff, and percent of teachers with master's degree) are related to output when both $\bar{Q}$ and σ are used. If only $\bar{Q}$ is used, then some (or all) of the inputs (depending on whether city, suburb, or town and rural samples are examined) are not statistically related to average achievement.

Where Do We Stand Now?

The lack of consistent results displayed in the preceding sections should not surprise anyone. Only in recent years has educational research begun to receive the attention it deserves, and the development of an educational production function has come into its own even more recently. It may therefore be unrealistic to expect uniform results across such idiosyncratic and situational conditions as exist in education at this point.

Nonetheless, it is unsettling to see the variation in results of input-output analyses as they have been reported in this chapter. While some school components, such as teacher experience, salary, and facilities, have been shown to be significant positive influences in a number of places and at a number of times, not all studies find this to be so.

Averch and his associates (1972) are forced to conclude the following after reviewing existing studies:

Research has not identified a variant of the existing system that is consistently related to students' educational outcomes.
  The term "a variant of the existing system" is used to describe the broad range of alternative educational practices that have been reviewed above. We specifically include changes in school resources, processes, organizations, and aggregate levels of funding.
  We must emphasize that we are not suggesting that nothing makes a difference, or that nothing "works." Rather, we are saying that research has found nothing that *consistently* and *unambiguously* makes a difference in students' outcomes. The literature contains numerous examples of educational practices that seem to have significantly affected students' outcomes.

The problem is that there are invariably other studies, similar in approach and method, that find the same educational practice to be ineffective. And we have no clear idea of why a practice that seems to be effective in one case is apparently ineffective in another.

We must also emphasize that we are not saying that school does not affect student outcomes. We have little knowledge of what student outcomes would be were students not to attend school at all. Educational research focuses on variants of the existing system and tells us nothing about where we might be without the system at all. (Pp. 154-55; italics in original)[10]

The answer lies not in giving up promising lines of research, but rather in refining measures of cognitive ability, finding ways to measure noncognitive functioning more adequately, better data collection, and more sophisticated data manipulation and analysis.

In a comprehensive synthesis of available studies of educational effectiveness undertaken for the New York State Education Department, Heim (1972) was able to present a slightly less ambiguous total view. Since most of the existing studies dealt with cognitive outputs, the preponderance of Heim's attention was upon such outcomes. He was particularly interested in those inputs that are amenable to policy manipulation, rather than those personal and demographic variables that cannot be changed by, or are not under the control of, educational policymakers.

With this frame of reference in mind, he indicated the "box scores" of those policy manipulable inputs that have been tested against cognitive outputs. Heim pointed out that five variables have been studied frequently, namely: (1) teacher degree status, (2) teacher experience, (3) interaction of noncognitive inputs and cognitive outputs, (4) class size (or student-teacher ratio), and (5) availability of special support staff.

Collapsed here into a single portrait, Heim paints the following in wide brush strokes.

In 83 percent of the studies reviewed, it was found that . . . the higher the average level of teacher education in the school, the more impressive was student performance . . . . Teacher experience is also commonly thought

10. There exists some evidence on this score. A study by Green et al. (1964) compared test performances by children whose schooling was interrupted for some years with performances by children from similar socioeconomic and locational backgrounds. The results clearly showed the importance of school: "It was found that the children whose schooling had been interrupted exhibited severe educational retardation, particularly on tests more closely related to school curriculums such as spelling and arithmetic. On an intelligence test the scores of these children were 15 to 30 points lower than those children in the adjacent county who had continued in school" (Mayeske et al., 1972: 113).

to influence student performance. However, the evidence is substantially less conclusive . . . . In the 23 studies reviewed, teacher experience was found to be significantly related to student performance only 57 percent of the time . . . . Persuasive evidence was reviewed which indicates that, in part, student achievement in the intellectual skills area is related to the level of a student's development in the noncognitive domain . . . . There seems to be little evidence to suggest that, within fairly broad limits class size (or its most often used proxy, teacher-pupil ratio) has any general effect upon cognitive or noncognitive school outputs . . . . Overall, the amount of special staff per pupil was found to have a significant effect on student achievement in fewer than half of the studies in which its effect was tested. (Pp. 98–102; see also Heim, 1973)

Again, the reader is cautioned not to assume that these variables are inoperative generally. It is rather stated that on the whole, only one out of five commonly tested school components is measured and shows positive impact consistently across different students in different settings.

Educational psychologists would readily point out that human development and learning are hypothetical constructs par excellence: they cannot be measured directly, but can only be inferred from a change in performance over time. A person in isolation would change over time through the sheer force of physical maturation. When one compounds complexity of the process by replacing isolation with the effects of socialization, physical and social deprivation, and a host of other potential factors, the relationship among inputs and outputs can become quite tenuous. The dilemma is exacerbated by the need to make comparisons not only of a given individual over time, but of different individuals with different hereditary and environmental interfaces in terms of a process that typically consumes not fewer than twelve calendar years and, commonly, longer.

While the timid might be given pause by the rich diversity of the human condition, drawing back from the effort is destined only to delay its solution. The solution is neither as simplistic as many would have hoped nor as insoluable as others would suggest. What is needed is the willingness to take small and tentative steps, to consolidate knowledge of past successes and failures, and to continually refine both the instruments and the processes.

APPLICATIONS OF THE PRODUCTION FUNCTION CONCEPT

Suppose we were able to estimate the educational production function so that the objections raised against it would be largely irrelevant.

Then it can be shown that an estimated production function may be used to improve resource allocation in schools. The type of application depends on the type of production function considered relevant and the existence (or lack of existence) of constraints.

Case I

The simplest case is one in which a linear production function is estimated, using a single output, with no constraints.[11] If Q is the output and x_1, x_2, . . . x_m are (m) school-related inputs, then our production function will yield estimated coefficients b_1, b_2, . . . , b_m such that

$$Q = a + b_1 x_1 + b_2 x_2 + \ldots + b_m x_m, \qquad (8.3)$$

where a represents the intercept and the effect of nonschool inputs.

Let the price of the inputs be denoted by p_1, p_2, . . . p_m. Then we calculate, for each input, the ratios b_1/p_1, b_2/p_2, . . . , b_m/p_m. Each of these ratios represents the contribution to output per dollar spent on the input. It follows that if the ratio b_i/p_i is highest for the ith input, then that input should be expanded indefinitely at the expense of other inputs.

A few empirical counterparts of Case 1 have been described in the literature. The best-known study is H.M. Levin (1970a), where production function results from Hanushek (1968) where combined with teacher input costs estimated by Levin. He shows that, for whites, a one point increase in a student's verbal achievement would cost $26 if the schools increased the average verbal facility of teachers and $128 if, instead, additional teacher experience was obtained. For black students, the figures are $26 and $253, respectively. The verbal facility input appears to be more cost-effective, having a higher ratio of marginal product to input cost. Levin's major conclusions are confirmed in a study by Boardman (1978).

A similar analysis was made by Harold Beebout in a study of Malaysia reported by Alexander and Simmons (1975: 31–37). Estimating the ratios of gains in achievement attributed to input factors divided by per unit cost of input (b_i/p_i), it is shown that reducing the number of untrained teachers is the most cost-effective policy, followed by changing the structure of schools from double to single sessions of instruction and, finally, by reducing class size.

Also, a study by Wolfe (1977), using Philadelphia data, shows the impact of an increase or decrease of $10 per pupil on achievement,

11. An exception is that *funds are limited*.

by type of pupil. Here the results are not quite so straightforward, for a change in one input may have the greatest impact on one student type whereas a change in another input may have the greatest impact on another student type. For instance, reducing class size in middle and high school to twenty-seven would have the largest impact on low and high achievement groups, but a nonsignificant effect on the middle achievement group. For the latter group, increasing the number of teachers trained in highly rated universities would be the input with the highest b/p ratio.

Case 2

This case is similar to Case 1 with the addition of resource constraints. It is quite likely that it will not be possible to expand use of the ith input without limit. For instance, if x_i is library books, it is not possible to expand the library indefinitely, due both to lack of adequate storage facilities and to lack of funds. Moreover, expansion of input i is frequently possible only to the extent that other inputs could be reduced, so that total expenditures on inputs will not change. It is likely, however, that other school inputs cannot be reduced to zero. For example, the number of teachers must be large enough to meet maximum class size standards as mandated by state law or collective bargaining agreements. Or educational level of instructional staff cannot be reduced beyond the minimum required for obtaining and maintaining teacher certification standards. Therefore, we cannot increase use of input i indefinitely, but can increase it only as much as possible at the expense of those inputs with the lowest b/p ratios. Moreover, it may be worthwhile to expand the input x_j for which b_j/p_j is next largest, at the expense of those inputs with lower b/p ratios. The same procedure would be followed until it is not possible to increase output any longer through input substitution.

An empirical counterpart of Case 2 is provided by Wolfe (1977). In addition to estimating additional output per $10 spent on resource inputs, she examines possible reallocation of resources when the budget remains constant and where maximum reallocation permitted is one-third of each input. In Scenario I, resources are allowed to be reallocated among the three achievement subgroups. In the second scenario, "up to one-third of most resources can be allocated either among achievement subgroups *or* among school inputs," where, again, the total budget remains constant (pp. 415–16; italics in original). Wolfe also considers the optimal manner by which a budget reduction of $30 per pupil could be affected.

Case 3

Now assume a nonlinear production function with no constraints.[12] Then we have:

$$Q = f(a, x_1, x_2, \ldots x_m). \tag{8.4}$$

Let the marginal productivities of the inputs be positive but diminishing. We can again obtain statistical estimates of the production coefficients (for certain types of nonlinear functions) and derive the inputs' marginal productivities. It can be shown that for maximum output, the following condition must hold:

$$MP_1/p_1 = MP_2/p_2 = \ldots = MP_m/p_m, \tag{8.5}$$

where MP_i is the marginal productivity of the ith input. Equation (8.5) requires that inputs should be combined such that the last dollar spent on each input should yield the same additional output as obtained by spending a dollar on any other input.

Case 4

Add to Case 3 resource constraints. Then it may not be possible to satisfy Equation (8.5), and the approach is to substitute inputs until it is no longer possible to add to output through input substitution. The general rule, again, is that inputs with higher MP/p ratios should be expanded, and inputs with lower MP/p ratios should be reduced.

Case 5

Consider now the case of multiple outputs. If there are n outputs with m manipulable inputs, then, in the linear case, we obtain the following reduced form set of linear equations:

$$
\begin{aligned}
Q_1 &= a_1 + b_{11}\, x_1 + b_{12}\, x_2 + \ldots + b_{1m}\, x_m \\
Q_2 &= a_2 + b_{21}\, x_1 + b_{22}\, x_2 + \ldots + b_{2m} x_m \\
&\quad\bullet \\
&\quad\bullet \\
&\quad\bullet \\
Q_n &= a_n + b_{n1} x_1 + b_{n2} x_2 + \ldots + b_{nm} x_m,
\end{aligned}
\tag{8.6}
$$

where the Qs are the outputs, the xs the inputs, the as represent the effect of the intercept term and nonmanipulable inputs, and the bs

12. Again, funds are in limited supply.

are the marginal products of the inputs. For example, b_{11} is the marginal product of input 1 used to produce Q_1, and in general, b_{ij} is the marginal productivity of the jth input in the production of the ith output.

We could again obtain the ratios of the marginal products per dollar spent on the inputs—namely, b_{ij}/p_j. This would make it possible to determine which input is most effective in augmenting a given output, but it is, of course, possible that different inputs will be most effective in augmenting different outputs. Unless we have some method by which additions to the various outputs can be compared, the production function concept will have only very limited applicability.

Case 6

Instead of seeking to find the input(s) that are most cost-effective in increasing output, it is possible to use mathematical programming models to minimize costs subject to satisfying varying constraints. In that case, we must first estimate the costs of inputs and then use linear (or other mathematical) programming techniques to estimate the optimal levels of inputs that would give us minimum costs. An example of such an exercise is provided by Boardman (1978), using the EEO survey data.

Case 7

Finally, we can use the multiple output model to obtain the optimal levels of inputs that would minimize deviations from target output levels. Again, relevant constraints are specified, but in addition, it is necessary to determine what should be the "target" levels of the outputs and whether the administrators are interested in achieving the target levels exactly or whether they are willing to over- or under-achieve the respective target values. The technique of goal programming may be used to compute the desired solution.

An empirical counterpart of this case, employing Pennsylvania data, is described in J.M. Morgan (1977), J.M. Morgan and Cohn (1977a, 1977b, 1977c), and Cohn and Morgan (1978b). A brief description of the model appears in Chapter 11 (below).

THE COST FUNCTION: THEORY, EMPIRICAL ESTIMATES, AND APPLICATIONS

Theory

The meaning of "cost" in economics differs in two important respects from conventional usage. First, economic costs include all opportunity costs, and therefore, economic costs are generally more inclusive. Second, and perhaps more importantly, economic costs are the minimum costs necessary to produce a given level of output. It is easy to show that private entrepreneurs have the necessary incentives to minimize costs, so that if all opportunity costs are included, it is likely that the minimum cost criterion will be satisfied. In education, however, the same incentives are lacking, and it is not clear whether expenditures are synonymous with costs.

We begin with a generalized production function, as described in Equation (8.1). It may be useful to add, explicitly, a school size variable (call it E), so we have instead of (8.1) the following:

$$f(Q, X, E/S) = 0, \tag{8.7}$$

where Q is a vector of outputs, X is a vector of manipulable variables, and S is a vector of nonmanipulable variables.

Next we estimate the prices of the X inputs, given by $p_1, p_2, \ldots, p_k$. Accounting costs of the X inputs are given by

$$\sum_{i=1}^{k} p_i x_i = p_1 x_1 + p_2 x_2 + \ldots + p_k x_k. \tag{8.8}$$

To obtain minimum costs for each level of output, it is necessary to follow a procedure by which the accounting costs are examined for different combinations of the Xs, all of which provide the same output. (This requires that inputs are substitutable in production.) After some manipulation (see Cohn and Riew, 1974: 411-12), we obtain the optimal input levels, x_1^*, x_2^*, and so forth, for which the economic costs of producing a given level of output are minimized. The economic costs are given by

$$C = \sum_{i=1}^{k} p_i x_i^*. \tag{8.9}$$

Since the x_i^* can be shown to depend both on the Q vector and on school size, E, it follows that C is a function of Q, E, the manipulable inputs, and their prices:

$$C = g(Q; E; p_1, p_2 \ldots, p_k; x_1, x_2, \ldots, x_k). \tag{8.10}$$

In practice, many of the input prices are identical in all school districts, so there is no need to include them in a cross-sectional regression equation. Also, in contrast to comments by H.M. Levin (1970b), the nonmanipulative inputs should not be included in the cost equations, as their effect on costs is transmitted through the effect they may have on output, Q.

It remains unclear from this analysis what shape Equation (8.10) must take. As is shown by Ferguson (1972), even a simple production function will produce a very complex cost formula, so that a linear approximation might be entirely unsatisfactory. It is recognized, however, that the correct theoretical form for Equation (8.10) cannot be determined until the shape of the production function is established, and we are clearly not in a position to provide an incontestable conclusion on this score. Empirical counterparts are, therefore, rather pragmatically oriented and have relied on curve-fitting methods to derive an implied shape for the cost function from observed data.

Economies of Scale. Suppose the per pupil cost function has the following form:

$$\frac{C}{E} = a + b_1 Q_1 + b_2 Q_2 + \ldots + b_n Q_n + c_1 x_1 + c_2 x_2 + \ldots$$

$$+ c_k x_k + d_1 E + d_2 E^2, \tag{8.11}$$

where a, the bs, the cs, and the ds are the coefficients of the cost functions, assumed to be constant, and C/E is per pupil costs. Then it can be shown that the cost-size relationship is U shaped—that is, when other things are equal, as school size increases, per pupil costs will decrease up to a point and then begin to increase. If we are dealing with a short-run cost function (i.e., during a time period too short to change the size of the school's plant), then the explanation for this shape of the cost function lies in the well-known "law of diminishing (marginal) returns" (that is, as we add more and more variable inputs to a fixed input—in this case the school's plant—the additions to output will, after some point, be successively smaller). In the long run (when it is possible to change all inputs, including the school's plant), the explanation for the U-shaped cost function has to do with economies and diseconomies of scale. That is, when the costs per pupil decline, we have economies of scale, and when costs per pupil increase, we have diseconomies of scale. In that case, there will be an optimal school size, given by that size at which costs per pupil are minimum. It can be shown that the level of E at which costs per pupil are minimum is given by $-d_1/2d_2$.[13]

It is possible, however, that a quadratic specification for E is inappropriate. An alternative specification, in which costs per pupil decline at all levels of school size, is (ignoring other variables included in Equation 8.11):

$$C/E = a + \ldots + d_3(1/E), \qquad (8.13)$$

where d_3 is a constant. The implied relationship between costs per pupil and school size is given by a rectangular hyperbola. In this case, the "optimal" school size is never attained, as costs continue to decrease when school size is increased.

Empirical Estimates

Elementary and Secondary Schools. A number of studies have appeared in which estimates of the "cost function" are presented. As is the case for production functions, however, the theoretical and empirical basis of the studies is extremely diverse, so that it is difficult to make valid comparisons.

One area of disagreement is the proper measure of school size. Is it enrollment in the entire district, the school, or the building? It appears that all three levels of aggregation are sensible. In the district level, some savings in costs may arise due to consolidation of administrative functions, lower costs of purchasing items, and so forth. At the school level, economies will occur through better utilization of teachers, other instructional and noninstructural personnel, and physical resources. The same kinds of economies could occur also at the building level, though with different intensities.

Cost functions were estimated, among others, by Riew (1966), Cohn (1968), Hettich (1968), Osburn (1970), and Sabulao and Hickrod (1971). In all of these studies, primary attention was centered on the question of scale economies. Although different functional forms were employed in these studies, the overwhelming conclusion has been that schools of a larger size can operate at lower per pupil costs, other things equal. The "optimal" school size varies from study to study, depending on the nature of the sample and the size measure used.

13. If Equation (8.11) applies, then

$$\partial (C/E)/\partial E = d_1 + 2d_2 E. \qquad (8.12)$$

Setting the results in Equation (8.12) equal to 0, we obtain $d_1 + 2d_2 E^* = 0$, or, $E^* = -d_1/2d_2$, where E^* is the optimal school size.

It should be noted that in at least two studies (Cohn, 1968, and Hettich, 1968) statistical analysis confirmed the allegation that the alternative specification in Equation (8.13) is superior to the one given in Equation (8.11). If this is true, then an "optimal" school size does not exist. The larger the school, the lower the per pupil costs appear to be. Generalization of such results is quite hazardous, however, since it requires extrapolation outside the range of empirical observations. The Cohn (1968) and Hettich (1968) studies may therefore be interpreted mainly in the context of questioning the alleged existence of diseconomies—that is, in placing an upper limit to school size.

Examples of optimum school size for studies using the quadratic specification (Equation 8.11) are 1,500 pupils in average daily attendance for Iowa high schools (Cohn, 1968); 1,675 for Wisconsin high schools (Riew, 1966); 2,244 for Missouri high schools (Osburn, 1970); 2,432 for unit districts, 874 for high school districts, and 336 for elementary districts in Illinois (Hickrod et al., 1975b).

In a study of Michigan secondary schools (Cohn and Hu, 1973), it was found that overall economies of scale did not appear to exist (in 1972). When costs by program are examined, however, it was found that economies of scale did exist for a number of programs. For example, mathematics, homemaking, general office clerk, stenographic and clerical, and electricity and electronics had significant scale effects, while other programs had scale effects that were not statistically significant, no scale effect, or even a reverse scale effect (a positive relationship between scale and costs, or in inverted U relationship).

Higher Education: The only comprehensive study on cost functions in the United States of which we are aware is Maynard (1971). Using data from a questionnaire sent to 123 institutions of higher education (IHEs) in thirteen states, cost per pupil functions were estimated and economies of scale appraised. Using the symbols defined above, Maynard's average cost function is:

$$C/E = a - 0.244E + 0.00002275E^2,$$

where a is a constant (assumed to be $1,500 by Maynard). Optimal school size is, therefore, $0.244/(2 \times 0.00002275) = 5,363$.

Other cost functions were also estimated by Southwick (1969) and Sengupta (1975) as parts of their studies described above.

For other countries, we have the comprehensive study on costs and outputs at British universities by Verry and Davies (1976). They show significant scale economies in a number of equations (disaggregated by field), although the scale effect is not always U shaped.

Applications

The most obvious application involves school reorganization, based upon scale effects. If, for instance, it can be shown that minimum per pupil costs occur when school size is 1,500, then it is clear that considerable savings can be reaped when schools smaller or larger than the optimal size reorganize until the 1,500 enrollment level is reached everywhere. The problem, of course, is that it is not always possible to reorganize without political action—that is, changes in school district boundaries or even in school area boundaries within a school system. Moreover, the full impact of transportation costs have not always been investigated in cost-size studies, so that consolidation may not be economical after all. A good illustration of this point is provided in a study by Holland and Baritelle (1975). Using linear and "seperable" programming techniques, they show that school consolidation in a sparsely populated rural area would have low benefits, because of increased transportation costs.

If it can be shown that consolidation or reorganization does have a reasonable payoff, then it might be worthwhile to exert pressure on school officials to change the scale of operations. A proposal to use state aid to education as a tool to capture scale economies has been made by this author in a recent paper (Cohn, 1975a; see also Cohn, 1974a: ch. 6).

Other uses of the cost function concept would be in identifying the impact of input utilization on school costs and in finding methods by which costs could be minimized. Cost functions are needed, for example, in carrying out linear-programming models such as Boardman (1978), discussed above, or extensions of the Morgan-Cohn goal-programming approach.

CONCLUDING COMMENTS

Proper estimation and interpretation of production and cost functions may be the most important contribution to education that economists could make. It is surprising, therefore, that very little has been done by economists in nurturing this field. Some reasons for this lack of leadership are explained by Maynard (1971), including data inadequacies, resistance to intrusion to educational data by educationists, the prevailing attitude that "nothing can be done about it anyway," and the economist's preoccupation with other sectors of the economy.

Despite the efforts that have been made, the state of the art is woefully inadequate. There is a need to develop production and cost models that are consistent with accepted economic and educational theory and to test the results against reliable data over time and space. Replication of the results is very important, since, as we have seen earlier, empirical studies have often arrived at diametrically opposite results.

The leadership for such an effort is not likely to come from individual scholars. It must come from the National Institute of Education, the U.S. Office of Education, National Science Foundation, or other large educational and scientific organizations. When the incentives to explore the area are present, the "law of the market" will insure that competent scholars will accept the challenge. Until then we must do with the information that has been produced to date.

LITERATURE GUIDE

Production Function
Overall reviews of the educational production function are provided in Alexander and Simmons (1975), Averch et al. (1972), Cohn with Millman (1975), Heim (1972, 1973), Heim and Perl (1974), Guthrie (1970), H.M. Levin (1970b), Lyle (1967), and Rossmiller and Geske (1976, 1977).

Specific production function studies include: Bane and Jencks (1972), Barnow (1975), Barron (1967), Boardman et al. (1973, 1974, 1977), Bowles (1969a, 1970c), Bowles and Levin (1968a, 1968b), Bieker and Anschal (1974), Bradley (1974), B.W. Brown and Saks (1975), Burkhead et al. (1967), Cain and Watts (1968, 1970), Cohn (1968, 1976b), Cohn with Millman (1975), Coleman (1968), Coleman et al. (1966), T.G. Fox (1969, 1971b), Goodman (1959), Green et al. (1964), Guthrie et al. (1969, 1971), Hanushek (1968, 1970, 1972), Hettich (1968), Jencks et al. (1972), Kass (1975), Katzman (1968, 1971), Kiesling (1967, 1969, 1970), Kuhns (1972), Leekley (1974), H.M. Levin (1968, 1970c), Lu and Tweeten (1973, 1976a, 1976b; see also comments by Zoloth, 1976a, 1976b), Maeroff (1977), Mayeske et al. (1972, 1973a, 1973b, 1975), Michelson (1970, 1972), Mollenkopf and Melville (1956), Mood (1970, 1973), Murnane (1975), O'Neill et al. (1972), Raymond (1968), M.S. Smith (1968), Summers and Wolfe (1975a, 1975b, 1977a), Thomas (1962, 1967, 1971), Tuckman (1971; see also comment by Hambor et al., 1973), Winkler (1975), and Wolfe (1977).

Critiques of the educational production function include H.M.

Levin (1974, 1976; see also comment by Hanushek, 1976), Luecke and McGuinn (1975), and B.W. Brown and Saks (1975). Studies related to the educational production of higher education include Astin (1968, 1973), Lumsden (1974), Sengupta (1975), Southwick (1967, 1969), and WICHE (1970). Information on countries other than the United States includes Alexander and Simmons (1975), Henderson et al. (1976), Simmons (1975, 1976), Verry and Davies (1976), Verry and Layard (1975), and Woodhall and Blaug (1965a, 1965b, 1968, 1969).

Cost Functions

Studies for elementary and secondary education include Cohn (1968), Cohn and Hu (1973), Cohn and Riew (1974), Hickrod et al. (1975b), Holland and Baritelle (1975), Holmes (1975), Jabbour (1975), Michelson (1972), Osburn (1970), Riew (1966, 1972), and Sabulao and Hickrod (1971). A related study is J. Jackson et al. (1974), and a critique of scale economies studies is contained in Niskanen and Levy (1974).

Cost function studies of higher education include Dunworth and Bottomely (1974), Levy (1969), Maynard (1971), Sengupta (1975), Southwick (1969), Verry and Davies (1976), and Verry and Layard (1975).

Related Areas

Other studies related to production and cost functions in education include H.F. Clark (1963), Cohn (1971b, 1974b), Cohn and Morgan (1978b), Comptroller General of the United States (1976), Garfinkel and Gramlich (1973), Green et al. (1964), Hamrin (1974), Hawthorne (1974), Haynes and Walker (1975), James (1969), Kershaw and McKean (1959), Klitgaard and Hall (1975), M. Knight (1977), Lazarus and Taylor (1977), Lessinger (1976), Lytton (1959), J.M. Morgan (1977), Morgan and Cohn (1977a, 1977b, 1977c), Nordell (1967), Redfern (1967), Welty (1971), and WICHE (1970).

✳ *Chapter 9*

Teachers' Salaries

> Public school teaching remains a calling with a rather low ceiling
> of pay relative to other fields that employ college graduates, and
> the immediate cause is that local school districts are more or less
> forced by the professional teachers' associations to award increments in
> pay to all teachers in approximately the same amounts. However adminis-
> trators may tinker with salary scales to obscure the process, the "across-
> the-board" raise is the usual thing in American School districts.
>
> Charles S. Benson, *The Cheerful Prospect*

Benson made this cogent observation in 1965. Today (1978),
it is no less true for the American public schools and is becoming
true also for American higher education.

This chapter will, therefore, explore the levels of teachers' salaries in the various hierarchies of American education. In addition,
the determinants of salary levels will be explored. Particular attention will be given to the effect of collective bargaining. In addition,
a framework designed to improve allocation of resources by awarding teachers' salaries on the basis of their implied productivity will
be presented.

TEACHERS' SALARIES IN ELEMENTARY
AND SECONDARY SCHOOLS

Data concerning both the structure and level of teachers salaries from
the turn of the twentieth century to the present are available from a
number of sources. The National Education Association has for

many years published data about teacher salaries. The United States Office of Education has provided information in its *Biennial Surveys of Education*, the *Digest of Educational Statistics* series, and the annual editions of *Projections of Educational Statistics*. These and other sources were utilized by many researchers in such works as Stigler's *Employment and Compensation in Education* and in *Teacher Shortages and Salary Schedules*, by Kershaw and McKean.

An analysis of average salaries of supervisors, principals, and teachers from 1900 to 1946 was made by Stigler (1950), portions of which are presented in Table 9-1. The table gives the average salaries for all personnel and for rural and urban personnel, respectively. It is seen that in the forty-six-year period, average wages have increased more than sixfold. At the same time, salaries in the urban communities continued to be much higher than in rural areas, although in relative terms, salaries have increased much faster in the rural areas.

As can be observed from the righthand columns of Table 9-1, the absolute rise in salaries was much greater than the rise in the purchasing power of these salaries. Using the 1935-1939 cost of living index to "deflate" the salary series, it is observed that urban salaries increased by 61.5 percent, as opposed to an absolute increase of 298.9 percent when no adjustment for price changes is made.

Further data appear in Table 9-2. Average salaries of instructional staff are given for the period 1929-1930 to 1974-1975 both in current prices and in purchasing power. Again, whereas absolute salaries increased by 750 percent during the period, the purchasing power of the salaries increased by 170.5 percent when deflated by the 1967 price level. It should also be pointed out that the pur-

Table 9-1. Average Salaries of Supervisors, Principals, and Teachers in Public Schools, 1900-1946 (selected years).

Year	Average Salary			Urban Salaries in 1935-1939 Purchasing Power
	All	*Rural*	*Urban*	
1900	$311	$215	$638	$1,213
1910	463	353	732	1,173
1920	871	638	1,222	903
1930	1,420	979	1,944	1,583
1940	1,441	959	1,955	1,963
1942	1,507	1,018	2,013	1,822
1946	1,995	1,508	2,545	1,959

Source: Adapted from Stigler (1950), pp. 19-23.

Table 9-2. Average Annual Salary of Instructional Staff in Full-Time Elementary and Secondary Schools—United States, 1929-1930 to 1974-1975.

Year	*In Current Prices*	*Consumer Price Index (1967 = 100)*	*In 1967 Prices*
	1	*2*	*3*
1929-30	$ 1,420	51.3	$2,768
1939-40	1,441	42.0	3,431
1949-50	3,010	72.1	4,175
1959-60	5,174	88.7	5,833
1969-70	8,840	116.3	7,601
1970-71	9,570	121.3	7,889
1971-72	10,100	125.3	8,061
1972-73	10,608	133.1	7,870
1973-74	11,185	147.7	7,573
1974-75	12,070	161.2	7,488

Sources: Column 1 from Grant and Lind (1976), Table 52, p. 54. Column 2 from *Economic Report of the President* (1976). Column 3 = (col. 1 ÷ col. 2) × 100.

chasing power of teachers' salaries declined from $8,061 in 1972 to $7,488 in 1975—a decline of 7.6 percent—as a result of high inflationary pressures in the United States during that period. The prevalence of high rates of inflation is likely to create significant problems in maintaining the trend of increased purchasing power of teachers' salaries.

Interstate and Regional Variations in Salaries

The average salaries reported above obscure considerable variations of salaries among states and regions in the United States. Such variations were extremely pronounced in earlier years. For example, in 1940, salaries in the South were only 57 percent of average salaries nationwide, whereas salaries in the Far West were 144.4 percent of (that is, 44.4 percent higher than) the national average. By 1970, the respective figures were 84.4 and 117.0 percent (the absolute differences, however, were much greater in 1970 than in 1940).[1]

Data on the regional and interstate variation in teachers' salaries are provided in Table 9-3. The difference between the highest and lowest average salaries is substantial—$8,568 ($16,906 for Alaska; $8,338 for Mississippi). Moreover, we find substantial variations within regions (compare, for example, New York and West Virginia

1. These calculations are based upon data in National Education Association (1970a: Table 2, p. 9).

Table 9-3. Interstate Variations in Salaries of Instructional Staff, U.S. Elementary and Secondary Schools, 1974-1975.

State	Average Salary	Deviation from U.S. Mean
United States	$12,070	—
New England		
Connecticut	12,151	$ 81
Maine	13,202	1,132
Massachusetts	12,468	398
New Hampshire	10,016	-2,054
Rhode Island	12,885	815
Vermont	9,206	-2,864
Middle Atlantic		
Delaware	12,110	40
District of Columbia	14,716	2,646
Maryland	13,282	1,212
New Jersey	na	na
New York	15,000	2,930
Pennsylvania	12,200	130
West Virginia	9,124	-2,946
South East		
Alabama	9,503	-2,567
Arkansas	9,021	-3,049
Florida	10,780	-1,290
Georgia	10,641	-1,429
Kentucky	9,240	-2,830
Louisiana	9,800	-2,270
Mississippi	8,338	-3,732
North Carolina	11,275	- 795
South Carolina	9,770	-2,300
Tennessee	9,878	-2,192
Virginia	11,279	- 791
Middle West		
Illinois	13,469	1,399
Indiana	11,358	- 712
Iowa	10,598	-1,472
Michigan	14,224	2,154
Minnesota	12,852	782
Missouri	10,257	-1,813
Ohio	11,100	- 970
Wisconsin	13,046	976
South West		
Arizona	11,168	- 902
New Mexico	10,200	-1,870
Oklahoma	9,208	-2,862
Texas	10,136	-1,934
North West		
Colorado	11,554	- 516
Idaho	9,573	-2,497
Kansas	9,770	-2,300
Montana	10,160	-1,910
Nebraska	9,715	-2,335
North Dakota	9,176	-2,894

Table 9-3. continued

State	Average Salary	Deviation from U.S. Mean
South Dakota	8,860	-3,210
Utah	10,150	-1,920
Wyoming	10,350	-1,720
Far West		
Alaska	16,906	4,836
California	14,915	2,845
Hawaii	13,665	1,595
Nevada	12,854	784
Oregon	10,958	-1,112
Washington	12,538	468

Source: Grant and Lind (1976), Table 52, p. 54.

na = not available

in the Middle Atlantic states; Missouri and Michigan in the Middle West; and Alaska and Oregon in the Far West).

Finally, even state averages obscure a good deal of variation within states, as will be explained in a subsequent section.

Variations by Level of School

Stigler (1950) notes that although secondary teachers appear to earn higher salaries than those in the elementary levels, "the difference between salaries of elementary and secondary school teachers in cities over 10,000 has been declining steadily over time" (p. 16). For example, while the ratio (in such cities) of secondary to elementary salaries in 1915 was 1.58, it declined to 1.48 in 1818, to 1.24 in 1928, and to 1.20 in 1938.

In Table 9-4, average salaries for elementary and secondary classroom teachers are given for the period 1955-1956 to 1974-1975. In column 5, the differences between secondary and elementary salaries are given, while in column 6, the ratio of secondary to elementary salaries is computed. We note that although the absolute differentials have persisted over time (and actually increased in recent years), the ratio of secondary to elementary salaries declined precipitously from 1956 to 1970. It has remained stable ever since. The main reason for the decline in the ratio appears to be the nearly universal adoption of the "single teacher salary schedule," in which salaries are determined only by the teacher's educational preparation and experience. Also, during that period, elementary schools began recruiting teachers with Master's degrees or other high qualifications. There may be an opposite trend in motion at the present

Table 9-4. Estimated Average Annual Salaries of Classroom Teachers, 1955–1956 to 1975–1976

School Year	Average Salary of Classroom Teachers			Salary Differential (col. 3 − col. 2)	Ratio of Secondary to Elementary Salaries (col. 3 ÷ col. 2)
	Elementary	Secondary	All Teachers		
1	2	3	4	5	6
1955–56	$ 3,852	$ 4,409	$ 4,055	$557	1.14
1959–60	4,815	5,276	4,995	461	1.13
1965–66	6,279	6,761	6,485	482	1.08
1969–70	8,412	8,891	8,635	479	1.06
1970–71	9,021	9,568	9,269	547	1.06
1971–72	9,424	10,031	9,705	607	1.06
1972–73	9,876	10,497	10,164	621	1.06
1973–74	10,507	11,077	10,778	570	1.05
1974–75	11,297	11,956	11,650	659	1.06
1975–76	12,130	12,844	12,524	714	1.06

Sources: Grant and Lind (1977), Table 55, p. 57.

time, as schools strive to reduce the costs of operation, and it is possible that an increase in the secondary-elementary salary ratio might ensue.

Comparisons With Other Occupations

Teacher salaries may be compared to salaries of workers in other occupations in several ways. It will be shown that different conclusions concerning the relative economic status of the teaching profession may be drawn from different comparison methodologies.

Ruml and Tickton. A fifty year comparison of teaching salaries with other occupations and industries was conducted in the mid-fifties by Ruml and Tickton (1955). Their basic methodology was as follows. First, current (1953) salaries were deflated to a base period (1904, 1929, and 1947) to account for changes in the value of the dollar. Second, the percent change from the base period to the present was computed. When this was done for both teaching and other professions, a comparison of relative change in economic status was possible.

This procedure was followed by Ruml and Tickton for various educational professions (teachers, professors, principals, and administrators) as well as for railway and industry positions. They found that for some educational professions, the absolute economic position has deteriorated—that is, deflated current salaries were less than those received during the base period. For example, principals of big city high schools in 1953 received an average "real" salary 30 percent lower than the average salary received in 1904, and teachers in big city high schools lost 1 percent in real purchasing power during the same period. Moreover, they found that, on the whole, teachers and educational administrators fared far worse than workers in railway and industry.

Stigler. Conclusions contrary to those found by Ruml and Tickton were given by Stigler (1950). His analysis follows a different methodological framework. First, Stigler argued that direct comparisons between teaching salaries and remuneration in other occupations could not be made because (1) teachers were entitled to personal income tax exemption prior to 1939; (2) teachers work for only a portion of the year; (3) fringe benefits, such as pensions, were much higher in public services during the first half of the twentieth century; (4) job security, in the form of tenure, has been much greater for the teaching profession than for industry in general; and (5) teacher salaries have been relatively equal, whereas salaries among other professions have shown much greater variation.

To compare teachers with other occupations, Stigler adjusted teaching salaries for (1) variations in the length of the school year; (2) exemption from income tax prior to 1939; and (3) value of fringe benefits (pensions). After such adjustments were made, Stigler found that, on the whole, teachers have fared far better than the average worker during the period 1900–1949, when teacher salaries increased much faster than per capita national income. Stigler notes, however, that from 1933 to 1949, per capita income increased faster than teacher salaries.

Stigler notes further that comparisons with other occupations are meaningless unless the types of jobs, average training, and so forth are similar in both teaching and the occupations with which comparisons are made. It is shown that between 1928 and 1949, the relative position of urban public school teachers vis-à-vis college teachers improved substantially. Further, when teacher salaries are compared to salaries of women hand bookkeepers in 1949, it is observed that teachers earned more than bookkeepers in all major cities in the United States.

Kershaw and McKean. Both nationwide and regional comparisons of teacher salaries with other occupations are given by Kershaw and McKean (1962) for 1960. Since their main thesis was that shortages in some teaching fields exist because of the uniformity of the salary structure in education, their comparisons are limited to calculating differential starting and top salaries between certain occupations and teachers. They also note that comparisons between teachers and other occupations, in general, are difficult to make because "of the difference in vacation arrangements [and] also because of the differences in other working conditions, fringe benefits, and so on" (p. 59).

It is observed that the differentials between starting salaries of science-engineering graduates and school teachers were larger than for those between liberal arts graduates and teachers. This differential is used to explain relative shortages in teaching. Further data on specific occupations classified by degree earned are also given. Compared with some occupations, teachers can expect top salaries higher than some professions, but in general, top teaching salaries, even for individuals holding advanced degrees, are shown to be far less than for other occupations (in 1960). Further analysis is given for regional variations in salaries of teachers and other occupations.

Recent Evidence. The National Education Association, in its annual report on the economic status of the teaching profession, provides comprehensive data on teacher salaries and remuneration in various other fields. Of particular interest is the comparison of teacher salaries with annual earnings of (1) wage and salary workers in all industries; (2) employees in manufacturing; and (3) civilian employees of the federal government. It is shown that the teaching profession has gained over all of the above-mentioned groups during the period 1929–1968. In fact, instructional salaries in 1963 were absolutely greater than those of workers in all industries and of manufacturing workers; in addition, the relative position of instructional staff vis-à-vis federal workers has improved considerably during the period.

It should be noted that the NEA data for salaries of instructional staff are transformed into "calendar year" estimates not by adjusting for vacation arrangements but "by adding 8/12 of the salary for one school year, January through August, to 4/12 of the salary for the following school year, September through December" (National Educational Association, 1970a: 23). This was done to make instructional salaries comparable with earnings data of other occupations, which are usually reported for a calendar year.

Alternatively, we can measure the change over time in the ratio of teachers' salaries to per capita personal income. This is done in Table 9-5 for the period 1929–1975. Wide fluctuations are observed in the ratio (column 5), showing improvements in the economic positions of teachers between 1929 and 1940, followed by a sharp deterioration between 1940 and 1950. There was again considerable improvement between 1950 and 1960. The situation in 1970 was less favorable than in 1960, but some progress was made between 1970 and 1971. From then on the teaching profession appears to have lost ground, and in 1975 the economic position of teachers was similar to what it was in 1929.

In conclusion, although the economic position of teachers did improve from time to time, it does not appear that significant progress has been made in increasing teachers' salaries relative to wages paid in other sectors of the economy or personal income per capita. Whereas it is true that teachers' salaries increased faster than wages in private industry for the period 1950–1970, the reverse is true for the period 1970–1975. During the latter period, teachers' salaries rose only by 13.9 percent, compared to an increase of 37.2 percent for wages of all nonagricultural workers in private industry.[2] What

2. Data on private-industry wages are from *Economic Report of the President* (1978, Table B-36, p. 299).

Table 9-5. Economic Status of the Teaching Profession, 1929-1975.

Year	Average Teachers' Salaries (dollars) 1	Personal Income (billions of current dollars) 2	Total Population (thousands) 3	Personal Income Per Capita (dollars) (col. 2 ÷ col. 3) 4	Ratio of Average Salaries to Per Capital Income (col. 1 ÷ col. 4) 5
1929	1,420	84.9	121,767	697	2.04
1940	1,441	77.8	132,122	589	2.45
1950	3,010	226.1	152,271	1,485	2.03
1960	5,174	399.7	180,671	2,212	2.34
1970	8,840	801.3	204,878	3,911	2.26
1971	9,570	859.1	207,053	4,149	2.31
1972	10,100	942.5	208,846	4,512	2.24
1973	10,608	1,052.4	210,410	5,002	2.12
1974	11,188	1,153.3	211,901	5,443	2.06
1975	12,070	1,249.7	213,540	5,852	2.06

Sources: Column 1 from Table 9-2, column 1; columns 2 and 3, from *Economic Report of the President* (1977), pp. 207, 217.

the data imply is that teachers are receiving a shrinking share of national income.

The Single Salary Schedule

Kershaw and McKean (1962) point out that the single schedule is a relatively recent phenomenon. About fifty years ago, salaries were arbitrarily determined by school administrators, who exercised wide discretionary powers. The movement toward the single salary schedule was definitely "a step forward in its time" (p. 2). It eliminated the personal (and allegedly arbitrary) determination of salaries by the school administrator, leaving the judgment to be based upon a number of objective factors related to the teacher's training and experience.

The typical single salary schedule calls for a basic salary—the amount paid to teachers with no previous teaching experience but who completed an accredited program of training. Increments are then paid (1) to those whose training exceeds the minimum required for the basic salary and (2) to those who have a given number of years of previous experience.[3] The precise nature of the required minimum training and the exact method by which additional wages are paid for extra schooling and/or experience vary among school systems.

Recent studies by the National Education Association (1969) indicate that the majority of salary schedules for reporting schools (in 1969-1970) were not based on a ratio or an index (using the "base salary" as a base for such index or ratio). In all, 22.8 percent of the schools based their schedules on such a ratio or index, the overwhelming choice (20.6 percent out of 22.8 percent of all reporting schools) for the base being the minimum salary that a teacher possessing a B.A. degree receives.

A great deal of variation exists among school districts in the United States regarding (1) minimum and maximum salaries for each education-experience cell; (2) the highest level of teacher preparation recognized in the schedule; (3) the number of "steps" in the schedule (i.e., the number of salary increments for additional experience); and other criteria.

Salary schedules show some variations by enrollment and geographic region. As is shown in Table 9-6, minimum and maximum salaries in the very large districts (Stratum 1) are larger than for other districts. And although minimum and maximum salaries do not

---

3. Additional compensation is sometimes provided for specialized services (e.g. coaching) and administrative responsibilities.

Table 9-6. 1969-70 Mean Sscheduled Salaries for Classroom Teachers, by Preparation Level, and by Enrollment of Reporting Systems.

Preparation Level	Enrollment Stratum					
	1 *100,000 or more*	*2* *50,000– 99,999*	*3* *25,000– 49,999*	*4* *12,000– 24,999*	*5* *6,000– 11,999*	*Total* *1 thru 5*
Number of systems reporting	26	52	93	307	664	1,142
Bachelor's degree (or 4 years)						
Minimum	$ 6,874	$ 6,363	$ 6,408	$ 6,420	$ 6,344	$ 6,383
Maximum	10,549	9,398	9,263	9,313	9,204	9,278
Master's degree (or 5 years)						
Minimum	7,540	6,972	7,064	7,132	7,010	7,058
Maximum	11,821	10,676	10,651	10,853	10,624	10,717
Six years						
Minimum	8,094	7,415	7,587	7,805	7,625	7,673
Maximum	12,761	11,642	11,814	12,237	11,914	12,002
Doctor's degree (or 7 years)						
Minimum	8,411	7,762	7,879	8,175	8,074	8,070
Maximum	13,147	12,037	12,084	12,633	12,446	12,452

Source: Reproduced by permission from NEA Research Division, *Salary Schedules for Teachers, 1969–70*, Table 3, p. 8 (Copyright © 1969 by the National Education Association. All rights reserved.)

show an entirely consistent pattern by enrollment levels, salary schedules are generally higher in larger districts.

While salary differences between classes of educational preparation could amount to 26 percent (compare the minima for Bachelor's and Doctor's degrees) or more, substantial variation are allowed within each preparation level as a reward for experience. As may be observed from Table 9-7, the number and amount of increments vary greatly among school systems. In fact, the maximum annual increments for Bachelor's degree holders reported in Table 9-7 is almost equivalent to the mean salary increment due to obtaining the Master's degree (see Table 9-6). Such aspects of the single salary schedule raise interesting questions about the economic value of a year's experience versus increments in educational preparation.

The Merit Pay Controversy

There are a number of serious shortcomings in the single salary schedule. For example, it limits the powers of the administrators to reward extraordinary talent and service, and it does not differentiate between areas of teaching, such as physical education and mathematics. In consequence, teachers do not have an incentive

Table 9-7. Mean and Median Number and Amount of Increments in 1969-1970 Salary Schedules, by Teacher Preparation Level.

Teacher Preparation Level	Number of Increments	Amount of Increments
Bachelor's degree		
Mean	11	$268
Median	11	280
Range: Low	2	45
High	24	604
Master's degree		
Mean	13	296
Median	13	308
Range: Low	3	50
High	25	693
Six years		
Mean	13	335
Median	13	343
Range: Low	3	50
High	25	733
Doctor's degree (or 7 years)		
Mean	13	330
Median	13	336
Range: Low	3	50
High	25	733

Source: National Education Association (1969, Tables 11 and 12).

to select teaching curricula in "difficult" subject matters. To overcome these and other difficulties with the single schedule, a number of alternative schedules have been proposed in recent years.

The main feature of any alternative schedule is the nonautomatic advance in salaries, the latter taking various shapes and forms. In some states, mandatory merit ratings were legislated; in others, pressure by the National Education Association resulted in the abandonment of merit pay statutes. A study by the NEA (1961) for 1960–1961 showed that out of 701 school districts 30,000 or more in population, only 58, or 8.3 percent, "authorize or require that superior service be rewarded with higher salaries" (p. 63). The study also showed that more and more schools abandoned the merit pay system in favor of the single salary schedule. The main reason cited for dropping merit pay plans is that "no satisfactory plan had been developed for selecting the superior teachers. The corollary . . . was that the plans had created dissension. Words such as ill will, friction, resentment, misunderstanding, and suspicion were used in reporting the negative reactions of the staff" (p. 62).

An entirely different picture is given by Mathis (1959). Mathis conducted a study, using questionnaires, in which teachers in ten suburban schools, five with merit systems and five without, were asked to comment on (1) self, (2) school, (3) community, (4) administration, and (5) policy. The schools were selected in such a fashion that they were as homogeneous as possible in all respects but for the existence of a merit rating system. The study revealed that although morale varied within each group, no statistically significant differences in morale were found between the two groups.

A proposal to eliminate the chance of favoritism and arbitrariness in merit rating was made by Lieberman (1959). His plan calls for the establishment of a national board to which teachers could subscribe, at a certain cost. The board would conduct written examinations and on-site inspections of teachers, awarding special recognition to deserving teachers. This would create the elite of teachers who could command spectacular salaries. Additionally, the rating would be done at no cost to the school systems, and moreover, national recognition would enable the teacher to shift positions among schools with relative ease. Such a proposal, if ever carried out, might solve some of the problems mentioned above (such as permitting high-salaried teaching personnel) but would leave unresolved other difficulties with the present schedule. Further, as Benson (1978) points out, creating an elite teachers' corps might only accentuate the dissatisfaction by some parents whose children will be taught by the "inferior" teacher.

The Benson plan for creating a "career schedule for teachers" is also interesting.[4] Its major contribution is in recognizing the fact that teachers, like any group of workers, are not homogeneous. His plan calls for the ranking of teachers first as apprentices, then as "classroom teachers," followed by two types of "specialist teachers." The first group is composed of new, inexperienced individuals. They would receive training and serve as teachers' aides for three years. Those who "graduate" become classroom teachers. After four years of teaching (i.e., seven years of service), a classroom teacher will be entitled to a sabbatical year, with full salary. Following the sabbatical, some teachers would be elevated to Specialist Teacher I; others would remain classroom teachers. Those elevated to Specialist I could subsequently draw another sabbatical and be elevated to Specialist Teacher II (one of whose duties is to supervise the apprenticeships). Such a system will create different ranks in subcollege education, higher ranks implying higher salaries (other things equal). The main drawbacks of the system are that it is not at all clear how teachers are to be ranked, upon whose shoulders rests the burden of ranking the teachers, and how the salary differentials among the various "ranks" and within each rank should be determined.

A comprehensive survey of the merit pay controversy would require many more pages, but the general points of the argument have been presented. A summary of the controversy could be given as follows: although the single salary schedule eliminates the aspect of arbitrariness and personal judgment in the determination of teacher salaries, as well as reducing the potential element of discord among teachers, it creates an intolerable situation in which talent and ability go unrewarded—resulting in loss of the most capable teachers. Our impression is that most scholars would not quarrel with the desirability of merit rating—if a "workable" scheme could be found. What separates the proponents and opponents of merit rating is a value judgment concerning the workability of the merit-rating systems currently employed or proposed.

FACULTY SALARIES AND COMPENSATION IN HIGHER EDUCATION

Historical Summary

Thorough analyses of past data on salaries in higher education were conducted by Stigler (1950) and Ruml and Tickton (1955). A brief survey of their findings follows.

4. Benson's plan is a variant of the "differentiated teaching staff" approach that has been adopted by the Temple City, California, school system.

Stigler. Both gross and "real" salaries are given by Stigler for the period 1908–1942. The data are limited to median salaries of college teachers in large public institutions; but the data are probably representative of general trends of salaries in higher education during the period. Some of Stigler's data are presented in Table 9–8.

A number of interesting observations regarding Table 9–8 may be made. First, except for instructors, the relative position of the respective ranks has not changed much. For example, salaries of associate professors fluctuated between 73.6 and 77.6 percent of full professors' salaries. The respective percentages for assistant professors are 61.4 and 63.6. Second, although gross salaries increased substantially between 1908 and 1940, much of the increase was absorbed by rising prices. For example, while current salaries of full professors increased by 67.8 percent during 1914–1940, real salaries increased by only 19.1 percent. The greatest increase was for instructors: 92.2 and 36.4 percent for current and real salaries, respectively. It should be noted, however, that the fraction of full professors declined from 35.0 to 20.9 percent from 1905–1945 in universities in New York, so average faculty salaries in large public institutions increased modestly from $1,658 in 1908 to $2,892 in 1942. Real wages increased even less.

Further evidence by Stigler shows that during the period 1942–1949 average salaries in land grant colleges increased from $2,892 to $4,217. Real wages, however, declined from $2,617 to $2,460 (in 1935–1939 dollars).

As was mentioned in the section on elementary and secondary salaries, teachers' salaries—in all levels of education—must be adjusted for a variety of factors to account for the unique job conditions, salary structures, and so forth prevailing in education. In higher education, the need to make some adjustments appears even stronger than is the case in other levels of education. In the first place, many faculty members earn income from nonuniversity sources (consulting, royalties, etc.). Second, sabbatical leaves with full pay are quite common. Third, "a variety of prerequisites," such as free or reduced cost housing, are sometimes available to faculty members. Finally, miscellaneous items, such as free tuition for the faculty member's family, free health services, and the like must be taken into account.

Concerning trends of salaries in higher education, such adjustments are necessary only to the extent that the real value of these increased or decreased during the period. But no such data are produced by Stigler.

Table 9-8. Median Salaries of College Teachers in Large Public Institutions, Selected Years, 1908-1942.

Year	Current Dollars				Dollars of 1935-1939 Purchasing Power			
	Professor	Associate Professor	Assistant Professor	Instructor	Professor	Associate Professor	Assistant Professor	Instructor
1908	2,279	1,646	1,451	891	3,506	2,532	2,232	1,371
1910	2,417	1,737	1,438	924	3,873	2,784	2,305	1,481
1920	3,262	2,447	2,022	1,508	2,411	1,809	1,494	1,115
1930	4,407	3,345	2,775	1,995	3,589	2,724	2,260	1,625
1935	3,775	2,903	2,449	1,769	3,924	3,018	2,546	1,839
1940	4,245	3,272	2,605	1,937	4,262	3,285	2,615	1,945
1942	4,302	3,324	2,645	1,862	3,893	3,008	2,394	1,685

Source: Adapted from Stigler (1950), Table 28, p. 42.

Ruml and Tickton. Data on salaries in large state universities are given by Ruml and Tickton for the period 1904–1953. For professors, average annual salaries at current prices increased from $2,000 in 1904 to $7,000 in 1953. In "real" purchasing power, however, the average salaries declined from $2,000 to $1,956 (a reduction of 2 percent). The data show a great deal of fluctuation in average real salaries, reaching a low of $1,399 in 1919 and a high of $2,839 in 1932.

For associate professors the picture was less gloomy. Average salaries at current prices increased from $1,500 in 1904 to $5,600 in 1953, with real purchasing power rising from $1,500 to $1,596. Again, considerable fluctuation in real salaries is observed, with a low of $1,051 in 1920 and a high of $2,129 in 1932. For assistant professors, wages at current prices rose from $1,300 to $4,600, and real wages increased from $1,300 to $1,338 during the period. Again, the low was $868 in 1920 with a high of $1,764 in 1932.

The group of teachers who appear to have gained most during the period are instructors. Their average salaries rose from $800 to $3,700 in current prices and from $800 to $1,106 in constant prices during the period. The lowest wages (in real terms) were given at $612 in 1919, while the highest real wages were $1,265 in 1933.

In percentage terms, real wages for associate professors increased by 6 percent during the period, 3 percent for assistant professors, and 38 percent for instructors. During the same period, the real salaries of university presidents decreased by 2 percent.

Recent Data and Trends

Two main data sources are utilized in this section: (1) NEA's *Salaries in Higher Education* and (2) annual reports of the American Association of University Professors (AAUP). Each source utilizes different samples to derive its statistics; hence, identity of results should not be expected.

NEA Reports. Information pertaining to over 1,000 colleges and universities surveyed by the NEA is available concerning salaries of instructional staff and other personnel by rank, type of institution, geographical location, and other categories. A quick summary of the NEA data for recent years is given in Table 9-9.

From Table 9-9 it is observed that salary differentials among ranks in higher education have been increasing during the period 1961–1962 to 1975–1976. During most of the period, professors' salaries increased faster than those of associate professors, who in turn saw their salaries rise faster than those of assistant professors. The sala-

Table 9-9.   Median Salaries in Four-Year Institutions of Higher Education by Rank, 1961-1962 through 1975-1976. (in current dollars)

Academic Year	All Ranks	Professors	Associate Professors	Assistant Professors	Instructors and Lecturers
1961-62	$ 7,436	$10,256	$ 8,167	$ 6,900	$ 5,582
1963-64	8,163	11,312	8,969	7,539	6,114
1965-66	9,081	12,953	10,058	8,417	6,761
1967-68	10,235	14,713	11,393	9,472	7,496
1969-70	11,745	16,799	12,985	10,698	8,416
1971-72	12,932	18,091	13,958	11,511	9,347
1973-74	14,373	19,897	15,331	12,644	10,221
1975-76	16,313	22,218	17,142	14,069	11,418

Source: National Education Association (1970b), pp. 9-12 and 64-65; and Grant and Lind (1976), Tables 105, 106, p. 103.

ries of assistant professors have increased in approximately the same rate as the salaries of instructors and lecturers (combined).

Median salaries of instructional personnel in two year institutions are also given for the period 1955-1956 to 1975-1976. During the early part of the period, median salaries in nonpublic institutions increased far faster than in public institutions, but salaries were still higher in the public institutions. Also, during the period 1967-1968 to 1975-1976, median salaries increased faster in the public institutions.

Additional data are given on salary variation by region cross-classified by rank and type of institution, distribution of salaries of administrative personnel, and other factors.

AAUP Data. A wealth of data on salaries in higher education have been provided annually by the AAUP. Of particular interest are two elements in the statistics that add further dimensions to the analysis of salaries in higher education: (1) salaries are adjusted to take account of movements in the Consumer Price Index: (2) estimates of fringe benefits are added to base salary to calculate compensation defined by the sum of salary plus fringe benefits.

As Table 9-10 indicates, average salaries in thirty-six institutions have risen rather sharply between 1939 and 1968. The real value of the salaries increased by far less than current salaries, but it is obvious that considerable gains have been made by the profession (employed by those institutions).

Another method by which the change in faculty salaries may be viewed is by calculating an index of salaries and comparing it to an index of personal income per capita. An example of the procedure

Table 9-10.   Average Salary All Ranks Combined and Average Salary Adjusted for Changes in the Consumer Price Index for the Thirty-Six Biennial Survey Institutions in Selected Years from 1939-1940 to 1968-1969 (Nine-month basis).

| | For all Ranks Combined | |
Selected Years	Average Salary in Current Dollars	Average Salary in 1939 Prices
1939-1940	$ 3,800	$3,800
1949-1950	5,310	3,100
1959-1960	8,660	4,130
1965-1966	11,840	5,210
1968-1969	14,070	5,620

Source: Reproduced by permission from *AAUP Bulletin* (June 1969), Appendix Table 12, p. 214.

is presented in Table 9-11 for selected years during the period 1957-1958 through 1972-1973. Notice that whereas salaries increased faster than per capita personal income during the period 1957-1969, the reverse was true for the later period, 1969-1972. More recent reports by the AAUP (e.g., Dorfman et al., 1976, 1977) show a slowing of the progress in faculty salaries, with salaries increasing by a slightly smaller percentage than the price level. Also, Howard Bowen, in a recent report in *The Chronicle of Higher Education* (March 31, 1978), argues that faculty salaries since 1969 have increased by about 6 percent per year, whereas pay raises for other workers averaged 8 percent per year. The relative position of academic salaries appears to be declining.

Salaries and Compensation.   It is important to investigate the level both of salaries and of compensation. Since fringe benefits are typically excluded from personal income tax liability, a person's purchasing power would rise if a larger portion of his real income would be in the form of fringe benefits, provided that he would have bought these fringe benefits anyway. For example, if every academic employee would desire to purchase retirement annuities equal to, say, 6 percent of his total income, then an increase in compensation through a fully vested 6 percent retirement benefit would be superior to a 6 percent increase in wages. This argument would lead one to expect that professors should seek to improve their well-being not necessarily through wage increases but through increases in total compensation. The data reported in Table 9-12 strongly support this view. It is observed that average fringe benefits increased from

Table 9-11. Average Salary, Salary Index, and Personal Income Per Capita Index, Selected Years, 1957-1958 through 1972-1973.

Academic Year	Average Salary	Salary Index (1957 = 100)	Index of Per Capital Personal Income (1957 = 100)
1957-1958	$ 7,760	100.0	100.0
1959-1960	8,660	111.6	105.7
1969-1970	14,980	193.0	181.3
1972-1973	16,830	216.9	218.9

Source: Steiner et al. (1973), Appendix Table 28, p. 213.

Table 9-12. Average Salaries, Compensation, and Fringe Benefits in Higher Education, 1967-1977 (in current dollars).

Academic Year	Average Salary	Average Compensation	Average Fringe Benefits	Fringe Benefits as a Percent of Average Compensation
1966-1967	$10,449	$11,316	$ 867	7.7%
1968-1969	11,825	13,030	1,205	9.2
1969-1970	12,511	13,955	1,444	10.3
1971-1972	13,662	15,457	1,795	11.6
1973-1974	14,984	17,188	2,204	12.8
1975-1976	16,763	19,458	2,695	13.8
1976-1977	17,601	20,587	2,986	14.5

Source: Dorfman et al. (1977), Table 21, p. 172.

$867, or 7.7 percent of compensation, in 1967 to $2,986, or 14.5 percent of compensation, in 1977. It is interesting to note that this increase in fringe benefits (both absolute and relative to total compensation) has occurred during the same period when significant advances have been made in faculty unionization. Although the evidence in Table 9-12 is surely insufficient to relate our findings to the increase in collective-bargaining activity, it is well known that labor unions frequently sought more vigorously to improve fringe benefits than wages. (The effect of faculty unions will be discussed in the next section.)

Faculty Salaries by Rank, Sex, and Other Factors. The AAUP reports provide further classification of faculty salaries and compensation by rank, region, sex, control, and "quality" of institution. Table 9-13 provides data for 1976-1977 regarding faculty salaries cross-classified by rank, sex, and control. The first, obvious, observation is that salaries vary by rank, with full professors

Table 9-13.   Average Academic Year (Nine months) Salaries for Faculty in Higher Education by Rank, Sex, and Control, 1976–1977 (in thousands of current dollars).

Rank	All Combined		Public		Private Independent		Church-related	
	M	F	M	F	M	F	M	F
Professor	24.3	22.2	24.3	22.6	25.8	22.4	20.4	18.3
Associate	18.3	17.5	18.7	18.1	18.2	16.9	16.3	14.9
Assistant	15.1	14.4	15.4	14.8	14.8	13.9	13.9	12.9
Instructor	12.3	15.4	12.4	11.8	12.1	11.4	11.8	10.8
All ranks	19.0	15.4	19.2	15.7	19.9	15.0	16.4	13.3

Source: Dorfman et al. (1977), Tables 18 and 19, pp. 169, 170.

earning, on the average, about twice as much as instructors. Second, church-related institutions appear to pay the lowest salaries. Public and private-independent institutions pay approximately the same salaries, with the latter paying higher salaries to male professors, while the former pay higher average salaries in all other categories. Finally, males are paid uniformly more than females, an observation that has caused a great deal of anxiety among supporters of the "equal pay for equal work" doctrine.

Lester (1976) argues that these male-female differentials could be misleading, insofar as males could have different attributes than females (e.g., educational preparation, continuous years of service, research publications, etc.), and hence, that such data should not be published. Dorfman (1976) retorts that whereas he agrees that one should not draw conclusions from the data regarding the question of sex discrimination in academe, the AAUP does have the obligation to report such data. Additional analysis regarding the effect of sex on salaries is deferred to another section.

It should be noted that the distribution of faculty by rank is much different for men and women. Whereas 30 percent of males are full professors, only 7 percent of women hold this rank. The rank of associate professor is held by 28 percent of the men compared to only 21 percent for women. Women, therefore, represent a much larger fraction of the lower ranks: 41 percent of males are instructors or assistant professors, while 67 percent of females are in these ranks. These facts explain (in part) why average salaries for all ranks combined are so much lower for females.

Variations by region and "quality" of institution are illustrated by Table 9-14. The AAUP definition of institutional categories

Table 9-14. Faculty Salaries in Higher Education by Region and AAUP Institutional Category, 1976-1977 (thousands of current dollars).

Region	AAUP Institutional Category				
	I	*IIA*	*IIB*	*III*	*IV*
Pacific	21.6	19.3	15.9	20.1	20.0
Mountain	18.9	16.4	15.2	14.2	15.0
West North Central	19.3	16.1	14.2	12.6	14.1
East North Central	19.9	17.2	15.2	16.5	16.6
Middle Atlantic	21.0	19.4	16.0	17.5	12.7
New England	20.8	16.8	15.6	14.2	12.0
West South Central	18.4	15.8	13.7	14.1	13.5
East South Central	17.6	15.1	12.7	12.3	11.8
South Atlantic	18.7	15.7	14.3	14.7	13.2

Source: Dorfman et al. (1977), Table 8, p. 159.

Note:
Category I includes institutions that offer the doctorate degree and that conferred in the most recent three years an annual average of fifteen or more earned doctorates covering a minimum of three nonrelated disciplines.
Category IIA includes institutions awarding degrees above the baccalaureate but not included in Category I.
Category IIB includes institutions awarding only the baccalaureate or equivalent degree.
Category III includes two year institutions with academic ranks.
Category IV includes institutions without academic ranks. (With the exception of a few liberal arts colleges, this category includes mostly two year institutions.)

cannot be accepted as a reliable proxy for quality, but it does classify institutions according to their general mission as two-year institutions, mainly four-year institutions, and two types of institutions offering graduate programs. Since the latter usually require more distinguished faculty, it is not surprising that institutions in categories I and IIA generally pay higher salaries. We also note the substantial regional variations in salaries, with highest salaries generally found in the Pacific and Northeast regions, while lowest salaries are generally found in the South.

In higher education, unlike elementary and secondary education, we find some variations in academic salaries across disciplines. NSF data reported by the Commission on Human Resources (1976a) provide annual salaries of doctoral scientists employed by educational institutions, by field, for 1975. The data, reported in row 1 of Table 9-15, show that salaries in educational institutions do vary somewhat by field of employment. Also, 1970 NSF data reported by Johnson and Stafford (1974a) indicate similar findings.

Table 9-15. Median Annual Salaries[a] of Doctoral Scientists and Engineers in the United States, by Type of Employer and Field of Employment, 1975.

					Field of Employment				
Type of Employer	All Fields	Mathe- matics	Physics	Chemist	Earth	Engineer	Bio- science	Phychol- ogy	Social Science
All Employees	$23,126	$21,790	$23,641	$23,885	$23,382	$25,133	$22,164	$22,020	$21,992
1. Educational Institution	21,370	20,740	21,977	20,513	20,907	23,476	20,843	20,851	21,004
2. Federal Government	26,231	26,129	25,517	26,105	27,363	26,557	25,369	26,600	28,838
3. State/Local Government	20,839	—b	—b	18,650	19,750	19,933	20,860	21,524	22,412
4. Hospital/Clinic	21,797	—b	—b	21,041	—b	—b	24,058	21,357	—b
5. Other Nonprofit Organization	24,794	26,321	24,531	23,043	23,658	25,884	22,758	24,603	28,433
6. Business/Industry	25,999	24,482	25,969	25,762	26,239	25,957	25,559	30,577	29,329

Souce: Commission on Human Resources (1976a), Table 8B, p. 23.
[a]Medians were computed for full-time employed civilians only. Academic salaries were multiplied by 11/9 to adjust for a full-year scale.
[b]Medians have not been calculated for cells with less than 20 cases reported.

Comparison With Other Occupations

As noted earlier, comparisons of teachers' salaries with other occupations require a number of adjustments in teachers' salaries. To the extent that other occupations are reported on an annual basis, teachers' salaries should be converted into annual equivalents. Further, the value of sabbatical leaves, reduced tuition for relatives of faculty members, health services, low cost housing, and so on should, in principle, be computed.

Since college professors and public school teachers have a great deal in common, Stigler (1950) attempted a comparison of the salaries earned by these groups. He showed that the large salary differential in the early part of the period 1900–1940 narrowed considerably by 1950: whereas in 1910 the ratio of college teachers' salaries to public school teachers' salaries was 2.4, it decreased to 1.6 by 1930 and to 1.5 by 1940. This narrowing of differentials is attributed by Stigler to a combination of factors. First, the formal education requirements for public school teachers increased considerably during the period. Second, a "convergence of teaching levels" is asserted to have occurred. Third, investment theory may be used to explain the narrowing of salary differentials: if the rate of return on investment in a profession involving college or university teaching is greater than for public school teaching, a relative shift from public school to college teaching should be expected. Such shifts are expected to reduce the relative attractiveness of college teaching. Indicative of this argument is the fact that during the period investigated by Stigler, data show a doubling of the number of teachers in public schools compared to a fivefold change in the number of college teachers.

Stigler proceeded to compare salaries of college teachers to other professions: law, medicine, and dentistry. The comparisons are made after several adjustments were made in each of the series. Stigler concluded that "in sum, . . . the evidence for 1941 suggests that the net financial advantages of college teaching were not much inferior to the more prosperous independent professions." (p. 63).

The data reported by Ruml and Ticketon (1955) provide a further basis for comparison, although it seems hardly justified to compare salaries in higher education to salaries of railroad workers or of employees in other industries. Nevertheless, the data indicate that, in general, workers in industry realized greater real gains in wages than college teachers. On the other hand, college teachers have on the whole fared better during 1904–1953 than, say, high school principals.

Information collected by the National Science Foundation (NSF) and analyzed by Melichar (1965) could be used to shed additional light on this issue. An analysis of economists' salaries, as of 1964, shows that when salaries are based on academic year, economists employed by educational institutions earned salaries lower than the national geometric mean. Percentage differences ranged from –3 percent for persons with twenty-five or more years of professional experience to –35 for persons with one year of experience. When calendar year salaries are used, the differences are reduced, and for persons with twenty or more years of experience, the differential is positive. Further, individuals with similar experience employed by the federal government earned consistently more than those employed in educational institutions but substantially less than those employed by industry or business.

Further analysis of economists' salaries (and salaries in other professions), based on NSF data for 1966, is given by Tolles and Melichar (1968). The data for 1966 also include supplemental income (in addition to salaries). When salaries are considered, it is shown that teachers in institutions of higher education received compensation far lower than independent professionals; employees of business and industry, nonprofit organizations, and the federal government; and research or administrative workers in higher education. The relative economic position of teachers is improved when supplemental income is considered, since the data show supplemental income to be a much larger proportion of total salary for employees of educational institutions than for all other types of employers. It should be emphasized that these relationships are discerned by Melichar using multiple regression analysis—that is, analysis in which other factors, such as age, sex, academic degree, and other factors are held constant.

Similar conclusions are obtained when NSF (1968) data for 1968 are examined. Median salaries, for all fields, of persons in educational institutions—using calendar year salaries—are slightly higher than the median for all scientists (which, incidentally, includes those in educational institutions with academic year salaries), but are less than those for employees of the federal government, nonprofit organizations, and industry and business and the self-employed. Salaries are lower in "other government"—that is, state and local government—and in "other." These conclusions hold, with minor exceptions, when the data are examined for each profession separately.

1970 NSF data, examined by G.E. Johnson and Stafford (1974a) show that, in general, annual earnings in academe are lower than what they are in the same fields of employment either in government or in private business. For example, an economist with twenty-five years of experience was expected to earn $37,110 in 1970 if employed in business, in comparison to $26,390 in government and $25,900 in academe. In biology, the differences were much less, with respective salaries of $27,730, $24,010, and $24,470. Other fields fall between these extremes.

In Table 9-15 we reproduce a portion of the data reported by the Commission on Human Resources of the National Research Council for 1975. The data in Row 1 are not strictly for faculty in institutions of higher education; they include doctoral scientists and engineers in other educational institutions as well as in nonacademic positions. Nevertheless, the bulk of the data in Row 1 does represent academic salaries, and hence a useful comparison could be made with other types of employment. We note that, in general, noneducational employments pay higher median annual salaries—with the exception of state and local governments. Higher wages are paid to employees of the federal government in all disciplines. Employees of business and industry also receive higher compensation—sometimes higher than in the federal government. Academic employment appears to pay higher wages only relative to employees of state and local governments, with the exception of psychology and social sciences.

A study by Siegfried and Scott (1977), using survey data for 1975, provides a contrasting conclusion for academic lawyers. They show that law school professors have a higher expected rate of return (in terms of their lifetime earnings) than the average practicing lawyer. The only group of nonacademic lawyers that appears to have superior earnings is the top quartile of practicing lawyers. They conclude thus:

> While it is not surprising to observe that the typical law school professor earns more than what is earned by 75 percent of all professionals, it seems striking that *average* academic lawyers earn more than *average* practicing attorneys. The conventional folklore is that academics earn less than practicing attorneys, but they are compensated in the form of more desirable non-pecuniary aspects of their jobs and living environment. (PP. 20-21; italics in original)

We can also extend Stigler's comparison between salaries of classroom teachers and faculty in higher education, employing data reported earlier. As is shown in Table 9-16, the ratio of salaries in higher education to salaries in elementary and secondary schools decreased from 1.53 in 1967 to 1.42 in 1970 and decreased further to 1.39 by 1974. The ratio increased, however, to 1.41 in 1975–1976, perhaps as a result of the relative glut in the market for teachers. The main conclusion is that salaries in higher education have

Table 9-16. A Comparison of Salaries in Elementary and Secondary Schools to Salaries in Higher Education, 1967-1976

	Average Salaries (current dollars)		*Salary Ratio (2) ÷ (1)*
	Classroom Teachers	*Higher Education*	
Academic Year	*1*	*2*	*3*
1966-1967	6,830	10,449	1.53
1969-1970	8,840	12,511	1.42
1973-1974	10,778	14,984	1.39
1975-1976	12,524	17,601	1.41

Sources: Column 1 from Grant and Lind (1977), Table 55, p. 57; Column 2 from Dorfman et al. (1977), Table 21, p. 172.

moved in roughly equal proportions to salaries in elementary and secondary schools during the period 1970-1976.

Finally, we can use calculations performed by Dorfman et al. (1977) of compensation indexes for faculty and nonagricultural employees. The "adjusted" indexes are reported in Table 9-17, where the adjustment made was for the effect of inflation. It can be seen that faculty in higher education fared better than nonagricultural employees from 1967 to 1970, but since then, the reverse has been true. Moreover, faculty compensation in 1974 was lower than it was in 1973, and by 1975 the faculty compensation index was below the 1968 level. The profession did not catch up by 1977, although a very slight improvement is noticed between 1976 and 1977. In contrast, compensation of nonagricultural employees has never regressed back to the 1968 level, and significant improvements were made between 1976 and 1977. The conclusion, already discussed earlier, is that average faculty salaries and compensation have not kept up recently either with inflation or with the pace of change in wages and compensation of other workers.

DETERMINANTS OF TEACHERS' AND FACULTY SALARIES

The preceding sections provided data on historical levels of salaries in education and compared them to wages in other professions. Although we have indicated from time to time that wages in education vary by region, sex, educational preparation, and many other factors, we made no attempt to provide a rigorous model that would help explain variations in salaries among individuals, educational organizations, or larger political jurisdictions. Of particular interest to us is

Table 9-17. Indexes of Compensation of Higher Education Faculty and Non-agricultural Employees, Adjusted for Inflation, 1966-67 Through 1976-77 (Indexes: 1967-68 = 100)

Academic Year	Index of Compensation of Faculty	Index of Compensation of Nonagricultural Employee
1966-1967	96.4	98.1
1967-1968	100.0	100.0
1969-1970	103.4	102.1
1972-1973	107.8	108.8
1973-1974	103.2	107.2
1974-1975	98.7	104.5
1975-1976	97.9	104.8
1976-1977	98.3	106.7

Source: Dorfman et al. (1977), Table 21, p. 172.

the effect that collective bargaining may have on faculty salaries and compensation. Such inquiries are developed in this section.

Elementary and Secondary Schools

Since the vast majority of school districts employ the single salary schedule, salary variations among individuals employed by the same school districts can be explained in terms of one's educational preparation and years of teaching experience. Questions of discrimination by race, sex, and so forth would not arise. We find, however, considerable variation between school districts. Such variations occur because of differences in the salary schedules and because of differences in the attribute mix of teachers in different schools. It is possible, for example, that unionization affects the salary schedule. It is also possible that racial minorities are excluded from schools in which better salaries are paid and thus that some discrimination by race might be discerned. It is possible, too, that discrimination by sex is excercised through hiring and promotional policies, even though in each school district men and women are paid according to a uniform schedule. These and other potential determinants of teachers' salaries have been investigated in a number of empirical studies.

One of the first attempts to study the determinants of teachers' salaries was conducted by the present writer (Cohn, 1971a). The unit for the analysis was the school district, and 1961-1962 data for 375 Iowa school districts were utilized. The dependent variable (the one that we seek to explain) was median teachers' salaries, and independent (or explanatory) variables included school size, the number of college hours per teaching assignment, distance from the nearest central city, and teachers' salaries in the central city. Employing the technique of multiple regression, the only statistically significant variable was the number of college hours, although a negative coefficient for the distance factor was found, implying that salaries are likely to be lower in school districts that are located further away from a central city. Additional explanatory variables were available for a subsample of the Iowa data, including average educational level of the adult population in the school district's community, median family income, and percent of families with income over $10,000. Both the first and last factors were found to be significant, although an unexpected negative coefficient for years of school was found.

Another study, conducted by H.M. Levin (1970a, Table 3), examined data from the Coleman study for 2,921 teachers. Factors influencing salaries include the teachers' verbal score, sex, years of schooling, type of college from which teachers graduated, years of experience, certification level, and the teachers' major in college. Other things equal, females earned almost $400 less than males, each extra year of experience was worth about $79, and each extra year of schooling was associated with an extra $400 in salary. Also, higher wages were earned by teachers with higher levels of certification, verbal score, those with a nonacademic major, and teachers who were dissatisfied with the racial mix of their students. Lower salaries were earned by graduates of teachers' colleges.

Effect of Unionization. Most of the other studies on the determinants of teachers' salaries were motivated by the desire to study the effect of unionization (or collective bargaining) on teachers' salaries. The first of these is Kasper (1970), who employed a cross-sectional model of the fifty states for 1967–1968. It was argued that a state's average salary is a function of the following variables: per capita income in the state (I); extent of urbanization (U); "proportion of total educational revenue provided by local (R_l), state (R_s), and federal sources (R_f);" per pupil current expenditures (E); "the relative mix of elementary and secondary teachers (P);" a discrete (zero-one) variable for the western states (W); and "the extent of teacher organization (O)" (1974 rprt: 221).

The "extent of organization" variable was measured by the ratio of instructional personnel in the state who are represented in school negotiations to the total number of classroom teachers. Multiple regression analysis indicated that higher salaries were significantly associated with higher values of I, U, E, and W, whereas lower salaries were significantly associated with higher levels of R_s, U^2, and R_l. The effect of urbanization is described by an inverted U shaped curve, with higher levels of urbanization associated with higher salaries until a point is reached when the reverse is true. The organization variable (0) had a modestly positive but statistically insignificant coefficient. Although Kasper recognizes deficiencies in his model and, especially, in the use of statewide averages, his results show a very small effect of extent of organization on average teachers' salaries.

Since the use of state averages obscures variations by school districts, other studies have appeared in which the school district serves as the unit of observation. A study by Thornton (1971) employs 1969-1970 data for school districts in cities with 100,000 or more population in the U.S. Four salary variables are investigated: minimum and maximum for holders of Bachelor's degrees and minimum and maximum for teachers with Master's degrees. Statistically significant factors include a collective bargaining effect, district size, and average wage in the area. The effect of collective bargaining (measured by the presence of a collective bargaining contract) varies greatly for the four salary measures, varying from an addition of 2.3 to 28.8 percent to teachers' salaries.

A similar approach was followed by Lipskey and Drotning (1973), using data for 700 districts in New York State. They argue that the effect of unionism is more likely to be felt shortly after collective bargaining was allowed to take place. Hence, their data for 1968 were collected approximately one year following the passage of the Taylor Law, which made it legal for teachers (and other public employees) to bargain collectively in New York. They also examined four different types of salaries: (1) base salary, (2) Bachelor's plus thirty college hours with seven years of experience, (3) Bachelors plus sixty college hours with eleven years of experience, and (4) mean salary. In addition to a variable measuring the extent of collective bargaining, they found a number of significant variables, such as district size, percent of teachers with advanced degrees, percent of teachers with three or fewer years of experience, the pupil-teacher ratio, "true" property value per pupil, tax effort, and debt service per pupil.

The collective bargaining variable was measured by the presence of a bargaining contract. It is shown to have an insignificant effect when the entire sample is examined. When a subsample for "small towns" is examined, the effect is significant but very small (from 0 to 3 percent). On the other hand, collective bargaining appears to have had a rather strong effect on salary changes, with unionized districts experiencing an average gain of 15 percent greater than nonunionized districts.

A study by Hall and Carroll (1973) was confined to 118 elementary school districts in Cook County, Illinois (which includes Chicago), for the year 1968–1969. They developed a simultaneous equation model designed to study the effect of collective bargaining on both salaries and class size. Significant variables include median family income, percentage of white collar workers in the district, district size, average teacher experience, proportion of per pupil expenditures derived from state aid, and average class size (measured by the student-teacher ratio). The effect of unionization (measured by the existence of a collective bargaining agreement) was significantly positive, showing an increase in salary of $613—again only a modest effect, consistent with the results obtained by Kasper, Thornton, and others.

Somewhat more pessimistic conclusions are obtained in a study by Balfour (1974), who used a cross-section of the states. None of three measures of unionization produced any significant impact on salaries. On the other hand, J.H. Bowman and Mikesell (1976) did obtain a significant effect of collective bargaining in Indiana (as a result of the 1973 law that required mandatory collective bargaining).

The strongest effect of collective bargaining was found by J.G. Chambers (1975a, 1975b, 1976b, 1977). He argues that the studies utilizing district data are not likely to get a strong union effect because other, nonunionized districts in the same region would have to adopt similar salary policies if they are to avoid unionization—what is known as the "threat effect." There are, in effect, "spillovers" from one district to another in the same region. Chambers hypothesized that one would find a strong effect of unionization on regional variations in salaries, depending on the extent of union coverage in each region, assuming that the "spillovers" would not extend to other regions.

Data from California and Missouri were used to test these hypotheses. For California, a sample of thirty-nine elementary and fifty unified districts located in the largest SMSAs were drawn. The results indicate that, on the average, teachers' salaries were increased by 5.7 and 12.2 percent, respectively, in unified and elementary districts. Almost all of the union effect was due to the regional effect as hypothesized. When the regional effect is ignored, results are similar to those obtained by Kasper, Balfour, and others. Chambers claims that his results are comparable to what H.G. Lewis (1963) obtained for the effect of unions in private industry.

The Missouri study (J.G. Chambers, 1976a) was undertaken for the 1974–1975 school year with a sample of 2,470 full-time employed school teachers in districts within the five largest SMSAs. As in California, the existence of bargaining on the district level appeared to have a negligible effect on salaries, and the impact of bargaining was greater in regions where a larger percentage of the teachers were involved in collective bargaining. Interestingly, collective bargaining was illegal in Missouri, but it was practiced nevertheless. Other variables that affected salaries significantly include district size and teacher-pupil ratios.

Monopsony Effects. Another area of inquiry has been the effect of "monopsony" on teachers' salaries.[5] Standard economic theory would predict that wages would be lower in larger school districts where administrators are able to influence wages, other things being equal.

The first empirical study that attempted specifically to isolate the effect of monopsony is by Landon and Baird (1971). They employ Census of Government data on 136 schools with at least 25,000 pupils. Starting salaries are shown to be positively related to the logarithm of the number of districts in the county, indicating that as the number of districts in the county is increasing, the relative power of monopsony dwindles. Other variables used in the regression model include per capita income, percent of revenues from local sources, the effective property tax rate, and discrete ("dummy") variables to capture regional effects.

The "monopsony effect" is shown to exist for district sizes up to 100,000 pupils. The authors explain the lack of monopsony effect for larger districts in terms of concentration of power: since such districts have so much power in the area, the existence of other small districts will make little difference. They test this assertion by substituting a "concentration" variable (measured by the percentage of students in the SMSA enrolled in the large school) into the regression equation. The results show a negative effect of concentration—the higher the concentration, the lower are salaries expected to be.

Other studies dispute the Landon and Baird findings, among them Thornton (1975) and J.G. Chambers (1976a). in Chamber's study of Missouri, larger districts tended to pay higher wages than did smaller districts. Also, higher salaries were found by Hall and Carroll for schools with larger average daily attendance. The conflicting results are probably a combination of the following (as well as other) factors: (1) Different controls were applied in different studies for various effects on salaries. (2) Schools in different areas and in different time

5. A monopsony is said to exist when there is a single buyer of a given factor of production (such as teachers' services). When there are a few such buyers, they are said to have some monopsony power.

periods use their monopsony power to a varying degree; although large districts may have *potential* monopsony powers, they may not wish to exercise such powers. (3) The effect of unionization goes in the opposite direction to the monopsony effect. But the larger districts have typically been unionized first. Moreover, teacher unions in very large school districts have immense power (especially through a strike) that they have used to exert wages much higher than exist elsewhere (e.g., Chicago, New York, and Philadelphia). It is not surprising, therefore, that the monopsony effect may be fully offset by collective bargaining in the large school districts. In fact, this kind of effect and countereffect could explain why in many studies we get neither a strong union effect nor a monopsony effect.

Sex Discrimination: The H.M. Levin study (1970a) showed large male-female earnings differentials. Could they be attributed to sex discrimination? As De Tray and Greenberg (1977) illustrate, a positive answer does not follow from Levin's results. Using data for Michigan, they obtain significantly negative coefficients for female teachers, even though the nature of the salary structure in Michigan convinced them that it must be a spurious statistical result, due to model misspecification. Their conclusion is reinforced when 1971–1972 data for San Diego are employed. They begin with an equation including just three explanatory variables: female, years of service, and Master's degree. It is shown that females earned $188 less than males. When the variable measuring educational preparation (Master's degree) was changed into five categories, the coefficient of the female variable showed that females earned only $7 less than males. The authors believe that this $7 difference would also disappear if teaching experience would have been entered in a more complicated form than just years of service.

Conclusion. There is evidence that factors other than educational preparation and years of service affect variations in teachers' salaries. Interdistrict and interstate models have shown that collective bargaining does have some, though quite modest, effect on salaries, although the extent of the effect varies from study to study. The effect of monopsony appears to be significant, although we have, again, conflicting results. Other variables that appear to be statistically significant are related to the school environment such as per capita income, tax effort, district property valuation per pupil, and the like. Because the various studies differ so much in scope, data sources, and model specification, it is impossible to provide a general estimate of the magnitudes of such effects in the salary structure of elementary and secondary schools.

Institutions of Higher Education

Early Studies. Stigler (1950) provides data for men's and coeducational colleges in 1927 showing salary variation by rank, enrollment, and region. This writer employed multiple regression analysis to isolate the effect of each of these factors on faculty salaries.

The analysis of Stigler's data indicates the following: (1) Holding enrollment and region constant, successively higher salaries are associated with promotion to a higher rank—for example, the net difference between instructor and assistant professor was $698, between assistant professor and associate professor $482, and between associate professor and full professor $730. (2) Holding rank and region constant, higher enrollments are associated with higher salaries—for example, colleges with enrollments of 500–1,000 offered salaries $231 higher than in colleges with enrollments under 500, and colleges with enrollments of 1,000 and over offered salaries $591 higher than colleges with enrollments of 500–1,000. (3) Holding rank and enrollment constant, salaries in New England and the Middle Atlantic states were significantly higher than salaries in the South, Middle West, and West. No significant differences among the latter three regions were observed.

Recent Studies. More than a dozen studies have appeared during the last ten years that attempt to investigate the structure of faculty salaries. The great majority of them use the individual faculty member as the unit of observation and utilize either large-scale survey data or data confined to a specific university or a department within a university. Others use the institution as a unit of observation, and except for this writer's study (Cohn, 1973a), their main focus is the effect of collective bargaining. For purposes of comparison, we shall discuss studies according to their focus.

Studies Using Large Sample Surveys of Faculty. Probably the first study of its kind was published in a supplement to the *American Economic Review* by Melichar (1968) based upon NSF data for 1966. Factors affecting salaries include highest academic degree, sex, profession (economist, mathematician, etc.), work activity (teaching, research, administration), base for salary (academic versus calendar year), and age. These factors, considered simultaneously, may be used to predict individual faculty salary. Location, community and college size, and other factors were not included in the model.

Another study, using 1970 NSF data, was published by G.E. Johnson and Stafford (1974b; see also 1974a). Variables in the model include predegree experience (all respondents held the doctorate), postdegree experience, citizenship status, whether the individual attended a department ranked at the top ten, and a number of interaction terms between sex and other variables. The two experience variables were entered in a quadratic form, to test the hypothesis of diminishing returns to professional experience. The authors were particularly interested in the male-female earnings differences.

The authors conclude that both pre- and postdegree experience follow the pattern of diminishing returns (first increasing at a decreasing rate, then decreasing). Also citizens usually earn more than noncitizens (this is not true in anthropology and mathematics), and faculty earning a degree from the prestigious universities almost always receive higher salaries (the exception is biology). Finally, substantial male-female differences are observed: After the receipt of one's degree, the differences are smallest (between 4 to 11 percent, depending on field of employment); "the differential grows most rapidly over the years 5–15, the years when child care is most prevalent" (p. 895); beyond that, however, male-female differentials are likely to narrow. The authors argue that such differentials may be attributed either to "differences in acquired skill and productivity between men and women" or to sex discrimination (p. 901). Their calculations suggest that about two-fifths of the male-female differentials are due to sex discrimination (p. 902). While Strober and Quester (1977) argue that the "human capital" argument for male-female differences is incorrect and that all of such differences are due to pure discrimination, work by Farber (1977) shows a narrowing of the male-female differential over time, generally supporting the Johnson-Stafford conclusions. G.E. Johnson and Stafford (1977) reiterate their acceptance of the existence of some discrimination, but continue to argue that human capital factors account for a large portion of male-female salary differences.

Tuckman and Tuckman (1976) use a 1972 sample of full-time faculty derived from a survey conducted by the American Council on Education (ACE). Utilizing the technique of multiple regression, they show that substantial returns to publication of journal articles are reaped by professors, although the extra returns from the publication of an additional article diminish with the number of articles published. There are lower returns to publication of books (ignoring any nonsalary earnings). Higher salaries are earned by both males and blacks. They also find differential returns by field, the differentials corresponding to the opportunities foregone (by choosing a professorial position rather than other positions for which the individuals are qualified). They also find high returns to age and experience, although the returns to age peak around age forty-nine. Finally, there are high returns to professors who have held past or present administrative positions.

Additional analysis of ACE data is reported by Tuckman et al. (1977). They show, again, considerable male-female salary differences and, moreover, that such differences do not disappear over time. As in the Tuckman and Tuckman (1976) study, they, too, show large, but diminishing, returns to article production and lower returns to book publication. They also show substantial returns to faculty who are regarded as "excellent" teachers.

Studies Using Faculty Data for a Single Institution. In this category we find the majority of published studies in this area. One of these was the study by Katz (1973) of the salary structure in the University of Illinois as of 1969-1970. Multiple regression analysis produced the following significant results: There was a higher return to books than articles, but "excellent" articles resulted in more than a fivefold increment to salaries than other types of articles. Chairing a dissertation also resulted in a handsome benefit. Some returns to committee work and public service were also found, along with a return to experience. Professors holding doctorates earned almost $2,000 more than others, while administrators earned $2,557 more. Females earned $2,410 less than males, and professors on eleven-month appointments earned $1,184 more than those on nine-month appointments. (In all of these cases, other factors are held constant). The results also indicate salary differences by field and that faculty receiving their undergraduate degrees from less prestigious schools tend to receive lower salaries. An interesting negative conclusion is that salaries were not significantly influenced by the ranking of the faculty member in teacher ratings compiled from student votes.

A more modest attempt was published by Siegfried and White (1973), employing information on faculty members in the Economics Department at the University of Wisconsin (Madison) for the year 1971-1972. The multiple regression results show a very large return to administrative duties ($5,209), high returns to experience and publication of journal articles, no significant returns to publication of monographs, and modest returns to other publications. The coefficient for a variable measuring teaching excellence is quite large, but not highly significant. The authors conclue that the most effective strategy to increase one's salary is through publication of journal articles.

The salary structure for an undisclosed "large urban university" is reported by N. Gordon et al. (1974). Regressions were run separately for males, females, and all employees. Returns to age are positive for males up to age fifty-five and for females only up to age forty-five. Unlike results in a number of other studies, whites are paid more than blacks. And as may be expected, completion of higher degrees implies higher salaries, with MDs earning the highest wages. Relative to assistant professors, higher salaries are earned by associates and full professors and less by lecturers and a group of faculty called "teachers." Variations by field are also shown, with the lowest salaries in fine arts whereas the highest salaries are shown for medicine. The authors calculate an average sex differential of 9.5 percent, but show that this varies by age, seniority, race, education, rank, and department.

Hoffman (1976) argues that the male-female differential found by Gordon et al. (1974) is too low, because they ignored the indirect effect of rank discrimination against females. Using data from the University of Massachusetts, Hoffman shows that when rank is omitted from the equation, the male-female differences more than double. The Massachusetts study also shows that blacks are paid more than whites and that considerable salary differences exist among fields.

There are two questionable aspects of the Hoffman study. First, it is not obvious that differences in the promotion of male and female faculty are due to discrimination. Second, the author calculates the residuals (amount of salary not explained by the set of explanatory variables) for separate equations run for males and females and argues that "any resulting difference in male and female average salaries which is not explained by differences in average characteristics, when the same salary structure is used for both groups, is attributed to discrimination" (p. 198). Then she shows that sex discrimination is responsible for up to 68 percent of the male-female salary differential. This procedure is questionable, however, because it is likely that attributes not included in the model might greatly reduce the apparent male-female differences, and the Hoffman model surely did not include all of the relevant faculty attributes.

Koch and Chizmar (1976a, 1976b) examine the salary structure at Illinois State University for 1972-1973 and 1973-1974. Of particular interest is their attempt to isolate the impact of affirmative action on male-female salary differentials. They claim that such differentials were positive in 1972-1973, but as a result of affirmative action, the male-female differentials were no longer statistically significant in 1973-1974. As we argue elsewhere (Cohn, 1978), there are serious questions concerning the model, and therefore, such results are at best tentative.

Other variables that appear to affect salaries significantly include rank, teaching excellence, service to university, and years of experience. Some of the variables are significant only for the year 1972–1973, including scholarly production, market demand for discipline, and whether the professor has a Ph.D. degree. The results imply that salary increments between the two sample years reduced variations among faculty salaries that hitherto could be explained in terms of such variables as scholastic productivity, market demand in the respective profession, or educational background.

Finally, Traynham (1977) reports results of a multiple regression analysis of 1975–1976 salaries at the University of North Florida. The results indicate that, on the average, blacks earn $502 more than whites, females earn $514 less than males, holders of the Ph.D. degree earn $1,646 more, and chairpersons earn $2,621 more than other faculty. Positive returns are shown for both academic and non-academic experience, plus a very modest return to publications. Considerable variations by field are apparent. As the author points out, the coefficients for race and sex were not statistically significant.

An Interinstitutional Study. This writer (Cohn, 1973a) employed 1970–1971 AAUP data (along with other information) to study the variations in faculty salaries and compensation between institutions of higher education. A sample of 204 four-year institutions was assembled for which all the desired information was available. Multiple regression analysis was employed to study the effect of a number of variables on faculty salaries and compensation for all ranks combined and by rank.

A common belief is that institutions classified as "universities" pay higher salaries than those classified as "colleges." Our analysis shows this to be not true. Also, although salaries in private, independent schools are generally higher than in public or church-related schools, the coefficients for the separate ranks are generally not statistically significant. Church-related schools are shown to pay generally lower salaries.

The "quality" of the institution does have significant effect on salaries. Variables that attempt to measure the elusive "quality" dimension include number of merit scholars in residence, percent of students pursuing professional or graduate studies following graduation, student-faculty ratio, and the AAUP classification (see Table 9-14, note).

The relationship between school size (measured by enrollment) and salaries is given by an inverted U curve: As enrollments increase up to approximately 30,000, so do salaries, though at a diminishing rate; beyond that point, average salaries appear to decline. Also, it was found that institutions of higher education located in states with higher per capita income are likely to pay higher faculty salaries.

A noteworthy aspect of the study is that different sets of variables are significant in the salary and compensation regressions. This suggests that the process of salary determination may be somewhat different from that of compensation.

Effect of Collective Bargaining.[6] A deficiency of the preceding study is the omission of a variable designed to isolate the effect of unionization (or collective bargaining). Prior to 1965, this would not have been a problem, since academic unions were virtually nonexistent. Unionism has increased, however, since 1965, so that by 1977 approximately 12 percent of all professional staff and over 20 percent of all full-time teaching faculty are now represented.

Faculty unions are found mainly in public colleges and universities, although there does exist a small but growing component in four year private schools. The strength of these unions can be traced directly to the type of union security agreement that is present. Union shop agreements are almost nonexistent, and even the agency shop is rare.[7] The absence of strong security agreements results in a weakening of the bargaining position of the individuals involved. In addition, fewer than 10 percent of the contracts contain any kind of union security clause, except for a dues checkoff, which exists in approximately 60 percent of the contracts negotiated (Virgo, 1977a).

One of the foremost considerations made when voting on unionization at a particular university is the composition of the bargaining unit. The type of people represented will have an effect not only on government and decisionmaking for the college, but also on the nature of collective bargaining itself. As a rule, the appropriate bargaining units are determined on the basis of the similarity of skills, working conditions, wages, bargaining history, duties, and the employees' wishes accruing to their professional status.

Three important variables are believed to have promoted collective bargaining on university campuses. First, as shown earlier, there has been a steady erosion of the real wages of faculty members in recent years. This fact, coupled with changing market conditions, due, in part, to a relative abundance of young Ph.D.s seeking academic positions, has resulted in less job security for professors. Whereas previ-

6. Margaret M. Capen assisted in the preparation of this section.

7. In union shop, all employees must join the union after a specified period of employment has elapsed. In the agency shop, employees do not have to join the union, but they must pay union dues (see Marshall, Cartter, and King, 1976, ch. 15, esp. pp. 398–403).

ously a professor could move if he was unsatisfied with his job, intense competition for existing jobs has greatly reduced the force of this option. Second, the increasing size of most universities has forced centralization, which has tended to remove the faculty member from a position where he was able to provide input into major decisions. Finally, exogenous forces such as the passage of legislation favorable to collective bargaining on campuses has made it easier to join unions by reducing the psychological and sociological barriers that previously existed.

The main bargaining agents for higher education faculty are the American Association of University Professors (AAUP), the National Education Association (NEA), and the AFT (American Federation of Teachers), affiliated with the AFL-CIO. As of 1975, thirty-four institutions were represented by the AAUP, twenty-nine by the NEA, twenty by the AFT, seven New York institutions (including the gigantic City University of New York, with eighteen campuses; and State University of New York, with twenty-four campuses) jointly by the AFT and NEA, and ten by independent bargaining agents. Due to its success in organizing multicampus systems, the NEA is probably the most successful bargaining agent at present.

Although there is a growing interest in the need to ascertain the impact of unionism, relatively few studies of faculty compensation in unionized institutions of higher education have been undertaken. Robert Birnbaum (1974), in one of the first of such studies, matched eighty-eight union with eighty-eight nonunion institutions. He found that the unionized institutions had a higher average salary of $777, with the largest differences occurring in four year public colleges, where the increase was about $1,200 greater than the salaries of faculty at comparable nonunion institutions. He did not control, however, for other determinants of faculty salaries.

An effort by William W. Brown and Courtenay C. Stone (1977) resulted in a less positive conclusion concerning the effects of collective bargaining. Unlike Birnbaum, the authors restricted their analysis to four year institutions whose faculty were covered by collective bargaining contracts. Comparisons of promotion and tenure rates as well as salary and compensation growth rates of faculty with those of national and regional averages failed to reveal any significant impact associated with the initiation of collective bargaining. Although their data did reveal net growth rates for salary in the upper ranks that was statistically significant, further analysis indicated that the gains observed in the upper rank salaries were not widespread, but were mainly accounted for by five Pennsylvania campuses that had several "unique" characteristics. In addition, growth in promotions to higher faculty ranks "occurred at an average rate slightly but not significantly greater" in colleges with collective bargaining agreements than would be implied by nationwide rates of promotion (p. 392). Again, the authors do not control for other factors.

Following Birnbaum, David Morgan and Richard Kearney (1977) matched forty-six union and nonunion college institutions in an attempt to estimate the levels of and changes in faculty compensation for the period 1969-1970 to 1974-1975. Multiple regression analysis was employed to control for certain variables such as per capita personal income, institutional control, and institutional "quality," measured by the Gourman index. Although they did not examine salaries by rank, they did divide their sample into three institutional categories. The authors concluded that faculties that were covered by collective bargaining had an average $265 differential over unorganized institutions. In addition, unionized faculty members were found to receive greater monetary fringe benefits as well. When change in compensation (1974-1975) was used as the dependent variable, the union-nonunion variable had the strongest effect in the equation. The authors argue that continued growth of collective bargaining is virtually certain, but that the long-run salary and compensation effect of academic unions cannot yet be determined.

In an extension of Morgan and Kearney's model, Larry Leslie and Teh-wei Hu (1977) focused on selected financial implications of collective bargaining. Using the sampling methods of Birnbaum, matched samples were obtained for 150 four and two year institutions. Two dependent variables were investigated: (1) faculty compensation and (2) institutional financial data obtained from the Higher Education General Information Survey files. The study used 1975-1976 average compensation data and compared the change in compensation that occurred during 1974-1975 and 1975-1976. Also, faculty compensation by rank was analyzed separately. The findings were as follows: (1) Average faculty compensation in unionized institutions during 1974-1975 was approximately $1,291 more than in nonunion institutions, controlling for other factors. This difference decreased, however, to around $800 in 1975-1976. This result would suggest that the effects of unionization on compensation may be more pronounced in the short run than in the long run. (2) the results also showed substantially higher benefits to senior faculty (full and associate professors) among unionized colleges and very low benefits to junior faculty (assistant professors and instructors).

Other variables affecting compensation include institutional control (public versus private), per capita income, institutional quality, and percent of faculty holding a doctorate degree. In addition, the authors find that type of union affiliation (AAUP versus NEA-AFT) could also affect the level of compensation, with the more aggressive NEA-AFT unions generally providing higher benefits than the AAUP unions.

Conclusion. Although studies on the effect of unionization provide conflicting results, we find a number of consistent patterns in the determinants of faculty salaries. Rank, sex, race, and control are almost always significant, with blacks typically earning more and women less. Private, independent schools usually pay higher wages than either public or church-related schools, and (on the average) faculty in higher ranks are always paid higher salaries than those in the junior ranks. Other things being equal, the breadth of degrees offered by universities and the quality of their students, faculty, and programs appear to be related to higher salaries. Productive attributes of faculty members provide some return, but the magnitudes of the returns vary between as well as within universities. Finally, variations by field are found to exist, and salaries are related to the economic environment of the state where colleges and universities are located.

A PRODUCTION FUNCTION APPROACH TO SALARY EVALUATION[8]

As noted earlier, the utilization of the single salary schedule is likely to lead to a number of undesirable results. At the same time, no operational alternative has so far been advanced. The analysis of this section is geared to answering the following questions:

1. Which teacher attributes should be considered when a salary schedule is formulated?
2. To what extent should individual salaries be adjusted according to the level of such attributes observed in the teacher?

The Educational Production Function

Our discussion of the preceding chapter concerning the educational production function may be used in answering the questions posed above. For the limited purposes of this discussion, it will be assumed that the set of outputs may be measured by a composite output index, Q, and that the set of inputs include the following: (1) teacher

8. This section is based on Cohn, "Methods of Teachers' Remuneration: Some Empirical and Theoretical Considerations," *1970 Business and Economic Statistics Section Proceedings of the American Statistical Association* (copyright © 1971 by the American Statistical Association), pp. 452–57.

inputs, t_1, t_2, . . . , t_h (h factors); (2) other (nonteacher) school inputs, v_1, v_2, . . . , v_m (m factors); and (3) student-related inputs s_1, s_2, . . . , s_n (n factors). In addition, it is assumed that the production function is linear, that is:

$$Q = \sum_{i=1}^{h} a_i t_i + \sum_{j=1}^{m} b_j v_j + \sum_{k=1}^{n} c_k s_k, \qquad (9.1)$$

where the coefficients a_i ($i = 1, . . . , h$), $b_j (j = 1, . . . , m)$, and c_k ($k = 1, . . . , n$) are constants to be estimated by least squares multiple regression analysis.

Teacher Characteristics

We have specified in the production function a separate set of teacher inputs or teacher characteristics. These include such factors as experience, education, verbal facility, and other measures of innate teaching ability, extracurricular activities, and so forth. Given a specific form of the educational production function, it is possible to estimate the effect of each of these factors on school outcomes. If the output, Q, is the variable that the school administration is striving to maximize, it follows that those characteristics that are shown to be conducive to the educational outcome should be rewarded accordingly. To illustrate, consider the teacher characteristics in Table 9–18. Each of these characteristics might be measured in standard units. For example, a "unit" of educational attainment might be fifteen semester hours beyond the highest degree, years of experience might be measured by the number of years the teacher has been with the present school system, and so forth

Suppose that the educational production function is given by Equation (9.1) and that the teacher inputs are given by Table 9–18. Further, assume that Q is a measure of achievement per student, measuring achievement in terms of equivalent years of schooling per pupil. Using whatever data might be available (such as a cross-section of students or schools in a state, region, or the nation as a whole), the coefficients in Equation (9.1) can be estimated using the statistical technique of multiple regression. Suppose that the partial regression coefficients for the five teacher variables are estimated as in Table 9–19.

The coefficients in Table 9–19 are purely hypothetical. They indicate that, other things equal: (1) an increase of one unit of educational attainment is associated with an increase on one-tenth of a

Table 9-18. Teacher Characteristics—An Example.

Variable	Characteristic
t_1	Educational attainment
t_2	Years of experience
t_3	Verbal facility
t_4	Extracurricular activity
t_5	Administrative responsibility

Table 9-19. Marginal Productivities of Teacher Characteristics—A Hypothetical Example.

Variable	Coefficient	Estimated value of coefficient
Educational attainment	a_1	0.10
Years of experience	a_2	0.05
Verbal facility	a_3	0.01
Extracurricular activity	a_4	0.02
Administrative responsibility	a_5	0.25

year of achievement per pupil; (2) an additional year of experience is associated with one-twentieth of a year of achievement; (3) one unit increase in verbal facility is associated with one-hundredth of a year of achievement; (4) one extra unit of extracurricular activity is associated with one-fiftieth of a year of achievement; and (5) one additional unit of administrative responsibility is associated with one-fourth of a year of achievement.

The coefficients provide the necessary weights for determining the reward associated with different teacher characteristics. Once it is determined how much any one factor listed in Table 9-18 should get for each additional unit of that factor, the determination for the remainder follows directly from Table 9-19. For example, if it is agreed that one year of additional experience is worth \$200, it follows that an additional unit of education is worth \$400, an additional unit of verbal facility, \$40, an additional unit of extracurricular activity, \$80, and an extra unit of administrative responsibility, \$1,000.

Our production function approach could be used to determine the dollar value of teacher characteristics even when no information is available regarding the proper value of a unit of any one of the teacher characteristics (experience, in the above illustration). In order to accomplish this, we need some information on the money value of a unit of achievement. Suppose that one extra unit of Q is worth X dollars; then the average value of an extra unit of t_i is Xa_i. Let the average salary be denoted by $\bar{S}$, individual salary by S_j (assuming there are N teachers: $j = 1, 2, \ldots, N$), so that t_{ij} represents the ith teacher characteristic of individual teacher j. Also, the average value of each factor, $t_{i\cdot}$, is given by:

$$t_{i\cdot} = \frac{\displaystyle\sum_{j=1}^{N} t_{ij}}{N}.$$

Then individual salary is given by:

$$S_j = \bar{S} + X[a_1(t_{1j} - t_{1\cdot}) + a_2(t_{2j} - t_{2\cdot}) + \ldots + a_5(t_{5j} - t_{5\cdot})] . (9.2)$$

The critical aspect of the approach is the estimation of X (the value of an extra unit of the output, Q). A plausible solution is to rely on recent studies on the economic value of education, as discussed in Chapters 3 and 6. Additional lifetime incomes due to education (properly discounted) have been calculated by ability level, years of education completed, geographic region, and other pertinent variables. When such data are used to estimate X, caution must be exercised to recognize (1) difficulties in obtaining reliable measures of income strictly due to education; (2) that the model presented here is imperfect, due to the fact that researchers have so far been unable to obtain reliable educational production functions; and (3) that the monetary value of education may seriously understate the social value of education. In any event, the procedure presented here may be used to suggest what relative salary differentials should be, on the basis of observed teacher characteristics, even if one is reluctant to go as far as suggesting absolute salary differentials on the basis of this model.

One principal difference between this approach and other merit pay proposals is that this approach establishes salary differences on the basis of observed differences in teacher characteristics, not on judgements regarding the teacher's behavior in the classroom. Questions of favoritism or lack of sufficiently sensitive instruments to properly measure "successful" classroom behavior would not arise. On the other hand, our model does not take into account variations among teachers who possess identical objective characteristics.

Another important feature of the model is the employment of a production function to ascertain the impact of teachers' inputs on educational output. The strength of the approach depends critically on the strength of the production function employed, and despite advances made in the production function domain in recent years, we are not yet ready to embrace the approach without reservation.

Finally, a similar approach has been proposed by this writer (1971d) to determine faculty salaries in institutions of higher education.

SUMMARY AND CONCLUSIONS

A number of interesting hypotheses were examined in this chapter. Of particular importance is the delineation of the structure of teachers' salaries, since the nature of the salary structure is likely to affect the movement of human and other resources into or out of education. The incentives embedded in the structure will surely determine, to some extent, the quality and types of teachers that the educational system will be able to recruit, as well as the effort and ingenuity that will be induced from those who choose education as a career.

Based on the data presented in this chapter, a number of observations may be briefly mentioned. We saw that the rise in the purchasing value of teachers' salaries has lagged behind the rise in money wages and, further, that the purchasing power of teachers at all levels has decreased in recent years. Also, teachers' salaries continue to lag behind salaries in the federal government, industry, and other areas.

It has been mentioned that comparison of teachers' salaries with other occupations necessitates numerous adjustments in the former. Longer vacations, outside earnings, fringe benefits, pleasant job conditions, and psychic income may be mentioned. Taking such factors into consideration will result in a much more favorable comparison between teachers' salaries and salaries in numerous other occupations.

An examination of the determinants of teachers' salaries at the elementary and secondary levels indicates that factors other than teaching experience and educational preparation account for interdistrict salary differentials. Collective bargaining is shown to have only a modest effect in most studies, although it is possible that the more substantial effects found by J.G. Chambers (1975a, 1975b, 1976b) are more accurate. Other factors influencing salaries include verbal facility of teachers, school size, district property value, tax effort, and other school and nonschool factors.

In higher education, we find conflicting evidence on the effect of collective bargaining. Even those studies showing a positive effect, however, indicate only a modest increase in wages as a result of unionization. Variables affecting individual salaries and compensation in institutions of higher education include rank, experience, sex, race, highest degree held, research publications, administrative responsibilities, field of employment, and in some cases, supervision of dissertations and teaching effectiveness. Variables affecting interinstitutional differences in salaries include control of institution, "quality" of institution, region, socioeconomic conditions in the area where the institution is located, and school size.

We have argued that a more rational teacher salary schedule should take into account teachers' productivity. Schedules in which salaries are arbitrarily set on the basis of such factors as educational background and seniority are likely to result in significant misuse of resources, as shown by Hanushek (1971). The proposed schedule, based upon the educational production function, offers a hope to alleviate this problem. But considerable experimentation and improvements in our ability to measure teachers' productivity—in all levels of education—should precede general utilization of the proposed scheme.

LITERATURE GUIDE

Elementary and Secondary Schools
Historical data are provided in various publications of the National Education Association (1969, 1970a, 1972, 1975), Kershaw and McKean (1962), Ruml and Tickton (1955), Stigler (1950), and in publications of the U.S. Office of Education (e.g., the *Biennial Surveys* and the *Digest*).

Discussion of the single salary schedule and the merit pay controversy may be found in Benson (1978: 235-46), Cohn (1971a, 1973b), Lieberman (1959), Mathis (1959), and National Educational Association (1961).

The effect of collective bargaining and other factors are discussed in Baird and Landon (1972, 1975), Balfour (1974), Cohn (1971a), Hall and Carroll (1973), J.G. Chambers (1975a, 1975b, 1976b, 1977), Kasper (1970, 1972), Landon and Baird (1971), H.M. Levin (1970a), Lipsky and Drotning (1973), G.A. Moore (1974), Pellegrino (1976), Rehmus and Wilner (1968), Thornton (1971, 1975), D.P. Wagner (1975), DeTray and Greenberg (1977), and Greenberg and McCall (1974a, 1974b).

Higher Education
Salary data may be found in the annual report of Committee Z of the AAUP, published each year in the summer issue of the *AAUP Bulletin*. Other sources of data include publications of the National

Science Foundation—for example, Commission on Human Resources (1976a, 1976b)—and the *Biennial Surveys* and *Digest* published by the U.S. Office of Education. Some historical data are also found in Ruml and Tickton (1955), Stigler (1950), and National Education Association (1970b).

Further discussion of such data and comparative analyses of faculty salaries may be found in Dorfman et al. (1976), Hendon (1969), G.E. Johnson and Stafford (1974a), Metcalf (1970), B. Rosenberg (1977), Siegfried and Scott (1977), Steiner et al. (1971, 1973), and Tolles and Melichar (1968).

The structure of faculty salaries—including the effects of collective bargaining or sex discrimination—is discussed in Bayer and Astin (1968), W.E. Becker (1975), Brown and Stone (1977), Cohn (1973a, 1978), Dorfman (1976), Farber (1977), N. Gordon, Morton, and Braden (1974), Hamovitch and Morgenstern (1975), Hoffman (1975, 1976), G.E. Johnson and Stafford (1974a, 1974b, 1977), Katz (1973), Koch and Chizmar (1976a, 1976b), Leslie and Hu (1977), Lester (1976), Melichar (1965, 1968), D.R. Morgan and Kearney (1977), Siegfried and White (1973), Traynham (1977), Tuckman and Tuckman (1976), and Tuckman, Gapinski, and Hageman (1977).

Miscellaneous

Other relevant readings include S.P. Smith (1976, 1977) on the structure of wages in the public sector; Cheng (1976), Garbarino (1975), Garbarino and Aussieker (1974), Cypert (1975), McLennan and Moskow (1970), and Virgo (1977a, 1977b) on the process of collective bargaining in education; Holtmann (1969) on the benefits of search; and Turnbull and Williams (1975) on teacher salaries in the United Kingdom. Studies showing the effect on wages of collective bargaining in other occupations include Ashefelter (1971), Ehrenberg (1973b), H.G. Lewis (1963), and Oaxaca (1975).

✳ *Chapter 10*

Financing Education

The expense of the institutions for education . . . may, . . . without injustice, be defrayed by the general contribution of the whole society. This expense, however, might perhaps with equal propriety, and even with some advantage, be defrayed altogether by those who receive the immediate benefit of such education and institution . . . .
Adam Smith, *The Wealth of Nations*

The wisdom of expending public and private funds on education is not to be measured by its direct fruits alone. It will be profitable as a mere investment, to give the masses of the people much greater opportunities than they can avail themselves of . . . .
Alfred Marshall, *Principles of Economics*

Schools and universities ought . . . to be made "a Publick Charge" so that the really able might be selected as scholars rather than let the "fond conceits" of privileged parents flood the schools and colleges with dullards.
Sir William Petty (Seventeenth Century)

There seems to be no special inevitability about the continuance of the present type of government role in education . . . . The proposal . . . that "social cohesion" is *the* sufficient condition for state-provided schooling is unsupported by the evidence.
E.G. West, *Education and the State*

Educational finance is probably the most controversial issue in the economics of education. There is disagreement not only on whether government should have any role in education, but also, for those (by far the majority) who agree that some role should be played by government, what role the government should take. Should the state provide subsidies, or should the state operate schools? If subsidization is desired, should the subsidies be paid to individuals or to institutions? Should subsidies be given as cash payments, subsidized loans, or perhaps in the form of a tax deduction or credits? Moreover, in a federal system, what roles, if any, should be played by local, state, and federal levels of government?

These and other questions are pondered in this chapter. After a discussion of the role of government in education, separate sections will be devoted to analyses of educational finance in (1) elementary and secondary schools and (2) institutions of higher learning. A brief discussion of the voucher plan is followed by a brief summary and an extensive literature guide.

THE ROLE OF GOVERNMENT IN EDUCATION

E.G. West (1970a) provides an in-depth examination of various reasons suggested by economists and others for an active government role in education. They include (1) state protection of minors, (2) the "neighborhood" or externality effect, (3) the role of education in making democracy work, (4) equality of opportunity, (5) the quest for "common values," and (6) the effect of education on economic growth.

Protection of Minors

Primary and secondary education largely involve children under eighteen years of age. As minors, children are not considered capable of making decisions for themselves. In the absence of a government role in education, parents are charged with decisionmaking regarding their children's education. The question posed is whether parents are sufficiently competent to make the "right" decision. What of a parent who has a bright child but decides to give him inferior education? Should the state intervene in the child's behalf and insure him an "adequate" upbringing? Arguments in favor of state intervention have been cast in terms of the Fourteenth Amendment to the United States Constitution, which requires that the state should not "deny to any person within its jurisdiction the equal protection of the laws," although the Supreme Court of the United States has held that the Fourteenth Amendment is not relevant in determining government's role in education.

The principal point of contention is whether parents should have the right to exercise free choice when it comes to their children's education. Compulsory attendance laws, now in force in most countries (and in all of the United States except for Mississippi, where such a law has recently been repealed), express the belief that parents should not have a free choice in the matter. There is a further reinforcement of the idea in the "uniform education clause" that appears in most state constitutions in the United States and requires the state to provide "uniform" education to all children.

Opponents of the protection of minors argument contend that if parents are not qualified to judge about their children's education, then they are also not qualified to judge about many other aspects of child rearing, such as proper nutrition, inculcation of religious beliefs, sanitation, and other psychological and physical aspects of the children's environment. Stretching the argument to its logical limit would require the state to remove children from parental custody to be raised by the state. Short of such a drastic action, why is it education that needs to be singled out?

Dismissing the argument against protection of minors does not preclude the role of government in providing subsidies to influence parental decisions. But one must look elsewhere for a justification for such subsidies.

External (or Neighborhood) Effects

Some space has already been devoted to this topic in preceding chapters. We have discussed the contention that positive external effects are associated with the acquisition of education. The main argument is that if such external effects exist, then a private market system in education will result in the production of less education than is socially desirable. Some public actions, in the form of either subsidies or direct provision by government, are then required.

The problem with the externality arguments is that, to date, no convincing empirical evidence has been brought to bear on the existence of such externalities, much less on their magnitudes. As West (1970a) points out, there are externalities associated with virtually every economic activity, yet few would suggest subsidization or nationalization of such activities.

The appeal of the externality argument cannot be dismissed very easily. There are some data to indicate, and, moreover, it is commonly believed, that education and crime are inversely related. It is also widely asserted, even if without adequate proof, that elementary and secondary education, especially training for basic literacy, provide social benefits far greater than those perceived by individuals. Given that compulsory attendance laws are in force, the policy implications of the externality argument are minimized. For higher education, however, government support is frequently justified (either implicitly or explicitly) in terms of external effects, and it is in this area of educational finance where evidence on the existence and magnitude of externalities is badly needed.

Education and Democracy

A variant of the externality argument, the "education for democracy" proposition, asserts that stable democracy cannot coexist with illiteracy. Moreover, higher education provides the leadership for a democratic society, and liberal arts education provides a broad understanding of various aspects of the sciences, literature, and arts that help in molding "well-rounded" people who are more likely to strive for the survival of democracy. Government provision and/or support of (especially liberal arts) education is therefore regarded as a means to perpetuate and strengthen democracy.

West (1970a) questions the validity of the assumption (implicit in the argument) that government interference will result in increased educational investment. Moreover, the validity of the assertion that literacy and further education are useful "in promoting political and economic communication" (p. 41) also must be examined. Furthermore, even if both assumptions are valid, it does not necessarily follow that government should provide education. Subsidization might accomplish the task more efficiently.

Equality of Opportunity

The banner of "equality of opportunity" has been raised in the United States to justify free and compulsory education at the K–12 level and free or subsidized education at higher levels. The argument is typically a hybrid of both allocative and redistributive aspects. The allocative aspects stress the supposition that some families could not afford to provide a given level of education for their children, resulting in loss of human resources not only to the individuals concerned but to society as a whole. Marshall's argument in favor of public support of education was that "the economic value of one great industrial genius is sufficient to cover the expenses of the education of a whole town . . . . All that is spent during many years in opening the means of highr education to the masses would be well paid for if it called out one more Newton or Darwin, Shakespeare or Beethoven (Marshall, 1961: I, 211).

The distributive aspect is concerned with income distribution. If additional education is required in order to obtain more income, and if the present (unequal) distribution of income is deemed undesirable, then providing education to children of the poor is one means by which future income distributions will become more equal. Increasing the equality of education will thus increase the opportunities people have to increase future income.

Both the allocative and distributive aspects are subject to serious reservations. First, as was stated earlier, it is not clear whether private benefits of education are substantially different from the social benefits. Second, although the income-education link is supported by a vast amount of empirical evidence, such evidence is by no means conclusive. Some studies show a relatively weak education-income association when a host of variables are taken into account, and moreover, all of the estimated earnings functions provide, at best, only a partial explanation of variations in income. Work by Levin H.M. (1977a) claiming that education has not been a vehicle for the reduction of poverty in the United States during the last decade casts doubt about the relevance of educational policy in reducing income equality.

The Quest for Common Values

Public education is a relatively modern institution. Up until the nineteenth century, the idea that education was a public function was practiced only in Prussia. In the United States, education was regarded as a private or semiprivate enterprise, funded, by and large, by the church and by parents. Even as government support was sought, it was mainly in the form of assistance, not in direct provision of education.

Public cognizance of and support for the needs of the "common school" in the United States began to coalesce firmly during the 1820s and 1830s. Under the leadership of such educational visionaries as Horace Mann, Gordon Carter, Henry Barnard, and others, the public was aroused by what has been called "the free school movement." The movement grew over time, until public provision was the dominant form of elementary and secondary education in the United States.

One important argument in favor of public schools was the need to provide a "melting pot" for the large number of immigrants arriving in the United States from a multitude of countries, each with a different language, cultural heritage, and mores. It was felt that the public school would provide "common values" necessary for the United States to survive as a nation. Another argument is the alleged need to provide for a separation of church and state. Since private education was provided largely through church-related schools, it was feared that the concept of the separation of the church from the state may not survive for long.

The strengths of both arguments appear much weaker today. Immigration to the United States affects only a very small number of people, and the principle of separation of church and state is deeply rooted in American folklore. Moreover, it is not at all clear that public provision of education would have any impact either on "common values" or on religious intrusion into the educational curriculum. For one, schools have successfully resisted attempts to homogenize the curriculum, so that to this day, a student in one school district might receive an entirely different set of "common values" than his counterpart in another school district. Also, despite legislation outlawing any church influence on the public schools, such influence persists, especially in small towns and in schools in relatively homogeneous neighborhoods.

More importantly, Should the state impose a set of "common values" on all pupils? Does the state have the right to dictate its own version of "what's right" to parents who may have a different set of values? Is it not the variability of ideas and values from which a rich culture is formed? If the answer to the first two questions is "no," and the answer to the last question is "yes," then the "common values" argument for public education is destroyed, and justification for the continued existence of public education must come from other sources.

Education and Economic Growth

The connection between economic growth and education has been described in considerable detail in Chapter 7. The evidence for the United States appears to support the contention that education is likely to enhance economic growth. If economic growth is a national goal, government intervention in education would be justified. Again, this does not require government control of schools; the same objective could be achieved via some form of subsidization.

It should be pointed out that not everyone is convinced of the relationship between education and economic growth. Moreover, some studies have shown a very weak relationship between education and growth in a number of countries. Finally, there are a growing number of people objecting to the very goal of economic growth on the grounds that economic growth inevitably results in environmental damage; the benefits from economic growth might be outweighed by the losses.

Other Factors

Two additional reasons for government intervention in education may be mentioned: (1) existence of monopoly power, and (2) efficiency in school operations.

Monopoly. For various reasons, educational institutions are likely to possess some monopoly power. This reduces the ability of the "customers" (parents and students) to substitute one school for the next, allowing the schools to charge higher prices and to provide less educational services. Government action to protect the customers from such monopoly power are no less justified in this case than in ordinary antitrust cases (and probably much more so). Furthermore, since many parents are unable to judge the true nature of the educational service purchased, some government control (e.g., accreditation) might be required to insure "product quality" and "truth in advertising."

Efficiency of Operation. Monopoly power, for one, typically results in socially inefficient operations. Moreover, the existence of scale economies in the operation of schools (as discussed in Chapter 8) precludes the private market for schooling from operating at the minimum cost point. Government operation of schools or subsidization would be needed to improve efficiency.

Who Should Pay for Educational Programs?

Once it is conceded that government should intervene in the financing and/or provision of educational services, the question remains: Which branch of government should be responsible for a given educational program? For example, who should shoulder the burdens of private and public elementary education, vocational education in high schools, community colleges, and undergraduate higher education?

From a theoretical point of view, answers to such questions are possible, although it must be recognized that the answers will not be simple. Consider the case of secondary education. It is recognized by most writers that universal secondary education is highly desirable—that is, we consider secondary education to be associated with substantial external benefits. But since the benefits of secondary education are in the main local or statewide, it may be argued that government involvement should be limited to state and local branches of government. This conclusion is based, in part, on data that show that the vast majority of persons receiving only secondary education are likely to remain in the state following graduation from high school. Interstate migration is far more common among persons who have had some college education. But the complexity of the issue becomes apparent even when it is assumed that the federal government has no role in secondary education. For it is far from clear how much of the burden should fall on the local and how much on the state government. The determination of the role of each branch would include an examination of the extent and direction of externalities and intrastate migration, fiscal capabilities, tax structures, and employment and other economic conditions. Moreover, since some of the educational effects are nationwide in scope, some federal involvement is justified. The desired extent of federal, state, and local involvement is obviously not easy to determine.

The roles of the different branches of government in the finance of education have shifted somewhat over the last twenty years. As is shown in Table 10-1, the share of local governments has decreased from 42.9 percent in 1956 to 28.5 percent in 1977. The share of both the state and federal governments increased precipitously during the period, the principal cause being the rise in the share of federal and state governments in the support of elementary and secondary schools. It is interesting that the changes occurring during the period were mainly intergovernmental, with federal and state levels taking over some of the responsibilities previously borne by the local governments, whereas the share of nongovernmental sources remained relatively constant.

The shift from local to state financing and from state to federal financing represents a departure from the highly decentralized structure of American education. Preference for decentralization is deeply rooted in American heritage, consistent with the philosophical concept of "subsidiarity"—that is, that decisions should be made at the level closest to the decision situation. Only those matters that cannot be handled through local governments should be pursued by the state and ultimately by the federal government. The increased role of state governments in financing local schools is a direct result of the successes of the educational finance reform movement, and further substitution of state for local funds is likely to continue in the near future.

Forms of Government Intervention

There would be few, if any, who would reject the notion that a combination of factors mentioned above would justify some sort of governmental intervention. What form government involvement should take in different cases is, usually, a matter of considerable controversy.

Table 10-1. Estimated Expenditures of Educational Institutions by Source of Funds—United States, 1955-1956, 1969-1970, and 1976-1977[a] (amounts in billions of dollars).

Source of Funds, by Level of Institution and Type of Control	1955-1956		1969-1970		1976-1977	
	Amount	Percent	Amount	Percent	Amount	Percent
All levels:						
Total public and nonpublic	$17.0	100.0	$70.4	100.0	$131.1	100.0
Federal	1.0	5.9	7.5	10.7	13.8	10.5
State	4.9	28.8	22.2	31.5	45.9	35.0
Local	7.3	42.9	22.6	32.1	37.4	28.5
All other	3.8	22.4	18.1	25.7	34.0	26.0
Total public	13.9	100.0	56.8	100.0	106.4	100.0
Federal	1.8	5.8	5.8	10.2	11.1	10.4
State	4.9	35.2	22.1	38.9	45.5	42.8
Local	7.3	52.5	22.5	39.6	37.3	35.1
All other	.9	6.5	6.4	11.3	12.5	11.7
Total nonpublic	3.1	100.0	13.6	100.0	24.7	100.0
Federal	0.2[b]	6.5	1.7	12.5	2.7	10.9
State	[b]	[c]	0.1	0.7	0.4	1.6
Local	[b]	[c]	0.1	0.7	0.1	0.4
All other	2.9	93.5	11.7	86.1	21.5	87.1
Elementary and secondary schools:						
Total public and nonpublic	12.8	100.0	45.7	100.0	81.9	100.0
Federal	0.5	3.9	3.4	7.4	6.4	7.8
State	3.8	29.7	15.8	34.6	31.0	37.9
Local	7.2	56.2	21.7	47.5	35.4	43.2
All other	1.3	10.2	4.8	10.5	9.1	11.1
Total public	11.5	100.0	41.0	100.0	72.9	100.0
Federal	0.5	4.3	3.4	8.2	6.4	8.8
State	3.8	33.1	15.8	38.6	31.0	42.5
Local	7.2	62.6	21.7	52.9	35.4	48.6
All other	—	—	0.1	0.3	0.1	0.1
Total nonpublic	1.3	100.0	4.7	100.0	9.0	100.0
Federal	—	—	—	—	—	—
State	—	—	—	—	—	—
Local	—	—	—	—	—	—
All other	1.3	100.0	4.7	100.0	9.0	100.0
Institutions of higher education:						
Total public and nonpublic	4.2	100.0	24.7	100.0	49.2	100.0
Federal	0.5	12.1	4.1	16.6	7.4	15.0
State	1.1	26.5	6.4	25.9	14.9	30.3
Local	0.1	3.0	0.9	3.6	2.0	4.1
All other	2.5	58.4	13.3	53.9	24.9	50.6

Table 10-1. continued

Source of Funds, by Level of Institution and Type of Control	1955-1956		1969-1970		1976-1977	
	Amount	Percent	Amount	Percent	Amount	Percent
Total public	2.4	100.0	15.8	100.0	33.5	100.0
Federal	0.3	11.5	2.4	14.9	4.7	14.0
State	1.1	45.6	6.3	39.7	14.5	43.3
Local	0.1	5.1	0.8	5.1	1.9	5.8
All other	0.9	37.8	6.3	40.3	12.4	36.9
Total nonpublic	1.8	100.0	8.9	100.0	15.7	100.0
Federal	0.2	12.8	1.7	18.8	2.7	17.0
State	b	1.6	0.1	1.6	0.4	2.3
Local	b	0.2	0.1	0.7	0.1	0.8
All other	1.6	85.4	7.0	78.9	12.5	79.9

Sources: Grant and Lind (1977) and earlier editions of the *Digest*.
[a]1955-56 data for estimated receipts, not expenditures.
[b]Less than $50 million.
[c]Less than 0.05 percent.

Where the "national interest" precludes private production and distribution—such as in matters of national security—it is almost universally agreed that production or provision by the government is indicated. Yet even in such cases, utilization of the market system may be desirable for purchases that do not involve confidential production. For example, the military could, and should, procure food, clothing, housing, and other supplies through the free market system whenever possible.

Where national security is not involved, the form of government intervention is more difficult to determine. Should the government operate public schools? Should the government subsidize accredited private schools? Or should the government give educational vouchers to parents, who could use them in an accredited school of their choice? Answers to such questions are far from simple. They involve, in addition to dispassionate economic rationale, value judgments concerning the appropriate role of government.

As noted earlier, the creation of public schools was largely a result of historical necessity. Our analysis does not provide an economic rationale for the continued existence of public schools. At best, economic analysis only suggests some form of subsidization. Given that elementary and secondary education is dominated by public schools and that the public-private mix is not likely to change in the foreseeable future, we must focus attention on other questions. For example, should the state provide subsidies to private schools? Should the state subsidize the schools (public or private) directly or indirectly through vouchers to parents? What should be the formula for state aid to education?

In the case of higher education, similar questions need to be asked. Again, public operation of institutions of higher education does not necessarily follow from the economic analysis. The proposition that government aid should be given to higher education, moreover, is not as strongly supported by the economic argument as is the case for elementary and secondary education, and there are numerous proponents of "full cost tuition." But if society chooses to provide aid to higher education, the questions of how, by whom, and to whom require answers.

Conclusion

Although there are a number of factors that would justify government intervention in education, our analysis indicates that a purely economic reason for a government role in education is far from conclusive. Moreover, there is no purely economic factor that would justify government operation of schools. The historical development of the educational system in the United States is a result of social, economic, and political forces, and one need not pursue a purely economic rationale for its present state.

Economic analysis can, however, assist in devising educational finance systems consistent with the aims of educational policy. For example, if equity in financing school districts is the aim, then economists can provide a framework to provide maximum equity, subject to financial and other constraints. Such an analysis would require a thorough examination of how "equity" may be defined, what are the alternative strategies to improve equity, and what are the expected consequences of the various strategies in reference to equity, efficiency, and total government aid required. Our focus in the remainder of the chapter is on questions of this type.

FINANCING ELEMENTARY AND SECONDARY SCHOOLS

A cursory examination of Table 10-1 indicates that public elementary and secondary schools are financed almost exclusively through government funds, whereas nonpublic schools receive no public aid. The lack of public support of nonpublic schools is based on the legal premise of separation between state and church and attempts to pass legislation permitting state aid to nonpublic schools have always resulted in court action declaring such aid unconstitutional. Some indirect aid to nonpublic schools is provided in some states, but its magnitude is negligible. The sections dealing with federal and state aid to education will, therefore, be confined to public schools. A brief discussion of the pros and cons of government aid to nonpublic schools will be provided later.

Federal Aid

Federal aid to elementary and secondary education may be direct or indirect. *Direct aid* includes funds that are specifically earmarked for local school districts. Three categories of direct aid are usually recognized: (1) aid for children of poor families (commonly known as "educationally disadvantaged"), given through provisions of Title I of the Elementary and Secondary Education Act (ESEA) of 1965 (and subsequent amendments); (2) aid for schools located in "federally Impacted Areas" (where large federal installations, such as military bases, are located); and (3) other "categorical" aid, consisting of vocational and other grant programs mandated by ESEA and the Vocational Education Act of 1963 (with subsequent amendments). Examples of discretionary (categorical) aid programs include school library resources, textbooks, and other instructional materials for school children; education of the handicapped; dropout prevention programs; and many others.

Indirect aid is given through federal grants to the states, portions of which are to be passed on to school districts. Also, programs such as the Revenue Sharing Act of 1972, funneling federal funds to the states, which, in turn, are required to pass them on to local governments (excluding school districts), relieve the states from using funds for nonschooling purposes, thus making it possible to provide additional funds for the support of schools.

In 1976–1977, $6.4 billion, or approximately 7.8 percent of elementary and secondary expenditures, came from federal sources. This contrasts with only 3.9 percent in 1955–1956—or a doubling of the role of the federal government. Nevertheless, the federal role remains quite limited, focused mainly on special purpose programs and special needs (such as students from poor families). Moreover, many federal programs require state or local matching, creating an inertia against use of federal funds.

Equalization. The concepts of "equity," "equalization," or "equality of opportunity" are frequently cited as the principal reasons for federal aid. But these concepts are difficult to define.

First, what needs to be equalized? Should we strive to equalize resources (inputs) or perhaps student achievement (output)? It is possible that even equalization of achievement is insufficient if equality of future income is desired. Second, among whom is equalization to be achieved? Is equalization to be achieved among states, school districts, schools (within a school district), classes (within schools), or pupils (within classes)? Moreover, what measures of equality are we to use? Finally, once all of the above questions are answered to our satisfaction (and it is doubtful that they will ever be), how should the equalization effort be carried out?

Suppose that the objective of federal aid is to increase the amount of resources available to school districts that have a large concentration of pupils from poor families. Then, according to a study by Ginsburg and Killalea (1977), it is found that much more federal aid per pupil went to districts with "most poverty" than to others. When only Title I ESEA funds are considered, the "most-poverty" areas appear to gain even more.

If the purpose of equalization is related to the assessed value of real property per pupil, from which property tax revenues could be raised (and it is well known that, in the United States, virtually all local educational revenues come from property tax proceeds), it is found that total federal aid to elementary and secondary education provides only a slightly larger per pupil aid to low property value districts than to middle and high property value districts. In fact, high property value districts appear to receive more aid per pupil than the middle group. This may be due to the fact that aid to districts in center cities is considerably higher than to suburban and nonmetropolitan districts, due to the large concentration of poor families in such areas, whereas assessed property value per pupil is relatively high in such cities. The latter phenomenon is due to three main factors: (1) the presence of considerable nonresidential property; (2) the flight of young middle and upper income families to the suburbs, leaving in the center cities the old and the poor; and (3) relatively large attendance in private schools of pupils from upper income families living in the cities. As a result, assessed property valuation per pupil is likely to be relatively high.

Ginsburg and Killalea conclude that "no single federal aid program is allocated in a way that satisfied the needs represented by all three grouping of districts studied: poverty, property wealth, and degree of urbanization" (p. 395). They argue that federal aid appears to focus on areas with large concentrations of poor families, disregarding low district property wealth as a "disadvantage" that needs to be equalized.

Federal aid can also be channeled through tax deduction or credits. The Internal Revenue Code currently permits deduction of state and local taxes from the federal income tax. As a result, a portion of the burden of taxes that, at least in part, are levied for the support of education, is shifted to the general (federal) taxpayer. Moreover, if federal funds are not returned to states and localities in proportion to income taxes paid, then some redistribution of the burden of education will be effected. A study by Guthrie and Lawton (1970) suggests that a significant redistribution does occur.

At present, the United States Congress is debating the merits of a tax credit scheme that would allow parents to receive a relatively small amount of tax credit for tuition charged by elementary and secondary schools. Another proposal for tax credit was presented by Riew (1971), arguing for federal tax credit of municipal income taxes. Such a scheme, it. is argued, would encourage enactment of municipal income tax laws, resulting in reduced reliance on the property tax and considerable relief to hard-pressed metropolitan areas (especially center cities).

State Aid

The notion of state aid to education is relatively new. The basic concept evolved from the works of Elwood P. Cubberley, George D. Strayer and Robert M. Haig, Paul R. Mort, Harlan Updegraff, and Henry C. Morrison, all writing in the period 1905–1933. Their basic argument was that substantial interdistrict vairations in educational expenditures represented differences in community wealth and tax efforts that create the intolerable situation that some pupils do not receive an adequate training (Cohn, 1974a: ch. 2).

The present emphasis on state aid to education is due to a number of factors: (1) There is a genuine interest in reducing disparities and improving the minimum quality of education available to every child. (2) The high burden of the property tax has resulted in a taxpayer's revolt in many areas, with voters turning down time and again proposals to increase the millage rate for educational purposes or voting down school bond elections for capital improvements. (3) Court actions, sponsored by the new reformers, have put increased pressure on legislators to reduce disparities in the educational finance structure of the states so that the structure would not be considered unconstitutional—as was the case in California, Texas, Minnesota, New Jersey, Connecticut, and other states.

It all boils down to a question of "equalization." To what extent are the interdistrict inequalities (in achievement, "needs," resources, or tax effort) so large as to arouse indignation and demand corrective action? That is no simple question, for not only is it difficult to define the concept of "equalization," it is also difficult to provide a measurement of inequality once the general concept of inequality has been defined.

A popular concept that has recently been coined is known as "wealth neutrality." Under the banner of wealth neutrality, an educational finance system will insure that every child will receive the same (or at least an acceptable minimum) education without regard to the wealth of the community in which he happens to reside. The concept, however, is by no means unambiguous, since the term "community wealth" is subject to different interpretations, and the meaning and measurement of what represents "the same education" are subject to all sorts of difficulties.

The NEFP Taxanomy. A useful classification of state aid systems has been developed by the National Education Finance Project (NEFP), as described in Johns and Salmon (1971):

1. Flat grants
   a. uniform flat grants
   b. variable flat grants
2. Equalization grants
   a. Strayer-Haig-Mort (foundation) programs
   b. percentage equalization or state aid ratio program
   c. guaranteed valuation program
3. Nonequalizing matching grants

Flat grants are funds that are channeled to school districts on a per student or classroom basis. In the case of uniform flat grants, account is taken of neither variation in educational needs nor community financial capacity. Variable flat grants similarly take no account of financial capacity; however, they do attempt to compensate for differing classroom needs. Most commonly, instructional units are weighted thus for secondary versus elementary instruction. Weights for other factors are found occasionally. Flat grants are often used in conjunction with other plans discussed below.

A majority of the states use equalizing plans to distribute the major portion of general (noncategorical, special purpose) funds, and of these, the foundation program or a variation of it is most popular. The basic foundation approach is to set a level for a minimum educational package and, within that level, to set limits for the state to provide whatever funds are required to bring local revenue at a mandated tax rate up to the foundation level per student.

Foundation programs may be either weighted or unweighted with regard to educational level or other factors.

A second type of equalizing plan is the percentage equalizing program. State aid increases with per pupil expenditures on education and is an inverse function of the relative wealth of the district. In a third equalizing approach, guaranteed valuation, the state guarantees a fixed yield from a mandated tax rate. The state pays the difference between what the tax produces and the guaranteed amount. The guaranteed valuation approach is, in effect, equivalent to the basic foundation approach.

In addition to flat grants and the various equalization grants, certain additional state funds are available on a matching basis, wherein the district must match dollar for dollar, or in some other proportion, all funds supplied by the subventor. Such grants are not equalizing with regard to financial capacity. However, since many of these grants are for special educational purposes, to that extent they could be described as differentially supplying funds for special educational needs.

Although the aid formulas within each type of plan vary among the states, it might be useful to provide fairly rigorous definitions of the plans in terms of their general characteristics.

The Foundation Plan. Equalization aid is typically computed according to the formula

$$EA_i = WADA_i \, (F - rV_i), \qquad (10.1)$$

where

EA_i = equalization aid to the ith district;
$WADA_i$ = weighted average daily attendance;
F = foundation level;
r = mandated tax rate; and
V_i = assessed valuation of property per pupil in the ith district.

If EA_i in Equation (10.1) is negative, equalization aid is zero.

The mandated tax rate, r, may be calculated on the basis of the tax levy that would yield the foundation level of support (F) in the wealthiest district. Then,

$$r = F/V_h, \qquad (10.2)$$

where V_h is the per pupil property valuation in the wealthiest district. Then Equation (10.1) becomes.

$$EA_i = WADA_i \cdot F(1 - V_i/V_h).\qquad(10.3)$$

One could also compute r on the basis of the necessary tax levy to yield F when average per pupil valuation in the state (V_s) is substituted for V_h. Then Equation (10.3) becomes

$$EA_i = WADA_i \cdot F(1 - V_i/V_s).\qquad(10.4)$$

When Equation (10.3) is used, all but the wealthiest districts would receive some equalization aid. When Equation (10.4) is used, only districts with per pupil valuations under the state average would receive equalization aid. In both cases, aid is given in inverse relation to the relative wealth of the districts.

The Guaranteed Valuation Plan. As noted previously, this plan is algebraically equivalent to the foundation plan. The guaranteed valuation plan specifies a given level of valuation, V_g, that all districts may use to compute the level of property tax revenues per pupil that the state will guarantee. Thus rV_g— where r is the mandatory tax rate—defines the guaranteed yield, which in the foundation plan has been called the minimum foundation support level, F. The guaranteed valuation plan provides for equalization aid on the basis of the following formula:

$$EA_i = WADA_i (rV_g - rV_i).\qquad(10.5)$$

Since rV_g, in effect, is equal to F, Equation (10.5) reduces to Equation (10.1), proving that the two plans are algebraically equivalent.

The equivalence of Equations (10.5) and (10.1) is contingent on the use of r as a mandated tax rate. If r is allowed to vary between districts, then the equivalence is no longer true. Moreover, the algebraic equivalence holds only to the extent that $F = rV_g$. Obviously, a change from one system to another, accompanied by changes in the implicit foundation level and/or other parameters in the formula would result in changes in state aid. A good example of this is the recent change in the state aid distribution system in Illinois, which permits districts to use either the old foundation approach or a new guaranteed valuation program (which is called a "resource equalization approach"—Hickrod and Hubbard, 1975, 1977a, 1977b).

The Percentage Equalizing Plan. Equalization aid is distributed according to the following formula:

$$EA_i = WADA_i (1 - xV_i/V_s) EXP_i,\qquad(10.6)$$

where EXP_i is local per pupil expenditures in the ith district, and x is a scalar between 0 and 1 indicating the extent to which the state is willing to share in educational expenditures. (A higher value of x indicates a smaller state share.)

For example, if V_i/V_s = 1/2 for district i, and if x = 0.25, the state will then pay a proportion $1 - 1/2(0.25) = 0.875$ (87.5 percent) of local expenditures. If, however, x = 0.5, the state will pay only $0.75 per dollar of expenditures.

It can also be shown that as the ratio V_i/V_s increases, state aid per dollar of expenditures decreases. For example, if x = 0.25, and V_i/V_s = 2, the state will pay $0.50, per dollar of local expenditures. If V_i/V_s = 4, the state will pay no equalization aid to that district.

As noted earlier, some states have combined such equalization plans with flat grants and other types of categorical grants. Also, states using the percentage equalization plan have stipulated maximum levels of EXP_i for the purpose of equalization aid, thus limiting the extent to which equalization could be achieved.

The District Power Equalizing Plan (DPE). In both the foundation and the percentage equalizing plans, per pupil expenditures in the individual districts remain a function of the district's wealth, measured by assessed valuation of property. Even if some wealthy districts receive no state aid whatever, they may still be able to raise more educational revenues for a given tax effort than other districts receiving state aid. It follows that the quality of the schools in a district (measured by per pupil expenditures) remains a function of wealth.

The power equalizing scheme, proposed by Coons and his colleagues (1970), calls for equal state aid to districts based on equal tax effort. That is, school districts that impose a given tax rate should be entitled to spend a given sum on education (per pupil) and no more. Any discrepancy between the amount the district can raise and that to which it is entitled will be filled by the state. Moreover, if a district can raise educational funds, for a given tax effort, in excess of the stipulated amount set by the state, the excess must be transferred to the state. This is known as a "recapture clause." In sum, any two school districts that impose the same property tax rate will have identical educational funds per pupil at their disposal, no matter how wealthy or poor the community is.

One method by which the concept may be implemented is to define state aid—both positive and negative—on the basis of the following formula:

$$EA_i = WADA_i[r_iV_s - r_iV_i] = WADA_i \ [r_i \ (V_s - V_i)] , \quad (10.7)$$

where r_i is the tax rate that residents of district i are willing to impose on themselves.

For example, if V_s = \$5,000, and V_i = \$3,000, aid will be given to the district on the basis of the formula $EA_i = r$ (\$2,000) $WADA_i$. If the district chooses a low rax rate, say 10 mills (r = 0.01), then per pupil aid is \$20. If it chooses a very high rate, say 100 mills (r = 0.1), per pupil aid would be \$200. For each additional mill, the district will get additional aid of \$2 per pupil in $WADA$.

On the other hand, if a district has a per pupil valuation (V_i) of \$6,000, it will pay the state negative aid based on the formula EA_i = r_i (-\$1,000). For each mill levied (yielding \$6 per pupil), the district will pay the state \$1. Hence, if the district chose to levy a tax of 10 mills, it will raise \$60 per pupil, pay the state \$10 per pupil, and retain \$50 per pupil. For the district in the preceding paragraph, local revenue for the 10 mill levy would be \$30 per pupil. Add to that the \$20 per pupil in state aid, and it is clear that both districts are left with \$50 per pupil despite the wide disparity in wealth between the two.

Instead of Equation (10.7), it is possible to formulate a specific schedule indicating the amount of educational revenues to which a district is entitled within a given range of tax levies. If revenue entitlement is denoted by RE, then state aid, positive or negative, is given by

$$EA_i = (RE - r_iV_i) \ WADA_i. \quad (10.8)$$

Note that RE in Equation (10.7) is simply r_iV_s, representing tax yield when the average property value in the state is taxed at the rate r_i.

Power-equalizing plans have become quite popular in recent years, as the pressure has mounted for "wealth neutrality" in the educational finance structure of the states. Few of the programs, however, carry the plan to its logical conclusion, especially in so far as the recapture clause is concerned. Without a recapture clause, the DPE plan is quite similar to the guaranteed valuation plan.

Full State Funding. It should also be mentioned that full state funding of educational expenditures has been advocated (e.g., Thomas, 1970; and Wise and Thomas, 1973). Under such a system, the state will assume all of the expenses of running local school districts. Likewise, the local property tax will be replaced with a statewide tax to generate the funds necessary to support the schools. At present, such systems operate in Hawaii and the District of Columbia.

Full state funding of schools does not necessarily eliminate all questions of equity. The Hobson versus Hansen case, concluded in the District of Columbia in 1971, concerned allegations that substantial interschool variations in the quality of instruction persisted in the District (Clune, 1972). This was achieved mainly through personnel policies, which allowed experienced teachers to transfer to more desirable neighborhoods, leaving the young and relatively inexperienced teachers in the less desirable, "ghetto" neighborhood schools. Since salaries paid to experienced teachers exceed those paid to inexperienced ones (see Chapter 9), it follows that operating expenditures per pupil are likely to be higher in the more desirable neighborhoods. This phenomenon is quite common to all of the larger urban school systems in the United States.

Moreover, critics of full state funding claim that full assumption of educational costs by the state will also mean complete control of the local schools, thus eliminating the possibility for local experimentation and provision of a variable educational program to meet local educational conditions, tastes, and preferences.

A Brief Description of Current (1978) State Aid Plans. Only two states, North and South Carolina, still operate on a flat basis. Moreover, South Carolina will begin implementation of a new foundation program in 1978–1979, leaving North Carolina the only state with a flat grant system. In contrast, twenty-six states operate under some version of the foundation program. The percentage equalizing plan is operating in five states (Alaska, Delaware, Pennsylvania, Rhode Island, and Vermont). The guaranteed yield (or "resource equalizer") plan is effective in eleven states; the district power equalizing plan in four states (Kentucky, Maine, Montana, and Utah), and full state funding is found only in Hawaii. Some changes in state aid plans have already been enacted (e.g., California), and additional changes are likely to be enacted in the near future. A summary of state aid to education is provided in Table 10–2.

It must be emphasized that the states vary greatly not only in the type of plan but also in how each state funds, modifies, and implements its plan. It is not surprising, therefore, that some basic support programs provide considerable equalization aid while others do not. This would be a function of (1) the level of the foundation support; (2) the use of flat grants; (3) the use of weightings in the formula; (4) the use of "save harmless" or other encumbering provisions; and (5) the method by which funds for programs other than the basic support program are distributed. These points are discussed in order.

Level of Foundation Support. It is obvious that the "foundation level" of support (F, in Formula 10.1) is critical. If in one state it is $500, while in another it is $1,500, other things being equal, the impact of state aid would vary substantially between the two states. The last three columns of Table 10-2 reveal considerable differences in the support levels of states using any one type of plan.

Flat Grants. The information in Table 10-2 reveals considerable differences among the states in the use of flat grants. In some states, flat grants are quite important and may be subtracted from the equalizing grant. If flat grants to district i are denoted by FG_i, then Formula (10.1) becomes:

$$EA_i = WADA_i\,(F - rV_i) - FG_i. \qquad (10.9)$$

This type of a foundation plan is considered to be less equalizing than one in which the same amount of state funds is channeled entirely through the distribution mechanism of Equation (10.1). Moreover, a number of states subtract from EA_i not only flat grants but also federal grants and/or other nonequalizing state funds. Similar adjustments may be made in the other finance plans.

Use of Weightings. In all of the formulas, aid per pupil is multiplied by $WADA_i$, not by unweighted ADA (average daily attendance) or ADM (average daily membership). In some states, differential weightings have been devised to take into account different "needs" of students. If the cost of education in high school is 50 percent higher than in the primary grades, than weightings of 1.5 and 1 might be used for secondary and primary grades, respectively. The same effect is obtained when funding is computed on a per class basis and the class size for funding purposes is varied among relevant educational levels. There is, however, considerable variation in the employment of weights, and moreover, in a number of states, no weighting is provided. The impact of state aid per dollar of state funds distributed would therefore vary among the states.

Table 10-2. General Characteristics of State Education Finance Systems, 1977-1978.

State	Type of Program	Flat Grants	State Aid as a Percent of Local and State Revenues 1975-1976	Equalizing Aid as a Percent of State Aid 1975-1976	Estimated Expenditures per Pupil
	1	2	3	4	5
Alabama	Foundation		75	87	$1,439[a]
Alaska	GV		78	75	3,341
Arizona	Foundation		61	94	1,436
Arkansas	Foundation	Save harmless[b]	62	19	1,193
California	Foundation[c]	$125 per pupil	45	49	1,720
Colorado	GV	$11.35 per mill per pupil	47	85	1,649
Connecticut	GV	$250 per pupil	28	0	2,089[a]
Delaware	PE	Most of state aid	76	3	2,138
Florida	Foundation		60	90	1,594
Georgia	Foundation		59	82	1,482[a]
Hawaii	Full State Funding		100	—	1,963
Idaho	Foundation		73	85	1,206
Illinois	Choice of Foundation or GV		52	80	2,058
Indiana	Foundation	$60 per pupil	55	89	1,449
Iowa	Foundation	Minimum basic grant	48	96	2,002
Kansas	GV	$200 per pupil	40	72	1,682
Kentucky	Foundation or DPE[d]		83	97	1,294
Louisiana	Foundation	$48 per pupil	58	88	1,481
Maine	DPE		50	99	1,562[a]
Maryland	Foundation		42	47	1,810
Massachusetts	PE	15 Percent of approved expenditures	28	76	na
Michigan	GV	$164 per pupil	41	82	1,975
Minnesota	Foundation		70	76	1,962
Mississippi	Foundation		75	81	1,220
Missouri	Foundation[e]		38	78	1,425
Montana	DPE[e]		60	96	1,972[a]
Nebraska	Foundation	Variable pupil and teacher grants	27	34	1,526
Nevada	Foundation and GV		48	100	1,526

State	Program				
New Hampshire	Foundation	$15.47 per pupil	6	20	1,366
New Jersey	GV		31	43	2,333
New Mexico	Foundation	$360 per pupil	87	92	1,476
New York	Foundation		40	98	2,527
North Carolina	Flat grants	$9,330–$14,230 per teacher	81	0	1,343
North Dakota	Foundation		67	85	1,343
Ohio	GV		46	61	1,581
Oklahoma	Foundation		50	68	1,461
Oregon	Foundation	$393 per pupil	20	18	1,929
Pennsylvania	PE	Minimum amount and save harmless[b]	50	79	2,079
Rhode Island	PE	30 percent of expenditures	36	94	1,846
South Carolina	Flat grants[f]	$7,487–$15,143 per teacher	65	0	1,271
South Dakota	Foundation		18	78	1,385
Tennessee	Foundation		44	90	1,209
Texas	Foundation	Save harmless[b]	51	75	1,352
Utah	DPE		72	74	1,363
Vermont	PE	$60 per pupil	36	75	1,550
Virginia	Foundation		35	52	1,560
Washington	Foundation		46	73	1,951
West Virginia	Foundation	$1200 per teacher and $36 per pupil	65	79	1,374
Wisconsin	GV		36	87	2,156[a]
Wyoming	Foundation	$90 per census persons age 0–21	35	100	2,007

Sources: Columns 1, 2, and 5 from Augenblick (1978b); Columns 3 and 4 from Tron (1976).

[a] Since 1977–1978 figures were not available, 1975–1976 data from Grant and Lind (1977) were multiplied by 1.2 to account for an expected increase in expenditures of about 20 percent.

[b] A "save harmless" provision guarantees to a district an amount of state aid equaling at least what is received in some previous year.

[c] Beginning with 1978–1979, the foundation program is replaced with a GV plan, which will become a DPE with full recapture in the 1980s.

[d] The DPE becomes effective only for districts imposing a tax rate above 30 mills.

[e] Excess funds above those required for the foundation program are not recaptured.

[f] A new foundation program is now in effect and is scheduled to be fully implemented within the next five years.

GV—guaranteed valuation; PE—percentage equalizing; DPE—district power equalizing.

Save Harmless and Other Encumbering Provisions. A "save harmless" clause typically guarantees a district a level of state aid at least as great as what it received in a given year (or, in some cases, minimum state aid in the current year is defined as some fixed proportion of last year's aid). Such provisions were frequently included in state aid plans to soften opposition to state aid reform. Such save harmless provisions have reduced the ability of the states to fully fund their equalization aid programs.

Other encumbering provisions are also occasionally attached to state aid plans. Most bothersome of these provisions are minimum and maximum amounts or percentages of total funds that districts can receive from the states. Such provisions may be so limiting that they could sap any strength a program might otherwise have.

Distribution of Other Funds. The information in Columns 1 and 2 of Table 10-2 pertains to the "basic support program." It ignores categorical aid to schools and other support services. For example, the state government assumes, in some cases, all of the capital costs under a full state funding system. In other states, capital costs are entirely borne by the school district. Various categorical grants may be made by the state with no regard to equity considerations, resulting in an overall equalizing impact different from what would be expected from the type and implementation of the basic support program.

In conclusion, the impact of state aid on equalization or degree of "wealth neutrality" cannot be discerned merely by noting the type of plan under which the basic support system operates.

Evaluation of State Support Programs. The amount of state aid funds, together with the method by which state funds are subvented to local school systems, determine the effect of state aid. Economic analysis typically is concerned with issues both of equity and of efficiency. Most of the educational finance literature has been concerned with equity alone. As pointed out earlier, however, even the issue of equity is so complex that a simple mode of evaluation is not likely to provide unambiguous answers.

The simplest form of evaluation would be to inspect data on per pupil expenditures within a state and to calculate the degree of variability in such expenditures. Several tools for analysis have been used, such as the range (difference between highest and lowest expenditures in the state), standard deviation, or interquartile range. If the variability shown is negligible (what is deemed "negligible" depends on one's judgement), then one could argue that the system works well.

The main problem with this approach is that it measures inequality on the basis of a single variable—expenditures. An evaluation of the state support system should also take into account the wealth (or fiscal capacity) of the school districts. Since wealthy districts can obtain more funds for a given tax effort, it is expected that higher expenditures will be found in wealthier school districts, other things being equal. If the objective of state aid is to reduce disparity in educational opportunity, defined as the ability to raise educational revenues, then an examination of the variability in educational expenditures must somehow be related to community wealth differences.

One alternative is the use of the Lorenz curve. The analysis would compare districts on a two dimensional scale, taking into account both "wealth" (or "fiscal capacity") and per pupil expenditures. One example of a Lorenz curve is displayed in Figure 10-1, where the

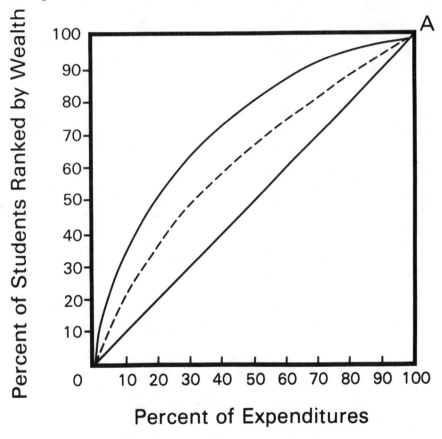

Figure 10-1. A Lorenz Curve: Inequality in School Finance.

percent of total (local plus state aid) expenditures in the state's districts is plotted against the percent of students ranked by "wealth" of the community. The diagonal line (OA) is the "ideal" situation, where an equal percent of total expenditures will be received by a given percentage of students. For example, the lowest 10 percent of students (in terms of wealth) would receive the same share of total expenditures as would the highest 10 percent. With no state aid, the solid curve is expected to prevail, with low wealth students receiving lower total per pupil expenditures. The reverse is true for high wealth students. If state aid is equalizing (but not perfectly so), then the dotted curve would prevail, indicating a reduction in the advantage of high wealth students. According to this method, "wealth neutrality" would occur when the dotted curve approaches the diagonal line OA.

One could also measure the degree of inequality using the Gini coefficient. It is defined as the area between the Lorenz curve and the diagonal line. In Figure 10-1, the Gini coefficient for the solid curve is larger (in absolute value) than the one for the dotted line. One could draw Lorenz curves for different states or for one state over time and compare the degree of inequality either in visual terms or through computation of the Gini coefficients. The Gini coefficient, as a summary statistic, has a number of limitations. One of the problems is that it takes into account only the total area between the Lorenz curve and the diagonal line, disregarding the shape of the curve. One could draw two or more significantly different Lorenz curves, all of which have the same Gini coefficient, implying equally good (or bad) distributions. However, one of these (call it distribution A) might represent great disadvantage for poor districts and relative advantage for wealthy districts, whereas another (call it B) might represent the reverse. With the objective of improving the lot of poor districts, the state might prefer distribution B to A. Moreover, the Lorenz curve might cross the diagonal line, in which case the Gini coefficient would indicate a good deal less inequality than actually exists (because the positive and negative deviations would cancel each other out). A modified Gini coefficient would overcome the last, but not the first, problem (Hickrod et al., 1975a).

The definition of "wealth neutrality" as represented by the diagonal line in the Lorenz diagram is not universally accepted. Missing from the analysis is the effort that is exerted by a district to raise local revenues, along with other factors that should perhaps be taken into account (such as number of high cost pupils, population density, cost of living, "municipal overburden," and the like). An alternative definition of wealth neutrality has been advanced as the situation where each school district is able to raise the same educational resources after allowance is made for wealth, tax effort, and other factors. The procedure requires a multivariate analysis, typically multiple regression. Recent work by Feldstein (1975) argues for further redefinition of wealth neutrality to include indirect effects of state aid on the "price of education" (defined as the local tax rate necessary to support educational expenditures).

In conclusion, evaluation of the equity impact of state aid is a complex matter. When efficiency aspects are considered, too, the task is formidable. But evaluation is necessary, and the best tools available should be used to do the job.

Fiscal Capacity and Wealth. Two important concepts that have been mentioned without explanation are "fiscal capacity" and community "wealth." Since education is financed locally almost exclusively through taxation of real property (mostly land and improvements), both fiscal capacity and wealth have been measured by assessed property valuation per pupil in the district. There are many problems with this measure, however. Some of the more significant problems are outlined here.

1. Although educational expenditures are derived from property taxation, the ability of a community to pay for educational services is a function of tangible and intangible assets as well as family income. A property poor but income rich community could afford to pay more per assessed valuation than another community which is both property poor and income poor. In other words, the local property tax effort required of local school districts should be directly related to family income in the community. Several states use an index of fiscal capacity including property value, personal income, and other economic variables.
2. Even if wealth and property value are considered to be identical, there are all sorts of problems with property assessment. First, there may not be uniform assessment practices throughout the state, creating a distortion in the true property value of districts. Second, even if assessment practices are uniform, it is well known that high-priced assets are more difficult to appraise than lower priced assets, especially in regard to residential housing. The tendency is, therefore, to undervalue expensive homes, reducing the assessed value of wealthier districts.
3. Even if assessed valuation is an acceptable proxy for community

wealth, fiscal capacity might vary among communities of identical wealth. One reason for this is "municipal overburden," which is related to the use of property tax revenues for purposes other than education. It has been argued that center cities of large metropolitan areas must provide services to workers commuting from the suburbs, resulting in substantial burdens placed upon the local property tax—the only source of local revenues in most cities. Also, the composition of the property (residential versus industrial) affects the ability of the school district to export some of the tax burden to the customers of the taxed industry, most of whom live outside the district (J.H. Bowman, 1973, 1974).

4. As mentioned earlier, if student characteristics and physical and economic conditions in the community result in increased costs of education per pupil vis-à-vis other districts, the fiscal capacity of the school districts is diminished. There is, therefore, some justification for modifying the basic support formula to account for differences in fiscal capacity.

5. Finally, there are strong arguments against the property tax per se as a "good" measure for raising revenues. First, it is considered to be regressive, with respect both to property value and to family income. That is, people possessing more property value (or earning higher income) are likely to pay a smaller proportion of their property value (or income) in taxes than those with lower property value (or income). The regressivity with respect to property value is due to the assessment problem already discussed. The regressivity with respect to income is due to the fact that the observed ratio of an individual's property value to family income decreases as income increases. Thus a uniform property tax (with fixed tax rates per dollar of assessed valuation) will result in higher income families paying a lower proportion of income in property taxes than would lower income families.

Other objections to the property tax include the argument that it is an "ugliness tax," discouraging landlords from improving properties; that it encourages land speculation; and that it discriminates against the poor and old who may have placed their lifetime's savings in a property. Some states have undertaken measures to improve the property tax, such as the use of a "circuit breaker," under which individuals with income under a prespecified level would be exempted from, or be subject to lower, property taxes. Such measures are, however, typically limited to the elderly, and the basic argument against the property tax has not yet fully been addressed.

Empirical Effects of State Aid. There are a number of interesting empirical questions related to state aid: (1) Does a change in the basic support system improve the equity of the system? (2) Does the state aid program provide property tax relief? (3) What effect does the state aid system have on educational expenditures derived from (a) local revenues and (b) total revenues? (4) What are the efficiency effects of state aid? For example, how does it affect school organization (scale effect) or resource allocation (e.g., class size)? Empirical studies have appeared in recent years in which these and other questions are addressed. A brief summary of some of the findings follows.

Effect on equity. In order to study the effect of state aid on equity, it is necessary to compare the degree of equity within a single system over time and space or cross-sectionally for a sample of the states. An example of a comparison within a state over time is the work of Hickrod and his associates on Illinois (Hickrod et al., 1975a, 1976). The general conclusion is that school finance reform in Illinois has reduced the degree of inequality. Also, a study by Hight (1974) suggests that the degree of inequality in Hawaii (measured by the correlation between per pupil expenditures and family income) was higher in 1970 than in a number of other states (including Michigan and Texas), despite the fact that it employed a full state funding plan. This is consistent with the argument made earlier that elimination of interdistrict variations will not necessarily eliminate also intradistrict differences. Also, a study by R.W. Clyde (reported in Cohn, 1974a: 83–91) of Pennsylvania counties (for 1970) shows a significant negative partial regression coefficient between relative property value and state aid per capita (suggesting that aid per capita is inversely related to district wealth, as would be expected from the Pennsylvania aid formula). And a study by Feldstein (1975) suggests that a district power equalizing plan is not likely to result in wealth neutrality. Using data from Massachusetts, he argues that some form of matching aid (as in the percentage equalizing plan) is necessary to achieve wealth neutrality.

Property Tax Relief. If a school district uses state aid funds to replace local revenues, then state aid, in effect, assumes the role of property tax relief. A number of studies show such a phenomenon. For example, Miner (1963), using 1959–1960 data for 1,127 school districts in twenty-three states, found a significantly negative effect of state aid on local expenditures. Studies by Brazer (1959), Renshaw (1960), Bishop (1964), Sacks and Harris (1964), Sacks (1972), and Cohn (1974a: ch. 5) suggest the same conclusion. Studies by McMahon (1970) and Hu and Booms (1971), however, suggest that, on the average, state aid may not provide any tax relief.

Effect on Expenditures. State aid may be defined as substitutive, dilutive, or stimulative. When state aid results in a reduction of expenditures from local revenue sources (but not in total expenditures), then state aid is substitutive. When state aid results in a reduction in total expenditures, it is dilutive. If, on the other hand, it results in an increase of total expenditures, then it is stimulative. Most of the studies mentioned in the preceding paragraph indicate that state aid is both substitutive and stimulative—that is, it encourages schools to increase total spending per pupil, while at the same time, it also results in reduced spending out of local revenues. The studies by McMahon (1970) and Hu and Booms (1971), however, suggest that state aid might be purely stimulative.

Effect on Efficiency. There is a dearth of published work on the efficiency effects of state aid to reducation. One attempt to study the effect of state aid on average school size was reported by this author (Cohn, 1974a: ch. 5). It was found that state aid was associated (*ceteris paribus*) with larger average school enrollments. Since in most states schools are generally too small, the findings do not reveal any adverse efficiency effects. The study was based, however, on state averages, which disregard intrastate variations in school size. Further work on the efficiency effects of state aid is obviously needed.

FINANCING HIGHER EDUCATION

The historical development of higher education followed a different pattern than elementary and secondary schooling. For one, the private sector of higher education has always been quite strong, and even in recent years, when the rapid expansion of public higher education put tremendous pressures on private schools, the private sector has continued to be viable and, at least in some segments, to thrive. Moreover, unlike the lower levels, public support of private institutions of higher education is common.

Another factor that distinguishes higher education from lower levels is the presence (with few exceptions) of tuition and fees in both public and private institutions of higher education. This shifts the focus of the analysis from the institution or the community to the student. Questions of equity are, therefore, typically directed to an individual or to groups of students. This is not to say, however, that questions of intercollege finance do not arise. As public IHEs proliferate, equity problems among public IHEs become more acute.

The rationale for the public support of higher education rests mainly on the externality argument. If higher education provides social benefits to society that individual students cannot capture, then the private demand for education will be less than the social demand, and underproduction of education will result. Public subsidies may be used to spur private demand for higher education. It has also been argued that individuals might not demand the type of education most needed by society. The overproduction of English and history majors, unable to find suitable employment, coupled with the underproduction of nurses, accountants, or computer analysts—where the demand for jobs exceeds the available supply—is often cited as a rationale for directing government subsidies in order to change the effective student demand. It should be noted that critics argue, in turn, that job shortages or surpluses would be eliminated, given sufficient time, through the effect on wages, unless major bottlenecks prevent the market from automatic adjustment (such as when artificial limits are placed on wages and salaries, the case of nurses being an example, or when ceilings on enrollments in a given field are placed by schools, a prime example of which is medicine).

It is quite fascinating—to some observers rather disturbing—that massive government aid to higher education is given on the basis of plausible yet unsupported assumptions regarding the existence of external benefits. As is seen from Table 10-1, $24.3 billion were granted to IHEs during 1976-1977 by federal, state, and local governments. Additional funds were given directly to individuals in the form of scholarships, loans, grants, and (indirectly) through tax deductions.

A breakdown of the current fund revenues of IHEs for 1974-1975 is reproduced in Table 10-3. It is noteworthy that tuition and fees account for only 20.3 percent of revenues, the remainder being funded from government, private sources, endowment income, and sales and services. Of course, the private sector relies much more heavily on nongovernment income, although federal grants account for 19.6 percent of private and only 15.8 percent of public IHEs revenues.

Federal Aid

Federal aid is given both to institutions and to individuals. The bulk of federal aid goes to IHEs under a number of categorical aid

Table 10-3. Current Fund Revenue of Institutions of Higher Education by Control of Institution and by Source of Revenue—United States, 1974-1975 (amounts in thousands of dollars).

	Current Fund Revenue, by Control of Institution					
	Public and Private		Public		Private	
Source	Amount	Percent	Amount	Percent	Amount	Percent
1	2	3	4	5	6	7
Total current fund revenue	$35,686,902	100.0	$24,004,864	100.0	$11,682,039	100.0
Tuition and fees from students	7,232,908	20.3	3,078,506	12.8	4,154,402	35.6
Federal government	6,072,554	17.0	3,786,094	15.8	2,286,461	19.6
Unrestricted appropriations	884,427	2.5	749,504	3.1	134,924	1.2
Unrestricted grants and contracts	548,464	1.5	279,437.	1.2	269,027	2.3
Restricted grants and contracts	3,558,078	10.0	2,269,674	9.5	1,288,404	11.0
Independent operations (FFRDC)[a]	1,081,585	3.0	487,479	2.0	594,106	5.1
State governments	10,857,376	30.4	10,608,449	44.2	248,925	2.1
Unrestricted appropriations	10,366,913	29.1	10,210,568	42.5	156,344	1.3
Unrestricted grants and contracts	84,348	0.2	67,987	0.3	16,361	0.1
Restricted grants and contracts	406,115	1.1	329,894	1.4	76,220	0.7
Local governments	1,424,392	4.0	1,336,841	5.6	87,550	0.7[b]
Unrestricted appropriations	1,228,603	3.4	1,226,004	5.1	2,599	[b]
Unrestricted grants and contracts	35,069	0.1	26,462	0.1	8,607	
Restricted grants and contracts	160,720	0.5	84,375	0.4	76,344	0.7
Private gifts, grants, and contracts	1,744,967	4.9	556,665	2.3	1,188,302	10.2
Unrestricted	708,030	2.0	47,114	0.2	660,917	5.7
Restricted	1,036,937	2.9	509,551	2.1	527,386	4.5
Endowment income	717,915	2.0	106,568	0.4	611,347	5.2
Unrestricted	403,987	1.1	50,673	0.2	353,314	3.0
Restricted	313,927	0.9	55,895	0.2	258,033	2.2
Sales and services	6,787,163	19.0	4,043,555	16.8	2,743,609	23.5
Educational activities	554,882	1.6	372,886	1.6	181,996	1.6
Auxiliary enterprises	4,080,202	11.4	2,548,498	10.6	1,531,705	13.1
Hospitals	2,152,079	6.0	1,122,171	4.7	1,029,908	8.8
Other sources	849,625	2.4	488,185	2.0	361,440	3.1

Source: Grant and Lind (1977), Table 123, p. 132.
[a]Generally includes only those revenues associated with major federally funded research and development centers.
[b]Less than 0.05 percent.

programs administered by all of the departments in the executive branch and also through grants from independent agencies of the federal government.

Restricted and unrestricted research grants and contracts accounted for 67.6 percent of federal aid to IHEs in 1974–1975. They represent, at least in part, purchase of services rendered by colleges and universities to the federal government, and therefore the label "aid" is somewhat misleading. It is clear, however, that without such grants and contracts, IHEs would not be able to retain the number and quality of faculty and other academic services (such as high speed advanced computers).

Large sums of federal aid to education in the United States have been directed to the advancement of science and engineering, in an effort to match advances by the Soviet Union. The National Defense Education Act of 1958 is a prime example. Library funds and other grants for university support were made available through the Higher Education Act of 1965 and subsequent amendments. Emphasis in recent years has shifted to student aid, especially for those considered to be "disadvantaged." For example, "educational opportunity grants" have been established in 1968, and by fiscal year 1977 they exceeded $1.1 billion. Likewise, the work study program was inaugurated around 1966, and by fiscal year 1977 more than $440 million were expended by the federal government. Furthermore, student loans increased from $40 million in 1960 to more than $1 billion in 1977 (Grant and Lind, 1977: ch. V).

The emphasis on student aid and research grants and contracts could be justified on economic grounds. Regarding student aid, the role of the federal government in income distribution is generally accepted. Income distribution policy, which is effected not through cash payments but rather through a student subsidization program that is designed to move the client out of poverty and into the mainstream of American life, has received widespread support. It is also consistent with our findings that substantial economic returns to investment in higher education could be reaped by individuals possessing adequate ability and motivation.

On the other hand, education subsidies as a tool of income distribution may be unfair, because only individuals willing and able to attend an IHE would be affected. It could also be inefficient, if the recipients of such aid would be enrolled in an IHE only to receive cash payments, returning to their original state of affairs after such payments cease. An alternative approach would be to give all poor families a certain cash grant, and it would be up to them to decide whether they want to use it to purchase college education or in an alternative manner.

The large sums given to IHEs as research grants and contracts are consistent with the hypothesis that the largest external returns generated by education are related to faculty and student research and postgraduate training. It is believed that scientific and industrial progress cannot proceed without the availability of highly skilled professionals, trained by graduate schools in colleges and universities. Since the private returns to graduate education are meager, while the costs of training postgraduate students are very high, large subsidies would be needed to attract postgraduate students. Moreover, since holders of advanced degrees are extremely mobile, it is unlikely that the individual states would be willing to provide sufficient subsidies to meet national needs for a highly skilled workforce. Federal subsidies are, therefore, justified.

Student Aid. There is much debate on the optimal means by which student aid should be provided. At present, such aid is provided through scholarships and other grants, loans, and limited tax deduction. A bill allowing modest tax credits for college tuition is now pending in Congress, but a presidential veto cannot be ruled out.

The principal bone of contention is whether student aid is a vehicle for increasing "equality of opportunity" or a means by which the externality issue may be addressed. If there are externalities, then outright subsidies are appropriate. If, however, the major problem is the lack of opportunities for the disadvantaged to obtain college education, then it appears that loans are appropriate. Most economists now argue that an adequate loan program is the answer to the problem, because evidence of the existence and magnitude of externalities is totally lacking.

Loans. If there were a perfect capital market, and if some form of servitude would be permissable, students should be able to obtain commercial loans to finance their higher education just as they use loans to finance homes, automobiles, or vacations. Capital markets, however, are imperfect. Moreover, commercial lenders cannot mortgate a person's future income and, in the event of default of the loan, sell his services to the highest bidder. It is no surprise that commercial lenders would be reluctant to float student loans without government guarantees.

Proceeding from the argument that student loans are necessary to insure equality of opportunity, the question then arises as to how such loans are to be provided. A number of possibilities have been investigated, including guarantee of commercial loans, conventional loans given by the government at a reduced rate of interest and with a stipulation that payments need not be made for a number of years following graduation, or some form of an income-contingent loan. A brief description of such loan programs follows.

Guaranteed Loans. As noted earlier, the purpose of such a program is to make available to students private loans that are guaranteed by the government. These loans may also contain a subsidy in the form of low interest charges repayable over relatively long periods. Obviously, the possibilities for variations are virtually infinite. The rationale for such loans is that their aggregate cost per student is relatively low, since the commercial lending institutions are equipped to handle such matters.

Among the many objections to guaranteed loans, two may be singled out. The first is that those students who need such loans most would be reluctant to borrow, due to the uncertainty concerning future earnings prospects. A "proof" of such reluctance has been cited by some authors, pointing out that only a fraction of available government-guaranteed loans has been tapped (Van Den Haag, 1956: 69–70). Although this "proof" may not be too convincing—due to the nature of these loans (generally designed to meet emergencies and providing only minor sums)—it is still probably true that such loan schemes may not be effective in attracting enough capable but poor students to higher education.

Second, if eligibility criteria for loans are not too restrictive, there is a danger that some students will borrow at these low rates of interest to finance noneducational ventures. The result will be that government subsidies will be used for purposes other than higher education. Given that interest charges on the loans are substantially lower than what one could obtain in the private market, an incentive for abusing educational loans is clearly present. A "means test" might reduce the severity of this problem, but arguments have also been advanced against such "means tests" (see H.R. Bowen, 1969). Under the Guaranteed Student Loans (GSL) program, more than $450 million were available in fiscal year 1977.

Government Loans. Direct loans by the federal government to students have increased over the years. The National Direct Student Loans (NDSL) program is by now well established, and in fiscal year 1977, the government appropriated approximately $333 million dollars for that program. The NDSL has replaced the National Defense Education Act loans established in 1958.

There are numerous areas for debate. For example, how should the loans be administered? Who should be eligible to receive loans?

What should be the terms for repayment? How can a loan program be designed to maximize the benefits derived therefrom per dollar of government investment? Should it be administered by an agency of the federal government, an independent agency, or by the individual IHEs?

Since the major purpose of loans is to enable able but poor individuals to obtain higher education, the need to examine the demand for loans is imperative. Brugel, Johnson and Leslie (forthcoming) provide one analysis of this kind, demonstrating student preference for loan schemes that offer more options for repayment, including income-contingent loans (described below). They also indicate that attitudes toward student loans do change in response to additional information provided about the features of the loan programs. Similar results were obtained in a study by Johnstone et. al. (1972).

Income-Contingent Loans. A proposal for such loans was made by Van Den Haag (1956). Although his proposal was for a self-financing loan program provided by IHEs, it is the forerunner of later proposals for government-financed income-contingent loans and therefore should be discussed at this point. Van den Haag argues that schools are the best judges of student talent, ability, and professional chances. Further, the loans are to be repaid not by any conventional repayment mechanism but by requiring the students to defray a portion of their future earnings. In this manner, only those students whose earnings are sufficiently large would be required to repay their loans. Moreover, since repayment is a function of future student earnings, schools will select those students who will, and offer such curricula to, maximize future earnings. To the extent that future earnings correctly indicate social educational benefits, such a scheme is likely to promote an optimal allocation of resources. At one and the same time, poor, through capable, students will be selected by the schools—because of the expected benefits—so that equality of opportunity will be enhanced. As a result, all deserving students will receive higher education. Of course, those students who are in a position to finance their own education may still do so. But there will no longer be an incentive for schools to attract rich but mediocre students.

The Educational Opportunity Bank (EOB). More than ten years after Van Den Haag's recommendations were published, a government panel (Zacharias, 1967, 1969) endorsed a federally based, massive loan program in which many of Van Den Haag's suggestions were incorporated. The system has been called the educational opportunity bank (EOB). The basic idea behind the EOB is that students may obtain substantial sums through the federal government to support their educational effort, repayment being made on the basis of future income. This latter feature is designed to encourage individuals to borrow for education: if the educational enterprise proves to be successful, a small additional tax on gross or net income would not be too difficult to absorb. If, on the other hand, expectations regarding educational benefits fail to materialize, the loan will be forgiven. Other features include an "opt out" provision—that is, individuals who wish to repay their loan through a more conventional repayment method, may do so by treating the loan as a conventional 6 percent loan. This will enable persons with exceptionally high future incomes to avoid repayment through income taxation that is far out of proportion to the amount of loan obtained. Other features include life and health incurance (also suggested by Van Den Haag), income insurance, and special provisions regarding repayment by women.

One distinct advantage of such a scheme over Van Den Haag's is that administration of the bank through the Internal Revenue Service guarantees low administrative costs and insures that earnings data will be accurate. At the same time, some of the allocative effects of the Van Den Haag scheme will not be realized through the EOB.

Karl Shell and his colleagues (1968) provide an in-depth analysis of the EOB with respect to its allocative and distributional effects, costs of operation, special features, and so on. They concur with the panel on the "opt out" option, but argue that their treatment of repayment by women has undesirable effects. They present an alternative repayment scheme for women. In addition, they discuss the fiscal impact of the bank on the federal budget, the desirability of contingent repayment loan programs (i.e., in which repayment is contingent upon future earnings), and the definition of income for repayment purposes.[1]

Income-contingent loans (ICLs) have become a subject of some controversy in recent years. Among those participating in the debate are R. Feldman (1976), Korczyk (1977), Nerlove (1975), and Raymond and Sesnowitz (1976a). One area of debate is the effect of such loans on (1) "adverse selection" and (2) "moral hazard." R. Feldman (1976), discussing the effect of ICLs on physicians' behavior

1. The EOB scheme is similar, in many respects, to a loan scheme proposed several years earlier by Vickrey (1962). The main difference between the EOB and the Vickrey proposal is that the former would base repayment on total income earned by individuals following graduation from school, where Vickrey proposed that repayment is based on extra (incremental) income that is due to the educational investment for which the loan was obtained (see also Shell, 1970).

argues that ICLs are likely to (1) adversely affect choice of speciality, resulting in fewer primary care physicians and more specialists; and (2) affect work disincentives significantly—the higher the rate of repayment, the more severe would work disincentives be. Since ICLs require higher repayment rates than flat rate loans, Feldman prefers the latter for financing medical education. In contrast, Raymond and Sesnowitz (1976a) argue that evidence of adverse selection or moral hazard is simply unconvincing or nonexistent.

Although the EOB proposal has never been implemented, Van Den Haag's plan has been adopted, in principle, by a number of institutions, most notably Yale University.

Tax Relief Measures.   Federal aid to students and/or their families may also be given indirectly via tax deductions, extra exemptions, or tax credits. At present, the scope for such aid is very limited, but if the current proposal for tax credits becomes law, it is likely that such tax relief measures would assume increasing importance in the future.

Tax Deductions and Extra Exemptions.   The Internal Revenue Service (IRS) code currently allows deduction of educational expenditures associated with a taxpayer's current employment. That is, if the current employer requires his employee to undertake a given educational investment as a condition for current or continuing employment, the expenses incurred are deductible. Expenses associated with children, or with one's desire to obtain different employment opportunities from those currently available to him by virtue of his education, are not deductible.

Several proposals have been advanced in recent years to change the IRS code. One proposal would allow parents to deduct fees and tuition charged to their dependents from their gross income. Maximum ceilings proposed vary from $600 to $2,000. Another proposal provides for the addition of one or two dependent exemptions per student to compensate for college expenses. The rationale for the latter is that deductions will result in greater subsidies to parents whose children go to private and/or more expensive schools, whereas additional exemptions will compensate all parents to the same extent. The implicit assumption is that more expensive colleges represent not additional social benefits but rather greater prestige and higher consumption benefits. Moreover, full cost deduction (up to some maximum) will encourage parents to send their children to the more expensive schools. This may not be in the best interest of society.

Goode (1962, 1976) argues against both deduction by parents of costs charged to their dependent's education and the extra exemptions. First, additional exemptions and/or deductions discriminate in favor of wealthier families (because they pay taxes at higher marginal rates and because poor families may not have enough income to enjoy any of the added exemptions or deductions). Second, he argues that the beneficiaries of the educational investment are the students themselves and that the contribution by parents should be considered as a gift. As an alternative, Goode suggests that persons should be allowed to amortize their direct educational costs against subsequent earnings. He concedes that there are several problems with his approach, one being that part of the educational investment is for consumption purposes. But he demonstrates that the aggregate economic effect of such a plan would be relatively negligible.

Tax Credits. A counterpart to the deduction by parents of educational expenses of dependents is the percentage credit plan. It is designed to overcome the objection noted earlier that double exemptions or deductions discriminate against poorer families. One variation of the percentage credit plan permits a 100 percent credit from tax liability for tuition and fees up to a certain ceiling. Ceilings varying from $100 to $300 have been proposed by R.A. Freeman (1965). Another variation provides for a flat percentage credit for educational expenses up to a maximum. The American Council on Education has proposed a 30 percent credit up to a maximum credit of $450. It should be noted that even though tax credits do not result in as large a discrimination against low income families as do additional exemptions and deductions, some discrimination remains. One plan that would reduce such discrimination further is the sliding tax credit plan, in which a percentage tax credit would be given for each range of fees paid. The lower ranges would have a higher percentage deductible. A maximum net tax credit would also be established.[2]

Although the sliding tax credit plan is less objectionable on equity grounds, it is still discriminatory, since families with no taxable income will receive no benefits therefrom—and it has other shortcomings. First, its economic effects would be relatively large, resulting in substantial loss of Treasury revenues. Second, since tax credits vary with school costs, institutions of learning could increase tuition and fees, shifting the educational burden to the federal taxpayer. Finally,

2. An Example given by R.A. Freeman (1965) is as follows:

Tuition and Fees	Credit (percent)
First $100	100
Next $400	30
Next $1000	20
Maximum net credit: $420	

high cost, private schools would clearly be favored; to the extent that high cost implies inefficiency, such a plan would help to perpetuate inefficient institutions.

It should be noted that all of the above-mentioned plans are likely to result in some redistribution of income from the poorer to the richer. This is based upon the fact that persons acquiring more education are more likely to come from higher income families. So the general taxpayer is asked to support the educational effort undertaken by the more affluent taxpayer. Such a policy could still be justified on the ground (1) that investment in the education of the richer person with funds raised, in part, from poorer taxpayers is likely to lead to social benefits that will more than compensate for the small loss to the poorer taxpayer; and (2) that the graduated income tax will redistribute the private educational benefits from those in whom investment is made to the general taxpayer. So, in effect, the poorer taxpayer is asked to make an investment that in turn, will benefit him in the long run.

The tax credit proposal now before Congress is a percentage tax credit plan, whereby a sum of up to $100 or $250 (depending on whether the House or Senate version is considered) may be credited against one's tax liability. Opponents of the tax credit proposals argue that (1) it is less satisfactory on equity grounds than other subsidy or loan programs where a means test can assure that government funds go to those who need the funds most; and (2) even if the initial program is modest, it is likely to be expanded in future years, costing the Treasury large sums while resulting in relatively little increase in student enrollments. Proponents of tax credits argue that low income students already receive adequate funding through scholarships, grants, and loans, while middle income students, who do not quality for them, have suffered the most and deserve some relief.

State Aid

State aid, in constrast to federal aid, is mostly in the form of unrestricted aid to IHEs on the basis of full-time equivalent (FTE) student enrollments and other criteria. While it has increased significantly in absolute terms over the last twenty years, the relative share of state aid in financing higher education has remained reasonably stable since 1960.

A summary of state aid to IHEs for 1977-1978 is provided in Table 10-4. We note significant variations in aid per student, with highest aid ($4,923) in Alaska and the lowest ($954) in New Hampshire. Average per pupil state aid in the United States is $1,735. This is 37 percent of per pupil direct costs of public IHEs (see Table 4-3)

Table 10-4. State Aid to Higher Education, 1977–1978.

	Total State Appropriations 1977-1978 (millions)	Enrollment in Public IHEs 1975-1976 (thousands)	Appropriations per Student: [(1) ÷ (2)] X 1,000 Amount	Rank
	1	2	3	4
Alabama	$ 311.0	146	$ 2,130	13
Alaska	64.0	13	4,923	1
Arizona	215.6	169	1,276	48
Arkansas	126.2	56	2,254	9
California	1,961.5	1,618	1,212	49
Colorado	220.9	136	1,624	37
Connecticut	164.5	94	1,750	29
Delaware	44.2	27	1,637	35
Florida	489.6	288	1,700	31
Georgia	302.9	143	2,118	14
Hawaii	109.6	43	2,549	4
Idaho	77.1	31	2,487	5
Illinois	740.2	444	1,667	32
Indiana	352.4	159	2,216	10
Iowa	244.3	84	2,908	2
Kansas	188.7	108	1,747	30
Kentucky	217.4	105	2,070	19
Louisiana	242.5	132	1,837	28
Maine	45.3	31	1,461	44
Maryland	266.1	177	1,503	42
Massachusetts	251.7	174	1,447	45
Michigan	660.4	437	1,511	41
Minnesota	380.9	149	2,556	3
Mississippi	186.6	90	2,073	18
Missouri	260.1	158	1,646	34
Montana	52.3	28	1,868	25
Nebraska	131.2	61	2,151	12
Nevada	45.5	30	1,517	40
New Hampshire	22.9	24	954	50
New Jersey	340.6	228	1,494	43
New Mexico	95.8	48	1,996	21
New York	1,298.8	614	2,115	15
North Carolina	460.9	201	2,293	8
North Dakota	61.2	28	2,186	11
Ohio	551.2	337	1,636	36
Oklahoma	173.3	124	1,398	46
Oregon	198.2	130	1,525	39
Pennsylvania	676.2	287	2,356	7
Rhode Island	66.7	32	2,084	17
South Carolina	227.1	108	2,103	16
South Dakota	41.1	22	1,868	25
Tennessee	230.6	140	1,647	33
Texas	1,050.4	542	1,938	22
Utah	117.1	57	2,054	20
Vermont	23.0	17	1,353	47
Virginia	330.6	215	1,538	38
Washington	380.3	203	1,873	24

297

Table 10–4.   continued

	Total State Appropriations 1977–1978 (millions)	Enrollment in Public IHEs 1975–1976 (thousands)	Appropriations per Student: [(1) ÷ (2)] × 1,000	
			Amount	Rank
West Virginia	126.3	68	1,857	27
Wisconsin	399.4	211	1,893	23
Wyoming	42.9	18	2,383	6
Total U.S.	15,267.3	8,798[a]	1,735	

Source: Coughlin (1977); and Grant and Lind (1977), Table 77.
[a]Excludes U.S. service schools.

and only 18 percent of the sum of direct costs plus earnings foregone per pupil (see Table 4–6).

There are many important issues regarding state aid to education. They include: (1) Should the states support undergraduate public education? (2) If the answer to (1) is in the affirmative, should the aid be given to students in grants and/or loans or to IHEs? (3) What proportion of school costs should be subsidized by the state? (4) In states with multiple public IHEs, how should state appropriations be divided among the institutions? Finally, (5) should the state provide direct subsidies to private IHEs?

Should the State Support Undergraduate Public Education?   One could extend the question to inquire whether public IHEs should exist at all. But even if one grants their right to exist, it does not necessarily follow that they should receive state subsidies. They could be financed through federal funds, endowment and other sources, and student tuition and fees.

The argument for state aid is that IHEs located in a state's boundaries provide external benefits. They are believed to improve the attractiveness of the state to business and to professionals whose skills are demanded in the state. It is often asserted that economic growth of a state depends critically on the quality of the educational (especially higher education) facilities available in the state. State subsidies are, therefore, regarded as an investment. In addition, state subsidies are a hidden form of tax rebate as well as a social welfare tool (as discussed in the section on federal aid).

The income distribution aspect of state aid to education has received considerable attention since the publication of the well-known work by Hansen and Weisbrod (1969a, 1969b). Using California data, they obtain results indicating that state subsidies benefit the rich relatively more than they benefit the poor. This is due to two main factors: (1) The more affluent students typically attend the more prestigious institutions, such as the University of California campuses, where state aid is relatively high, whereas lower income students typically attend the less prestigious IHEs, such as the community colleges or the state college system (now state university system), where state aid is much lower. (2) A much larger fraction of the well to do attend the state-aided system.

The Hansen-Weisbrod findings have been freely debated, with successive studies affirming or debunking their conclusions. The most persistent critic has been Pechman (1970, 1971, 1972), who reanalyzed the Hansen-Weisbrod data and obtained opposite conclusions. Also, Rubin (1975) argues that the Hansen-Weisbrod method has severe shortcomings and employes data from New Jersey to show that subsidies to IHEs do not have adverse redistributive impact. Other contributors to the debate include Cohn (1970a), Crean (1975), Hartman (1970), Hight and Pollock (1973), J.W. McGuire (1976), and Sharkansky (1970). A theoretical analysis by Conlisk (1977) supports the Pechman position.

There is a growing number of economists supporting full cost funding of IHEs through student tuition and charges. One of the earliest argument in favor of full cost tuition was made by Danière (1964). The trend in state aid to IHEs, however, continues to show strong state support, with state aid increasing 20 percent during the period 1975–1976 to 1977–1978 (6 percent when adjusted for inflation; see Coughlin, 1977).

Institutional versus Student Aid. Given that current beliefs in the United States support the argument that higher education deserves state support because of equity and/or efficiency considerations (i.e., the desire to help able but poor students; and the need to subsidize higher education to offset external effects), it remains unclear whether such support should be given directly to students (in the form of scholarships, grants, or loans) or to IHEs. The question also involves, of course, the treatment of nonpublic IHEs, but it would be preferable to confine the discussion at this point to public IHEs.

The basic arguments in favor of direct student support include (1) giving students more choice as to where their subsidy could be spent; (2) providing a market type process of accountability by IHEs, since those IHEs that do not provide quality education would lose enrollments; and (3) minimizing the interference of the state in the internal affairs of the IHEs. Proponents of institutional grants argue, on the other hand, that students are not competent to make rational choices when it comes to higher education (being a highly invisible product) and, thus, that the efficiency of the higher educational system might be impaired if institutional grants are replaced by student grants. Moreover, institutional funding provides a leverage through which the state could direct the development of academic and other programs in the best interest of the state.

Although some state aid is given through scholarships, grants, and loans, by far most of the state funds are given to educational institutions. There are no visible signs for a change in the trend in the foreseeable future.

Amount of State Aid. If it is accepted that state aid should be given to IHEs, what should be the amount of aid? If cost per pupil is $X, what proportion of X should be funded by the state and what by the student? Since the students are likely to benefit from their education, there is a justification for student charges.

The question involves, once more, both equity and efficiency aspects. If only efficiency matters, then state support should be equal to the proportion that external benefits are of total benefits. The problem, however, is not only to measure average external benefits, but also to calculate the benefits from and costs of different educational packages. Variable tuition and subsidy rates should then be determined by discipline and degree program. And whereas some data on costs of education by discipline and degree programs are available, there is virtually no information on the existence and magnitude of external benefits.

The equity issue also requires differential tuition and subsidies. In the absence of other sources of student support (such as federal grant and loan programs), subsidies should vary inversely with a student's family income. A variable tuition program was, in fact, instituted at Michigan State University, but was subsequently discontinued. The major reason for the lack of support for such programs is the tremendous administrative difficulties involved.

It is not surprising, therefore, that the amount of state aid per pupil or per program varies substantially. While in some states aid is determined on the basis of a funding formula, in others state appropriations are still determined by direct negotiations between the respective IHEs and the legislature.

Formula Funding. The number and type of IHEs has increased greatly during the past twenty years. There are multiple public IHEs in all of the states, requiring some procedure by which state aid to higher education is to be divided between the IHEs. There are still some states in which each IHE negotiates a separate deal with the legislature. But some form of formula finance has become commonplace in many states.

There are two major types of formulas: (1) base formulas and (2) functional formulas. In base formulas, direct expenditures for instruction are first determined, and other expenses are calculated as a percentage of the base (i.e., instructional costs). In functional formulas, on the other hand, costs of services are estimated "through a consideration of factors directly relevant to the activity itself" (J.L. Miller, 1965: 106). A combination of the two is also possible. Also, some form of program budgeting has been used to generate appropriation requests.

The 1978-1979 funding formula in South Carolina is an example of the base formula. It consists of the following steps:

1. Estimate student credit hours by level (undergraduate, master's, and doctoral) and academic area.
2. Calculate number of FTE (full-time equivalent) students, where one FTE student equals fifteen credit hours of undergraduates, eleven of masters, and nine of doctoral students.
3. Using a table, calculate the number of FTE faculty. The table shows how many FTE students equal one FTE faculty for each level and discipline. Student-teacher ratios in the table vary from a low of 4:1 in textile science for doctoral students to a high of 26:1 for law.
4. Divide FTE teaching positions into regular faculty and teaching assistants. For the former, the number of FTE teachers are multiplied by the highest average salary for institutions of a given class (for example, $17,808 for Clemson and University of South Carolina) plus an improvement factor. For the latter, FTE teaching assistant positions are multiplied by $6,633 (plus an improvement factor). The two sums are then added.
5. For instructional costs other than teacher salaries, add 40, 35, or 30 percent depending on type of institution. When items 4 and 5 are summed, we get an estimate of "total instructional costs" (TIC).
6. Add 10 percent of TIC for library costs.
7. Add allowable costs for operation and maintenance of plant and utilities. This is not related to TIC.
8. Add 26 percent of TIC to cover general administration, student services, and other activities. The sum of items 4, 5, 6, 7, and 8 are equal to the costs of "basic educational and general operations" (BEGO) of each IHE.

9. Subtract from BEGO the required "fee income deduction" ($300 or $200 per FTE student, depending on type of IHE). The result is "the lump-sum state appropriation request for basic educational and general operations, subject to adjustments for actual fall 1978 enrollments" (South Caroline Commission on Higher Education, 1978: 45).

In addition to these steps, (1) expenditures for research are supported separately, including a $250 supplement per FTE graduate student; and (2) capital funds are provided entirely separately from the funding formula.

Additional funding may be requested for continuing or one-time expenditures of a special nature. Moreover, the state legislature has the final authority to appropriate funds, and individual IHEs can (and usually do) attempt to receive additional funds. Finally, the legislature has not always fully funded the appropriation requests by the Higher Education Commission for each IHE.

The South Carolina example (modeled after the Oklahoma formula) illustrates the various possible combinations and permutations that might be employed to change the base formula. This can be achieved by changing the definitions of FTE student or faculty or by employing different salary levels to obtain the TIC (for example, the average salary in the region could be used), and of course, the various "add ons" are completely arbitrary.

The alternatives to base formula—functional formula or program budgeting—are less arbitrary because they base funding on present costs of activities or expected program performance. But their implementation requires a lot more information, along with a coordinating agency capable of evaluating and monitoring programs of this kind.

Subsidies to Private IHEs. Direct state aid to private IHEs amounted to $400 million in 1976-1977. From a purely economic point of view, if state support to public IHEs is justified according the externality argument, the same rationale can be used to justify state aid to private IHEs. Moreover, the argument concerning subsidization of churches loses its force when only private-independent IHEs are considered for state aid.

A serious consequence of the reluctance to provide state aid to private IHEs has been the increased competitive advantage of public IHEs. If students could get an equally good education at a public IHE, why enroll in a private IHE where tuition and charges must be higher (to offset state aid received by public IHEs)? The result should be predictable: private IHEs would opt to become public institutions, so that they, too, would be able to receive state aid. Examples of this phenomenon abound: University of Pittsburgh, University of Buffalo (now SUNY at Buffalo), and many others. Only the truly outstanding private IHEs can continue to favorably compete with the public IHEs. What is almost astounding is that despite the unfavorable competitive situation, private IHEs have been able to maintain enrollments (though their share of total enrollments has decreased over time; see Table 1-1, above).

Aid to students (scholarships, loans, etc.) is generally made available on the basis of need or merit, regardless of where the individual enrolls. Student aid, moreover, is generally not included in the basic support formula and is handled entirely separately. Nevertheless, the private IHEs require higher aid per student, other things equal, placing them at a disadvantage in recruiting low and especially middle income students.

THE VOUCHER PLAN

Government aid to education in the United States and other countries is focused on educational institutions. Although some aid is given directly to students or indirectly through tax relief, the great majority of government funds is disbursed to institutions. Proponents of the educational voucher plan claim that government aid should be given to students or their parents, who in turn will decide where to enroll.

As E.G. West (1967) observes, the voucher idea dates back to the eighteenth century and Tom Paine (in his book, *The Rights of Man*). Paine's basic proposal included the following elements: (1) every family would receive £4 per child under fourteen years of age; (2) the parents will be required to send the children to school; (3) local ministers will certify compliance with the requirement; and (4) children in rural areas will receive a special allowance.

The reasons for supporting such a scheme include the following: (1) administration of the plan would be simple; (2) it will ensure competition among schools so that schools and teachers would have to be accountable for their actions; (3) "decentralized education would counter the prevailing desire of the aristocrats to maintain their power by depending on ignorance" (West, 1967: 382); (4) "Paines proposals contained the independent aim of abolishing the pernicious effects of the poor law" (id.). Moreover, the use of ministers as inspectors was the answer to anticipated criticism that parents would be unable to choose the "right" educational medium.

The modern development of the voucher plan is generally credited to Milton Freidman (1955, 1962). Friedman's arguments parallel those of Paine, but do not include the use of ministers or "inspectors." Instead, vouchers would be paid only to parents sending their children to accredited schools. Also, a major purpose of Friedman's plan was to enable parents to spend extra funds for their children's education. Under the present public school system, if, say, per pupil expenditures are $1,000 and a parent wishes to spend $1,200 on his child's education, then he would have to pay an increment of $1,200, not $200, by enrolling the child in a private school (which receives no state aid). The parent would have to pay state and local taxes for education regardless of whether the child is enrolled in a public or a private school. Such a system clearly discourages parents from choosing a slightly more expensive educational program and results in an underinvestment in education. The voucher plan, on the other hand, would permit parents to supplement the voucher by choosing educational programs costing more than that covered by the vouchers.

Interestingly, the voucher plan has received support form individuals holding divergent political beliefs. Thus Milton Friedman is joined by Christopher Jencks and others in support of the voucher system (Jencks, 1971; Jencks et al., 1970). Jencks and his colleagues supported the voucher plan primarily because they saw in it an opportunity to increase community control over the schools. Also, the Jencks plan contains various modifications of the original plan to eliminate the alleged impact it would have on pupils from poor families and minorities.

Opponents of the Friedman system retort with a number of counterarguments. First, they contend that parents are not sufficiently aware or informed of educational matters and may choose a school on the basis of advertisement rather than quality of educational program. Further, it is argued that progress made by the civil rights movement in school integration will be entirely eliminated. Another common objection is the fear that such a system will lead to loss of cohesion in society and to the sort of fragmentation in society against which the public school system in the United States has been devised in the first place. It is also feared that poor persons who are unable to provide transportation to locations where superior schools might be established will be forced to accept substandard schooling. Also, teachers' unions object out of fear that seniority rights, tenure, and other benefits now enjoyed in the public school system may be changed drastically when a substantial portion of the educational enterprise will be run by private business. Finally, it is pointed out that a shift from public to private or to mixed public-private schooling will result in the idling of much plant and equipment, at a staggering cost to the taxpayer.

Most of these counterarguments have been addressed by the Jencks modified voucher proposals. Under the modified proposals, the amount of the vouchers would vary with the type of student, with "disadvantaged" students receiving more. This would encourage schools to seek out the disadvantaged. Moreover, schools could be required to accept a fixed proportion of the minority students applying for admission, and free or subsidized transportation could be made available to transport students to areas where good schools are located.

The voucher plan was quite popular in the United States during the late 1960s and early 1970s. The idea of a voucher was even entertained by the Congress of the United States, and pilot experimental programs were approved. The best-known and most-analyzed one is the experimental program that took place in Alum Rock, California, under the auspices of the Office of Economic Opportunity (OEO). Other voucherlike experimental programs were carried out in Oregon and New Hampshire.

There is a considerable amount of literature on the design and effect of the various voucher programs. The problem, however, is that none of these programs even remotely resembled the Friedman or Jencks voucher systems. Most importantly, none incorporated any nonpublic schools. The Alum Rock plan allowed students to choose any school among those participating in the program, but since surrounding schools refused to participate, the choice was extremely limited. As Cohen and Farrar (1977) observe, the desire to give parents more power may have actually resulted in more power usurped by the local educational system, simply because the latter was much better organized and motivated and was strongly opposed to educational reform.

Nonpublic School Finance

The crux of the matter is the issue of government aid to nonpublic schools. So long as such aid is prohibited by state or federal constitutions, a true voucher system is a myth. Moreover, there are no signs to indicate massive political support behind a movement to make such aid legal. Nevertheless, considerable support for tax credits against tuition charges in nonpublic elementary and secondary schools has been observed in recent congressional proceedings.

It was noted earlier that economic theory can hardly be used to support the argument against state aid to nonpublic schools. The arguments usually rest on moral and philosophical tenents, and these have been debated over time and space. The point is that until nonpublic school aid is permitted, a bona fide test of the voucher plan is impossible.

Resistance by Local Education Agencies

Equally damaging to the voucher plan is the staunch opposition by public school teachers and administrators alike. The opposition is understandable, but hardly to be applauded. Yet the strength of the local education lobby is so great as to seriously diminish the prospects for a voucher plan.

This is unfortunate, because the voucher plan holds great promise in eliminating sources of inefficiency in American education. Coupled with safeguards to insure the continuation and strengthening of equality of opportunity, the voucher system is one of the most important innovations promulgated in school finance. As matters stand now, only a strong, positive outcome of a research and demonstration (R&D) project could save the plan from extinction, and even prospects for such an R&D plan appear remote at this juncture.

Family Power Equalization

An alternative plan has been suggested by Coons et al. (1970) in which the level of the voucher will vary according to the rate at which each family is willing to tax itself. Thus, the power to buy educational services will rest on the tax effort only, not on financial ability. Those families that are willing to tax themselves at higher rates would be entitled to purchase more educational services. The system would be quite similar to the "district power equalizing" scheme discussed above, except that the decision unit will be the family instead of the school district.

A potential difficulty with the family power equalization scheme is the possibility that the marginal utility of income (i.e., the subjective valuation of an extra dollar of income) is very high for low income people, so that even if low income families place a relatively high value on education, they might be reluctant to impose high tax rates upon themselves. A modification of the plan, in which family power equalization will commence only at some (relatively high) income level, might be more attractive.

CONCLUSIONS

The role of government in education is based on two main pillars—equalization and externalities. Equalization is difficult to define and measure, but operationally it has meant the desire to improve the lot of property and income poor families and communities. Government aid would be designed to reduce the degree of income and wealth inequality. Programs of federal and state aid to elementary and secondary education have been shown to be generally consistent with this aim, while some disagreement remains about the income distributional effects of state aid to IHEs. The externality argument is that education bestows social benefits to society that individual students are unable to appropriate. Lack of government aid would therefore result in underinvestment in education. Federal and state support are needed to offset the external effects. Unfortunately, virtually no empirical support of the argument has surfaced to date.

It has been emphasized throughout that even if the arguments in favor of government involvement in education are accepted, economic theory does not provide a rationale for government-controlled schools and IHEs. In fact, the voucher system, which provides for support of both public and private schools through aid to students, appears to be extremely attractive from an economic point of view.

In financing elementary and secondary schools, the federal government has focused on low income pupils while states have focused on property poor districts. Despite equalization efforts by both federal and state governments, there remains considerable variation in per pupil expenditures among the states and among school districts within states. In addition, it may not be the type of state aid plan that is of paramount importance, but rather the total amount of state aid provided and the proportion of state aid included in the equalization formula.

The finance of IHEs is more complex, as both students and IHEs receive state and federal aid. Further, not all states use a formula to appropriate funds to IHEs, and individual IHEs continue to lobby for aid in excess of recommended amounts. Federal funds, moreover, are mainly for research, and it is virtually impossible to disentangle pure aid from payment for services provided. In addition, both federal and state funds are provided (directly or indirectly) to private IHEs, increasing the complexity of the funding system. It was noted, however, that the predominance of state aid to public IHEs gives them a competitive advantage, creating financial difficulties for the less prestigious, private IHEs. As more private IHEs are forced to close or to reduce the quality of instruction (in an effort to reduce costs), the pressure will surely mount for another look at the question of state aid to private IHEs. It is this area where the prospects for a voucher system appear brightest.

LITERATURE GUIDE

There is an overwhelming quantity of material on educational finance, and a careful taxonomy by topic and subtopic would require a tremendous effort. The breakdown here follows generally the topical divisions in the chapter.

Role of Government in Education

Studies discussing the role of government, especially regarding issues of equity and external effects, include ACIR (1973), Alchian (1967), Alchian and Allen (1968), Buchanan and Devletoglou (1970), Cohn (1972c: ch. 4; 1974a: ch. 1), J.R. Davis (1970), Friedman (1955, 1962), Hirsch and Marcus (1969), Hirsch, Segelhorst, and Marcus (1964), Holland (1974), Peackock and Weisman (1964), Riew (1974b), Weisbrod (1962, 1964), and West (1970a). General statements on the role of government in the economy may be found in Bator (1958), Buchanan (1965), Buchanan and Stubblebine (1962), P. Feldman (1971), and R.A. Musgrave (1959).

The role of government in higher education is discussed in Daniére (1964, 1969, 1973), Friedman (1968), Cheit (1977), Kerr (1969), Kirkwood and Mundel (1975), Leslie (1973), Leslie and Johnson (1974), Leslie, Johnson, and Carlson (1977), Machlup (1973), Merrett (1967), Michaeli (1972), Mundel (1973), Page (1973), and Rivlin and Weiss (1969). See also M.J. Bowman (1973), R.E. Clark (1973), Dresch (1973), R.B. Freeman (1973), Hansen (1973), and Hartman (1973).

Intergovernmental Relations

Revenue sharing is discussed in Bradford and Oats (1971), Goetz (1972), Joint Economic Committee (1967), McLure (1971), Neenan (1976), and Whitman (1977). Other aspects of intergovernmental relations are discussed in ACIR (1974a, 1976, 1977a, 1977b), Brazer (1970a), and McGuire (1971).

Elementary and Secondary Schools

Federal Aid. See, for example, Bedenbaugh and Alexander (1971), Berke (1974), Berke and Kirst (1972), Ginsburg and Killalea (1977), Guthrie and Lawton (1970), R.L. Johns and Lindman (1972), Magers (1977), Riew (1971, 1974c), Tiedt (1971), and Wynkoop (1976).

State Aid. Useful summaries of state aid to education may be found in Harris (1975), Augenblick (1977a, 1978b), T.L. Johns

(1972), and Tron (1976). Texts covering educational finance in general and state aid in particular include Benson (1963, 1978), Cohn (1974a), and R.L. Johns and Morphet (1975). The work of the National Education Finance Project includes R.L. Johns et al. (1970); R.L. Johns, Alexander, and Stollar (1971); and R.L. Johns and Alexander (1971), as well as volumes 1 (*Dimensions of Educational Need*) and 3 (*Planning to Finance Education*), which are not listed in the bibliography.

Additional material on state aid to education includes K. Alexander (1977), K. Alexander and Jordan (1973), Augenblick (1977b), Benson et al. (1965), Berke, Campbell, and Goettel (1972), Callahan and Wilken (1972), Chambers (1976a), Cohn (1973c, 1975a), Commission on Alternative Design for Funding Education (1973), Coons et al. (1970), Cummins (1973), Doyle et al. (1977) Eleven School Finance Models (1972), Feldstein (1975), Firestine (1977), Firestine et al. (1973), Fleischman Commission (1973), Garms and Smith (1970), Gilmer (1975), Gilmer and Morgan (1973, 1975), Goettel and Firestine (1975), Hartman and Reischauer (1974), Hettich (1968), Hickrod (1972, 1973a, 1973b) Hickrod et al. (1973, 1975a, 1975b, 1976), Hickrod, Chaudhari, and Hubbard (1977), Hickrod and Hubbard (1975, 1977a, 1977b, 1978), Hickrod, Hubbard, and Yang (1975), Hickrod Laymon, and Hubbard (1974), Hickrod and Sabualo (1969), Hubbard and Hickrod (1975), Hou (1977), Hou and Carson (1977), Jargowsky et al. (1977), R.L. Johns (1971, 1975, 1976, 1977a, 1977b), R.L. Johns and Burns (1971), R.L. Johns and Salmon (1971), T.L. Johns (1973, 1976, 1977), Jones (1971), Kindl (1971), Kirst (1973), Levi (1975), B. Levin (1975, 1977), B. Levin, Muller, and Scanlon (1972), H.M. Levin (1971a, 1975b, 1977b) Lows and Tcheng (1971), Lydall (1964), McLoone (1974), Meltsner et al. (1973), D.C. Morgan (1973, 1974), Pogrow and Swift (1977), Netzer (1975), Nielsen et al. (1975), Oakland (1976), O'Brien (1971), Riew (1970a, 1970b, 1974, 1974b), Riew and Fox (1974), Sacks (1972), School Finance Study Unit (1973), Skloot (1977), Sparkman (1977), Stewart (1973), Strayer and Haig (1923), Stubblebine and Teeples (1974), Talley (1974, 1976), Thomas (1970, 1974), Tron (1975), Wagner and Stollar (1971), Weischdale (1977), S.J. Weiss (1970), S.G. Weiss and Driscoll (1972), West (1964, 1968), Wilkin and Porter (1977), Winokur (1976), A.E. Wise (1976), and A.E. Wise and Thomas (1973). See also Bezeau (1977), Brazer (1975), J.B. Conant (1972), Elliot (1976), Flora (1976), Geske and Rossmiller (1977), Grubb and Michelson (1974), Hale (1975), and Lindman (1977).

The issue of *taxation* (especially property taxation) as it relates to state aid is examined in the following: ACIR (1974b, 1975), K. Alexander (1977), Bergstron (1973), J.H. Bowman (1973, 1974), Fiske (1975), Gensemer (1976), Hamilton (1976a, 1976b), Harriss (1974), Ladd (1975, 1976), LeRoy and Brockschmidt (1972), Levi (1975), D.O. Moore (1971), Netzer (1966, 1970), Pechman (1965, 1977), Riew (1971, 1974, 1974b), and Yang and Chaudhari (1976).

The *Tiebout Hypothesis* is described in Tiebout (1956) and examined in Barlow (1973), Edelson (1973), Hamilton (1976a), Hogan and Shelton (1973), Oates (1969, 1973) and Pollakowski (1973).

Aid to nonpublic schools is discussed in Goddard and Goffman (1973), Landynski (1969), D.J. Sullivan (1974), West (1976a), and West et al. (1976). Other issues concerning public and private school finance are discussed in Barzel (1973), Pauly (1967), and Riew and Fox (1974).

The issue of *"fiscal capacity"* is included in many of the items previously mentioned, but special focus is placed on this matter in ACIR (1971), Akin and Auten (1976), Briley (1971), R.L. Johns (1977b), Odden (1977, 1978), and Riew (1970a, 1970b).

Court cases relating to state aid to education are discussed in M.D. Alexander and Hudgins (1977), M.D. Alexander and McCarthy (1977), Browning (1973), Browning and Lehtman (1972), Clune (1972), Education Commission of States (1977), Horton et al. vs. Meskill et al. (1974), Lawyers' Committee for Civil Rights Under Law (1976, 1977), B. Levin (1977), Odden et al. (1976), O'Neill et al. (1972), Michelson (1972), Shannon (1973), Summers (1973), Summers and Wolfe (1976), and Teeples (1975).

Determinants of public education expenditures, including effect of state aid on expenditures, are discussed in G.A. Bishop (1964), Booms and Hu (1973), Brazer (1959, 1970b), O.A. Davis (1965), Denzau (1975), Fisher (1964), R.A. Freeman (1953), Hickrod (1971), Hirsch (1959a, 1959b, 1960, 1961), Hu and Booms (1971), Hu, Lee, and Stromsdorfer (1968), James et al. (1966), McMahon (1970), Miner (1963), Renshaw (1960a), Sacks (1972), Sacks and Harris (1964), Shapiro (1962), Sharkansky (1967), Stern (1973), and F.C. White and Miller (1976). See also Henderson (1968), Hickrod and Sabulao (1969), Horowitz (1968), Morss (1966), and Morss et al. (1967).

Other contributions include Akin and YoungDay (1976), Ashline et al. (1976), B. Brown (1971), Coleman (1970), Coombs (1968), Crane (1972), Denison (1970), Edwards and Edwards (1974), Gensemer (1975), and Hight (1974).

Higher Education
Student Loans. Studies include Alloway and Cordasco (1976),

H.R. Bowen (1969), Brugel, Johnson, and Leslie (forthcoming), Carlsson (1970), Dresch and Goldberg (1972), R. Feldman (1976), R.W. Hartman (1971, 1972), Hinson (1968a, 1968b), Johnstone (1972), Johnstone et al. (1972), Korczyk (1977), Krueger (1972), Nerlove (1975), Raymond and Sesnowitz (1976a), Shell (1970), Shell et al. (1968), Solmon (1970b), Van Den Haag (1956), Vickrey (1962), and Zacharias (1967, 1969).

Tuition. See Bolch and Hinshaw (1977), H.R. Bowen (1969), Eckstein (1960), F. P. Johnson (1975), Shechter (1976), and Windham (1972a).

Tax Relief. See Congressional Budget Office (1977, 1978), R.A. Freeman (1969), Goode (1962), O.E. Johnson (1968), Maeroff (1978), McNulty (1973), and UPI (1977). An excellent treatment of the federal income tax and a discussion of exemptions, deductions, and tax credits is contained in Goode (1976).

Formula Funding. See Augenblick (1978a), Berdahl (1971), J.L. Miller (1965), Rutledge and Stafford (1977), and South Carolina Commission on Higher Education (1978).

Income Distributional Effects of State Aid to Public Education. The basic work is Hansen and Weisbrod (1969a, 1969b). See also Cohn (1970a), Conlisk (1977), Crean (1975), Hansen and Weisbrod (1971a), R.W. Hartman (1970), Hight and Pollack (1973), K.S. Lyon (1974), J. McGuire (1976), Pechman (1970, 1971, 1972), Rubin (1975), and Sharkansky (1970).

Other Topics. Issues in the economics and financing of higher education are included in W. Adams (1977), R.E. Anderson (1975), Astin and Galvin (1972), Ben-David (1972), Bolton (1969), F. Bowen (1976), R. Bowen and Minter (1975), W.G. Bowen (1969, 1977), Boyd (1971), Brovender (1974), D.G. Brown (1967), Budig (1977), Burn et al. (1971), Burns and Chiswick (1970), Carnegie Commission on Higher Education (1968, 1970a, 1970b, 1970c, 1971a, 1971b, 1972a, 1973a, 1973b), M.M. Chambers (1970), Clotfelter (1976a), Cheit (1971), *Economics of Higher Education* (1967), Farmer (1970), Godwin and Mann (1972), Greenwood (1973), Gustman and Pidot (1973), Hansen (1974, 1977a), Hansen and Lampman (1974), Hansen and Weisbrod (1971b), S.E. Harris (1960, 1962, 1964, 1965, 1969, 1972), L. Hartman (1969), Hinson (1971), Hodgkinson (1971), Hudson (1974), Hyde (1978), Kaysen (1960), Knight (1960), Kottis and Kottis (1973, 1974), Leslie (1972), Machovec (1972), Magarrell (1974, 1976), Mood et al. (1972), Mushkin (1969), Orlans (1972), Pelzman (1973), Quindry and Mastern (1976), Schultz (1968, 1972b), Segal (1969), "Some Trends in . . ." (1976), Spies (1973), Tollison and Willet (1972, 1973), Weathersby and Nash (1974), West (1974), Wilson (1972), Wilson and Mills (1972), Windham (1970, 1972b, 1976b), and Wolfle (1954, 1971, 1972). See also Coughlin (1977), Folger (1977), H.G. Johnson (1972), Thackery (1969), and Tobin and Ross (1969a, 1969b).

The Voucher Plan

Entries are divided into four groups—Journal articles selected by ERIC, ERIC documents, articles in *Times Educational Supplement*, and other references.

ERIC Journal Articles. Alloway and Cordasco (1976), Bushnell (1973), Coons and Sugarman (1973), Flygare (1973), Foster (1973), Golden (1971-1972), Jenkins (1973), J.M. Levin (1973a, 1973b, 1974), McClure (1976), Maltby (1973), Mason (1975), Overlan (1975), Pickard and Richards (1976), J.B. Robinson (1974), Sage and Guarino (1974), Schimmels (1974), Sears (1975), Selden (1975), Spillane (1973), Stigler (1973), Sugarman (1974), J. Walsh (1973), Warren (1976), and P.T. West (1974).

ERIC Documents. Abramowitz (1976), Blackman (1975), Bridge (1974), Dunning (1976a, 1976b), Dunning and Unger (1975), Esposito and Thompson (1976), Gutierrez and Chacon (1974), Haggart and Furry (1974), Honey and Hartle (1975), Levinson (1976), Newton et al. (1975), Nirenberg (1976), O'Reilly and Sheridan (1975), Paller et al. (1975), Rasmussen (1976), Richardson and Sharp (1974, 1975), Vanecko (1974), Warren (1974), Weiler et al. (1974), and Weiner (1974).

Times Educational Supplement. Bogdanor (1976), Boyson (1976), D. Mandel (1976), McCurdy (1974), and Wallace (1976).

Other. A convenient collection of essays is La Noue (1972). See also Areen and Jencks (1972), Arons (1971), Blum (1958), Carlson (1964), Carr and Hayward (1970), Cohen and Farrar (1977), Coons et al. (1970), Erickson (1970), Friedman (1955, 1962), Ginzberg (1971), Glennan (1971), Havinghurst (1970), Horobin and Smith (1960), Jencks (1971), Jencks et al. (1970), Katzman (1972), Klitgaard (1974), Laird and Schilson (1965), D.W. Lyon (1971), McCann and Areen (1971), Megel (1971), Mecklenburger and Hostrop (1972), Mill (1972), Parish (1963), Peacock and Weisman (1964), *Phi Delta Kappan* (1970), Poindexter v. Louisiana Financial Assistance Commission (1967), and Wiseman (1959, 1960).

Other Literature

Additional literature on educational finance or related areas includes: Haveman (1976b), Heddinger (1971), Henning and Tussing (1974), Bruno (1969b), Gertmenian (1975), Hatley and Croskey (1977), J.A. Maxwell (1977), Michigan Department of Education (1974, 1976), President's Commission on School Finance (1972), Reifman (1964), Van Fleet and Boardman (1971), Wiseman (1966), and Peston (1966).

There are very few studies of educational finance in countries other than the United States. Exceptions include Cook (1976) and MacLennan (1967)—on the United Kingdom—and Michaeli (1972)—on Israel.

Chapter 11

Educational Planning

THE RATIONALE FOR PLANNING

In a private market system, where adequate "signals" exist to monitor changes in demand (tastes, preferences, level of income, prices of goods and services) and supply (factor costs, prices of goods and services, and production possibilities), central economic planning is regarded by most economists as unnecessary. We have seen, however, that the education industry differs from other markets on several scores. First, the types of signals available in the market economy (prices, profits, etc.) are either not observable in the educational case or must be calculated in some manner. So long as such calculations cannot be made with any degree of certainty, or if mass dissemination of such calculations is either too expensive or impractical, optimal allocation of resources cannot be guaranteed. This is true even if some government action, in the form of subsidies, loans, tax credits, and so forth, is taken to account for external effects, income distribution goals, and other factors.

It is argued that due to the lack of appropriate signals, "manpower needs" or "manpower requirements" will differ from available manpower. What is meant, exactly, by "requirements" or "needs" will be clarified later, but for the present one might accept the argument that the possibility exists that optimal allocation of resources will not be achieved due to the lack of knowledge concerning the profitability of various educational investments. It is also pointed out that when individuals make their own calculations, they cannot predict in advance the precise demand for positions in the future. Since educational investments involve lengthy training periods, substantial "wastage" is predicted to occur—unless some remedial action, whether in the form of planning or otherwise, is taken.

Moreover, suppose that all potential students are aware of the opportunities available and the expected net returns from each educational investment. Individuals would then be expected to maximize the net present value of their lifetime earnings. This may or may not be consistent with society's economic and social targets. That is to say, so long as it is recognized that educational decisions have some bearing on several policy goals, society may want to manipulate both the demand for and the supply of education in such a manner that these goals may be maximized. While such educational plans are bound to infringe on the individuals' freedom of choice, it is asserted that such infringements are necessary in order that society's goals may be reached.

A further rationale for planning concerns microeducational elements—such as a school district, academic department, college, or a university. The argument is again (1) that lack of market information makes it impossible for the educational unit to assure an optimal allocation of its resources and (2) that some schools may wish to maximize a given goal (such as "excellence"), so that educational planning could be used to suggest strategies that will assist the policymaker in attaining his goals.

In summary, whether one subscribes to the thesis that educational cost-benefit information is either deficient because of such factors as outlined in Chapter 6 and/or due to the lack of sufficient information (because of data limitations, etc.), or whether it is the maximization of certain goals through education that one is concerned with, educational planning, both on aggregate (macro) and small (micro) scales, is a tool that may be used to further one's goals.

APPROACHES TO EDUCATIONAL PLANNING

Manpower Requirements
The presumed goal of educational planning is to promote productivity by matching expected demand for skills with the supply. The chief purpose of the approach is to forecast manpower needs by skill categories and then to transform manpower requirements into edu-

cational requirements. The educational system can then adapt it-self·to these forecasts (Parnes, 1962).

The typical manpower forecasting approach would be to estimate the demand for manpower by occupation for each sector of the economy by assuming (1) a given target for national income (e.g., GNP), (2) given average labor output coefficients (the inverse of the average productivity of labor), and (3) mutually exclusive occupational categories. The target of GNP, for example, may be set according to a five year plan that envisages, let us say, a 5 percent annual growth in real per capita income. The average productivity of labor may be measured for each occupation by (1) average productivity attained in another country or in the most progressive industry in the country under study; (2) observing past trends and extrapolating them in some manner to the future; and (3) surveying industrial estimates of productivity changes and manpower needs based on given assumptions concerning future market conditions.

Given that manpower forecasts by occupation could be made, these must then be translated into educational requirements. Eckaus (1964) has proposed two measures, one relating to general education requirements, the other to specific vocational training. For the first, each job is placed in a given general educational development (GED) category, which is translated into the number of equivalent school years necessary to achieve such an educational level. Similarly, each job is ranked according to the specific vocational reparation (SVP) categories, which are translated into training time (from zero to seven years). Given the GED and SVP requirements for each job, manpower forecasts may then be translated into educational and training requirements.

Several other possibilities are outlined by Parnes (1962). One method is to forecast future manpower needs by occupation and to translate the latter into educational needs by utilizing the current distribution of educational attainment by occupation. Another method is to use data on educational distribution by occupation for another country at a given period in time to approximate the future educational distribution envisaged for the country under study.[1] Combined with forecasts of manpower requirements, educational requirements may thus be calculated.

A more ambitious analysis is suggested by Parnes in which analysis of "educational development" indexes is made. This method,

1. This method was utilized by M.K. Bacchus (1968) to assess educational requirements in Guyana by 1975. The countries used as "models" for Guyana were Jamaica and Trinidad.

entitled job analysis, analyzes each job according to the competence required of workers in such areas as reasoning, mathematics, and languages. These may then be translated into equivalent educational requirements for each job. Parnes admits that such a method is quite difficult to implement.

A final alternative suggested by Parnes is to survey a sample of firms and industries. Each employer will be asked to furnish facts and estimates concerning present educational qualifications for each job, hiring standards, adequacy of present employees' job preparations, optimal and minimal levels of preparation for each job, and expectations of future changes in these or any other relevant factors. Needless to say, such an analysis requires considerable investment and must be updated periodically. From such information, educational requirements for each job may be delineated.

A Critique of the Manpower Requirements Approach.[2]   Eckaus, in support of his manpower forecasting model, presents a strong critique of the cost-benefit approach discussed in Chapters 3–6 above. He questions the validity of rate of return studies in education and proceeds to argue that (1) profitability does not matter, since lower levels of education are compulsory; (2) national income as a measure of economic welfare is far from satisfactory; (3) consumption cannot be separated from investment; and (4) externalities must be recognized and measured. Clearly, these objections are accurate. At the same time, the methods suggested by Eckaus, Parnes, and others are subject to several serious criticisms, some of which, ironically, were used by Eckaus to criticize the rate of return approach.

The first critical comment, perhaps the most important of all, concerns the usual assumption that labor productivity is given by some parameter (determined according to one of the possible methods outlined earlier). This implies that the economy is characterized by a fixed coefficients type of production function—that is, in which labor productivity is invariant with respect to other factors of production, including other types of labor. A world in which no substitutabilities exist among factors of production is not likely to be found.

Second, the methods outlined for converting manpower needs into educational requirements are highly suspect. (1) It could be that any one job could be staffed by persons possessing varying amounts of education. For example, using Eckaus's model, there

---

2. Much of the material in this subsection is based on Mark Blaug (1967a).

might be some substitutability between the GED and SVP requirements. (2) The conversion of manpower requirements into educational requirements by "years of schooling" leaves a great deal to be desired. Not only do we need some information on vocational and/or on the job training requirements (Eckaus's SVP index comes close to this), but it must be recognized that length of formal or informal schooling, by itself, is highly inadequate. (This type of criticism is usually recognized by the proponents of manpower forecasting.) Finally, (3) there is a strong possibility that educational "requirements" vary with the availability of education manpower. That is to say, what employers consider as "essential" may depend, to a large extent, on what type of manpower is available. It is argued that upgrading of the labor force, in terms of educational qualification, is likely to occur when the supply of educated manpower is increased relative to the demand for labor. And although Parnes's last two suggestions regarding the conversion of manpower requirements into educational needs are designed to overcome this objection, such schemes have not been actively pursued in any of the educational plans that have been designed in recent years.

Third, the manpower requirements approach assumes that the labor market is, or will be, at a point of disequilibrium; it is designed to reduce the likelihood of such a disequilibrium in the future. If currently there is a disequilibrium, however, forecasts made on current or past information are likely to predict, once more, points of disequilibrium.

Fourth, if it is conceded that the economy is characterized by a production function in which substitution among factors of production is not possible, any erroneous forecast would result in irreparable damage (due to the assumed inability of the system to automatically adjust itself). It follows that either forecasts are not very important —when it is assumed that substitutability among productive factors is possible—or that they should not be made unless they can be made with a high degree of accuracy. The record shows that the typical manpower forecast was far off the mark.

Fifth, manpower forecasts are typically of the "single value" variety—that is, they give a single prediction of expected manpower and educational needs. Such a forecast is extremely hazardous inasmuch as it ignores changes in supply. Since an equilibrium situation requires a given interaction of both supply and demand forces, changes in factors affecting educational supply should be taken into account. A multivalued forecast, in which several predictions are made, each with respect to a different set of assumptions concerning both supply and demand conditions, is both more useful and less likely to lead to inflexible educational policy that may cause irremediable damage.

Sixth, Eckaus's objection to the use of national income as a measure of welfare is just as relevant to manpower forecasting, unless the goal according to which manpower projections are made is something other than target GNP or the like. Although Eckaus does not explicitly state that the goal of manpower forecasting is the maximization of income, his article implicitly assumes such a goal—despite statements to the contrary concerning reasons for education other than increased output. If income is not an appropriate goal for rate of return studies, it should not be used for manpower planning for the same reason. If it is accepted that national income is the best measure available for economic welfare, an important element in the critique against the rate of return approach is removed.

Last, Eckaus objects to rate of return studies on the ground that distinctions between "consumption" and "investment" components of education are virtually impossible to make. If such a criticism is valid, it becomes, at the same time, a powerful criticism of the manpower-forecasting approach. Indeed, it seems that the distinction between investment and consumption is even more crucial in the planning context. Educational requirements are given by equivalent years of schooling, but since years of schooling include education for both investment and consumption, manpower forecasting is bound to suggest substantial overinvestment in education. To some extent, this is also true of the rate of return approach. But if government involvement in education is limited to financing or otherwise influencing only those aspects of education for which government involvement is justified (see Chapter 10), the chances for over- (or for that matter, under-) investment are minimized.

Social Demand

Instead of concentrating on the potential demand for manpower —and hence for educational services—by industries, one might want to plan the educational system so that the projected demand by students for places in the various levels of education is met. In other words, whereas the manpower requirements approach concentrates on meeting the demand by industry for manpower, the social demand approach is based upon the notion that planning should be used to affect the supply of educated manpower, irrespective of market demand. The social demand approach would call for the projection of private demand for education, so that educational institutions may adapt themselves to the expected demand. Such projections would be useful for planning capital expansion, teacher-training programs, and so on. Moreover, social demand projections might be useful in that industry could be made aware of the potential pool of manpower; rational choices involving such matters as more or less capital-intensive methods of operation, and the adoption of highly modern techniques of operation might be facilitated by such projections.

Such an approach to educational planning was endorsed by the Robbins Committee on Higher Education (1963; named after its distinguished chairman, Lord Robbins) in Great Britain. The committee's rationale in choosing this method (and rejecting the manpower requirements approach) was their belief that "all young persons qualified by ability and attainment to pursue a full-time course in higher education should have the opportunity to do so" (p. 49).

Although the social demand approach has never been formally endorsed in the United States, in reality it has been practiced in many states, and a number of state governments now make periodic projections of student demand for places. The main problem with such projections is that they are likely to depend not only on demographic factors, but also on socioeconomic factors and government action regarding such variables as tuition, loans, location and type of public institutions, admissions policies, and efforts to stabilize the economy. A number of studies appearing during the last fifteen years have employed various sources of data to estimate the effect of such variables on college choice (with regard to lower levels of education, it is usually agreed that demographic factors are most important). As is described in a survey of such studies (Cohn and Morgan, 1978a), the vast majority of studies indicate a significant, negative effect of tuition on the propensity to attend college. Also, the higher the costs of attendance, the lower would be the propensity to enroll. And socioeconomic factors, such as parental income, education, occupation, and the like, are usually significantly related to the propensity to attend college.

Despite the availability of such studies, projections of student demand are usually made on the basis of a time trend analysis. That is, either student enrollments or the ratio of student enrollments to a given population cohort (such as ages eighteen to twenty-four) are projected into the future on the basis of past trends. This is the technique employed by the United States Office of Education in its *Projections of Educational Statistics* (Frankel and Harrison, 1977: 91–98) and by the various state agencies (e.g., Kinard and Krech, 1977, for South Carolina). The major reasons for not using a causal model (in which various factors combine to explain student demand) are (1) that government agencies frequently lack the expertise to formulate and run such models; (2) that economists are not in full agreement as to what constitutes a "correct" causal model; and (3) that even if a "correct" model can be formulated, there is a lack of data to implement it, especially in regard to future years. That is to say, in order to predict enrollments t years hence, it is necessary, first, to project the levels of the explanatory variables (parental income, education, occupation, rates of unemployment, levels of tuition, other costs of education, availability of student loans, campus locations, etc.) t years into the future. That may be an impossible task.

It is of no surprise that Blaug (1967a) condemns the social demand approach precisely because approaches to measure student demand are usually based on a time trend analysis. Moreover, it is not at all obvious that society should provide space to all those who are able and desire to attend. It is possible, indeed likely, that the marginal social benefits will not exceed the marginal social costs of attendance for all students. A nation may not wish, therefore, to follow a strict social demand approach.

Moreover, the social demand approach completely disregards the availability of job vacancies. In a perfectly flexible economy, supply-demand mismatches would not arise or would be cleared away rather quickly. In many economies, however, labor markets are extremely rigid, and overproduction of high level manpower could result in long-term unemployment, or at least underemployment,[3] of such manpower. Examples of such phenomena have been observed in many underdeveloped countries (see UNESCO, 1968), and the sight of Ph.D's driving taxis in New York City (which is a case of underemployment) illustrates that even in a highly capitalistic economy, severe supply-demand disequilibria could create considerable waste in the employment of human resources.

The Rate of Return Approach

A great deal of space has already been devoted to the concept of the net returns to education. This general methodology may be used as a planning tool in the following way: For each educational program for which data are available, the net present value of future income streams is calculated. Those programs for which net present values are positive are to be stimulated by the planning authorities; those for which net present values are zero or negative should be reduced in size or at least should receive less resources in proportion

---

3. Underemployment occurs when workers are employed in positions in which their maximum productivity cannot be attained.

to total expenditures on education. Such a policy, when continuously reappraised, may lead to the ultimate outcome in which the net present value, at a given rate of discount, of all educational programs will approach zero.[4]

All of the objections cited in Chapters 3 and 6 relative to the returns to education approach apply here. In addition, for long-run planning purposes, information about the future is required. Rate of return studies, by their very nature, employ past data to predict present relationships. A projection of such data to the distant future may not be justifiable. And although the manpower requirements and the social demand approaches also utilize past and present data, it appears that manpower demand forecasts or projections of private demand for education may be made with a much higher degree of confidence that rate of return projections. But, clearly, the distinction is a matter of degree only.

Other Approaches

Blaug's Synthesis of the Three Approaches. Instead of choosing one approach as opposed to another, Blaug (1967a) suggests a synthesis in which all three approaches may be utilized hand in hand. Manpower forecasts, especially for short horizons such as three to five years, may be made, together with studies designed to determine the degree of substitutability in industry among different types of manpower and of capital versus various types of labor. At the same time, calculations of the private demand for education may also be made, making use of rate of return studies to establish the sensitivity of enrollments to changes in the "price of education." All of these pieces of information could be placed together in the context of a mathematical or a programming model so that an optimal distribution of educational manpower might be found, given society's targets. Such a model should, according to Blaug, be complemented by actions to make the curriculum more, rather than less, general—so that errors in prediction could be ameliorated more quickly through diminished time lags in training for any specific occupation. Also, attempts should be made to make the economy more, rather than less, automatic, so that errors in prediction could be more self-correcting. Finally, Blaug proposes an "active manpower policy," in which manpower retraining, distribution of labor market information, and so on are pursued.

4. When limited budgets preclude investment in education up to the point where the net present value of each program is zero, allocations should be made according to the ranking of investments derived from Formula (5.11) in Chapter 5.

Harbison and Myers—Strategies of Human Resource Development. This approach to educational planning is based on the premise that both intra- and intercountry relationships should be considered for educational planning. Harbison and Myers (1964) developed an index of human resource development for each country. It is shown that this index—given by the sum of "(1) enrollment at the second level of education as a percentage of the age group 15 to 19, adjusted for length of schooling, and (2) enrollment at the third level of education as a percentage of the age group, multiplied by a weight of 5" (pp. 31–32)—is highly correlated among seventy-two countries with GNP per capita. In other words, countries with a higher score on the index typically have higher per capita GNPs.

Harbison and Myers argue that educational planning should take into account the level of development, the role of agriculture in the economy, and both the quantity and quality of education and other human resource development. Strategies for achieving economic development—in terms of educational planning—are suggested for each of four groups of countries, where each country is classified into a given group according to its score on the human resource development index. These strategies vary for each country according to population growth, employment and unemployment, institutional factors, and shortages or surpluses in certain sectors.

Although the approach has the advantage of planning educational systems on the basis of a far wider framework than any of the other methods outlined above, it suffers from a number of inadequacies, such as the definition of the index (shown by Sen [1966a] to virtually maximize the correlation between it and per capita income) and some of the specific recommendations made by the authors.

Mathematical Programming. Educational planning is frequently viewed as an exercise in resource allocation. The planner attempts to achieve some goals (or objectives), subject to various constraints. For example, under the social demand approach, the goal is to provide adequate spaces to all able persons desiring such a space. Constraints include legal, financial, and institutional factors. Likewise, the manpower-forecasting approach may be cast in programming terms. The program provides a "solution vector" to be employed so that the goal is obtained in an optimal manner.

Educational planners are not always concerned with global goals. In decentralized systems, such as exist in the United States, the educational planner is typically an agent of a school district or a university. Planning often takes place at the lowest hierarchy, such as the school building or college department. In such cases, the goals or objectives may be to maximize faculty positions, maximize scholastic achievement or departmental "excellence," or minimize fluctuations in enrollments. As will be shown later, multiple objectives frequently characterize the educational planning problems, requiring sophisticated apparatuses for their solutions.

A Note on the Definition of Shortages[5]

One of the principal aims of manpower and educational planning is to avoid "shortages" and "surpluses" in various occupations. But the meaning of a "shortage" or a "surplus" is not unambiguous. Several definitions are given below.

1. From the point of view of economic statics, we have a situation of "shortage" whenever the demand by industry for manpower of a given kind, *given the wage levels offered in the labor market*, exceeds the supply of manpower that will be forthcoming at these wages. A solution to such a shortage is not necessarily an increase in the supply of such manpower. The shortage could also be diminished or eliminated by increasing the wages paid for that type of manpower. If this is the type of shortage contemplated by the manpower forecasters, wage policy may be more effective than educational planning. Of course, it is conceivable that institutional rigidities do not permit one to alter wage levels in certain occupations (teaching, for example), so that educational planning that is designed to increase the supply of, say, teachers at given wage levels may be justified.

2. A "shortage" is often defined to exist when an insufficient supply of manpower is expected to be forthcoming, at given wage levels, to achieve a given target or end. For example, it has been argued that a shortage of physicians is certain to occur if current enrollments in medical schools do not double in the near future and, importantly, if current physician-population proportions are to remain constant. That is, the forecast of physician shortages is based on the assumption that the number of physicians per, say, 100,000 of population that will be required ten years from now is no different from the current ratio or, what amounts to the same thing, that no change in medical technology regarding the delivery of health services is contemplated.

3. Another definition of "shortages" concerns the possibility that while in the aggregate the supply of a given type of manpower is sufficient to meet the demand for it, there may be some "bottleneck areas" in which a shortage in the sense of definitions 1 or 2

5. See Leibenstein (1965), Hansen (1964, 1965, 1967a), Holtmann (1968), and Yett (1970).

above exist. For instance, while there may be enough physicians in the United States to satisfy a given ratio of physicians to total population, there exist several areas—especially rural—in which the ratio of physicians to the population falls short of the national average by a wide margin. Such "shortages" are cited as reasons for some planning, whether educational or of other form.

4. W. Lee Hansen (1965) argues that shortages in the sense of definitions 1 through 3 are not meaningful at all. Suppose that the supply of and the demand for manpower are sensitive to the wage rates and, further, that persons move into and out of an occupation, on the margin, according to expected net lifetime income, properly discounted. Then, according to Hansen, it may be shown that some "surplus" occupations are not really in surplus and some "shortage" occupations are not really in shortage. Further, Hansen's data indicate that some professions that were earlier classified as "shortage" occupations, due to the high internal rates of return that investment in these professions entailed, are no longer classified in this manner, due to the changes that have occurred in the relative profitability of investment in these occupations. In fact, Hansen observed fluctuations of certain occupations from shortage to surplus, the reason for fluctuation being based, according to Hansen, on "overshooting the mark" by prospective entrants. Hansen argues, thus, that shortages and surpluses tend to disappear over time; manpower forecasting or projections of social demand for education are, therefore, unnecessary.

5. A final definition of shortages and surpluses is given by Arrow and Capron (1959). Shortages are alleged to exist, as in definition 1, when demand exceeds supply at a given price. But their model does not end with such a static statement. The dynamics of resolving the given shortage or surplus are investigated. A shortage would truly exist only to the extent that such shortages cannot be speedily eliminated through interaction of supply and demand adjustments. The model, thus, attempts to discover, in the first place, whether an adjustment process leading to a market-clearing equilibrium is possible, and second, the "market reaction speed" with which such an adjustment takes place. This reaction speed is measured by an index that is based upon "the time it takes the firm to recognize the existence of a shortage at the current salary level, the time it takes to decide upon the need for higher salaries and the number of vacancies at such salaries, and either the time it takes employees to recognize the salary alternatives available and to act upon this information or the time it takes the firm to equalize salaries without outside offers" (p. 325).

The implications of these definitions of "shortages" are quite obvious. Educational planning, justified under the guise of eliminating shortages and/or surpluses, may be entirely unnecessary or even harmful to achieving equilibrium in the labor market. In any event, it is not enough to state that "shortages" will thus be reduced or eliminated. A clear and explicit explanation of what is meant by the term "shortage" is clearly required.

SOME MACROMODELS OF EDUCATIONAL PLANNING

In recent years, considerable work in the theory and application of educational planning has taken place. Educational planning models have been conveniently grouped into four categories by K.A. Fox and Sengupta (1968) as follows:

A. Models with few sectors (usually two sectors) with national output as an exogenous variable. . . ;
B. Models with several sectors based on open-dynamic input-output models . . . ;
C. Programming models with investment in education as a component of aggregate national investment. . . ; and
D. Recursive models with specific variables relating to a particular component of the overall educational system. . . . (P. 667)

In this section we shall discuss one variant per each category.

Tinbergen and Bos—The "Econometric Approach"

One relatively simple model, belonging to category A, though far more sophisticated than the manpower forecasting approach as devised by Parnes and others, is the econometric approach of Tinbergen and Bos (1964). The model seeks to formalize the relationship between the educational system and the economy's manpower requirements through an aggregate production function describing the effect of both educational and noneducational outputs on aggregate national product. A fundamental difference between this model and the manpower forecasting approach is that the former does not study present manpower conditions but rather concentrates on predicting future demands for skills in light of production possibilities. The stated purpose of their exercise is "to describe the demand flows for various types of qualified manpower to be expected from the organizers of production and of education . . . and to aid in the process of planning for education for labour-market policies" (p. 148).

The model, in its simplest form, considers the following "basic facts" in constructing the model:

1. Economic life needs a stock of qualified manpower; the flow of new graduates from educational establishments represents a very small proportion of this stock in view of human longevity;
2. education often consists of a series of successive stages, each depending on the former for its supply of new recruits, e.g., expansion at university level would be impossible if sufficient secondary-level graduates were not available;
3. part of the stock of qualified manpower must be used in the education process itself—as seed is used in agriculture;
4. qualified manpower may be imported. (Pp. 147–48)

The simplest form of the model consists of six basic equations:

Equation (1).   The labour force with a secondary education is used for production only and must develop proportionally with the volume of national production;

Equations (2) and (5).   The labor force consists of those already in it one time unit earlier and those who have joined it during the previous 6 years. It is assumed that a proportion $[\lambda_2]$ and $[\lambda_3]$ respectively of those already in the labour force one time unit earlier has dropped out owing to death or retirement;

Equation (3).   The number of newcomers to the labour force with a secondary education is equal to the number of students one time unit earlier minus the number of students now in third-level education;

Equation (4).   The number of newcomers to the labour force with a third-level education is equal to the number of third-level students one time unit earlier;

Equation (6).   The labour force with a third-level education consists of those employed in production, and is assumed to be proportional in numbers to the volume of production, and of those teaching at both levels of education and assumed to be proportional to the respective student numbers. (P. 149)

The model takes primary enrollments for granted and presumes these to be no bottleneck for secondary level expansion or production increases. These equations are used over a time period of six years, where various coefficients, such as λ_2 and λ_3, are either assumed to be of a given magnitude or are periodically estimated from statistical data. The ability to estimate the coefficients from statistical analyses is considered by the authors to be an important virtue of the model.

An essential element of the model is the assertion that education causes economic development. Clearly, whereas education might be one of the forces influencing economic growth, the evidence only indicates correlation between education and development. It could be that expansion of the educational system is the effect of economic development, not its cause. Another difficulty with the model is its reliance on the "balanced growth" concept: "The ideal development of the educational system is one of regular growth parallel to the desired growth of the economy. If the economic variables develop with a constant rate of growth, it is possible to find one path of development of the educational variables showing the same rate of growth" (p. 150). This concept, coupled with assumptions about the aggregate production function, is shown by Bombach (1964) to lead to very curious results. Other criticisms of the model include Sen's (1964) allegation that the model incorrectly assesses educational training time periods, that it treats human depreciation in an odd manner, and finally, that it ignores the fact that humans are different from machines in so far as workers "learn by doing." Several extensions of the model are proposed by the various critics.

Stone's Model

As Fox and Sengupta note, the Tinbergen-Bos model, as a representative of category A models, is developed around the assumption that there are two sectors in the economy—education and noneducation. The education sector is considered as one unit. The model developed by Stone (1965, 1966) is an extension of the former in that a multisectoral model of the educational system is considered. Instead of confining oneself to first, second, and third levels of education only, the Stone model considers various forms of education and training. The model contains a system of flow equations (a system that "is basically similar to that of an open-dynamic input-output model") where "a given year's activity levels expressed in terms of students are shown as functions of future vectors of graduate leavers who are potential entrants to the labor force" (Fox and Sengupta, 1968: 670). The essential function of the model is, once more, its ability to generate the desired growth path of the educational system as a function of the desired future output levels and structure of skilled manpower.

The Stone model contains a number of interesting features. After defining the educational system, by drawing a boundary around the various educational processes or activities in the various educational institutions, Stone utilizes an input-output matrix to represent student flows. The equations take into account attrition due to all sorts of reasons. Then the demand for places in higher education is regarded as a series of epidemic processes in which changes in the demand for places depend on (1) the number "infected" (carriers) and (2) the number not yet "infected" (potential catchers). Stone classifies economic inputs into (1) intermediate inputs, (2) capital goods, and (3) labor. These inputs are in turn determined by the activity levels. The initial activity levels are determined from demographic data, but beyond the level of compulsory education, the "epidemic" model is used to predict the demand for places: students and their advisors are presumed to make educational decisions, which are influenced by the economic prospects of specialization; these decisions determine the number of students enrolled in each sector of the system at each stage. These demand influences determine future mixes of graduate leavers that in turn determine current activity levels in the different processes.

The calculation of activity levels enables the determination of the requirements for various inputs, such as teachers, buildings, equipment, and supplies. The effects of technical change or changes in educational technology on learning processes or economic inputs may also be introduced into the model.

One of the difficulties with the model is its inability to analyze the implicit opportunity costs of alternative educational policies. Further, "there is a need to distinguish between 'capacity' variables and accounting variables." That is, the effect of certain inputs on (1) current output and (2) future output through indirect stimuli should be delineated. A final point is that the nature of the variables in the model, describing the processes of the educational system, must be clarified if such effects as scale economies are to be determined (Fox and Sengupta, 1968: 673-74). A model in which the first of these objections is overcome belongs to category C, to be discussed next.

Adelman's Linear Programming Model

Adelman (1966) considers three different objectives for the economy:

1. Maximize the discounted value of GNP over a given horizon;
2. Maximize the growth rate of the economy;
3. Minimize the discounted sum of net foreign capital inflow.

The economy is then divided into an education sector and nine noneducational sectors, each of which is characterized by a set of linear constraints concerning initial supplies, social and other factors influencing enrollments, the satisfaction of "production functions for the educational system, which specify the 'technological' conditions for the transformation of matriculants of a given school level into graduates" (p. 387), as well as several constraints pertaining to the "productive" sectors of the economy.

A linear programming model for four periods of five years each is used with data partially characterizing Argentina's economy. The solutions of the model serve to indicate not only the "best" setup for the educational system but also relevant policy formulas for other sectors of the economy. Further, the "dual" of the program permits an assessment of the "shadow prices" of various education and training programs. That is, the implicit marginal social benefit (productivity) of each educational investment may be computed from the program, indicating the relative merits of each program. Further, marginal social costs are alleged to be computable from the model; Adelman claims "that the major elements [of school costs] are the opportunity cost of student and teacher time and the opportunity cost of school buildings" (p. 407). Using the shadow prices for the most remunerative opportunity of student, teacher, or building use, these costs may be calculated from the data. It follows that a cost-benefit analysis may be conducted simultaneously with the programming analysis, which is designed to delineate the optimal activity vector.

The outcomes of the model for the Argentina case are rather curious. For example, it is found that only university graduates or dropouts should be trained. Another outcome is that commercial and vocational schools are not "utilized in the optimal school network." These results are probably due to Adelman's assumption that the productivity of university graduates is three and one half times that of secondary school graduates—which, as Bowles (1966) notes, is rather unlikely to be true.

Even if the curious outcomes are not the result of the nature of the model itself (but rather peculiar to the set of assumptions and data given by Adelman), several difficulties exist that should be recognized. Regarding the shadow prices, they are "strongly conditioned by the way the coefficients of the objective function and of the restraints are set up. . . . To that extent the statistical sensitivity to errors in specification or estimation presents quite a complicated problem" (Fox and Sengupta, 1968: 676). Second, the linearity of the relationships (both the objective function and the constraints) implies a constant and permanent rate of substitution among various inputs; thus, structural changes in the economy over the planning horizons cannot be incorporated into the model. To overcome this objection, Fox and Sengupta suggest that the linear model should be replaced with a nonlinear, perhaps quadratic model, in which rates of substitution among inputs will be allowed to vary over the horizon. A final criticism of the model is Adelman's reliance on the optimal solution alone; no attempt has been made to assess the sensitivity of the solutions to marginal changes in the coefficients of the relations. Several suggestions on this score are given by Fox and Sengupta. One of these is to compute, in addition to the optimal (first best) solution, also the second best and third best solutions. The range of variation among these solutions will provide some basis for assessing the sensitivity of the results to marginal changes in the coefficients.

The Bowles Model

The models in category D typically consider the education sector separately from the entire economy (in what is termed "partial equilibrium analysis") but, unlike the Adelman model, consider the sensitivity of the optimal vector to some changes in the coefficients. The Bowles (1967) model is an example of this category.

In Bowles's model, the objective function is the maximization of the additional lifetime earnings, properly discounted, that are attributable to the educational process. These discounted lifetime income estimates are used as weights for enrollments of various educational levels in forming the objective function. The constraints include "what can be called an intertemporal production possibility set for the educational system," availability of various educational inputs, and "boundary conditions [that] limit the policy instruments to values which are judged to be politically and administratively feasible" (pp. 191–92).

The model is designed to simulate the functioning of the educational system over several years, with relationships used to express intertemporal connections in the educational system. Bowles argues that the model should use a year as the time unit and "be operated on a year-by-year sequential basis." The optimal solution of the model determines the activity level of the instrument variables (i.e., those subject to government manipulation), given the objective function and the set of constraints. Thus, for each year during the planning horizon, the model yields: (1) optimal enrollment patterns and optimal input use in the various educational levels; (2) "levels of recruitment of new inputs . . . to the system"; (3) the most promising educational techniques; and (4) the implicit marginal productivities (shadow prices) of the various educational investments (p. 194).

An important feature of the Bowles model is his attempt to test the sensitivity of the optimal solution to changes in the coefficients of the linear relations. Using Nigerian data, Bowles demonstrates that "reasonable" changes in the parameters do not significantly affect the final result. Another important feature of the model is that, unlike other planning models, it "is based on the assumption that each category of educated labor is highly substitutable both vis-à-vis other types of labor and vis-à-vis capital." Finally, unlike the Adelman model, it considers explicitly both the benefits and the costs of various educational processes (p. 190).

The simplicity and lack of computational problems in this model are due, in some measure, to simplifying assumptions made by Bowles, such as (1) that observed income differentials are attributed solely to educational differences; (2) that social marginal productivity is not considered; and (3) that educational effects consist of only increments in income; effects in the form of satisfaction not reflected in income (consumption benefits) are ignored. Nevertheless, the utility of a model should not be measured by the realism of its assumptions, but rather by how close the model comes to predicting the real world. The main reason for questioning the manpower forecasting or the social demand approaches is that their record of predictability has been shown to be rather dismal.

The four models discussed in this section are, in some respects, typical of the four categories outlined above. Several other planning models, each with different sets of assumptions and structures, have been proposed in recent years, but space limitations preclude us from discussing them all.

It should also be noted that several authors prefer a "disaggregated" approach, in which the inputs in the aggregate production function for the economy are broken down into finer categories.[6] Although such an approach may be useful, it still leaves the production function at a highly aggregative state. For this reason (and others), many would prefer an approach in which planning is car-

6. See, e.g., Svennilson (1964), Haavelmo and Kaldor (1964), and Tinbergen and Bos (1964: 161–63).

ried out on a small scale (microanalysis) where the planning unit is a school district, an academic department, a college, or a university.

MICROMODELS OF EDUCATIONAL PLANNING

In addition to the understandable desire of many economists for planning that is based on as small units as possible—to avoid problems connected with aggregation—there is also a clear need for small-scale planning of educational institutions if the educational targets of each community are to be met at the least possible expense. Models of educational planning relating to schools and universities have been designed in recent years. In this section we shall discuss one model of planning in a high school system and one model concerning planning of an academic department in a university.

Resource Allocation in Secondary Schools

Objectives are usually stated in terms of maxima or minima. In educational planning, most of the models strive either to maximize a given goal ("excellence," achievement, GNP, etc.) or to minimize costs. In all of these cases, some variant of mathematical programming has been employed.

When there are multiple objectives of an educational system, but where it is impossible to assign weights by which these objectives might be added, the technique of linear programming cannot be used. It is possible, however, to use goal programming, in which the objective becomes to minimize *deviations* from target goal (or output) levels. It is still necessary, however, to obtain a ranking of the goals, although the ranking may be based on ordinal rather than cardinal measurement. (That is, if there are two goals, say A and B, we only need to know whether A is preferred to B, B is preferred to A, or whether A and B are equally satisfactory; we do not have to know the *intensity* of preference.)

A model of this type was recently developed by Morgan and Cohn (1977a, 1977b, 1977c; see also Morgan, 1977, and Cohn and Morgan, 1978b) and applied to Pennsylvania data. The model consists of an objective function and a system of constraints.

The objective function seeks to minimize both negative and positive deviations from target output levels and desired levels of inputs, where the twelve outputs and eighteen inputs described in Tables 8-1 and 8-2 were employed. Target output levels were defined as the output mean plus three standard deviations. Further, a "preemptive priority factor" was attached to each output, based upon a summary of preferences voiced by school administrators, to guide the program in determining which output deviations are to be minimized first, second, and so forth. Also, "coefficients of regret" were calculated from the administrators' responses to guide priority selection in case two or more outputs (or inputs) held the same priority level.

Three main sets of constraints were invoked. The first may be called a technological constraint, reflecting the estimated production relations of the twelve outputs. This set was derived from the simultaneous production function estimates reported in Cohn with Millman (1975). The second set defines the desired levels of the inputs as being equal to the actual input levels plus or minus any deviation from the desired values. The final set provides for resource availability constraints (you cannot have an input greater than what is available) and nonnegativity restrictions (to eliminate nonsensical solutions).

Using the Pennsylvania data, the model was implemented, providing an input vector that, if adopted, would minimize deviations from target output levels. It is shown that, financial constraints aside, it is possible to achieve ten out of the twelve target output levels. And sensitivity analysis showed that while some elements in the solution vector do change as a result of changes in the parameters of the model, the degree to which the system can achieve the target output levels is not changed materially.

Allocation of Resources in a University Department

A comprehensive planning model, encompassing a period of four years, has been developed by Plessner, Fox, and Sanyal (1968). Although the model is applied to a university department in a state-related institution—with its peculiar constraints and relationships —it is, in principle, also applicable to public school districts or to larger units in higher education, such as a college or an entire university.

The state of affairs at the Department of Economics at Iowa State University (Ames, Iowa) as of 1965 is taken as the basis for the development of the model. The department has been involved in both undergraduate and graduate teaching, awarding B.S., M.S., and Ph.D. degrees, as well as in research and extension activities.

The objective function is presumed to be the maximization of additional discounted lifetime income of graduating students over the four year period. Five categories of students are recognized— students receiving the B.S. degree, students receiving the M.S. degree, and three types of Ph.D. graduates: (1) those who receive no university support; (2) those receiving support for teaching services (instructors); and (3) those who receive support for research services in the department. The extra lifetime income of each of these graduates, discounted at 4.3 percent, less foregone earnings, provides for the objective function coefficients c_j, $j = 1, 2, \ldots, 5$. Other elements in the objective function with nonzero coefficients include new faculty hired, research by existing faculty, research by new faculty, and office space addition. For new faculty hired, the coefficient, c_6, was computed by assuming the "starting salary of a new faculty member, and [computing] his total discounted salary from the time he entered the system until the end of the program." The coefficients for faculty research, c_7 and c_8, were defined "as the total research expenditures, other than faculty and student salaries, per hour of faculty research"; c_9, the coefficient of new office space, is not defined, but it probably is the cost per unit of such facilities (pp. 263–64).

The authors note that the first five elements (students' income) constitute what one may call "economic" returns, whereas the other variables, such as research time, represent outputs that cannot easily be converted into dollars and cents—therefore they may be termed "noneconomic." The procedure employed by the authors was to set a given range within which research activities are to take place. The model will thus take into account the fact that increased research time, for instance, reduces faculty time available for teaching. Optimal research levels within the range stipulated by the decisionmaker could then be determined from the optimal solution. The only other alternative would have been to assign an explicit price per unit to research (however a "unit" is defined), but lack of even tenuous data as of 1965 prevented the authors from choosing this course.

There are a total of sixteen constraints. They include (1 and 2) manpower for undergraduate and graduate teaching; (3 and 4) pools of existing and new manpower; (5 and 6) manpower for undergraduate and graduate administration; (7) office space; (8 and 9) admission of undergraduates and graduates; (10 and 11) ratios of Ph.D. (student) instructors to undergradutes and of M.S. to total graduates; (12) manpower of research assistants (Ph.D.); (13) dissertation supervision requirements; (14) existing manpower transferable to undergraduate teaching; (15) new manpower transferable to administration; and (16) manpower available for research activities.

Several assumptions relevant to the constraints are given: (1) "the extension functions of the department are predetermined"; (2) "tuition policy and admission standards are prescribed"; (3)

"there are no student drop-outs or, if there are, they will be offset by student transfers from other curricula and by the addition of students whose major was previously undecided" (p. 261); (4) institutional factors regarding manpower transferability and ratios of students in various categories determine constraints 10, 11, and 14-16. Departmental data sources were utilized to estimate some of the coefficients in a number of the constraints.

The model, which is "based on the use of parametric linear programming," was applied using two alternative sources of data for estimating the coefficients $c_1, \ldots, c_5$ (the net discounted additional lifetime earnings of students in the five categories): (1) 1964 starting salaries for economists based on NSF data, as reported in a 1965 supplement to the *American Economic Review* (AER), and (2) salary data collected for the specific department. The values of c_js are provided in Table 11-1.

Despite the substantial differences between the two sets of estimates, it is shown that the optimal solution is quite similar in both cases. The major reasons for this insensitivity are (1) the model's requirement that M.S. candidates must always be a given proportion of all graduate students (25 percent); (2) the constancy of admission standards, which clearly defines the undergraduate student body; and (3) the various institutional requirements concerning such matters as the ratio of graduate instructors to undergraduate students.

In principle, the model yields a four year plan that must be updated each year: "For example, undergraduates are admitted each year. In specifying our restrictions for Years 1, 2, 3, and 4, we must accommodate the freshman class of Year 0-2 until it graduates at the end of Year 1; Year 0-1 freshmen till the end of Year 2; and Year 0 freshman till the end of Year 3. Similar considerations apply to graduate students admitted in Year 0 or earlier . . . . When student admissions, faculty recruitment and other data relating to Year 1 have become firm, the model should be applied to Years 2, 3, 4, and 5" (p. 265).

Table 11-1. Estimates of Discounted Lifetime Earnings for B.S., M.S., and Ph.D. Graduates.

Degree	Coefficient	Discounted Lifetime Earnings	
		AER Data	*Departmental Data*
B.S.	c_1	$57,700	$36,000
M.S.	c_2	–6,075	9,000
PH.D.	c_3, c_4, c_5	10,017	43,000

Source: Plessner, Fox, and Sanyal (1968).

The implicit value per hour of research is computed through its effect on the cost of replacing one hour of teaching with one hour of research. There are two components. The first takes into account the fact that hiring of a new faculty member will add to the teaching program only a fraction of the faculty member's time (a further allegation is that the new member will need more time than an existing one to handle the same teaching load at the existing quality standard).[7] The second component considers the costs of supporting services (office space, secretarial help, and supplies). Changes in starting salaries of new faculty and/or "the percentage of new faculty members' time allocated to research" will affect the first component (p. 268). Similarly, changes in the cost of supporting services will alter the value of research measured by the second component.

The novel aspect of the model lies in its ability to suggest not merely the optimum number of students in each degree program, but also the allocation of the existing teaching staff between teaching, research, and other activities, the allocation of teaching time between graduate and undergraduate courses, and the optimal allocation of resources to (and of) new faculty.

Although many aspects of the model have been glossed over, most are quite specific to the state of affairs in the specific institution anyway. But the model clearly indicates that fruitful efforts aimed at developing and implementing intertemporal models for microplanning in education are definitely possible. A discussion of the model's limitations and several suggestions for improvements are given by the authors.

A noteworthy feature of this study is that it was initiated and co-authored by the policymaker responsible for the department involved (Fox), who had served as its head for over a decade and was also well versed in economic theory and econometric methods. In such a setting, it is not likely that the model solutions would be implemented uncritically; also, the relatively small scale of the model permits the department head and his colleagues to check "unreasonable" solutions by direct reasoning and by more detailed analysis of department operations at the level of subprograms, fields, and individual courses.

The particular model described should be regarded simply as one member of a class of programming models that can be applied quite flexibly to illuminate resource allocation problems at the level of a university department and its subprograms. The models

7. The authors assumed that new faculty members would be recruited exclusively at the new Ph.D. level with little or no previous experience in teaching.

are small enough and close enough to the daily experience of the faculty members that they can be used in a participatory context —for example, in discussing proposed changes in the graduate program of the department or alternative patterns for staffing undergraduate courses. To the extent that coefficients in the objective function are uncertain (as salaries of graduates must be), the effects of alternative values of these coefficients can be calculated and compared.

SUMMARY AND CONCLUSIONS

Although some scholars strongly object to educational (as well as other) planning—especially on a macro level—on philosophical or practical grounds,[8] most would agree that some planning is desirable. This position is taken primarily because it is recognized that various imperfections in the economic system, and the lack of a pricing system in education, prevent the educational system from reaching the point of maximum efficiency without some external interference. As we have seen, the major source of disagreement is how to plan, not whether we should plan.

We have discussed a number of approaches to macroplanning and have presented in some detail four specific planning schemes. Each is subject to some criticism. Some would rather choose a simple model, even if some realism is thereby lost. Others would prefer to construct a model that is capable of approximating the real world as closely as possible. In general, the latter appears to be the more desirable approach. But to the extent that making the model more realistic creates, at the same time, the need for a more refined set of data—which at present may not exist—its application may be delayed. In the meantime, it may be argued that some planning, even if it is imperfect, may be superior to no planning. If this is the case, some less rigorous models might be well worth considering.

But when such models as the simple manpower forecasting approach are utilized, care must be exercised so that irreparable damage will not be done. For example, instead of single forecasts, based upon a single set of assumptions, multivalued forecasts, involving a number of assumption sets (considering such matters as supply conditions, productivity, etc.) should be attempted. Then the policy-maker could have some idea as to the sensitivity of the predictions

8. A good example is Stein (1977).

to various changes in the assumptions and, hence, the likelihood that miscalculation would lead to serious errors.

It is inevitable that we will be forced to use models that are less than ideal, due to lack of data and/or inability to construct ideal models. But lack of data should not discourage us from developing more sophisticated models, ones that would enable us to do a better job of planning. For the collection of data is frequently made in response to "need," such as when a new model is erected for which new data are required.

We have come a long way in the past twenty years, but further progress in model development and collection of data sources is clearly desirable. Moreover, planning educational systems in a macro sense may be inadequate on the ground that "the allocation of resources as implied by the solution to the centralized model may not correspond to the allocation arrived at by a decentralized decision-making process" (Plessner, Fox, and Sanyal, 1968: 258). Since the American educational system is characterized by and large by a "decentralized decision-making process," there is a clear justification for the intensification of planning efforts at the micro level.

LITERATURE GUIDE

Texts, Surveys, and Other General Items

Texts and collections of readings include Ahmed and Blaug (1973), Correa (1963, 1969, 1975a), Fox (1972), Hartley (1968), OECD (1964a, 1965, 1969, 1973a, 1974b), Sengupta and Fox (1969), and UNESCO (1968). Two surveys are Correa (1975b) and Fox and Sengupta (1968). Bibliography is given in Hüfner (1968). Finally, two items on linear programming include Dorfman (1953); and Dorfman, Samuelson, and Solow (1958). See also Blaug (1967a, 1968, 1969, 1970) and Eckaus (1964).

Planning Models

Macroplans. See Adelman (1966), Aarrestad (1975), Bowles (1966, 1967, 1969b), Carnoy and Thais (1972), Correa (1975c, 1975d), Correa and Leonardson (1975), DeVoretz (1969), Haavelmo and Kaldor (1964), Harbison and Myers (1964, 1965), Kleindorfer (1975), C.J. Lee (1974), OECD (1965, 1969, 1973c, 1973d, 1974b), Parnes (1962), Puntasen (1977), Schiefelbein and Davis (1974), Sen (1964, 1966a), Stone (1965, 1966), Svennilson (1961), Tinbergen and Bos (1964), Tu (1969b), and Windham (1975, 1977c).

Microplans. See Balderston (1974), Boardman (1978), Boardman and Horowitz (1978), Culyer (1970), Cyert (1975), K.A. Fox (1972, 1974, 1975), Gaunt and Haight (1977), Gruver (1972), Holtmann (1968), J.M. Morgan (1977), J.M. Morgan and Cohn (1977a, 1977b, 1977c), J.M. Morgan, McMeekin, and Cohn (1977), Plessner, Fox, and Sanyal (1968), Sengupta and Fox (1970), Szekely et al. (1968), Thomas-Hope (1975), and H. Williams (1966).

Input Substitutability. On the question of whether labor inputs can be substituted for one another and whether labor and capital are substitutable, see Bowles (1970a), Groenveld and Kuipers (1976), King (1973), Psacharopoulos and Hinchliffe (1972), and Ritzen (1977).

Definition of "Shortages"

A discussion of the meaning and measurement of "shortages" is contained in Arrow and Capron (1959), Bumas (1968), Hansen (1964, 1965, 1967a), Holtmann (1968), Leibenstein (1965), and Yett (1970).

Social Demand

Studies on Demand-Supply Factors in Higher Education. See Barnes (1974, n.d.), Barnes and Erickson (1976), Bishop (1977), Bishop and Van Dyk (1977), Breneman (1974, 1975), Campbell and Siegel (1967), Clay (1974), Cohn (1976c), Conroy (1970), Corazzini et al. (1972), Crean (1973), Dodd (1976), Dresch (1975), Feenberg (1977), Feldman and Hoenack (1969), R.B. Freeman (1971, 1975, 1976, 1977a), Freiden and Staaf (1973), Galper and Dunn (1969), Handa and Skolnik (1972), Hight (1975), Hoenack and Weiler (1975), Hyde (1978), Kohn, Manski, and Mundel (1976), Korczyk (1975), Lehr (1975), Leslie, Johnson, and Carlson (1977), Medsker and Trent (1965), Mundel (1974), Radner and Miller (1970), Strom (1948), Trent and Medsker (1968), Tuckman and Ford (1972), von Zur-Muehlen (1972), and Young (1975). Two surveys are Cohn and Morgan (1978a) and Jackson and Weathersby (1975).

Enrollment Projections. The most comprehensive projections for the United States are given in Frankel and Harrison (1977). See also Abramson (1975), B.W. Brown and Savage (1975), Cartter (1966), Cohn and Wilder (1975, 1978), T.G. Fox (1971), and Kinard and Krech (1977).

Related Items. See also Clotfelter (1976b) on private school enrollment, Edwards (1975, 1976) on teenage enrollment rates and school retention, Rosenzweig (1976) on the demand for education in farm areas, and Panitchpakdi (1974) on supply-demand models for a cross-section of underdeveloped countries.

Other Items

Additional work in, or related to, educational planning includes: Ahmed (1975), Balogh (1969), Barnes, Jud, and Walker (1977), Bottomley (1966), M.J. Bowman (1964a), Brembeck and Thompson (1973), Coombs (1968), Coombs and Ahmed (1974), Ewald and Kiker (1970), Gerwin (1969), Hobbs and Anderson (1971), D.B. Johnson and Holzman (1975), Lassiter (1976), Leff (1967), Lindert (1977), Manning (1976), Reisman and Taft (1969), Ritzen and Balderston (1975), Sanyal and Yacoub (1975), Schiefelbein (1975), Scoville (1966), Sewell (1972), Somers (1968), Southwick and Zionts (1969), Stein (1977), C.K. Tanner (1971), Weathersby and Balderston (1971), Wells (1976), and Willingham (1970).

✳ *Chapter 12*

Summary, Conclusions, and Suggestions
for Further Research

> Scientific activity is the only one which is obviously and un-
> doubtedly cumulative and progressive.
>
> George Sarton, *The History of Science and the History*
> *of Civilization* (1930).

OVERALL SUMMARY AND
MAJOR CONCLUSIONS

This volume is based on an examination of the literature in the economics of education generated primarily during the past twenty years.
It is obvious that enormous progress has been made both in the development of the theoretical structure of the discipline and in the empirical work conducted to test various hypotheses and theories. Yet
we have been forced to withhold final judgement in many problem
areas because the field is still in flux. There are numerous areas still
starving both for theoretical and empirical analyses. Solutions are
sought not merely for esthetic and purely scientific purposes but also
for important policy guidelines.

Education As an Industry

It has been shown that education in the United States is an enormous "industry," enrolling nearly sixty million pupils, employing at
least three million teachers, with total expenditures estimated to be
more than $130 billion in 1977 (and total resource costs of $230
billion). Questions of resource allocation are, therefore, of great

343

significance, as inoptimal use of resources would have important social welfare implications.

Education in Early Writings
A brief examination of early contributions to the theory of human capital and the economics of education points to the recognition of human capital in early writings. Education and human capital, however, rarely became the focus of attention and were frequently ignored altogether.

Benefits of Education
Measurement of the benefits of education was shown to require a complex taxonomy and difficult theoretical and empirical aspects. One important issue is how to measure the returns that are strictly due to education. Although the "earnings function" approach appears to be most promising, the questions raised by proponents of the "labor market segmentation" and "screening" hypotheses must be addressed. Moreover, estimation of nonmonetary and external benefits is required if a comprehensive measurement of educational benefits is to be had.

Costs of Education
The costs of education were divided into "direct" and "indirect" categories. By far the major component of direct costs is expenditures by educational institutions, whereas the major component of indirect costs is earnings foregone. A number of issues have been discussed with regard to the measurement of foregone earnings, costs of tax exemptions, and estimates of other cost categories.

Benefit-Cost Analysis
The general theory of benefit-cost analysis was briefly outlined, including a discussion of the three most popular decision criteria (net present value, benefit-cost ratio, and internal rate of return). Conceptual and measurement problems were also reviewed.

Benefit-Cost Analysis in Education
The benefit-cost framework was applied to education, and results of numerous studies, related both to the United States and to other countries, were briefly summarized. The results indicate relatively high returns to education across most levels and regions or countries, although the returns do vary significantly by level, student ability, and other personal characteristics, as well as by country. These results suggest that a government contemplating changes in educational

policy should carefully review the potential benefits and costs of the policy.

Education and Economic Growth

It is frequently asserted that education causes economic growth. Our examination of available evidence suggests a positive correlation between education and economic growth insofar as the United States is concerned. The evidence is not quite so strong when the relationship between economic growth and education is examined for other countries. Moreover, it is quite difficult to establish causation—rather than just correlation—between education and economic growth. In addition, the issue of how to measure the effect of education on economic growth has been discussed in some detail, and we have shown considerable variation in the results depending on which method is used.

Production and Cost Functions

As the "accountability" movement became stronger in the United States, greater attention has been placed on the relationship between school inputs and educational outcomes (outputs). A survey of several studies spanning the period 1956–1977 leads to ambiguous conclusions. There is, unfortunately, a lack of consensus on whether (or which) school inputs matter. This is due to variations in data, methods of analysis, and other peculiar nuances associated with the various studies. Despite the lack of consensus, we find an encouraging ray of light stemming from recent studies, indicating that better methods of analysis and more comprehensive data demonstrate that schools and teachers do matter. Applications of the production function results have also been discussed. In addition, the cost-size relationship was examined, showing, in general, the existence of scale economies (at least up to a certain point) in the operation of schools and universities. Policy implications and other applications were also examined.

Faculty Salaries

In addition to providing data on salaries and compensation of teachers and faculty, we have examined the relative position of teachers vis-à-vis other professions. Our examination reveals a serious deterioration in the relative economic positions of teachers in all educational levels, especially during the last five years. Our data indicate, further, that teacher salaries have not kept pace with inflation, resulting in reduction in the purchasing power of teacher salaries.

Considerable space has been devoted to the determinants of teacher and faculty salaries, with primary focus on the effect of collective bargaining on salaries. Although the results are mixed, it does not appear that collective bargaining has increased wages much. Other determinants of teacher and faculty salaries have also been examined. A particularly interesting question is the alleged sex bias in faculty salaries, for which, again, mixed results have been obtained.

Educational Finance

There is probably as much literature on educational finance as there is for all other topics combined. We have glossed over numerous issues, such as the practical aspects of property tax assessment, financing of special services in elementary and secondary schools, or operation of endowment funds in private universities. Our focus was placed upon federal and state aid to education, provided to individuals and to institutions. Our initial task was to query whether government aid or operation of schools are justified on economic grounds. It has been argued that the existence of externalities provides a justification for government aid but not necessarily for government operation of schools. A similar conclusion is derived when the equity argument is raised.

To the extent that equity reasons are used to justify federal aid to education, an analysis of federal aid to elementary and secondary education does show a distribution favoring more "needy" pupils. Federal aid is not designed, however, to reduce the effect of wealth differences among school districts. That being the primary purpose of the state equalization formulas, we provided a detailed examination of state aid plans and percentage distribution of aid in the fifty states. We concluded that it may not be the type of plan that is most important, but rather, the percentage of funds going toward equalization and the basic level of state support.

In higher education, federal funds are provided primarily for student aid and institutional research. An examination of alternative student aid programs was provided, along with a discussion of the merits of tax deduction, exemption, and credits. Also, information on state aid to higher education was provided, along with a brief outline of state formula finance in higher education. It was followed by a brief discussion of the pros and cons of the voucher system.

Educational Planning

Finally, the rationale for educational planning was discussed, together with a few macro and micro plans. Arguments in favor of and against the manpower forecasting and social demand approaches were entertained. The macro and micro plans discussed illustrate the range of possible approaches available to assist decisionmakers at all levels in improving resource allocation. It has been argued that microplans are to be preferred, since the danger of irreparable damage caused by erroneous decisions is much less significant in the case of microplans.

An Assessment

Mark Blaug (1976b) is critical of recent developments in human capital theory and the economics of education. He claims that despite significant strides that have been made, human capital theory fails to explain convincingly such phenomena as the private demand for education, the "screening" hypothesis, and many others. "Worse still, is the persistent resort to *ad hoc* auxiliary assumptions to account for every perverse result, culminating in a certain tendency to mindlessly grind out the same calculations with a new set of data, which are typical signs of degeneration in a scientific research program" (p. 849). This is a harsh criticism of the field, moderated somewhat by Blaug's admission that "the human-capital research program . . . has no genuine rival of equal breadth and rigor." We do not agree with such a conclusion. True, ad hoc explanations and assumptions are made frequently, and the quality of the research is not always satisfactory. But this is generally true of all applied social sciences, where rigorous theoretical development must eventually give way to empirical, including ad hoc, analysis. Also, the interface of economists, sociologists, and educatimists leads to a hybrid of research designs and frameworks. We do not share the view that a deterioration is occurring. On the contrary, we observe a surge in the development of more sophisticated models replacing relatively simple ones and a greater emphasis on empirical research based upon accepted social science theory. Our assessment of the emerging literature is that it will become even more theoretical and sophisticated, making it much more difficult to comprehend than has been the case hitherto. Students of the economics of education will have to learn new and more complicated tools if they are to follow the new developments in the field.

SUGGESTIONS FOR FURTHER RESEARCH

Readers who followed closely the various issues discussed in this volume will need no direction in finding a plethora of areas requiring additional research. It might be convenient, however, to provide a short list of research problems which, it is believed, are of primary interest.

Externalities.   It has been stated numerous times that we do not have adequate information on the existence and magnitude of external benefits and costs of education. Yet educational finance plans and government-supported programs are frequently justified (vaguely) on the basis of externalities. Information on external effects is clearly needed.

Education and Earnings.   There are many issues requiring solution or reaffirmation, including the empirical validity of the "screening" and "labor market segmentation" hypotheses and the effect of ability, motivation, race, sex, and other personal attributes on the relationship between education and earnings.

Nonwage Benefits.   Little is known about the variation in nonwage benefits and educational attainment. Studies on nonwage benefits should explore various monetary fringe benefits (employer's share of health and life insurance costs, retirement benefits, and other paid benefits), along with nonmonetary benefits such as use of a private secretary or company car and other job-related conditions that affect one's level of satisfaction.

Costs of Education.   There are several areas needing study, including external costs, foregone earnings, the question of tax exemption and data needed to calculate such costs, better estimates of costs of books and supplies, and estimates of the educational costs of formal and informal programs occurring outside the established school system.

Profitability of Education.   Additional, and improved, studies on the returns to education are warranted. Such studies are needed to assess the value of education over time and space and for educational decisionmaking both by governments and individuals.

Education and Economic Growth.   There is a need to refine the tools employed to study the relationship between education and growth and to monitor the education-growth relationship over time and space. More disaggregated studies would be especially useful.

Production and Cost Functions.   This is an area where substantial improvements are needed, for example, better data and improved methods. The record of inconsistent results over time and space begs for correction. A longitudinal research program, which will have to be supported by major private and/or public organizations, is required for studying the long-term effects of schools on their pupils. A research and demonstration type program might be most effective. Even without such a massive program, researchers should continue to apply available analytical tools to new data and improved tools to available (and new) data. Work on learning processes would be especially welcome.

Teacher Salaries. Since ambiguous results have been obtained on the effect of collective bargaining on salaries, further work is in order. Replication over time and space could shed considerable light on this issue. Likewise, although we already have a fairly good idea about the factors that affect faculty salaries in IHEs, it would be desirable to continue along the lines of past and present research, providing both more and improved estimates. Moreover, the work done by NEA and AAUP Committee Z should continue and, hopefully, improve, so that it will be possible to observe the movement in salaries of teachers and faculty. Also, E.G. West (1973) has suggested that the theory of the bureaucracy be used to investigate faculty salaries.

State Aid to Education. This is an area where possibilities for research are virtually unlimited. Most obvious are the efficiency and equity implications of the various state aid plans, *ceteris paribus.* Research on the measurement and definition of equalization has come a long way but needs further work both in quantity and quality. Research should also be directed to the merits of various "modifiers" in state aid formulas, regarding such issues as cost of living, declining enrollments, municipal overburden, cost of special student services, or sparsely populated areas. It might also be worthwhile to explore the use of state aid as a tool to improve efficiency in school operations along the lines suggested by this writer (Cohn, 1974a, 1975a).

Student Aid in Higher Education. Choice of grants, loans, or tax relief measures are available. Although there is already abundant literature on the topic, the question of the optimal mix of student aid programs still requires scrutiny. Of some interest, for example, is the rate of default on loans, raising some questions about the real difference between grants and loans. Further, the empirical effects of alternative educational finance programs need to be explored.

Educational Vouchers. We noted that no real tests of the voucher plan ever took place, so that it is far from clear what the effects of a voucher plan might be. We suggested a research and demonstration program in one or more areas, which should involve both public and private institutions, in accordance with the Friedman (1955) or Jencks et al. (1970) models. Experimentation would be useful at both the elementary and secondary and higher educational levels.

Formula Finance in State Aid to IHEs. There is a dearth of information on the equity-efficiency aspects of state aid to IHEs. There appears to be a fertile area for research, relating to the type of formula finance, use of equalizing and nonequalizing components, and a study of their effects using empirical research. Such studies may then be used to recommend alternative funding formulas.

Educational Planning. Further study of educational planning, at both the macro and micro levels, is warranted. Improvements in forecasting and projection techniques, studies of the reliability of past forecasts and success or failure of educational plans, and development of educational plans to meet the needs of varying types of circumstances all should prove to be useful.

LITERATURE GUIDE

This final literature guide is divided into three parts: (1) research agenda; (2) data sources; and (3) miscellaneous items not covered elsewhere.

Research Agenda
In addition to Blaug's (1976b) critique, from which a number of research topics immediately emerge, consult Rivlin (1962), Solmon (1973c), and Thorp (1962).

Data Sources

Referenced Items. U.S. Office of Education publications include *Biennial Survey* (up to 1962), *Digest of Educational Statistics* (annual), *Projections of Educational Statistics* (annual), and *Statistics of State School Systems.* The Bureau of Census in the Department of Commerce publishes a great deal of data, for example, U.S. Bureau of the Census (1973). Other sources include the *Economic Report of the President* (annual), *Employment and Training Report of the President* (annual; formerly entitled *Manpower Report . . .*); Naylor and Gattis (1974), OECD (1974-1975), Research Triangle Institute

(1976), National Education Association (1969, 1970a, 1970b, 1972, 1975), and *National Comparison of Local School Costs* (annual).

Nonreferenced Items. Data sources not listed in the bibliography include other publications of the National Center for Educational Statistics in the U.S. Office of Education (e.g., *Statistics of Local Public School Systems, Financial Statistics of Institutions of Higher Education, Higher Education Basic Student Charges*, or *Fall Enrollment in Higher Education*); Census Bureau publications, including the *Census of Governments* (issued every five years), *Current Population Survey* series (providing current data on the basis of a sample survey) available both in publications and a public use tape, and other data derived from the decennial census; Bureau of Labor Statistics, providing data on cost of living, employment, wages; and other useful data, some of which are published regularly in the *Monthly Labor Review;* various publications by the National Education Association on teachers, faculty, and financial conditions of schools; Organization for Economic Cooperation and Development (OECD), providing economic and educational data in its various media; UNESCO and other United Nations agencies, providing social and economic data (including the U.N. *Yearbook*); and two outstanding sources of micro data: the Michigan Income Dynamics, collected by the Research Survey Center of the University of Michigan, and the National Longitudinal Survey, collected by the Center for Human Resource Research at Ohio State University (both of which are available on tape). Finally, some of the Bureau of Census data are published in the *Statistical Abstract of the United States* (annual) and in the *Historical Statistics of the United States to Colonial Times.*

Miscellaneous Items

Studies of interest not listed elsewhere include Hawkins, Ritter, and Walter (1973) on "quality" of economics journals; Huffman (1974) on the role of human capital in allocative efficiency; Stollen and Gnuschke (1977) on ratings of economics departments; Tideman and Tullock (1976) and Vickrey (1960) on social choice mechanisms; Tinbergen (1959) on trend movements; Toda (1976) on estimation of cost functions for Soviet manufacturing industries; Tuckman (1970) on migration of college students; Tuckman and Leahey (1975) on the value of a journal article; Tullock (1973) on the salary structure in higher education; Wegner and Sewell (1970) on the probability of graduation from college; Weinstein (1974) on the economic effects of migration in the Bible; Yeager (1976) presenting an outstanding essay on capital theory; and Zuckerman (1974) on the evaluation of human life.

Bibliography

Aarrestad, J. 1975. "On the Optimal Allocation of Labour to the Educational Sector." *Swedish Journal of Economics* 77: 303-17.

AAUP. 1969. "The Threat of Inflation Erosion: The Annual Report on the Economic Status of the Profession." *AAUP Bulletin* 55 (June): 192-253.

AAUP Committee Z. 1970. *The Annual Report on the Economic Status of the Profession, 1969-70.* Washington: AAUP.

Abramovitz, M. 1962. "Economic Growth in the United States." *American Economic Review* 52 (September): 762-82.

Abramowitz, S. 1976. "The Effects of Mini-School Size on the Organization and Management of Instruction." Report No. ED 122 396. Eugene, Oregon: ERIC.

Abramson, E.W. 1975. "Projected Demand for and Supply of Ph.D. Manpower, 1972-85." *Monthly Labor Review* 98 (December): 52-53.

Abt, C.C. 1969. "Design for an Education System Cost-Effectiveness Model." *Socio-Economic Planning Sciences* 2 (April): 300-416.

——. 1970. "Reforming Urban Education with Cost-Effectiveness Analysis." *Educational Technology* 10 (September).

Abu-Laban, B., and Abu-Laban, S.M. 1976. "Education and Development in the Arab World." *Journal of Developing Areas* 10 (April): 285-304.

Acharya, S.N. 1971. "Unemployment, Excess Capacity, and Benefit-Cost Investment Criteria: A Comment." *Review of Economics and Statistics* 53 (February): 103-105.

Adams, A.V., and Nestel, G. 1976. "Interregional Migration, Education, and Poverty in the Urban Ghetto: Another Look at Black-White Earnings Differentials." *Review of Economics and Statistics* 58 (May): 156-66.

Adams, W. 1977. "Financing Public Higher Education." *American Economic Review* 67 (February): 86-89.

Adelman, I. 1966. "A Linear Programming Model of Educational Planning: A Case Study of Argentina." In Adelman and Thorbecke (1966: 385-412).

Adelman, I., and Thorbecke, E., eds. 1966. *The Theory and Design of Economic Development.* Baltimore: Johns Hopkins Press.

Adkins, D.L. 1975. *The great American degree machine: An economic analysis of the human resource output of higher education.* A Technical Report Sponsored by The Carnegie Commission on Higher Education. Berkeley, Calif.: Carnegie Commission on Higher Education.

Advisory Commission on Intergovernmental Relations (ACIR). 1965. *Federal-State Coordination of Personal Taxes.* Washington: ACIR.

———. 1971 (1972 for M-58R). *Measuring the Fiscal Capacity and Effort of State and Local Areas.* ACIR Report M-58 (also Revised Tables M-58R). Washington, D.C.: ACIR.

———. 1973. *Financing Schools and Property Tax Relief—A State Responsibility.* Report No. A-40. Washington, D.C.: ACIR, January.

———. 1974a. *Federal-State-Local Finances: Significant Features of Fiscal Federalism.* Report No. M-79. Washington, D.C.: ACIR, February.

———. 1974b. *The Property Tax in a Changing Environment: Selected State Studies.* Report No. M-83. Washington, D.C.: ACIR, March.

———. 1975. *Property Tax Circuit Breakers: Current Status and Policy Issues.* Report No. M-87. Washington, D.C.: ACIR, February.

———. 1976. *Significant Features of Fiscal Federalism, 1976 Edition.* Vol. I. *Trends,* Washington: ACIR.

———. 1977a. *Significant Features of Fiscal Federalism, 1976-77.* Vol 2. *Revenue and Debt.* Washington: ACIR.

———. 1977b. *Significant Features of Fiscal Federalism, 1976-77.* Vol. 3. *Expenditures.* Washington, D.C.: ACIR.

Agnello, R.J., and Hunt, J.W., Jr. 1976. "The Impact of a Part-Time Graduate Degree and Early-Career Earnings on Late-Career Earnings." *Journal of Human Resources* 11 (Spring): 209-18.

Ahmed, B., and Blaug, M., eds. 1973. *The Practice of Manpower Forecasting.* San Francisco: Jossey Bass.

Ahmed, M. 1975. *The Economics of Nonformal Education: Resources, Costs and Benefits.* New York: Praeger Publishers.

Akin, J.S., and Auten, G.E. 1976. "City Schools and Suburban Schools: A Fiscal Comparison." *Land Economics* 52 (November): 452-66.

Akin, J.S., and Kniesner, T.J. 1976. "Proxies for Observations on Individuals Sampled from a Population." *Journal of Human Resources* 11 (Summer): 411-412.

Akin, J.S., and YoungDay, D.J. 1976. "The Efficiency of Local School Finance." *Review of Economics and Statistics* 58 (May): 255-58.

Alchian, A.A. 1967. *Pricing and Society.* London: Institute of Economic Affairs.

Alchian, A. A., and Allen, W.R. 1968. "What Price Zero Tuition?" *Michigan Quarterly Review* 7 (October): 269-72.

Alexander, K. 1976. "The Value of an Education." *Journal of Education Finance* 1 (Spring): 429-67.

———. 1977. "The Wealth Tax as an Alternative Revenue Source." *Journal of Education Finance* 2 (Spring): 451-80.

Alexander, K.; Hamilton, O.; and Forth, D. 1971. "Classification of State School Funds." In R.L. Johns, Alexander, and Stollar (1971: 29-48).

Alexander, K., and Jordan, D.F., eds. 1973. *Constitutional Reform of School Finance.* Lexington, Mass.: Heath Lexington Books.

Alexander, L., and Simmons, J. 1975. "The Determinants of School Achievement in Developing Countries: The Educational Production Function." Staff

Working Paper No. 201. Washington, D.C.: International Bank for Reconstruction and Development, March.

Alexander, M.D., and Hudgins, H.C. 1977. "Finance Law Reviews." *Journal of Education Finance* 2 (Winter): 396–406.

Alexander, M.D., and McCarthy, M.M. 1977. "Finance Law Reviews." *Journal of Education Finance* 3 (Summer): 129–41.

Alloway, D.N., and Cordasco, F. 1976. "Student Loans and Higher Education: A Way Out." *Intellect* 104 (January): 301–302.

Alternative Measures of Local Wealth and Effort. 1977. Springfield, Ill.: Illinois Office of Education.

Alwin, D.F. 1974. "College Effects on Educational and Occupational Attainments." *American Sociological Review* 39 (April): 210–23.

Alwin, D.F., and Hauser, R.M. 1975. "The Decomposition of Effects in Path Analysis." *American Sociological Review* 40 (February): 37–47

American Association of University Professors. 1968. "On the Financial Prospects for Higher Education." *AAUP Bulletin* 54 (Summer): 182–237.

———. 1969. "The Threat of Inflationary Erosion: The Annual Report on the Economic Status of the Profession, 1968–1969." *AAUP Bulletin* 55 (Summer): 192–253.

"Analysis of Senate Bill 72: School Finance Program in Utah." 1973. Unpublished memorandum.

Anderson, C.A., and Bowman, M.J., eds. 1965. *Education and Economic Development.* Chicago: Aldine Publishing Company.

Anderson, C.A.; Bowman, M.J.; and Tinto, V. 1972. *Where Colleges are and Who Attends.* New York: McGraw-Hill.

Anderson, R.E. 1975. "Private/Public Higher Education and the Competition for High Ability Students." *Journal of Human Resources* 10 (Fall): 500–11.

Andrisani, P., and Kohen, A.I. 1975. *Career thresholds: A longitudinal study of the educational and labor market experience of male youth.* Vol. 5. Columbus: Center for Human Resource Research, The Ohio State University.

Annable, J.E., Jr., and Fruitman, F.H. 1973. "An Earnings Function for High-Level Manpower." *Industrial and Labor Relations Review* 26 (July): 1107–21.

Antos, J.R., and Rosen, S. 1975. "Discrimination in the Market for Public School Teachers." *Journal of Econometrics* 3 (May): 123–50.

"Application of Washington's School Finance system to Seattle Held Unconstitutional." 1977. In *Committee Report* (April), pp. 3, 5. Washington: Lawyers' Committee for Civil Rights Under Law.

Areen, J., and Jencks, C. 1972. "Education Vouchers: A Proposal for Diversity and Choice." In La Noue (1972: 49–57).

Arons, S. 1971. "Equity, Option, and Vouchers." *Teachers College Record* 72 (February): 337–63. Reprinted in La Noue (1972: 71–97).

Arrow, K.J. 1971. *Essays in the Theory of Risk-Bearing.* Chicago: Markham Publishing Co.

———. 1973. "Higher Education as a Filter." *Journal of Public Economics* 2 (July): 193–216.

Arrow, K.J., and Capron, W.M. 1959. "Dynamic Shortages and Price Rises: the Engineer-Scientist Case." *Quarterly Journal of Economics* 73: 292–308. Reprinted in Blaug (1968: 318–37).

Arrow, K.J., and Lind, R.C. 1970. "Uncertainty and the Evaluation of Public Investment Decisions." *American Economic Review* 60 (June): 364–78.

Arrow, K.J., et al. 1961. "Capital-Labor Substitution and Economic Efficiency." *Review of Economics and Statistics* 43 (August): 225-50.

Ashenfelter, O. 1971. "The Effect of Unionization on Wages in the Public Sector." *Industrial and Labor Relations Review* 24 (January): 191-202.

Ashenfelter, O., and Mooney, J.D. 1968. "Graduate Education, Ability, and Earnings." *Review of Economics and Statistics* 50 (February): 78-86.

———. 1969. "Some Evidence On the Private Returns to Graduate Education." *Southern Economic Journal* 35 (January): 247-56.

Ashline, N.F.; Pezzullo, T.R.; and Norris, C.I.; eds. 1976. *Education Inequality, and National Policy*. Lexington, Mass.: Heath Lexington Books.

Associated Press. 1976. "Study: College Grads Can Find Satisfying Jobs." *The Columbia Record* 77 (December 16): 13B.

———. 1977. "Student Attitudes Tested in Pennsylvania Program." *The Columbia Record* (April 11).

Astin, A.W. 1968. "Undergraduate Achievement and Institutional 'Excellence'." *Science* 161 (August 16): 661-68.

———. 1973. "Measurement and Determinants of the Outputs of Higher Education." In Solmon and Taubman (1973: 107-27).

Astin, A.W., and Galvin, B.T.L. 1972. *The Invisible Colleges*. New York: McGraw-Hill.

Astin, A.W., and Panos, R.J. 1968. *The Educational and Vocational Development of American College Students*. Washington, D.C.: American Council on Education.

Atkinson, A.B. 1970. "On the Measurement of Inequality." *Journal of Economic Theory* 2 (September): 244-63.

Augenblick, J. 1977a. *School Finance at a Second Glance*. Denver: Education Commission of the States.

———. 1977b. *Systems of State Support for School District Capital Expenditures: Issues Related to Capital Outlay and Debt Service*. Report No. F76-8. Denver: Education Commission of the States, May.

———. 1978a. "Financing Community Colleges: Simulation of an Equalizing Formula in New Jersey." *Journal of Education Finance* 3 (Winter): 315-32.

———. 1978b. *School Finance at a Third Glance*. Denver: Education Commission of the States.

Aukrust, O. 1959. "Investment and Economic Growth." *Productivity Measurement Review* (February): 35-50. Reprinted in Kiker (1971: 83-100).

Averch, H.A.; Carroll, S.J.; Donaldson, T.S.; Kiesling, H.J.; and Pincus, J. 1972. *How Effective is Schooling? A Critical Review and Synthesis of Research Findings*. Santa Monica, Calif.: The Rand Corporation.

Axelrod, S.J., ed. 1964. *The Economics of Health and Medical Care*. Ann Arbor: University of Michigan.

B

Babcock, D.L. 1975. "Continuing Education of Professional Employees—A Benefit-Cost Model." *Engineering Economics* 20 (Summer): 281-93.

Bacchus, M.K. 1968. "A Quantitative Assessment of the Levels of Education Required in Guyana by 1975." *Social and Economic Studies* 17 (June): 178-96.

———. 1969. "Patterns of Educational Expenditure in an Emergent Nation—A

Study of Guyana 1945-65." *Social and Economic Studies* 18 (September): 282-301.

Bailey, D., and Schotta, C. 1972. "Private and Social Rates of Return to Education of Academicians." *American Economic Review* 62 (March): 19-31.

Baird, L.L., and Holland, J.L. 1969. "The Flow of High School Students to Schools, Colleges and Jobs." *Journal of Human Resources* 4 (Winter): 22-37.

Baird, R.N., and Landon J.H. 1972. "The Effect of Collective Bargaining on the Public School Teachers' Salaries: Comment." *Industrial and Labor Relations Review* 25 (April): 410-16.

——. 1975. "Monopsony and Teachers' Salaries: Some Contrary Evidence: Reply." *Industrial and Labor Relations Review* 28 (July): 576-77.

Balderston, F.E. 1974. *Managing Today's University.* San Francisco: Jossey-Bass.

Baldwin, R.E., and Weisbrod, B.A. 1974. "Disease and Labor Productivity." *Economic Development and Cultural Change* 22 (April): 414-35.

Balfour, G.A. 1974. "More Evidence That Unions Do Not Achieve Higher Salaries for Teachers." *Journal of Collective Negotiations in the Public Sector* 3 (Fall): 289-303.

Balogh T. 1969. "Education and Agrarian Progress in Developing Countries." In Hüfner and Naumann (1969: 259-68).

Balogh, T., and Streeten, P.P. 1963. "The Coefficient of Ignorance:" *Bulletin of the Oxford University Institute of Economics and Statistics* (May): 97-107. Reprinted in Blaug (1968: 383-95).

Bane, M.J., and Jencks, C. 1972. "The Schools and Equal Opportunity." *Saturday Review* (October): 37-42.

Banghart, F.W. 1969. *Education Systems Analysis.* Toronto: The Macmillan Company.

Barkume, A.J. 1977. "Tax-Prices and Voting Behavior: The Case of Local Educational Financing." *Economic Inquiry* 15 (October): 574-86.

Barlow, R. 1970. "Efficiency Aspects of Local School Finance." *Journal of Political Economy* 78 (September–October): 1028-40.

——. 1973. "Efficiency Aspects of Local School Finance: Reply." *Journal of Political Economy* 81 (January–February): 199-202.

Barnes, G.T. 1974. Remarks on "Recent Developments in the Understanding of the Determinants of Demand for Postsecondary Education." Presented to the Annual Meeting of the Southern Economic Association, November 14-16.

——. n.d. (ca. 1976). "Determinants of the College Going and College Choice Decision." Unpublished manuscript, Department of Economics, University of North Carolina at Greensboro.

Barnes, G.T., and Erickson, E.W. 1976. "Advances Needed in Analysis of the Demand for Higher Education and the Need for Student Financial Aid." Paper read at the 1976 meeting of the Southern Economic Association.

Barnes, G.T.; Jud, G.D.; and Walker, J.L. 1977. "Manpower Forecasting for Small Regions." *Growth and Change* 8 (April): 15-23.

Barnow, B.S. 1975. "The Production of Primary Education in Pennsylvania." Working Paper No. 14, Department of Economics, University of Pittsburgh, May.

Barnow, B.S., and Cain, G.G. 1977. "A Reanalysis of the Effect of Head Start on Cognitive Development: Methodology and Empirical Findings." *Journal of Human Resources* 12 (Spring): 177-97.

Barron, W.E. 1967. "Measurement of Educational Productivity." In Gauerke and Childress (1967: 279-308).

Barsby, S.L. 1972. *Cost-Benefit Analysis and Manpower Programs.* Lexington, Mass.: Lexington Books.

Barth, M.C. 1977. "Generating Inequality: A Review Article." *Journal of Human Resources* 12 (Winter): 92-102.

Barzel, Y. 1973. "Private Schools and Public School Finance." *Journal of Political Economy* 81 (January-February): 174-86.

Bator, F.M. 1957. "The Simple Analytics of Welfare Maximization." *American Economic Review* 47 (March): 22-59.

———. 1958. "The Anatomy of Market Failure." *Quarterly Journal of Economics* 72: 351-79.

Baumol, W.J. 1970. "On the Discount Rate for Public Projects." In Haveman and Margolis (1970: 273-90).

Baxter, N. 1977. "Payoffs and Payments: The Economics of a College Education." *Occupational Outlook Quarterly* (Summer).

Bayer, A.E., and Astin, H.S. 1968. "Sex Differences in Academic Rank and Salary Among Science Doctorates in Teaching." *Journal of Human Resources* 3 (Spring): 191-200.

Becker, G.S. 1960. "Underinvestment in College Education?" *American Economic Review (Papers and Proceedings)* 50 (May): 345-54.

———. 1962. "Investment in Human Capital: A Theoretical Analysis." *Journal of Political Economy* 70 (Supplement: October): 9-49.

———. 1964. *Human Capital—A Theoretical and Empirical Analysis, with Special Reference to Education.* New York: National Bureau of Economic Research.

———. 1967. *Human Capital and the Personal Distribution of Income: An Analytical Approach.* W.S. Woytinsky Lecture no. 1. Ann Arbor: Institute of Public Administration, University of Michigan.

———. 1972. "Comment." *Journal of Political Economy* 80 (Supplement: May-June): S252-55.

Becker, W.E., Jr. 1975. "The University Professor as a Utility Maximizer and Producer of Learning, Research, and Income." *Journal of Human Resources* 10 (Winter): 107-15.

Bedenbaugh, E.H., and Alexander, K. 1971. "Financial Equalization Among the States from Federal Aid Programs." In R.L. Johns, Alexander, and Stollar (1971: 251-92).

Beeby, C.E. 1966. *The Quality of Education in Developing Countries.* Cambridge, Mass.: Harvard University Press.

———. 1969. *Qualitative Aspects of Educational Planning.* Paris: International Institute for Educational Planning.

Beers, J.S. 1970. *The Ten Goals of Quality Education: Rationale and Measurement.* Harrisburg: Pennsylvania Department of Education.

Bell, E.B. 1975. "Student Choice of Undergraduate Major Field of Study and Private Internal Rates of Return: Comment." *Industrial and Labor Relations Review* 28 (January): 282-84.

Ben-David, J. 1972. *American Higher Education.* New York: McGraw-Hill.

Bendick, M., Jr. 1975. "Essays on Education as a Three-Sector Industry." Ph.D. dissertation, Department of Economics, University of Wisconsin. Also an Urban Institute Working Paper.

Benewitz, M.C., and Zucker, A. 1968. "Human Capital and Occupational Choice—A Theoretical Model." *Southern Economic Journal* 34 (January): 406-409.

Benham, L. 1974. "Benefits of Women's Education Within Marriage." *Journal of Political Economy* 82 (March-April, pt. 2): S 57-71.

Bennett, N. 1970. "Primary Education in Rural Communities: An Investment in Ignorance?" *Journal of Development Studies* 6 (July): 92–103.

———. 1975. *Problems of Financing the Thai Educational System During the 1960s and 1970s.* International Institute for Educational Planning, Financing Educational Systems. Country Case Studies no. 3. Paris: Unesco Press; distributed by Unipub, New York.

Ben-Porath, Y. 1966. "Lifetime Income and Economic Growth: Comment." *American Economic Review* 56 (September): 869–72.

———. 1967. "The Production of Human Capital and the Life Cycle of Earnings." *Journal of Political Economy* 75 (August): 352–65.

Benson, C.S., ed. 1963. *Perspectives on the Economics of Education.* Boston: Houghton Mifflin Co.

———. 1967. "The Rationale Behind Investment in Education." *Education Age* (March–April).

———. 1978. *The Economics of Public Education.* 3rd ed. New York: Houghton Mifflin Co.

Benson, C.S.; Ritzen, J.M.M.; and Blumenthal, I. 1974. "Recent Perspectives on the Economics of Education." *Social Science Quarterly* 55 (September): 244–61.

Benson, C.S., et al. 1965. *State and Local Fiscal Relationships in Public Education in California.* Sacramento, Calif.: Senate of the State of California.

Berdahl, R.O. 1971. *Statewide Coordination of Higher Education.* Washington, D.C.: American Council on Education.

Berg, I. 1970. *Education and Jobs: The Great Training Robbery.* New York: Praeger.

Berg, I., and Freedman, M. 1977. "The American Workplace: Illusions and Realities." *Change* 9 (November): 24–30, 62.

Berg, I.; Freedman, M.; and Freeman, M. 1978. *Managers and Work Reform: A Limited Engagement.* New York: Free Press.

Bergstron, T. 1973. "A Note on Efficient Taxation." *Journal of Political Economy* 81 (January–February): 187–91.

Berk, R.A. 1977. "A Comment on Summers and Wolfe." *Journal of Human Resources* 12 (Summer): 401–405.

Berke, J.S. 1974. *Answers to Inequality: An Analysis of the New School Finance.* Berkeley, Calif.: McCutchan Publishing Company.

Berke, J.S.; Campbell, A.K.; and Goettel, R.J. 1972. *Financing Equal Educational Opportunity.* Berkeley, Calif.: McCutchan Publishing Co.

Berke, J.S., and Kirst, M.W., eds. 1972. *Federal Aid to Education: Who Benefits? Who Governs?* Lexington, Mass.: Heath Lexington Books.

Berls, R.H. 1969a. "An Exploration of the Determinants of Effectiveness in Higher Education." In Joint Economic Committee (1969: 207–60).

———. 1969b. "Higher Education Opportunity and Achievement in the United States." In Joint Economic Committee (1969: 145–204).

Besen, S.M. 1968. "Education and Productivity in U.S. Manufacturing: Some Cross-Section Evidence." *Journal of Political Economy* (May–June): 494–97.

Bezeau, L.M. 1977. "A Closer Look at the Weighted Pupil." *Journal of Education Finance* 2 (Spring): 509–12.

Bieda, K. 1970. "The Pattern of Education and Economic Growth." *Economic Record* 46 (September): 368–79.

Bieker, R.F. 1970. "Social and Economic Determinants of the Educational Achievement of Selected Eleventh Grade Students in Rural Kentucky: An Exploratory Study." Doctoral dissertation, West Virginia University.

Bieker, R.F., and Anschel, K.R. 1973. "Estimating Educational Production Functions for Rural High Schools: Some Findings." *American Journal of Agricultural Economics* 55 (August): 515-19.

——. 1974. "Estimating Educational Production Functions for Rural High Schools: Reply." *American Journal of Agricultural Economics* 56 (November): 835-36.

Biennial Survey of Education. Biannual. Published by the U.S. Office of Education until its replacement by the *Digest of Educational Statistics* in 1962. Washington, D.C.: Government Printing Office.

Birnbaum, H. 1976. "Career Origins, On-the-Job Training, and Earnings." *Southern Economic Journal* 42 (April): 587-99.

Birnbaum, R. 1974. "Unionization and Faculty Compensation." *Educational Record* 55 (Winter): 29-33.

Bishop, G.A. 1964. "Stimulative versus Substitutive Effects of State School Aid in New England." *National Tax Journal* 17 (June): 133-43.

Bishop, J. 1974. "The Private Demand for Places in Higher Education: A Study of the Response of Project Talent High School Students to Variations in the Cost of Attending College." Ph.D. dissertation, University of Michigan.

——. 1977. "The Effect of Public Policies on the Demand for Higher Education." *Journal of Human Resources* 12 (Summer): 285-307.

——. 1978. "Union Power and the Returns to Schooling." In Ehrenberg (1978).

Bishop, J., and Van Dyk, J. 1977. "Can Adults Be Hooked on College? Some Determinants of Adult College Attendance." *Journal of Higher Education* 48 (January–February): 39-62.

Blackman, J. 1975. *Voucher Schools: Who Participates?* Report No. ED 117257. Eugene, Ore.: ERIC.

Blandy, R. 1967. "Marshall on Human Capital: A Note." *Journal of Political Economy* 75 (December): 874-75.

Blaug, M. 1965. "The Rate of Return on Investment in Education in Great Britain." *The Manchester School* 33: 205-51.

——. 1967a. "Approaches to Educational Planning." *Economic Journal* 77 (June): 262-87.

——. 1967b. "The Private and the Social Returns on Investment in Education: Some Results for Great Britain." *Journal of Human Resources* 2 (Summer): 330-46.

——, ed. 1968. *Economics of Education 1*. Baltimore: Penguin Books.

——, ed. 1969. *Economics of Education 2*. Baltimore: Penguin Books.

——. 1970. *An Introduction to the Economics of Education*. London: Allen Lane the Penguin Press.

——. 1971. *The Rate of Return to Investment in Education in Thailand*. Bangkok: Ford Foundation.

——. 1974. "An Economic Analysis of Personal Earnings in Thailand." *Economic Development and Cultural Change* 23 (October): 1-31.

——. 1976a. "Review of *Schooling in Capitalist America* by Bowles and Gintis." *Challenge* 19 (July–August): 59-61.

——. 1976b. "The Empirical Status of Human Capital Theory: A Slightly Jaundiced Survey." *Journal of Economic Literature* 14 (September): 827-55.

——. 1976c. "Review of *Schooling, Experience and Earnings* by Jacob Mincer." *Economic Development and Cultural Change* 25 (October): 166-71.

——. 1976d. *Economics of Education: A Selected Annotated Bibliography*. 3rd ed. New York: Pergamon Press.

———. 1976e. "The Rate of Return on Investment in Education in Thailand." *Journal of Development Studies* 12 (January): 270-83.

Blinder, A.S. 1976. "On Dogmatism in Human Capital Theory." *Journal of Human Resources* 11 (Winter): 8-22.

Blinder, A.S., and Weiss, Y. 1976. "Human Capital and Labor Supply: A Synthesis." *Journal of Political Economy* 84 (June): 449-72.

Blitz, R.C. 1962a. "The Nation's Education Outlay." In Mushkin (1962b: 147-69).

———. 1962b. "A Calculation of Income Foregone by Students: Supplement to 'The Nation's Educational Outlay.'" In Mushkin (1962b: 390-403).

———. 1968a. "Education, the Nature of Man, and the Division of Labor." In Bowman et al. (1968: 37-39).

———. 1968b. "Education in the Writings of Malthus, Senior, McCulloch, and John Stuart Mill." In Bowman et al (1968: 40-49).

Bloch, F., ed. 1977. *Evaluating Manpower Training Programs.* Greenwich, Conn.: JAI Press.

Block, N.J., and Dworkin, G., eds. 1976. *The IQ Controversy.* New York: Pantheon Books.

Bloom, G., and Northrup, H. 1969. *Economics of Labor Relations.* Homewood, Ill.: Richard D. Irwin.

Blum, V.C. 1958. *Freedom of Choice in Education.* New York: Macmillan. Excerpt reprinted in La Noue (1972: 21-28).

Boardman, A.E. 1978. "Policy Models for the Management of Student Achievement and Other Educational Outputs." *TIMS Studies in the Management Sciences* 8.

Boardman, A.E.; Davis, O.A.; and Lloyd, A. 1974. "A Simultaneous Equations Model of the Educational Process Restructured." Paper presented at the North American Meeting of the Econometric Society, San Francisco.

Boardman, A.E.; Davis, O.A.; and Sanday, P.R. 1973. "A Simultaneous Equations Model of the Educational Precess: The Coleman Data Revisited with an Emphasis upon Achievement." In *1973 Social Statistics Section Proceedings of the American Statistical Association*, pp. 62-71.

———. 1977. "A Simultaneous Equations Model of the Educational Process." *Journal of Public Economics* 7 (February): 23-49.

Boardman, A.E., and Horowitz, D.A. 1978. "The Potential of Social Science Research for Educational Management and Policy—Theory and Practice." *Urban Education* 12 (January): 363-87.

Boardman, A.E., and Schinnar, A.P. 1977. "Educational Resources Multipliers for Use in Local Public Finance: An Input-Output Approach." Paper presented at the American Economic Association Meetings, New York, December.

Bogdanor, V. 1976. "Defending Equal Rights." *Times Educational Supplement* (London) (May 28): 20-21.

Bolch, B.W., and Hinshaw, C.E. 1977. "A Prepaid Tuition Plan for Private Higher Education." *Journal of Education Finance.* 3 (Summer): 101-106.

Bolton, R.E. 1969. "The Economics and Public Financing of Higher Education: An Overview." In Joint Economic Committee (1969: 11-104).

Bombach, G. 1964. "Comments on the Paper by Messrs. Tinbergen and Bos." In OECD (1964a: 70-179).

Booms, B.H., and Hu, T-w. 1971. "Toward a Positive Theory of State and Local Public Expenditures: An Empirical Example." *Public Finance* 26: 419-36.

———. 1973. "Economics and Social Factors in the Provision of Urban Public Education." *American Journal of Economics and Sociology* 32 (January): 35-43.

Borus, M.E. 1977. "A Cost-Effectiveness Comparison of Vocational Training for Youth in Developing Countries: A Case Study of Four Training Modes in Israel." *Comparative Education Review* 21 (February): 1-13.

Borus, M.E., and Nestel, G. 1973. "Response Bias in Reports of Father's Education and Socioeconomic Status." *Journal of the American Statistical Association* 68 (December): 816-20.

Bottomley, A. 1966. "Optimum Levels of Investment in Education and Economic Development." *Zeitschrift für die Gesamte Staatswissenschaft* 122 (April): 237-46. Reprinted in Wykstra (1971b: 458-67).

Bowen, F. 1976. "State Fiscal Stringency and Public Higher Education." *The Research Reporter* 10, no. 1: 1-4 (Berkeley: Center for Research and Development in Higher Education, University of California).

Bowen, H.R. 1969. "Tuitions and Student Loans in the Finance of Higher Education." In Joint Economic Committee (1969: 618-31).

———. 1977. *Investment in Learning.* San Francisco: Jossey-Bass.

Bowen, R., and Minter, W. 1975. *Private Higher Education; First Annual Report on Financial and Educational Trends in the Private Sector of American Higher Education.* Washington, D.C.: Association of American Colleges.

Bowen, W.G. 1964. *Economic Aspects of Education: Three Essays.* Princeton: Princeton University, Department of Economics, Industrial Relations Section.

———. 1969. "Economic Pressures on the Major Private Universities." In Joint Economic Committee (1969: 399-439).

———. 1977. "Economic Problems Confronting Higher Education: An Institutional Perspective." *American Economic Review* 67 (February): 96-100.

Bowen, W.G., and Finegan, T.A. 1969. *The Economics of Labor Force Participation.* Princeton: Princeton University Press.

Bowlby, R.L., and Schriver, W.R. 1970. "Nonwage Benefits of Vocational Training: Employability and Mobility." *Industrial and Labor Relations Review* 23 (July): 500-509.

———. 1973. "Academic Ability and Rates of Return to Vocational Training." *Industrial and Labor Relations Review* 26 (April): 980-90.

Bowles, S. 1966. "Comment." In Adelman and Thorbecke (1966: 412-17).

———. 1967. "The Efficient Allocation of Resources in Education." *Quarterly Journal of Economics* 81 (May): 189-219.

———. 1969a. *Educational Production Functions.* Final Report to the U.S. Office of Education under cooperative research contract OEC-1-7-00451-2651.

———. 1969b. *Planning Educational Systems for Economic Growth.* Cambridge, Mass.: Harvard University Press.

———. 1970a. "Aggregation of Labor Inputs in the Economics of Growth and Planning: Experiments with a Two-Level CES Function." *Journal of Political Economy* 78 (January-February): 68-81.

———. 1970b. "Migration as Investment: Empirical Tests of the Human Investment Approach to Geographical Mobility." *Review of Economics and Statistics* 52 (November): 356-62.

———. 1970c. "Towards an Educational Production Function." In Hansen (1970a: 11-61).

———. 1972a. "Schooling and Inequality from Generation to Generation." *Journal of Political Economy* 80 (Supplement: May-June): S219-51.

———. 1972b. "Unequal Education and the Reproduction of the Hierarchical

Division of Labor." In *The Capitalist System*, ed. R.C. Edwards, M. Reich, and T.E. Weisskopf, pp. 218-29. Englewood Cliffs, N.J.: Prentice-Hall, Inc., 1972.

——. 1972c. "Unequal Education and the Social Division of Labor." In Carnoy (1972: 36-66).

——. 1974. "The Integration of Higher Education into the Wage Labor System." *Review of Radical Political Economics* 6 (Spring): 100-33.

Bowles, S., and Gintis, H. 1975. "The Problem with Human Capital Theory— A Marxian Critique." *American Economic Review* 65 (May): 74-82.

——. 1976. *Schooling in Capitalist America: Educational Reform and the Contradictions of Economic Life.* New York: Basic Books, Inc.

Bowles, S.; Gintis, H.; and Simmons, J. 1976. "The Impact of Education on Poverty: The U.S. Experience." *International Development Review* 18, no. 2: 6-10.

Bowles, S., and Levin, H.M. 1968a. "The Determinants of Scholastic Achievement: An Appraisal of Some Recent Findings." *Journal of Human Resources* 3 (Winter): 3-24.

——. 1968b. "More on Multicollinearity and the Effectiveness of Schools." *Journal of Human Resources* 3 (Summer): 393-400.

Bowman, J.H. 1973. "Cost and Benefit Spillouts as Factors Affecting Local Taxation for Public Schools." In *Proceedings of the Sixty-Sixth Annual Conference on Taxation*, pp. 494-503. Columbus, Ohio: National Tax Association— Tax Institute of America, 1973.

——. 1974. "Tax Exportability, Intergovernmental Aid, and School Finance Reform." *National Tax Journal* 27 (June): 163-73.

Bowman, J.H., and Mikesell, J.L. 1976. "The Effect of Mandated Collective Bargaining on Teacher Compensation and School Budgets With Frozen Tax Levies." Paper presented to the Annual Meeting of the Southern Economic Association.

Bowman, M.J. 1962. "Social Returns to Education." *International Social Science Journal* 14: 647-60.

——. 1964a. "Perspectives on Education and Development." *International Development Review* 6 (September): 3-7. Reprinted in Wykstra (1971b: 425-34).

——. 1964b. "Schultz, Denison, and the Contribution of 'Eds' to National Income Growth." *Journal of Political Economy* (October): 450-64.

——. 1966a. "The Costing of Human Resource Development." In Robinson and Vaizey (1966: ch. 14).

——. 1966b. "The New Economics of Education." *International Journal of Educational Sciences* 1: 29-46.

——. 1970a. "An Economist's Approach to Education." *International Review of Education* 16.

——. 1970. "Education and Economic Growth." In Johns et al. (1970: 83-120).

——. 1973. "Selective Remarks and Some Dicta." In Solmon and Taubman (1973: 381-92).

——. 1974. "Postschool Learning and Human Resource Accounting." *Review of Income and Wealth* 20 (December): 483-99.

Bowman, M.J., and Anderson, C.A. 1963. "Concerning the Role of Education in Development." In *Old Societies and New States*, ed. C. Geertz, pp. 247-70. New York: The Free Press of Glencoe, 1963.

———. 1969. "Relationship among Schooling, 'Ability', and Income in Industrialized Societies." In Hüfner and Naumann (1969: 97-119).

Bowman, M.J., and Myers, R.G. 1967. "Schooling, Experience, and Gains and Losses in Human Capital Through Migration." *Journal of the American Statistical Association* 62 (September): 875-98. Reprinted in Kiker (1971: 485-516).

Bowman, M.J., et al., eds. 1968. *Readings in the Economics of Education.* Paris: UNESCO.

Boyd, J.D., et al. 1971. *Comprehensive Information Systems for Statewide Planning in Higher Education.* Iowa City: The American College Testing Program.

Boyson, R. 1976. "More Power to Parents." *Times Educational Supplement* (London), May 28, p. 21.

Bradford, D.F., and Oates, W.E. 1971. "The Analysis of Revenue Sharing In A New Approach to Collective Fiscal Decisions." *Quarterly Journal of Economics* 85 (August): 416-39.

Bradley, M. 1974. "Estimating Educational Production Functions for Rural High Schools: Comment." *American Journal of Agricultural Economics* 56 (November): 833-34.

Brandl, J.E. 1970. "Comment on 'Towards an Educational Production Function'." In Hansen (1970a: 61-65).

Brazer, H.E. 1959. *City Expenditure in the United States.* Occasional Paper 66. New York: National Bureau of Economic Research.

———. 1970a. "Federal, State, and Local Responsibility for Financing Education." In Johns et al. (1970: 235-64).

———. 1970b. "The Variable Cost Burdens of State and Local Governments." In *Financing State and Local Governments,* pp. 93-106. Boston: Federal Reserve Bank of Boston, 1970.

———. 1975. "Adjusting for Differences Among School Districts in the Costs of Educational Inputs: A Feasability Report." In Tron (1975: 89-133).

Brazer, H.E., and David, M. 1962. "Social and Economic Determinants of the Demand for Education." In Mushkin (1962b: 21-42).

Brazziel, W.F. 1966. "Effects of General Education in Manpower Programs." *Journal of Human Resources* 1 (Summer): 39-44.

Brembeck, C.S., and Thompson, T.J., eds. 1973. *New Strategies for Educational Development: The Cross-Cultural Search for Nonformal Alternatives.* Lexington, Mass.: Heath Lexington Books.

Breneman, D.W. 1974. "Conceptual Issues in Modeling the Supply Side of Higher Education." Paper prepared for the Annual Meeting of the Southern Economic Association, Atlanta, November 15.

———. 1975. "Predicting the Response of Graduate Education to No Growth." *New Directions for Institutional Research* 2 (Summer): 77-87.

Brewster, K., Jr. 1972. "Should Colleges Retain Tenure?" *The Wall Street Journal,* October 2.

Bridge, R.G. 1974. "Parental Decision Making in an Education Voucher System." Report No. ED 098656. Eugene, Ore.: ERIC.

Bridgman, D.S. 1930. "Success in College and Business." *The Personnel Journal* (June).

———. 1960. "Problems in Estimating the Monetary Value of College Education." *Review of Economics and Statistics* 42: 180-84.

Briley, W.P. 1971. "Variation Between School District Revenue and Financial Ability." In R.L. Johns, Alexander, and Stollar (1971: 49-118).

Brovender, S. 1974. "On the Economics of a University: Toward the Determination of Marginal Cost of Teaching Services." *Journal of Political Economy* 82 (May–June): 657-64.

Brown, B. 1971. "Minorities and Public Education." *The American Journal of Economics and Sociology* 30 (January): 1-14.

Brown, B.W. 1970. "Achievement, Costs, and the Demand for Public Education." *Western Economic Journal* 10.

Brown, B.W., and Saks, D.H. 1975. "The Production and Distribution of Cognitive Skills Within Schools." *Journal of Political Economy* 83 (June): 571-93.

———. 1977. "Review of *Schooling in Capitalist America*, by S. Bowles and H. Gintis." *Journal of Economic Issues* 11 (March): 158-62.

Brown, B.W., and Savage, I.R. 1975. "Statistical Studies in Prediction of Attendance for a University." In Correa (1975a: 171-98).

Brown, C. 1976. "A Model of Optimal Human-Capital Accumulation and the Wages of Young High School Graduates." *Journal of Political Economy* 84 (April): 299-316.

Brown, D.G. 1967. *The Mobile Professors.* Washington, D.C.: American Council on Education.

Brown, G.D. 1976. "How Type of Employment Affects Earnings Differences by Sex." *Monthly Labor Review* 99 (July): 25-30.

Brown, K.M. 1972. "The Short Reign of Academic Economism." *Journal of Political Economy* 80 (September–October): 1074-76.

Brown, S.E., and Moran, R.H. 1978. "Educational Expenditures as Related to Property Tax Collection." *Journal of Education Finance* 3 (Winter): 297-304.

Brown, W.W., and Stone, C.C. 1977. "Academic Unions in Higher Education: Impacts on Faculty Salary, Compensation and Promotions." *Economic Inquiry* 15 (July): 385-96.

Browning, R.S. 1973. "School Finance Litigation in a Post-Rodriguez Era." Paper presented at the National Symposium on School Finance Reform, Silver Spring, Maryland, November 26.

Browning, R.S., and Lehtman, M. 1972. "Law Suits Challenging State School Finance Systems." Washington, D.C.: Lawyers' Committee for Civil Rights Under Law.

Brugel, J.F.; Johnson, G.P.; and Leslie, L.L. In press. "The Demand for Student Loans in Higher Education: A Study of Preferences and Attitudes." *Journal of Research in Higher Education.*

Bruno, J.E. 1969a. "An Analytical Approach to Salary Evaluation for Educational Personnel." *International Journal of Educational Sciences* 3 (October): 161-72.

———. 1969b. "A Mathematical Programming Approach to School Finance." *Socio-Economic Planning Sciences* 3 : 1-12.

———. 1969c. "An Alternative to the Use of Simplistic Formulas for Determining State Resource Allocation in School Finance Programs." *American Educational Research Journal* 6 (November): 479-500.

———. 1970. "An Alternative to the Fixed Step Salary Schedule." *Educational Administration Quarterly* 6 (Winter): 26-46.

———. 1971. "Compensation of School District Personnel." *Management Science* 17 (June): B569-87.

Buchanan, J.M. 1965. *The Public Finances.* Rev. ed. Homewood Ill.: Richard D. Irwin.

Buchanan, J.M., and Devletoglou, N.E. 1970. *Academia in Anarchy.* New York: Basic Books.

Buchanan, J.M., and Stubblebine, W.C. 1962. "Externality," *Economica* (N.S.) 29: 371–84.

Budig, G. 1977. "A Gubernatorial View of Public Higher Education." Normal, Ill.: Center for the Study of Educational Finance, Illinois State University, June.

Bumas, L.O. 1968. "The Economics of Engineering and Scientific Man-Power: A Comment." *Journal of Human Resources* 3 (Spring): 246–52.

Bureau of the Census. Various eds. *Census of Governments.* Washington, D.C.: Government Printing Office.

———. annual. *The Statistical Abstract of the United States.* Washington, D.C.: Government Printing Office.

Bureau of Labor Statistics. 1976. *Educational Attainment of Workers, March 1976.* Special Labor Force Report 193. Washington, D.C.: U.S. Department of Labor.

Burkhead, J., with Fox., T.G., and Holland, J.W. 1967. *Input and Output in Large-City High Schools.* Syracuse, N.Y.: Syracuse University Press.

Burkhead, J., and Miner, J. 1971. *Public Expenditure.* Chicago: Aldine Publishing Company.

———. 1974. "The Economics of Education in British Perspective—A Review Article." *Journal of Human Resources* 9 (Summer): 390–97.

Burn, B.B., with others. 1971. *Higher Education in Nine Countries.* New York: McGraw-Hill.

Burns, J.M., and Chiswick, B.R. 1970. "Analysis of the Effects of a Graduated Tuition Program at State Universities." *Journal of Human Resources* 5 (Spring): 237–45.

Bushnell, D.S. 1973. "Needed: A Voucher Plan for Adults." *Education* 94 (September–October): 3–11.

Butter, Irene H. 1966. *Economics of Graduate Education: An Exploratory Study.* Cooperative Research Project No. 2852, Contract No. OE-5-10-244. Washington: U.S. Office of Education, Bureau of Research. (Available through ERIC Document Reproduction Service, ED 010 639.)

C

Cain, G.G. 1976. "The Challenge of Segmented Labor Market Theories to Orthodox Theory: A Survey." *Journal of Economic Literature* 14 (December): 1215–57.

Cain, G.G., and Dooley, M.D. 1976. "Estimation of a Model of Labor Supply, Fertility, and Wages of Married Women." *Journal of Political Economy* 84 (Supplement: August): S179–99.

Cain, G.G., and Watts, H.W. 1968. "The Controversy about the Coleman Report: Comment." Journal of Human Resources 3 (Summer 1968): 389–92.

———. 1970. "Problems in Making Inferences from the Coleman Report." *American Sociological Review* 35 (April): 228–42.

Callahan, J.J., Jr., and Wilken, W.H. 1972. *Revision, Relief, and Redistribution of the Connecticut State and Local Tax Structure.* Hartford: Connecticut Education Association, December.

Campbell, J.M., Jr. and Curtis, T.D. 1975. "Graduate Education and Private Rates of Return: A Review of Theory and Empiricism." *Economic Inquiry* 13 (March): 99–118.

Campbell, R., and Siegel, B.N. 1967. "The Demand for Higher Education in the United States, 1919–1964." *American Economic Review* 57 (June): 482–94.

Cardell, N.C., and Hopkins, M.M. 1977. "Education, Income, and Ability: A Comment." *Journal of Political Economy* 85 (February): 211-15.

Carliner, G. 1976. "Returns to Education for Blacks, Anglos, and Five Spanish Groups." *Journal of Human Resources* 11 (Spring): 172-84.

Carlson, R.D. 1964. "Environmental Constraints and Organizational Consequences: The Public School and Its Clients." In *Yearbook* of the National Society for the Study of Education, ed. Daniel Griffiths, vol. 63, pt. II. Chicago: The Society, 1964.

Carlsson, R.J. 1970. "A Federal Program of Student Loans." *American Journal of Economics and Sociology* 29 (July): 263-76.

Carnegie Commission on Higher Education. 1968. *Quality and Equality: New Levels of Federal Responsibility for Higher Education.* New York: McGraw-Hill.

——. 1970a. *Higher Education and the Nation's Health: Policies for Medical and Dental Education.* New York: McGraw-Hill.

——. 1970b. *The Open-Door Colleges: Policies for Community Colleges.* New York: McGraw-Hill.

——. 1970c. *Quality and Equality: Revised Recommendations: New Levels of Federal Responsibility for Higher Education.* New York: McGraw-Hill.

——. 1971a. *The Capitol and the Campus: State Responsibility for Post-Secondary Education.* New York: McGraw-Hill.

——. 1971b. *Less Time, More Options: Education Beyond the High School.* New York: McGraw-Hill.

——. 1972a. *Instructional Technology in Higher Education.* New York: McGraw-Hill.

——. 1972b. *The More Effective Use of Resources.* New York: McGraw-Hill.

——. 1973a. *Higher Education: Who Pays? Who Benefits? Who Should Pay?* New York: McGraw-Hill.

——. 1973b. *Priorities for Action.* New York: McGraw-Hill.

Carnoy, M. 1967. "Rates of Return to Schooling in Latin America." *Journal of Human Resources* 2 (Summer): 359-74.

——, ed. 1972. *Schooling in a Corporate Society.* New York: David McKay.

——. 1975a. "The Economic Costs and Returns to Educational Television." *Economic Development and Cultural Change* 23 (January): 207-48.

——. 1975b. "The Social Benefits of Improving Pupil Performance." in Correa (1975a: 122-47).

——. 1977. Education and Economic Development: The First Generation." *Economic Development and Cultural Change* 25 (Special Supplement: Essays on Economic Development and Cultural Change in Honor of Bert F. Hoselitz, ed. M. Nash; January).

Carnoy, M., and Levin, H.M. 1975. "Evaluation of Educational Media: Some Issues." *Instructional Science* 4 (October): 385-406.

Carnoy, M., and Marenbach, D. 1975. "The Return to Schooling in the United States, 1939-69." *Journal of Human Resources* 10 (Summer): 312-31.

Carnoy, M., and Thais, H. 1972. "Educational Planning with Flexible Wages: A Kenyan Example." *Economic Development and Cultural Change* 20 (April): 438-73.

Carpenter, M.B., and Haggart, S.A. 1970. "Cost-Effectiveness Analysis for Educational Planning." *Educational Technology* (October).

Carr, R.H., and Hayward, G.C. 1970. "Education by Chit: An Examination." *Education and Urban Society* 2: 179-92.

Carroll, A.B., and Ihnen, L.A. 1967. "Costs and Returns for Two Years of

Postsecondary Technical Schooling: A Pilot Study." *Journal of Political Economy* 75 (December): 863-73.

Carroll, S.J. 1976. "School District Expenditure Behavior." *Journal of Human Resources* 11 (Summer): 317-27.

Carter, C.F., and Williams, B.R. 1963. "Proposals for Reform in University Finance." *The Manchester School of Economics and Social Studies* 31 (September): 255-60.

Cartter, A.M. 1959. *Theory of Wages and Employment.* Homewood, Ill.: Richard D. Irwin.

———. 1965. "Economics of the University." *American Economic Review* 55 (May): 491-94.

———. 1966. "The Supply of and Demand for College Teachers." *Journal of Human Resources* 1 (Summer): 22-38.

Cass, J., and Birnbaum, M. 1964. *Comparative Guide to American Colleges.* New York: Harper and Row.

Caswell, E.A. 1917. *The Money Value of Education.* Washington, D.C.: Government Printing Office.

Center for Educational Research and Innovation. 1972. *Alternative Educational Futures in the United States and In Europe.* Paris: OECD.

Chamberlain, G. 1977. "Education, Income and Ability Revisited." *Journal of Econometrics* 5: 241-57.

Chamberlain, G., and Griliches, Z. 1975. "Unobservables with a Variance-Components Structure: Ability, Schooling and the Economic Success of Brothers." *International Economic Review* 16 (June): 422-49.

———. 1976. "More on Brothers." Discussion Paper No. 469, Harvard Institute of Economic Research, April.

Chamberlain, N.W. 1967. "Some Second Thoughts on the Concept of Human Capital." *Proceedings of the Twentieth Annual Winter Meeting of the Industrial Relations Research Association,* December 28-29, pp. 1-13. Reprinted in Wykstra (1971b: 205-15).

Chambers, J.G. 1975a. "The Impact of Collective Bargaining for Teachers on Resource Allocations in Public School Districts: The California Experience." Paper presented at the meetings of the Southern Economic Association in New Orleans, November.

———. 1975b. "The Impact of Collective Negotiations for Teachers on Resource Allocation in Public School Districts." Ph.D. dissertation, Stanford University.

———. 1976a. "Educational Price Differentials: A clarification of the Issues." Presented at the American Educational Finance Conference, Nashville, March.

———. 1976b. "The Impact of Bargaining on the Earnings of Teachers: A Report on California and Missouri." Presented at the U.K.-U.S. Conference on Teacher Markets, University of Chicago.

———. 1976c. "An Economic Analysis of Decision Making in Public School Districts." Manuscript, University of Rochester School of Education.

———. 1976d. "A Model of Resource Allocation in Public School Districts: A Theoretical and Empirical Analysis." Manuscript, University of Rochester, School of Education.

———. 1977. "The Impact of Collective Bargaining for Teachers on Resource Allocation in Public School Districts." *Journal of Urban Economics* (June): 324-39.

———. n.d. "Educational Cost Differentials: The Conceptual Framework and an Empirical Analysis for School Districts in the State of Missouri." Prepared for the Educational Finance Committee of the Governor's Conference on Education in the State of Missouri.

Chambers, M.M. 1968. *Higher Education: Who Benefits? Who Gains?* Danville, Ill.: Interstate Printers and Publishers.

———. 1970. *Higher Education in the Fifty States.* Danville, Ill.: Interstate Printers and Publishers.

Chan, L.K. 1975. "Nonpecuniary Returns to Work: Theory and Empirical Evidence Based on the Value of Commutation Time." Ph.D. dissertation, University of California, Berkeley.

Chau, T.N., and Caillods, F. 1975. *Educational Policy and its Financial Implications in Tanzania.* International Institute for Educational Planning, Financing Educational Systems: Country Case Studies No. 4. Paris: UNESCO Press.

Cheit, E.F. 1971. *The New Depression in Higher Education.* New York: Carnegie Commission on Higher Education (McGraw-Hill).

———. 1977. "The Benefits and Burdens of Federal Financial Assistance to Higher Education." *American Economic Review* 67 (February): 90-95.

Cheng, C.W. 1976. *Altering Collective Bargaining: Citizen Participation in Educational Decision Making.* New York: Praeger Publishers.

Chervin, S.M. 1975. "The Spatial Effects of Institutional Location on the Price of Senior College Attendance and on Senior College Enrollment Rates Among Tennessee and Kentucky Counties." Ph.D. dissertation, University of Tennessee (Knoxville).

Chiswick, B.R. 1970. "An Interregional Analysis of Schooling and the Skewness of Income." In Hansen (1970a: 157-84).

———. 1971. "Earnings Inequality and Economic Development." *Quarterly Journal of Economics* 85 (February): 21-39.

———. 1972. "Schooling and Earnings of Low Achievers: Comment." *American Economic Review* 62 (September): 752-54.

———. 1973. "Schooling, Screening, and Income." In Solomon and Taubman (1973: 151-58).

Chiswick, B.R., and Mincer, J. 1972. "Time-Series Changes in Personal Income Inequality in the United States from 1939, with Projections to 1985." *Journal of Political Economy* 80 (May-June, Supplement): S34-66.

Christensen, S.; Melder, J.; and Weisbrod, B.A. 1975. "Factors Affecting College Attendance." *Journal of Human Resources* 10 (Spring): 174-88.

Cicirelli, V.G., et al. 1969. *The Impact of Head Start: An Evaluation of the Effects of Head Start on Children's Cognitive and Affective Development.* Vols. I and II. Report presented to the Office of Economic Opportunity pursuant to Contract B89-4536 by Westinghouse Learning Corporation and Ohio University. Springfield, Va.: Clearinghouse for Federal Scientific and Technical Information, U.S. Department of Commerce.

Clark. H.F. 1937. *Life Earnings in Selected Occupations in the United States.* New York: Harper and Brothers.

———. 1963. *Cost and Quality in Public Education.* Syracuse: Syracuse University Press.

Clark, K.E. 1973. "A Slightly Different Approach." In Solmon and Taubman (1973: 317-20).

Clay, J.P. 1974. "Factors Causing Changes in the Undergraduate Enrollment at the Kansas Regents' Institutions of Higher Education." Ph.D. dissertation, Kansas State University.

Clement, M.O., and Gustman, A.L. 1975. "Enrollments in Vocational Education Programs—A Cross State Analysis." In Leiter (1975: 33-59).

Clotfelter, C.T. 1976a. "Public Spending for Higher Education: An Empirical Test of Two Hypotheses." *Public Finance* 31, no. 2: 177-95.

——. 1976b. "School Desegregation, 'Tipping,' and Private School Enrollment." *Journal of Human Resources* 11 (Winter): 28-50.

Clune, W.H., III. 1972. "Law and Economics in Hobson v. Hansen: An Introductory Note." *Journal of Human Resources* 7 (Summer): 275-82.

Clurman, M. 1969. "Does Higher Education Need More Money." In Joint Economic Committee (1969: 632-51).

Cobb, C.W., and Douglas, P.H. 1928. "A Theory of Production." *American Economic Review* (Supplement) 18: 139-65.

Cochrane, J.L., and Kiker, B.F. 1970. "An 'Austrian' Approach to the Theory of Investment in Human Beings." *Southern Economic Journal* 36 (April):385-89.

Cohen, D.K., and Farrar, E. 1977. "On the Education Voucher Fiasco." *The Public Interest* 33 (Summer): 72-97.

Cohen, N. 1958. *Vocational Training Directory of the United States.* Arlington, Va.: Potomac Press.

Cohn, E. 1968. "Economies of Scale in Iowa High School Operations." *Journal of Human Resources* 3 (Fall): 422-34.

——. 1970a. "Benefits and Costs of Higher Education and Income Redistribution." *Journal of Human Resources* 5 (Spring): 222-26.

——. 1970b. "Engel's Formula for Estimating the Costs of Producing an Individual: A Note." *Journal of Political Economy* 78 (July–August): 778-81.

——. 1971a. "Methods of Teachers' Remuneration: Some Empirical and Theoretical Considerations." In *1970 Proceedings of the Business and Economic Statistics Section of the American Statistical Association*, pp. 452-57. Washington: American Statistical Association, 1971.

——. 1971b. "Economic Rationality in Secondary Schools." *Planning & Changing* 1 (January): 166-74.

——. 1971c. "Health, Education, and Poverty." In *Child Health and Welfare Programs: A Cost-Effectiveness Study*, ch. 3. University Park, Pa.: Institute for Research on Human Resources, The Pennsylvania State University, 1971.

——. 1971d. "The Structure of Teacher Salaries in Higher Education." Paper presented at the Winter Meeting of the Econometric Society in New Orleans, La., December 27-29.

——. 1972a. "On the Net Present Value Rule for Educational Investments." *Journal of Political Economy* 80 (March–April): 418-20.

——. 1972b. "Investment Criteria and the Ranking of Educational Investments." *Public Finance* 27, no. 3: 355-60.

——. 1972c. *Public Expenditure Analysis—With Special Reference to Human Resources.* Lexington, Mass.: Heath Lexington Books.

——. 1973a. "Factors Affecting Variations in Faculty Salaries and Compensation in Higher Education." *Journal of Higher Education* 44 (February): 124-36.

——. 1973b. "A Production Function Approach to Evaluate Teachers' Salaries." *Planning and Changing* 3 (Winter): 35-43.

——. 1973c. *An Economic Analysis of State Aid to Education.* Final Report, Project No. R020628, Grant No. OEG-0-72-1417. Washington: National Institute of Education, June.

———. 1974a. *Economics of State Aid to Education.* Lexington, Mass.: Heath Lexington Books.

———. 1974b. "Suboptimization as a Tool to Improve Decision Making in Public Education." *Marquette Business Review* 18 (Spring): 28-36.

———. 1975a. "A Proposal for School Size Incentives in State Aid to Education." *Journal of Education Finance* 1 (Fall): 216-25.

———. 1975b. *The Economics of Education.* 1972; rprt: Cambridge, Mass.: Ballinger Publishing Co.

———. 1976a. What is the Economics of Education?" *Educational Economics* 1 (February): 5-8.

———. 1976b. "Input-Output as a Management Tool in Public Education." *Educational Economics* 1 (May-June): 17-22, 25.

———. 1976c. "The Demand for Higher Education: A Survey and Some Additional Results." Working Papers in Human Resources, No. 67-6, Columbia, S.C.: Center for Studies in Human Resource Economics, University of South Carolina. (A summary of the paper appeared in the *American Journal of Economics and Sociology* 37 [April 1978]: 193-94.)

———. 1977a. "Economic Benefits of Education and Investment in Human Resources." In *Economic and Social Perspectives on Adult Illiteracy* (1977: 4-23).

———. 1977b. "The Costs of Formal Education in the United States, 1950-1975." *Journal of Education Finance* 3 (Summer): 70-81.

———. 1977c. "On Adjustment for Unemployment in Calculation of Foregone Earnings." Department of Economics, University of South Carolina. Mimeograph.

———. 1978. "On the Structure of Faculty Salaries in Higher Education." *Economic Inquiry* 16 (January): 150-53.

Cohn, E. and Hu, T-w. 1973. "Economies of Scale, by Program, in Secondary Schools." *Journal of Educational Administration* 11 (October): 302-13.

Cohn, E.; Hu, T-w.; and Kaufman, J.J. 1972. *The Costs of Vocational and Nonvocational Programs: A Study of Michigan Secondary Schools.* University Park, Pa.: Institute for Research on Human Resources, The Pennsylvania State University.

Cohn, E., with Millman, S.D. 1975. *Input-Output Analysis in Public Education.* Cambridge, Mass.: Ballinger Publishing Company.

Cohn, E., and Morgan, J.M. 1978a. "The Demand for Higher Education: A Survey of Recent Studies." *Higher Education Review* 1 (Winter): 18-30.

———. 1978b. "Improving Resource Allocation Within School Districts: A Goal Programming Approach." *Journal of Education Finance* 4 (Summer): 89-104.

———. Forthcoming. "Determinants of Enrollments in Institutions of Higher Education: Some Additional Results." *1978 Proceedings of the Social Statistics Section, American Statistical Association.*

Cohn, E., and Riew, J. 1974. "Cost Functions in Public Schools." *Journal of Human Resources* 9 (Summer): 408-14.

Cohn, E., and Wilder, R.P. 1975. "Enrollment Projections for Post-Secondary Education in South Carolina to 1985," Report submitted to the South Carolina Commission on Higher Education, Columbia, S.C.

———. 1978. "Forecast of Enrollments for Post-Secondary Education in South Carolina, 1977-1985." *Business and Economic Review* 25.

Cohn, E., et al. 1977. "Urban Labor Markets and Labor Force." In *Selected Readings in Quantitative Urban Analysis,* ed. S.J. Bernstein, pp. 37-61. New York: Pergamon Press, 1977.

Colberg, M.R. 1975-1976. "Age-Human Capital Profiles for Southern Men." *Review of Business and Economics Research* 11 (Winter): 63-73.

Colberg, M.R., and Windham, D.M. 1970. "Age-Income Profiles and Invidious Comparisons." *Mississippi Valley Journal of Business and Economics* 5 (Winter): 28-40.

Coleman, J.S. 1968. "Equality of Educational Opportunity: Reply to Bowles and Levin." *Journal of Human Resources* 3 (Spring): 237-46.

———. 1970. Forward. In Coons, Clune, and Sugrman (1970: vii-xvi).

Coleman, J.S., et al. 1966. *Equality of Educational Opportunity*. Washington, D.C.: Government Printing Office.

Comay, Y. 1970. "The Benefits and Costs of Study Abroad and Migration." *Canadian Journal of Economics* 3 (May): 300-308.

Comay, Y.; Melnik, A.; and Pollatschek, M.A. 1973. "The Option Value of Education And the Optimal Path for Investment in Human Capital." *International Economic Review* 14 (June): 421-35.

———. 1976. "Dropout Risks, Option Values, and Returns to Investment in Schooling." *Canadian Journal of Economics* 9 (February): 45-56.

Commission on Alternative Design for Funding Education. 1973. *Financing the Public Schools: A Search for Equality*. Bloomington, Ind.: Phi Delta Kappa.

Commission on Human Resources. 1976a. *Doctoral Scientists and Engineers in the United States, 1975 Profile*. Washington, D.C.: National Academy of Sciences.

———. 1976b. *Employment Status of Ph.D. Scientists and Engineers, 1973 and 1975*. Washington: National Academy of Sciences.

Comptroller General of the United States. 1976. *The National Assessment of Educational Progress: Its Results Need to Be Made More Useful*. Washington, D.C.: General Accounting Office, July 20.

Conant, E.H. 1973. *Teacher and Paraprofessional Work Productivity: A Public School Cost-Effectiveness Study*. Lexington, Mass.: Heath Lexington Books.

Conant, J.B. 1972. "Full State Funding." In *Financing Public Schools* (1972: 111-18.

Congressional Budget Office. 1977. *Postsecondary Education: The Current Federal Role and Alternative Approaches*. Washington, D.C.: U.S. Government Printing Office.

———. 1978. *Federal Aid to Postsecondary Students: Tax Allowance and Alternative Subsidies*. Washington, D.C.: United States Congress.

Conlisk, J. 1969. "Determinants of School Enrollment and School Performance." *Journal of Human Resources* 4 (Spring): 140-57.

———. 1971. "A Bit of Evidence on the Income-Education-Ability Interrelation." *Journal of Human Resources* 6 (Summer): 358-62.

———. 1976. "The Science and Politics of I.Q.: A Review Article." *Journal of Human Resources* 11 (Fall): 561-67.

———. 1977. "A Further Look at the Hansen-Weisbrod-Pechman Debate." *Journal of Human Resources* 12 (Spring): 147-63.

Conroy, J.D. 1970. "The Private Demand for Education in New Guinea: Consumption or Investment?" *The Economic Record* 46 (December): 497-516.

Conta, D.J. 1978. "Fiscal Incentives and Voluntary Integration: Wisconsin's Effort to Integrate Public Schools." *Journal of Education Finance* 3 (Winter): 279-96.

Cook, W.R. 1976. "How the University Grants Committee Determines Allocations of Recurrent Grants—A Curious Correlation." *Journal of the Royal Statistical Society* 139, pt. 3: 374-84.

Coombs, P.H. 1968. *The World Educational Crisis.* New York: Oxford University Press.

———. 1969. *What is Educational Planning? Fundamentals of Educational Planning—1.* Paris: International Institute for Educational Planning.

Coombs, P.H., and Ahmed, M. 1974. *Attacking Rural Poverty—How Nonformal Education Can Help.* Baltimore: The Johns Hopkins University Press.

Coombs, P.H., and Hallak, J. 1972. *Managing Educational Costs.* New York: Oxford University Press.

Coons, J.E.; Clune, W.H. III; and Sugarman, S.D. 1970. *Private Wealth and Public Education.* Cambridge, Mass.: Belknap Press of Harvard University.

Coons, J.E., and Sugarman, S.D. 1973. "Vouchers for Public Schools." *Inequality in Education* 15 (November): 60-62.

Coons, J.E.; Sugarman, S.D.; and Clune, W.H., III. 1971. "Reslicing the School Pie." *Teachers College Record* 72 (May): 485-93. Reprinted in La Noue (1972: 59-67).

Corazzini, A.J. 1967. "When Should Vocational Education Begin." *Journal of Human Resources* 2 (Winter): 41-50.

———. 1968. "The Decision to Invest in Vocational Education: An Analysis of Costs and Benefits." *Journal of Human Resources* 3 (Supplement): 88-120.

Corazzini, A.J.; Dugan, D.J.; and Grabowski, H.G. 1972. "Determinants and Distributional Aspects of Enrollment in U.S. Higher Education." *Journal of Human Resources* 7 (Winter): 39-59.

Corbo, M. 1974. "Schooling, Experience, and Wages in Santiago, Chile." Ph.D. dissertation, University of Chicago.

Correa, H. 1963. *The Economics of Human Resources.* Amsterdam: North-Holland Publishing Company.

———. 1969. *Quantitative Methods of Educational Planning.* Scranton, Pa.: International Textbook Company.

———. 1970. "Sources of Economic Growth in Latin America." *Southern Economic Journal* 37 (July): 17-31.

———. ed. 1975a. *Analytical Models in Educational Planning and Administration.* New York: David McKay.

———. 1975b. "A Survey of Models in Education and Educational Planning and Administration." In Correa (1975a: 1-41).

———. 1975c. "Models for Forecasting Flows of Students and the Human and Physical Resources Required with and without Technologically Assisted Education." In Correa (1975a: 45-82).

———. 1975d. "Quantitative Analysis of the Implementation of Educational Plans in Latin America." *Socio-Economic Planning Sciences* 9: 247-55.

Correa, H., and Leonardson, G. 1975. "An Empirical Test of Different Methods for Estimating the Educational Structure of the Labor Force Required to Achieve Economic Targets." In Correa (1975a: 110-21).

Coughlin, E.K. 1977. "State Tax Funds for Higher Education top $15-Billion." *Chronicle of Higher Education* 15 (October 25): 9-11.

Craft, J.A. 1975. "Human Resource Accounting and Manpower Management: A Review and Assessment of Current Applicability." *Journal of Economics and Business* 28 (Fall): 23-30.

Crane, J.S. 1972. "The Public School Finance Cases, Part One." Washington, D.C.: The Appalachian Regional Commission, Current Issue Report No. II, September.

Crary, L.J., and Leslie, L.L. 1977. "The Private Costs of Postsecondary Education." Manuscript, August.

Crean, J.F. 1972. "Expected Rate of Return and the Demand for Education: Some Empirical Evidence." *Industrial Relations* 27 (August).

———. 1973. "Foregone Earnings and the Demand for Education: Some Empirical Evidence." *Canadian Journal of Economics* 6 (February): 23–42.

———. 1975. "The Income Redistributive Effects of Public Spending on Higher Education." *Journal of Human Resources* 10 (Winter): 116–23.

Culen, E., ed. 1977. "Changing Patterns of Higher Education." *Road Maps of Industry*, nos. 1800 and 1801. New York: The Conference Board, February.

Culyer, A.J. 1970. "A Utility-Maximising View of Universities." *Scottish Journal of Political Economy* 17 (November): 349–68.

Cummins, J. 1973. "Utah's Schools Get $216 Million, New Methods to Spend." *The Salt Lake Tribune*, March 11, p. A5.

Cyert, R.M. 1975. *The Management of Non-Profit Organizations: With Emphasis on Universities*, ed. L. Benton. Lexington, Mass.: Heath Lexington Books, 1975.

Cypert, C.L. 1975. "An Economic Analysis of the Public Education Sector of the State of Michigan for the Period 1965–69." Ph.D. dissertation, University of Oklahoma.

Cypress, B.K. 1976. *Pupil Participation, Staffing and Expenditures in Federally Aided Programs Operated by School Districts, 1973*. Consolidated Program Information Report—CPIR. NCES 76-300. Washington, D.C.: Government Printing Office.

D

D'Aeth, R. 1975. *Education and Development in the Third World*. Lexington, Mass.: Heath Lexington Books.

Daigle, R.R. 1975. "A Factor-Analytic Study of the Relationship Between Students' Level of Economic Understanding and Selected Personal and Psychometric Characteristics." Ph.D. dissertation, Clark University.

Danielsen, A.L. 1970. "Some Evidence on the Private Returns to Graduate Education—Comment." *Southern Economic Journal* 36 (January): 334–38.

———. 1972. "Subjective Expected Rates of Return to Education." *Mississippi Valley Journal of Business and Economics* 7 (Spring): 11–20.

Danielsen, A.L., and Okachi, K. 1971. "Privage Rates of Return to Schooling in Japan." *Journal of Human Resources* 6 (Summer): 391–97.

Danière, A. 1964. *Higher Education in the American Economy*. New York: Random House.

———. 1969. "The Benefits and Costs of Alternative Federal Programs of Financial Aid to College Students." In Joint Economic Committee (1969: 556–98).

———. 1973. "Economics of Higher Education: The Changing Scene." In Solmon and Taubman (1973: 365–80).

Danière, A., and Mechling, J. 1970. "Direct Marginal Productivity of College Education in Relation to College Aptitude of Students and Production Costs of Institutions. *Journal of Human Resources* 5 (Winter): 51–70.

Darling, H.B., Jr. 1975. "An Investigation of the Potential Benefits of a Productive Education Industry in an Underdeveloped Area and the Explicit Costs of a Maximum Subsidy or Bill of Rights for Continuing Education for all Public School Teachers and Supervisors of the SMSA Concerned." Ph.D. dissertation, University of Arkansas.

Dauterive, J.W., and Jonish, J.E. 1975. "The Structure of Wage Rates Among Black and White Career Women." Paper presented at the annual meetings of the Southern Economic Association at New Orleans, November 15.

David, M. 1969. "Time-Series Versus Cross Section Lifetime Patterns in Different Occupational Groups." *1969 Proceedings of the American Statistical Association,* pp. 664-74.

Davis, J.R. 1970. "The Social and Economic Externalities of Education." In R.L. Johns et al. (1970: 59-82).

Davis, J.R., and Morrall, J.F., Ill. 1974. *Evaluating Educational Investment.* Lexington, Mass.: Heath Lexington Books.

Davis, O.A. 1965. "Empirical Evidence of Political Influence Upon the Expenditure Policies of Public Schools." In Margolis (1965: 91-111).

Davis, R.G., and Lewis, G.M. 1975. *Education and Employment: A Future Perspective of Needs, Policies and Programs.* Lexington, Mass.: Heath Lexington Books.

Deane, R.T. 1975. "Rate of Return to the Ph.D. in Economics: Comment." *Industrial and Labor Relations Review* 28 (January): 288-91.

Decker, R.L. 1975. "The Demand for Economics Ph.D.'s in Community Colleges." *Journal of Economic Education* 6 (Spring): 127-28.

Deitch, K.M. 1960a. "Economic Aspects of American Higher Education, 1960-1970." Ph.D. Dissertation, Harvard University.

———. 1960b. "Some Observations on the Allocation of Resources in Higher Education." In S.E. Harris (1960: 192-98).

Deitch, K.M., and McLoone, E.P. 1966. *The Economics of American Education: A Bibiography.* Bloomington, Ind.: Phi Delta Kappa.

Delaplaine, J.W., and Hollander, E.D. 1970. "Federal Spending for Human Resources Helps the Growth Rate." *Growth and Change* 1 (January): 28-33.

De Mello E Souza, A. 1975. "Rates of Return, Occupational Mobility and the Labor Market for Industrial Workers: A Study of Two Brazilian States." Ph.D. dissertation, University of Michigan.

Denison, E.F. 1962. *The Sources of Economic Growth in the United States.* New York: Committee for Economic Development.

———. 1964a. "Measuring the Contribution of Education (and the Residual) to Economic Growth." In Organization for Economic Cooperation and Development (1964a: 13-55).

———. 1964b. "Proportion of Income Differentials Among Education Groups due to Additional Education." In Organization for Economic Cooperation and Development (1964a): 86-100.

———. 1967. *Why Growth Rates Differ?* Washington, D.C.: The Brookings Institution.

———. 1969a. "Some Major Issues in Productivity Analysis: An Examination of Estimates by Jorgenson and Griliches." *Survey of Current Business* 49 (May, pt. 2): 1-28. Reprinted in *Survey of Current Business* 52 (May 1972, pt. 2): 37-64.

———. 1969b. "The Contribution of Education to the Quality of Labor: Comment." *American Economic Review* 59 (December): 935-43.

———. 1970. "An Aspect of Inequality of Opportunity." *Journal of Political Economy* 78 (September-October): 1195-1202.

———. 1971. "Welfare Measurement and the GNP." *Survey of Current Business* 51 (January): 13-16, 19.

———. "Final Comments." 1972. *Survey of Current Business* 52 (May, pt. 2): 95-110.

———. 1974. *Accounting for United States Economic Growth, 1929-1969.* Washington, D.C.: The Brookings Institution.

Denzau, A.T. 1975. "An Empirical Survey of Studies on Public School Financing." *National Tax Journal* 28 (June): 241-49.

Despain, L.K. 1975. "Education Accountability: The Rate of Return to Nursing Education at Mesa Community College." Ph.D. dissertation, University of Arizona.

DeTray, D.N., and Greenberg, D.H. 1977. "On Estimating Sex Differences in Earnings." *Southern Economic Journal* 44: 348-53.

DeVoretz, D. 1969. "Alternative Planning Models For Philippine Educational Investment." *The Philippine Economic Journal* 8 (Second Semester): 99-116.

Dewey, D. 1965. *Modern Capital Theory.* New York: Columbia University Press.

De Wolff, P., and Van Slijpe, A.R.D. 1973. "The Relation between Income, Intelligence, Education and Social Background." *European Economic Review* 4 (October): 235-64.

Dick, D.T., and Medoff, M.H. 1976. "Filtering by Race and Education in the U.S. Manufacturing Sector: Constant-Ratio Elasticity of Substitution Evidence." *Review of Economics and Statistics* 58 (May): 148-55.

Digest of Educational Statistics. Annual. Published by the National Center for Educational Statistics, U.S. Office of Education. Washington, D.C.: Government Printing Office.

Do Teachers Make a Difference? 1970. Washington, D.C.: Government Printing Office.

Dodd, P.A. 1976. "A Quantitative Analysis of the Determinants of College Choice." Ph.D. dissertation, Georgia State University.

Dodge, D.A. 1972a. "Occupational Wage Differentials, Occupational Licensing, and Returns to Investment in Education: An exploratory Study," In Ostry (1972: 133-76).

———. 1972b. *Returns to Investment in University Training: The Case of Canadian Accountants, Engineers, and Scientists.* Kingston, Ontario: Industrial Relations Centre, Queen's University.

Dodge, D.A., and Stager, D.A.A. 1972. "Economic Returns to Graduate Study in Science, Engineering and Business." *Canadian Journal of Economics* 5 (May): 182-98.

Dodge, J. 1904. "The Money Value of Technical Training." *Transactions of the American Society of Mechanical Engineers* 24.

Doeringer, P.B., and Piore, M.J. 1971. *Internal Labor Markets and Manpower Analysis.* Lexington, Mass: D.C. Heath.

———. 1975. "Unemployment and the dual labor market." *The Public Interest* 38 (Winter): 67-79.

Donaldson, L. 1976. *Policy and the Polytechnics: Pluralistic Drift in Higher Education.* Lexington, Mass.: Heath Lexington Books.

Dorai, G.C. 1969. "A Cost-Benefit Analysis of the International Flow of Students." *Indian Economic Journal* 17 (October-December): 234-49.

Dorfman, R. 1953. "Mathematical or 'Linear' Programming: A Non-mathematical Exposition." *American Economic Review* 43 (December): 797-825.

———. 1976. "The AAUP Salary Survey: Reply." *AAUP Bulletin* 62 (Summer): 158-59.

Dorfman, R.; Samuelson, P.A.; and Solow, R.M. 1958. *Linear Programming and Economic Analysis.* New York: McGraw-Hill.

Dorfman, R., et al. 1976. "Nearly Keeping Up: Report on the Economic Status of the Profession, 1975-76." *AAUP Bulletin* 62 (Summer): 195-284.

——. 1977. "No Progress This Year: Report on the Economic Status of the Profession, 1976-1977." *AAUP Bulletin* 63 (August): 146-228.

Doyle, D.P.; Cunningham, R.; and Abramowitz, S. 1977. "School Finance and Declining Enrollment: Less Than Meets the Eye." Paper presented at the annual meeting of the American Education Finance Association, March 20-21.

Doyle, K.O., Jr., 1975. *Student Evaluation of Instruction*. Lexington, Mass.: Heath Lexington Books.

Dresch, S.P. 1973. "Blindered Economics: Higher Education and Public Policy." In Solmon and Taubman (1973: 335-40).

——. 1975. "Demography, Technology, and Higher Education: Toward a Formal Model of Educational Adaptation." *Journal of Political Economy* 83 (April): 535-69.

Dresch, S.P., and Goldberg, R.D. 1972. "Variable Term Loans for Higher Education—Analytics and Empirics." *Annals of Economic and Social Measurement* 1 (January): 59-92.

Dublin, L.I., and Lotka, A.J. 1946. *The Money Value of A Man*. New York: The Ronald Press Company.

Duncan, G.J. 1976. "Earnings Functions and Nonpecuniary Benefits." *Journal of Human Resources* 11 (Fall): 462-83.

Dunning, B.B. 1976a. *Occupational Choices and Vocational School Selections: Experiences with the Portland Win Voucher Training Program*. Report No. ED134638. Eugene Ore. ERIC.

——. 1976b. "Occupational and School Selections: Experience with the Portland WIN Voucher Training Program." Report No. ED134639. Eugene, Ore.: ERIC.

Dunning, B.B., and Unger, J.L. 1975. *Schools' Responses to Vouchered Vocational Training: Experiences with the Portland WIN Voucher Training Program*. Report No. ED114916. Eugene, Ore.: ERIC.

Dunworth, J., and Bottomley, A. 1974. "Potential Economies of Scale At The University of Bradford." *Socio-Economic Planning Science* 8: 47-55.

Durbin, E. 1970. "Comment." *American Economist* 14 (Spring): 19-21.

Dyal, J.T. 1975. "Efficiency of Investment in Graduate Education." Ph.D. dissertation, University of Illinois.

E

Ebel, R.L. 1977. "For: They Reflect the Real World." *New York Times*, Spring Survey of Education, sec. 12 (May 1) pp. 1, 23.

Eckaus, R.S. 1962. "Education and Economic Growth." In Mushkin (1962b: 102-28).

——. 1964. "Economic criteria for Education and Training." *Review of Economics and Statistics* 46 (May): 181-90.

——. 1973. *Estimating the Returns to Education: A Disaggregated Approach*. Berkeley, Calif.: The Carnegie Corporation.

Eckstein, O. 1960. "The Problem of Higher College Tuition." *Review of Economics and Statistics* 42 (August): 61-72.

——. 1961. "A Survey of the Theory of Public Expenditure Criteria." In *Public Finances: Needs, Sources and Utilization*. ed. J.M. Buchanan, pp. 439-94. Princeton: Princeton University Press.

——. 1968. "Interest Rate Policy for the Evaluation of Federal Programs." Testimony before the Subcommittee on Economy in Government, Joint Economic Committee, *Hearings*, 90th Cong., 2nd sess., pp. 50–57. Washington, D.C.: Government Printing Office. Reprinted in Wykstra (1971b: 149–57).

Economic Report of the President. 1977. Washington, D.C.: Government Printing Office.

Economic Report of the President (together with *The Annual Report of the Council of Economic Advisers*). 1978. Washington, D.C.: Government Printing Office.

Economic and Social Perspectives on Adult Illiteracy: A Conference Report. 1977. Tallahassee: Florida Department of Education.

The Economics of Higher Education. 1967. New York: College Entrance Examination Board.

Edelson, N.M. 1973. "Effeciency Aspects of Local School Finance: Comments and Extensions." *Journal of Political Economy* 81 (January–February): 158–73.

Edding, F. 1966. "Expenditures on Education: Statistics and Comments." In E.A.G. Robinson and Vaizey (1966: ch. 2).

Eden, P. 1972. "U.S. Human Capital Loss in Southeast Asia." *Journal of Human Resources* 7 (Summer): 384–94.

Education Commission of the States, Education Finance Center. 1977. *Finance Facts* 2 (June).

Educational Quality Assessment in Pennsylvania: The First Six Years. 1973. Harrisburg: Pennsylvania Department of Education.

Edwards, L.N. 1975. "The Economics of Schooling Decisions: Teenage Enrollment Rates." *Journal of Human Resources* 10 (Spring): 155–73.

——. 1976. "School Retention of Teenagers over the Business Cycle." *Journal of Human Resources* 11 (Spring): 200–208.

Edwards, L.N., and Edwards, F.R. 1974. "School Expenditures and Educational Discrimination Under the Fourteenth Amendment." *Journal of Economic Issues* 8 (March): 159–66.

Edwards, R.C. 1976. "Individual Traits and Organizational Incentives: What Makes a 'Good' Worker?" *Journal of Human Resources* 11 (Winter): 51–68.

Eggers, H.C. 1971. "The Evaluation of Human Assets." *Management Accounting* 53 (November): 28–30.

Ehrenberg, R.G. 1973a. "The Demand for State and Local Government Employees." *American Economic Review* 63 (June): 366–79.

——. 1973b. "Municipal Government Structure, Unionization, and the Wages of Fire Fighters. *Industrial and Labor Relations Review* 27 (October): 36–48.

——. ed. 1977. *Research in Labor Economics.* Vol. 1. Greenwich, Conn.: JAI Press.

——. ed. 1978. *Research in Labor Economics.* Vol. 2. Greenwich, Conn.: JAI Press.

Ehrlich, I. 1975. "On the Relation Between Education and Crime." In Juster (1975: 313–38).

"Eleven School Finance Models." 1972. *Compact* 6 (April): 41.

Elifoglu, I.H. 1975. "The Allocation of Educational Resources in Large American Cities, 1965–1971." Ph.D. dissertation, New School for Social Research.

Elliott, D.S. 1976. "The Determination of Expenditures on Primary and Secondary Education in Minnesota From the School District's Own Sources, 1970–71." Ph.D. dissertation, University of Minnesota.

Employment and Training Report of the President. 1976. Washington, D.C.: Government Printing Office.

Engel, E. 1883. *Der Werth des Menschen.* Berlin: Verlag von Leonard Simion.

English, J.M., ed. 1968. *Cost-Effectiveness.* New York: John Wiley and Sons.

Epstein, E.H., and Weisbrod, B.A. 1974. "Parasitic Diseases and Academic Performance of School children." *Social and Economic Studies* 23 (December): 551-70.

Erickson, D.A. 1970. "Education Vouchers: Nature and Funding." *Theory into Practice* 11, no. 2: 108-16.

Esposito, A.J., and Thompson, W.B. 1976. *Parents' Choice. A Report on Education Vouchers in East Hartford, Connecticut.* Report No. ED133870. Eugene, Ore.: ERIC.

Evaluating Compensatory Education. 1976. An Interim Report on the NIE Compensatory Education Study. Washington, D.C.: National Institute of Education.

Evdokimova, L. 1971. "Economic Forecasts of the Development of Higher Education." *Problems of Economics* 13 (April): 78-85.

Evenson, J.A. 1975. "Economic and Statistical Analysis of Human Capital." Ph.D. dissertation, Colorado State University.

Ewald, A.A., and Kiker, B.F. 1970. "A Model for Determining the Input Cost of University Degrees." *Socio-Economic Planning Science* 4: 331-40.

———. 1971. "Input Costs of Producing University Degrees: A Case Study." *Decision Sciences* 2 (October): 481-98.

Eysenbach, M.L. 1974. "Voucher Plans, Voting Models, and the Efficiency of Local School Finance." *Journal of Political Economy* 82 (July-August): 863-71.

F

Fägerlind, I. 1975. *Formal Education and Adult Earnings: A Longitudinal Study on the Economic Benefits of Education.* Stockholm: Almqvist and Wiksell International.

Fallon, P.R., and Layard, P.R.G. 1975. "Capital-skill Complementarity, Income Distribution, and Output Accounting." *Journal of Political Economy* 83 (April): 279-301.

Fane, G. 1975. "Education and the Managerial Efficiency of Farmers." *Review of Economics and Statistics* 57 (November): 452-61.

Farber, S. 1977. "The Earnings and Promotion of Women Faculty: Comment." *American Economic Review* 67 (March): 199-206.

Farmer, J. 1970. *Why Planning, Programming, Budgeting Systems for Higher Education?* Boulder, Colo.: Western Interstate Commission for Higher Education.

Farr, W. 1853. "Equitable Taxation of Property." *Journal of the Royal Statistical Society* (March): 1-45.

Farrell, C.H., III. 1974. "Forced Busing and the Demand for Schooling." Ph.D. dissertation, North Carolina State University.

Featherman, D.L., and Hauser, R.M. 1976a. "Sexual inequalities and Socioeconomic Achievement in the U.S. 1962-1973." *American Sociological Review* 41 (June): 462-83.

———. 1976b. "Changes in Socioeconomic Stratification of the Races." *American Journal of Sociology* 82 (November): 621-51.

Feenberg, D. 1977. "What Price Graduate School? A note." *American Economist* 21 (Spring): 73-75.

Feldman, K.A., and Newcomb, T.M. 1969. *The Impact of College on Students.* Vol. I. San Francisco: Jossey-Bass.

Feldman, P. 1971. "Efficiency, Distribution, and the Role of Government in a Market Economy." *Journal of Political Economy* 79 (May-June): 508-26.

Feldman, P., and Hoenack, S.A. 1969. "Private Demand for Higher Education in the United States." In Joint Economic Committee (1969: 375-95).

Feldman, P., and Singer, N.M. 1970. "Benefit-Cost Analysis of Public Programs for Education and Training." *Socio-Economic Planning Sciences* 4 (June).

Feldman, R. 1976. "Some More Problems With Income—Contingent Loans: The Case of Medical Education." *Journal of Political Economy* 84 (December): 1305-11.

Feldstein, M.S. 1973. *Lowering the Permanent Rate of Unemployment.* A Study for the Joint Economic Committee, U.S. Congress. Washington, D.C.: Government Printing Office.

———. 1975. "Wealth Neutrality and Local Choice in Public Education." *American Economic Review* 65 (March): 75-89.

Ferguson, C.E. 1972. *Microeconomic Theory.* 3rd ed. Homewood, Ill.: Richard D. Irwin.

Fetters, W.B. 1975. *National longitudinal study of the high school class of 1972: Comparative profiles one and one-half years after graduation.* NCES 76-220. Washington, D.C.: G.P.O.

———. 1976. *National longitudinal study of the high school class of 1972— Base year study: Student questionnaire and test results by academic ability, socioeconomic status, and region.* Tabular reports series. NCES 76-235. Washington, D.C.: G.P.O.

Fields, G.S. 1975. "Higher Education and Income Distribution in a Less Developed Country." *Oxford Economic Papers* 27 (July): 245-59.

Figà-Talamanca, L. 1974. "Private and Social Rates of Return to Education of Academicians: A Note." *American Economic Review* 64 (March): 217-19.

Financing Public Schools. 1972. Boston: Federal Reserve Bank of Boston.

Firestine, R.E. 1977. "Income and Wealth in a Multivariate Classification of School Districts." *Journal of Education Finance* 3 (Fall): 214-37.

Firestine, R.E.; Carvellas, J.; and LaMacchia, T. 1973. *A Data Capability for School Finance Aid Simulations.* Syracuse, N.Y.: Syracuse University Research Corporation, October.

Firestone, O.J. 1968. "Education and Economic Development-The Canadian Case." *Review of Income and Wealth* 14 (December): 341-85.

Fishelson, G. 1971. "Returns to Human and Research Capital in the Non-South Agricultural Sector of the United States, 1949-1964." *American Journal of Agricultural Economics* 53 (February): 129-31.

Fisher, G.W. 1964. "Interstate Variation in State and Local Government Expenditure." *National Tax Journal* 17 (March): 57-74.

Fishlow, A. 1966. "Levels of Nineteenth Century American Investment in Education." *Journal of Economic History* 26 (December): 418-36.

Fiske, E.B. 1975. "School Tax: Can Reform Aid Quality?" *New York Times,* November 18.

———. 1977a. "Dilemma Growing Over Inequities in Financing School Systems Through Property Taxes." *New York Times,* February 17, p. 16c.

———. 1977b. "Controversy Over Testing Flairs Again." *New York Times,* Spring Survey of Education, May1, sec. 12, pp. 1, 14.

——. 1977c. "Quality of Test Questions is at Center of Debate." *New York Times,* Spring Survey of Education, May 1, sec. 12, p. 15.

——. 1977d. "A College Degree Still Maintains Its Aura." *New York Times,* July 20, p. 35.

Flanagan, J.C., et. al. 1966. *Project Talent One-Year Follow-Up Studies.* U.S. Office of Education Cooperative Research Report No. 2333. Pittsburgh: University of Pittsburgh.

Fleischmann Commission. 1973. *Report on the Quality, Cost, and Financing of Elementary and Secondary Education in New York State.* New York: Viking Press.

Flemming, J.S., and Wright, J.F. 1971. "Uniqueness of the Internal Rate of Return: A Generalization." *Economic Journal* 81 (June): 256-63.

Flora, J.L. 1976. "Equity in Financing Primary and Secondary Education: A Midwestern Example." *American Journal of Economics and Sociology* 35 (April): 175-89.

Flygare, T.J. 1973. "An Abbreviated Voucher Primer." *Inequality in Education* 15 (November): 53-56.

Fogel, W. 1966. "The Effect of Low Educational Attainment on Incomes: A Comparative Study of Selected Ethnic Groups." *Journal of Human Resources* 1 (Fall): 22-40.

Folger, J.K. 1967. "The Balance Between Supply and Demand for College Graduates." *Journal of Human Resources* 2 (Spring): 143-69.

——. 1977. "Prospects for Higher Education Finance in the Next Decade." *Journal of Education Finance* 3 (Fall): 187-98.

Folger, J.K., and Nam, C.B. 1967. *Education of the American Population.* Washington, D.C.: U.S. Government Printing Office.

Foster, B., Jr. 1973. "Financing Education: The Case for Vouchers." *Black Scholar* 4 (May–June): 8-13.

Fountain, M.C. 1968. "What Is An Education Worth?" *Occupational Outlook Quarterly* 12 (December).

Fox, K.A., ed. 1972. *Economic Analysis for Educational Planning: Resource Allocation in Nonmarket Systems.* Baltimore: The Johns Hopkins University Press.

——. 1974. *Social Indicators and Social Policy: Elements of an Operational System.* New York: John Wiley and Sons.

——. 1975. "Practical Optimization Models for University Departments." In Correa (1975a: 220-57).

Fox, K.A., and Kumar, T.K. 1965. "The Functional Economic Area:Delineation and Implications for Economic Analysis and Policy." *Papers of the Regional Science Association* 15: 57-85.

Fox, K.A., and Sengupta, J.K. 1968. "The Specification of Econometric Models for Planning Educational Systems: An Appraisal of Alternative Approaches." *Kyklos* 21: 665-94.

Fox, T.G. 1969. "School System Resource Use in Production of Interdependent Educational Outputs." Paper presented at joint meeting of American Astronautical Society and Operations Research Society.

——. 1971a. "Long-Run Planning For Undergraduate-Higher Education Capacity Needs: Basing Enrollment Projections on Partial-College-Potential vs. Full-College-Potential." *Socio-Economic Planning Science* 5: 1-23.

——. 1971b. "The Use of Mutually Interdependent vs. Mutually Independent School System Outputs in Estimating Education Production Functions." *Pro-*

ceedings of the Social Statistics Section, American Statistical Association, pp. 306–10.

Frankel, M.M., and Harrison, F.W. 1977. *Projections of Educational Statistics to 1985–86.* Washington, D.C.: Government Printing Office.

Franklin, G.S., Jr., and Sparkman, W.E. 1978. "The Cost Effectiveness of Two Program Delivery Systems for Exceptional Children." *Journal of Education Finance* 3 (Winter): 305–14.

Frederiksen, N., and Schrader, W.B. 1951. *Adjustment to College: A Study of 10,000 Veteran and Non-Veteran Students in Sixteen American Colleges.* Princeton, N.J.: Educational Testing Service.

Freedman, M.D. 1976. *Labor Markets: Segments and Shelters.* Montclair, N.J.: Allanheld, Osmun and Co.

Freeman, R.A. 1953. "State Aid and Support of Our Public Schools." *State Government* 26 (October): 237–40, 252–53.

———. 1965. *Crisis in College Finance?* Washington, D.C.: The Institute for Social Science Research.

———. 1969. "Federal Assistance to Higher Education Through Income Tax Credits." In Joint Economic Committee (1969: 665–83).

Freeman, R.B. 1971. *The Market for College-Trained Manpower.* Cambridge, Mass.: Harvard University Press.

———. 1973. "On Mythical Effects of Public Subsidization of Higher Education: Social Benefits and Regressive Income Redistribution." In Solmon and Taubman (1973: 321–28).

———. 1974. "Occupational Training in Proprietary Schools and Technical Institutes." *Review of Economics and Statistics* 56 (August): 310–18.

———. 1975. "Overinvestment in College Training?" *Journal of Human Resources* 10 (Summer): 287–311.

———. 1976. *The Overeducated American.* New York: Academic Press.

———. 1977a. "Investment in Human Capital and Knowledge." In *Capital for Productivity and Jobs*, ed. E. Shapiro and W.L. White, pp. 96–123. New York: The American Assembly, Columbia University, 1977. Distributed by Prentice-Hall.

———. 1977b. "The Decline in the Economic Rewards to College Education." *Review of Economics and Statistics* 59 (February): 18–29.

Freiden, A., and Staaf, R.J. 1973. "Scholastic Choice: An Economic Model of Student Behavior." *Journal of Human Resources* 8 (Summer): 396–404.

Freiman, M.P. 1976. "Empirical Tests of Dual Labor Market Theory and Hedonic Measures of Occupational Attainment." Ph.D. dissertation, University of Wisconsin, Madison.

Frey, D.E. 1973a. "The Distribution of Educational Resources in Large American Cities: A Comment." *Journal of Human Resources* 8 (Fall): 516–18.

———. 1973b. "Wage Determination in Public Schools and the Effects of Unionization." Presented at the Conference on Labor in Non-Profit Industry and Government. Princeton: Industrial Relations Section, Princeton University.

Friedman, M. 1955. "The Role of Government in Public Education. In *Economics and the Public Interest*, ed. R.A. Solo, pp. 123–53. New Brunswick, N.J.: Rutgers University Press.

———. 1962. *Capitalism and Freedom.* Chicago: University of Chicago Press.

———. 1968. "The Higher Schooling in America." *The Public Interest* 24 (Spring): 108–12.

Friedman, M., and Kuznets, S. 1945. *Income from Individual Professional Practice.* New York: National Bureau of Economic Research.

Froomkin, J. 1969. "Cost-Effectiveness and Cost-Benefit Analysis of Educational Programs." *Socio-Economic Planning Sciences* 2 (April): 381-88.

Froomkin, J.; Jamison, D.T.; and Radner, R.; eds. 1976. *Education as an Industry.* Cambridge, Mass.: Ballinger Publishing Company (for National Bureau of Economic Research).

Fuerst, A.M. 1975. "Economic Development with Special Attention to the Role Played by Human Capital: The Cases of Israel and Puerto Rico Selected Observations." *American Economist* 19 (Fall): 38-42.

Fuller, W.A. 1962. "Estimating the Reliability of Quantities Derived from Empirical Production Functions." *Journal of Farm Economics* (February 1962): 85-86.

G

Gallaway, L. 1965. "The Foundations of the 'War on Poverty.'" *American Economic Review* 55 (March): 121-31.

Galper, H., and Dunn, R.M., Jr. 1969. "A Short-Run Demand Function for Higher Education in the United States." *Journal of Political Economy* 77 (September–October): 765-77.

Garbarino, J.W. 1975. "Faculty Union Activity in Higher Education—1974." *Industrial Relations* 14 (February): 110-11.

Garbarino, J.W., and Aussieker, M.W. 1974. "Faculty Unionism In Institutions of Higher Education." *Monthly Labor Review* (April): 48-52.

Garfinkel, I., and Gramlich, E.M. 1973. "A Statistical Analysis of the OEO Experiment in Educational Performance Contracting." *Journal of Human Resources* 8 (Summer): 275-305.

Garms, W.I. 1971. "A Benefit-Cost Analysis of the Upward Bound Program." *Journal of Human Resources* 6 (Spring): 206-20.

Garms, W.I., and Smith, M.C. 1970. "Educational Need and Its Application to State School Finance." *Journal of Human Resources* 5 (Summer): 304-17.

Garner, W.F. 1973. "The Identification of an Educational Production Function by Experimental Means." Paper presented at the American Educational Research Association Annual Meeting.

Gasson, R.M.; Haller, A.O.; and Sewell, W.H. 1972. *Attitudes and Facilitation in the Attainment of Status.* Washington: American Sociological Association.

Gauerke, W.E., and Childress, J.R., eds. 1967. *The Theory and Practice of School Finance.* Chicago: Rand McNally.

Gaunt, R.N., and Haight, M.J. 1977. "Planning Models in Higher Education Administration." *Journal of Education Finance* 2 (Winter): 305-23.

Gay, R.S. 1975. "The Impact of Unions on Relative Real Wages: New Evidence on Effects Within Industries and Threat Effects." Ph.D. dissertation, University of Wisconsin, Madison.

Gensemer, B.L. 1975. "Equalizing Educational Opportunity: Analysis of Proposed Reforms in Ohio State Aid to Public Schools." Paper delivered at the 1975 annual meeting of the Ohio Association of Economists and Political Scientists in Columbus, Ohio, April 18-19.

———. 1976. "Personal Income Variations Among Ohio School Districts and Their Implications for the Guaranteed Yield Formula." In *Preliminary Report to the Education Review,* General Assembly, State of Ohio, 1976.

Gerking, S.D. 1976. "Input-Output as a Simple Econometric Model." *Review of Economics and Statistics* 58 (August): 274-82.

Gertmenian, L.W. 1975. "The Economics of Education in the Urban Ghetto." Ph.D. dissertation, University of Southern California.

Gerwin, D. 1969. *Budgeting Public Funds.* Madison: University of Wisconsin Press.

———. ed. 1974. *The Employment of Teachers: Some Analytical Views.* Berkeley, Calif.: McCutchan Publishing Corporation.

Geske, T.G., and Rossmiller, R.A. 1977. "The Politics of School Fiscal Reform in Wisconsin." *Journal of Education Finance* 2 (Spring): 513-32.

Ghazalah, I.A. and Pejovich, S. 1973. "The Economics of Vocational and Technical Education: A Report on Three Studies." *Review of Social Economy* 31 (October): 191-98.

Gilmer, R.W. 1975. "Predicting the Cost of Fiscal Equalization in School Finance." *Public Finance Quarterly* 3 (July): 261-74.

Gilmer, R.W., and Morgan, D.C. 1973. "The Equivalence of Flat Grants and Foundation Programs in State Aid Formulas." *Public Finance Quarterly* 1 (October): 437-47.

———. 1975. "The Equalization Equivalence of Flat Grants and Foundation Programs: A Reply and Extended Analysis." *Public Finance Quarterly* 3 (January): 86-96.

Gilpatrick, E. 1975. "Education for Work: A Full Employment Strategy." *Annals of the American Academy of Political and Social Science* 418 (March): 147-55.

Gilroy, C.L. 1975. "Investment in Human Capital and Black-White Unemoyment." *Monthly Labor Review* 98 (July): 13-21.

Ginsburg, A.L., and Killalea, J.N. 1977. "Patterns of Federal Aid to School Districts." *Journal of Education Finance* 2 (Winter): 380-95.

Gintis, H. 1971. "Education, Technology, and Characteristics of Worker Productivity." *American Economic Review* 61 (May): 266-79.

———. 1972. "Towards a Political Economy of Education: A Radical Critique of Ivan Illich's Deschooling Society." *Harvard Educational Review* 42 (February): 70-96.

Ginzberg, E. 1966. *The Development of Human Resources.* New York: McGraw-Hill.

———. 1971. "The Economics of the Voucher System." *Teacher College Record* 72 (February): 373-82. Reprinted in La Noue (1972: 99-108).

———. 1975. *The Manpower Connection: Education and Work.* Cambridge, Mass.: Harvard University Press.

Gisser, M. 1968. "On Benefit-Cost Analysis of Investment in Schooling in Rural Farm Areas." *American Journal of Agricultural Economics* 50 (August): 621-29.

Glennan, T.K. 1971. "OEO Experiments in Education." *Compact* 5 (February): 3-5.

Goddard, F.O., and Goffman, I.J. 1973. "The Public Financing of Non-Public Education." *Review of Social Economy* 31 (October): 152-66.

Godwin, W.L., and Mann, P.B., ed. 1972. *Higher Education: Myths, Realities and Possibilities.* Atlanta: Southern Regional Education Board.

Goettel, R.J., and Firestine, R.E. 1975. "Declining Enrollments and State Aid: Another Equity and Efficiency Problem." *Journal of Education Finance* 1 (Fall): 205-15.

Goetz, Charles J. 1972. *What is Revenue Sharing?* Washington, D.C.: The Urban Institute.

Goffman, I.J. 1977. "Social Benefits and Non-Quantifiable Returns." In *Economic and Social Perspectives on Adult Illiteracy* (1977: 81-84).

Goldberger, A.S. 1964. *Econometric Theory.* New York: John Wiley and Sons.

———. 1976a. "Jensen on Burks." *Educational Psychology* 12: 64-78.

———. 1976b. "On Jensen's Method for Twins." *Educational Psychology* 12: 79-82.

———. 1976c. "Mysteries of the Meritocracy." In Block and Dworkin (1976: 265-79).

Goldberger, A.S.; Nagar, A.L.; and Odeh, H.S. 1961. "The Covariance Matrices of Reduced-Form Coefficients and of Forecasts for a Structural Econometric Model." *Econometrica* 29 (October): 556-73.

Golden, C.J., Jr. 1971-1972. "Education Vouchers: The Fruit of the Lemon Tree." *Stanford Law Review* 24: 687-711.

Goldfeld, S.M. and Quandt, R.E. 1972. *Nonlinear Methods in Econometrics.* Amsterdam: North-Holland Publishing Company.

Golladay, M.A. 1976. *The Conditions of Education: A Statistical Report on the Condition of Education in the United States.* NCES 76-400. Washington, D.C.: Government Printing Office.

Goode, R. 1962. "Educational Expenditures and the Income Tax." In Mushkin (1962b: 281-304). Reprinted in Kiker (1971: 563-89).

———. 1976. *The Individual Income Tax.* Rev. ed. Washington, D.C.: The Brookings Institution.

Goodman, S.M. 1959. *The Assessment of School Quality.* Albany: The University of the State of New York, State Education Department.

Gordon, M.M., ed. 1974. *Higher Education and the Labor Market.* New York: McGraw-Hill.

Gordon, N.; Morton, T.; and Braden, I. 1974. "Faculty Salaries: Is There Discrimination by Sex, Race, and Discipline?" *American Economic Review* 64 (June): 419-27.

Gordon, R.H. 1976. "Essays on the Causes and Equitable Treatment of Differences in Earnings and Ability." Ph.D. dissertation, Massachusetts Institute of Technology.

Gordon, R.J. 1969. "$45 Billion of U.S. Private Investment Has Been Mislaid." *American Economic Review* 59 (June): 221-38.

———. 1973. "The Welfare Costs of Higher Unemployment." *Brookings Papers on Economic Activity* 1: 133-95.

Gorseline, D.E. 1932. *The Effect of Schooling Upon Income.* Bloomington: Graduate Council of Indiana University.

Gramlich, E.M., and Koshel, P.P. 1975. *Educational Performance Contracting: An Evaluation of an Experiment.* Washington, D.C.: Brookings.

Grant, W.V., and Lind, C.G. 1976. *Digest of Educational Statistics, 1975 ed.* Washington, D.C.: Government Printing Office.

———. 1977. *Digest of Educational Statistics, 1976 Edition.* Washington, D.C.: Government Printing Office.

Grayson, L.P. 1972. "Costs, Benefits, Effectiveness: Challenge to Educational Technology." *Science* 175 (March).

Green, R.L., et al. 1964. *The Educational Status of Children in a District without Public Schools.* Report to the U.S. Office of Education under cooperative research project 2321.

Greenberg, D., and McCall, J.J. 1974a. *Analysis of the Educational Personnel*

System: VII. Teacher Mobility in Michigan. R-1343-HEW. Santa Monica, Calif.: The Rand Corporation.

———. 1974b. "Teacher Mobility and Allocation." Journal of Human Resources 9 (Fall): 480-502.

Greenwood, M.J. 1973. "The Geographic Mobility of College Graduates." Journal of Human Resources 8 (Fall): 506-15.

Griliches, Z. 1963a. "Estimates of the Aggregate Agricultural Production Function from Cross-Sectional Data." Journal of Farm Economics 45 (May): 419-28.

———. 1936b. "The Sources of Measured Productivity Growth: United States Agriculture, 1940-1960." Journal of Political Economy 71 (August): 331-46.

———. 1964. "Research Expenditures, Education, and Aggregate Agricultural Production Function." American Economic Review 54 (December): 961-74.

———. 1967. "Production Functions in Manufacturing: Some Preliminary Results." In The Theory and Empirical Analysis of Production, ed. M. Brown, pp. 275-322. New York: National Bureau of Economic Research, 1967.

———. 1970. "Notes on the Role of Education in Production Functions and Growth Accounting." In Hansen (1970a: 71-115).

———. 1974 "Errors in Variables and Other Unobservables." Econometrica 42 (November): 971-98.

———. 1976. "Wages of Very Young Men." Journal of Political Economy 84 (Supplement: August): S69-85.

———. 1977a. "Estimating the Returns to Schooling: Some Econometric Problems." Econometrica 45 (January): 1-22.

———. 1977b. "The Changing Economics of Education." In Resource Allocation and Economic Policy, ed. M. Allingham and M.L. Burstein. New York: Macmillan, 1977.

———. 1977c. "Rejoinder to Cardell and Hopkins." Journal of Political Economy 85 (February): 215.

Griliches, Z., and Mason, W.M. 1972. "Education, Income, and Ability." Journal of Political Economy 80 (May-June, pt. 2): S74-103.

Groenveld, K., and Kuipers, S.K. 1976. "Some Further Evidence on the Substitution Possibilities between Graduate and Other Labour." Kyklos 29: 531-39.

Gronau, R. 1974. "Wage Comparisons—A Selectivity Bias" Journal of Political Economy 82 (November-December): 1119-43.

Grossman, M. 1972. Demand for Health. Occasional Paper 119. New York: National Bureau of Economic Research.

Groves, H. 1961. Education and Economic Growth. Washington, D.C.: National Education Association.

Grubb, W.N., and Michelson, S. 1974. States and Schools: The Political Economy of Public School Finance. Lexington, Mass.: Heath Lexington Books.

Grubel, H.G., and Scott, A.D. 1966. "The International Flow of Human Capital." American Economic Review 56 (May): 268-74.

Gruver, G. 1972. "Goal Programming and Efficiency in Decision Models for Educational Institutions." In K.A. Fox (1972: 179-87).

Gurin, G. 1971. "The Impact of the College Experience." In Withey (1971: 25-54).

Gustman, A.L. 1973a. "On Estimating the Rate of Return to Education." Applied Economics 5 (June): 89-99.

———. 1973b. "On the Appropriate Model for Analyzing Investment in Human Capital Where the Capital Market is Imperfect." Review of Income and Wealth 19 (September): 303-305.

Gustman, A.L., and Clement, M.O. 1977. "Teachers' Salary Differentials and Equality of Educational Opportunity." *Industrial and Labor Relations Review* 31 (October): 61-70.

Gustman, A.L., and Pidot, G.B., Jr. 1973. "Interactions Between Educational Spending and Student Enrollment." *Journal of Human Resources* 8 (Winter): 3-23.

Gustman, A.L., and Segal, M. 1977. "Interstate Variations in Teachers' Pensions." *Industrial Relations* 16 (October): 335-44.

———. 1978. "Teachers' Salary Structures—Some Analytical and Empirical Aspects of the Impact of Collective Bargaining." In *Proceedings of the Industrial Relations Research Association*, 1978.

Gustman, A.L., and Stafford, F.P. "Income Expectations and the Consumption of Graduate Students." *Journal of Political Economy* 80 (November-December): 1246-58.

Guthrie, J.W. 1970. "A Survey of School Effectiveness Studies." In *Do Teachers Make a Difference?*, pp. 25-54.. Washington, D.C.: Government Printing Office. 1970.

Guthrie, J.W.; Kleindorfer, G.B.; Levin, H.M.; and Stout, R.T. 1971. *Schools and Inequality*. Cambridge, Mass.: MIT Press.

Guthrie, J.W., and Lawton, S.B. 1970. "The Distribution of Federal School Aid Funds." *Educational Administration Quarterly* 6 (Winter): 47-61.

Guthrie, J.W., et al. 1969. *Schools and Inequality*. Washington, D.C.: The Urban Coalition.

Gutierrez, F., and Chacon, G. 1974. "The Educational Voucher Intrigue: An Analysis of its Impact on the Alum Rock Community." Report No. ED 100578. Eugene, Ore.: ERIC.

Gwartney, J.D. 1970. "Discrimination and Income Differentials." *American Economic Review* 60 (June): 396-408.

———. 1972. "Discrimination, Achievement, and Payoffs of a College Degree." *Journal of Human Resources* 7 (Winter): 60-70.

H

Haavelmo, T. 1960. *A Study in the Theory of Investment*, Chicago: University of Chicago Press.

Haavelmo, T., and Kaldor, N. 1964. "Comments." In OECD (1964a: 161-63).

Haggart, S.A., and Furry, W.S. 1974. "Resource Allocation and Budgeting for the 1972-73 Mini-Schools of the Alum Rock Voucher Demonstration, Analysis of the Education Voucher Demonstration." Report No ED106894. Eugene, Ore.: ERIC.

Halbert, M.H. 1969. "The Soft Data Problem: A Case Study of Education." Paper (no. IB1) presented at the Joint National Meeting of the American Astronautical Society and the Operations Research Society, June.

Hale, J.A. 1975. "School Finance Reform in New Mexico, 1974." In Tron (1975: 235-45).

Haley, W.J. 1973. "Human Capital: The Choice Between Investment and Income." *American Economic Review* 63 (December): 929-43.

———. 1976. "Estimation of the Earnings Profile from Optimal Human Capital Accumulation." *Econometrica* 44 (November): 1223-38.

Hall, W.C., and Carroll, N.E. 1973. "The Effect of Teachers' Organizations on Salaries and Class Size." *Industrial and Labor Relations Review* 26 (January): 834-41.

Hallak, J. 1969. *The Analysis of Educational Costs and Expenditures.* Paris: International Institute for Educational Planning.

——. 1974. *A Qui Profite L'Ecole?* Paris: Presses Universitaires de France.

Hambor, J.C.; Phillips, L.; and Votey, H.L. 1973. "High School Inputs and Their Contribution to School Performance: A Comment." *Journal of Human Resources* 8 (Spring): 260-63.

Hamilton, B.W. 1976a. "The Effects of Property Taxes and Local Public Spending on Property Values: A Theoretical Comment." *Journal of Political Economy* 84 (June): 647-50.

——. 1976b. "Capitalization of Intrajurisdictional Differences in Local Tax Prices." *American Economic Review* 66 (December): 743-53.

Hamovitch, W., and Morgenstern, R.D. 1975. "The Principal Casue of Salary Differentials: Research Output or Experience?: Comment." *American Economic Review* 65 (June): 484-85. (See also "Reply," by D.A. Katz, p. 486.)

Hamrin, R.D. 1979. "OEO's Performance-Contracting Project: Evaluation Bias in a Social Experiment." *Public Policy* 22 (Fall): 467-88.

Handa, M.L., and Skolnik, M.L. 1972. "Empirical Analysis of the Demand for Education in Canada." In Ostry (1972: 5-44).

Hanoch, G. 1967. "An Economic Analysis of Earnings and Schooling." *Journal of Human Resources* 2 (Summer): 310-29.

Hansen, W.L. 1963. "Total and Private Rates of Return to Investment in Schooling." *Journal of Political Economy* 71 (April): 128-40.

——. 1964. "'Shortages' and Investment in Health Manpower." In Axelrod (1964: 75-91).

——. 1965. "Human Capital Requirements for Educational Expansion: Teacher Shortages and Teacher Supply." In C.A. Anderson and Bowman (1965).

——. 1967a. "The Economics of Scientific and Engineering Manpower." *Journal of Human Resources* 2 (Spring): 191-215 (see also discussion pp. 215-20).

——, ed. 1967b. "Symposium on Rates of Return to Investment in Education." *Journal of Human Resources* 2 (Summer): 291-374.

——, ed. 1970a. *Education, Income, and Human Capital.* New York: Columbia University Press (for National Bureau of Economic Research).

——. 1970b. "Income Distribution Effects of Higher Education." *American Economic Review* 60 (May): 335-40.

——. 1973. "On External Benfits and Who Should Foot the Bill." In Solmon and Taubman (1973): 329-34.

——. 1974. "The Financial Implications of Student Independence," In *Who Pays? Who Benefits? A National Invitational Conference on the Independent Student,* pp. 10-26. New York: College Entrance Examination Board, 1974.

——. 1977a. "Financing Higher Education: A Look Toward the 1980's." Paper presented to the 1977 Western Economic Association Conference.

——. 1977b. "Education and Economics." *Comparative Education Review* 21 (June-October).

Hansen, W.L.; Kelley, A.C.; and Weisbrod, B.A. 1970. "Economic Efficiency and the Distribution of Benefits from College Instruction." *American Economic Review* 60 (May): 364-69.

Hansen, W.L., and Lampman, R.J. 1974. "Basic Opportunity Grants for Higher Education." *Challenge* 17 (November-December): 46-51.

Hansen, W.L., and Weisbrod, B.A. 1969a. *Benefits, Costs, and Finance of Public Higher Education.* Chicago: Markham Publishing Company.

———. 1969b. The Distribution of Costs and Direct Benefits of Public Higher Education: The Case of California." *Journal of Human Resources* 4 (Spring): 176-91.

———. 1969c. "The Search for Equity in the Provision and Finance of Higher Education." In Joint Economic Committee (1969: 107-23).

———. 1971a. "On the Distribution of Costs and Benefits of Public Higher Education: Reply." *Journal of Human Resources* 6 (Summer): 363-74.

———. 1971b. "A New Approach to Higher Education Finance." In Orwig (1971: 117-42).

Hansen, W.L.; Weisbrod, B.A.; and Scanlon, W.J. 1970. "Schooling and Earnings of Low Achievers." *American Economic Review* 60 (June): 409-18.

Hansen, W.L., et al. 1977. "The Market for New PhD Economists: An Econometric Model." Paper presented at the 1977 Annual Meetings of the American Economic Association.

Hanushek, E.A. 1968. "The Education of Negroes and Whites." Doctoral dissertation, Massachusetts Institute of Technology.

———. 1970. *The Value of Teachers in Teaching.* Santa Monica, Calif.: The RAND Corporation.

———. 1971. "Teacher Characteristics and Gains in Student Achievement: Estimation Using Micro Data." *American Economic Review* (Papers and Proceedings) 61 (May): 280-88.

———. 1972. *Education and Race.* Lexington, Mass.: D.C. Heath Co.

———. 1976. "Comment." In Froomkin, Jamison, and Radner (1976: 191-96).

Harberger, A.C. 1965. "Investment in Man Versus Investment in Machines: The Case of India." In C.A. Anderson and Bowman (1965: 11-50).

Harbison, F. 1969. "Education and Economic Development in Advanced Countries." In Hüfner and Naumann (1969: 223-30).

Harbison, F., and Myers, C.A. 1964. *Education, Manpower, and Economic Growth.* New York: McGraw-Hill.

———, eds. 1965. *Manpower and Education.* New York: McGraw-Hill.

Hardin, E. 1975. "Human Capital and the Labor Market Success of New Parolees." In *1975 Proceedings of the Business and Economic Statistics Section of the American Statistical Association,* pp. 330-35.

Hardin, E. and Borus, M.E. 1971. *The Economic Benefits and Costs of Retraining.* Lexington, Mass.: Heath Lexington Books.

———. 1972. "Benefits and Costs of MDTA-ARA Retraining." *Industrial Relations* 11 (May): 216-28.

Harris, M., and Raviv, A. 1978. "Some Results on Incentive Contracts with Applications to Education and Employment, Health Insurance, and Law Enforcement." *American Economic Review* 68 (March): 20-30.

Harris, M.A. 1976. "School Finance at a Glance, December 1975." Denver: Education Commission of the States.

Harris, S.E., ed. 1960. *Higher Education in the United States.* Cambridge, Mass.: Harvard University Press.

———. 1962. *Higher Education: Resources and Finance.* New York: McGraw-Hill.

———. 1964. *Economic Aspects of Higher Education.* Paris: Organization for Economic Cooperation and Development.

———, ed. 1965. *Education and Public Policy.* Berkeley, Calif.: McCutchan Publishing Corporation.

——. 1969. "Financing Higher Education: An Overview." In Joint Economic Committee (1969: 467-506).

——. 1972. *A Statistical Portrait of Higher Education.* New York: Carnegie Commission on Higher Education (McGraw-Hill).

Harrison, B. 1970. "Education and Earnings in Ten Urban Ghettos." *American Economist* 14 (Spring): 12-18.

——. 1972a. "Education and Underemployment in the Urban Ghetto." *American Economic Review* 62 (December): 796-812.

——. 1972b. *Education, Training, and the Urban Ghetto.* Baltimore: The Johns Hopkins University Press.

Harrison, F.W., and McLoone, E.P. 1965. *Profiles in School Support: Decennial Overview.* Washington, D.C.: U.S. Government Printing Office.

Harrison, R.S. 1976. *Equality in Public School Finance.* Lexington, Mass.: Heath Lexington Books.

Harriss, C.L. 1974. "Property Taxation: What's Good and What's Bad about It?" *American Journal of Economics and Sociology* 33 (January): 89-102.

Harrod, R.F. 1939. "An Essay in Dynamic Theory." *Economic Journal* (March).

Hartley, H.J. 1968. *Educational Planning-Programming-Budgeting: A Systems Approach.* Englewood Cliffs, N.J.: Prentice-Hall.

Hartman, L. 1969. *Graduate Education: Parameters for Public Policy.* Washington, D.C.: National Science Foundation.

Hartman, R.W. 1970. "A Comment on the Peachman-Hansen-Weisbrod Controversy." *Journal of Human Resources* 5 (Fall): 519-23.

——. 1971. *Credit for College: Public Policy for Student Loans.* New York: McGraw-Hill.

——. 1972. "Equity Implications of State Tuition Policy and Student Loans." *Journal of Political Economy* 80 (May–June): S142-71.

——. 1973. "The Rationale for Federal Support for Higher Education." In Solmon and Taubman (1973: 271-92).

Hartman, R.W., and Reischauer, R.D. 1974. "The Effect of Reform in School Finance on the Level and Distribution of Tax Burdens," In Pincus (1974: 107-50).

Hartog, J. 1976. "Ability and Age-Income Profiles." *Review of Income and Wealth* 22 (March): 61-74.

Haskew, L.D. 1977. "1975 Texas Legislative Processing of Foundation Program Measurements and Technologies." *Journal of Education Finance* 3 (Summer): 107-13.

Hatley, R.V., and Croskey, F.L. 1977. "Socioeconomic Variables as Predictors of School Financial Referenda Voting Behavior." *Journal of Education Finance* 2 (Spring): 481-98.

Hause, J.C. 1971. "Ability and Schooling as Determinants of Lifetime Earnings, or If You're So Smart, Why Aren't you Rich?" *American Economic Review* 61 (May): 289-98.

——. 1972. "Earnings Profile: Ability and Schooling." *Journal of Political Economy* 80 (May–June): S108-38.

——. 1975a. "The Theory of Welfare Cost Measurement." *Journal of Political Economy* 83 (November–December): 1145-82.

——. 1975b. "An Analysis of the Covariance Structure of Earnings and the On the Job Training Hypothesis." Manuscript, University of Minnesota, August.

Hauser, R.M. 1972. "Disaggregating A Social-Psychological Model of Educational Attainment." Working Paper 7209, Social Systems Research Institute, University of Wisconsin, Madison.

——. 1973. "Socioeconomic Background and Differential Returns to Education." In Solmon and Taubman (1973: 129-46).

Hauser, R.M., and Daymont, T.N. 1976. "Schooling, Ability and Earnings: Cross-Sectional Findings 8 to 14 years After High School Graduation." Working Paper 76-19, Center for Demography and Ecology, University of Wisconsin, Madison.

Hauser, R.M., and Featherman, D.L. 1976. "Equality of Schooling: Trends and Prospects." *Sociology of Education* 49 (April): 99-120.

Hauser, R.M., and Sewell, W.H. 1976. "On the Effects of Families and Family Structure on Achievement." Working Paper 76-32, Center for Demography and Ecology, University of Wisconsin, Madison.

Hauser, R.M.; Sewell, W.H.; and Alwin, D.F. 1974. "High School Effects on Achievement." Working Paper 74-24, Center for Demography and Ecology, University of Wisconsin, Madison.

Haveman, R.H. 1976a. "Benefit-Cost Analysis and Family Planning Programs." *Population and Development Review* 2 (March): 37-64.

——. 1976b. *The Economics of the Public Sector*, 2nd ed. New York: Wiley/Hamilton.

Haveman, R.H., and Margolis, J., eds. 1970. *Public Expenditures and Policy Analysis.* Chicago: Markham Publishing Company.

——. 1977. *Public Expenditure and Policy Analysis*, 2nd ed. Chicago: Rand McNally.

Haveman, R.H., and Weisbrod, B.A. 1975, "Defining Benefits of Public Programs: Some Guidance for Policy Analysts." *Policy Analysis* 1, no. 1: 169-96.

Havighurst, R.J. 1970. "The Unknown Good: Education Vouchers." *Phi Delta Kappan* 52 (September): 52-53.

Hawkins, R.G.; Ritter, L.S.; and Walter, I. 1973. "What Economists Think of Their Journals." *Journal of Political Economy* 81 (July-August): 1017-32.

Hawthorne, P. 1974. *Legislation by the States: Accountability and Assessment in Education.* Madison: Division for Management and Planning Services, Wisconsin Department of Public Instruction.

Hay, G.A. 1976. *Educational Finance and Educational Reform in Peru.* International Institute for Educational Planning, Financing Educational Systems. Country Case Studies no. 5. Paris: UNESCO.

Haynes, J.L., and Walker, C. 1975. *Operating an Objective-Referenced Testing Program: Florida's Approach to Large-Scale Assessment.* Denver: Cooperative Accountability Project, Report No. 28.

Heckman, J.L. 1976. "A Life-Cycle Model of Earnings, Learning, and Consumption." *Journal of Political Economy* 84 (Supplement: August): S11-44.

Heckman, J.L., and Polachek, S. 1974. "Empirical Evidence on the Functional Form of the Earnings-Schooling Relationship." *Journal of the American Statistical Association* 69 (June): 350-54.

Heddinger, F.M. 1971. "New Leverage for Funding Agencies." *Compact* 5 (February): 35-37.

Heim, J.J. 1972. *Variables Related to Student Performance and Resource Allocation Decisions at the School District Level.* Albany: The University of the State of New York, State Education Department, Bureau of School Programs Evaluation.

——. 1973. *What Research Says About Improving Student Performance.* Albany, N.Y.: State Education Department.

Heim, J.J., and Perl, L. 1974. *The Educational Production Function.* Ithaca, N.Y.: Institute of Public Employment, Cornell University.

Heinemann, H.N., and Sussna, E. 1971. "Criteria for Public Investment in the Two-Year College: A Program Budgeting Approach." *Journal of Human Resources* 6 (Spring): 181-84.

Heller, W.W. 1957. "Economics and the Applied Theory of Public Expenditures." *Federal Expenditure Policy for Economic Growth and Stability.* Washington, D.C.: Joint Economic Committee.

——. 1966. *New Dimensions of Political Economy.* Cambridge, Mass.: Harvard University Press.

——. 1968. "A Sympathetic Reappraisal of Revenue Sharing." In *Revenue Sharing and the City,* ed. Harvey S. Perloff and Richard P. Nathan. Baltimore: Johns Hopkins Press, 1968.

Henderson, J.M. 1968. "Local Government Expenditures: A Social Welfare Analysis." *Review of Economics and Statistics* 50 (March): 156-63.

Henderson, J.M. and Quandt, R.E. 1958. *Microeconomic Theory.* New York: McGraw-Hill.

Henderson, P.D. 1968. "Investment Criteria for Public Enterprises." In Turvey (1968: 86-169).

Henderson, V.; Mieszkowski, P.; and Sauvageau, Y. 1976. *Peer Group Effects and Educational Production Functions.* Ottawa: Economic Council of Canada.

Hendon, W.S. 1969. "Faculty Compensation and the Cost of Living." *Social Science Quarterly* 50 (September): 396-400.

Henning, J.A., and Tussing, A.D. 1974. "Income Elasticity of the Demand for Public Expenditures in the United States." *Public Finance* 29 (November 3): 325-41.

Herrnstein, R.J. 1973. *I.Q. in the Meritocracy.* Boston: Little, Brown and Company.

Hershkowitz, M., and Sussman, Z. 1971. "Growth, Induced Changes in Final Demand, Educational Requirements, and Wage Differentials." *Review of Economics and Statistics* 53 (May): 169-75.

Hettich, W. 1968. "Equalization Grants, Minimum Standards, and Unit Cost Differences in Education." *Yale Economic Essays* 8 (Fall): 5-55.

——. 1971. "Consumption Benefits from Education." In Ostry (1972: 177-98).

Hickrod, G.A. 1971. "Local Demand for Education: A Critique of School Finance and Economic Research Circa 1959-1969." *Review of Educational Research* 41: 35-49.

——. 1972. *Definition, Measurement, and Application of the Concept of Equalization in School Finance.* Illinois State Superintendent's Advisory Committee on School Finance (Occasional Paper), February.

——. 1973a. "Demur on Full State Funding." In Hickrod et al. (1973): 105.

——. 1973b. *Alternative Fiscal Solutions to Equity Problems in Public Schools.* Gainsville, Fla.: National Education Finance Project.

Hickrod, G.A.; Chaudhari, R.; and Hubbard, B.C. 1977. "School Finance Reform and Suburban Districts: A Few Facts, Several Research Design Questions, and Some Policy Considerations." Normal, Ill.: Center for the Study of Educational Finance, Illinois State University, September.

Hickrod, G.A., and Hubbard, B.C. 1975. "Research Agenda for School Finance Reform in Illinois." Research Report 1-HH-75. Normal, Ill.: Center for the Study of Educational Finance, Department of Educational Administration, University of Illinois.

——. 1977a. "Illinois School Finance Research: Some Knowns and Unknowns." Paper prepared for the Midwest Administration Center, University of Chicago, for the Conference on Dilemmas in School Finance: Illinois and the Nation, February.

————. 1977b. "Return to the 'Two-Tier' Funding Notion in Illinois: A Re-examination of the Basic Rationale for the School Finance Reform of 1973." Normal, Ill.: Center for the Study of Educational Finance, Illinois State University, October.

————. 1978. "The Concept of Fiscal Effort in the Illinois General Purpose Educational Grant-in-Aid: Some Legal and Measurement Problems." *Journal of Education Finance* 3 (Winter): 272-78.

Hickrod, G.A.; Hubbard, B.C.; and Yang, T.W. 1975. "The 1973 Reform of the Illinois General Purpose Education Grant-in-Aid: A Description and an Evaluation." In Tron (1975: 1-87).

Hickrod, G.A.; Laymon, R.L.; and Hubbard, B.C. 1974. "Towards a Political Theory of School Finance Reform in the United States." *Journal of Educational Administration* 12 (October): 57-70.

Hickrod, G.A., and Sabulao, C.M. 1969. *Increasing Social and Economic Inequalities among Suburban Schools.* Danville, Ill.: The Interstate Printers and Publishers, Inc.

Hickrod, G.A., et al. 1973. *Final Report of the Superintendant's Advisory Committee on School Finance.* Springfield, Ill.: Office of the Superintendent of Public Instruction, State of Illinois, April.

————. 1975a. "Measurable Objectives for School Finance Reform: A Further Evaluation of the Illinois School Finance Reforms of 1973." Paper presented to the 1975 annual meeting of the American Educational Research Association, Washington, D.C. April 1.

————. 1975b. "Cost-Size Relationship Among School Districts in Illinois, 1974." Research Paper 2-HCYH-75. Normal, Ill.: Center for the Study of Educational Finance, Department of Educational Administration, Illinois State University.

————. 1976. *The 1973 Reform of the Illinois General Purpose Grant-in-Aid: An Evaluation After Three Years.* Normal, Ill.: Center for the Study of Educational Finance, Department of Educational Administration, Illinois State University.

Hight, J.E. 1974. "Full State Funding and the Distribution of Educational Resources in Hawaii," *National Tax Journal* 27 (March): 1-28.

————. 1975. "The Demand for Higher Education in the U.S. 1927-72: The Public and Private Institutions." *Journal of Human Resources* 10 (Fall): 512-20.

Hight, J.E., and Pollock, R. 1973. "Income Distribution Effects of Higher Education Expenditures in California, Florida, and Hawaii." *Journal of Human Resources* 8 (Summer): 318-30.

Hill, C.R. 1976. *Education and Earnings: A Review of the Evidence.* Technical Analysis Paper. Washington, D.C.: Education Planning Staff, Office of the Assistant Secretary for Planning and Evaluation, U.S. Office of Education.

————. In press. "Capacities, Opportunities and Educational Investments: The Case of the High School Dropout." *Review of Economics and Statistics.*

Hill, C.R., and Stafford, F.P. 1974. "Allocation of Time to Preschool Children and Educational Opportunity." *Journal of Human Resources* 9 (Summer): 323-41.

————. 1977. "Parental Care of Children: Time Diary Estimates of Quantity, Predictability and Variety." Manuscript, Department of Economics, University of South Carolina and University of Michigan, December.

Hill, P., et al. 1977. *Compensatory Education Service*. Washington, D.C.: National Institute of Education.

Hinchliffe, K. 1976. "Earnings Determinants in the Nigerian Textile Industry." *Comparative Education Review* 20 (February): 48-60.

Hines, F.; Tweeten, L.; and Redfern, M. 1970. "Social and Private Rates of Return to Investment in Schooling, by Race-Sex Groups and Regions." *Journal of Human Resources* 5 (Summer): 318-40.

Hinson, J.P. 1968a. "Student Loan Programs for Higher Education . . . Part 1." *New England Business Review* (June): 2-11.

———. 1968b. "Student Loan Programs for Higher Education . . . Part 2." *New England Business Review* (July): 2-15.

———. 1971. "Higher Education—How to Pay." *New England Economic Review* (March-April): 3-22.

Hirsch, W.Z. 1959a. *Analysis of the Rising Costs of Public Education*. Washington, D.C.: Joint Economic Committee, Study Paper No. 4.

———. 1959b. "Expenditure Implications of Metropolitan Growth and Consolidation." *Review of Economics and Statistics* 41 (August): 232-40.

———. 1960. "Determinants of Public Education Expenditures." *National Tax Journal* 13 (March): 29-40.

———. 1961. "Income Elasticity of Public Education." *International Economic Review* 2 (September): 330-39.

Hirsch, W.Z., and Marcus, M.J. 1969. "Intercommunity Spillovers and the Provision of Public Education." *Kyklos* 22: 641-60.

Hirsch, W.Z., and Segelhorst, E.W. 1965. "Incremental Income Benefits of Public Education." *Review of Economics and Statistics* 47 (November): 392-99.

Hirsch, W.Z.; Segelhorst, E.W.; and Marcus, M.J. 1964. *Spillover of Public Education Costs and Benefits*. Los Angeles: Institute of Government and Public Affairs, University of California.

Hirshleifer, J. 1966. "Investment Decision Under Uncertainty: Applications of the State-Preference Approach." *Quarterly Journal of Economics* 60 (May): 252-77.

———. 1976. *Price Theory and Applications*. Englewood Cliffs, N.J.: Prentice-Hall.

Hirshleifer, J., and Shapiro, D.L. 1970. "The Treatment of Risk and Uncertainty." In Haveman and Margolis (1970: 291-313).

Hirshleifer, J., et al. 1960. *Water Supply*. Chicago: University of Chicago Press.

Hobbs, W.C., and Anderson, G.L. 1971. "The Operation of Academic Departments." *Management Science* 18 (December): B134-44.

Hodgkinson, H.L. 1971. *Institutions in Transition*. New York: McGraw-Hill.

———. 1972. "How Can We Measure the 'Value Added' to Students by a College Education?" *The Chronicle of Higher Education*. November 13, p. 10.

Hoenack, S.A. 1971. "The Efficient Allocation of Subsidies to College Students." *American Economic Review* 61 (June): 302-11.

Hoenack, S.A., and Weiler, W.C. 1975. "Cost-Related Tuition Policies and University Enrollments." *Journal of Human Resources* 10 (Summer): 332-60.

Hoerr, O.D. 1974. "Educational Returns and Educational Reform in Ethiopia." *East Africa Economic Review* 6 (December): 18-34.

Hoffman, E.P. 1975. "An Econometric Study of University of Massachusetts Faculty Salary Differentials." Ph.D. dissertation, University of Massachusetts.

———. 1976. "Faculty Salaries: Is There Discrimination by Sex, Race, and Discipline? Additional Evidence." *American Economic Review* 66 (March): 196-98.

Hogan, J.C. 1974. *The Schools, the Courts, and the Public Interest.* Lexington, Mass.: Heath Lexington Books.

Hogan, T., and Shelton, R. 1973. "A Note on Barlow's Local School Finance." *Journal of Political Economy* 81 (January-February): 192-98.

Holcombe, R. 1975. "A Public Choice Analysis of Millage Elections for Financing Public Schools." Ph.D. dissertation, Virginia Polytechnic Institute.

Holland, D.W. 1974. "The Impact of Benefit Spillovers upon Economic Efficiency in Public School Finance." *American Journal of Agricultural Economics* 56 (May): 300-305.

Holland, D.W., and Baritelle, J.L. 1975. "School Consolidation in Sparsely Populated Rural Areas: A Separable Programming Approach." *American Journal of Agricultural Economics* 57 (November): 567-75.

Holmes, A.B. 1975. "An Empirical Estimation of a Cost Function for Elementary and Secondary Education." Ph.D. dissertation, State University of New York, Binghamton.

Holt, G. 1975. "Human Capital Investment under Constrained Optimization." *Quarterly Review of Economics and Business* 15 (Spring): 47-51.

Holtmann, A.G. 1968a. "Linear Programming and the Value of an Input to a Local Public School District." *Public Finance* 23, no. 4: 429-40.

———. 1968b. "The 'Shortage' of School Teachers and the Principle of Equal Net Advantage." *Journal of Economic Issues* 2 (June): 211-18.

———. 1969. "Teacher Salaries and the Economic Benefits of Search." *Journal of Human Resources* 4 (Winter): 99-103.

Holtmann, A.G., and Bayer, A.E. 1970. "Determinants of Professional Income Among Recent Recipients of Natural Science Doctorates." *Journal of Business* 43 (October): 410-18.

Honey, J.C., and Hartle, T.W. 1975. *A Career Education Entitlement Plan: Administrative and Political Issues.* Report No. ED110752. Eugene, Ore.: ERIC.

Hopkins, T.D. 1974. "Higher Education Enrollment Demand." *Economic Inquiry* 12 (March): 53-65.

Horobin, G.W., and Smith, R.L. 1960. "The Economics of Education: A Comment." *Scottish Journal of Political Economy* 7: 69-74. Reprinted in Blaug (1969: 373-78).

Horowitz, A.R. 1968. "A Simultaneous-Equation Approach to the Problem of Explaining Interstate Differences in State and Local Government Expenditures." *Southern Economic Journal* 34 (April): 459-76.

Horton, B., et al., versus Meskill, T.J., et al. No. 18 52 83. *Memorandum of Decision,* Superior Court, County of Hartford, CT, December 26, 1974.

Hou, J.D. 1977. "Effects of Various Income Weightings on the Distribution of Illinois State Aid to Education." In *Alternative Measures of Local Wealth and Effort* (1977: 1-20).

Hou, J.D., and Carson, W.B. 1977. "Various Income-Weighted Operating Tax Rates and Illinois State Aid to Education." In *Alternative Measures of Local Wealth and Effort* (1977: 21-41).

Houthakker, H.S. 1959. "Education and Income." *Review of Economics and Statistics* 41 (February): 24-28.

Hu, S.C. 1976. "Education and Economic Growth." *Review of Economic Studies* 43 (October): 509-18.

Hu, T-w. 1973. *Econometrics: An Introductory Analysis*. Baltimore: University Park Press.

Hu, T-w., and Booms, B.H. 1971. "A Simultaneous Equation Model of Public Expenditure Decisions in Large Cities." *Annals of Regional Science* 5 (December): 73–85.

Hu, T-w.; Kaufman, J.J.; Lee, M.L.; and Stromsdorfer, E.W. 1971. "Special Problems in the Economic Analysis of Education." In Wykstra (1971b: 158–75).

Hu, T-w.; Lee, M.L.; and Stromsdorfer, E.W. 1968. "An Econometric Study of Demand for and Supply of Public Expenditures on Education." *1968 Business and Economic Statistics Section Proceedings of the American Statistical Association*, pp. 397–402.

———. 1971. "Economic Returns to Vocational and Comprehensive High School Graduates." *Journal of Human Resources* 6 (Winter): 25–50.

Hu, T-w.; Lee, M.L.; Stromsdorfer, E.W.; and Kaufman, J.J. 1969. *A Cost-Effectiveness Study of Vocational Education*. University Park, Pa.: Institute for Research on Human Resources, The Pennsylvania State University.

Hu, T-w., and Stromsdorfer, E.W. 1973. *Demand and Supply of Higher Education in Massachusetts*. A study submitted to the Massachusetts Board of Higher Education. Boston: Board of Higher Education.

Hubbard, B.C., and Hickrod, G.A. 1975. "A Look at Comparing State Aid to Local School Districts on an Interstate Basis." Speech 1-HH-75. Normal, Ill.: Center for the Study of Educational Finance, Department of Educational Administration, Illinois State University.

Hubbell, L.K., and Olson, G.W. 1976. "Alternative Methods for Funding Property Tax Financed Services: Kansas City." *National Tax Journal* 29 (March): 86–96.

Hudson, B.M. 1974. "Regional Economic Effects of Higher Education Institutions." *Socio-Economic Planning Sciences* 8: 181–94.

Huffman, W.E. 1974. "Decision Making: The Role of Education." *American Journal of Agricultural Economics* 56 (February): 85–97.

———. 1977. "Allocative Efficiency: The Role of Human Capital." *Quarterly Journal of Economics* 91 (February): 59–79.

Hüfner, K. 1968. "Economics of Higher Education and Educational Planning." *Socio-Economic Planning Sciences* 2: 66–88.

Hüfner, K., and Naumann, J., eds. 1969. *Economics of Education in Transition*. Stuttgart: Ernst Klett Verlag.

Hull, C.H., ed. 1899. *Economic Writing of Sir William Petty*. Cambridge: University Press.

Hunt, S.J. 1963. "Income Determinants for College Graduates and the Return to Educational Investment." *Yale Economic Essays* 3 (Fall): 305–57.

Husén, T. 1969a. *Talent, Opportunity, and Career*. Stockholm: Almqvist and Wiksell.

———. 1969b. "Some Views of Cross-National Assessment of the 'Quality of Education'" In Hüfner and Naumann (1969: 87–96).

———. 1972. *Social Background and Educational Career*. Paris: OECD.

———. 1975. *Social Influences on Educational Attainment*. Paris: OECD.

Hussain, K.M., ed. 1977. *Management Information Systems for Higher Education*. Paris: OECD.

Hyde, W.D., Jr. 1978. "The Effect of Tuition and Financial Aid on Access and Choice in Postsecondary Education." Papers in Education Finance, No. 1. Denver: Education Commission of the States, January.

Hyman, H.H.; Wright, C.R.; and Reed, J.S. 1975. *The Enduring Effects of Education.* Chicago: University of Chicago Press.

I

Illich, I. 1971. *Deschooling Society.* New York: Harper and Row.
———. 1972. "Why We Must Disestablish Schools." In Carnoy (1972: 250–71).
Inman, R.P. 1978. "Optimal Fiscal Reform of Metropolitan Schools: Some Simulation Results." *American Economic Review* 68 (March): 107–22.
Ishikawa, T., 1975. "A Note on the Optimal Spacing Properties in a Sample Jevonian Model of Education Investment." *Quarterly Journal of Economics* 89 (November): 633–42.

J

Jabbour, A.G. 1975. "The Interrelationships Among Size, Expenditure Level and Quality in Nonpublic Schools: The Case of Seventh Day Adventists." Ph.D. dissertation, Catholic University.
Jackson, G.A., and Weathersby, G.B. 1975. "Individual Demand for Higher Education: A Review and Analysis of Recent Empirical Studies." *Journal of Higher Education* 46 (November–December): 623–52.
Jackson, J.; McDougall, G.; and Wright C. 1974. "Economies of Scale and Optimum City Size In the Provision of Local Public Services." Claremont Economic Papers, No. 99, May.
Jaggi, B., and Lau, H.S. 1975. "Toward a Model for Human Resource Valuation: A Reply." *Accounting Review* 50 (April): 348–50.
James, H.T. 1969. *The New Cult of Efficiency and Education.* Pittsburgh: University of Pittsburgh Press.
James, H.T.; Kelley, J.; and Garms, W.I. 1966. *Determinants of Educational Expenditures in Large Cities of the United States.* Stanford: School of Education, Stanford University.
Jargowsky, P.; Moskowitz, J.; and Sinkin, J. 1977. "School Finance Reform: Decoding the Simulation Maze." *Journal of Education Finance* 3 (Fall): 199–213.
Jencks, C. 1966. "Is the Public School Obsolete?" *The Public Interest* 35: 18–27.
———. 1971. "Giving Parents Money for Schooling." *Compact* 5 (February): 25–27.
Jencks, C., et al. 1970. *Education Vouchers: A Report on Financing Elementary Education by Grants to Parents.* Cambridge, Mass.: Center for the Study of Public Policy.
———. 1972. *Inequality: A Reassessment of the Effects of Family and Schooling in America.* New York: Basic Books.
Jenkins, E. 1973. "Debate Intensifies: Stand by for Vouchers." *Compact* 7 (November): 7–9.
Jenny, H.H., and Wynn, R. 1969. "Short-Run Cost Variations in Institutions of Higher Learning." In Joint Economic Committee (1969: 261–94).
Jensen, A.R. 1969. "How Much Can We Boost IQ and Scholastic Achievement?" *Harvard Educational Review* 39 (Winter): 1–123.

——. 1972. *Genetics and Education.* New York: Harper and Row.

——. 1973. *Educability and Group Differences.* New York: Harper and Row.

——. 1975. "The Meaning of Heritability in the Behavioral Sciences." *Educational Psychology* 11: 171-83.

Johns, R.L. 1971. "The Development of State Support for the Public Schools." In R.L. Johns, Alexander, and Stollar (1971: 1-27).

——. 1975. "An Index of Extra Costs of Education Due to Sparsity of Population." *Journal of Education Finance* 1 (Fall): 159-204.

——. 1976. "Improving the Equity of School Finance Programs." *Journal of Education Finance* 1 (Spring): 540-49.

——. 1977a. "Analytical Tools in School Finance Reform." *Journal of Education Finance* 2 (Spring): 499-508.

——. 1977b. "Response to 'Alternative Measures of School District Wealth' by Allan Odden." *Journal of Education Finance* 3 (Summer): 98-100.

Johns, R.L., and Alexander, K. 1971. *Alternative Programs for Financing Education.* Gainesville, Fla.: National Education Finance Project.

Johns, R.L.; Alexander, K.; and Jordan, F., eds. 1972. *Financing Education: Fiscal and Legal Alternatives.* Columbus, Ohio: Charles E. Merrill.

Johns, R.L.; Alexander, K.; and Stollar, D.H., eds. 1971. *Status and Impact of Educational Finance Programs.* Gainesville, Fla.: National Education Finance Project.

Johns, R.L., and Burns, J.A. 1971. "Comparison of Revenues for Different Population Classifications of School Districts." In R.L. Johns, Alexander, and Stollar (1971: 193-208).

Johns, R.L., and Lindman, E. 1972. "Federal Responsibilities for Financing Educational Programs." In Johns, Alexander, and Jordan (1972).

Johns, R.L., and Morphet, E.L. 1975. *The Economics and Financing of Education: A Systems Approach.* 3rd ed. Englewood Cliffs, N.J.: Prentice-Hall, 1975.

Johns, R.L., and Salmon, R.G. 1971. "The Financial Equalization of School Support Programs in the United States for the School Year, 1968-69." In R.L. Johns, Alexander, and Stollar (1971: 119-91).

Johns, R.L., et al, eds. 1970. *Economic Factors Affecting the Financing of Education.* Gainesville, Fla.: National Education Finance Project.

Johns, T.L., ed. 1972. *Public School Finance Programs, 1971-72.* Washington, D.C.: Government Printing Office.

——. 1973. "School Finance Reform in 1973—An Overview." Address delivered at the National Symposium on School Finance Reform, Silver Spring, Md., November 26.

——. 1976. "1975 School Aid Legislation: A Look at Three States." *Journal of Education Finance* 1 (Winter): 397-406.

——. 1977. "Alternative Approaches to Equity in School Finance." In *Economic and Social Perspectives on Adult Illiteracy* (1977: 85-92).

Johnson, E.A.J. 1964. "The Place of Learning, Science, Vocational Training and 'Art' in Pre-Smithian Economic Thought." *Journal of Economic History* 24 (June): 129-44. Reprinted in M. J. Bowman et al. (1968: 25-34).

Johnson, D.B., and Holzman, A.G. 1975. "A Statistical Decision-Theory Model of the College-Admission Process." In Correa (1975a: 199-219).

Johnson, F.C., and Dietrich, J.E. 1971. "Cost Analysis of Instructional Technology," In *To Improve Learning,* ed. S.G. Tickton, New York: R.B. Bowker, 1971.

Johnson, F.P. 1975. "Differential Tuition Determined by Differential Unit Cost for Higher Education." Ph.D. dissertation, Colorado State University.

Johnson, G.E. 1970. "The Demand for Labor by Educational Category." *Southern Economic Journal* 37 (October): 190-204.

Johnson, G.E., and Stafford, F.P. 1973. "Social Returns to Quantity and Quality of Schooling." *Journal of Human Resources* 8 (Spring): 139-55.

———. 1974a. "Lifetime Earnings in a Professional Labor Market: Academic Economists." *Journal of Political Economy* 82 (May-June): 549-70.

———. 1974b. "The Earnings and Promotion of Women Faculty." *American Economic Review* 64 (December): 888-903.

———. 1977. "The Earnings and Promotion of Women Faculty: Reply." *American Economic Review* 67 (March): 214-17.

Johnson, G.E., and Youmans, K.C. 1971. "Union Relative Wage Effects By Age and Education." *Industrial and Labor Relations Review* 24 (January): 171-79.

Johnson, H.G. 1972. "The Alternatives Before Us." *Journal of Political Economy* 80 (May-June, pt. 2): S280-89.

Johnson, J.N., and Peterson, H.L. 1978. "The Cost to Colleges of Individualizing Teacher/Student Relationships." *Journal of Education Finance* 3 (Winter): 333-43.

Johnson, O.E. 1968. "Tax Credits and Scholarships for Education." *Business and Government Review* (University of Missouri) 9 (September-October): 31-38.

Johnson, T. 1970. "Returns from Investment in Human Capital." *American Economic Review* 60 (September): 546-60.

Johnson, T., and Hebein, F.J. 1974. "Investment in Human Capital and Growth in Personal Income 1956-1966." *American Economic Review* 64 (September): 604-15.

Johnson, W.R. 1977. "Estimating the Economic Effect of Schooling Vintage: A Test of The Screening Hypothesis." Paper presented to the 1977 Annual Meeting of the Western Economic Society.

Johnston, J. 1972. *Econometric Methods*. Rev. ed. New York: McGraw-Hill.

Johnstone, D.B. 1972. *New Patterns for College Lending: Income-Contingent Loans*. New York: Columbia University Press.

Johnstone, D.B.; Wackman, D.B.; and Ward, S. 1972. "A Survey of Student Attitudes Toward Income Contingent Loans." *Journal of Financial Aid* 2 (March): 11-27.

Joint Economic Committee, U.S. Congress. 1967. *Revenue Sharing and Its Alternatives*. Hearings Before Subcommittee on Fiscal Policy. Washington, D.C.: Government Printing Office.

———. 1969. *The Economics and Financing of Higher Education in the United States*. Washington, D.C.: Government Printing Office.

Jones, T.H. 1971. *Review of Existing State School Finance Programs*. Vol. 1. Washington, D.C.: President's Commission on School Finance.

Jorgenson, D. 1966. "The Embodiment Hypothesis." *Journal of Political Economy* 74 (February): 1-17.

Jorgenson, D.W., and Griliches, Z. 1967. "The Explanation of Productivity Change." *Review of Economic Studies* 34 (July): 249-83. Reprinted in *Survey of Current Business* 49 (May 1969, pt. 2): 31-64; and reprinted again in *Survey of Current Business* 52 (May 1972, pt. 2): 3-36.

———. 1972a. "Issues in Growth Accounting: A Reply to Edward F. Denison." *Survey of Current Business* 52 (May, pt. 2): 65-94.

———. 1972b. "Final Reply." *Survey of Current Business* 52 (May): 111.

Joshi, N.U. 1973. "Validity of International Comparisons of Relationship between Economic Development and Human Resource Development." *Indian Economic Review* 8 (April): 90-92.

Juster, F.T., ed. 1975. *Education, Income and Human Behavior.* New York: McGraw-Hill.

K

Kalachek, E., and Raines, F. 1976. "The Structure of Wage Differences Among Mature Male Workers." *Journal of Human Resources* 11 (Fall): 484-506.

Kaser, M. 1969. "Some Macroeconomics of Education." In Hüfner and Naumann (1969: 139-54).

Kasper, H. 1970. "The Effect of Collective Bargaining on Public School Teachers' Salaries." *Industrial and Labor Relations Review* 24 (October): 57-72. Reprinted in Gerwin (1974: 216-38).

———. 1972. "The Effect of Collective Bargaining on the Public School Teachers' Salaries: Reply." *Industrial and Labor Relations Review* 25 (April): 417-23.

Kass, H.A. 1975. "The Relationship Between Economic Inputs and Student Test Performance at the Primary Level of Education in New Jersey." Ph.D. dissertation, Rutgers University.

Kastner, H.H., Jr. 1964. "School Dropouts and the National Economy." *The American School Board Journal* (April): 11-14.

———. 1976. "Cost/Benefit Analysis of Community College Education. *Community College Review* 4 (winter): 17-26.

Katz, D.A. 1973. "Faculty Salaries, Promotions, and Productivity at a Large University." *American Economic Review* 63 (June): 469-77.

Katzman, M.T. 1968. "Distribution and Production in a Big City Elementary School System." *Yale Economic Essays* 8: 201-56.

———. 1971. *The Political Economy of Urban Schools.* Cambridge, Mass.: Harvard University Press.

———. 1972. "Pricing Primary and Secondary Education." In *Public Prices for Public Products*, ed. S.J. Mushkin, pp. 371-94. Washington, D.C.: The Urban Institute, 1972.

Kauffman, R.V. 1975. "A Study of the Educational Production Function." Ph.D. dissertation, Colorado State University.

Kaysen, C. 1960. "Some General Observations On the Pricing of Higher Education." *Review of Economics and Statistics* 42 (August): 55-60.

Kendrick, J.W. 1974. "The Accounting Treatment of Human Investment and Capital." *Review of Income and wealth* 20 (December): 439-68.

Kerr, C. 1969. "Federal Aid to Higher Education through 1976." In Joint Economic Committee (1969: 599-617).

Kershaw, J.A., and McKean, R.N. 1959. *Systems Analysis and Education.* Memorandum RM-2473-FF. Santa Monica, Calif.: The Rand Corporation.

———. 1962. *Teacher Shortages and Salary Schedules.* New York: McGraw-Hill.

Kershaw, J.A., and Mood, A.M. 1970. "Resource Allocation in Higher Education." *American Economic Review* 60 (May): 341-46.

Kiesling, H.J. 1967. "Measuring a Local Government Service: A Study of

School Districts in New York State." *Review of Economics and Statistics* 49 (August): 356-67.

———. 1969. *The Relationship of School Inputs to Public School Performance in New York State*. Santa Monica, Calif.: The Rand Corporation.

———. 1970. *A Study of Cost and Quality of New York School Districts*. Final Report, Project No. 8-0264. Washington, D.C.: U.S. Department of Health, Education, Welfare, Office of Education, February.

Kiker, B.F. 1966. "The Historical Roots of the Concept of Human Capital." *Journal of Political Economy* 74 (October): 481-99.

———. 1967. "The Concept of Human Capital in the History of Economic Thought." *The Indian Economic Journal* 14 (March): 481-99.

———. 1968a. *Human Capital: In Retrospect*. Columbia: Bureau of Business and Economic Research, University of South Carolina.

———. 1968b. "Marshall on Human Capital: Comment." *Journal of Political Economy* 76 (September-October): 1088-90.

———. 1969. "Von Thünen on Human Capital." *Oxford Economic Papers* 21 (November): 341-43.

———. ed. 1971. *Investment in Human Capital*. Columbia: University of South Carolina Press.

———. 1974. "Nicholson on Human Capital." *Scottish Journal of Political Economy* 21 (June): 171-76.

Kiker, B.F., and Birkeli, J. 1972 "Human Capital Losses Resulting from U.S. Casualties of the War in Vietnam." *Journal of Political Economy* 80 (September-October): 1023-30.

Kiker, B.F., and Cochrane, J.L. 1973. "War and Human Capital in Western Economic analysis." *History of Political Economy* 5 (Fall): 375-98.

Kiker, B.F., and Liles, W.P. 1974. "Earnings, Employment, and Racial Discrimination: Additional Evidence." *American Economic Review* 64 (June): 492-501.

———. In press. "Earnings, Education, and Ability: Additional Evidence." *Eastern Economic Journal*.

Kiker, B.F., and Su, T.T. 1969. "Evaluation of Investment in Training." *Metroeconomica* 21 (May-August): 187-92.

Kiker, B.F., and Wilder, R.P. 1975. "Economic Aspects of Educational Television in the MBA Program." *AACSB Bulletin* 11 (April): 1-10.

Kinard, F.E., and Krech, A.S. 1977. *Projected Degree-Credit Enrollments Through 1985 in South Carolina Colleges and Universities*. Columbia: South Carolina Commission on Higher Education, May.

Kindl, D.L. 1971. "State Dollars to School Districts." *Business Review* (Federal Reserve Bank of Philadelphia) (June): 3-11.

King, A.G. 1973. "A Comment on Bowles' Model of Educational Planning." *Economics of Planning* 13: 131-35.

Kirkwood, J.B., and Mundel, D.S. 1975. "The Role of Tax Policy in Federal Support for Higher Education." *Law and Contemporary Problems* 39 (Autumn): 117-55.

Kirst, M.W. 1973. "Future Directions for School Finance Reform." Paper presented to the National Symposium of School Finance Reform, Silver Spring, Maryland, November 26.

Klarman, H.E. 1964. "The Increased Cost of Hospital Care." In Axelrod (1964: 237-39).

———. 1965. *The Economics of Health.* New York: Columbia University Press.

Kleindorfer, G.B. 1975. "Educational Planning with Combined Network and State Variable Models." In Correa (1975a: 83-109).

Klevmarken, A., and Quigley, J.M. 1976. "Age, Experience, Earnings, and Investments in Human Capital." *Journal of Political Economy* 84 (February): 47-72.

Klinov, R. 1975. "Is it Age or Experience that Matter?" *Kyklos* 29: 866-69.

Klinov-Malul, R. 1966. *The Profitability of Investment in Education in Israel.* Jerusalem: The Maurice Falk Institute for Economic Research.

Klitgaard, R.E. 1974. *Achievement Scores and Educational Objectives.* Report No. R-1217-NIE. Santa Monica, Calif.: Rand Corporation.

———. 1975. "Going Beyond the Mean in Educational Evaluation." *Public Policy* 23 (Winter): 59-79.

Klitgaard, R.E., and Hall, G.R. 1975. "Are There Unusually Effective Schools?" *Journal of Human Resources* 10 (Winter): 90-106.

Klochkov, V. 1975. "'Human Resources' in Bourgeois Political Economy." *Problems of Economics* 17 (February): 89-106.

Knapp, C.B. 1977. "Education and Differences in Postschool Human Investment." *Economic Inquiry* 15 (April): 283-89.

Knapp, C.B., and Hansen, W.L. 1976. "Earnings and Individual Variations in Postschool Human Investment." *Journal of Political Economy* 84 (April): 351-58.

Knight, D.M., ed. 1960. *The Federal Government and Higher Education.* Englewood Cliffs, N.J.: Prentice-Hall.

Knight, M. 1977. "Suburbs Losing Control of Schools." *New York Times,* July 18, pp. C1, 18.

Koch, J.V. 1975. "Student Choice of Undergraduate Major Field of Study and Private Internal Rates of Return: Reply." *Industrial and Labor Relations Review* 18 (January): 286-87.

Koch, J.V., and Chizmar, J.F., Jr. 1976a. "Sex Discrimination and Affirmative Action in Faculty Salaries." *Economic Inquiry* 14 (March): 16-24.

———. 1976b. *The Economics of Affirmative Action.* Lexington, Mass.: Heath Lexington Books.

Kohen, A.I.; Nestel, G.; and Karmas, C. 1976. *Success and Failure in College: A New Approach to Persistence in Undergraduate Programs.* Columbus: Ohio State University, College of Administrative Science, Center for Human Resource Research.

Kohn, M.G.; Manski, C.F.; and Mundel, D.S. 1976. "An Empirical Investigation of Factors Which Influence College-Going Behavior." *Annals of Economic and Social Measurement* 5 (Fall): 391-419.

Korczyk, S.M. 1975 "A Model of College Demand." Ph.D. dissertation, Washington University, St. Louis.

———. 1977. "The Microeconomics of Student Loans." Paper presented to the 1977 Conference of the Western Economic Association.

Kothari, V.N. 1967. "Returns to Education in India." Unpublished manuscript. Cited in Nalla Gounden (1967: 353).

———. 1970. "Disparities in Relative Earnings Among Different Countries." *Economic Journal* 80 (September): 605-16.

Kottis, A.P., and Kottis, G.C. 1973. "Who Benefits from Higher Education Subsidies: A Reconsideration." *Tijdschrift Voor Economie* 18, no. 3: 492-501.

———. 1974. "Public Subsidies to Higher Education: A Mathematical Analysis of the Impact on the Supply and Salaries of College Graduates." *Finanzarchiv* 32, no. 2: 305-12.

Kraft, R.H.P. 1976. *Cost-Value Analysis: A Unified Approach.* Manuscript. Tallahassee, Fla.: Florida State University, College of Education.

Krueger, A.O. 1972a. "Comment." *Journal of Political Economy* 80 (May-June, pt. 2): S31-33.

———. 1972b. "Rates of Return to Turkish Higher Education." *Journal of Human Resources* 7 (Fall): 482-99.

Krutilla, J.V., and Eckstein, O. 1958. *Multiple Purpose River Development.* Baltimore: Johns Hopkins Press.

Kuhns, R.J. 1972. "Input-Output Analysis of Secondary Schools in Pennsylvania." Doctoral dissertation, The Pennsylvania State University.

Kuo, C.-Y. 1976. "The Effect of Education on The Earnings of Indian, Eskimo, Métis, and White Workers in the Mackenzie District of Northern Canada." *Economic Development and Cultural Change* 24 (January): 387-98.

L

Ladd, H.F. 1975. "Local Education Expenditures, Fiscal Capacity, and the Composition of the Property Tax Base." *National Tax Journal* 28 (June): 145-58.

———. 1976. "State-Wide Taxation of Commercial and Industrial Property for Education." *National Tax Journal* 29 (June): 143-53.

Laird, W.E., and Schilson, D.L. 1965. "Financing Investment in Education." *Journal of General Education* 17: 55-61.

Lampman, R.J. 1966. "Toward an Economics of Health, Education, and Welfare." *Journal of Human Resources* 1 (Summer): 45-53.

Lando, M.E. 1975. "The Interaction Between Health and Education." *Social Security Bulletin* 38 (December): 16-22.

Landon, J.H., and Baird, R.N. 1971. "Monopsony in the Market for Public School Teachers." *American Economic Review* 61 (December): 966-71.

Landynski, J.W. 1969. "Governmental Aid to Non-Public Schools: The Constitutional Conflict Sharpens." *Social Research* 36 (Autumn): 333-56.

La Noue, G.R. 1971. "The Politics of Education." *Teachers College Record* 73 (December): 128-45.

———. ed. 1972. *Educational Vouchers: Concepts and Controversies.* New York: Teachers College Press, Columbia University.

Lassiter, R.L., Jr. 1965. "The Association of Income and Education for Males by Region, Race, and Age." *Southern Economic Journal* 32 (July): 15-22.

———. 1966. *The Association of Income and Educational Achievement.* Social Sciences Monograph No. 30. Gainsville, Fla.: University of Florida Press.

———. 1976. *Instructional Productivity and the Utilization of Faculty Resources in the State University System of Florida.* Gainsville, Fla.: Institute of Higher Education, University of Florida.

Lawyers' Committee for Civil Rights Under Law. 1976. *Update on State-wide School Finance Cases.* Washington, D.C.: The Committee, January.

———. 1977. *Summary of State-Wide School Finance Cases Since 1973.* Washington: The Committee, February.

Layard, P.R.G., ed. 1972. *Cost-Benefit Analysis: Selected Readings.* Baltimore: Penguin Education.

———. 1973. "Denison and the Contribution of Education to National Income Growth: A Comment." *Journal of Political Economy* 81 (July-August): 1013-16.

Layard, P.R.G., and Psacharopoulos, G. 1974. "The Screening Hypothesis and the Returns to Education." *Journal of Political Economy* 82 (September-October): 985-98.

Layard, P.R.G., et al. 1971. *Qualified Manpower and Economic Performance.* London: Penguin.

Lazarus, M., and Taylor, E.F. 1977. "Against: They Don't Measure Learning." *New York Times*, Spring Survey of Education, May 1, sec. 12, pp. 1, 22.

Lazear, E. 1976. "Age, Experience, and Wage Growth." *American Economic Review* 66 (September): 548-58.

———. 1977a. "Academic Achievement and Job Performance: Note." *American Economic Review* 67 (March): 252-54.

———. 1977b. "Education: Consumption or Production?" *Journal of Political Economy* 85 (June): 569-97.

———. 1977c. "Schooling as a Wage Depressant." *Journal of Human Resources* 12 (Spring): 164-76.

Lecht, L.A. 1974. *Evaluating Vocational Education—Policies and Plans for the 1970s: With An Annotated Bibliography.* New York: Paeger.

Ledebur, L.C. 1977. *The Economic Development Context of Population Distribution Issues.* Washington, D.C.: Economic Development Administration, Department of Commerce.

Lee, A.J. 1976. "The Economics of Compulsory Schooling: A Theoretic and Empirical Investigation." Ph.D. dissertation, University of Wisconsin, Madison.

Lee, C.J. 1974. "A Goal Programming Model for Analyzing Educational Input Policy with Application for Korea." Ph.D. dissertation, Florida State University.

Lee, E. 1969. "Education and Migration in the United States." In Hüfner and Naumann (1969: 231-38).

Lee, R.D., Jr., and Johnson, R.W. 1973. *Public Budgeting Systems.* Baltimore: University Park Press.

Leekley, R.M. 1974. "A Multiple Output Approach to Public Education." Ph.D. dissertation, Michigan State University.

Lefocowitz, M.J. 1973. "Poverty and Health: A Reexamination." *Inquiry* (March): 3-13.

Leff, N. 1967. "A Note on the Quality-Quantity Problem in Educational Planning." *Indian Economic Journal* 15: 67-74.

Leftwich, R.H. 1976. *The Price System and Resource Allocation.* 6th ed. Hinsdale, Ill.: The Dryden Press.

Lehr, D.K. 1975. "Analysis of the Demand for Higher Education: Case Study—The State of Oregon." Ph.D. dissertation, University of Oregon.

Leibenstein, H. 1965. "Shortages and Surpluses in Education in Under-developed Countries: A Theoretical Foray." In C.A. Anderson and Bowman (1965: ch. 3).

Leibowitz, A. 1974. "Home Investments in Children." *Journal of Political Economy* 82 (March-April, pt. 2): S 111-31.

———. 1976. "Years and Intensity of Schooling Investment." *American Economic Review* 66 (June): 321-34.

Leigh, D.E. 1976a. "Job Experience and Earnings Among Middle-Aged Men." *Industrial Relations* 15 (May): 130-46.

———. 1976b. "Occupational Advancement in the Late 1960s: An Indirect Test of the Dual Labor Market Hypothesis." *Journal of Human Resources* 11 (Spring): 155-71.

Leiter, R.D., ed. 1975. *Costs and Benefits of Education*. Boston: Twayne Publishers.

Lerner, A.P. 1944. *The Economics of Control*. New York: Macmillan.

LeRoy, S.F., and Brockschmidt, P. 1972. "The Property Tax and School Finance." *Monthly Review* (Federal Reserve Bank of Kansas City), December, pp. 3-13.

Leslie, L.L. 1972. *The Rationale for Various Plans for Funding American Higher Education*. Report No. 18. University Park: Center for the Study of Higher Education, The Pennsylvania State University.

———. 1973. *The Trend Toward Government Financing of Higher Education Through Students: Can the Market Model be Applied?* Report No. 19. University Park: Center for the Study of Higher Education, The Pennsylvania State University.

Leslie, L.L., and Hu, T-w. 1977. "The Financial Implications of Collective Bargaining." *Journal of Education Finance* 3 (Summer): 32-53.

Leslie, L.L., and Johnson, G.P. 1974. "The Market Model and Higher Education." *Journal of Higher Education* 45 (January): 1-20.

Leslie, L.L.; Johnson, G.P.; and Carlson, J. 1977. "The Impact of Need-Based Student Aid." *Journal of Education Finance* 2 (Winter): 269-85.

Lessinger, L.M. 1976. "Quality Control and Quality Assurance in Education." *Journal of Education Finance* 1 (Spring): 503-15.

Lester, R.A. 1976. "The AAUP Salary Survey: Comments and Suggestions." *AAUP Bulletin* 62 (Summer): 156-58.

Lethem, F.J. 1974. "Innovation in Education in Western Africa." *Finance and Development* 11 (December): 26-28, 42.

Lev, B., and Schwartz, A. 1971. "On the Use of the Economic Concept of Human Capital in Financial Statements." *The Accounting Review* 46 (January): 103-12.

Levhari, D., and Weiss, Y. 1974. "The Effect of Risk on The Investment in Human Capital." *American Economic Review* 64 (December): 950-63.

Levi, J.H. 1975. "Financing Education and the Effect of the Tax Laws." *Law and Contemporary Problems* 39 (Autumn): 75-116.

Levin, B., ed. 1975. *Future Directions for School Finance Reform*. Lexington, Mass.: Heath Lexington Books.

———. 1977. "New Legal Challenges in Educational Finance." *Journal of Education Finance* 3 (Summer): 54-69.

Levin, B.; Muller, T.; and Scanlon, W.J. 1972. *Public School Finance: Present Disparities and Fiscal Alternatives*. vol. II. Washington, D.C.: The Urban Institute.

Levin, H.M. 1968. "What Difference Do Schools Make?" *Saturday Review*, January 20, pp. 57-58, 66, 67.

———. 1970a. "A Cost-Effectiveness Analysis of Teacher Selection." *Journal of Human Resources* 5 (Winter): 24-33.

———. 1970b. "The Effect of Different Levels of Expenditure on Educational Output." In Johns et al. (1970: ch. 6).

———. 1970c. "A New Model of School Effectiveness." In *Do Teachers Make a Difference?* (1970: 55-78).

———. 1971a. "Review of *Private Wealth and Public Education*, by Coons et al." *Planning and Changing* 1 (January): 194-99.

———. 1971b. "Cost-Effectiveness Analysis of Instructional Technology: The Problems." In *To Improve Learning—An Evaluation of Instructional Technology*, Vol. II, ed. S. Tickton, pp. 999-1006. New York: R.R. Bowker, 1971.

———. 1972. "The Social Science Objectivity Gap." *Saturday Review/ Education* (December): 49–51.

———. 1974. "Measuring Efficiency in Educational Production." *Public Finance Quarterly* 2 (January): 3–24.

———. 1975a. "Cost-Effectiveness Analysis in Evaluation Research." In *Handbook of Evaluation Research*, ed. M. Guttentag, and E. Struening., pp. 89–122. Beverly Hills: Sage Publications, 1975.

———. 1975b. "Education, Life Chances, and the Courts: The Role of Social Science Evidence." *Law and Contemporary Problems* 39 (Spring): 217–40.

———. 1976. "Concepts of Economic Efficiency and Educational Production." In Froomkin, Jamison, and Radner (1976: 149–91).

———. 1977a. "A Decade of Policy Developments in Improving Education and Training for Low-Income Populations." In *A Decade of Federal Antipoverty Programs*, ed. R.H. Haveman. New York: Academic Press, 1977.

———. 1977b. "A Radical Critique of Educational Policy." *Journal of Education Finance* 3 (Summer): 9–31.

Levin, H.M., and Osman, J.W. 1970. *Alternative Methods of State Support For Independent Higher Education in California.* Phase III of a Study of State Aid to Private Higher Education. Calif.: Coordinating Council for Higher Education, February.

Levin, J.M. 1973a. "Alum Rock: Vouchers Pay off." *Inequality in Education* 15 (November): 57–59.

———. 1973b. "Educational Alternatives Within the Public School System." *Educational Horizons* 52 (Fall): 26–31.

———. 1974. "Alum Rock After Two Years: You, Dear Reader, Have a Choice." *Phi Delta Kappan* 56 (November): 201–204.

Levinson, E. 1976. "The Alum Rock Voucher Demonstration: Three Years of Implementation." Report No. ED 122430. Eugene, Ore.: ERIC.

Levy, F.K. 1969. "Sources of Economies of Scale in Universities." In Joint Economic Committee (1969: 295–302).

Lewis, H.G. 1963. *Unionism and Relative Wages in the United States.* Chicago: University of Chicago Press.

———. 1974. "Comments on Selectivity Biases in Wage Comparisons." *Journal of Political Economy* 82 (November–December): 1145–55.

Lewis, W.A. 1962. "Education and Economic Development." *International Social Science Journal* 14: 685–99.

Lieberman, M. 1959. "A Foundation Approach to Merit Pay." *Phi Delta Kappan* 41 (December): 118–22.

Lillard, L.A. 1977. "Inequality: Earnings vs. Human Wealth." *American Economic Review* 67 (March): 42–53.

Lindert, P.H. 1977. "Sibling Position and Achievement." *Journal of Human Resources* 12 (Spring): 198–219.

Lindholm, R.W., ed. 1974 *Property Taxation and the Finance of Education.* Madison: University of Wisconsin Press.

Lindley, R.M. 1975. "The Demand For Apprentice Recruits By The Engineering Industry, 1951–71." *Scottish Journal of Political Economy* 22 (February): 1–24.

Lindman, E.L. 1977. "A Correction Factor for One Dimension of the Municipal Overburden Problem." *Journal of Education Finance* 3 (Fall): 254–58.

Lindsay, C.M. 1971. "Measuring Human Capital Returns." *Journal of Political Economy* 79 (November–December): 1195–1215.

———. 1973. "Real Returns to Medical Education." *Journal of Human Resources* 8 (Summer): 331–48.

———. 1976. "More Real Returns to Medical Education." *Journal of Human Resources* 11 (Winter): 127–30.

Link, C.R. 1975a. "Black Education, Earnings, and Interregional Migration: A Comment and Some New Evidence." *American Economic Review* 65 (March): 236–40.

———. 1975b. "The Quantity and Quality of Education and Their Influence on Earnings: The Case of Chemical Engineers." *Review of Economics and Statistics* 55 (May): 241–47.

———. 1975c. "Graduate Education, School Quality, Experience, Student Ability, and Earnings." *Journal of Business* 48 (October): 477–91.

Link, C.R., and Ratledge, E.C. 1975. "Social Returns to Quantity and Quality of Education: A Further Statement." *Journal of Human Resources* 10 (Winter): 78–89.

Link, C.; Ratledge, E.; and Lewis, K. 1976. "Black-White Differences in Returns to Schooling: Some New Evidence." *American Economic Review* 66 (March): 221–23.

Lipsky, D.B., and Drotning, J.E. 1973. "The Influence of Collective Bargaining on Teachers' Salaries in New York State." *Industrial and Labor Relations Review* 27 (October): 18–35.

Lipsey, R.G., and Lancaster, K. 1956-1957. "The General Theory of Second Best." *Review of Economic Studies* 24, no. 1: 11–32.

Long, C. 1958. *The Labor Force Under Changing Income and Employment.* Princeton: Princeton University Press.

Long, C.S., and Liles, W.P. 1976. "Evidence on the Functional Form of the Earnings-Schooling Relationship in Human Capital Models." Working Papers in Human Capital, No. 76-3. Center for Studies in Human Capital, College of Business Administration, University of South Carolina.

Lord, E.W. 1928. *The Relation of Education and Income.* Indianapolis: Alpha Kappa Psi Fraternity.

Lows, R., and Tcheng, M.T. 1971. "Penalty and Equity in Funding Separate Elementary and Secondary School Districts." *Planning and Changing* 1 (January): 175–85.

Lu, Y.-C., and Tweeten, L. 1973. "The Impact of Busing on Student Achievement." *Growth and Change* 4 (October): 44–46.

———. 1976a. "The Impact of Busing on Student Achievement: Reply." *Growth and Change* 7 (July): 48–49.

———. 1976b. "The Impact of Busing on Student Achievement: Retort." *Growth and Change* 7 (July): 52.

Luecke, D.F., and McGinn, N.F. 1975. "Regression Analyses and Education Production Functions: Can They Be Trusted?" *Harvard Educational Review* 45 (August): 325–50.

Lumsden, K., ed. 1974. *Efficiency in Universities: The La Paz Papers.* Amsterdam: Elsevier.

Luytjes, J.B. 1971. "Note on the Impact of Increased Educational Funds in Lagging Areas." *Growth and Change* 22 (January): 38–41.

Lydall, H.F. 1964. "The Economics of State Aid to Education." *Economic Record* 40 (June): 260–67.

Lyle, J.R. 1967. "Research on Achievement Determinants in Educational Systems: A Survey." *Socio-Economic Planning Sciences* 1: 143–55.

Lyon, D.W. 1971. "Capitalism in the Classroom: Education Vouchers."

Business Review (Federal Reserve Bank of Philadelphia), December, pp. 3-10.
  Lyon, K.S. 1974. "The Valuation of Income Redistribution Impacts."
American Journal of Agricultural Economics 56 (May): 444-47.
  Lytton, H.D. 1959. "Recent Productivity Trends in the Federal Government:
An Exploratory Study." *Review of Economics and Statistics* 41 (November):
341-59.

M

  Maass, A. 1966. "Benefit-Cost Analysis: Its Relevance to Public Investment
Decisions." *Quarterly Journal of Economics* 80 (May): 208-26. Reprinted in
Wyksra (1971b:132-48).
  Machlup, F. 1963. *The Production and Distribution of Knowledge in the
United States.* Princeton, N.J.: Princeton University Press.
  ———. 1970. *Education and Economic Growth.* Lincoln: University of Ne-
braska Press.
  ———. 1973. "Perspectives on the Benefits of Postsecondary Education."
In Solmon and Taubman (1973: 353-64).
  ———. 1975. *Education and Economic Growth.* New York: New York
University Press.
  Machovec, F.M. 1972. "Public Higher Education in Colorado: Who Pays
the Costs? Who Receives the Benefits? *Intermountain Economic Review* 3
(Fall): 24-35.
  MacLennan, B. 1967. "The Finance of Grant-Aided Schools in Scotland."
Scottish Journal of Political Economy 14 (June): 156-74.
  Maeroff, G.I. 1977. "A Look at How Class Size Affects Learning." *New
York Times,* June 22, sec. C.
  ———. 1978. "Census Bureau Disputes Theory of College Squeeze on In-
comes." *New York Times,* March 13, p. A14.
  Magarrell, J. 1974. "State Support: Up 29 percent in 2 Years." *The Chronicle
of Higher Education* 9 (October 21): 1, 8-10.
  ———. 1976. "State Appropriations Up 24 Percent in Two Years." *Chronicle
of Higher Education* 13 (October 25): 9-11.
  Magers, D.A. 1977. "Two Tests of Equity Under Impact Aid Public Law
81-874." *Journal of Education Finance* 3 (Summer): 124-28.
  Magnusson, L. 1973. "Cost-Benefit Analysis of Investment in Higher Educa-
tion: Some Swedish Results." *Swedish Journal of Economics* 75 (June): 119-27.
  Malassis, L. 1969. "Education and Agricultural Development." *International
Social Science Journal* 21: 244-55.
  Maldonado, R. 1976. "Education, Income Distribution and Economic
Growth in Puerto Rico." *Review of Social Economy* 34 (April): 1-12.
  Maltby, G.P. 1973. "Aid to Individuals Versus Aid to Institutions: A Discus-
sion of Basic Issues." *Notre Dame Journal of Education* 4 (Fall): 258-67.
  Mandel, A.S. 1975. *Resource Distribution Inside School Districts.* Lexington
Mass.: Heath Lexington Books.
  Mandel, D. 1976. "Schools on the Market." *Times Educational Supplement*
(London) (May 21): 20-1.
  Manheim, L.M. 1975. "Health, Health Practices, and Socio-economic Status:
The Role of Education." Ph.D. dissertation, University of California, Berkeley.
  Manning, R. 1975. "Optimal Aggregative Development of a Skilled Work-
force." *Quarterly Journal of Economics* 89: 504-11.

———. 1976. "Issues in Optimal Educational Policy in the Context of Balanced Growth." *Journal of Economic Theory* 13 (December): 380-95.

Mantell, E.H. 1973. "Labor Markets for Engineers of Differing Ability and Education." *Industrial and Labor Relations Review* 27 (October): 63-73.

———. 1974. "Discrimination Based On Education In the Labor Market for Engineers." *Review of Economics and Statistics* 56 (May): 158-66.

Margolis, J., ed. 1965. *The Public Economy of Urban Communities.* Washington, D.C.: Resources for the Future, Inc.

Marin, A., and Psacharopoulos, G. 1976. "Schooling and Income Distribution." *Review of Economics and Statistics* 58 (August): 332-38.

Marinelli, J.J. 1975. "Critical Issues in the Financing of Education for the Handicapped." *Journal of Education Finance* 1 (Fall): 246-49.

Marriner, L.S. 1977. "The Cost of Educating Handicapped Pupils in New York City." *Journal of Education Finance* 3 (Summer): 82-97.

Marsh, J., and Stafford, F.P. 1967. "The Effect of Values on Pecuniary Behavior: The Case of Academicians." *American Sociological Review* 32 (October): 740-54.

Marshall, A. 1961. *Principles of Economics.* 9th (varorium) ed. Ed. C.W. Guillebaud. 2 vols. London: The Macmillan Co.

Marshall, F.R.; Cartter, A.M.; and King, A.G. 1976. *Labor Economics: Wages, Employment and Trade Unionism.* 3rd ed. Homewood, Ill.: Richard D. Irwin.

Mason, P. 1975. "Educational Vouchers Under Test." *Oxford Review of Education* 1:159-67.

Masters, S.H. 1969. "The Effect of Family Income on Children's Education: Some Findings on Inequality of Opportunity." *Journal of Human Resources* 4 (Spring): 158-75.

———. 1974. "The Effect of Educational Differences and Labor-Market Discrimination on the Relative Earnings of Black Males." *Journal of Human Resources* 9 (Summer): 342-60.

Masters, S.H., and Ribich, T.I. 1972. "Schooling and Earnings of Low Achievers: Comment." *American Economic Review* 62 (September): 755-60.

Mathis, C. 1959. "The Relationship Between Salary Policies and Teacher Morale." *Journal of Educational Psychology* 50 (December): 275-79.

Maurizi, A. 1975. "Rates of Return to Dentistry and the Decision to Enter Dental School." *Journal of Human Resources* 10 (Fall): 521-28.

Maxwell, J.A. 1977. *Financing State and Local Governments,* 3rd ed. Washington, D.C.: The Brookings Institution.

Maxwell, L. 1970. "Some Evidence on Negative Returns to Graduate Education." *Western Economic Journal* 8 (June): 186-89.

Mayeske, G.W., and Beaton, A.E. 1975. *Special Studies of our Nation's Students.* Washington, D.C.: U.S. Office of Education.

Mayeske, G.W., et al. 1972. *A Study of our Nation's Schools.* Washington, D.C.: U.S. Office of Education.

———. 1973a. *A Study of the Achievement of Our Nation's Students.* Washington, D.C.: U.S. Office of Education.

———. 1973b. *A Study of the Attitude Toward Life of Our Nation's Students.* Washington, D.C.: U.S. Office of Education.

Maynard, J. 1971. *Some Microeconomics of Higher Education: Economies of Scale.* Lincoln: University of Nebraska Press.

Mayshar, J. 1977. "Should Government Subsidize Risky Private Projects?" *American Economic Review* 67 (March): 20-28.

McCann, W., and Areen, J. 1971. "Vouchers and the Citizen—Some Legal Questions." *Teachers College Record* 72 (February): 389-404. Reprinted in La Noue (1972: 111-26).

McClelland, D. 1966. "Does Education Accelerate Economic Growth?" *Economic Development and Cultural Change* (April): 257-278.

McClure, P. 1976. "Grubstake: A Radical Proposal." *Change* 8 (June): 30, 38-44.

McCulloch, J.R. 1849. *Principles of Politics and Economics.* Edinburgh: Adam and Charles Black.

McCurdy, J. 1974a. "A Market System." *Times Educational Supplement* (London), April 12, p. 24.

———. 1974b. "Shop Around Scheme Shows Few Benefits." *Times Education Supplement* (London), August 16, p. 9.

McDowell, G.R. 1975. "Whose Preferences Count? A Study of the Effects of Community Size and Characteristics on the Distribution of the Benefits of Schooling." Ph.D. dissertation, Michigan State University.

McGuire, J.W. 1976. "The Distribution of Subsidy to Students in California Public Higher Education." *Journal of Human Resources* 11 (Summer): 343-53.

McGuire, M.C. 1971. "Cost Versus Performance Subsidies As Tools of Intergovernment Finance." *National Tax Journal* 24 (March): 13-18.

McInnis, M. 1970. "Age, Education, and Occupational Differentials in Interregional Migration." *Demography* 8: 195-204.

McIntyre, M.C. 1969. "Determinants of Expenditures for Public Higher Education." *National Tax Journal* 22 (June): 262-72.

McKean, R.N. 1958. *Efficiency in Government through Systems Analysis.* New York: John Wiley and Sons.

McKenzie, R.B. 1972. "The Economics of Reducing Faculty Teaching Loads." *Journal of Political Economy* 80 (May–June): 617-19.

McLennan, K., and Moskow, M.H. 1970. "Public Education." In *Emerging Sectors of Collective Bargaining,* ed. S.L. Wolfbein, pp. 219-60. Morristown, N.J.: General Learning Corporation, 1970.

McLoone, E.P. 1974. *Profiles in School Support, 1969-1970.* Washington, D.C.: Government Printing Office.

McLure, C.E., Jr. 1971. "Revenue Sharing: Alternative to Rational Fiscal Federalism?" *Public Policy* 19 (Summer): 457-78.

McMahon, W.W. 1970. "An Economic Analysis of Major Determinants of Expenditures on Public Education." *Review of Economics and Statistics* 52 (August): 242-52.

———. 1974. *Investment in Higher Education.* Lexington, Mass.: Heath Lexington Books.

———. 1975. "Economic and Demographic Effects on Investment in Higher Education." *Southern Economic Journal* 41 (January): 506-14.

———. 1976. "Influences on Investment by Blacks in Higher Education." *American Economic Review* 66 (May): 320-23.

McNulty, J.K. 1973. "Tax Policy and Tuition Credit Legislation: Federal Income Tax Allowance for Higher Education." *California Law Review* 61 (January): 1-80.

Mecklenburger, J. 1972. "Vouchers at Alum Rock." *Phi Delta Kappan* 54 (September): 23-25.

Mecklenburger, J., and Hostrop, R., eds. 1972. *Educational Vouchers: From Theory to Alum Rock.* Homewood, Ill.: ETC Publications.

Medsker, L.L., and Trent, J.W. 1965. *The Influence of Different Types of Public Higher Institutions on College Attendance from Varying Socioeconomic and Ability Levels.* Berkeley: University of California, Center of the Study of Higher Education.

Megel, C.J. 1971. "Education Vouchers." *Compact* 5 (February): 31–32.

Melichar, E. 1965. "The Net Influence on Economists' Salaries of Each of Seven Characteristics: A Regression Analysis." *American Economic Review* 55 (Supplement: December): 63–70.

——. 1968. "Factors Affecting 1966 Basic Salaries in the National Register Professions." *American Economic Review* 58 (Supplement: December): 56–79.

Meltsner, A.J., et al. 1973. *Political Feasibility of Reform in School Financing: The Case of California.* New York: Praeger Publishers.

Merewitz, L., and Sosnick, S.H. 1971. *The Budget's New Clothes: A Critique of Planning-Programming-Budgeting and Benefit-Cost Analysis.* Chicago: Markham.

Merrett, S. 1966 "The Rate of Return to Education: A Critique." *Oxford Economic Papers* 18, N.S. (November): 289–303.

——. 1967. "Student Finance in Higher Education." *Economic Journal* 77 (June): 288–302.

——. 1971. "The Education-Occupation Matrix: An Indian Case Study." *International Labour Review* 103 (May): 499–510.

Metcalf, D. 1970. "University Salaries: Faculty Differentials." *Economica* 37 (November): 362–72.

——. 1973. "The Rate of Return to Investing In A Doctorate: A Case Study." *Scottish Journal of Political Economy* 20 (February): 43–51.

Michael, R.T. 1972. *The Effect of Education on Efficiency in Consumption.* New York: Columbia University Press (for National Bureau of Economic Research).

——. 1973a. "Education in Non-Market Production." *Journal of Political Economy* 81 (March–April): 306–27.

——. 1973b. "Education and the Derived Demand for Children." *Journal of Political Economy* 81 (March–April, pt. 2): S 128–64.

Michaeli, M. 1972. "On the Economics of Higher Education." *Ma'ariv* (January 14): 19 (in Hebrew).

Michelson, S. 1969. "Rational Income Decisions of Negroes and Everybody Else." *Industrial Labor Relations Review* 23 (October): 15–28.

——. 1970. "The Association of Teacher Resourceness with Children's Characteristics." In *Do Teachers Make a Difference?* (1970: 120–68).

——. 1972. "For the Plaintiffs—Equal School Resource Allocation." *Journal of Human Resources* 7 (Summer): 283–306.

Michigan Department of Education. 1974. *Compensatory Education: The Program in Michigan.* Lansing, January.

——. 1975. *Chapter 3 Summary Report.* Lansing; June.

——. 1976. "Chapter 3 of the State School Aid Act." Lansing.

Milhaud, M. 1969. "Human Resources, Social Charges And Productivity In Industry." *Annals of Public and Co-operative Economy* 40 (October–December): 411–33.

Mill, J.S. 1909. *Principles of Political Economy,* ed. W.J. Ashley. New York: Longmans, Green, and Company.

——. 1972. "On Liberty." Reprinted in La Noue (1972: 3–6).

Miller, A.V. 1974. "The Optimal Allocation of Time Over the Life Cycle with an Age-Dependent Utility Function: Implications for the Female Investment in Education." Ph.D. dissertation, Northwestern University.

Miller, H.P. 1960. "Annual and Lifetime Income in Relation to Education: 1939-1959." *American Economic Review* 50 (December): 962-86.

———. 1965. "Lifetime Income and Economic Growth." *American Economic Review* 55 (September): 834-44.

Miller, J.L., Jr. 1965. *State Budgeting for Higher Education: The Use of Formulas and Cost Analysis.* Ann Arbor: Institute of Public Administration, The University of Michigan.

Miller, W.L. 1966. "The Economics of Education in English Classical Economics." *Southern Economic Journal* 32 (January): 294-309.

———. 1967. "Education as a Source of Economic Growth." *Journal of Economic Issues* (December): 280-96.

Millman, S.D., and Toombs, W. 1972. *The Quality of Graduate Studies: Pennsylvania and Selected States.* Report No. 14. University Park: Center for the Study of Higher Education, The Pennsylvania State University.

Mincer, J. 1962. "On-the-Job Training: Costs, Returns and Some Implications." *Journal of Political Economy* (Supplement) 70 (October): 50-79.

———. 1970. "The Distribution of Labor Incomes: A Survey With Special Reference to the Human Capital Approach." *Journal of Economic Literature* 8 (March): 1-26.

———. 1974. *Schooling, Experience and Earnings.* New York: Columbia University Press.

Mincer, J., and Polachek, S. 1974. "Family Investments in Human Capital: Earnings of Women." *Journal of Political Economy* 82 (March-April, pt. 2): S76-108.

Miner, J. 1963. *Social and Economic Factors in Spending for Public Education.* Syracuse: Syracuse University Press.

Mishan, E.J. 1970. "Criteria for Public Investment: A Reply." *Journal of Political Economy* 78 (January-February): 178-89.

———. 1970. *Technology and Growth: The Price We Pay.* New York: Praeger Publishers.

———. 1971. "Evaluation of Life and Limb: A Theoretical Approach." *Journal of Political Economy* 79 (July-August): 687-705.

———. 1976. *Cost-Benefit Analysis.* 2nd ed. New York: Praeger Publishers.

Mollenkopf, W.G., and Melville, S.D. 1956. "A Study of Secondary School Characteristics as Related to Test Scores." Princeton, N.J.: Educational Testing Service.

Mood, A.M. 1967. "On Some Basic Steps in the Application of Systems Analysis to Instruction." *Socio-Economic Planning Sciences* 1: 19-26.

———. 1969. "Macro-Analysis of the American Educational System." *Operations Research* (September-October): 770-84.

———. 1970. "Do Teachers Make a Difference?" In *Do Teachers Make a Difference?* (1970: 1-24).

———. 1973. "Forward." In Mayeske et al. (1973b: iii-iv).

Mood, A.M., et al. 1972. *Papers on Efficiency in the Management of Higher Education.* Berkeley, Calif.: Carnegie Commission on Higher Education.

Moody, R.E. 1974. "Inadequacy of The Cost-Benefit Ratio As A Measure of the Public Interest." *American Journal of Agricultural Economics* 56 (February): 188-91.

Moore, D.O. 1971. "Local Nonproperty Taxes for Schools." In R.L. Johns, Alexander, and Stollar (1971: 209-22).

Moore, G.A. 1974. "Some Salary Effects of Professional Negotiations in the Public Schools: The Nebraska Experience." Ph.D. dissertation, University of Nebraska.

Moore, P.R. 1975. "Optimal Investment in Higher Education by State and Local Governments: A Human Capital Approach." Ph.D. dissertation, University of Illinois.

Moore, W.J. 1972. "The Relative Quality of Economics Journals: A Suggested Rating System." *Western Economic Journal* 10 (June): 156-69.

Morgan, C.L. 1976. "Psychological, Sociological, and Economic Aspects of Occupational Choice: A Review." Working Papers in Human Capital, Center for Studies in Human Capital, College of Business Administration, University of South Carolina.

Morgan, D.C., Jr. 1973. "The Impact of 'No Wealth Discrimination' on Equal Educational Opportunities in Urban Areas." Presented at the annual meeting of the Southern Economic Association in Houston, November 10.

————. 1974. "The Arithmetic of 'No Wealth Discrimination.'" *Social Science Quarterly* 55 (September): 310-30.

Morgan, D.R., and Kearney, R.C. 1977. "Collective Bargaining and Faculty Compensation: A Comparative Analysis." *Sociology of Education* 50 (January).

Morgan, J.M. 1977. "Goal Programming and Resource Allocation Within the Pennsylvania Secondary School System." Ph.D. Dissertation, University of South Carolina.

Morgan, J.M., and Cohn E. 1977a. "Goal Programming and Resource Allocation Within Educational Systems." Working papers in Human Resources, Center for Studies in Human Resource Economics, College of Business Administration, University of South Carolina.

————. 1977b. "Resource Allocation Within Secondary Schools: A Goal Programming Approach." In *1977 Proceedings of the Social Statistics Section, American Statistical Association*, pp. 646-652.

————. 1977c. "A Static Resource Optimization Model for Secondary Education." Paper presented at the 1977 meetings of the Southern Economic Association.

Morgan, J.M.; McMeekin, G.C.; and Cohn, E. 1977. "Value-Restricted Preferences and Educational Planning." Manuscript. Bowling Green: Department of Economics, Western Kentucky University.

Morgan, J.N., and David, M.A. 1963. "Education and Income." *Quarterly Journal of Economics* 77 (August): 424-37.

Morgan, J.N., and Lininger, C. 1964. "Education and Income: Comment." *Quarterly Journal of Economics* 78 (May): 346-47.

Morgan, J.N., and Sirageldin, I. 1968. "A Note on the Quality Dimension in Education." *Journal of Political Economy* 76 (September–October): 1069-77.

Morgan, J.N., et al. 1962. *Income and Welfare in the United States.* New York: McGraw-Hill.

Morgenstern, R.D. 1973. "Direct and Indirect Effects on Earnings of Schooling and Socio-Economic Background." *Review of Economics and Statistics* 55 (May): 225-33.

Morris, J. 1976. "Some Simple Tests of the Direct Effect of Education on Preferences and on Nonmarket Productivity." *Review of Economics and Statistics* 58 (February): 112-17.

Morse, L.D. 1974. "Schooling and Discrimination in the Labor Markets." *Journal of Human Resources* 9 (Summer): 398-407.

Morse, W.J. 1975. "Toward a Model for Human Resource Valuation: A Comment." *Accounting Review* 50 (April): 345–47.

Morss, E.R. 1966. "Some Thoughts on the Determinants of State and Local Expenditures." *National Tax Journal* 19 (March): 95–103.

Morss, E.R.; Fredland, J.E.; and Saul, H.H. 1967. "Fluctuations in State Expenditures: An Econometric Analysis." *Southern Economic Journal* 33 (April): 496–517.

Mortimer, K.P., and Lozier, G.G. 1972. *Collective Bargaining: Implications for Governance.* Report No. 17. University Park: Center for the Study of Higher Education, The Pennsylvania State University.

Muchinski, P.M., and Finch, M.K. 1975. "Subjective Expected Utility and Academic Preference." *Organizational Behavior and Human Preference* 14 (October): 217–26.

Muhsam, H.V., ed. 1975. *Education and Population—Mutual Impacts.* New York: Ordina Editions.

Mundel, D.S. 1973. "Whose Education Should Society Support?" In Solmon and Taubman (1973: 293–316).

———. 1974. "Recent Developments in the Understanding of the Determinants of Demand for Postsecondary Education." Paper presented to the annual meeting of the Southern Economic Association, November 14–16.

Murnane, R.J. 1975. *The Impact of School Resources on the Learning of Inner City Children.* Cambridge, Mass.: Ballinger Publishing Company.

Murphy, D.R. 1974. "Equality of Educational Opportunity and Educational Finance: A Question of the Applicability of the Serrano v. Priest Decision." Ph.D. Dissertation, Iowa State University.

Musgrave, J.C. 1976. "Fixed Nonresidential Business and Residential Capital in the United States, 1925–1975." *Survey of Current Business* 56 (April): 46–52.

Musgrave, R.A. 1959. *The Theory of Public Finance.* New York: McGraw-Hill.

———. 1969. "Cost-Benefit Analysis and the Theory of Public Finance." *Journal of Economic Literature* 7 (September): 797–806.

Mushkin, S.J. 1962a. "Health as an Investment." *Journal of Political Economy* 70 (October, pt. 2): 129–57.

———. ed. 1962b. *Economics of Higher Education.* Washington, D.C.: U.S. Office of Education, 1962.

———. 1969. "A Note on State and Local Financing of Higher Education." In Joint Economic Committee (1969: 518–40).

———. 1977. "Direct Economic Benefits of Education." In *Economic and Social Perspectives on Adult Illiteracy* (1977: 40–51).

N

Nalla Gounden, A.M. 1967. "Investment in Education in India." *Journal of Human Resources* 2 (Summer): 347–58.

Nam, C.B. 1964. "Impact of the 'GI Bills' on the Educational Level of the Male Population." *Social Forces* 43 (October): 26–32.

Nassau, W.S. 1939. *An Outline of the Science of Political Economy.* New York: Farrar and Rinehart.

National Comparison of Local School Costs, For the 1975–76 School Year. 1975. Westport, Conn.: Market Data Retrieval, Inc.

National Comparison of Local School Costs, for the 1976-77 School Year. 1977. Westport, Conn.: Market Data Retrieval, Inc.

National Education Association. 1961. "Why Few Schools Systems Use Merit Ratings." *N.E.A. Research Bulletin* (May 1961).

———. 1969. *Salary Schedules for Teachers, 1969-70.* Washington, D.C.: The Association.

———. 1970a. *Economic Status of the Teaching Profession, 1969-70.* Washington, D.C.: The Association.

———. 1970b. *Salaries in Higher Education, 1969-70.* Washington, D.C.: The Association.

———. Committee on Educational Finance. 1972. *Financial Status of the Public Schools, 1972.* Washington, D.C.: The Association.

———. 1975. *Estimates of School Statistics.* Washington, D.C.: The Association.

National Register of Scientific and Technical Personnel. 1970. *Summary of American Science Manpower, 1968.* Washington, D.C.: National Science Foundation, NSF 70-5, January.

National Science Board. 1969. *Toward A Public Policy for Graduate Education in the Sciences.* Washington, D.C.: National Science Foundation.

National Science Foundation. 1968. *Review of Data on Science Resources.* NSF 69-5. Washington, D.C.: Government Printing Office.

Naylor, T.H., and Gattis, D.R. 1974. "Financial Planning and Budgeting Models for Higher Education." Paper prepared for the annual meeting of the Southern Economic Association, Atlanta, November 15.

Needham, D. 1975. "The Economics of Reducing Faculty Teaching Loads: Comment." *Journal of Political Economy* 83 (February): 219-23.

Neenan, W.B. 1976. "Revenue Sharing as a Redistributional Program." *State and Local Government Review* 8 (September): 54-61.

Nelson, R.R., and Phelps, E.S. 1966. "Investment in Humans, Technological Diffusion, and Economic Growth." *American Economic Review* 56 (May): 69-75.

Nerlove, M. 1975. "Some Problems in the Use of Income-Contingent Loans for the Finance of Higher Education." *Journal of Political Economy* 83 (February): 157-83.

Netzer, D. 1966. *Economics of the Property Tax.* Washington, D.C.: The Brookings Institution.

———. 1970. "Impact of the Property Tax: Its Economic Implications for Urban Problems." In *State and Local Finance,* ed. W.E. Mitchell and I. Walter, pp. 138-74. New York: Ronald Press.

———. 1975. "State Education Aid and School Tax Efforts in Large Cities." In Tron (1975: 135-232).

Newton, J.N., et al. 1975. *Developing an Empirical Test of the Impact of Vouchers on Elasticity of Demand for Post-Secondary Education and on the Financing of Higher Education; and Economic Efficiency in Post-Secondary Education.* Report No. ED132958. Eugene, Ore.: ERIC.

Nichols, A., and Soper, J.C. 1972. "Economic Man in the Classroom." *Journal of Political Economy* 80 (September-October): 1069-73.

Nicholson, J.S. 1891. "The Living Capital of the United Kingdom." *Economic Journal* 1 (March 1891): 95-107. Reprinted in Bowman et al (1968: 227-34).

Nielsen, D.A.; Turner, K.K.; and Blair, R.F. 1975. "Financial Determinants of Disparities in Educational Opportunity Among Nebraska School Districts." *Nebraska Journal of Economics and Business* 14 (Winter): 19-38.

Niemi, A.W., Jr. 1974. "Racial and Ethnic Differences in Returns on Educational Investment in California and Texas." *Economic Inquiry* 12 (September): 398-402.

———. 1975a. "Racial Differences in Returns to Educational Investment in the South." *American Journal of Economics and Sociology.* 34 (January): 87-94.

———. 1975b. "Sexist Differences in Returns to Educational Investment." *Quarterly Review of Economics and Business* 15 (Spring): 17-25.

———. 1975c. "Journal Publication Performance During 1970-1974: The Relative Output of Southern Economics Departments." *Southern Economic Journal* 42 (July): 97-106.

———. 1976. "Racial and Ethnic Differences in Returns on Educational Investment in California and Texas: Reply." *Economic Inquiry* 14 (December): 610-12.

Nirenberg, J. 1976. *Education Vouchers—The Connecticut Experience: A Critical Appraisal.* Report No. ED130386. Eugene, Ore.: ERIC.

Niskanen, W.A., and Levy, M. 1974. *Cities and Schools: A Case for Community Government in California.* Working Paper No. 14. Berkeley: Department of Economics, University of California.

Nollen, S.D. 1974. "The Supply and Demand for College-Educated Labor." Ph.D. dissertation, University of Chicago.

———. 1975. "The Economics of Education: Research—Results and Needs." *Teachers College Record* 77 (September): 51-77.

Nordell, L.P. 1967. *A Dynamic Input-Output Model of the California Educational System.* Office of Naval Research, Technicians Report No. 25, Center for Research in Management Science, University of California, Berkeley.

Norman, V.D. 1976. *Education, Learning and Productivity.* Oslo: Universitetsforlaget (Distributed by Columbia University Press).

Noto, N.A., and Raiff, D.L. 1977. "Philadelphia's Fiscal Story: The City and the Schools." *Business Review* (Federal Reserve Bank of Philadelphia), March-April, pp. 3-47.

O

Oakland, W.H. 1970. "Criteria for Public Investment: A Comment." *Journal of Political Economy* 78 (January-February): 175-77.

———. 1976. "Incidence and Other Fiscal Impacts of State Assumption of Education Costs: Baltimore." *National Tax Journal* 29 (March): 73-85.

Oates, W.E. 1969. "The Effects of Property Taxes and Local Public Spending on Property Values: An Empirical Study of Tax Capitalization and the Tiebout Hypothesis." *Journal of Political Economy* 77 (November-December): 957-70.

———. 1973. "The Effects of Property Taxes and Local Public Spending on Property Values: A Reply and Yet Further Results." *Journal of Political Economy* 81 (July-August): 1004-1008.

Oaxaca, R.L. 1975. "Estimation of Union-Nonunion Wage Differentials within Occupational/Regional Subgroups." *Journal of Human Resources* 10 (Fall): 529-37.

O'Brien, T. 1971. "Grants-in-Aid: Some Further Answers." *National Tax Journal* 24 (March): 65-77.

Odden, A. 1977. "Alternative Measures of School District Wealth." *Journal of Education Finance* 2 (Winter): 356-79.

———. 1978. "Alternative Measures of School District Wealth: A Rejoinder." *Journal of Education Finance* 3 (Winter): 344-45.

Odden, A.; Augenblick, J.; and Vincent, P.E. 1976. *School Finance Reform in the States, 1976-1977: An Overview of Legislative Actions, Judicial Decisions and Public Policy Research.* Denver, Colo.: Education Commission of the States.

O'Donoghue, M. 1971. *Economic Dimensions in Education.* Chicago: Aldine-Atherton.

O'Neill, D.M. 1970. "The Effect of Discrimination on Earnings: Evidence from Military Test Score Results." *Journal of Human Resources* 5 (Fall): 475-86.

O'Neill, D.M.; Gray, B.; and Horowitz, S. 1972. "For the defendants—Educational Equality and Expenditure Equalization Orders." *Journal of Human Resources* 7 (Summer): 307-25.

Orcutt, G.H., et al. 1977. "Does Your Probability of Death Depend on Your Environment? A Microanalytic Study." *American Economic Review* 67 (February): 260-64.

O'Reilly, R.C., and Sheridan, T.M. 1975. "An Analysis of the Public Attitude Toward the Financing of Public Education as Reported in the Gallup Poll of Attitudes toward Education, 1969-1974." Report No. ED105613. Eugene, Ore.: ERIC.

Organization for Economic Cooperation and Development. 1961. *Policy Conference on Economic Growth and Investment in Education.* Paris.

———. 1963. *Higher Education and the Demand for Scientific Manpower in the United States.* Paris.

———. 1964a. *The Residual Factor and Economic Growth.* Paris.

———. 1964b.*Economic Aspects of Higher Education.* Paris.

———. 1965. *Econometric Models of Education.* Paris.

———. 1969. *Systems Analysis for Educational Planning.* Paris.

———. 1973a. *Costs and Potential Economies.* Studies in Institutional Management in Higher Education, University of Bradford. Paris.

———. 1973b. *Decision, Planning and Budgeting.* Studies in Institutional Management in Higher Education, University of Copenhagen. Paris.

———. 1973c. *Long-Range Policy Planning in Education.* Paris.

———. 1973d. *The Utilization of Highly Qualified Personnel.* Paris.

———. 1974a. *Indicators of Performance of Educational Systems.* Paris.

———. 1974b. *Mathematical Models for the Education Sector.* Paris.

———. 1974-1975. *Educational Statistics Yearbook.* Vol. I—International Tables; Vol. II—Country Studies. Paris.

———. 1975a. *Education, Inequality and Life Chances.* 2 vols. Paris.

———. 1975b. *Participatory Planning in Education.* Paris.

———. 1976. *Review of National Policies for Education.* A series of country studies: Norway (March); Canada (July); Netherlands (September); and Austria (November). Paris.

Orlans, H. 1972. *The Nonprofit Research Institute.* New York: McGraw-Hill.

Orvis, C.C. 1976. "An Analysis of Demand for Post-Secondary Education in Minnesota." Ph.D. dissertation, University of Minnesota.

Orwig, M., ed. 1971. *Financing Higher Education: Alternatives for the Federal Government.* Iowa City: American College Testing Program.

Osberg, L. 1976. "Tinbergen and the 'Blurring' of the Human Capital Paradigm: A Review." *Review of Income and Wealth* 22 (March): 93-97.

Osborn, T.N., II. 1976. *Higher Education in Mexico: History, Growth and*

Problems in a Dichotomized Industry. Inter-American Studies. El Paso: University of Texas, Texas Western Press and Center for Inter-American Studies.

Osburn, D.D. 1970. "Economics of Size Associated with Public High Schools." *Review of Economics and Statistics* 52 (February): 113-15.

Ostry, S., ed. 1972. *Canadian Higher Education in the Seventies.* Ottawa: Economic Council of Canada.

Ott, D.J., and Ott, A.F. 1971. "Economic Analysis and Public Expenditures." *Public Policy* 19 (Summer): 535-38.

Oulton, N. 1974. "The Distribution of Education and the Distribution of Income." *Economica* 41 (November): 387-402.

Overlan, S.F. 1975. "Is There A Future For Education Vouchers?" *Independent School Bulletin* 34 (May): 37-41.

Owen, J.D. 1972. "The Distribution of Educational Resources in Large American Cities." *Journal of Human Resources* 7 (Winter): 26-38.

P

Packer, A.H. 1975. "Financing Health Care and Education: Consumer Units and Resource Allocation." *Public Policy* 23 (Winter): 39-58.

Padmanabhan, C.B. 1968. "Recent Trends in Economics of Education and Economics of Educational Planning." *Asian Economic Review* 10 (August): 476-82.

Page, E.B. 1973. "Effects of Higher Education." In Solmon and Taubman (1973: 147-50).

Paller, A., et al. 1975. *Designing A Transportation System For A Parent Choice School District: A Transportation Supervisor's Handbook.* Report No ED116307. Eugene, Ore.: ERIC.

Palm, G. 1968. "International Comparisons of Educational Outlay: Problems and Approaches." *International Social Science Journal* 20, no. 1: 98-198.

Palmer, S.K. 1975. "An Empirical Investigation of the Determinants of the Length of Full-Time Schooling." Ph.D. dissertation, North Carolina State University.

Panke, H.H. 1954. "Factors Affecting the Proportion of High School Graduates Who Enter College." *Bulletin of the National Association of Secondary School Principals* 28 (November).

Panitchpakdi, S. 1974. *Educational Growth in Developing Countries: An Empirical Analysis.* Rotterdam: Rotterdam University Press.

Parden, R. J. 1971. "Planning, Programming, Budgeting Systems." *Liberal Education* 57: 202-10.

Parish, R.M. 1963. "The Economics of State Aid to Education." *Economic Record* 39 (September): 292-304.

Park, S.H., and Bielefeld, J. 1976. "The Effect of Schooling, Postschool Investments, and Unemployment on the Earnings of Engineers: A Human Capital Approach." *Quarterly Review of Economics and Business* 16 (Autumn): 45-50.

Parks, R.P. 1975. "Assistant Professors Should be Discriminated Against, or the Less Productive I am, the More I should Be Paid." *Journal of Political Economy* 83 (February): 225-26.

Parnes, H.S. 1962. *Forecasting Educational Needs for Economic and Social Development.* Paris: OECD.

Paroush, J. 1976. "The Risk Effect and Investment in Human Capital." *European Economic Review* 8 (December): 339-47.

Parsons, D.O. 1972. "Specific Human Capital: An Application to Quit Rates and Layoff Rates." *Journal of Political Economy* 80 (November–December): 1120–43.

——. 1974. "The Cost of School Time, Foregone Earnings, and Human Capital Formation." *Journal of Political Economy* 82 (March–April): 251–66.

——. 1975. "Intergenerational Wealth Transfers and the Educational Decisions of Male Youth." *Quarterly Journal of Economics* 89 (November): 603–17.

Patel, M. 1977. "Return to Engineering Degrees." Paper presented to the 1977 Conference of the Western Economic Association.

Paul, S. 1972. "An Application of Cost-Benefit Analysis to Management Education." *Journal of Political Economy* 80 (March–April): 328–46.

Pauly, M.V. 1967. "Mixed Public and Private Financing of Education: Efficiency and Feasibility." *American Economic Review* 57 (March): 120–30.

——. 1970. "Risk and the Social Rate of Discount." *American Economic Review* 60 (March): 195–98.

Peacock, A.T., and Wiseman, J. 1964. *Education for Democrats.* London: Institute of Economic Affairs.

Peaslee, A. 1969. "Education's Role in Development." *Economic Development and Cultural Change* 17 (April): 293–318.

Pechman, J.A. 1965. "Financing State and Local Governments." In *Proceedings of a Symposium on Federal Taxation.* American Bankers Association, 1965.

——. 1970. "The Distributional Effects of Public Higher Education in California." *Journal of Human Resources* 5 (Summer): 361–70.

——. 1971. "The Distribution of Costs and Benefits of Public Higher Education: Further Comments." *Journal of Human Resources* 6 (Summer): 375–76.

——. 1972. "Note on the Intergenerational Transfer of Public Higher-Education Benefits." *Journal of Political Economy* 80 (May–June, pt. 2): S 256–59.

——. 1977. *Federal Tax Policy.* 3rd ed. Washington, D.C.: The Brookings Institution.

Pellegrino, A.J. 1976. "Collective Wage Bargaining by Public Teachers in Springfield, Massachusetts and Adjacent School Districts." Ph.D. dissertation, University of Massachusetts.

Pelzman, S. 1973. "The Effect of Government Subsidies-in-kind on Private Expenditures: The Case of Higher Education." *Journal of Political Economy* 81 (January–February): 1–27.

Peppard, D.M., Jr. 1975. "Public Expenditures Incidence in Michigan, 1970." Ph.D. dissertation, Michigan State University.

Perl, L.J. 1973. "Family Background, Secondary School Expenditure, and Student Ability." *Journal of Human Resources* 8 (Spring): 156–80.

Perlman, R. 1973. *The Economics of Education: Conceptual Problems and Policy Issues.* New York: McGraw-Hill.

Peston, M. 1966. "The Theory of Spillovers and Its Connection with Education." *Public Finance* 21: 184–205.

Petty, W. (Sir). 1699. *Political Arithmetick, or A Discourse Concerning the Extent and Value of Lands, Buildings, etc.* London.

Phi Delta Kappan. 1970. Special Issue on Educational Vouchers. Vol. 2 (September).

Phillips, J.; Votey, H.L., Jr.; and Maxwell, D. 1972. "Crime, Youth, and the Labor Market." *Journal of Political Economy* 80 (May–June, pt. 1): 491–504.

Pickard, B.W., and Richards, D.M. 1976. "Educational Vouchers." *Canadian*

Administrator 15 (January): 1-5.

Pigou, A.C. 1920. *The Economics of Welfare.* London: Macmillan and Co.

Pincus, J., ed. 1974. *School Finance in Transition: The Courts and Educational Reform.* Cambridge, Mass.: Ballinger Publishing Company.

Pinera, J.S. 1976. "The Economics of Education in Developing Countries: A Collection of Essays." Ph.D. dissertation, Harvard University.

Piore, M.J. 1971. "The Dual Labor Market: Theory and Implications." In *Problems in Political Economy: An Urban Perspective,* ed. D.M. Gordon. Lexington, Mass.: D.C. Heath and Company, 1971.

——. 1972. "Notes for a Theory of Labor Market Stratification." Working Paper No. 95. Cambridge, Mass.: MIT Department of Economics, October.

Plessner, Y.; Fox, K.A.; and Sanyal, B.C. 1968. "On the Allocation of Resources in a University Department." *Metroeconomica* 20 (September–December 256-71).

Ploughman, T.; Darnton, W.; and Heuser, W. 1968. "An Assignment Program to Establish School Attendance Boundaries and Forecast Construction Needs." *Socio-Economic Planning Science* 1: 243-58.

Plowden Report. 1967. *Children and Their Primary Schools.* Report cf the Central Advisory Council on Education. London: Her Majesty's Stationery Office.

Pluta, J.E. 1974. "Growth and Patterns in U.S. Government Expenditures, 1956-1972." *National Tax Journal* 27 (March): 71-87.

Pogrow, S., and Swift, D. 1977. "New Mexico School Finance Revisited: The Politics of Revising a Weighted-Pupil Formula." *Journal of Education Finance* 3 (Summer): 114-23.

Poindexter v. Louisiana Financial Assistance Commission. 1967. 175 F. Supp. 833, U.S. District Court E. D. Louisiana, August 26, 1967. Reprinted in La Noue (1972: 31-45).

Poirier, D.J. 1975. "On the Use of Bilinear Splines in Economics." *Journal of Econometrics* 3 (February): 23-34.

Pollakowski, H.O. 1973. "The Effects of Property Taxes and Local Public Spending on Property Values: A Comment and Further Results." *Journal of Political Economy* 81 (July–August): 994-1003.

Preece, P.F.W. 1970. "The Economics of Education." *Science and Society* 34 (Fall): 303-18.

President's Commission on School Finance. 1972. *Schools, People, and Money.* Washington, D.C.: Government Printing Office.

Prest, A.R., and Turvey, R. 1965. "Cost-Benefit Analysis: A Survey." *Economic Journal* 75 (December): 683-735.

Projections of Educational Statistics. Annual. Published by the National Center for Educational Statistics. Washington, D.C.: Government Printing Office.

Psacharopoulos, G. 1969. *The Rate of Return on Investment in Education at the Regional Level: Estimates for the State of Hawaii.* Honolulu: Economic Research Center, University of Hawaii.

——. 1970. "Estimating Shadow Rates of Return to Investment in Education." *Journal of Human Resources* 5 (Winter): 34-50.

——. 1974. "College Quality as a Screening Device?" *Journal of Human Resources* 9 (Fall): 556-58.

——. 1975. *Earnings and Education in OECD Countries.* Paris: OECD.

Psacharopoulos, G., and Hinchliffe, K. 1972. "Further Evidence on the lasticity of Substitution Among Different Types of Educated Labor." *Journal f Political Economy* 80 (July–August): 786-92.

Psacharapoulos, G., Assisted by Hinchliffe, K. 1973. *Returns to Education: An International Comparison.* San Francisco: Jossey-Bass.

Pugh, R.C. 1968. "The Partitioning of Criterion Score Variance Accounted for in Multiple Correlation." *American Educational Research Journal* 5 (November): 639-46.

Puntasen, A. 1977. "Manpower and Educational Planning for Higher Education in Thailand." *Economic Development and Cultural Change* 25 (January): 279-92.

Pyun, C.S. 1968. "The Monetary Value of a Housewife." *American Journal of Economics and Sociology* 28 (July): 271-84.

Q

Quandt, R.E. 1976. "Some Quantitative Aspects of the Economics Journal Literature." *Journal of Political Economy* 84 (August): 741-55.

Quindry, K.E., and Mastern, J.T. 1976. "Financing Postsecondary Education, 1950-1972." *Journal of Education Finance* 1 (Spring): 516-33.

Quinn, R.P., and de Mandilovitch, M.S.B. 1975. *"Education and Job Satisfaction: A Questionable Payoff.* Ann Arbor: Survey Research Center, University of Michigan.

R

Rabinovitch, Y. 1975. "Measurement of the Effects of Socioeconomic Variables on College Student Employment: A Test of Applicable U.S. 1970 Census Data." Ph.D. dissertation, University of Florida.

Radner, R., and Miller, L.S. 1970. "Demand and Supply in U.S. Higher Education: A Progress Report." *American Economic Review* 60 (May): 326-34.

Ramsey, J.B. 1970. "The Marginal Efficiency of Capital, the Internal Rate of Return, and Net Present Value: An Analysis of Investment Criteria." *Journal of Political Economy* 78 (September–October): 1017-27.

Ramsey, R. 1974. "The Social Return on Selected Programs at the University of Kentucky." Ph.D. dissertation, University of Kentucky.

Rasmussen, R.L. 1976. "The Organization and Management of Schools under a System of Parent Choice." Report No. ED-125121. Eugene, Ore.: ERIC.

Rasmussen, R.L.; Abramowitz, S.; and Levinson, E. 1977. *Organization, Management and Incentives in the Alum Rock Schools.* Report No. WN-9244-NIE. Santa Monica, Calif.: Rand Corporation, May.

Rawlins, V.L. 1974. "Discrimination, Achievement and Payoffs of a College Degree: A Comment." *Journal of Human Resources* 9 (Summer): 415-20.

Rawlins, V.L., and Ulman, L. 1974. "The Utilization of College-Trained Manpower in the U.S." In M.M. Gordon (1974: 195-235).

Raymond, R.D. 1968. Determinants of the Quality of Primary and Secondary Public Education in West Virginia." *Journal of Human Resources* 3 (Fall): 450-70.

Raymond, R.D., and Sesnowitz, M.L. 1975. "The Returns to Investments in Higher Education: Some New Evidence." *Journal of Human Resources* 10 (Spring): 139-54.

———. 1976a. "On the Repayment Burden of Income-Contingent Student Loans." *Public Policy* 24 (Summer): 423-36.

———. 1976b. "Comment on Racial and Ethnic Differences in Returns on Educational Investments in California and Texas." *Economic Inquiry* 14 (December): 604-609.

Razin, A. 1972. "Optimum Investment in Human Capital." *Review of Economic Studies* 34: 455-60.

———. 1976. "Lifetime Uncertainty, Human Capital and Physical Capital." *Economic Inquiry* 14 (September): 439-44.

———. 1977. "Economic Growth and Education: New Evidence." *Economic Development and Cultural Change* 25 (January): 317-24.

Reagan, B., and Maynard, B. 1974. "Sex Discrimination in Universities: An Approach Through Internal Labor Market Analysis." *AAUP Bulletin* 60 (Spring): 11-21.

Reder, M.W. 1967. "Gary Becker's Human Capital: A Review Article." *Journal of Human Resources* 2 (Winter): 97-104.

Redfern, P. 1967. *Input-Output Analysis and Its Application to Education and Manpower Planning.* CAS Occasional Paper, No. 5. London: Her Majesty's Stationery Office.

Reed, R.H., and Miller, H.P. 1970. "Some Determinants of the Variation in Earnings for College Men." *Journal of Human Resources* 5 (Spring): 177-90.

Rees, A. 1968. "Spatial Wage Differentials in a Large City Labor Market." In Industrial Relations Research Association, *Proceedings of the Twenty-first Annual Meeting,* pp. 1-11. Madison: IRRA, 1968.

———. 1974. "Low-Wage Workers in Metropolitan Labor Markets." In *The Future of the Metropolis: People, Jobs, and Income,* ed. E. Ginzberg pp. 131-43. Salt Lake City: Olympus Press, 1974.

Rehmus, C.M., and Wilner, E. 1968. *The Economic Results of Teacher Bargaining: Michigan's First Two Years.* Research Paper in Industrial Relations in Human Resources. Ann Arbor and Detroit: Institute of Labor and Industrial Relations, University of Michigan and Wayne State University.

Reich, M.; Gordon, D.M.; and Edwards, R.C. 1973. "Dual Labor Markets: A Theory of Labor Market Segmentation." *American Economic Review* 50 (May): 359-65.

Reifman, L., ed. 1964. *Financing of Education for Economic Growth.* Paris: OECD.

Reisman, A., and Taft, M.I. 1969. "A Systems Approach to the Evaluation and Budgeting of Educational Programs." *Socio-Economic Planning Science* 3: 245-77.

Renshaw, E.F. 1960a. "A Note on the Expenditure Effect of State Aid to Education." *Journal of Political Economy* 68 (April): 170-74.

———. 1960b. "Estimating the Returns to Education" *Review of Economics and Statistics* (August): 318-24.

———. 1972. "Are We Overestimating the Returns from a College Education?" *School Review* 80 (May).

Research Triangle Institute. 1976. *National Longitudinal Study of the High School Class of 1972: A Capsule Description of First Followup Survey Data.* NCES 76-216. Washington, D.C.: Government Printing Office.

Ribich, T.I. 1968. *Education and Poverty.* Washington, D.C.: The Brookings Institution.

———. 1970. "The Effect of Educational Spending on Poverty Reduction." In Johns et al. (1970: 207-34).

Ribich, T.I., and Murphy, J.L. 1975. "The Economic Returns to Increased Educational Spending." *Journal of Human Resources* 10 (Winter): 56-77.

Richardson, A., and Sharp, L.M. 1974. "The Feasibility of Vouchered Training in WIN: Report on the First Phase of a Study." Report No. ED 105144. Eugene, Ore.: ERIC.

Richardson, A., and Sharp, L.M. 1975. "The Early Experience in Vouchering on-the-Job Training: A Report on Progress in the Portland Voucher Project." Report No. ED 120483. Eugene, Ore.: ERIC.

Riew, J. 1966. "Economies of Scale in High School Operations." *Review of Economics and Statistics* 48 (August): 280-87.

——. 1970a. "Metropolitan Disparity and Fiscal Federalism." In *Financing and Metropolis: Public Policy in Urban Economics*, ed. J.P. Crecine. Vol. 4 of *Urban Affairs Annual Review*, pp. 137-61. Beverly Hills: Sage Publications, 1970.

——. 1970b. "State Aids for Public Schools and Metropolitan Finance." *Land Economics* 46 (August): 297-304.

——. 1971. "The Case for a Federal Tax Credit of Municipal Income Tax." *Public Policy* 19 (Summer): 479-87.

——. 1972. "Scale Economies In Public Schools." *Review of Economics and Statistics* 54 (February): 100.

——. 1973. "Migration and Public Policy." *Journal of Regional Science* 13, no. 1: 65-76.

——. 1974a. "Assigning Collections of a Statewide Uniform Rate Land Tax to Finance Local Education." In Lindholm (1974: 77-89).

——. 1974b. "Finance of Education with a Statewide Land Tax." In *Property Taxation and the Finance of Education* (TRED-7), ed. R.W. Lindholm, pp. 77-89. Madison: University of Wisconsin Press, 1974.

——. 1974c. "Financing Public Schools and the Federal Government." Manuscript. University Park: Department of Economics, The Pennsylvania State University.

Riew, J., and Fox, T.G. 1974. "Public Financing of Public Schools: Some Reflections." Manuscript. University Park: Department of Economics, The Pennsylvania State University.

Riley, J.G. 1976a. "Information, Screening and Human Capital." *American Economic Review* 66 (May): 254-60.

——. 1976b. "Towards A Test of the Educational Hypothesis." Discussion paper, University of California, Los Angeles, Department of Economics, January.

Ritzen, J.M.M. 1977. *Education, Economic Growth and Income Distribution.* Amsterdam: North-Holland Publishing Company.

Ritzen, J.M.M., and Balderston, J.B. 1975. *Methodology for Planning Technical Education—With a Case Study of Polytechnics in Bangladesh.* New York: Praeger Publishers.

Rivlin, A.M. 1962. "Research in the Economics of Higher Education: Progress and Problems." In Mushkin (1962b: 357-83).

——. 1975. "Income Distribution—Can Economists Help?" *American Economic Review* 65 (May): 1-15.

Rivlin, A.M., and Weiss, J.H. 1969. "Social Goals and Federal Support of Higher Education—The Implications of Various Strategies." In Joint Economic Committee (1969: 543-55).

Rizzuto, R.J. 1977. "The Economic Returns to the Quality of Schooling." Paper presented to the 1977 Western Economic Association Conference.

Robbins, L., Sir. Chairman. Committee on Higher Education. 1963. *Higher Education.* London: Her Majesty's Stationery Office.

Roberts, D.B. 1975. "Incidence of State and Local Taxes in Michigan." Ph.D. dissertation, Michigan State University.

Robinson, A.J. 1967. "The Economic Implications of Increased University Enrollments in Canada." *International Journal of Educational Sciences* 2: 51-60.

———. 1971. "Government Subsidy to Higher Education: The Benefits, Costs, and Non-Economic Value of the Policy." *The American Journal of Economics and Sociology* 30 (July): 259-74.

Robinson, E.A.G., and Vaizey, J.E., eds. 1966. *The Economics of Education.* New York: St. Martin's Press.

Robinson, H.F. 1970. "Human Resources: Discussion." *American Journal of Agricultural Economics* 52 (December): 733.

Robinson, J. 1972. "The Second Crisis of Economic Theory." *American Economic Review* 62 (May): 1-9.

Robinson, J.B. 1974. "Little Room Left to Maneuver." *Journal of Law and Education* 3 (January): 123-28.

Rogers, D.C. 1969. "Private Rates of Return to Education in the U.S.: A Case Study." *Yale Economic Essays* 9 (Spring): 89-134.

Rogers, D.C., and Ruchlin, H.S. 1971. *Economics and Education: Principles and Applications.* New York: The Free Press.

Rosen, S. 1972. Learning and Experience in the Labor Market." *Journal of Human Resources* 7 (Summer): 326-42.

———. 1974. Review of "Theories of Poverty and Unemployment" by David M. Gordon. *Journal of Political Economy* 82 (March–April): 437-39.

———. 1975. "Measuring the Obsolescence of Knowledge." In Juster (1975: 199-232).

———. 1976. "A Theory of Life Earnings." *Journal of Political Economy* 84 (Supplement: August): S45-67.

Rosenberg, B., with editorial assistance by P.E. Vincent. 1977. *Retrenchment in Education: The Outlook for Women and Minorities.* Report No. F76-9. Denver: Education Commission of the States, May.

Rosenberg, S. 1975. "The Dual Labor Market: Its Existence and Consequences." Ph.D. dissertation, University of California, Berkeley.

Rosenzweig, M.R. 1976a. "The Demand of Farm Families for the Quantity and Quality of Schooling for Their Children in the United States." *American Journal of Agricultural Economics* 58 (December): 842-47.

———. 1976b. "Nonlinear Earnings Functions, Age, and Experience: A Nondogmatic Reply and Some Additional Evidence." *Journal of Human Resources* 11 (Winter): 23-27.

———. 1977. "Farm-Family Schooling Decisions: Determinants of the Quantity and Quality of Education in Agricultural Populations." *Journal of Human Resources* 12 (Winter): 71-91.

Rosenzweig, M.R., and Morgan, J. 1976. "Wage Discrimination: A Comment." *Journal of Human Resources* 11 (Winter): 3-7.

Ross, M.H. 1975. "Student Choice of Undergraduate Major Field of Study and Private Internal Rates of Return: Comment." *Industrial and Labor Relations Review* 28 (January): 285-86.

Rossman, J.S., and Kirk, B. 1968. "Factors Related to Persistence and Withdrawal Among University Students." *Journal of Counselling Psychology* 76 (May–June): 327-47.

Rossmiller, R.A., and Geske, T.G. 1976. "Toward More Effective Use of School Resources." *Journal of Education Finance* 1 (Spring): 484-502.

———. 1977. "Economic Analysis of Education: A Conceptual Framework." Theoretical Paper No. 68. Madison: Wisconsin Research and Development Center for Cognitive Learning, University of Wisconsin, October.

Rowley, C.K. 1969. "The Political Economy of British Education." *Scottish Journal of Political Economy* 16 (June): 152-76.

Rubin, I.J. 1975. "Some Income Distribution Effects of Higher Education: The Case of New Jersey." Ph.D. dissertation, Duke University.

Rubinfeld, D.L. 1975. "The Determination of Equalized Valuation: A Massachusetts Case Study." *Public Finance Quarterly* 3 (April): 153-61.

———. 1977. "Voting in a Local School Election: A Micro Analysis." *Review of Economics and Statistics* 59 (February): 30-42.

Rude, R. 1954. "Assets of Private Nonprofit Institutions in the United States." Manuscript, New York: National Bureau of Economic Research, April. Cited in Schultz (1960, Table 3).

Ruml, B., and Tickton, S. 1955. *Teaching Salaries Then and Now.* New York: The Fund for the Advancement of Education.

Russell, N.F. 1971. *Pupil, School, and Community Conditions: Definition and Measurement.* Harrisburg: Pennsylvania Department of Education.

Rutledge, V.B., and Stafford, J.H. 1977. "Unit Cost Funding for University Systems." *Journal of Education Finance* 2 (Winter): 324-34.

Ryder, H.E.; Stafford, F.P.; and Stephan, P.E. 1976. Labor, Leisure and Training over the Life Cycle." *International Economic Review* 17 (October): 651-74.

S

Sabulao, C.M., and Hickrod, G.A. 1971. "Optimum Size of School District Relative to Selected Costs." *Journal of Educational Administration* 9 (October): 178-91.

Sacks, S. 1972. *City School, Suburban School: A History of Conflict.* Syracuse, N.Y.: Syracuse University Press.

Sacks, S., and Harris, R. 1964. "The Determinants of State and Local Government Expenditures and Intergovernmental Flows of Funds." *National Tax Journal* 17 (March): 75-85.

Sage, D.D., and Guarino, R. 1974. "Unintended Consequences: A Law Which Purports to Aid Handicapped Children." *Phi Delta Kappan* 55 (April): 533-35.

Samuelson, P.A. 1961. *Economics: An Introductory Analysis.* New York: McGraw-Hill.

———. 1976. "Economics of Forestry in an Evolving Society." *Economic Inquiry* 14 (December): 466-92.

Sandmo, A. 1972. "Discount Rates for Public Investment Under Uncertainty." *International Economic Review* 13 (June): 287-302.

Sanyal, B.C., and Yacoub, E.A. 1975. *Higher Education and Employment in the Sudan.* Paris: International Institute for Educational Planning.

Schaafsma, J. 1976. "The Consumption and Investment Aspects of the Demand for Education." *Journal of Human Resources* 11 (Spring): 233-42.

Schaffer, W.A. 1970-1971. "Education In Regional Economics." *Review of Regional Studies* 1 (Winter): 7-16.

Scheffler, R.M. 1974. "The Market for Paraprofessionals: The Physician Assistant." *Quarterly Review of Economics and Business* 14 (Autumn): 47-60.

———. 1975. "Physician Assistants: Is There a Return to Training?" *Industrial Relations* 14 (February): 78–89.

Schiefelbein, E. 1975. "An Approach to Introducing Quality in Educational Models." In Correa (1975a: 148–68).

Schiefelbein, E., and Davis, R.G. 1974. *Development of Educational Planning Models and Applications in the Chilean School Reform.* Lexington, Mass.: Heath Lexington Books.

Schimmels, C. 1974. "New Cloth for Old Tunics." *Journal of Thought* 9 (July): 191–94.

School Finance Study Unit. 1973. "New School Finance Laws in Maine and Montana." Washington, D.C.: Department of Health, Education and Welfare, August 23. Mimeographed.

Schultz, T.W. 1960. "Capital Formation by Education." *Journal of Political Economy* 68 (December): 571–83.

———. 1961a. "Investment in Human Capital." *American Economic Review* 51 (March): 1–17.

———. 1961b. "Education and Economic Growth." In *Social Forces Influencing American Education*, ed. N.B. Henry, pp. 46–88. Chicago: University of Chicago Press, 1961. Abridged version reprinted in M.J. Bowman (1968): 277–89, 298–312.

———. 1962. "Reflections on Investment in Man." *Journal of Political Economy* 70 (Supplement: October): 1–8.

———. 1963. *The Economic Value of Education.* New York: Columbia University Press.

———. 1967. "The Rate of Return in Allocating Investment Resources to Education." *Journal of Human Resources* 2 (Summer): 293–309.

———. 1968. "Resources for Higher Education: An Economist's View." *Journal of Political Economy* (May–June): 327–47.

———. 1971. *Investment in Human Capital.* New York: The Free Press.

———. 1972a. *Human Resources.* New York: Columbia University Press (for National Bureau of Economic Research).

———. 1972b. "Optimal Investment in College Instruction: Equity and Efficiency." *Journal of Political Economy* 80 (May–June, pt. II): S2–30.

———. ed. 1973. *New Economic Approaches to Fertility.* Chicago: University of Chicago Press. Also published as a Supplement to the *Journal of Political Economy* 81 (March–April, pt. II).

Schwartz, A. 1976. "Migration, Age and Education." *Journal of Political Economy* 84 (August): 701–19.

Schwartzbaum, A.M., and Cross, M. 1970. "Secondary School Environment and Development; The Case of Trinidad and Tobago." *Social and Economic Studies* 19 (September): 368–88.

Schweitzer, S.O. 1971. "Occupational Choice, High School Graduation, and Investment in Human Capital." *Journal of Human Resources* 6 (Summer): 321–32.

Scitovsky, T. 1951. *Welfare and Competition.* Homewood, Ill.: Richard D. Irwin.

Scoville, J.G. 1966. "Education and Training Requirements for Occupations." *Review of Economics and Statistics* 48 (November): 387–94.

Scully, G.W. 1969. "Human Capital and Productivity in U.S. Manufacturing." *Western Economic Journal* 7: 334–40.

Seagraves, J.A. 1970. "More on the Social Rate of Discount." *Quarterly Journal of Economics* 84 (August): 430–50.

Sears, D.W. 1975. "The Recreation Voucher System: A Proposal." *Journal of Leisure Research* 7: 141-45.

Seeborg, M.C. 1976a. "Student Choice of Major and Its Labor Market Consequences." Ph.D. dissertation, University of Utah.

———. 1976b. "Student Choice of Major: A Theoretical Appraisal." *Intermountain Economic Review* 7 (Fall): 26-40.

Segal, D. 1969. "'Equity' Versus 'Efficiency' in Higher Education." In Joint Economic Committee (1969: 135-44).

Selby-Smith, C. 1969. "Benefits to British Employers from Post-Secondary Education." *Journal of the Royal Statistical Society* 132: 408-17.

———. 1970. "Costs and Benefits in Further Education: Some Evidence from a Pilot Study." *Economic Journal* 80 (September): 583-601.

———. 1975. "Rates of Return to Post-Secondary Education in Australia." *Economic Record* 51 (December): 455-85.

Selden, D. 1975. "Education Vouchers: A Critic Changes his Mind." *Nations Schools and Colleges* 2 (June): 44-46.

Seligman, B.B. 1966. "Introduction." In *Poverty as a Public Issue*, ed. Ben B. Seligman. New York: The Free Press, 1966.

Selowsky, M. 1969. "On the Measurement of Education's Contribution to Growth." *Quarterly Journal of Economics* 83 (August): 449-63.

———. 1976. "A Note on Preschool-Age Investment in Human Capital in Developing Countries." *Economic Development and Cultural Change* 24 (July): 707-20.

Sen, A.K. 1964. "Comments on the Paper by Messrs. Tinbergen and Bos." In OECD (1964a: 188-97).

———. 1966a. "Economic Approaches to Education and Manpower Planning." *Indian Economic Review* 1: 11-21. Reprinted in Blaug (1969: 67-75).

———. 1966b. "Education, Vintage, and Learning by Doing." *Journal of Human Resources* 1 (Fall): 3-21.

———. 1977. "Social Choice Theory: A Re-Examination." *Econometrica* 45 (January): 53-89.

Sengupta, J.K. 1975. "Cost and Production Functions in the University Education System: An Econometric Analysis." In Correa (1975a: 258-75).

Sengupta, J.K., and Fox, K.A. 1969. *Economic Analysis and Operations Research: Optimization Techniques in Quantitative Economic Models.* Amsterdam: North Holland Publishing Company.

———. 1970. "A Computable Approach to Optimal Growth of an Academic Department." *Zeitschript Für Die Gesamte Statswissenschaft* 126 (January): 97-125.

Senior, N.W. 1939. *An Outline of the Science of Political Economy.* New York: Farrar and Rinehart.

Senna, J. 1975. "Schooling, Job Experience, and Earnings in Brazil." Ph.D. dissertation, Johns Hopkins Unniversity.

Servelle, P. 1975. "Effects of Pricing Policies on Enrollment Demand and the Distribution of Enrollment Between the Private and Public Sectors of Higher Education." Ph.D. Dissertation, Claremont College.

Sewell, D.O. 1967. "A Critique of Cost-Benefit Analysis of Training." *Monthly Labor Review* 29 (September).

Sewell, D. 1972. "Educational Planning Models and The Relationship between Education and Occupation." In Ostry (1972: 45-74).

Sewell, W.H. 1971. "Inequality of Opportunity for Higher Education." *American Sociological Review* 36 (October): 793-809.

Sewell, W.H.; Haller, A.O.; and Ohlendorf, G.W. 1970. "The Educational and Early Occupational Status Attainment Process: Replication and Revision." *American Sociological Review* 35 (December): 1014-27.

Sewell, W.H.; Haller, A.O.; and Portes, A. 1969. "The Educational and Early Occupational Attainment Process." *American Sociological Review* 34 (February): 82-92.

Sewell, W.H., and Hauser, R.M. 1972. "Causes and Consequences of Higher Education: Models of the Status Attainment Process." *American Journal of Agricultural Economics* 54 (December): 851-61.

———. 1975. *Education, Occupations and Earnings: Achievement in the Early Careers.* New York: Academic Press.

———. 1976. "Recent Developments In the Wisconsin Study of Social and Psychological Factors in Socioeconomic Achievement." Working Paper 76-11, Center for Demography and Ecology, University of Wisconsin, Madison.

Sewell, W.H.; Hauser, R.M.; and Featherman, D.L., eds. 1976. *Schooling and Achievement in American Society.* New York: Academic Press.

Sewell, W.H., and Shah, V.P. 1967. "Socioeconomic Status, Intelligence, and the Attainment of Higher Education." *Sociology of Education* 40 (Winter): 1-23.

———. 1968. "Social Class, Parental Encouragement, and Educational Aspirations." *American Journal of Sociology* 73 (March): 559-72.

Shaffer, H.G. 1961. "Investment in Human Capital: Comment." *American Economic Review* (September): 1026-35.

Shannon, T.A. 1973. "Rodriguez: A Dream Shattered or a Call for Finance Reform?" *Phi Delta Kappan* 54 (May): 587-88, 640-41.

Shapiro, S. 1962. "Some Socioeconomic Determinants of Expenditures for Education: Southern and other States Compared." *Comparative Education Review* 6 (October): 160-66.

Sharkansky, I. 1967. "Some More Thoughts about the Determinants of Government Expenditure." *National Tax Journal* 20 (June): 171-79.

———. 1970. "Benefits and Costs of Higher Education and Income Redistribution: A Comment." *Journal of Human Resources* 5 (Spring): 230-36.

Sharma, D., and Ram, R. 1974. "Suggestions for Treatment of Human Capital in National Accounts—with Illustrations from Indian Data." *Review of Income and Health* 20 (December): 501-41.

Sharp, L.M. 1966. "Graduate Study and Its Relation to Careers: The Experience of a Recent Cohort of College Graduates." *Journal of Human Resources* (Fall): 41-58.

Shaycoft, M.F. 1967. *The High School Years: Growth in Cognitive Skills.* Pittsburgh, Pa.: American Institute for Research and School of Education, University of Pittsburgh.

Shechter, Z. 1976. "A Graduated Tuition in Higher Education Faculties." *Ma'ariv*, September 16 (published in Israel, in Hebrew).

Sheehan, J. 1973. *The Economics of Education.* London: George Allen and Unwin.

Shell, K. 1970. "Notes on the Educational Opportunity Bank." *National Tax Journal* 23 (June): 214-20.

Shell, K., et al. 1968. "The Educational Opportunity Bank: An Economic Analysis of a Contingent Repayment Loan Program for Higher Education." *National Tax Journal* 21 (March): 2-45.

Sherman, J.D., et al. 1977. *Underfunding of Majority-Black School Districts in South Carolina.* Washington, D.C.: School Finance Project, Lawyers' Committee for Civil Rights Under Law.

Sheshinski, E. 1968. "On the Individual's Lifetime Allocation Between Education and Work." *Metroeconomica* 20 (January): 42–49.

Shipunov, V. 1973. "Effectiveness of Vocational Technical Training of Workers." *Problems of Economics* 16 (August): 82–94.

Shryock, H.S., Jr., and Nam, C.B. 1965. "Education Selectivity of Inter-regional Migration." *Social Forces* 43 (March): 229–310.

Shokla, S. 1967. "Educational Techniques and Educational Planning." *International Journal of Educational Sciences* 2: 13–24.

Siegfried, J.J. 1971. "Rate of Return to the Ph.D. in Economics." *Industrial and Labor Relations Review* 24 (April): 420–31.

———. 1972. "The Publishing of Economic Papers and Its Impact on Graduate Faculty Ratings, 1960–1969." *Journal of Economic Literature* 10 (March): 31–49.

———. 1975. "Rate of Return to the Ph.D. in Economics: Reply." *Industrial and Labor Relations Review* 28 (January): 291–92.

Siegfried, J.J., and Scott, C.E. 1977. "The Financial Returns to Law School Faculty." Paper presented to the 1977 Conference of the Western Economic Association.

Siegfried, J.J., and White, K. 1973. "Financial Rewards to Research and Teaching: A Case Study of Academic Economists." *American Economic Review* 63 (May): 309–15.

Simmons, J. 1975. "How Effective is Schooling in Promoting Learning? A Review of the Literature." Staff Working Paper No. 200. Washington, D.C.: International Bank for Reconstruction and Development.

———. 1976. "Retention of Cognitive Skills Acquired in Primary School." *Comparative Education Review* 20 (February): 79–93.

Simms, C. 1975. "A Decision Model for Intradistrict Allocation of Educational Resources." Ph.D. dissertation, Stanford University.

Simon, H. 1957a. *Administrative Behavior.* 2nd ed. New York, Macmillan.

———. 1957b. *Models of Men: Social & Rational.* New York: John Wiley and Sons.

Simon, K.A., and Grant, W.V. 1972. *Digest of Educational Statistics.* 1971 ed. Washington, D.C.: Government Printing Office.

Simon, K.A., and Frankel, M.M. 1976. *Projections of Educational Statistics to 1984–85.* Washington, D.C.: Government Printing Office.

Sims, E.C., Jr., and Pinches, G.E. 1973. "Factors Related to the Performance of College Endowment Funds." *Journal of Economics and Business* 25 (Spring-Summer): 198–205.

Singer, N., and Feldman, P. 1969. "Criteria for Public Investment in Higher Education." In Joint Economic Committee (1969: 124–34).

Sinha, B.K.; Gupta, S.K.; and Sisson, R.L. 1969. "Toward Aggregate Models of Educational Systems." *Socio-Economic Planning Science* 3: 25–36.

Sirageldin, I.A. 1969. *Non-Market Components of National Income.* Ann Arbor: Survey Research Center, Institute for Social Research, The University of Michigan.

———. ed. 1978. *Research in Human Capital and Development.* Vol. 1. Greenwich, Conn.: JAI Press.

Sjaastad, L.A. 1962. "The Costs and Returns of Human Migration." *Journal of Political Economy* 70 (October, pt. 2): 80–93.

Skloot, F. 1977. "School Finance Reform in a Time of Fiscal Stringency: The Illinois Situation." *Journal of Education Finance* 2 (Spring): 533–42.

Skolnik, A.M., and Dales, S.R. 1974. "Social Welfare Expenditures, 1972–73." *Social Security Bulletin* 37 (January): 3–18.

Sloan, F.A. 1970. "Lifetime Earnings and Physicians' Choice of Specialty." *Industrial and Labor Relations Review* 24 (October): 47–56.

——. 1976. "Real Returns to Medical Education: A Comment." *Journal of Human Resources* 11 (Winter): 118–26.

Smith, A. 1952. *The Wealth of Nations.* Chicago: Encyclopedia Britannica.

Smith, J.P. 1975. "On the Labor-Supply Effects of Age-Related Income Maintenance Programs." *Journal of Human Resources* 10 (Winter): 25–43.

Smith, J.P., and Welch, F. 1977. "Black-White Male Wage Ratios: 1960–1970." *American Economic Review* 67 (June): 323–38.

Smith, M.S. 1968. "Equality of Educational Opportunity: Comments on Bowles and Levin." *Journal of Human Resources* 3 (Summer): 384–89.

Smith, R.D. 1969. "Integrated Information Systems for Higher Education: A Heuristic Approach." *International Journal of Educational Sciences* 3: 69–82.

Smith, S.P. 1976. "Government Wage Differentials by Sex." *Journal of Human Resources* 11 (Spring): 185–99.

——. 1977. *Equal Pay in the Public Sector: Fact or Fantasy.* Princeton, N.J.: Department of Economics, Industrial Relations Section, Princeton University.

Smith, W.H. 1975. "An Analysis of State Aid to Local School Districts for Pupil Transportation in Kansas with Proposals for Modification." Ph.D. dissertation, Kansas State University.

Smyth, D.J. 1972. "Tertiary Education, Investment, and Growth." Claremont Economic Papers, No. 46, The Claremont College, November.

Snodgrass, M.M. 1974. "Off-Campus Work and Study Experience Programs for Undergraduate Students in Agricultural Economics and Agricultural Business Management." *American Journal of Agricultural Economics* 56 (December): 1153–62.

Solmon, L.C. 1970a. "Opportunity Costs and Models of Schooling in the Nineteenth Century." *Southern Economic Journal* 37 (July): 66–83.

——. 1970b. "A Note on Equality of Educational Opportunity," *American Economic Review* 60 (September): 768–71.

——. 1971. "Capital Formation by Expenditures on Education, 1960." *Journal of Political Economy* 79 (November–December): 1412–17.

——. 1973a. "Schooling and Subsequent Success." In Solmon and Taubman (1973: 13–34).

——. 1973b. "The Definition and Impact of College Quality." In Solmon and Taubman (1973: 77–102).

——. 1973c. "Prerequisites for Further Research on the Effects of Higher Education." In Solmon and Taubman (1973: 403–10).

——. 1975. "The Relation Between Schooling and Savings Behavior: An Example of the Indirect Effects of Education." In Juster (1975: 253–94).

Solmon, L.C., and Taubman, P.J. eds. 1973. *Does College Matter?* New York: Academic Press.

Solow, R.M. 1959. "Investment and Economic Growth: Some Comments." *Productivity Measurement Review* (November): 62–68. Reprinted in Kiker (1971: 101–108).

——. 1962. "Technical Progress, Capital Formation, and Economic Growth."

American Economic Review 52 (Proceedings: May): 76-92. Reprinted in Wykstra (1971b: 81-92).

"Some Trends in State Revenue Appropriations for Higher Education." 1976. *The Research Reporter* 10, no. 1: 8. Berkeley: Center for Research and Development in Higher Education, University of California.

Somers, G.G. 1968. "The Response of Vocational Education to Labor Market Changes." *Journal of Human Resources* 3 (Supplement): 32-58.

Somers, G.G., and Stromsdorfer, E.W. 1970. *A Cost-Effectiveness Study of the In-School and Summer Neighborhood Youth Corps.* Madison, Wisc.: Industrial Relations Research Institute.

——. 1972. "A Cost-Effectiveness Analysis of In-School and Summer Neighborhood Youth Corps: A Nationwide Analysis. *Journal of Human Resources* 7 (Fall): 446-59.

South Carolina Commission on Higher Education. 1978. *Annual Report.* Columbia, S.C.: The Commission.

Southwick, L. Jr. 1967. "The University as a Firm." *Carnegie Review* (October): 3-8, 25-29.

——. 1969. "Cost Trends in Land Grant Colleges and Universities." *Applied Economics* 1 (August): 167-82.

Southwick, L., Jr., and Zionts, S. 1969. "A Control Theory Model of an Education Decision: Education, The Negative Income Tax, and Public Policy." Paper presented at the 36th national meeting of the Operations Research Society of America, Miami Beach, November.

Sparkman, W.E. 1977. "The Relationship Between Socioeconomic Variables and State Effort for Education." *Journal of Education Finance* 2 (Winter): 335-55.

Spence, D. 1973. "Job Market Signaling. *Quarterly Journal of Economics* 87 (August): 355-74.

Spengler, J.J. 1977. "Adam Smith on Human Capital." *American Economic Review* 67 (February): 32-36.

Spiegleman, R.G. 1968. "A Benefit/Cost Model to Evaluate Educational Programs." *Socio-Economic Planning Sciences* 1:443-60.

Spies, R.R. 1973. *The Future of Private Colleges.* Princeton: Industrial Relations Section, Princeton University.

Spillane, R.R. 1973. "Fostering Consumerism in Education: New Rochelle Examines the Voucher Plan." *Phi Delta Kappan* 55 (November): 180-82.

Srivastava, R.C. 1976. "Planning for Post-Graduate Employment." *Economic Affairs* 21 (May): 193-95.

Staaf, R.J., and Tullock, G. 1973. "Education and Equality." *Annals of the American Academy of Political and Social Science* 409 (September): 125-34.

Stafford, F.P. 1969. "Student Family Size in Relation to Current and Expected Income." *Journal of Political Economy* 77 (July-August): 471-77.

Stager, D.A.A. 1972a. "Allocation of Resources in Canadian Education." In Ostry (1972: 199-238).

——. 1972b. "Economics of Continuing Education in the Universities." In Ostry (1972: 265-90).

Standing, G. 1976. "Education and Female Participation in the Labour Force." *International Labour Review* 114 (November-December): 281-97.

Stapleton, D.C. 1976. "External Benefits of Education: An Assessment of the Effect of Education on Political Participation." Paper presented to the Annual

North American Meetings of the Econometric Society, September. Revised version will appear in *Sociological Methodology*, 1978.

Starler, N.H., and Thomas, R.W. 1973. "Intergovernmental Education Grants and the Efficiency of Resource Allocation in School Districts." *Applied Economics* 5: 181-92.

Stauss, J.H. 1969. "Endowment as a Source of Increased Revenue." In Joint Economic Committee (1969: 507-17).

Stein, H. 1977. "National Planning: Loch Ness Monster." *MBA [Master in Business Administration]* 11 (February): 56, 61.

Steinberg, B.E. 1976. "Social Class Background as a Determinant of Labor Earnings." Ph.D. dissertation, University of Michigan.

Steiner, P.O., et al. 1971. "At the Brink: Report on the Economic Status of the Profession, 1970-71." *AAUP Bulletin* 57 (June): 223-85.

———. 1973. "Surviving the Seventies: The Economic Status of the Profession, 1972-73." *AAUP Bulletin* 59 (June): 188-258.

Stephan, P.E. 1976. "Human Capital Production: Life-Cycle Production with Different Learning Technologies." *Economic Inquiry* 14 (December): 539-57.

Stephens, John B. 1974. "Information and Efficiency in Cost-Benefit Studies: A Suggested Procedure." *Scottish Journal of Political Economy* 21 (February): 55-66.

Stephens, K. 1972. "The Role of Education in Economic Growth: A Cobb-Douglas Analysis." *Marquette Business Review* 16 (Winter): 199-206.

Stern, D. 1973. "Effects of Alternative State Aid Formulas on the Distribution of Public School Expenditures in Massachusetts." *Review of Economics and Statistics* 55 (February): 91-97.

Stewart, G. 1973. *A Measure of Local Effort*. Harrisburg: Bureau of Information Systems, Pennsylvania Department of Education.

Stigler, G.J. 1950. *Employment and Compensation in Education*. New York: National Bureau of Economic Research.

———. 1973. "Absurd Culprits: Professors Supressing Freedom?" *Compact* 7 (November-December): 15-17.

Stiglitz, J.E. 1973. "Education and Inequality." *Annals of the American Academy of Political and Social Science* 409 (September): 135-45.

———. 1975. "The Theory of 'Screening,' Education, and the Distribution of Income." *American Economic Review* 65 (June): 283-300.

Stoikov, V. 1977. "On Some Models of the Educational Decision." *Kyklos* 30: 74-87.

Stollen, J.D., and Gnuschke, J.E. 1977. "Reflections on Alternative Rating Systems for University Economics Departments." *Economic Inquiry* 15 (April): 277-82.

Stone, R. 1965. "A Model of the Educational System." *Minerva* 3 (Winter): 172-86.

———. 1966. *Mathematics in the Social Sciences and Other Essays*. Cambridge, Mass.: The MIT Press.

Strayer, G.D., and Haig, R.M. 1923. *The Financing of Education in the State of New York*. New York: The Macmillan Co.

Streeten, P. 1969. "Economic Development and Education." In Hüfner and Naumann (1969: 183-98).

Strober, M.H., and Quester, A.O. 1977. "The Earnings and Promotion of Women Faculty: Comment." *American Economic Review* 67 (March): 207-13.

Strom, R.J. 1948. *A Study of Disabled Veterans in Colleges and Universities*. Washington, D.C.: American Council on Education.

Stromsdorfer, E.W.; Hu, T-w.; and Lee, M.L. 1968. "Theoretical and Empirical Problems in the Analysis of the Economic Costs of Vocational Education. *1968 Social Statistics Section Proceedings of the American Statistical Association,* pp. 144-152.

Stroup, R.H., and Hargrove, M.B. 1969. "Earnings and Education in Rural South Vietnam." *Journal of Human Resources* 4 (Spring): 215-25.

Stubblebine, W.C., and Teeples, R.K. 1964. "California and the Finance of Education: Alternatives in the Wake of Serrano v. Priest." In Lindholm (1974: 163-78).

Sugarman, S.D. 1974. "Family Choice: The Next Step in the Quest for Equal Educational Opportunity?" *Law and Contemporary Problems* 38 (Winter-Spring): 513-65.

Sullivan, D.J. 1974. *Public Aid to Nonpublic Schools.* Lexington, Mass.: Heath Lexington Books.

Sullivan, G.E. 1971. "Modeling the University Budget." *Management Accounting* 53 (November): 47-51.

Summers, A.A. 1973. "Equity in School Financing: The Courts Move in." *Business Review* (Federal Reserve Bank of Philadelphia), March, pp. 3-13.

Summers, A.A., and Wolfe, B.L. 1975a. "Which School Resources Help Learning? Efficiency and Equity in Philadelphia Public Schools." *Business Review* (Federal Reserve Bank of Philadelphia), February, pp. 4-28.

——. 1975b. "Some School Resources Help Some Students to Learn—But Which? *Tax Review* 36 (September): 37-40.

——. 1976. "Intradistrict Distribution of School Inputs to the Disadvantaged: Evidence for the Courts." *Journal of Human Resources* 11 (Summer): 328-42.

——. 1977a. "Do Schools Make a Difference?" *American Economic Review* 67 (September): 639-53.

——. 1977b. "Reply." *Journal of Human Resources* 12 (Summer): 406-409.

Surridge, O. 1975. "Fever Pitch: Signs of Vouchers Catching on in Kent." *Times Education Supplement,* October 24, p. 10.

Suval, E.M., and Hamilton, C.H. 1965. "Some New Evidence on Educational Selectivity in Migration to and from the South." *Social Forces* 43 (May): 536-47.

Svennilson, I. 1964. "Economic Growth and Technical Progress." In OECD (1964a: 103-32).

Svennilson, I., et al. 1961. "Targets for Education in Europe in 1970." *Policy Conference on Economic Growth and Investment in Education.* Paris: OECD.

Swift, W.J., and Weisbrod, B.A. 1965. "On the Monetary Value of Education's Intergeneration Effects." *Journal of Political Economy* 73 (December): 643-49.

Szekely, M; Stankard, M.; and Sisson, R. 1968. "Design of a Planning Model for an Urban School District." *Socio-Economic Planning Science* 1: 231-42.

T

Tachibanaki, T. 1976. "Quality Change in Labor Input: Japanese Manufacturing." *Review of Economics and Statistics* 58 (August): 293-99.

Talley, W.K. 1974. "The Equivalence of Flat Grants and Foundation Programs in State Education Aid Formulas: A Comment." *Public Finance Quarterly* 2 (October): 493-96.

———. 1976. "The Equilization Equivalence of Flat Grants and Foundation Programs: A Further Comment." *Public Finance Quarterly* 4 (April): 239-44.

Tannen, M.B. 1976. "The Distribution of Family Incomes: A Reexamination." *Southern Economic Journal* 42 (April): 666-74.

Tanner, C.K. 1971. *Design for Educational Planning: A Systemic Approach.* Lexington, Mass.: Heath Lexington Books.

Taubman, P.J. 1972. "Comment." *Journal of Political Economy* 80 (May-June, pt. 2): S104-107.

———. 1973. "Introduction." In Solmon and Taubman (1973: 1-9).

———. 1975. *Sources of Inequality of Earnings.* Amsterdam: North Holland Publishing Company.

———. 1976a. "Earnings, Education, Genetics, and Environment." *Journal of Human Resources* 11 (Fall): 447-61.

———. 1976b. "The Determinants of Earnings: Genetics, Family, and Other Environments: A Study of White Male Twins." *American Economic Review* 66 (December): 858-70.

Taubman, P.J., and Wales, T.J. 1972a. *Education as an Investment and a Screening Device.* New York: National Bureau of Economic Research.

———. 1972b. *Mental Ability and Higher Educational Attainment in the Twentieth Century.* Occasional Paper No. 118. New York: National Bureau of Economic Research.

———. 1973. "Higher Education, Mental Ability, and Screening." *Journal of Political Economy* 81 (January-February): 28-55.

———. 1974. *Higher Education and Earnings.* New York: McGraw-Hill.

Taussig, M.K. 1968. "An Economic Analysis of Vocational Education in the New York City High Schools." *Journal of Human Resources* 3 (Supplement): 59-87.

Teeples, R.K. 1975. "The Meaning of Serrano Criteria for California Public School Finance." Claremont Economic Papers, No. 140, The Claremont Colleges, July.

Thackrey, R.I. 1969. "Youth Endowment?" *New Republic* 160 (June 7): 30-32.

Theil, H. 1967. *Economics and Information Theory.* Amsterdam: North-Holland Publishing Company.

Thias, H., and Carnoy, M. 1972. *A Cost-Benefit Analysis in Education: A Case Study for Kenya.* Baltimore: Johns Hopkins University Press.

Thomas, J.A. 1962. "Efficiency in Education: A Study of the Relationship between Selected Inputs and Mean Test Scores in a Sample of Senior High Schools." Doctoral dissertation, Stanford University.

———. 1967. "Efficiency Criteria in Urban School Systems." Paper presented to the American Educational Research Association. February.

———. 1970. "Full State Funding of Education." *Administrator's Handbook* 18 (May): 1-4.

———. 1971. *The Productive School.* New York: John Wiley and Sons.

———. 1974. "Trends in Public School Finance." *New York University Education Quarterly* 6 (Fall): 2-10. Reprinted in *Educational Economics* 1 (February 1976): 10-19.

Thomas-Hope, E. 1975. "An Approach to the Delimitation of School Districts: The Example of Primary Schools in the Parish of St. Ann, Jamaica." *Social and Economic Studies* 24 (September): 320-40.

Thornton, R.J. 1971. "The Effects of Collective Bargaining on Teachers' Salaries." *Quarterly Review of Economics and Business* 11 (Winter): 37-46.

——. 1975. "Monopsony and Teachers' Salaries: Some Contrary Evidence: Comment." *Industrial and Labor Relations Review* 28 (July): 574-75.

Thorp, W.L. 1962. "101 Questions for Investigation." In Mushkin (1962b: 345-56).

Thurow, L.C. 1970. *Investment in Human Capital.* Belmont, Calif.: Wadsworth Publishing Company.

——. 1972. "Education and Economic Inequality." *The Public Interest* 28 (Summer): 66-81.

——. 1975. *Generating Inquality: Mechanisms of Distribution in the U.S. Economy.* New York: Basic Books.

Tideman, T.N., and Tullock, G. 1976. "A New and Superior Process for Making Social Choices." *Journal of Political Economy* 84 (December): 1145-59.

Tiebout, C.M. 1956. "A Pure Theory of Local Expenditures." *Journal of Political Economy* 64 (October): 416-24.

Tiedt, S. 1971. "Historical Development of Federal Aid Programs." In R.L. Johns, Alexander, and Stollar (1971: 223-50).

Tinbergen, J. 1959. "On the Theory of Trend Movements." In *Selected Papers.* Amsterdam: North Holland Publishing Company.

Tinbergen, J., and Bos, H.C. 1964. "A Planning Model for the Educational Requirements of Economic Development." In OECD (1964: 147-69).

Tobin, J., and Ross, L. 1969a. "A National Youth Endowment." *New Republic* 160 (May 5): 18-21.

——. 1969b. "In Reply." *New Republic* 160 (June 7): 32-33.

Toda, Y. 1976. "Estimation of a Cost Function When the Cost is Not Minimum: The Case of Soviet Manufacturing Industries, 1958-1971." *Review of Economics and Statistics* 58 (August): 259-68.

Tolles, N.A., and Melichar, E. 1968. *Studies of the Structure of Economist's Salaries and Income.* Published as a supplement to the *American Economic Review* 58 (December, pt. 2).

Tolley, G.S., and Olson, E. 1971. "The Interdependence between Income and Education." *Journal of Political Economy* 79 (March-April): 460-80.

Tollison, R.D., and Willett, T.D. 1972. "A Proposal for Marginal Cost Financing of Higher Education." *Public Finance* 27: 375-80.

——. 1973. "The University and the Price System." *Journal of Economics and Business* 25 (Spring-Summer): 191-97.

Tomaske, J.A. 1974. "Private and Social Rates of Return to Education of Academicians: Note." *American Economic Review* 64 (March): 220-24.

Toombs, W. 1972. *Productivity and the Academy: The Current Condition.* Report No. 16. University Park: Center for the Study of Higher Education, The Pennsylvania State University.

Toomey, D. 1968. "Parents' Preferences in Secondary Education: An Australian Case." *International Journal of Educational Science* 2: 141-48.

Traynham, E.C., Jr. 1977. "An Examination of the Role of Merit, Market, and Non-Merit Factors in Determining Faculty Salaries." Paper presented to the Western Economic Association Meeting, June.

Trent, J.W., and Medsker, L.L. 1968. *Beyond High School.* San Francisco: Jossey-Bass.

Tron, E.O., ed. 1975. *Selected Papers in School Finance, 1974.* Washington, D.C.: U.S. Office of Education.

——. ed. 1976. *Public School Finance Programs, 1975-76.* Washington, D.C.: Government Printing Office.

Trotter, G.J. 1976. "The Economic Rationale for Educational Planning." *South African Journal of Economics* 44 (December): 343-77.

Tu, P.N.V. 1969a. "The Classical Economists and Education." *Kyklos* 22: 691-716.

——. 1969b. "Optimal Educational Investment in an Economic Planning Model." *Canadian Journal of Economics* 2: 52-64.

——. 1970. "A Multisectoral Model of Educational and Economic Planning." *Metroeconomica* 22: 207-26.

Tuckman, B.H., and Tuckman, H.P. 1976. "The Structure of Salaries at American Universities." *Journal of Higher Education* 47 (January-February): 51-64.

Tuckman, H.P. 1970. "Determinants of College Student Migration." *Southern Economic Journal* 37 (October): 184-89.

——. 1971. "High School Inputs and their Contribution to School Performance." *Journal of Human Resources* 6 (Fall): 490-509.

Tuckman, H.P., and Ford, W.S. 1972. *The Demand for Higher Education: A Florida Case Study.* Lexington, Mass.: Lexington Books.

Tuckman, H.P.; Gapinski, J.H.; and Hagemann, R.P. 1977. "Faculty Skills and the Reward Structure in Academe: A Market Perspective." *American Economic Review* 67 (September): 692-702.

Tuckman, H.P. and Leahey, J. 1975. "What is an Article Worth?" *Journal of Political Economy* 83 (October): 951-67.

Tullock, G. 1973. "Universities Should Discriminate Against Assistant Proressors." *Journal of Political Economy* 81 (September-October): 1256-57.

Turnbull, P., and Williams, G. 1975. "Supply and Demand in the Labour Market for Teachers: Qualification Differentials in Teachers' Pay." *British Journal of Industrial Relations* 13 (July): 215-22.

Turvey, R. 1963. "Present Value Versus Internal Rate of Return—An Essay in the Theory of the Third Best." *Economic Journal* 73 (March): 93-98.

——. ed. 1968. *Public Enterprise.* Baltimore: Penguin Books.

Tyler, R.W. 1969. "The Changing Structure of American Institutions of Higher Education." In Joint Economic Committee (1969: 305-20).

U

UNESCO. 1968. *Manpower Aspects of Educational Planning.* Paris.

——. 1975. *Statistical Yearbook.* Paris.

UPI. 1977. "Tuition Tax Credits Proposed." *The Columbia Record*, September 26, p. 17-A.

U.S. Bureau of the Census. 1973. *Census of Population:* 1970. Vol. 1—*Characteristics of the Population*, Part 1, United States Summary, Section 2. Washington, D.C.: Government Printing Office.

U.S. Office of Education. 1930. *Land Grant College Survey.* Bulletin No. 9, Vol. I. Washington, D.C.: Office of Education.

——. Various eds. *Statistics of State School Systems.* Washington, D.C.: Government Printing Office.

Uzawa, H. 1965. "Optimal Technical Change in an Aggregative Model of Economic Growth." *International Economic Review* 6 (January): 18-31.

V

Vaizey, J. 1962. *The Economics of Education.* London: Farber and Farber.
———. 1973. *The Economics of Education.* London: MacMillan.
Vaizey, J., and Chesswas, J.D. 1967. *The Costing of Educational Plans.* Paris: International Institute for Educational Planning.
Van Den Haag, E. 1956. *Education as an Industry.* New York: Augustus M. Kelley.
Vanecko, J.J. 1974. "Teachers' Reactions to the First Year of the Alum Rock Voucher Demonstration." Report No. ED105586. Eugene, Ore.: ERIC.
Van Fleet, D.S., and Boardman, G. 1971. "The Relationship Between Revenue Allocation and Educational Need as Reflected by Achievement Test Scores." In R.L. Johns, Alexander, and Stollar (1971: 293-318).
Vanzetti, N.R., and Bessell, J.E. 1974. "Education and the Development of Farming in Two Areas of Zambia." *Journal of Development Studies.* 11 (October): 41-54.
Verdon, W.A. 1974. "Rates of Return to Investment in Education at all Levels in the State of Nebraska." Ph.D. dissertation, University of Nebraska.
Verry, D.W., and Davies, B. 1976. *University Costs and Outputs.* Amsterdam: Elsevier.
Verry, D.W., and Layard, P.R.G. 1975. "Cost Functions for University Teaching and Research." *Economic Journal* 85 (March): 55-74.
Vickrey, W. 1960. "Utility, Strategy, and Social Decision Rules." *Quarterly Journal of Economics* 74 (November): 507-35.
———. 1962. "A Proposal for Student Loans," In Mushkin (1962b: 268-80).
Virgo, J.M. 1977a. "Evolving Professional Unionism." *Atlantic Economic Journal* 5 (March): 1-12.
———. 1977b. "An Empirical Analysis of Collective Bargaining on the University Campus." Paper presented to the 1977 Western Economic Association Conference.
Von Thünen, H. 1968. "Costs of Education as Formation of Productive Capital." In Bowman et al. (1968: 393-94).
von Zur-Muehlen, M. 1972. "The Ph.D. Dilemma in Canada: A Case Study." In Ostry (1972: 75-132).
Voronina, E. 1974. "Effectiveness of Social Expenditures on Education." *Problems of Economics* 16 (April): 77-92.

W

Wachtel, P. 1976. "The Effect of Earnings of School and College Investment Expenditures." *Review of Economics and Statistics* 58 (August): 326-31.
Wachter, M. 1974. "The Primary and Secondary Labor Market Mechanism: A Critique of the Dual Approach." *Brookings Papers on Economic Activity* 3: 637-80.
Wagner, D.P. 1975. "An Econometric Analysis of the Labor Market for School Teachers." Ph.D. dissertation, Vanderbilt University.
Wagner, J.F., and Stollar, D.H. 1971. "Intent and Effect of Title I ESEA in the Financial Equalization of Public Elementary and Secondary Education." In R.L. Johns, Alexander, and Stollar (1971: 319-36).

Wagner, L. 1975. "Television Videotape Systems for Off-Campus Education: A Cost Analysis of SURGE." *Instructional Science* 4 (October): 315–32.

Waldman, E. 1969. "Educational Attainment of Workers." *Monthly Labor Review* 92 (February): 14–22.

Wales, T.J. 1973. "The Effects of College Quality on Earnings: Results from the NBER-Thorndike Data." *Journal of Human Resources* 8 (Summer): 306–17.

Wallace, R.G. 1976. "A Choice Myth." *Times Educational Supplement* (London), May 21, pp. 20–21.

Wallace, R.L. 1976. "Comments on the Impact of Collective Bargaining on Administrative and Faculty Roles in Academe." *Michigan Academician* 9 (Summer): 7–14.

Wallace, T.D., and Ihnen, L.A. 1975. "Full-Time Schooling in Life-Cycle Models of Human Capital Accumulation." *Journal of Political Economy* 83 (February): 137–55.

Walras, L. 1954. *Elements of Pure Economics.* Translated by William Jaffé. Homewood, Ill.: Richard D. Irwin.

Walsh, J. 1973. "PSAC: Last Hurrah From Panel on Youth." *Science* 182 (October): 141–45.

Walsh, J.R. 1935. "Capital Concept Applied to Man." *Quarterly Journal of Economics* 49 (February): 255–85. Reprinted in Bowman et al. (1968: 453–74).

Walsh, T.J. 1974. "An Exploration of the Effects of Sponsored Research on Higher Education." Ph.D. dissertation, University of California, Los Angeles.

Warren, C. 1974. "Educational Vouchers: Panacea of Pandora's Box?" Report No. ED103544. Eugene, Ore.: ERIC.

Warren, J. 1976. "Alum Rock Voucher Project." *Educational Researcher* 5 (March): 13–15.

Wasserman, W. 1963. *Education Price and Quantity Indexes.* Syracuse: Syracuse University Press.

Watson, J.O. 1977. "Estimated Rates of Return to Investment in Public and Proprietary Post-Secondary Vocational Education and the Desirability of Subsidizing Proprietary Institutions." Paper presented to the 1977 Western Economic Association Conference.

Watts, H.W. 1976. "Comment." In Froomkin, Jamison, and Radner (1976: 197–98).

Weathersby, G.B., and Balderston, F.E. 1971. *PPBS in Higher Education Planning and Management.* Berkeley: Office of Analytic Studies, University of California.

Weathersby, G.B., and Nash, D., eds. 1974. *A Context for Policy Research in Financing Postsecondary Education.* Washington, D.C.: National Commission on the Financing of Postsecondary Education, June.

Webb, L.D. 1976. "Cost-Benefit Analysis: An Accountability Asset." *Journal of Education Finance* 2 (Fall): 209–33.

——. 1977. "Savings to Society by Investing in Adult Education." In *Economic and Social Perspectives on Adult Illiteracy* (1977: 52–73).

Webster, W.J. 1976. "Cost and Effect Analysis: An Educational Example." *Educational Economics* 1 (May–June): 10–14.

Webster's New World Dictionary of the American Language. 1962. College ed. Cleveland: The World Publishing Company.

Wegner, E.L., and Sewell, W.H. 1970. "Selection and Content as Factors Affecting the Probability of Graduation from College." *American Journal of Sociology* 75 (January): 665–79.

Weiler, D., et al. 1974. *A Public School Voucher Demonstration: The First Year at Alum Rock.* Report No. R-1495-NIE. Santa Monica, Calif.: Rand Corporation.

Weiner, S.S. 1974. "Implementing the 'Voucher' Demonstration in Alum Rock, or Taking the 'Ouch' out of Vouchers." Report No. ED091804. Eugene, Ore.: ERIC.

Weinstein, R. 1974. "Human Migration: A Survey of Preclassical Literature." *Journal of Political Economy* 82 (March–April): 433–36.

Weintraub, S., ed. 1973. *Income Inequality.* Published as a special issue of *The Annals of the American Academy of Political and Social Science* 409 (September).

Weisbrod, B.A. 1961. "The Valuation of Human Capital." *Journal of Political Economy* 69 (October): 425–36.

———. 1962. "Education and Investment in Human Capital." *Journal of Political Economy* 70 (October, Supplement): 106–23.

———. 1964. *External Benefits of Public Education: An Economic Analysis.* Princeton: Industrial Relations Section, Princeton University.

———. 1965a. "Geographical Spillover Effects and the Allocation of Resources to Education." In Margolis (1965: 192–206).

———. 1965b. "Preventing High School Dropouts." In *Measuring Benefits of Government Investments,* ed. Robert Dorfman, pp. 117–49. Washington, D.C.: The Brookings Institution, 1965.

———. 1966. "Investing in Human Capital." *Journal of Human Resources* 1 (Summer): 5–21.

———. 1968. "Income-Redistribution Effects and Benefit-Cost Analysis of Government Expenditure Programs." In *Problems in Public Expenditure Analysis,* ed. Samuel B. Chase, pp. 177–209. Washington, D.C.: The Brookings Institution, 1968.

———. 1972. "Comment." *Journal of Political Economy* 80 (May–June): S139–41.

Weisbrod, B.A., and Hansen, W.L. 1968. "Measuring Economic Welfare." *American Economic Review* 58 (December): 1315–29.

Weisbrod, B.A., and Karpoff, P. 1968. "Monetary Returns to College Education, Student Ability, and College Quality." *Review of Economics and Statistics* 50 (November): 491–97.

Weischdale, D.E. 1977. "New Jersey: A Case Study in the Politics of Public School Finance." *Journal of Education Finance* 3 (Fall): 259–64.

Weiss, L., and Williamson, J.G. 1972. "Black Education, Earnings, and Interregional Migration: Some New Evidence." *American Economic Review* 62 (June): 372–82.

———. 1975. "Black Education, Earnings, and Interregional Migration: Even Newer Evidence," *American Economic Review* 65 (March): 241–44.

Weiss, R.D. 1970. "The Effect of Education on the Earnings of Blacks and Whites." *Review of Economics and Statistics* 52 (May): 150–59.

Weiss, S.J. 1970. "The Need for Change in State Public School Finance Systems." *New England Economic Review* (January–February): 3–22.

Weiss, S.J., and Driscoll, D. 1972. "Comparative School Finance Data, New England States vs. California." In *Financing Public Schools* (1972: 16–43).

Weiss, Y. 1971a. "Ability and Investment in Schooling: A Theoretical Note." *Journal of Economic Literature* 19 (June): 459–61.

———. 1971b. "Investment in Graduate Education." *American Economic Review* 61 (December): 833–52.

———. 1972a. "The Effect of Education on the Earnings of Blacks and Whites." *Review of Economics and Statistics* 52 (May): 150-59.

———. 1972b. "The Risk Element in Occupational and Educational Choices." *Journal of Political Economy* 80 (November–December): 1203-13.

Welch, F. 1967. "Labor-Market Discrimination: An Interpretation of the Income Differences in the Rural South." *Journal of Political Economy* 75 (June): 225-40. Reprinted in Kiker (1971: 540-62).

———. 1970. "Education in Production." *Journal of Political Economy* 78 (January): 35-59.

———. 1973a. "Education and Racial Discrimination." In *Discrimination in Labor Markets*, ed. O. Ashenfleter and A. Rees. Princeton: Princeton University Press, 1973.

———. 1973b. "Black-White Differences in Returns to Schooling." *American Economic Review* 67 (December): 893-907.

———. 1975. "Human Capital Theory: Education, Discrimination, and Life Cycles." *American Economic Review* 65 (May): 63-73.

Wells, S. 1976. *Instructional Technology in Developing Countries: Decision-Making Processes in Education.* New York: Praeger Publishers.

Welty, G.A. 1971. "Educational Benefit-Cost Analysis and the Problem of Scale." Paper presented at the American Educational Research Association Annual Meeting, February.

Wenning, P. 1975. "Kent May Try Out Voucher System." *Times Education Supplement*, January 17, p. 3.

Wessel, R.H. 1971. "Ability and the Returns on Graduate Education." *Western Economic Journal* 9 (June): 208-10.

———. 1978. "Why Guaranteed Yield Failed in Ohio." *Journal of Education Finance* 3 (Winter): 265-71.

West, E.G. 1964. "Private Versus Public Education: A Classical Economic Dispute." *Journal of Political Economy* 72 (October): 465-75.

———. 1967. "Tom Paine's Voucher Scheme for Public Education." *Southern Economic Journal* 33 (January): 378-82.

———. 1968. *Economics, Education, and the Politician.* London: The Institute of Economic Affairs.

———. 1970a. *Education and the State.* 2nd ed. London: Institute of Economic Affairs.

———. 1970b. "Resource Allocation and Growth in Early Nineteenth-Century British Education." *Economic History Review* 23 (April): 65-95.

———. 1973. "Review of *The Economics of Education*, by E. Cohn." *Journal of Economic Literature* 11 (December): 1416-17.

———. 1974. "Differential Versus Equal Student Subsidies in Post-Secondary Education: A Current Canadian Dispute." *Higher Education* 3: 25-42.

———. 1975a. "Educational Slowdown and Public Intervention in the 19th-Century England: A Study in the Economics of Bureaucracy." *Explorations in Economic History* 12 (January): 61-87.

———. 1975b. *Education and the Industrial Revolution.* New York: Barnes and Noble.

———. 1976a. "An Economic Analysis of the Law and Politics of Non-Public 'Aid'." *Journal of Law and Economics* 19 (April): 70-101.

———. 1976b. "The Radical Economics of Public School Breakdowns: A Critique." *Review of Social Economy* 34 (October): 125-46.

West, E.G., et al. 1976. *Nonpublic School Aid: The Laws, Economics, and Politics of American Education.* Lexington, Mass.: Heath Lexington Books.

West, P.T. 1974. "Wild in the Schools." *Thrust for Education Leadership* 4 (October): 3-7.

White, F.C., and Miller, B.R. 1976. "Implication of Public School Finance Reform with Local Control." *American Journal of Agricultural Economics* 58 (August): 415-24.

White, R.D. 1974. "School Finance Reform: Courts and Legislatures." *Social Science Quarterly* 55 (September): 331-46.

Whitman, R.D. 1977. "Federal Revenue Sharing and Education." *Journal of Education Finance* 3 (Fall): 238-53.

WICHE. 1970. *Outputs of Higher Education: Their Identification, Measurement, and Evaluation.* Boulder: Western Interstate Commission for Higher Education.

———. 1977. *Annual Report, 1976.* Boulder: Western Interstate Commission on Higher Education.

Wilkin, W.H., and Porter, D.O. 1977. *State Aid for Special Education: Who Benefits?* Washington, D.C.: National Foundation for the Improvement of Education.

Wilkinson, B.W. 1966. "Present Values of Lifetime Earnings for Different Occupations." *Journal of Political Economy* 64 (December): 556-72.

Wilkinson, G.L. 1973. "Cost Evaluation of Instructional Strategies." *Audiovisual Communication Review* 21 (Spring).

Williams, B.R. 1963. "Capacity and Output of Universities." *The Manchester School of Economic and Social Studies* 31 (May): 185-202.

Williams, G.; Blackstone, T.; and Metcalf, D. 1974. *The Academic Labor Market: Economic and Social Aspects of a Profession.* Amsterdam: Elsevier.

Williams, H. 1966. *Planning for Effective Resource Allocation in Universities.* Washington, D.C.: American Council on Education.

Willingham, W.W. 1970. *Free-access Higher Education.* New York: College Entrance Examination Board.

Wilson, L. 1972. *Shaping American Higher Education.* Washington, D.C.: American Council on Education.

Wilson, L. with Mills, O., eds. 1972. *Universal Higher Education: Costs, Benefits Options.* Washington, D.C.: American Council on Education.

Windham, D.M. 1970. *Education, Equality, and Income Distribution.* Lexington, Mass.: Heath Lexington Books.

———. 1972a. "Tuition, the Capital Market, and the Allocation of Subsidies to College Students." *School Review* 80 (August): 603-18.

———. 1972b. "The Efficiency/Equity Quandary and Higher Educational Finance." *Review of Educational Research* 42 (December): 541-60.

———. 1975. "The Macro-Planning of Education: Why it Fails, Why it Survives, and the Alternatives." *Comparative Education Review* 19 (June): 187-236.

———. 1976a. "Economists and the Economic Analysis of Education." *The Review of Education* (January-February): 26-34.

———. 1976b. "Social Benefits and the Subsidization of Higher Education: A Critique." *Higher Education* 5 (August): 237-52.

———. 1976c. "The Economics of Higher Education." *In Comparative Higher Education: Bibliography and Analysis.* ed. P.G. Altbach, pp. 183-221. New York: Praeger Publishers, 1976.

Windham, D.M., ed. 1977a. *Economic Perspectives on Education.* Stanford: National Academy of Education.

———. 1977b. "Economic Analysis and Public Support of Higher Education: The Divergence of Theory and Policy." In Windham (1977a).

———. 1977c. "Microeducational Decisions as a Basis for Macroeducational Planning." Paper presented at the IIEP Seminar on "New Tasks in Educational Planning: Changing Concepts and Practices," June.

Winkler, D.R. 1975. "Educational Achievement and School Peer Group Composition." *Journal of Human Resources* 10 (Spring): 189-204.

Winokur, H.S., Jr. 1976. "Expenditure Equalization in the Washington, D.C. Elementary Schools." *Public Policy* 24 (Summer): 309-35.

Winsborough, H.H. 1975. "Age, Period, Cohort, and Education Effects on Earnings by Race." In *Social Indicator Models,* ed. K.C. Land and S. Spilerman, pp. 201-17. Russell Sage Foundation, 1975.

Wise, A.E. 1976. "Minimum Educational Adequacy: Beyond School Finance Reform." *Journal of Education Finance* 1 (Spring): 468-83.

Wise, A.E., and Thomas, J.A. 1973. "Full State Funding." in Hickrod et al. (1973: 67-76).

Wise, D.A. 1975. "Academic Achievement and Job Performance." *American Economic Review* 65 (June): 35–66.

Wiseman, J. 1959. "The Economics of Education." *Scottish Journal of Political Economy* 6 (February): 48-58. Reprinted in Blaug (1969: 360-72).

———. 1960. "Rejoinder." *Scottish Journal of Political Economy* 7: 76-76. Reprinted in Blaug (1969: 379-81).

———. 1965. "Cost-Benefit Analysis in Education." *Southern Economic Journal* 32 (July): 1-14. Reprinted in Wykstra (1971b: 177-93).

———. 1966. "Public Finance and Education: A Summary of the Issues." *Public Finance* 21: 316-24.

Withey, S.B., ed. 1971. *A Degree and What Else?* New York: McGraw-Hill.

Witmer, D.R. 1970. "Economic Benefits of College Education." *Review of Educational Research* 40 (October): 511-23.

———. 1972. "Cost Studies in Higher Education." *Review of Educational Research* 42 (Winter).

Wittstein, T. 1867. *Mathematische Statistik und deren Anwendung auf National-Ökonomie und Versicherung-wissenschaft.* Hanover: Hahn'sche Hofbuchlandlung.

Wolfe, B. 1977. "A Cost-Effectiveness Analysis of Reductions in School Expenditures: An Application of an Educational Production Function." *Journal of Education Finance* 2 (Spring): 407-18.

Wolfe, D. 1954. *America's Resources of Specialized Talent.* New York: Harper.

———. 1971. *The Uses of Talent.* Princeton: Princeton University Press.

———. 1972. *The Home of Science: The Role of the University.* New York: McGraw-Hill.

———. "To What Extent do Monetary Returns to Education Vary with Family Background, Mental Ability, and School Quality?" In Solomon and Taubman (1973: 65-74).

Wolfe, D., and Smith, J. 1965. "The Occupational Value of Education for Superior High-School Graduates." *Journal of Higher Education* (April): 201-13.

Wolpin, K.I. 1974. "Education, Screening, and the Demand for Labor of Uncertain Quality." Ph.D. dissertation, City University of New York.

———. 1977. "Education and Screening." *American Economic Review* 67 (December): 949-58.

Wood, W., and Campbell, D.H.F. 1970. *Cost-Benefit Analysis and the Economics of Investment in Human Resources: An Annotated Bibliography.* Ontario: Industrial Relations Center, Queen's University.

Woodhall, M. 1972. *Economic Aspects of Education: A Review of Research in Britain.* Windsor, U.K.: National Foundation for Educational Research in England and Wales.

Woodhall, M., and Blaug, M. 1965a. "Productivity Trends in British University Education, 1938-62." *Minerva* 3 (Summer): 483-98.

———. 1965b. "Productivity Trends in British University Education: Reply." *Minerva* 3 (Autumn): 101-105.

———. 1968. "Productivity Trends in British Secondary Education, 1950-63." *Sociology of Education* 41 (Winter): 1-35.

———. 1969. "Variations in Costs and Productivity of British Primary and Secondary Education." In Hüfner and Naumann (1969: 69-86).

Wright, E.O., and Perrone, L. 1977. "Marxist Class Categories and Income Inequality." *American Sociological Review* 42, no. 1: 32-55.

Wykstra, R.A., ed. 1971a. *Education and the Economics of Human Capital.* New York: The Free Press.

———, ed. 1971b. *Human Capital Formation and Manpower Development.* New York: The Free Press.

Wynkoop, R.J. 1976. "A New Rationale for a Federal Foundation Program." *Journal of Education Finance* 1 (Spring): 550-58.

Y

Yang, C.S.W., and Sewell, W.H. 1976. "Residence, Migration, and Earnings." Working Paper 76-28, Center for Demography and Ecology, University of Wisconsin, Madison.

Yang, T.W., and Chaudhari, R. 1976. "A Study of the Relationship Between Selected Socio-Economic Variables and Local Tax Effort to Support Public Schools in Illinois." Report to the Technical Task Force on School Finance, Illinois Office of Education, December.

Yeager, L.B. 1976. "Toward Understanding Some Paradoxes in Capital Theory." *Economic Inquiry* 14 (September): 313-46.

Yett, D.E. 1970. "The Chronic 'Shortage' of Nurses: A Public Policy Dilemma." In *Empirical Studies in Health Economics,* ed. H.E. Klarman, pp. 357-89. Baltimore: The Johns Hopkins Press, 1970.

You, J.K. 1976. "Embodied and Disembodied Technical Progress in the United States, 1929-1968." *Review of Economics and Statistics* 58 (February): 123-27.

Young, A.M. "Going Back to School at 35 and Over." *Monthly Labor Review* 98 (December): 47-50.

Z

Zacharias, J.R., Chairman, 1967. *Educational Opportunity Bank:* A Report of the Panel on Educational Innovation to the U.S. Commissioner on Education Harold Howe II and others. Washington: U.S. Government Printing Office.

———. 1969. "Educational Opportuntiy Through Student Loans: An Approach to Higher Education Financing." In Joint Economic Committee (1969: 652-63).

Zeckhauser, R. 1970. "Uncertainty and the Need for Collective Action." In Haveman and Margolis (1970: 96-116).

Ziderman, A. 1969. "Costs and Benefits of Adult Retraining in the United Kingdom." *Economica* 36 (November): 363-76.

———. 1973a. "Rates of Return on Investment in Education: Results for Britain." *Journal of Human Resources* 8 (Winter): 85-97.

———. 1973b. "Does it Pay to Take a Degree? The Profitability of Private Investment in the University Education in Britain." *Oxford Economic Papers* 25 (July): 262-74.

Zoloth, B.S. 1976a. "The Impact of Busing on Student Achievement: Reanalysis." *Growth and Change* 7 (July): 43-47.

———. 1976b. "The Impact of Busing on Student Achievment: Rejoinder." *Growth and Change* 7 (July): 50-51.

Zuckerman, G.J. 1974. "An Economic Study Concerned with the Valuation of Human Life in Court Cases Involving the Accidental Death of Females." Ph.D. dissertation, North Carolina State University.

Zymelman, M. 1976. *The Economic Evaluation of Vocational Training Programs.* Baltimore: The John Hopkins University Press.

Index

About the Author

ELCHANAN COHN is Professor of Economics at the University of South Carolina. From 1968 to 1974 he was assistant and then associate professor of economics at The Pennsylvania State University (University Park), where he also was a Research Associate with the Institute for Research on Human Resources. His interest in the economics of education dates back to 1967 when he wrote his Doctoral dissertation on the quality of high school education in Iowa. Since then, he has written four books and numerous articles, reviews, and research reports on this topic. The first edition of The Economics of Education (originally published in 1972) received wide acclaim. His other books are *Public Expenditure Analysis* (1972), *Economics of State Aid to Education* (1974), and *Input-Output Analysis in Public Education* (1975). He is presently engaged in research on mathematical-programming models of education, and is cooperating in the completion of a book-length manuscript on the use of goal programming to improve resource allocation in public schools.